Gale Contextual Encyclopedia of World Literature

Gale Contextual Encyclopedia of World Literature

VOLUME 4

S–Z

GALE
CENGAGE Learning™

Detroit • New York • San Francisco • New Haven, Conn • Waterville, Maine • London

**Gale Contextual Encyclopedia
of World Literature**

Project Editors: Anne Marie Hacht and Dwayne
D. Hayes

Editorial: Ira Mark Milne

Rights Acquisition and Management: Kelly Quin,
Tracie Richardson, and Robyn Young

Composition: Evi Abou-El-Seoud

Manufacturing: Wendy Blurton

Imaging: Lezlie Light

Product Design: Pam Galbreath and Jennifer Wahi

For product information and technology assistance, contact us at
Gale Customer Support, 1-800-877-4253.
For permission to use material from this text or product,
submit all requests online at **www.cengage.com/permissions.**
Further permissions questions can be emailed to
permissionrequest@cengage.com

Cover photographs reproduced by permission. Blake, William, painting by John
Linnell. Source unknown; Austen, Jane, print; Marquez, Gabriel Garcia, 1982, photograph.
AP Images; Shakespeare, William, illustration. The Library of Congress; Frank, Anne,
photograph. The Library of Congress; Aristotle, engraving. The Library of Congress;
Achebe, Chinua, 1988, photograph. AP Images; Borges, Jorge Luis, photograph. The
Library of Congress; Dickens, Charles, photograph. The Library of Congress; Allende,
Isabel, photograph. AP Images; Shelley, Mary Wollstonecraft, illustration. Source
unknown; Wiesel, Elie, photograph. AP Images; Chaucer, Geoffrey, illustration; Verne,
Jules, 1904, photograph.

While every effort has been made to ensure the reliability of the information
presented in this publication, Gale, a part of Cengage Learning, does not guarantee the
accuracy of the data contained herein. Gale accepts no payment for listing; and
inclusion in the publication of any organization, agency, institution, publication, service,
or individual does not imply endorsement of the editors or publisher. Errors brought to
the attention of the publisher and verified to the satisfaction of the publisher will be
corrected in future editions.

Editorial Data Privacy Policy. Does this publication contain information about you as
an individual? If so, for more information about our editorial data privacy policies,
please see our Privacy Statement at www.gale.com.

Library of Congress Cataloging-in-Publication Data

Gale contextual encyclopedia of world literature / editorial, Anne Marie Hacht,
Dwayne D. Hayes.
    p. cm.
    Includes bibliographical references and index.
    ISBN 978-1-4144-4870-1 (set) -- ISBN 978-1-4144-3135-2 (vol. 1) --
ISBN 978-1-4144-3136-9 (vol. 2) -- ISBN 978-1-4144-3137-6 (vol. 3) --
ISBN 978-1-4144-3138-3 (vol. 4)
    1. Literature--Encyclopedias. I. Hacht, Anne Marie. II. Hayes, Dwayne D.
III. Title: Encyclopedia of world literature.

PN41.G36 2009
803--dc22   2008032003

Gale
27500 Drake Rd.
Farmington Hills, MI, 48331-3535

978-1-4144-4870-1 (set)   1-4144-4870-8 (set)
978-1-4144-3135-2 (vol. 1)   1-4144-3135-X (vol. 1)
978-1-4144-3136-9 (vol. 2)   1-4144-3136-8 (vol. 2)
978-1-4144-3137-6 (vol. 3)   1-4144-3137-6 (vol. 3)
978-1-4144-3138-3 (vol. 4)   1-4144-3138-4 (vol. 4)

This title is also available as an e-book.
ISBN-13: 978-1-4144-4871-8 ISBN-10: 1-4144-4871-6
Contact your Gale, a part of Cengage Learning sales representative for ordering
information.

Printed in the United States of America
1 2 3 4 5 6 7 13 12 11 10 09

Contents

Contents

VOLUME 2

D-E

Graham Greene 745

Nicolás Guillén 748

H-J

Thomas Hardy 753

Jaroslav Hašek 756

Gerhart Hauptmann 760

Václav Havel 763

Bessie Head 767

Seamus Heaney 771

Lafcadio Hearn 774

George Herbert 777

Robert Herrick 781

James Herriot 784

Hermann Hesse 787

Nazim Hikmet 791

Rolf Hochhuth 794

Fritz Hochwaelder 798

Peter Hoeg 800

Homer 803

Gerard Manley Hopkins 806

Nick Hornby 810

A. E. Housman 812

Ted Hughes 816

Victor Hugo 819

Aldous Huxley 823

Henrik Ibsen 826

Eugene Ionesco 830

Christopher Isherwood 834

Kazuo Ishiguro 837

Kobayashi Issa 840

Alfred Jarry 841

Elfriede Jelinek 844

Juan Ramón Jiménez 847

Samuel Johnson 851

Ben Jonson 855

James Joyce 859

VOLUME 3

K-L

M

VOLUME 4

S

Introduction

How to Use This Book

The *Gale Contextual Encyclopedia of World Literature* is a resource for students who seek information beyond the simple biographical details of an author's life or a brief overview of the author's major works. This book is designed to offer a comprehensive view of how an author's work fits within the context of the author's life, historical events, and the literary world. This allows for a greater understanding of both the author's work and the cultural and historical environment in which it was created.

The *Gale Contextual Encyclopedia of World Literature* is divided into entries, each focused on a particular writer who has made significant contributions to world literature. In some cases, these individuals may be known primarily for contributions outside the realm of literature. Karl Marx and Mohandas Gandhi, for example, are two figures famous for their political activism; in another realm, Jean Cocteau and Pier Paolo Pasolini are two writers better known in modern times for their ground-breaking work in film. However, all of these figures have, aside from their other accomplishments, created significant works of literature that have stood the test of time and affected readers beyond the borders of their own cultures.

This book is best used not just to locate the facts of a writer's life and work, but as a way to understand the social, literary, and historical environment in which the writer lived and created. By understanding the context of the writer's work, you are more likely to recognize key themes and stylistic traits as elements of larger trends in the literary world, as well as understand the impact of historical events from a new and unique perspective.

Sections Found within Each Entry in This Book

Each entry in this book is divided into three main parts: Works in Biographical and Historical Context; Works in Literary Context; and Works in Critical Context. These sections are discussed below.

In addition, each entry includes: a Key Facts section, containing birth/death date information as well as a list of major works; a Responses to Literature section, containing discussion and writing activities related to the author in question; a Further Reading section that includes bibliographic citations as well as reputable sources of additional material about the author in the form of books, periodicals, or Web sites; a Literary and Historical Contemporaries sidebar, listing several famous contemporaries of the author; and a Common Human Experience sidebar, offering examples of other literary or artistic works that share themes or techniques with those by the subject of the entry.

Works in Biographical and Historical Context In this section, you will find information about how events and concerns in the author's life helped to shape the author's work. For example, Russian author Aleksandr Solzhenitsyn's experiences in a Soviet labor camp led him to write *The Gulag Archipelago* (1973), while his experiences battling cancer inspired his novel *Cancer Ward* (1968). This section also includes information on historical events or trends that had an effect on the author. For example, the scientific and technological advancements of the nineteenth century greatly influenced the subject matter of the works of Jules Verne, which primarily focused on "fanciful" scientific achievements such as a journey to the moon.

Works in Literary Context In this section, you will find information about how the author's work fits within the context of the body of literature as a whole. This may include a description of a stylistic trait exhibited in the author's writing; for example, the literary technique known as "stream of consciousness" is a defining characteristic of much of the fiction of Virginia Woolf, and information on the technique—as well as examples of how the author used it—can be found in her entry. This section may also include a discussion of the writer's work as it exists within a specific genre, such as Gothic fiction or Surrealist poetry. Finally, the Works in Literary Context section may contain information of specific themes commonly found in the author's work. The writings of Aimé Césaire, for example, frequently address the theme of race relations in colonial regions.

Works in Critical Context In this section, you will find a survey of critical and popular opinion related to the author and the author's most important works. The emphasis is on contemporary opinions, or those formed by readers and critics at the time the author's work was first published. In some cases, critical or popular opinion from the time of publication may not be available; this may be due to the passage of time, as with some ancient Greek and Roman authors, or due to the writer's lack of fame during his or her own lifetime. This section also includes information on how critical or popular opinion on an author has changed over time. Joseph Conrad and Rudyard Kipling, for example, have been taken to task by some modern critics for their depictions of race in their most highly regarded works. Some authors popular during their own time, such as Samuel Richardson, have fallen from favor among modern readers, while others virtually unknown during their lifetimes have become part of the classic literary canon.

Other Information Contained in This Book

In addition to the entries for individual authors, this book also contains a chronology that indicates some major historical events related to the development of world literature. At the end of the book, you will find a glossary of terms—primarily literary and historical in nature—that are used in various entries throughout the book, along with a brief explanation of each term.

Advisory Board

Robert Todd Felton

is a freelance writer and educational consultant. He holds a BA in English from Cornell University and an MA from Syracuse University. He taught high school English for nine years.

Allen Michie

has graduate degrees from Oxford University and Emory University, and he has taught British literature at Coastal Carolina University, the University of North Carolina, Wake Forest University, and Iowa State University. He is currently a Program Director for the Texas Higher Education Coordinating Board.

Alicia Baker Elley

taught undergraduate and high school literature, composition, and technical writing classes for over ten years. She is currently district librarian for the Harmony Independent School District in Texas.

Roger K. Smith

has been a teacher of English, writing, and other humanities courses at such institutions as Ithaca College, Rutgers, and Edward R. Murrow High School (Brooklyn). He holds a BA from Swarthmore College and an MA from New York University.

Chronology

This chronology contains a brief overview of some of the major events in the history of world literature. This includes the development of technologies and tools that advanced the writing and publishing process, as well as some significant historical events that had an impact on the development of literature.

2100 BCE–499 CE

c. 2100 BCE

The earliest existing fragments of the *Epic of Gilgamesh*, widely recognized as the first epic documented in written form, are recorded on clay tablets by ancient Sumerians.

c. 1600 BCE

The first known example of a literary story documented on papyrus, a durable paper-like material made from the fibrous stem of the papyrus plant, is written by ancient Egyptians.

c. 1050 BCE

The Phoenician alphabet, the first widely used alphabetic writing system in the world, is developed from older scripts that included Egyptian hieroglyphics.

c. 850 BCE

Homer, credited as the author of the first ancient Greek epics in written form, the *Iliad* and *Odyssey*, is believed to have lived.

472 BCE

Aeschylus's play *The Persians*, the oldest surviving example of an ancient Greek tragedy, was first performed.

425 BCE

The Acharnians, a play by Aristophanes and the oldest surviving example of ancient Greek comedy, is first performed.

c. 190 BCE

The production of parchment, a writing surface derived from animal skin, is refined into an easily produced method in the ancient Greek city of Pergamum, effectively ending the dominance of papyrus.

c. 300 CE

Kâlidâsa, Indian playwright and one of the foremost literary figures of the Sanskrit language, is believed to have lived.

397 CE Augustine of Hippo, a North African bishop, begins publication of his *Confessions*, generally regarded as the first autobiography and the first example of confessional literature.

500–1499

c. 794 The first paper mill begins operation in Baghdad, in modern-day Iraq. Over the course of several centuries, wood pulp-based paper replaces parchment as the dominant writing surface throughout the world.

868 The *Diamond Sutra* is published in China; printed using woodblock printing methods, this publication is the oldest known printed book in existence.

1021 *The Tale of Genji*, a Japanese work attributed to Murasaki Shikibu, is published. The work becomes a landmark in Japanese literature and is often cited as one of the earliest books to resemble the modern novel.

1048 Omar Khayyam, a Persian mathematician and poet, is born. His poetic works are later collected—along with some works of suspect attribution—in *The Rubaiyat of Omar Khayyam*, a key work of Persian literature.

c. 1220 Snorri Sturluson creates the first comprehensive written collection of Norse mythology with the completion of the *Prose Edda*.

1265 Italian poet Dante Alighieri, creator of the epic known as *The Divine Comedy*, is born.

1439 German metalworker Johann Gutenberg creates the first functional printing press, resulting in the ability to mass-produce copies of literature easily and cheaply instead of by hand.

1500–1799

1558 Queen Elizabeth I assumes the throne of England, marking the beginning of the Elizabethan Age, a period of forty-five years during which significant advancements in English poetry and drama occurred.

1564 William Shakespeare, generally acknowledged by modern readers as the greatest dramatist in the history of the English language, is born.

1605 The first volume of *Don Quixote* by Miguel de Cervantes is published. Written in Spanish, *Don Quixote* is widely considered to be the first modern novel.

1649 The Puritan-led British Commonwealth Parliament, in control after the overthrow of the British monarchy, bans theatrical productions throughout England due to the purported indecency of dramatic works. The ban would last until 1680, and would be followed by an explosion of theatrical development during the period known as the Restoration.

1719 *The Life and Strange Surprising Adventures of Robinson Crusoe* by Daniel Defoe is published; this book is often regarded as the first true novel of the English language.

1798 *Lyrical Ballads, with a Few Other Poems*, a poetic collection by William Wordsworth and Samuel Taylor Coleridge, is published, marking for many the beginning of the Romantic movement in English literature.

1800–Today

1856 Gustave Flaubert's novel *Madame Bovary* is published in serial form, leading to an obscenity trial over its contents. *Madame Bovary* is considered by many to be the key work that launched the Realism movement in literature.

1857 Novelist Charles Dickens founds *All the Year Round*, one of many inexpensive British serial magazines that make literature available to virtually all levels of social class; *All the Year Round* subsequently features the first publication of the Dickens novels *Great Expectations* and *A Tale of Two Cities*.

1873 Production begins on the first commercially successful typewriter by E. Remington and Sons, which will allow writers to produce work substantially more quickly and more neatly than writing by hand.

1922 James Joyce's novel *Ulysses* and T. S. Eliot's poem "The Waste Land" are both published, defining for many the Modernist literary movement.

1924 André Breton publishes his *Surrealist Manifesto*, launching an avant-garde literary and artistic movement characterized by a celebration of the irrational.

1932 Joseph Stalin, dictatorial leader of the Soviet Union, decrees that socialist realism—an artistic style in which the working class and government leaders are praised—is the only government-approved art style. Writers and artists who create controversial works are censored and placed into labor camps; a secret distribution system known as *samizdat* is created to preserve and share censored works among dissenting intellectuals.

1950 Eugène Ionesco's play *The Bald Soprano* debuts in Paris, launching the theatrical movement known as Theater of the Absurd.

1992 The World Wide Web, an interlinking structure designed by Sir Tim Berners-Lee for viewing cross-referenced multimedia documents from any location through data transfer, is officially released.

S

⬙ Thomas Sackville

BORN: *1536, Sussex, England*

DIED: *1608, London, England*

NATIONALITY: *British*

GENRE: *Drama, poetry*

MAJOR WORKS:

The Tragedy of Gorboduc (1562)

"Induction" (1563)

"Complaint" (1563)

Overview

Thomas Sackville was by no means a prolific poet. Only four of his poems have survived, and one of those was only very recently discovered. Yet Sackville's fellows and followers in the art of poetry were in no doubt as to the quality and importance of his work. Edmund Spenser himself, the arch-poet of Elizabethan England, praised Sackville's "golden verses." Spenser was particularly impressed by Sackville's "Induction," one of the two poems he contributed to the second edition of William Baldwin's compilation *A Mirror for Magistrates* in 1563. This is the poem that is best known and most appreciated today as a pinnacle of Elizabethan poetry.

Works in Biographical and Historical Context

Royal Ties and Inherited Wealth   Throughout the sixteenth century, England underwent a number of cultural and artistic transformations, often collectively referred to by scholars as the English Renaissance or the golden age in English history. During this time of change, William Shakespeare composed his now famous plays and the Protestant Reformation became the dominant religious trend among the people. Sackville was born in 1536 in the Sussex village of Buckhurst, from which he took the title Baron Buckhurst when Queen Elizabeth I raised him to the peerage in 1567. Queen Elizabeth I described Sackville as her "beloved kinsman," for indeed Sackville was related to the queen; her mother, Anne Boleyn, was a cousin of his father, Sir Richard Sackville. It was this royal connection and the wealth that he inherited upon his father's death in 1566 that confirmed him in his career as a courtier and statesman. In this role, first under Elizabeth and then James I, Sackville was named the first Earl of Dorset in 1605. It was a career for which his birth and breeding had always intended him, but as a young man—indeed, as a boy—he seems to have intended for himself the career of a poet.

Oxford Education and the Inns of Court   Very little is known of Sackville's education, but he attended Oxford before settling, at about age seventeen, in London in 1553. The next year he was married to Cecily, daughter of Sir John Baker, and a year later he was admitted to the Inner Temple, where his father was one of the governors. The Inner Temple was one of the Inns of Court, institutions that functioned both as law colleges and finishing schools for young gentlemen intending the sort of political career that Sackville was eventually to take. The Inns of Court were also the center of literary life in mid-Tudor London. Jasper Heywood, in his translation of Seneca's *Thyestes* (1560), includes Sackville among the best of the Inns of Court writers. In Heywood's work "Sackville's sonnets, sweetly sauced" are singled out for praise. These sonnets were probably about love: in "Sackville's Old Age" the poet tells the reader that his "lusty pen" has written many a "sweet complaint of woeful lover's wrong." But none of them are now extant, and it is on his "tragical" poetry that Sackville's reputation now stands.

Commentator on Literature: A Protector of the Arts   After having written a number of poems by the year 1559, Sackville wrote little, apart from the last two acts of *Gorboduc* (1562), during the rest of his life. In 1561, he contributed a commendatory sonnet to Sir Thomas Hoby's translation of Baldassare Castiglione's *Book of the Courtier*. It returns to the old theme of

Sir Thomas Sackville   *Archive Photos / Getty Images*

worldly pomp that fuels the tragedies in "Bochas," and Sackville demeans the gorgeous palaces that "royal kings" erect and elevates the virtues of good courtiership: "what in Court a courtier ought to be." More important, one sees here Sackville taking up a marginal position in the literary world: a praiser of other men's works who does not undertake anything considerable himself. So, for example, in 1571 he wrote a commendatory letter regarding Bartholomew Clerke's translation of Castiglione's book into Latin. Indeed, later poets praise Sackville for his support of literature and learning. In 1602 Thomas Campion dedicated his *Observations in the Art of English Poesy* to Sackville, calling him "the most honorable protector of all industrious learning." And in 1608 Joshua Sylvester dedicated to him part of his translation of Guillaume de Salluste, Seigneur du Bartas's *Divine Weeks and Works*, including him among the "noble host/Of learned friends to learning."

Farewell to Poetry But Sackville had bade farewell to poetry long before. His last poem, written between 1566 and 1574, is the recently discovered "Sackville's Old Age." Here he returns to the theme of the transience of life. He also discusses his reading habits as a younger man (he was still only in his mid-thirties) and lists his favorite English authors: Chaucer, "my guide, my master"; Surrey, especially his "English Virgil"; and Wyatt's translations of the Psalms. But, he wrote, it was time to say

good-bye to poetry: "O trifles past, adieu, I ye forsake." He was good to his word, and no other poems of his have been discovered. Characteristically, Sackville died while working at the Council Table in London on April 19, 1608.

Works in Literary Context

Although Sackville's overall literary production is small, since he opted instead for a career in diplomacy and statesmanship, his works are recognized for their historical, if not literary, value. His only play, *The Tragedy of Gorboduc* (1565), cowritten by Thomas Norton, is considered the first English neoclassical tragedy, and the opening sequence of his poem "Induction" established a humanistic model for a *hiemal chronographia*, or description of winter, which succeeding generations of writers sought to emulate.

Tragedy as Drama The idea that tragedy was a kind of drama was still a new one in mid-Tudor England. In fact it was Sackville himself, in collaboration with a fellow Inner Templar, Thomas Norton, who wrote the first neoclassical tragic drama in English, *The Tragedy of Gorboduc*, which was performed at the Inner Temple in 1562. *Gorboduc* is an important milestone in the history of English "vernacular humanism," the enrichment of the native literary tradition by incorporating into it material and forms from classical literature, in this case the plays of the Latin tragic dramatist Seneca.

The drama as tragedy is an extremely important development in literature, if for no other reason than that it was the preferred form of William Shakespeare. Some of Shakespeare's most highly acclaimed works—*Hamlet*, *King Lear*, *Macbeth*, and a slew of others—are all considered dramatic tragedies, a form that did not really exist in English literature before Sackville collaborated on *The Tragedy of Gorboduc* with Thomas Norton.

But throughout the sixteenth century the word *tragedy* was also used in its medieval sense to refer to a short narrative poem dealing with the fall of some great man or woman into misery. This conception of tragedy found its fullest expression in John Lydgate's translation of Giovanni Boccaccio's *De casibus virorum illustrium* as *The Fall of Princes* (1431–1438). And it was with this kind of tragedy, and indeed this book, that Sackville's short poetic career began.

In the early part of 1555, the printer John Wayland determined to bring out a new edition of Lydgate's "Bochas" and procured Baldwin and seven others to undertake an appendix dealing with English princes. The book, which appeared in 1559, has a notoriously difficult publishing history, but it seems that the young Sackville—a lad of nineteen years or so at the time—was appointed to write the tragedy of Henry Stafford, Duke of Buckingham, one of the henchmen of Richard III. Baldwin collected nineteen tragedies, and the book went to press, but it was halted in mid-print on orders from the government.

Hiemal Chronographia The "Induction" begins with a traditionally medieval description of a winter landscape, in which the poet Sackville wanders, and where, overtaken by the sudden fall of night, he muses on the mutability of fortune. It was these three stanzas that most haunted the minds of Sackville's Elizabethan followers. The opening description of a winter landscape, with its "blustering blasts," "small fowls flocking," and "naked twigs ... shivering all for cold," is in itself entirely conventional; every detail can be traced to several earlier poems. But the skill and sensitivity with which these details were knit together made Sackville's three stanzas the "classic" example of a hiemal chronographia, the one that later poets imitated when they wished to write their own descriptions of winter. Spenser, to take only the most prestigious of Sackville's imitators, for example, modeled the landscape of his "January" eclogue (1579) on Sackville's poem.

Works in Critical Context

Although critical evaluation of Sackville's body of work has varied greatly throughout the four and a half centuries since his productive period, it is difficult to challenge the importance of Sackville in the history of English literature. While some modern critics find his verse artificial, his influence on esteemed authors such as Shakespeare and Spenser, in addition to the laudatory comments of his contemporaries, mark it as exceptional. Sackville's *Gorboduc* shares much the same fate: admired by his contemporaries for its innovation and appreciated by scholars for the same, it is now rarely considered an outstanding piece of literature outside of these considerations of its revolutionary form.

Gorboduc Even so, *Gorboduc* is the first English drama to receive serious literary criticism. Sir Philip Sidney in his *Defence of Poesie* praised its "stately speeches and well-sounding phrases, climbing to the height of Seneca's style, and full of notable morality." However, deploring its lack of unities of place and time, he declared it could not be "an exact model" for all tragedies. Nonetheless, Sackville's *Gorboduc* has come to be esteemed as a landmark in the history of English literature. Irby B. Cauthen Jr. noted that "not only is it the first 'regular' English tragedy (one that follows classical rules), but it is marked by innovations that were to become traditional."

"Induction" Sackville's contemporaries enthused about his literary contributions; for instance, Edmund Spenser lauded Sackville's "golden verses." However, in light of the small quantity of Sackville's writings, some twentieth-century critics have questioned the value of his literary achievement. "Sackville's reputation owes too much to an interpretative treatment of literary history," wrote J. Stewart. "Whether such a treatment regards his

---

LITERARY AND HISTORICAL CONTEMPORARIES

Sackville's famous contemporaries include:

William Shakespeare (1564–1616): English dramatist and poet who utilized the tragedy drama frequently in his body of work.

Miguel de Cervantes (1547–1616): Spanish author whose *Don Quixote* is often regarded as the first novel.

Michel de Montaigne (1533–1592): French author who pioneered the essay as a genre of writing.

Elizabeth I (1533–1603): Queen of England and of Ireland from 1558 until her death in 1603.

Takeda Shingen (1521–1573): Prominent Japanese feudal lord who sought control over all of Japan during the "warring states" period.

Andrea Andreani (1540–1623): Italian wood engraver who was among the first to use chiaroscuro, a technique in which light colors are contrasted with darker ones.

---

work as the last flower of medievalism or as a prelude to Spenser, is immaterial." Nonetheless, Sackville's "Induction" remains most appreciated today as "one of the first truly great Elizabethan poems," according to Alan T. Bradford.

Responses to Literature

1. Although Sackville helped pioneer the tragic drama, he did not define its limitations nor even produce the most notable examples of the form. Read *Gorboduc* and, in a short essay, compare it in style, theme, and content with another popular tragedy—something from Shakespeare or Marlowe's *The Tragical History of Doctor Faustus*. Can you find elements of Sackville's work that seem to have influenced Shakespeare and Marlowe?

2. Thomas Sackville was in his mid-thirties when he considered himself an old man. Indeed, Shakespeare, too, wrote about being an old man when he was also in his thirties. Using the Internet and the library, research life expectancies and living standards during Thomas Sackville's lifetime. Then, in a short essay or story, explore the following question: What role does an author's life expectancy play in shaping his or her work? How would your life be different if you viewed your thirties as "old age"? Would your plans for the next ten years change? If so, how?

3. The hiemal chronographia—the description of winter—at the beginning of Sackville's "Induction" inspired a number of poets after Sackville. Read

COMMON HUMAN EXPERIENCE

It would be difficult to overestimate the importance of tragedy in the history of literature. Only forty years after Sackville helped write *Gorboduc*, Shakespeare wrote what is arguably the premier example of the form, *Hamlet*. Here are a few more examples of literary tragedies:

> *Death of a Salesman* (1949), a play by Arthur Miller. In this work, Miller describes the slow and painful demise of title character Willy Loman under the weight of the "American Dream."
>
> *A Doll's House* (1879), a play by Henrik Ibsen. In this work, Ibsen explores and, indeed, criticizes the norms of marriage in the nineteenth century.
>
> *The Tragical History of Doctor Faustus* (1604), a play by Christopher Marlowe. In this work, Faust (whose Latin name is Faustus) sells his soul to the devil for knowledge and power.

"Induction." One of the marks of effective poetry is that it enables you to see clearly what is being described. Do the opening lines of "Induction" qualify? Try it out. When you read these lines, what do you picture? Now, make a drawing, painting, or sculpture of what you see when you read these lines. Then, in a short essay, reflect on the connection between the written words and what you've produced—think about which descriptions inspired which images.

4. Critics have argued that as Sackville's career advanced, his work decreased in literary merit. Read *Gorboduc*, "Induction," and "Complaint," then respond to this criticism of Sackville's work. Do you agree or disagree? In your response, cite examples from the texts to support your argument.

BIBLIOGRAPHY

Books

Baker, Howard. *Induction to Tragedy, a Study in the Development of Form in* Gorboduc, The Spanish Tragedy, *and* Titus Andronicus. Baton Rouge: Louisiana State University Press, 1939.

Berlin, Normand. *Thomas Sackville*. Boston: Twayne, 1974.

Clemen, Wolfgang. *English Tragedy before Shakespeare*. London: Methuen, 1961.

Doran, Madeleine. *Endeavors of Art: A Study of Form in Elizabethan Drama*. Reading, Mass.: Addison-Wesley, 1994.

Herrick, M. T. *Studies in Speech and Drama in Honor of Alexander M. Drummond*. Ithaca, N.Y.: Cornell University Press, 1944.

Lewis, C. S. *English Literature in the Sixteenth Century, Excluding Drama*. Oxford University Press, 1954.

Ribner, Irving. *The English History Play in the Age of Shakespeare*. London: Methuen, 1965.

Talbert, Ernest W. *Studies in Honor of Dewitt T. Starnes*. Austin: University of Texas Humanities Research Center, 1967.

◈ Antoine de Saint-Exupéry

BORN: *1900, Lyons, France*

DIED: *1944, France*

NATIONALITY: *French*

GENRE: *Fiction, nonfiction*

MAJOR WORKS:

Southern Mail (1929)

Night Flight (1931)

Wind, Sand, Stars (1939)

The Little Prince (1943)

Overview

While best known in the United States for what has become a classic in children's literature, the fable *The Little Prince* (1943), Antoine de Saint-Exupéry is recognized in his native country of France for the humanism and reflection shown in his adventurous tales of aviation. Largely autobiographical, his work depicts not only the freedom and dangers of flight but also the importance of comradeship and dedication to duty. With a distinctive lyrical, poetic prose style, Saint-Exupéry shares his philosophy of life: individuals should always endeavor to reach their true potential.

Works in Biographical and Historical Context

Privileged Upbringing Saint-Exupéry was born in Lyons, France, on June 29, 1900, into an aristocratic family. After his father, an insurance salesman, died of a stroke in 1904, Saint-Exupéry's mother moved with her children to Le Mans in 1909. As a child, he attended a Jesuit school in Le Mans, followed by two private schools, one in France, the other in Switzerland. After failing his final exam at a university preparatory academy, he entered the École des Beaux Arts to study architecture.

Seeking Flight A turning point in Saint-Exupéry's life came in 1921, when he began military service in the second regiment of Chasseurs (a French military unit, usually light infantry) and began training as a pilot. Flying was not entirely new to him. He had flown for the first

Antoine de Saint Exupéry   © *Mary Evans Picture Library / Alamy*

time when he was twelve. After making his first solo flight in July 1921 and receiving his pilot's license in 1922, Saint-Exupéry studied at the school for air cadets and at Avord Air Base. That same year he had a serious crash, the first of many.

During the time of his flight training, Saint-Exupéry had become engaged to Louise de Vilmorin, later known as a writer in her own right for such novels as *Madame de* (1951). Because Vilmorin's family objected to his career in the air force, Saint-Exupéry took a position with a tile manufacturing company in Paris, a job his fiancée's family procured for him. After Vilmorin ended their engagement in 1923, Saint-Exupéry held various jobs over the next several years—bookkeeper, journalist, and truck salesman. In the meantime, his first work, "L'Aviateur," was published in a small-press magazine in 1926. Already evident in this story are what would become recurring aviation themes in Saint-Exupéry's work: the connection between a pilot and his plane and his fellow aviators.

Flying Postal   Flying a postal route for the commercial airline Aéropostale, Saint-Exupéry was instrumental in establishing mail routes across the African deserts and the Andes Mountains in South America. By 1928, Saint-Exupéry became the director of the remote post at Cape Juby in the Spanish Sahara, surrounded by rebel tribes.

This experience proved to be of utmost importance to his development as a writer, as the desert would become the background for *The Little Prince* and *The Wisdom of the Sands* (1948). During these years at Cape Juby, Saint-Exupéry wrote his first novel, *Southern Mail* (1929), which celebrated the postal pilots who regularly flew dangerous missions as quickly as possible so as to win a commercial advantage over railway and steamship mail carriers.

On July 14, 1929, Saint-Exupéry and a friend broke the transatlantic speed record. That same year, Saint-Exupéry received a French Legion of Honor Award for peaceful negotiations with the Moors and Spaniards in Morocco. He assumed a post in South America, where he met his future wife, Consuelo Suncin, widow of an Argentine journalist whose literary friends included French playwright Gabriele D'Annunzio. In 1931, Saint-Exupéry published *Night Flight*, a novel that praises the heroism of those pilots who pioneered flying at night on the South American postal routes.

Crashes   By 1934, Saint-Exupéry was a publicity agent for Air France and, beginning in 1935, served as a foreign correspondent for an assortment of newspapers. Toward the end of 1935, the Air Ministry sponsored a contest to reward the pilot who could break the time record between Paris and Saigon. Saint-Exupéry took to the air with his mechanic, André Prévot. On the leg from Benghazi to Cairo, the duo was disoriented by a head wind that slowed their progress, and they crashed in the Libyan desert. Near death, they were found by Bedouins five days later. One of the best-known sections of Saint-Exupéry's memoir *Wind, Sand, and Stars* (1939) recounts their struggle to survive without provisions. In 1937, Saint-Exupéry and Prévot were seriously injured in yet another plane crash, this one in Guatemala, an additional experience captured in *Wind, Sand, and Stars.*

Wartime   By the time *Wind, Sand, and Stars* was published, Europe was being engulfed in what would become World War II. Nazi Germany, led by Adolf Hitler, expanded its military and expressed territorial ambitions beginning in the mid-1930s. While countries like France and Great Britain practiced a policy of appeasement when Germany annexed parts of Czechoslovakia and Austria in 1938, they declared war after Germany invaded Poland and took it over in 1939. Hitler and Germany's imperial ambitions became clearer in 1940, when many other European countries were conquered by Germany. France was one of the countries that came under Nazi control, though free French forces fought on the side of the Allies (Great Britain, France, and, later, the United States and the Soviet Union).

After the fall of France in World War II, Saint-Exupéry was decorated with the Croix de Guerre for his part in a reconnaissance mission over German-occupied territory. At the end of 1940, he lived in self-imposed exile in New York for two years, a time of productivity during

LITERARY AND HISTORICAL CONTEMPORARIES

Saint-Exupéry's famous contemporaries include:

Amelia Earhart (1897–1937): Earhart was the first woman to pilot a plane over the Atlantic Ocean. She disappeared over the Pacific Ocean while attempting to circumnavigate the earth in 1937.

George Orwell (1903–1950): Novelist Orwell exhibited a contempt for authority in his books. His most popular works are the political satires *Animal Farm* (1945) and *1984* (1949).

Louis Armstrong (1901–1971): A gifted jazz trumpeter and singer, Armstrong pioneered the scat technique, a method of singing in which meaningless syllables are improvised, often in imitation of the sounds of a musical instrument.

Jorge Luis Borges (1899–1986): Exploring time and reality, Borges wrote fiction of imagination, philosophy, and dream that changed Latin American literature. His publications include the short story collections *Ficciones* (1944) and *The Aleph and Other Stories* (1949).

Charles Lindbergh (1902–1974): American pilot who rose to international fame after making the first solo transatlantic flight in 1927.

Emperor Hirohito (1901–1989): Japan's longest-reigning emperor (1921–1989), Hirohito oversaw his country's military invasion of China and defeat in World War II as well as Japan's postwar transformation into an economic superpower.

which he worked on *Flight to Arras* (1942), *The Little Prince* (1943), *Letter to a Hostage* (1950), and *The Wisdom of the Sands* (1950). All four of these works reveal Saint-Exupéry's belief that moral values were necessary for the rebuilding of Europe. Saint-Exupéry returned to active duty with the army in 1943. On July 31, 1944, he was reported missing in action, presumably shot down somewhere over the Mediterranean. In 2004, divers found the tailpiece of the plane Saint-Exupéry was flying three miles off the French coast between the cities of Marseille and Cassis.

Works in Literary Context

Diverse Influences Influenced by André Gide, Henri Bergson, and André Breton, Saint-Exupéry nevertheless is recognized as an innovator in literature due to a distinctive vision that transcends ordinary perception. The effect that reading Plato had on Saint-Exupéry's life and writing is also clear. He agreed with the philosopher that courage is the basest virtue, as it is composed of vanity, anger, and stubbornness. Saint-Exupéry's greatest inspi-

ration, though, was his experience as a pilot. Multiple crashes, defying death in the desert, the exhilaration of flight, and connecting with other pilots all form the foundation for his work.

Universality Characterized by a childlike altruism and a universal approach to the purpose of life, Saint-Exupéry's works surpass their immediate topics. Although much of his writing focuses on aviation, a deeper humanistic message is nonetheless recognizable. Saint-Exupéry shuns psychological jargon, thereby avoiding an overly moralistic tone. Instead, truth subtly appears in his stories, almost as if it is there by accident, which is most likely what Saint-Exupéry, believing that essential things are invisible to the eyes, intended.

Personal Enlightenment In *The Little Prince*, Saint-Exupéry presents his recurring theme of personal enlightenment through the exploration of both the outside world and one's inner world. Saint-Exupéry warns against being narrow-minded and judgmental, as these qualities can only result in ignorance. From the story's onset, the narrator emphasizes the fact that adults are uninteresting, superficial, and self-righteous in their assumption that their limited perspective is the only one possible. Children are clearly more imaginative because they are open-minded and receptive to the beauty and mystery of the universe. As the little prince travels from planet to planet, the grown-ups he meets reveal characteristics that are contradictory and shallow, and it is the little prince who points out their shortcomings. Through the symbolic little prince, Saint-Exupéry shows that a willingness to seek what is unknown and unseen in the world is the key to understanding life itself.

Introspection and spiritual growth, too, require honest exploration of not only the physical world but also one's own feelings. A most important lesson to be learned from *The Little Prince* is at once simple and complex: recognizing one's responsibilities to the world as a whole leads to one's understanding of the responsibilities involved in maintaining a relationship with another person. When, for example, the fox asks to be tamed even though he knows how to tame himself, he explains to the little prince that being willing to give a part of oneself to another person makes the recipient, as well as everything associated with that person, more valuable to the world and to the self. The essence of man, Saint-Exupéry writes in *Flight to Arras*, is a "knot of relationship with others." Despite the emotional commitment involved, creating ties with another person enriches the meaning of the world.

Works in Critical Context

At the time of their publication, Saint-Exupéry's books were generally acclaimed by critics. Much of what he wrote, however, with the exception of *The Little Prince* fell out of favor with critics and scholars after his death. Since the 1950s, *The Little Prince* has been treated by critics and the general public alike as a work of children's literature, while his novels and nonfiction have been relegated to the categories of "aviation history" or "World War II literature." Thus, his works have generally been overlooked in the canon of twentieth-century literature. Since the 1980s, there has been a renewed, though still limited, interest among English-speaking critics in the author and his books. Since the mid-1980s, critics have gradually returned to the assessment made by the author's own countrymen during his lifetime: that Saint-Exupéry wrote in a style and voice both distinctive and impressive and that his observations and metaphors have an enduring relevance and power beyond their historical setting.

The Little Prince When *The Little Prince* was published, Saint-Exupéry's fans were dismayed by what one critic described as "his sudden trajectory into absurdity." Years later, however, even the harshest critics of *The Little Prince* began to consider it Saint-Exupéry's most insightful work due to the sophisticated philosophical concepts that are wrapped in a seemingly simple package.

Evaluating the story's autobiographical components and Saint-Exupéry's concern for the fate of Europe under fascist control, scholars have commented on his motives for writing the fable. While some critics have argued that such political elements place *The Little Prince* in a category other than children's literature, others generally recognize it as an allegory that can be enjoyed by children as well as adults. Maxwell A. Smith has commented:

> Because of its poetic charm...its freshness of imagery, its whimsical fantasy, delicate irony and warm tenderness, it seems likely that *The Little Prince* will join that select company of books like La Fontaine's *Fables*, Swift's *Gulliver's Travels*, Carroll's *Alice in Wonderland* and Maeterlinck's *Blue Bird*, which have endeared themselves to children and grown-ups alike throughout the world.

Responses to Literature

1. Saint-Exupéry wrote *The Little Prince* after France had been captured by the Nazis during World War II. What symbols of war and exile can you find in the fable? Research major occurrences that took place during World War II. Create a timeline showing events that were occurring in the United States during Saint-Exupéry's lifetime.

2. Investigate the disappearances of famous aviators during flight. What are some explanations you can think of that would account for their vanishing? Choose one of these individuals and write a newspaper article reporting his or her disappearance. Also, write a newspaper obituary for the person you chose. Because your purpose for each piece is different, make sure you use appropriate diction and style in both.

COMMON HUMAN EXPERIENCE

For Saint-Exupéry, flight was more than a feeling of exhilaration. It provided spiritual enlightenment. Other works that feature aviators who find freedom and divinity in the air are:

I Was Amelia Earhart (1996), a novel by Jane Mendelsohn. In this book, Mendelsohn writes in the voice of Amelia Earhart, who tells what happened after Earhart and her navigator, Fred Noonan, disappeared off the coast of New Guinea in 1937.

The Spirit of St. Louis (1953), a nonfiction book by Charles A. Lindbergh. Lindbergh won a Pulitzer Prize in 1954 for his account of his adventurous journey across the Atlantic in his single-engine plane.

West with the Night (1942), a memoir by Beryl Markham. British-born adventurer Markham was a horse trainer on her family's farm in Kenya before becoming the only female bush pilot in Africa. In 1936 she achieved fame for being the first woman to fly across the Atlantic solo from west to east.

---

3. What distinguishes children from adults in *The Little Prince*? Do you think the difference is based on age or on something else? Why do you think the little prince wants to return home instead of remaining with the pilot, especially given their friendship? Create a presentation based on your findings and conclusions.

4. While some characters in *The Little Prince* see Drawing Number One as a hat, others think it illustrates an elephant inside a boa constrictor. What is the meaning and significance of these different perspectives? What view do you have? Write a paper that offers your interpretation.

BIBLIOGRAPHY

Books

Rumbold, Richard, and Lady Margaret Stewart. *The Winged Life: A Portrait of Antoine de Saint-Exupéry, Poet and Airman*. New York: McKay, 1953.

Schiff, Stacy. *Saint-Exupéry: A Biography*. New York: Knopf, 1994.

Smith, Maxwell A. *Knight of the Air: The Life and Works of Antoine de Saint-Exupéry*. London: Pageant, 1956.

Periodicals

Schiff, Stacy. "Saint-Exupéry Lands at Last." *New York Times*, April 11, 2004.

Shattuck, Kathryn. "A Prince Eternal." *New York Times*, April 3, 2005.

Web Sites

"Antoine de Saint-Exupéry." Books and Writers. Retrieved April 14, 2008, from http://www.kirjasto.sci.fi/exupery.htm.

◈ Saki

BORN: *1870, Akyab, Burma*

DIED: *1916, Beaumont-Hamel, France*

NATIONALITY: *French*

GENRE: *Fiction*

MAJOR WORKS:
Reginald in Russia (1910)
The Chronicles of Clovis (1912)
Beasts and Super-Beasts (1914)
The Watched Pot (1914)

Overview

The reputation of Hector Hugh Munro (pen name: Saki) rests primarily on his short stories, which convey whimsical humor, fascination with the odd and eerie, and worldly disillusionment with hypocrisy and banality. Written between the end of Queen Victoria's reign and the beginning of World War I, Munro's works memorialize the luxurious world of the upper class. The stories present characters who, through capriciousness or eccentric behavior, get into odd situations from which they usually escape by means of their quick wits; at the same time, their clever remarks and cynical views expose the arbitrariness and artificiality of their society.

Works in Biographical and Historical Context

From the Far East to Victorian England Munro was born in the Far East, where his father was a colonel in the British military police. Upon the death of his mother, Munro and his two siblings were sent to live with their grandmother and aunts in Devon, England. The aunts, Charlotte and Augusta, squabbled endlessly over trivialities, involved the children in their petty jealousies, and enforced on their young charges a strict Victorian regimen. Munro, being the youngest, quite delicate and pale, escaped the worst of the aunts' tyranny, and he soon became adept at devising ways to bend their inflexible and contradictory rules. Reginald, Clovis Sangrail, and Comus Bassington, witty and self-absorbed comic heroes in Munro's future work as Saki, clearly developed from his own experiences.

Government Service When Munro was seventeen years old, his father retired and returned to England to look after his nearly grown children. Over the next few years, they traveled as a family throughout the Continent. Munro followed in his father's footsteps and subsequently spent about a year as part of the Indian Imperial Police in Burma. He returned to England in 1894 because of failing health. He worked at the British Museum and published only a short story, "Dogged," during the next six years. Munro wrote a historical study, *The Rise of the Russian Empire*, in 1900 and, from 1902 to 1909, was a foreign correspondent for the *Morning Post* in the Balkans and Paris.

Career as a Writer While working as a foreign correspondent, Munro published his first collection of stories, titled *Reginald* (1904). In 1910, his second collection of short fiction was published, misleadingly titled *Reginald in Russia*—only the title story concerns Reginald. The rest of the tales continue Saki's satiric examination of upper-class country life or venture into fable-like lessons. This successful collection was followed by *The Chronicles of Clovis* (1912), which introduced two of his more popular characters, Clovis Sangrail and Bertie Van Tahn.

In 1912, Munro published a novel, *The Unbearable Bassington*, whose hero, Comus Bassington, resembles Reginald with an undeniable mean streak. Munro continued writing stories for newspapers. These works were

H. H. Munro, also known as, Saki   *Munro, H. H., aka Saki, photograph. Source unknown.*

collected in *Beasts and Super-Beasts* (1914); as the title suggests, animal stories take up a large part of the collection. Munro's second novel, *When William Came: A Story of London under the Hohenzollerns* (1914), is a fantasy about life in England under German occupation led by Kaiser Wilhelm. It is one of the first examples of "invasion literature," a genre that emerged with the onset of World War I and dealt with the anxieties of invading foreign powers.

The Watched Pot and Other Drama Although he is best known for his fiction, drama seems to be the genre best suited to Munro's abilities. His plays show his strengths—witty dialogue, complexity of plot, and energetic pace—to advantage, while his weaknesses, which appear in his fiction as gratuitous witticisms and pompous asides in the narrative, are absent. For example, in 1914, he wrote *The Watched Pot*, a comedy of manners centered on several women who are determined to marry a wealthy man and are thwarted by his territorial aunt.

World War I Less than a month after war was declared in early August 1914, Munro enlisted in the cavalry. Munro saw the declaration of war as a chance to act nobly and heroically in an unquestionably good cause. Hoping to get into the fighting more quickly, Munro transferred into the infantry, joining the Royal Fusiliers. He enjoyed being a soldier, hiking for miles with heavy backpacks, serving long hours as camp orderly, and expressing contempt for those who had not enlisted. Proud of his ability to keep up with much younger men, Munro rose to the rank of corporal and eventually lance sergeant, but he refused offers of a commission as an officer, content to be a simple soldier among his comrades.

He was shipped off to France in 1915, and his wit and macabre sense of humor survived the horrific conditions he found on the battlefield. In her "Biography of Saki," Ethel Munro recalled that at Christmas 1915 her brother sent her this version of a carol: "While Shepherds watched their flocks by night / All seated on the ground / A high-explosive shell came down / And mutton rained around."

In June 1916, Munro spent a short leave in London with his sister and brother. He then returned to the front to fight in several battles, during which time he suffered a return of his old malaria. On November 14, he received a fatal wound while in no man's land during a night march. Two collections of Munro's stories appeared posthumously, *The Toys of Peace* (1919) and *The Square Egg* (1924).

Works in Literary Context

Respected as a master of the short story during his own lifetime, Munro has been ranked with the Frenchman Guy de Maupassant and the American O. Henry as a craftsman of the first order. As A. J. Langguth has pointed out in *Saki: A Life of Hector Hugh Munro, With Six Short Stories Never Before Collected*, some of Munro's

---

LITERARY AND HISTORICAL CONTEMPORARIES

Saki's famous contemporaries include:

Wilhelm II (1859–1941): The last German kaiser (emperor), Wilhelm reversed the careful diplomacy of his grandfather Wilhelm I and his advisor Otto von Bismarck in favor of a more forceful, bellicose policy. These changes upset the diplomatic of the European powers and led to the outbreak of World War I. At the end of the war, he abdicated the throne and lived out his life in exile.

L. Frank Baum (1856–1919): American author of children's fantasy, Baum is most noted for the Oz series, which began with the classic *The Wonderful Wizard of Oz* (1900).

Theodore Roosevelt (1858–1919): The twenty-sixth President of the United States and a leading Progressive politician, Roosevelt made a name for himself with his exploits as a soldier and naturalist. His larger-than-life personality made him a popular and much-admired public figure; the teddy bear was created in his honor.

Hermann Hesse (1877–1962): A German author, Hesse wrote about the pursuit of enlightenment in such books as *Siddhartha* (1922) and *Journey to the East* (1932). These themes led to a revival of interest in his work among American counterculture readers during the 1960s.

W. B. Yeats (1865–1939): The first Irishman to win the Nobel Prize for Literature, Yeats stands as one of the central figures of Irish literature in the twentieth century. Both his poetry and his work with the Abbey Theatre as dramatist and manager were hugely influential in their respective fields.

---

efforts reflect the influence of the master of the trick ending, O. Henry. However, Saki's stories are not innocent or sentimental like O. Henry's, but mix wit with outrageousness, humor with seemingly justified malice.

Wit and Irony, with a Touch of Lyric Epigrammatic wit, a strong dramatic sense, and a satiric concern with the ironies of social life mark Munro's stories, in which the traditions of the comedy of manners give dialogues central importance. However, in turning to the uncanny, Munro at times moved beyond satire altogether, yet even then he often returned to irony and further extended the comedy of manners by transforming the supernatural and the animal into subjects of a social wit. The descriptive developments in Munro's later fiction likewise accommodate a pervasive sense of the ironies of human life—even if a lyrical voice emerges briefly, at the end, from the battlefield.

Suppressed Sexuality Significantly, women in Munro's work are usually hateful guardian aunts or elderly duchesses; they only rarely are young attractive girls of sexual interest to the main characters. Munro remained a bachelor throughout his life, and this fact, plus some suggestiveness in his work, has led modern readers to conclude he was homosexual. Moreover, rumors of Munro's homosexuality circulated in publishing circles during his lifetime. But sexuality is kept far below the surface in Munro's work. While the artist in Munro learned much from Oscar Wilde's writing, he also may have learned from Wilde's notorious trial and imprisonment in 1895—which concerned Wilde's homosexuality—what kind of public behavior would not be tolerated by English society.

Fairy Tale Cruelty? Readers and critics often mention the apparent cruelty and heartlessness in Munro's stories. Writing in 1940 in the *Atlantic Monthly*, Elizabeth Drew explained and justified this lack of fellow feeling: "The cruelty is certainly there, but it has nothing perverted or pathological about it.... It is the genial heartlessness of the normal child, whose fantasies take no account of adult standards of human behaviour, and to whom the eating of a gypsy by a hyena is no more terrible than the eating of Red Ridinghood's grandmother by a wolf. The standards of these gruesome tales

are those of the fairy tale; their grimness is the grimness of Grimm.... He deliberately chose a pseudonym for his writings—Saki, the cupbearer whose 'joyous errand' was to serve the guests with wine in the *Rubaiyat* of Omar Khayyam. He never sought intimacy with his readers, or gave them his confidence." To see the cruelty in Saki as fantasy, and to set it next to the unsparing details of nursery rhymes and fairy tales, is to understand that even though in Saki's stories terribly unfair things happen, he provides a satisfying sense of justice done and human decency restored that can appeal to children and adults alike.

Influence Popular and respected as a master of the short story during his lifetime, throughout the twentieth century Saki has been ranked with the Frenchman Guy de Maupassant and the American O. Henry as a craftsman of the first order. Funny, original, sometimes bizarre, and at times creepily frightening, Saki's work clearly has left its mark on the British writer P. G. Wodehouse, whose farcical stories of well-heeled, empty-headed young men about town are reminiscent of the Reginald stories. The world of Wodehouse's characters Bertie and Jeeves is essentially the same as that of Reginald and Clovis. In these worlds, it is always about the turn of the century; England is the unquestioned center of the universe; life has been made comfortable for one by others; and a young man need only think about his social life, the quality of the food, drink, and entertainment provided, and the fun he can dream up.

Works in Critical Context

Some literary critics in the 1960s and 1970s argued that there is a serious side to Munro that goes beyond mere entertainment to explore weighty moral issues. Certainly some of his stories can be analyzed to discover serious concerns. But it would be misleading to maintain that Saki's greatness rests on the breadth of his moral imagination. For better or worse, his genius resides in his stories, in which the qualities defined by Coward as "the verbal adroitness of Saki's dialogue and the brilliance of his wit" shine most brightly.

Perhaps responding to the strain of seriousness in Munro's writings, the English critic J. W. Lambert, in a 1956 essay in the *Listener*, noted Saki's affinities to Kipling and to two other English writers, William Makepeace Thackeray and, surprisingly, George Orwell: "All four had Anglo-Indian backgrounds and divided childhoods. They were all fascinated by the social display and organization of life 'at home'; their works [express] the colonial mentality, a little disappointed, sometimes more than a little embittered. Thackeray's self-conscious moralizing bubbled up often in Saki; so did Kipling's emotional afflatus.... The same feelings, in different generations, drove Orwell to prodigies of bleak panache and turned his snobberies upside down, and drove Saki in 1914 not only to join the Army when well over age but consistently to refuse a commission."

Responses to Literature

1. Contrast Munro's use of irony to that of O. Henry's. Choose a story from each author that features an ironic twist or ending and, in an essay, discuss how their literary techniques—in both the build-up to and the payoff of the ironic twist—are similar and different.

2. With a classmate, discuss how Munro's journalistic experience seems to inform his literary style. Use examples from a text to support your ideas.

3. Choose two Munro stories that feature eerie or supernatural elements. In an essay, analyze his use of these elements in his story and compare them to supernatural elements used in two stories by H. P. Lovecraft, another master of short horror.

4. With a classmate, discuss the significance of the hyena in Munro's "Esme." What do you feel the author is satirizing in this tale? Report your findings to the rest of the class.

BIBLIOGRAPHY

Books

Gillen, Charles H. *H. H. Munro (Saki)*, Boston: Twayne, 1969.

Langguth, A. J., *Saki: A Life of Hector Hugh Munro, With Six Short Stories Never Before Collected*, New York: Simon & Schuster, 1981.

Ullmann, Carol, ed. "The Interlopers." *Short Stories for Students*, vol. 15. Detroit: Gale, 2002.

Wilson, Kathleen, ed. "The Open Window." *Short Stories for Students*, vol. 1. Detroit: Gale, 1997.

Periodicals

Atlantic Monthly (July 1940).

English Literature in Transition, vol. 9, no. 1(1966), vol. 11, no. 1 (1968).

Modern British Literature, vol. 4 (1979).

New York Times (August 25, 1981).

Spectator (May 30, 1952; December 21, 1956).

Times Literary Supplement (November 21, 1963; May 13, 1989).

◈ George Sand

BORN: *1804, Paris, France*

DIED: *1876, Nohant, France*

NATIONALITY: *French*

GENRE: *Fiction, nonfiction*

MAJOR WORKS:

Consuelo (1842)

The Devil's Pool (1846)

La Petite Fadette (1849)

She and He (1859)

Le Marquis de Villemer (1860)

Overview

George Sand was a celebrated yet controversial French writer whose personal life oftentimes overshadowed her creative production. Known for its blend of romance and realism, her writing was effortlessly spontaneous and prolific without sacrificing style and form. Sand stated that the primary happiness in life was to be in love, and so she focused on relationships in most of her novels as she tackled the complexities of politics, society, and gender.

Works in Biographical and Historical Context

Aristocratic Upbringing in Berry Sand was born Armandine Aurore Lucille Dupin in Paris on July 1, 1804, to parents from very different backgrounds. Her father, Maurice Dupin, was an aristocratic soldier, while her mother, Sophie Delaborde, was the daughter of a bird trainer. After her father's death, the four-year-old Sand was entrusted to her paternal grandmother at the family estate of Nohant in Berry, a historical region in France that would later be the setting of several of her novels.

George Sand *Mansell / Time Life Pictures / Getty Images*

Reached Maturity in Paris When her grandmother died, Sand, then seventeen, was reclaimed by her mother and taken to Paris. At eighteen, Sand married Casimir Dudevant, a local army officer, and later gave birth to two children. Unmoved by her coarse, unromantic husband, Sand grew restless and left her husband and children in 1831 to pursue aspirations of a literary career in Paris. Because divorce in France was illegal at this time, she battled in court for a legal separation that included property rights and custody of one of her children. She eventually prevailed, and Michel de Bourges, who advised her during her legal proceedings, became her lover. Supportive of her strength of character, Bourges persuaded Sand to express herself politically. His influence colored the remainder of Sand's writing, which increasingly reflected her feminist and political concerns.

The failure of the 1830 revolution in France had coincided with the failure of Sand's marriage. The three-day 1830 revolution saw the removal of King Charles X, an ultraroyalist who had ruled since 1824. Charles wanted to restore the absolute powers of the monarchy and the supremacy of the Catholic Church. Leftist forces allied with the upper bourgeoisie to replace Charles with Louis Philippe of the house of Orléans as a "citizen-king," who agreed to be ruled by the desires of the rising industrial plutocracy.

An Unconventional Woman Free from the social restrictions of marriage, Sand actively pursued life as a writer, moving in literary circles, selling articles, and being mentored by writers, such as Henri de Latouche and Charles Sainte-Beuve. Sand began an affair with Jules Sandeau, a young intellectual who embraced an exciting life that took advantage of Paris's cultural offerings. Encouraged by her daring partner, Sand began dressing as a man to gain access to venues that were usually closed to women.

Though the identity of the young cross-dresser was soon public knowledge, Sand enjoyed shocking the Parisian cultural scene and continued to elicit gossip with her dress and her habit of smoking in public (considered scandalous for a woman). While these actions endangered her reputation, they also gained her literary and social fame. Inspired by Sandeau's own literary output, she continued to write, collaborating with Sandeau and eventually publishing her first solo novel, *Indiana* (1832), under the male pseudonym George Sand.

Failure in Love Affects Writing Jealous of her success, Sandeau broke with Sand, who was thrust into a period of despair. Disillusioned with men and love, she wrote *Leila* (1833), a novel exploring women's inability to follow their true desires. Soon after, she began a relationship with a young poet, Alfred de Musset, and joined him in his travels throughout Italy.

Sand, a would-be anarchist, candidly admitted that she hated all political factions and said that had she been born a man, she would be dangerous. Shortly after the failed 1830 revolution she wrote *Une Conspiration en 1537*, in which she dramatized the anarchist she herself could not be: the Renaissance prince Lorenzo de Medici, who assassinated his cousin Duke Alexander de Medici of Florence in 1537. When Sand gave Musset *Une Conspiration en 1537* as a gift in 1833, Musset rewrote the play into his masterpiece, *Lorenzaccio* (1834), preserving Sand's main characters and events.

Lovers Abroad Though her liaison with Musset ended when she fell in love with the doctor who was tending to Musset during an illness, Sand's time in Italy with Musset sparked her first autobiographical writing, a series of Italian travel vignettes published as *Letters of a Traveler* in 1847. With a talent for observation, Sand explored the nature of travel and the customs of Italy through a series of vivid portrayals of cultural life abroad.

For nine years, Frédéric Chopin was Sand's next famous lover. During Sand and Chopin's time together in relative seclusion in Majorca, Spain, both artists enjoyed a period of great creative productivity. Sand completed another novel before turning to a literary investigation of socialism, a growing movement in the nineteenth century that criticized the Industrial Revolution for creating inequality and poverty while advocating for the even distribution of wealth. Her dream for a more egalitarian society was reflected in *Horace* (1842). Sand, who believed that country people had a better understanding of democracy, idealized provincial life, an approach that would influence writers from Thomas Hardy to Leo Tolstoy. However, her provincial idealism also gained criticism for its patronizing tone and its rustic, historically inaccurate portrayals.

Autobiographical Novel Sand's next work demonstrated a more autobiographical feel. Though she denied it was drawn from her own life, her 1859 novel *She and He* depicts her tumultuous relationship with Musset. The work was immediately attacked for its depiction of Musset, who had died two years earlier, and Sand was criticized for using men to her advantage. *She and He* even provoked Musset's brother to write a novel in response, and *Lui et Elle* (He and She) appeared just six weeks after Sand''s book.

Though Sand was criticized for her "unfeminine" affairs and her carefree, dismissive attitude toward convention, she was still held in high regard, and her 1860 novel *Le Marquis de Villemer* appeared to great fanfare. Along with several of Sand's other works, it was later adapted for the stage. As a result, Sand began writing plays with rustic settings, creations that were extremely popular and reinvented Sand in the eyes of French society.

Retired to Nohant After her 1872 retirement from the world of Paris theater, Sand settled at the family estate in Nohant. There, she spent time caring for her granddaughters, for whom she wrote several stories and novels emphasizing self-confidence, acceptance, and change. She grew less concerned with politics, preferring to enjoy the company of family and friends, including authors Gustave Flaubert and Ivan Turgenev. After suffering from a stomach ailment that was most likely cancer, Sand died in her bedroom on June 9, 1876.

Works in Literary Context

Social Explorations Sand is best known for bold statements about the rights of women in nineteenth-century society, her exploration of contemporary social and philosophical issues, and her depiction of the lives and language of French provincials. Each period of her literary career focused on specific themes and had its own set of influences. Her rustic novels are perhaps the truest representation of her form as an author.

Rebellion Against Marriage The works of her first period reflect her rebellion against the bonds of marriage and deal largely with the relationships between men and women. Clearly influenced by English poet Lord Byron and French philosopher Jean-Jacques Rousseau, Sand wrote romantic novels full of passionate personal revolt and ardent feminism, attitudes that went against societal conventions and outraged her early British and American critics. These early novels, including *Indiana*, *Lelia*, and *Jacques* (1834), were extremely successful and established Sand as an important literary voice for her generation.

Philosophical Concerns The works of Sand's second period—such novels as *Consuelo* (1842–1843) and *The Miller of Angibault* (1845)—reveal Sand's increasing concern with contemporary social and philosophical problems. These novels were strongly influenced by French philosopher and politician Pierre Leroux and deal specifically with humanitarianism, Christian socialism, and republicanism. Considered by many to be her least credible works, their tone is often didactic and their plots obviously contrived.

Pastoral Novels Sand's pastoral novels, which depict rural scenes and peasant characters, form the last phase of her career. Set in Berry, where she grew up, *The Haunted Marsh* (1846) and *Francis the Waif* (1847–1848) were inspired by her love of the French countryside and her sympathy with the peasants. Realistic in background detail and distinguished by their gentle idealism, these pastoral works are considered by many critics to be Sand's finest novels. Although she continued writing until her death, few of the works written after her pastoral period are remembered today.

Influence Sand's work is recognized as an important step in the development of the French novel, influencing writers like George Eliot and Thomas Hardy with their provincial idealization and portrayal of rustic lifestyles. An admired colleague of Victor Hugo and Alexandre

Dumas, Sand was also an inspiration to Gustave Flaubert, with whom she had a meaningful literary friendship. Opposites in most every regard, she and Flaubert shared ongoing intellectual arguments over their conflicting literary philosophies.

Works in Critical Context

Considering the moral climate during her lifetime and her open defiance of social standards, it is not surprising that Sand became better known for her personal life than for her literary accomplishments. From the onset of her career, Sand's flamboyant lifestyle colored serious critical evaluation of her work. Reception to Sand's literature was oftentimes hostile, with critics dismissing her "adolescent" work based on what they perceived to be her lack of morality.

Criticism through the Years When several of her novels were adapted for the stage, Sand enjoyed great popular success, and many of her books were reissued to a receptive audience. In spite of this, much of Sand's work was dismissed as autobiographical and beneath literary notice. After her death in 1876, Sand's literary popularity declined. There is evidence that Sand's most

COMMON HUMAN EXPERIENCE

Sand's novels idealized country life as simple, democratic, and egalitarian. Here are other works of literature and art that explore pastoral life:

Lyrical Ballads (1798), a poetry collection by William Wordsworth and Samuel Taylor Coleridge. Wordsworth and Coleridge were major figures in the Romantic movement. Romantic poetry often featured pastoral figures such as milkmaids and shepherds.

So Big (1924), a novel by Edna Ferber. Ferber's novel, which won a Pulitzer Prize in 1925 and has been adapted for film multiple times, follows the life of a young woman of Dutch descent living in an Illinois farming community.

Sunrise (1927), a film by F. W. Murnau. This movie shows a man's reconciliation with his country wife after his affair with a city woman.

ardent attackers could have been motivated by gender bias, professional or personal jealousy, or genuine aversion to her art and politics. Whatever their driving force, Sand's critics succeeded in diminishing her accomplishment, and she fell into obscurity. Sand's work was rediscovered in the 1950s and began to receive serious attention from feminist critics who have since redefined her place in the French literary canon.

Indiana Marked by Sand's critique of marriage and her incipient feminism, *Indiana* outraged some early British and American critics, but was extremely popular with the general reading public, prompting early reviewers to speculate about the author's sex by identifying both masculine and feminine qualities in the novel's language and characterizations. More recently, critics have argued the extent to which *Indiana* can be interpreted as a feminist novel, and many have studied Sand's manipulation of conventional gender categories through her transformations of Ralph and Raymon. The work has also been read as a critique of bourgeois domesticity and its circumscription of women within the household or private sphere. Modern scholarship has also noted that Sand crafted the central personalities in *Indiana* from stock characters of romance. Raymon, for example, is a Don Juan type.

Many critics have offered interpretations of the novel, including Carol V. Richards. In *George Sand Papers: Conference Proceedings, 1978*, Richards interprets the novel as "not the failure of love . . . but the triumph of an ideal love which wins for the heroine the happiness she missed in her loveless marriage."

Responses to Literature

1. Sand's scandalous personal life often influenced public reception of her novels. Can you think of other public figures who are known more for their lifestyles than their work? Write an essay that compares such figures to Sand.

2. Sand's childhood in rural France doubtlessly influenced her pastoral novels. In what ways does Sand's work fit into the broader tradition of pastoral art? Create a presentation that demonstrates this link.

3. Though Sand publicly denounced marriage and scorned tradition in her personal life, she was ambiguous as to whether women should have the right to vote. In a paper, address the following questions: Do you think this fact influences whether Sand should be considered a feminist writer? Why or why not? What reasons can you think of for Sand's ambivalence in regard to this monumental issue in women's rights?

4. Sand's pen name was adopted from the last name of her lover. Research the origins of other famous pen names such as Lewis Carroll or Mark Twain. Create a pseudonym for yourself and explain why you chose that particular name in a paper.

5. Sand's personal relationships with literary and cultural figures influenced her work and life. In an essay, address these questions. Can you find common characteristics that her lovers shared? Why do you think Sand seemed not to stay in love with one person for long? How is such behavior classified in the realm of psychology?

BIBLIOGRAPHY

Books

Crecelius, Kathryn J. *Family Romances: George Sand's Early Novels.* Bloomington: Indiana University Press, 1987.

Dickinson, Donna. *George Sand: A Brave Man, the Most Womanly Woman.* Oxford, U.K.: Berg, 1988.

Richards, Carol V. "Structural Motifs and the Limits of Feminism in *Indiana*." In *George Sand Papers: Conference Proceedings, 1978.* Edited by Natalie Datlof et al. New York: AMS Press, 1982.

Schermerhorn, Elizabeth W. *The Seven Strings of the Lyre: The Romantic Life of George Sand.* Whitefish, Mont.: Kessinger, 2003.

Seyd, Felicia. *Romantic Rebel: The Life and Times of George Sand.* New York: Viking, 1940.

Web Sites

The George Sand Association. Retrieved March 16, 2008, from http://people.hofstra.edu/david_a_powell/gsa.

◨ Sappho

BORN: *Between 630 and 612 BCE, Lesbos, Greece*

DIED: *c. 570 BCE, Lesbos, Greece*

NATIONALITY: *Greek*

GENRE: *Poetry*

MAJOR WORKS:

*Sappho: A Garland; the Poems and Fragments of
Sappho* (1993)

Overview

Regarded by ancient commentators as the equal of
Homer, the ancient Greek poet Sappho expressed human
emotions with honesty, courage, and skill. Sappho has
been the subject of controversy, and most of her work has
been lost over the centuries or deliberately destroyed. It is
clear from the existing verses, however, that she deserved
her reputation, and her work warrants continued study
and appreciation.

Works in Biographical and Historical Context

Native of Lesbos Very few details of Sappho's life
survive, and many classicists note that these accounts have

Sappho *Sappho, photograph. The Library of Congress.*

been thoroughly interwoven with legend, myth, and sup-
position. The only standard—but unreliable—source of
information about Sappho is the *Suidas*, a Greek lexicon
compiled at around the end of the tenth century. Based
on earlier lexicons, scholarly commentaries, and excerpts
from the works of historians, grammarians, and biographers, the *Suidas* records that Sappho was a native of
Lesbos, an island northeast of Athens in the Aegean
Sea, and that she was probably born in either the city of
Eresus or Mytilene. Her father's name is given as Sca-
mandronymus and her mother's as Cleis. Evidence also
suggests that Sappho had three brothers and that her
family belonged to the upper class. According to traditional accounts, she lived briefly in Sicily around 600 BCE,
having been forced into exile by political strife on Lesbos.

After returning to her homeland, Sappho married a
wealthy man named Cercylas, had a daughter named
Cleis, and spent the rest of her life in Mytilene. There
she organized and ran a *thiasos*, or academy for unmarried
young women. The school was devoted to the cult of
Aphrodite and Eros, where beauty and grace were held as
the highest values. Ancient commentary attests that this
thiasos ranked as one of the best, and Sappho enjoyed
great renown as its dedicated teacher and spiritual leader.
Some legends of Sappho's life indicate that she lived to
old age, but others relate that she fell hopelessly in love
with Phaon, a young sailor, and, disappointed by their
failed love affair, leaped to her death from a high cliff—a
story that has been largely discredited by modern
scholars.

The Tenth Muse In antiquity, Sappho was regularly
counted among the greatest of poets and was often
referred to as "the Poetess," just as Homer was called
"the Poet." Plato hailed her as "the tenth Muse," and
she was honored on coins and with civic statuary. Her
principal work consisted of nine books, which the grammarians of Alexandria arranged according to meter. The
earliest surviving texts date from the third century BCE
Because the first book contained 1,320 lines, it can be
surmised that Sappho left approximately 12,000 lines,
700 of which have survived, pieced together from several
sources. Only one complete poem remains, quoted by
Dionysius of Halicarnassus, the rest ranging in completeness from several full lines to one word. Many of the lines
lack beginning, middle, or end because they have survived on mummy wrapping in Egyptian tombs, the papyrus having been ripped crosswise of the roll, lengthwise of
the poem. The long rolls of papyrus, made from the stalks
of a water plant, also survived in battered condition in the
dry Egyptian climate in garbage dumps and as stuffing in
the mouths of mummified crocodiles.

In 1898 knowledge of Sappho's works increased
dramatically when scholars discovered third-century BCE
papyri containing additional verse fragments. In 1914
archaeologists excavating cemeteries in Oxyrhynchus,
Egypt, unearthed papier-mache coffins composed of

LITERARY AND HISTORICAL CONTEMPORARIES

Sappho's famous contemporaries include:

Nebuchadrezzar II (630–562 BCE): The Babylonian king who plays a significant part in the biblical *Book of Daniel*, Nebuchadrezzar II is also remembered for the construction of the Hanging Gardens of Babylon.

Solon (638–558 BCE): Credited with laying the foundations of Athenian democracy, Solon's reforms were brought about by a crisis in the Athenian city-state during the 590s. Solon opened up Athenian politics to a wider range of citizens and strengthened the city's economic and social structures.

Zedekiah (sixth century BCE): The last king of Judah, Zedekiah was installed by Nebuchadnezzar II as a puppet ruler but led his country in revolt against Babylon.

Anaximander (610–546 BCE): A Greek pre-Socratic philosopher, Anaximander was one of the first Greek thinkers to place primary importance on science and mathematics; his teachings would bear fruit in his protégé Pythagoras, who would espouse a philosophy that "all was number."

scraps of paper containing fragments of literary writings, including some by Sappho. These findings sparked renewed interest in Sappho and inspired new critical studies of her texts.

Scandalous Love Poet Sappho's works have been admired for their stylistic merit from her own time onward, and while her literary merit remains secure, Sappho's personal reputation has been controversial even to the point of sometimes overshadowing her status as a poet. Her passionate verses and attitudes toward love have attracted a great deal of attention and garnered rumors about her sexual preference. In fact, the opinion that Sappho's sexual orientation was lesbian is so entrenched that the term itself is derived from the name of her homeland.

Works in Literary Context

Lyric Poetry Sappho wrote poetry at a time when Greek literature was dominated by the influence of Homer and the epic narrative. Yet the tradition of lyric poetry was even older and had played an important part in Greek history. During Sappho's time, lyric poetry enjoyed a successful revival. Sappho seems to have been not only familiar with Homer but also with the poets Terpander and Alcaeus, both from Mytilene, and Archilochus, a poet from the nearby island of Paros. As was typical of Greek lyric poetry in general, Sappho's verses

were highly personal, conveying deeply felt emotion in a simple, translucent style. Her emphasis was on emotion, on subjective experience, and on the individual.

Sappho's Love Songs Music, too, as in all early Greek lyric poetry, served an important function in her works: Most of Sappho's poems are monodies, songs composed for solo singers and intended to be sung to the accompaniment of the lyre. Much of Sappho's poetry commemorated a certain event taking place in her *thiasos*, but she also composed narrative poetry, hymns, and epithalamia, or marriage songs. Sources from antiquity have recorded that Sappho was especially famous for the latter and that she was a frequent guest at weddings where she would sing a song composed especially for the couple. Scholars contend that Sappho's epithalamia raised this ancient folk tradition to a new level of artistic excellence.

Highly Personal Voice Most commentators regard her eloquence, the individual voice revealing itself and communicating with the reader, as the hallmark of Sappho's style. The speaker in the poems, generally assumed to be Sappho herself, displays a wide range of emotion, from tender protectiveness and friendship to erotic longing and jealousy; from playful chiding of her pupils to extreme anger toward those who have proven disloyal; and outright vilification of the headmistress of a rival *thiasos*. Scholars also praise Sappho's ability to analyze her feelings even as she is enacting them, sacrificing none of the immediacy and intensity of the moment but demonstrating remarkable insight into her own situation. Commentators emphasize, however, that the spontaneous tone of Sappho's verse is deliberate rather than accidental.

Sapphic Meter Although she employed a less refined language, Sappho's poetry evinces an innate verbal elegance, the result of her writing in the melodic Aeolic dialect and of her development of the graceful Sapphic meter. Consisting of four lines, the Sapphic verse form calls for three lines of eleven syllables each and a fourth line of five syllables. This construction dictates the use of three spondees (a foot composed of two accented syllables) in each line, with variations allowed in the fourth and eleventh syllables of the first three lines, and in the final syllable of the fourth line. It is unknown whether Sappho invented the meter that bears her name, but she probably perfected and popularized it; thus, it clearly came to be connected with her.

Works in Critical Context

Many critics consider Sappho the greatest female poet of the classical world and the most accomplished and influential of a group of lyric poets who were active in Greece between 650 BCE and 450 BCE—a period often designated the Lyric Age of Greece. Although little remains of her work, Sappho's poetry has been acclaimed since antiquity for its emotional intensity, directness, simplicity, and revealing personal tone. It has also been the subject of much critical controversy, however, with various scholars debating the precise nature of the eroticism typical of Sappho's verses.

Influential Muse Throughout the centuries, Sappho has remained a fascinating subject for poets, novelists, dramatists, and biographers. David M. Robinson claimed, "[N]early every thought in her fragments…has been borrowed or adapted by some ancient Greek or Roman poet or some modern poet in English, Italian, French, German, or modern Greek." Despite the fact that only a minuscule portion of Sappho's canon remains, fragments of her verses continue to have a powerful effect on readers and critics alike. Guy Davenport, one of Sappho's most prominent translators, remarked that "many of the fragments are mere words and phrases, but they were once a poem and, like broken statuary, are strangely articulate in their ruin."

Willis Barnstone, another eminent translator of Sappho's works, observed that "there is no veil between poet and reader. . . . Sappho makes the lyric poem a refined and precise instrument for revealing her personal and intense experience of life." For example, unlike her literary counterparts, who mainly depict their immediate natural surroundings, Sappho concentrates instead on how such scenes affect her emotionally and on the associations it calls forth in her. She uses the same direct and personal tone in frankly portraying her attraction to some of the young women in her *thiasos*. While some readers have lauded her passion, eroticism, and lack of self-consciousness, others have faulted it as grossly indelicate.

Modern Reputation In the nineteenth century, Sappho emerged as the symbol of passion, especially among the Romantics. In 1816 the German classicist Friedrich Gottlieb Welcker published "Sappho von einem herrschenden Vorurtheil befreit," an essay that laid to rest controversies surrounding Sappho's personal life and redirected the focus of criticism to her works. During the last two centuries, scholars have concentrated on analyzing the elements of Sappho's style, and studies by such critics as John Addington Symonds, C. M. Bowra, and Hilda Doolittle, among others, now complement the exegeses of Dionysius of Halicarnassus, Plutarch, and Longinus, who, centuries earlier, acknowledged the extraordinary qualities in Sappho's poetry. Yet all assessments of her work remain intrinsically inconclusive because so few of her poems survive. Addressing this difficulty, Peter Green commented that "all study of [Sappho's] work is, must be, a frantic raking over the scrapheap whence some verbal splinter may shine out golden before the darkness closes in once more." As scholarly speculation about the circumstances surrounding Sappho's poetry continues, so does critical admiration and appreciation. Critics unanimously praise Sappho's sincerity, intensity, simple yet effective style, and ability to communicate intimately with the reader. Sappho, as

---

COMMON HUMAN EXPERIENCE

Sappho's love poetry was part of a movement in ancient poetry that began in the sixth century BCE in which attention was turned away from heroic epics and focused on images and metaphors of love. Here are some other works with the same theme:

Love's Season (sixth century BCE), a poem by Ibykos. A transitional work, this love poem does not focus on personal experience but rather describes the actions of the god Aphrodite (here called Kypris) and her son Eros, combining erotic and mythical themes.

Eclogue II (42–35 BCE), a poem by Virgil. The Romans carried forward the tradition of Greek love poetry, as in this, one of the famous Roman poet's well-known bucolic poems, the story of unrequited love between two shepherd boys, a not uncommon theme in ancient poetry.

"Negress" (270 BCE), a poem by Asklepiades. Third-century Alexandria was as cosmopolitan as modern-day Manhattan, with people of many different races and creeds intermingling freely. In this love poem, Asklepiades considers his love for an African woman, rejecting the traditional ancient Greek prejudice against dark skin, turning it into a positive attribute.

Bowra concludes, "stands in her own right as the most gifted woman who has ever written poetry."

Responses to Literature

1. In small groups, read several of Sappho's poems aloud. Then discuss the author's attitudes toward love and intimacy.

2. Express Sappho's veneration of friendship with other women, particularly her daughter.

3. Comment on Sappho's influence on Catullus, Ovid, and other Roman poets.

4. Select at least two or three translations of Sappho's poem "Hymn to Aphrodite" and compare the translations. Note the differences in word choice and discuss the varying connotations that are created with different translations.

BIBLIOGRAPHY

Books

Bowie, Angus M. *The Poetic Dialect of Sappho and Alcaeus.* New York: Ayer Co., 1981.

Doolittle, Hilda (H.D.). *Notes on Thought and Vision & The Wise Sappho.* Ed. Anne Janowitz. San Francisco: City Lights Books, 1982.

Duban, Jeffrey M. *Ancient and Modern Images of Sappho.* Lanham, Mich.: University Press of America, 1983.

Grahn, Judy. *The Highest Apple: Sappho and the Lesbian Poetic Tradition.* San Francisco: Spinsters Ink, 1985.

"Hymn to Aphrodite." *Poetry for Students.* Ed. Anne Marie Hacht. Vol. 20. Detroit: Gale, 2004.

"Lepidopterology." *Poetry for Students.* Ed. Anne Marie Hacht. Vol. 23. Detroit: Gale, 2006.

Snyder, Jane McIntosh. *The Woman and the Lyre: Women Writers in Classical Greece and Rome.* Carbondale: Southern Illinois University Press, 1989.

José Saramago

BORN: *1922, Azinhaga, Portugal*

NATIONALITY: *Portuguese*

GENRE: *Novels, drama*

MAJOR WORKS:
The Year of the Death of Ricardo Reis (1984)
The Stone Raft (1986)

José Saramago   *Saramago, Jose, photograph. AP Images.*

Blindness (1995)
All the Names (1997)
The Double (2004)
Seeing (2006)

Overview

José Saramago is a Portuguese author of fiction, poetry, plays, and essays. An accomplished writer and storyteller, he is most highly regarded for his novels, which vary in theme and subject matter and tend to explore the values and priorities in modern society. Saramago, an outspoken Communist and atheist, is known as the voice of the common person, a role he undertakes with newspaper and radio commentaries as well as in his fiction. He is the first Portuguese-language author to win the Nobel Prize in Literature.

Works in Biographical and Historical Context

A "Wild Radish" of Portugal José Saramago was born on November 16, 1922, to José de Sousa and Maria de Piedade in the provincial town of Azinhaga, Portugal. "Saramago," which is Portuguese for "wild radish," was actually a nickname of his father's family, and it was accidentally included in his name in the registry of births. In 1924, the family moved from the province to the city of Lisbon, which gave Saramago the rare opportunity to receive an education. While in school, where he excelled in all of his subjects, he made time for his grandfather's farm back in Azinhaga, helping to take care of the land. After attending Lisbon's grammar schools, unfortunately, Saramago was forced to drop out due to the family's dwindling finances.

During his teen years, Saramago attended a technical school for mechanics that offered other academic courses on the side. Saramago took full advantage of the opportunity and studied literature and French with the aim of mastering the art of literary translator. Though he never finished formal schooling, he later obtained several honorary doctorates from various universities.

In 1944, Saramago met Ilda Reis, one of Portugal's best engravers, and they had one daughter, Violante. While working mechanical jobs, he wrote and published a short novel, *Land of Sin.* He later traded in his mechanical jobs and worked as an editor for a small Lisbon newspaper. When he lost his job, he turned to translating French manuscripts, and it was not long before he returned to writing his own stories.

Literary Success In 1977, Saramago published what he considers to be his first novel, *Manual of Painting and Calligraphy.* This was followed by two more books in quick succession: *Quasi Objects* (1978) and *Raised from the Ground* (1980). *Raised from the Ground* was well received in literary circles and in the press, earning Saramago some degree of recognition. His 1982 novel, *Memorial do convento* translated into English as *Baltasar and Blimunda*, was the first of his works to be translated and is often ranked foremost among his artistic triumphs.

During the 1980s, Saramago dedicated his time to several more novels: *The Year of the Death of Ricardo Reis* released in 1984, *The Stone Raft* (1986), and *The History of the Siege of Lisbon* (1989).

Offending the Church In 1991, Saramago published *The Gospel According to Jesus Christ*, a novel that was condemned by the Catholic Church. Portugal's conservative government contested the novel's entry into the running for the European Literary Prize under the pretext that the book was offensive to Catholics. Saramago and his second wife, whom he married in 1988, left Lisbon and moved to Lanzarote in the Canary Islands. In 1995, he published the novel *Blindness* and in 1997 *All the Names*. His hard work and perseverance paid big dividends as he went on to win several awards, including the Nobel Prize in Literature in 1998, cementing his reputation as one of Europe's most highly regarded literary figures.

Works in Literary Context

Although Portuguese is spoken in three continents by between 140 million and 200 million people, Saramago was the first writer in that language to win the Nobel Prize in Literature. In 1998, the Nobel Committee presented the award to the seventy-four-year-old Saramago, "who with parables sustained by imagination, compassion and irony continually enables us once again to apprehend an elusory reality," according to the official Nobel Foundation Web site.

Free-Flowing Prose

With his engaging storytelling and a unique style of writing, Saramago has carved himself a niche as one of Europe's most important literary figures. Saramago uses a distinctive narrative voice that is undeniably his own. Stylistically, he uses run-on sentences and pages of endless paragraphs, refusing to follow conventional rules of punctuation. Thematically, he balances dread and hope and portrays human resilience amid unbearable misery.

Fantasy and Parable

Saramago's works often rely upon fantastic elements to tell a tale that illustrates a point or delivers a message. In *The Stone Raft*, for example, the peninsula that contains Spain and Portugal breaks free from Europe and begins drifting across the Atlantic Ocean. In *The Year of the Death of Ricardo Reis*, a fictional persona of Portuguese poet Fernando Pessoa continues living after the poet himself has died. In *Blindness*, nearly all the citizens of an unspecified city are struck by a plague that results in blindness; the novel deals largely with the aftermath, and how the afflicted adjust to a society without sight. In each of these tales, the setting is clearly a realistic world in which an element of fantasy has been introduced.

LITERARY AND HISTORICAL CONTEMPORARIES

Saramago's famous contemporaries include:

Gabriel García Márquez (1927–): Hailing originally from Colombia, García Márquez is one of Latin America's most famous authors; he was recognized for his contribution to twentieth century literature in 1982 when he was awarded the Nobel Prize.

Jorge Luis Borges (1899–1986): This Argentine author was one of Latin America's most original and influential prose writers and poets; his short stories revealed him as one of the great stylists of the Spanish language.

Harold Pinter (1930–): English playwright and author of *The Birthday Party* who received the Nobel Prize in Literature in 2005.

Julio Cortázar (1914–1984): Argentine author famous for his influential postmodern novels and stories, especially *Hopscotch* (1963).

Works in Critical Context

Through the years, José Saramago's works have had a place in Portuguese—and European—literary history, starting with *Raised from the Ground*, which was one of Saramago's first works to earn considerable literary recognition in Portugal. With regard to *Blindness*, Andrew Miller of the *New York Times Book Review* has called it "a clear-eyed and compassionate acknowledgment of things as they are, a quality that can only honestly be termed wisdom." The novel helped Saramago gain the respect of readers and critics alike, laying the foundation for the awards he received later. *The Library Journal*, meanwhile, praised *All the Names*, saying it is "in turns claustrophobic, playful, farcical, and suspenseful." The world immediately took notice of Saramago's unique writing talent, which won him the Nobel Prize for Literature in 1998.

The Double Critical reception of the novel *The Double* was also favorable, with Merle Rubin of the *Los Angeles Times* praising the way it "[intrigues] us, proceeds to entertain, charm and engage, and ultimately manages to disturb." Amanda Hopkinson, writing for *The Independent*, even called it "his most practiced and polished" work, that it is "philosophy and thriller rolled into one with—as ever—a tight cast of characters." Finally, Philip Graham of the *New Leader* considers it as "a deft reworking of a timeless theme and a virtuoso exercise in voice—from a writer who seems to produce masterpiece after masterpiece like clockwork."

Seeing *Seeing* also gained the respect of critics, although some thought that its storytelling "is so hazy that it's hard to see the point," according to Troy

<table>
<tr><td>

COMMON HUMAN EXPERIENCE

Identity formation, or the way in which an individual comes to distinguish his or herself as a separate entity, is a key theme explored in Saramago's novel *The Double*. Other works that explore this theme include:

> *The Life and Opinions of Tristram Shandy, Gentleman* (1759–1767), a novel by Laurence Sterne. Considered by some to be the first postmodern novel, this work purports to tell the story of the protagonist's life, although Tristram struggles to explain himself so much that the telling of his birth is not reached until the third volume of the work.
>
> *Invisible Man* (1952) a novel by Ralph Ellison. This story is about the travels of a narrator, a nameless African American. In the novel, Ellison explores the influences of various cultural and political forces, particularly with regard to race, on identity formation.
>
> *Identity* (1998), a novel by Milan Kundera. In this short work, Kundera explores the questions of identity within the context of romantic love.

</td></tr>
</table>

Patterson of *Entertainment Weekly*, and that, in the words of *Publishers Weekly*, "[t]he allegorical blindness/sight framework is weak and obvious." Jack Shreve of *Library Journal* countered by saying that "Saramago's clear eye for acknowledging things as they are barrages us with valuable insights suggesting that the dynamics of human governance are not as rational as we like to think." Also, Sarah Goldman of *Salon* maintains that Saramago "is a deliberate, attentive writer; he knows exactly what his words mean, and all of them—despite what he may have thought more than a half-century ago—are completely worthwhile." Finally, Julian Evans of *The Independent* recalled that no novel has told more "with such arresting humor and simplicity, about the imposture of the times we live in" as *Seeing* did.

Responses to Literature

1. What questions does Saramago's *The Double* raise about identity while following Tertuliano Maximo Afonso's search for his double? Cite specific examples from the novel.

2. Discuss the role of namelessness in *Blindness*. How is namelessness important to the theme?

3. What role does "stream of consciousness" play in *Blindness*? Why does Saramago choose this particular technique to include in this work?

4. How does Saramago's unconventional use of sentence structure and punctuation affect you as a reader? In a small group, discuss why Saramago would want to break the rules of punctuation. How does his writing style contribute to the themes he addresses?

BIBLIOGRAPHY

Books

Bloom, Harold, ed. *José Saramago*. Philadelphia: Chelsea House, 2005.

———. *The Varieties of José Saramago*. Lisbon: Fundação Luso-Americana, 2002.

Periodicals

Bloom, Harold. "The One with the Beard Is God, the Other Is the Devil." *Portuguese Literary & Cultural Studies* 6 (2001): 155–66.

Costa, Horácio. "Saramago's Construction of Fictional Characters: From Terra do pecado to Baltasar and Blimunda." *Portuguese Literary & Cultural Studies* 6 (2001): 33–48.

Daniel, Mary Lou. "Ebb and Flow: Place as Pretext in the Novels of José Saramago." *Luso-Brazilian Review*, 27 2 (1990): 25–39.

———. "Symbolism and Synchronicity: José Saramago's Jangada de Pedra". *Hispania*, 74 3 (1991): 536–41.

Frier, David. "Ascent and Consent: Hierarchy and Popular Emancipation in the Novels of José Saramago". *Bulletin of Hispanic Studies*, 71 1 (1994): 125–138.

———. "In the Beginning Was the Word: Text and Meaning in Two Dramas by José Saramago." *Portuguese Studies* 14 (1998): 215–26.

———. "José Saramago's Stone Boat: Celtic Analogues and Popular Culture." *Portuguese Studies* 15 (1999): 194–206.

———. "Writing Wrongs, Re-Writing Meaning and Reclaiming the City in Saramago's Blindness and All the Names." *Portuguese Literary & Cultural Studies* 6 (2001): 97–122.

Krabbenhoft, Kenneth. "Saramago, Cognitive Estrangement, and Original Sin?" *Portuguese Literary & Cultural Studies* 6 (2001): 123–36.

Martins. "José Saramago's Historical Fiction." *Portuguese Literary & Cultural Studies* 6 (2001): 49–72.

Maurya, Vibha. "Construction of Crowd in Saramago's Texts." *Colóquio/Letras* 151–152 (1999): 267–278.

Sabine, Mark J. L. "Once but No Longer the Prow of Europe: National Identity and Portuguese Destiny in José Saramago's The Stone Raft." *Portuguese Literary & Cultural Studies* 6 (2001): 185–203.

Tesser, Carmen Chaves, ed. "A Tribute to José Saramago." *Hispania*, 82 1 (1999): 1–28.

Jean-Paul Sartre

BORN: *1905, Paris, France*

DIED: *1980, Paris, France*

NATIONALITY: *French*

GENRE: *Nonfiction (philosophy), novels, drama, criticism*

MAJOR WORKS:

Nausea (1938)

Being and Nothingness (1943)

No Exit (1944)

The Roads to Freedom (1945, 1947, 1949)

Critique of Dialectical Reason (1960)

Overview

French philosopher and man of letters, the versatile writer Jean-Paul Sartre ranks as the dominant influence in three decades of French intellectual life. As scholar Lynn-Dianne Beene noted, "Sartre challenged not only contemporary ideas about freedom and human liberation, but also the oppression he found in Western capitalism. His relentless search for freedom gave rise to a process of existential inquiry and reflection."

Works in Biographical and Historical Context

Sartre's literary and philosophical careers are inextricably bound together and are best understood in relation to one another and to their biographical and historical context.

Defiant, Precocious Beginnings Jean-Paul Sartre was born in Paris on June 21, 1905. His father Jean-Baptiste, a naval officer, died while on a tour of duty in Indochina (then part of the French colonial empire) before Sartre was two years old. His mother took her young son to live at her parents' house, where she and her son were treated as "the children." Later Sartre would describe his unnatural childhood as a spoiled and precocious boy. Lacking companions his own age, he found "friends" exclusively in books. Reading became

Jean-Paul Sartre *Sartre, Jean-Paul, photograph. AP Images.*

his first passion, and he soon decided to be a writer. According to *The Words*, the autobiography of his youth, this decision was made in conscious opposition to the wishes of his grandfather.

School and Simone de Beauvoir

When his mother remarried, Sartre moved from Paris to La Rochelle with her and his stepfather, a solemn professional man with whom he felt little in common. There Sartre followed the path of a professional, finishing his studies at Lycée Henri IV in Paris, and entering the École Normale Supérieure in 1924. While there he became a student of and was influenced by Émile Auguste Chartier, a humanist and materialist philosopher and essayist. It was also at Normale Supérieure where he met feminist intellectual novelist Simone de Beauvoir, who would become Sartre's lifelong companion, though by no means his only love interest. Sartre earned his doctorate, taking first place in the *agrégation* of philosophy in 1929. De Beauvoir finished second, affirming the pair's intellectual bond and sealing their emotional one.

Introduction to Phenomenology

After completing compulsory military service as a conscript in the French army from 1929 to 1931, Sartre took a teaching job at a school in Le Havre, and from 1933 to 1935 he was a research student on a grant at the Institut Français in Berlin and in Freiburg. Having read over the years philosopher Henri Bergson's works as well as those of Georg Wilhem Friedrich Hegel, Martin Heidegger, Edmund Husserl, and Immanuel Kant, he began to form his first philosophical writings with respect to phenomenology, the philosophical examination of the nature of individual consciousness. A series of works on consciousness resulted. He also wrote his first novel, *Nausea* (1938), which some critics have called the century's most influential French novel, and produced *The Wall* (1939), a first-rate volume of short stories.

World War II and the Resistance

World War II intervened, and Sartre was called up by the army. He served briefly on the Eastern front as a meteorologist. Captured by Germans in 1940 at Padoux, he was taken prisoner to Nancy and then *Stalag* 12D, Trier. There he wrote his first play and read more Heidegger, which would inform his first major work on phenomenological thought, *Being and Nothingness* (1943). After nine months, in April 1941, he secured his release by noting his bad eyes interfered with his balance. He returned to teaching at *Lycée Pasteur* near Paris, moving into the Hotel Mistral near Montparnasse. While he was given a new position at Lycée Condorcet, Sartre joined with Maurice Merleau-Ponty, de Beauvoir, and others to form the underground intellectual resistance group, Socialisme et Liberté. The coalition, begun in May of 1941, was finished by August due to lack of support by the undecided André Gide and André Malraux and others.

Sartre returned to writing, penning the now classic dramas *The Flies* (1942) and *No Exit* (1944), contributing to literary magazines, and evading German censorship for both plays and legitimate and underground writings. *No Exit* was clearly molded by Sartre's experiences in occupied France. It is a serious, disturbing play about personal accountability in an irrational world, a theme that resonated with Parisian audiences forced to live under Nazi rule. In fact, the play's one-act structure is a direct response to that rule: Sartre had to make the play short so Parisian audiences could watch it and still get home before the German-imposed curfew.

The Role of the Intellectual

After the war, Sartre abandoned teaching altogether, determined to support himself by writing. Intellectuals, he thought, must take a public stand on every great question of their day. He thus became fundamentally a moralist, both in his philosophical and literary works, and subsequently would be considered by critics and scholars alike as the greatest philosopher of his time. He wrote full time, creating the influential trilogy *The Roads to Freedom* (1945–1949), a number of comedies, and more plays. He founded and edited *Les Temps Modernes* (*Modern Times*), a literary and political monthly. And he became an active contributor to *Combat*, the newspaper created covertly by the eminent philosopher and author Albert Camus.

Though never a member of the Communist Party, Sartre usually sympathized with the political views of the far left. Whatever the political issue, he was quick to publish his opinions, often combining them with public acts of protest. He, de Beauvoir, and Camus shared sympathies, and thus maintained a close camaraderie—until 1951 when Camus had clearly turned away from communism. Criticized by Camus for being a writer who resisted and not a resistor who wrote, and by other philosophers for his lack of political commitment, Sartre returned to philosophy in 1960.

In *Being and Nothingness* he declared man to be "a useless passion," condemned to strive for meaningless freedom. But now his new interest in social and political questions and his reestablishment with Marxist thought led him to more optimistic and activist views. He published his first volume of *Critique of Dialectical Reason* (1960), a modified version of his existentialism by way of Marxist ideas.

A Change of Mind About the Futility of Life

In his early work, Sartre pointed to the futility of life. His actions in the 1960s show a change of mind. Sartre was a vocal supporter of the Algerian efforts to be free of French colonial rule. Likewise, he was a vocal critic of U.S. actions in Vietnam, which many saw as imperialist rather than anti-Communist. Sartre headed the Organization to Defend Iranian Political Prisoners, beginning in 1964. He also sought out audiences with Cuban president Fidel Castro and Marxist revolutionary leader Ernesto "Che" Guevara. It is evident Sartre began to believe human actions mattered. In another about-face, Sartre seemed to ease the strict atheism of his early career as he neared the end of his life. In a 1974 interview with de Beauvoir, Sartre mused that he did not feel like "a speck of dust in the universe" and said that perhaps a "Creator" had a role in mind for him.

As Sartre worked on his final major efforts, including *The Family Idiot* (1971), his failing eyesight progressed to blindness and his health deteriorated. In Paris on April 15, 1980, Sartre died.

Works in Literary Context

Sartre was primarily influenced by the works of philosophers Søren Kierkegaard, Edmund Husserl, and Martin Heidegger. His work and thought was also profoundly influenced by his contemporaries, such as Merleau Ponty and Simone de Beauvoir, and was informed and driven further by revolutions and several wars, which pushed his political philosophies and antagonized his themes of freedom and choice. In turn, Sartre was one of the most influential intellectuals of the twentieth century, doubtless the greatest of his immediate generation in France.

Existentialism Existentialism is the term used to describe a philosophy that holds that there is no meaning in life other than what individuals create for themselves. This somewhat bleak perspective is associated with fiction that portrays characters coming to grips with reality and experiencing feelings of malaise, boredom, and alienation. Perhaps no writer is as strongly associated with existentialism as Sartre, but he was by no means the first writer to posit the idea of humankind's essential meaningless. Critics point out that existentialist tendencies can be seen in the work of nineteenth-century Russian author Fyodor Dostoevsky as well. Dostoevsky's early fiction, particularly his "Petersburg" tales, exhibit strong existentialist traits in keeping with the antireligious radical philosophy he espoused. His characters feel alienated from both society and themselves. Existentialism, as Sartre proposed it, stresses the primacy of the thinking person and of concrete individual experience as the source of knowledge. It also emphasizes the anguish and solitude inherent in the individual's freedom and responsibility in making choices.

Works in Critical Context

Of Sartre's body of work in general, the scholars and critics agree: Sartrean scholars Michel Contat and Michel Rybalka called him, "uncontestably the most outstanding philosopher and writer of our time." Scholar Henri Peyre described him as "the most powerful intellect at work . . . in the literature of Western Europe," the "Picasso of literature." And author Iris Murdoch explained that "to understand Jean-Paul Sartre is to understand something important about the present time."

Sartre's comedies, critics like Henry Peyre claimed, "reveal . . . him as the best comic talent of our times." His letters, compiled in several different volumes, illuminate

---

LITERARY AND HISTORICAL CONTEMPORARIES

Sartre's famous contemporaries include:

Albert Camus (1913–1960): Philosophical writer, second-youngest Nobel Prize recipient who, while associated with existentialism, actually rejected the title for, more accurately, "nihilism."

Sir Winston Churchill (1874–1965): Twice prime minister of the United Kingdom, this statesman and acclaimed orator was also a Nobel Prize-winning author.

Simone de Beauvoir (1908–1986): French author and philosopher best known for her 1949 treatise *The Second Sex.*

Ernest Hemingway (1899–1961): American writer known for his spare, modernist style.

Hiroshi Inagaki (1905–1980): Japanese filmmaker best known for his *Samurai* trilogy.

---

the private life and pre-novel thoughts of the philosopher, relate to the early years of such interpersonal dynamics as the unconventional Sartre–de Beauvoir love relationship, and reveal what America's Peter T. Conner identified as "an intimate portrait of the precocious philosopher emerging into a kind of intellectual and spiritual maturity." Sartre's most telling writing, however, affirming all the critical commentary, is in such works as *Nausea.*

Nausea (1938) Sartre's first fiction work, *Nausea,* is what many critics have called the century's most influential French novel. The title indicates the hero's reaction toward existence: when he discovers that life is absurd, he feels repulsed. Nothing, it would seem, can save him, except the discovery that he might be able to write a novel that would have internal necessity and be a rival to life. Thus, he proposes to save himself through an act of aesthetic creation. Sartre said in *The Words:* "At the age of thirty, I executed the masterstroke of writing in *Nausea*—quite sincerely, believe me—about the bitter unjustified existence of my fellow men and of exonerating my own."

Nausea was received with praise and had considerable success. In *Esprit,* reviewer Armand Robin called *Nausea* "undoubtedly one of the distinctive works of our time." While it illustrates what de Beauvoir dubbed Sartre's "opposition aesthetics"—his desire to use literature as a critical tool—the work also later prompted critics like Anthony Richards Manser to call it "that rare thing: a genuinely philosophic novel."

Responses to Literature

1. Sartre said he would choose *Critique of Dialectical Reason* to be remembered by. As you read it, try to

Leak, Andrew. *Jean-Paul Sartre*. Chicago: Reaktion Books, 2006.

McBride, William. *Sartre's French Contemporaries and Enduring Influences*. New York: Garland, 1997.

Rowley, Hazel. *Tête-à-Tête: Simone de Beauvoir and Jean-Paul Sartre*. New York: HarperCollins, 2005.

Periodicals

Choice (July–August 1993): 1786.

Chronicle of Higher Education (November 21, 2003): 10–13.

Web sites

Books and Writers. *Jean-Paul Sartre (1905–1980)*. Retrieved February 14, 2008, from http://www.kirjasto.sci.fi/sartre.htm

Nobel Prize. *The Nobel Prize in Literature, 1964: Jean-Paul Sartre*. Retrieved February 17, 2008, from http://nobelprize.org

Sartre Online. Retrieved February 14, from http://www.geocities.com/sartresite

COMMON HUMAN EXPERIENCE

Here are a few titles by writers whose work includes existential themes or thought:

City of Glass (1986), a novel by Paul Auster. Playing with language, scene, and structure, Auster brings readers one of the earliest postmodern novels to combine detective fiction, existentialism, and intellectual literature.

Rhinoceros (1959), a play by Eugene Ionesco. Ionesco's bizarre, somewhat comical play shows the inhabitants of a French town turning, one by one, into rhinoceroses.

Notes from the Underground (1864), a novel by Fyodor Dostoevsky. Dostoevsky's book is considered by many literary historians to be the first existential novel.

Fight Club (1996), a novel by Chuck Palahniuk. A profound study of doubles in a questionable reality marked by violence and moral murkiness.

find reasons why Sartre chose this particular book as a testament to his decades of philosophical writing.

2. What areas of thought (philosophical, social, psychological, etc.) does Sartre cover in *Critique of Dialectical Reason*? Where do these areas come together? Where do they diverge?

3. In *Nausea*, the idea of sex and sexuality disgusts the main character, Roquentin. Why do you think this is? Do you think Roquentin is a misogynist, or woman-hater? Examine his relations with women and write about how you think those affect his attitude toward sex.

4. In *Nausea*, Roquentin is unmarried and lonely. How does his loneliness influence his perception of the outside world? Do you think he would feel the same way if he were married?

BIBLIOGRAPHY

Books

Cranston, Maurice. *The Quintessence of Sartrism*. New York: Harper, 1971.

Cumming, Robert D. *The Philosophy of Jean-Paul Sartre*. New York: Random House, 1965.

de Beauvoir, Simone. *Adieux: A Farewell to Sartre*. New York: Pantheon, 1984.

Hayman, Ronald. *Sartre: A Life*. New York: Simon & Schuster, 1987.

Lapointe, François, and Claire Lapointe. *Jean-Paul Sartre and His Critics*. Bowling Green, Ohio: Philosophy Documentation Center, Bowling Green State University, 1980.

Siegfried Sassoon

BORN: *1886, Brenchley, United Kingdom*

DIED: *1967, Warminster, United Kingdom*

NATIONALITY: *British*

GENRE: *Poetry, fiction, nonfiction*

MAJOR WORKS:

The Old Huntsman, and Other Poems (1917)

The War Poems of Siegfried Sassoon (1919)

Memoirs of an Infantry Officer (1930)

Sherston's Progress (1936)

Overview

Best remembered for the angry, compassionate poems that chronicled World War I, British poet Siegfried Sassoon became internationally famous for his satiric tone and his antiwar beliefs. Though the war was a topic of many great poets of the age, Sassoon's verse avoids sentimentality and patriotism, instead mocking the officials whose blind obedience led to one of the most violent wars in history. While his later poems were not as widely appreciated as his early work, Sassoon won major awards and acclaim for a fictionalized semiautobiographical work that is widely recognized as an outstanding portrait of his time.

Works in Biographical and Historical Context

Privileged Upbringing Sassoon was born in Brenchley, Kent, England, on September 8, 1886. Born into a wealthy Jewish family who had made their fortune in colonial India, Sassoon was the child of a marriage

Siegfried Sassoon   *George C. Beresford / Hulton Archive / Getty Images*

particularly in eastern Europe. The alliances aligned as war was declared. Britain fought on the side of Russia and France, with the United States joining them later. They fought against Germany, Austria-Hungary, and the Ottoman Empire (Turkey).

When World War I broke out, Sassoon was one of the first British poets to enlist, leaving for France with the Royal Welch Fusiliers in 1915. Although his poetry would later attack the brutality and destruction of war, Sassoon earned a reputation as a courageous soldier. Nicknamed "Mad Jack" by his fellow fighters, he received a Military Cross for his actions on the battlefield, which included saving a wounded soldier during a battle. Sassoon was considered for another medal of honor after he captured a German trench position single-handedly. (Much of the war was fought in trenches on the Western front.)

Joined Antiwar Movement Sassoon himself was wounded several times, and while recuperating in England, he met individuals who were active in the antiwar movement. Their views soon infiltrated his opinion of combat. Believing "this War is being deliberately prolonged by those who have the power to end it," Sassoon made a public protest in 1917 against the continuation of the war by throwing his Military Cross into a river and, in what Sassoon called a "wilful defiance of military authority," writing an open letter to the War Department that was published in newspapers and read in the British House of Commons at the urging of pacifist philosopher Bertrand Russell. Sassoon expected to be court-martialed for his actions. Because fellow poet Robert Graves insisted that Sassoon was ill and in need of hospitalization, Sassoon's open act of defiance was believed to be the result of shell shock (what would be called combat stress reaction today), and charges were not brought against him. Instead, he was sent to the Craiglockhart War Hospital in Edinburgh, Scotland, where he became close friends with Wilfred Owen, another war poet.

Sassoon's volume of poetry *The Old Huntsman, and Other Poems* (1917) had been published the year before and began to receive increased notice due to his public stand against the war. His next book, *Counter-Attack, and Other Poems*, appeared in 1918 to fierce public reaction. The book, which contained war poems inspired by Sassoon's experience in combat and in the hospital, was graphically violent and realistic. Sassoon was criticized for being unpatriotic and extreme, and even his influential pacifist friends complained about the explicit details of the verses. Critics and authors of the time disliked Sassoon's shocking methods and complained that he was writing propaganda, not poetry. Nevertheless, the book sold well, and Sassoon became well-known for both his poetry and his political stance.

Postwar Work Sassoon, who had been sent back to battle in 1918 despite his protests, was shot in the head and discharged before the war came to an end. By the

between a Gentile mother and a Jewish father. Though the couple eventually separated and Sassoon's father died young, Sassoon enjoyed the cultured, comfortable life of a country gentleman in the years leading up to World War I. He was taught at home by private tutors and attended law school at Marlborough College before going to Cambridge, where he studied history.

Interest in Poetry Sassoon left school without taking a degree, however, preferring to focus on his new pursuit: poetry. When his mother introduced him to several of society's literary figures, including Rupert Brooke, Edmund Gosse, and Edward Marsh, Sassoon soon began to publish his poems privately. Sassoon's early poetry reflects the influence of the Pre-Raphaelite movement, characterized by romance, melodrama, and old-fashioned language. Literary critics have generally dismissed this work as unimportant and too similar to that of John Masefield, one of Sassoon's literary influences.

War As Sassoon reached maturity, World War I engulfed Europe. The war began when Archduke Franz Ferdinand, the heir to the throne of Austria-Hungary, was assassinated by a Bosnian terrorist in Serbia. Ferdinand's death had a domino effect as much of Europe was divided by entangling alliances. The late nineteenth and early twentieth centuries had been marred by increasing tensions over control of territory and sovereignty issues,

LITERARY AND HISTORICAL CONTEMPORARIES

Sassoon's famous contemporaries include:

E. M. Forster (1879–1970): This English novelist and essayist wrote *A Room with a View* (1908) and *Howard's End* (1910), both successfully adapted as films.

Archduke Franz Ferdinand of Austria (1863–1914): The assassination of this heir to the throne of Austria-Hungary led to the outbreak of the First World War.

Charlie Chaplin (1889–1977): This British-born comedic actor was known for his humorous silent roles. His films include *The Kid* (1921) and *The Great Dictator*.

Vaslav Nijinsky (1889–1950): This Polish ballet dancer and choreographer is known as one of the greatest dancers of all time. He choreographed ballets, such as *Jeux* (1913).

Marie Curie (1867–1934): This Polish-born French physicist and chemist discovered radium and polonium. In 1932, she founded the Radium Institute in Warsaw.

Margaret Sanger (1879–1966): American activist Sanger was an advocate for birth control and founded the American organization eventually known as Planned Parenthood.

conclusion of World War I, more than eight hundred thousand Britons had been killed, and many more were injured. Following the war, Sassoon became involved in politics, supporting his pacifist friends and lecturing on pacifism. Though he continued to write, critics widely acknowledge that his work had lost the relevance and prophetic quality that it had displayed during the First World War. Sassoon's anger and his hatred of combat did not resound with the new set of social and political problems facing England and Europe in the 1920s and beyond. In Great Britain, for example, the economic and human losses brought on serious disturbances in society. By the 1930s, the United Kingdom, like many countries in the world, was immersed in the a deep economic depression resulting in the unemployment of millions of workers.

In the meantime, Sassoon was achieving success as a prose writer. He published a trilogy of semiautobiographical novels, *Memoirs of a Fox-Hunting Man* (1928), *Memoirs of an Infantry Soldier* (1930), and *Sherston's Progress* (1936), published together as *The Complete Memoirs of George Sherston* in 1937. In addition to relating a barely fictionalized account of Sassoon's experiences during World War I, these works contrast the pleasures of country life with the brutality of war. The novels were well received, with some readers asserting that Sassoon's

prose was better than his poetry. In 1948, Sassoon also wrote a respected critical biography of Victorian novelist George Meredith, titled *Meredith*.

Later Life After a period in which his spiritual life became of increasing concern, Sassoon converted to Catholicism in 1957. Though his religious poetry is considered inferior to his other writing, his book *Sequences* (1956), which appeared soon before his conversion, is considered among the century's most impressive religious poetry. Sassoon's later life was solitary, though he married (and quickly divorced) Hester Gatty in 1933 and had a son, who visited him often during his later years. He died on September 3, 1967.

Works in Literary Context

The Modern Epoch Though Sassoon had a varied literary career, he is best remembered for his striking portraits of life in World War I, an event that affected nearly the whole of his output. His works depict a generation's transformation from the pastoral simplicity of the past to the violent uncertainty of a modern epoch. Sassoon was among the ranks of other war poets, such as Wilfred Owen, Rupert Brooke, Isaac Rosenberg, Edmund Blunden, and Robert Graves.

Early Verse Unlike his wartime poetry, Sassoon's early verse is written in the Georgian style, a return to the pastoral literary tradition in reaction to the reason and realism of the Victorian age. Sassoon was influenced by an expansive reading list, which included classic literature, the Romantic poets, the Pre-Raphaelites, and the plays of William Shakespeare. In general, Sassoon's early poems favored conventional romantic themes and archaic language. "The Old Huntsman" is appreciated for its serene, humorous reminiscences of the changes undergone by both the title character and the world. Overall, however, the poetry from Sassoon's early career is considered inferior to his later work.

"Happy Warrior" Poetry Even in *The Old Huntsman, and Other Poems*, which is regarded as the epitome of Sassoon's romantic poetry, one can see signs that Sassoon belongs to a generation of realistic war poets, as this volume also contains several short poems that express his anger toward the war. Before Sassoon had been in the trenches himself, he had remarked, after reading Robert Graves's war poems, that war should not be depicted so realistically. The war poems in *The Old Huntsman, and Other Poems* are sometimes referred to as "happy warrior" verse because they are idealistic and employ the same language and structure as his pastoral work.

War Poetry World War I inspired the production of poignant and terrifying poetry that captured the awfulness of trench warfare and death, often experienced firsthand by the poets themselves. Indeed, it was Sassoon's experiences during World War I that changed not only his poetic style but also his outlook on life forever. The harsh realities of death, destruction, injury, and desperation that Sassoon faced in the trenches gave immediacy to his war poetry, which was characterized by some readers as a shocking assault on the senses—clearly a break from the romantic idealization found in most Georgian poetry. "Deliberately written to disturb complacency," Sassoon said of his writing during this time, which became satirical, unsentimental, frank, and stylistically colloquial and informal. Occasionally, though, he had the ability to transcend his anger. During such a period, for example, he wrote "Everyone Sang," a joyful lyric expressing relief at the armistice ending World War I.

Influence   In documenting the era of the First World War, Sassoon's satiric mockery of warfare established an influential model for other writers in the twentieth century, many of whom became lifelong friends.

Works in Critical Context

War Protest   Combined with the influence of his pacifist friends, Sassoon's aversion to warfare resulted in emotionally charged pleas against a war he thought would never end. His poetry about combat has been recognized as a chronicle of his times, almost documentary in presentation. As is the case with any form of protest, Sassoon's war poetry elicited mixed reactions, though it is generally regarded as the highlight of his career. His ability to capture the nuances of emotion experienced by a whole generation of soldiers in a few biting lines earned him much admiration in his time. However, Sassoon has never received as much critical attention as other great poets of the twentieth century, perhaps due to his strong identification with antiwar poetry.

War Poetry   While some critics praise Sassoon's controversial war poems for their common language, human interaction, concrete details, and sarcastic self-mockery, they are simultaneously criticized for their unpatriotic antiwar messages and shocking nature. Designed to convey the disturbing brutality of combat, Sassoon's poems were abrasive, filthy, and morally ambiguous, presenting images of suicide, cowardice, and horror that contrasted sharply with pro-war propaganda of the time. Many critics, including some of Sassoon's friends and fellow poets, have condemned his presentation of warfare, maintaining that his poetry deals with only the immediate, startling aspects of war without any attempt toward artistic value. These critics contend that Sassoon's rage appeals exclusively to the senses, to visceral response. The *Times Literary Supplement* critic wrote, for example, "The dynamic quality of his war poems was due to the intensity of feeling which underlay their cynicism."

A number of scholars throughout the years have felt that Sassoon's need to express the ugly reality of war

COMMON HUMAN EXPERIENCE

Siegfried Sassoon's poems address the horrors of war. Here are other antiwar pieces of art:

The Red Badge of Courage (1895), a novel by Stephen Crane. In this book, a young man struggles with the horrors of war—and his desire to flee from battle—during the American Civil War.

All Quiet on the Western Front (1929), a novel by Erich Maria Remarque. This work delivered such a powerful antiwar message that it was banned in Nazi Germany.

Gallipoli (1981), a film directed by Peter Weir. This film, starring Mel Gibson, follows the fate of two young Australian men who both serve in the disastrous Battle of Gallipoli during World War I.

Three Kings (1999), a film directed by David O. Russell. Depicting innocents who suffered the effects of chaotic and random combat, this movie questions the rationale of Operation Desert Storm.

overshadowed his own poetry. According to fellow war poet Wilfred Owen, Sassoon's poems limit the reader to a momentary reaction instead of translating the intensity and horror of war into a universal human context. John Middleton Murry agreed with Owen that Sassoon's work is typified by a negativity that terrifies and then numbs readers to the extent that they are denied any aesthetic quality, the result of which is "a lack of finished artistry." Virginia Woolf concurred, stating that Sassoon "deserted art in a compulsion to express the intolerable."

Responses to Literature

1. Sassoon's antiwar sentiments almost had him arrested. Instead, he was hospitalized for "shell shock" (or what today is called combat stress reaction) an ailment similar to post-traumatic stress disorder (PTSD). Research shell shock and PTSD, including their effects, treatment, and how many people are estimated to suffer from them, and summarize your findings in a PowerPoint presentation.

2. Sassoon is known for his barely fictionalized novels of British country life. This genre is sometimes known as "roman à clef." Research the characteristics of this kind of literature and write a paper on your findings. Do you think this genre is merely entertaining or does it have deeper implications?

3. Sassoon's war poetry is known for its brutal portrayal of death, suicide, cowardice, blood, and gore. Why do you think these images were so controversial to English audiences during World War I? Consider the

videos the United States receives from terrorist organizations showing the beheading of Americans they have captured. Compare public reaction to these videos with the images presented in Sassoon's poems in a paper. Do you feel that our society has become too desensitized to violence as a result of our country's movie and video game industries?

4. Sassoon was a friend and mentor of Wilfred Owen, who eventually became more well-known than his teacher. How would the friendship between Sassoon and Owen have affected both poets' work? Find other examples of students whose work surpassed that of their mentors and create a presentation of your findings. What reasons can you give for this success? How do you think the mentors reacted?

BIBLIOGRAPHY

Books

Moeyes, Paul. *Scorched Glory: A Critical Study*. New York: Palgrave Macmillan, 1997.

Roberts, John Stuart. *Siegfried Sassoon*. London: John Blake, 2000.

Thorpe, Michael. *Siegfried Sassoon: A Critical Study*. London: Oxford University Press, 1966.

Wilson, Jean Moorcroft. *Siegfried Sassoon: The Making of a War Poet*. London: Duckworth, 2004.

Periodicals

Times Literary Supplement, July 11, 1918; June 3, 1926; November 1, 1947; September 18, 1948; January 4, 1957; December 7, 1973.

Marjane Satrapi   *Satrapi, Marjane, photograph. AP Images.*

Marjane Satrapi

BORN: *1969, Rasht, Iran*

NATIONALITY: *Iranian, French*

GENRE: *Graphic novels, children's stories*

MAJOR WORKS:

Persepolis: The Story of a Childhood (2003)
Persepolis 2: The Story of a Return (2004)

Overview

Marjane Satrapi is an Iranian graphic novelist, illustrator, animated film director, and children's book author based in France. She is critically acclaimed for her graphic novels *Persepolis: The Story of a Childhood* and *Persepolis 2: The Story of a Return*, where she artistically narrates her childhood and teenage experiences of growing up in Iran and later immigrating to Europe.

Works in Biographical and Historical Context

A Girl in the Revolution   Born on November 22, 1969, in Rasht, Iran, Marjane Satrapi grew up in Tehran in a progressive upper-middle-class family. The early years of her youth were spent under the rule of Mohammad Reza Shah Pahlavi, who sat on the throne from World War II onward and oversaw dramatic changes in the form of modernization and relaxation of Muslim influence on the government. These changes included voting rights for women and the transfer of land ownership from the wealthy to individual farmers. While the Shah was arguably regarded by the Western world as a positive force in Iran, opposition within the country—particularly among religious fundamentalists led by Ayatollah Ruhollah Khomeini, who saw the Shah's efforts at modernization as an affront to Islamic traditions—continued to grow throughout his rule. As the economic situation in Iran worsened during the 1970s, opposition forces gained the support of the public in their attempts to overthrow the Shah. This happened in 1979, and although there was general agreement that the end of the monarchy was a positive event, there was much dispute over what should take its place. Khomeini and his followers, some of whom used tactics of violence against those who opposed them and came to be known as the Hezbollah, assumed control of the government and instituted stricter adherence to Muslim traditions, such as the wearing of headscarves by females and the prohibition of alcohol. Khomeini's regime purged thousands of government employees that it viewed as too Westernized, or that were suspected of rejecting Islam. It was this transition to a fundamentalist climate that Satrapi experienced as a girl and later documented in her graphic novels.

To Europe and Back Satrapi studied at the Lycée français, and then moved to a boarding school in Vienna to finish high school. She returned to Iran for college, where she met her first husband, a man named Reza, and married him at the age of twenty-one. They were divorced a year later and she went on to study visual communication, gaining a master's degree from the School of Fine Arts in Tehran's Islamic Azad University. In 2001 she received an Angoulême Coup de Coeur Award for the original French version of *Persepolis*, and an Angoulême Prize for Scenario for *Persepolis 2* the following year. *Poulet aux Prunes*, or *Chicken with Plums*, received an Angoulême Best Comic Book Award in 2005. *Persepolis* was adapted into an animated movie in 2007 and was awarded a Jury Prize at the Cannes Film Festival.

Satrapi currently lives in Paris with her husband, Mattias Ripa, working as a graphic artist, illustrator, children's book author, and a contributor to various magazines and newspapers worldwide, including the *New Yorker* and the *New York Times*.

Works in Literary Context

In contrast to the majority of graphic novels that are published by large comic companies, Satrapi's memoir was published in graphic novel form by mainstream publishing houses. As a result, Satrapi's graphic novels are among the most popular of the genre, with *Persepolis* selling more than 450,000 copies worldwide. Its success ultimately led to the adaptation of the story to animated film. In 2007 *Persepolis* was released, despite objections from the Iranian government, at the Cannes Film Festival, where it won the Jury Prize.

The Persian Culture Virtually all of Satrapi's works focus on Persian culture, its traditions, and its place in the modern world. Both *Persepolis* and *Persepolis 2* deal with the event of the Islamic Revolution in Iran, a country that was once known as Persia. The titles of these works refer to the ancient city of Persepolis, which was the capital of the Persian Empire. The characters in *Persepolis* make up a broad spectrum of Persian culture and provide different perspectives on the modern history of Iran. *Chicken with Plums* concerns an Iranian man—the author's great-uncle—who stops eating after his *tar*, an Iranian lute, is destroyed and cannot be replaced.

Women's Issues Another important theme in Satrapi's work is the concerns and rights of women. In *Persepolis*,

---

LITERARY AND HISTORICAL CONTEMPORARIES

Satrapi's famous contemporaries include:

Mohammad Reza Pahlavi (1919–1980): Exiled during the Iranian Revolution of 1979, this monarch of Iran was the second of the Pahlavi House and the last shah of Iran.

Gulrukhsor Safieva (1947–): This highly regarded artist is Tajikstan's national poet and particularly known for her modern Persian folksongs and poetry.

Simin Daneshvar (1921–): In 1949 this Iranian author became the first woman in Iran to publish a book of short stories and, later, in 1969, the first woman to publish a novel, *Mourners of Siyavosh*.

Margaret Atwood (1939–): An award-winning Canadian fiction writer, Atwood is known best for her novels, poetry, and feminist activism.

Art Spiegelman (1948–): American comic author and artist who won the Pulitzer Prize for his stylized graphic memoir *Maus* (1973–1991), which told the tale of his father's experiences as a Jew during the Holocaust and his later life.

Khaled Hosseini (1965–): American author born in Afghanistan who drew upon his childhood knowledge of his native country for his novel *The Kite Runner* (2003).

Marji's mother protests against the newly instituted rule requiring women to wear headscarves—a protest that ends in violence. Marji herself dares to rebel against the fundamentalists who police the streets by wearing Western clothes. *Embroideries* (2006) focuses exclusively on the lives and concerns of Iranian women. The book centers on a gathering of women at the home of the author's grandmother; there, they share stories about their lives.

Works in Critical Context

With only a handful of works to her credit, Marjane Satrapi's reputation rests largely on her first graphic novel, *Persepolis*, and its sequel. The critical response for these works was overwhelmingly positive, and mainstream popular success followed—an unusual occurrence for works that some might view as "comics." Although her follow-up works have not attained the same level of success, they have still enjoyed great popularity and have drawn many new readers into the realm of the graphic novel.

Persepolis Known as "the most significant new talent in the world of the graphic novel," Satrapi has wooed critics and received largely positive attention for

COMMON HUMAN EXPERIENCE

Foremost among Satrapi's themes is the cultural changes brought to Iran by the Islamic Revolution, during which the monarchy ruled by Mohammad Reza Shah Pahlavi was overthrown and replaced by an Islamic republic under Ayatollah Ruhollah Khomeini. For example, as the narrator explains in *Persepolis*, shortly after the revolution in 1979, women were ordered to wear veils in schools. Other works that explore the cultural impact of political change include:

The Tempest (1610–11), a play by William Shakespeare. In this classic tragedy, argued by some scholars to be about the moment of revolution in the colonies, the "good servant" Ariel and the rebellious Caliban trade arguments about the projected effects of a revolt against Prospero.

The Eighteenth Brumaire of Louis Napoleon (1852), a nonfiction study by Karl Marx. Political philosopher Karl Marx's famous consideration of the successes and, mostly, the failures of France's revolution of 1848; he was particularly dismissive of Louis Bonaparte's role, noting that great historical events occur for the first time as tragedy and the second as farce.

The House of Spirits (1982), a novel by Isabel Allende. This novel concerns the lives of a Trueba family during major sociopolitical upheavals of postcolonial Latin America.

Persepolis. London's *Independent* called her the "Princess of Darkness" for her trademark monochrome style in graphic novels. Luc Sante in the *New York Times Book Review* commented that "the graphic form, with its cinematic motion and its style as personal as handwriting, endows it with a combination of dynamism and intimacy uniquely suited to a narrative at once intensely subjective and world-historical." *Publishers Weekly* added that the novel was "a universally insightful" bildungsroman. Also, Satrapi has followed such notables as Art Spiegelman's *Maus* in proving that graphic novels can be of serious content. As noted in a *USA Today* article, "The fact that [Satrapi] is able to portray such a vast range of emotions with a few simple strokes of a pen is impressive. That she does this consistently for 153 pages is a mighty achievement."

Chicken with Plums "Satrapi's deceptively simple, remarkably powerful drawings match the precise but flexible prose she employs in adapting to her multiple roles as educator, folklorist, and grand-niece," the *New Yorker* noted in a review for *Chicken with Plums*. *Harvard Book Review*'s Noah Hertz-Bunzl, however, believes otherwise, arguing that though the piece is "full of charming incidents and anecdotes, it lacks clear direction and pur-

pose." Critics may be divided on accepting the novel, but its Angoulême Best Comic Book Award in 2005 certainly indicates that the Iranian artist has created yet another significant piece of literature.

Responses to Literature

1. Discuss the ways in which people struggle for freedom in *Persepolis: The Story of a Childhood*. Paying particular attention to specific acts of rebellion, identify the different kinds of freedom that are valued by the people in Satrapi's memoir.

2. How important is gender to the people in *Persepolis*? Compare and contrast the ways in which gender influences several different characters in this story.

3. What role does story-telling play in the lives of Satrapi's narrators? Compare and contrast the concept of a "national history" with that of a "personal history." What is the author communicating to readers about them and their relationship with one another? Support your answer using specific examples from the text.

4. Consider Satrapi's choice to use the graphic novel to communicate her story. How significant are the illustrations? Why do you think she chose this medium over others?

BIBLIOGRAPHY

Web Sites

"Author Biography," Pantheon Graphic Novels, http://www.randomhouse.com/pantheon/graphicnovels/satrapi.html February 25, 2008.

"Marjane Satrapi: On Writing Persepolis," Pantheon Graphic Novels, http://www.randomhouse.com/pantheon/graphicnovels/satrapi2.html February 25, 2008.

"Marjane Satrapi Returns," Powells.com, http://www.Powells.com.

◈ Friedrich von Schiller

BORN: *1759, Marbach, Germany*

DIED: *1805, Weimar, Germany*

NATIONALITY: *German*

GENRE: *Poetry, fiction, nonfiction*

MAJOR WORKS:

The Robbers (1781)

Intrigue and Love (1784)

Wallenstein (1800)

Maria Stuart (1801)

Wilhelm Tell (1804)

Friedrich von Schiller   *Schiller, Friedrich von, engraving. The German Information Center.*

Overview

To this day, many regard Friedrich Schiller as the greatest dramatist in all of German history. More brilliantly than any of his predecessors, he revealed the power of drama and poetry in expressing a philosophy that emphasized both his idealism and his concern for human freedom. Schiller was also esteemed as an adept lyricist and theoretician whose works are informed by his conviction that the writer should strive not only to entertain, but also to instruct and improve his audience.

Works in Biographical and Historical Context

Birth and Education Johann Christoph Friedrich von Schiller was born on November 10, 1759, in Marbach, Germany, to an army captain and an innkeeper's daughter. He initially wanted to be a clergyman and enrolled in the Latin School at Ludwigsburg in 1766. Against his parents' wishes, however, Schiller was drafted into the Karlsschule, an elite military academy, in 1773. Karlsschule was located in Stuttgart (a city in Württemberg) and was a rigidly disciplined academy established to train the sons of German army officers for public service. At the time, Germany remained fragmented into more than three hundred principalities, bishoprics, and free

cities, including Württemberg. By this time, Prussia had emerged to first rank among the German territories, especially through the military brilliance of Frederick the Great, who ruled Prussia from 1740 until 1786.

At the Karlsschule, Schiller was educated in an intensely disciplined atmosphere, and, although he was being trained in medicine, Schiller spent much of his time secretly reading the works of Jean-Jacques Rousseau, Seneca, and William Shakespeare, along with the revolutionary works of Friedrich Gottlieb Klopstock. Even before he graduated in 1780 and was appointed a medical officer in the military of Duke Karl Eugen (who ruled Württemberg with an iron fist), Schiller had begun writing *The Robbers* (1781), his first dramatic work.

Poverty and Early Plays Though Schiller had completed his play, he was unable to find a publisher and eventually self-published despite his pitiful salary, beginning a cycle of debt that would characterize his entire early career. In 1782, Schiller attended the performance of *The Robbers* at a theater in Mannheim, a production that earned him both public acclaim and the wrath of Duke Eugen, who insisted that he work only on medical texts from then on. This conflict forced Schiller to flee Stuttgart in 1782, launching a period of financial deprivation and uncertainty.

Schiller was financially desperate, but not without acquaintances. A friend gave him a post at the Mannheim Theater in 1783, and he was offered generous financial assistance by patron and friend Christian Gottfried Körner. His appointment at the Mannheim lasted a single year because the management wanted drama that avoided the extravagances of Schiller's *The Robbers* and *Intrigue and Love* (1784), his next major play. Around the same time, Schiller founded the literary journal *Rheinland Thalia*. Appearing in the publication was his poem "An die Freude" (1786), which would later inspire Ludwig van Beethoven's "Ode to Joy" (from the last movement of his Ninth Symphony).

Literary Friendships Schiller continued his dramatic pursuits, publishing and producing several plays and completing *Don Carlos, Infante of Spain* in 1787. With its historical setting and its use of blank verse to explore a theme of love versus duty, this play would prove important to Schiller's dramatic development. It featured a noblewoman character based on his friend, Charlotte von Kalb. When Schiller visited Frau von Kalb at her Weimar home in 1787 after publishing the play, he met Johann Wolfgang von Goethe, a dramatist and poet of growing importance, who became his close friend and collaborator in classicism. Schiller launched into a period of productivity that ensured his fame and social position. Schiller's historical work on the revolt of the Netherlands against Spain (the 1568–1648 revolt of seventeen provinces in the Netherlands against the Spanish Empire, which controlled them), as well as Goethe's support, earned him a professorship in history at the University

LITERARY AND HISTORICAL CONTEMPORARIES

Schiller's famous contemporaries include:

Johann Wolfgang von Goethe (1749–1832): This German poet and philosopher was Schiller's close friend. It was Schiller who encouraged Goethe to continue with his work on *Faust* (1808, 1832) after he had abandoned the future masterpiece.

Wolfgang Amadeus Mozart (1756–1791): This Austrian composer was hailed for his large musical output as well as his musical genius. His compositions include the "Paris" Symphony (1778) and the opera *The Marriage of Figaro* (1786).

Benjamin Franklin (1706–1790): A founding father of the United States, Franklin was also a prolific writer and inventor. His publications include *Poor Richard's Almanack* (1733–1758).

Christoph Martin Wieland (1733–1813): The German author wrote both the educational novel *Geschichte des Agathon* (1766–1767) and the romantic poem *Oberon* (1780). He also collaborated with both Goethe and Schiller in Weimar.

Maria Gaetana Agnesi (1718–1799): This Italian mathematician was known for her solution to an algebraic equation and wrote the first book that discussed both differential calculus and integral calculus. Her books include *Instituzioni analitiche ad uso della gioventu italiana* (1748).

Denmark Vesey (1767–1822): This West Indian slave plotted a rebellion in Charleston, South Carolina, and along the Carolina coast, which was supposed to happen on July 14, 1822. The plan failed, and he was convicted and hanged for his role in the conspiracy.

of Jena in 1789, a position he would hold for the next decade.

Early in 1790, Schiller married Charlotte von Lengefeld, also a gifted writer. He was named a nobleman in 1803. Around this time, he became interested in Immanuel Kant's aesthetic philosophy. He began to write philosophical treatises and poems, including "The Artists" (1789), a work in which he celebrates art as a power that could create world harmony, overcome human desire, and awaken the artist to the mystery and beauty of the universe. His 1796 essay "On Naïve and Sentimental Poetry" is considered the basis for modern poetry criticism. These philosophical musings would affect the remainder of Schiller's work and have a lasting impact on criticism and literature itself.

Late Work and Death After completing a tragic trilogy based on the Thirty Years' War (the 1618–1648)

war of religion between Protestants and Catholics fought mainly in Germany but involving most of the major powers in Europe) that critics have compared with the dramas of Shakespeare, Schiller's correspondence with Goethe flourished, and Schiller eventually joined Goethe in Weimar, which was known as the "German Athens" because its ruler, Karl August, had succeeded in making it a center of art and culture. Schiller's most popular play, *Maria Stuart*, was completed in 1800, and he wrote several other important plays during this time. In 1804, Schiller published his greatest literary achievement, *Wilhelm Tell*, a powerful blend of history and heroic fiction. Although he completed other works before his death, Schiller's literary output was interrupted by illness, and he died in Weimar on May 9, 1805.

Works in Literary Context

German Significance Though the reverence Germany has bestowed upon Schiller might seem excessive, the cultural, artistic, and historical opinion of the country that influenced his writing during the eighteenth century helps provide an explanation. Schiller's work surfaced at a time when art and literature were dominated by the immense accomplishments of English, French, and Italian artists and writers. Even the German language itself was the cause of considerable debate, as some scholars asserted that the German tongue was not fit to be an agent of literary expression. Schiller, however, proved that Germany could compete with—and in some ways surpass—the creative and intellectual achievements of any other country. He was greatly influenced in his work by the writers he favored while in school (Rousseau, Seneca, Shakespeare, and Klopstock), the German theater, history, and ideas of natural philosophy as well as his friendship with Goethe.

Sturm und Drang The overemphasis on reason in the Age of Enlightenment led to a reaction in favor of the emotional and imaginative aspects of human personality and personal freedom. The result was the Sturm und Drang, or "Storm and Stress," movement that swept German literature in the late eighteenth century. This literary tendency, characterized by passion, turbulence, and melodrama, was embraced by both Schiller and Goethe early in their writing careers.

Central to Schiller's first three dramas is the question of freedom: *The Robbers*, in which the play's hero escapes corrupt society by fleeing to the Bohemian forests and becomes a type of German Robin Hood; *Fiesco; or, The Genoese Conspiracy* (1783), a tragedy with the theme of struggle against oppression; and *Intrigue and Love*, another tragedy that calls for freedom of the individual amidst political and social opposition. Schiller's Sturm und Drang work, however, mellowed with age, and his later pieces are well-planned, reasoned, and articulate expressions of neoclassical ideals and philosophical exploration.

Innovations in Drama   Published in 1787, *Don Carlos* marks Schiller's break with his youthful rebellion and his movement toward German classicism. During this shift, Schiller established the tradition of a new type of drama, the *Ideendrama*, or drama of ideas. *Don Carlos* also set a precedent for the verse form of the German classical drama: Shakespearean blank verse. Schiller's intent in the play was to concentrate his passion for morality in a more theatrically dramatic—as opposed to reactive—fashion in order to present the tragic defeat of idealism by conspiracy and deception. While *Don Carlos* does contain Sturm und Drang subject matter, it is overshadowed by the play's elements of classical tragedy.

Legacy   Though Schiller has tended to fall under the shadow of Goethe, his famous friend, he continues to hold an important place in German literature. Schiller's intellectual superiority and creative passion were cause for national pride; for instance, his birthday was declared a national holiday, streets and schools were named after him, and his works were adopted as part of Germany's educational curriculum. Schiller's appeal has continued in part because of his association with great music, having inspired Beethoven's "Ode to Joy" and operas by Rossini and Verdi. Thinkers such as Carl Gustav Jung, Friederich Nietzsche, Friederich Hegel, and Karl Marx were also indebted to the ideas Schiller set forth in his philosophical and aesthetical works.

Works in Critical Context

National Icon   Schiller's reputation as a boldly original thinker and artist was established with his controversial but highly successful first play, *The Robbers*. With the production of *The Minister*, he was recognized as one of the great masters of German drama. During his lifetime, he was lauded as one of the figures who raised the stature of German literature. Critics marveled at his ability to portray with immediacy and complexity human suffering and the triumph of the human spirit. He was regarded as a national icon on his death, and the attention paid to his works by German literary critics is comparable to Shakespeare in the English-speaking world.

In the nineteenth century, critics admired Schiller's taste and feeling and his concern for human freedom. Contemporary critics have suggested that Schiller's dramas are less accessible to modern readers due to their flamboyant, sometimes bombastic language. Nevertheless, most commentators agree that Schiller's themes and concerns, including political and individual freedom, the complexity of human endeavor, and the struggle between the rational and sensual aspects of the self are remarkably prescient of twentieth- and twenty-first-century concerns. Contemporary critics also tend to stress the

---

COMMON HUMAN EXPERIENCE

Schiller's plays often drew on historical events for both content and emotion. Here are a few examples of other writings based on historical events:

> *A Tale of Two Cities* (1859), a novel by Charles Dickens. This well-known classic portrays human involvement in the events leading up to the bloody French Revolution.
> *Kristin Lavransdatter* (1920), a novel by Sigrid Undset. Filled with dramatic events, romantic intrigue, and political conspiracy, this work helped win its author the 1928 Nobel Prize.
> *The Other Boleyn Girl* (2003), a novel by Philippa Gregory. This work of historical fiction is told from the perspective of Anne Boleyn's sister Mary, who was King Henry VIII's mistress before he married Anne.
> *Braveheart* (1995), a film directed by Mel Gibson. This movie depicts life and war in thirteenth-century Scotland.

---

philosophical underpinnings of Schiller's plays and poetry as well as the political themes in his works.

Wilhelm Tell   Since its debut in 1804, *Wilhelm Tell* has remained a work that is frequently performed and read. Critic H. B. Garland believes that *Wilhelm Tell* is "probably Schiller's most popular play, rich in qualities which no other of his works displays in equal degree," although, according to W. G. Moore, evaluation of the work "really rests upon a decision as to whether Schiller was predominantly a thinker, writing to present an argument about freedom, or a dramatist, presenting a case of notable conflict and a revelation of the mystery of life." Whatever their approach, critics continue to praise Schiller's ability to control the dramatic action of *Wilhelm Tell* through characterization, setting, and language.

Responses to Literature

1. Though Schiller's importance is now widely recognized, he was better known as Goethe's contemporary for many years. Select another famous literary friendship and analyze in an essay how the relationship affected each writer's work, as well as how each other's work affected their relationship.

2. Schiller's work inspired important pieces of music, from Beethoven's "Ode to Joy" to Rossini's *William Tell Overture*. Find at least three other pieces of music—any style, any time period—that were inspired by literature and create a presentation of your findings. Do you think adapting an existing text to song form makes for a successful piece of music?

3. Schiller's discovery of Immanuel Kant greatly influenced his later work. What were Kant's primary beliefs? How might these have influenced Schiller's writings? Write an essay that outlines your conclusions.

4. Schiller moved from romantic poetry to a quieter and more measured style as he grew older. Compare the early and later works of one of your favorite authors in a paper. What criteria would you use to assess the different bodies of work?

5. Schiller was rescued from poverty by the patronage of a friend. In a paper, address these questions: How would the lack of a patron affect an author's literary output? What benefits does patronage provide? What solutions would you suggest for an aspiring artist who does not have a patron?

BIBLIOGRAPHY

Books

Carlyle, Thomas. *The Life of Friedrich Schiller*. London: Camden House, 1992.

Garland, H. B. *Schiller: The Dramatic Writer*. Oxford: Clarendon, 1969.

Stahl, Ernst L. *Friedrich Schiller's Drama: Theory and Practice*. Oxford: Clarendon, 1954.

Witte, W. *Schiller*. Oxford: Blackwell, 1949.

Olive Schreiner

BORN: *1855, South Africa*

DIED: *1920, South Africa*

NATIONALITY: *South African*

GENRE: *Fiction, nonfiction*

MAJOR WORKS:

The Story of an African Farm (1888)
Trooper Peter Halket of Mashonaland (1897)
Woman and Labour (1911)
From Man to Man (1927)

Overview

South African author Olive Schreiner was an important feminist and social critic. Her fiction, set in her native South Africa, brought that country's natural beauty, people, and racial problems to the world's attention. Modern feminists consider Schreiner one of the most important voices of the movement's early days. Her pioneering essays on the repressed plight of women and South African blacks have influenced many writers around the world.

Works in Biographical and Historical Context

Child of Missionaries Olive Emilie Albertina Schreiner was born on March 24, 1855, at a remote Wesleyan mission station, Wittebergen, on the border of

Olive Schreiner *Schreiner, Olive, 1901, photograph. Mansell / Mansell / Time and Life Pictures / Getty Images.*

Basutoland in Cape Colony, South Africa. (At the time, Cape Colony was controlled by the United Kingdom, which annexed much of the territory that became South Africa in the nineteenth century.) The ninth of Gottlieb and Rebecca Lyndall Schreiner's dozen children, Olive was one of the seven who survived to adulthood. To supplement the meager salary he earned as a missionary, her father resorted to private trading, a violation for which he was expelled from the London Missionary Society. Financially unable to provide for his family as a storekeeper, Gottlieb Schreiner sent his two youngest children, eleven-year-old Olive and her nine-year-old brother, Will, to live with their older brother Theo, a school headmaster in Cradock. With her family dispersed, Schreiner boarded with relatives and friends until 1874, when she began to work as a governess for up-country Boer farming families. (Boers were Dutch farmers. The Dutch had begun settling what became South Africa in the mid-seventeenth century and soon began establishing farms. Boers and British settlers sometimes came into conflict over territory.)

Launched Writing Career Self-educated and well read, Schreiner took five teaching posts in the Cape Colony over the next seven years. She began writing fiction and saving her wages for a trip abroad, hoping to find a publisher and to study medicine. In 1881, at the age of twenty-six, Schreiner traveled to London with three manuscripts, including one she at first called *Thorn Kloof*, then *Lyndall*, before finally deciding on *The Story of an African Farm*. Writer George Meredith, a reader for the publisher Chapman & Hall, recommended its publication. The novel appeared to acclaim in January 1883 under the pseudonym Ralph Iron. Critics soon revealed that the best-selling work had been penned by a woman, making the ideas it espoused all the more controversial.

Breaking with Tradition Prevented from studying medicine by worsening asthma, Schreiner forged a career as a writer, moving in progressive political and literary circles, planning an edition of Mary Wollstonecraft's *A Vindication of the Rights of Woman* (1792), and agitating for suffrage. At the time, women did not have the right to vote in Great Britain, though the Isle of Man had granted property-owning women the right to vote in 1881. Despite her upbringing by missionary parents, she gradually repudiated their traditional religious and social beliefs and formed friendships with freethinkers like Havelock Ellis, Eleanor Marx, and Karl Pearson.

Schreiner had little regard for prevailing fashions. With her marked disdain for hats, gloves, and restraining undergarments, Schreiner endured the constant disapproval of those who adhered to the rigid code of Victorian decorum. Her apparent disregard for appearances and adoption of the New Woman's reformed dress stemmed from more than a desire for comfort in her native South African climate. It was a deliberate statement on the severely limited boundaries of the woman's sphere. By emphasizing her "strong square figure" in shapeless suits, Schreiner physically asserted the feminist beliefs that formed the basis of her writing.

Return to South Africa In 1889, Schreiner returned to South Africa and, five years later, married farmer-politician Samuel C. Cronwright. Defying tradition, she retained her maiden name, while he hyphenated his to Cronwright-Schreiner. Their marriage was intermittently happy, marked by frequent and lengthy separations and marred by the death of their only child soon after her birth in 1895. As the nineteenth century drew to a close and the twentieth century began, Great Britain cemented its power in South Africa after winning the second Boer War in 1902. The British fought the Boers, largely farmers of Dutch descent, who were concerned that the British wanted to exert total dominance over the Boer states of Transvaal and the Orange Free State, which had been annexed by Great Britain after the First Boer War in 1877, but enjoyed limited self-government; it turned out they were right to be concerned. The war was unpopular even in Britain, where the military's brutal actions in South Africa were viewed as naked imperialism. Great Britain gained control of the region with the signing of the Treaty Vereeninging.

During her marriage, she published collections of allegories and stories, articles on South African politics,

and her most influential writing on women's lives, *Woman and Labour* (1911). Gathering evidence from the animal world and women's history, Schreiner argued that the roles played by men and women were "neither universal nor innate." In the future, she maintained, both sexes would shed outer pretenses and emerge as equal "comrades and co-workers." As a result, Schreiner rejected the prevailing Victorian doctrine of separate spheres for the sexes and emerged as an advocate of egalitarian cooperation.

Yet in a society with such a fixed social and political hierarchy, she was by and large an outsider often unwell, and frequently short of funds. Schreiner feared at times that she was "only a broken and untried possibility" as a writer, citing her literary gifts, her unfinished works, and her difficult private life.

Novels Published after Death Throughout her life, Schreiner worked in spite of ill health and self-doubt to expose and remedy what she called "the desolating emptiness and barrenness of the majority of middle-class women's lives," paving the way for feminists who followed. After a return to England in 1914, she went back to South Africa shortly before her death in 1920. Schreiner's other novels—*From Man to Man* (1927) and *Undine* (1929)—had feminist themes and appeared posthumously.

Works in Literary Context

Questioning Established Beliefs Schreiner's experiences growing up in South Africa as the daughter of Christian missionary parents provided much inspiration to her writings and her life. While she eventually rebelled

COMMON HUMAN EXPERIENCE

Schreiner is often associated with the feminist movement. Her literary portrayals of women who were equal partners with the men in their lives were inspiring and, at the time, uncommon. Here are some other works that focus on the role of women in difficult times:

A Room of One's Own (1929), an essay by Virginia Woolf. In this extended essay, Woolf claims that women must have money, time, and space if they want to write.

The Feminine Mystique (1963), a nonfiction book by Betty Friedan. This popular book challenged the idea that women mainly belong in the home.

The Handmaid's Tale (1985), a novel by Margaret Atwood. In Atwood's futuristic society, women's main purpose is to produce children or to be wives.

Fried Green Tomatoes at the Whistle Stop Café (1987), a novel by Fannie Flagg. In this novel, which was made into a popular film, a group of southern American women explore their various social and sexual roles and try to change them.

against these beliefs as well as many of the values of Victorian society, the background gave her something to react against. Schreiner was also self-educated, and the many books she read also influenced her as a writer.

Women and Children All of Schreiner's novels are concerned with women's search for equality, love, and fulfillment. They share characteristics common to Victorian fiction: the tendency to ramble and to appeal to the emotions rather than to the intellect. Schreiner drew credible characterizations of children, but her depictions of adults, and especially her male characters, are often considered unrealistic. In her *Story of an African Farm*, however, the characters are sketched so vividly, so concretely, that most readers will remain attentive when the farm's isolation or the descriptions of nature lead a character to some philosophical or mystical musing. Clearly the young children's attempts to think through the demands of conventional religion are touching; the children are stunted and controlled by these restrictions.

The Natural World and the World of Mind Set in the landscape of Schreiner's childhood, *The Story of an African Farm* recounts the tale of two orphaned cousins, one a domestic, unimaginative sort, the other the most outspoken feminist to appear until then in British fiction. The novel combines several haunting, evocative descriptions of nature with many explorations of each character's own point of view. Many of the philosophical musings on religion, life, death, sexual roles, and the purpose of life

may have seemed profound to Schreiner, who was only twenty when she began to work on the isolated Fouche farm, Klein Ganna Hoek, in the Cape Colony.

Influence Modern feminists consider Schreiner one of the most important voices of the movement's early days. Her role as an influence upon other writers is also widely acknowledged. D. H. Lawrence's early novels owe much to Schreiner's daring treatment of human sexuality.

Works in Critical Context

Pioneer An unconventional woman, Schreiner was a pioneer in her treatment and depiction of women and in her vivid portrayal and use of the African landscape. As a novelist, short-story writer, and political essayist, she was both acclaimed and derided during her lifetime for her pioneering views on the role of women, her rejection of Christian convention, her anti-imperialist stance, and her pacifism during World War I.

Many critics contend that Schreiner is best appraised as something other than a fiction writer. In her novels, the artist often gives way to the social reformer, and Schreiner's bold, lively, and realistic style takes on a quasi-biblical aura in her short stories. These stories offer vibrant, optimistic visions of life, contrasting sharply with her novels in style and tone. Based upon readings of Schreiner's stories, some critics have described her as essentially a poet and a prophet and not a fiction writer. Today, Schreiner's works are read and studied by a new generation of feminists who ascribe to her a leadership role in the advancement of women's rights.

The Story of an African Farm When the public discovered that the author of *African Farm* was a woman, Schreiner's fame turned to notoriety, and the book was reassessed as un-Christian and antifeminine by many critics. While Henry Norman of the *Fortnightly Review* believed the novel was written by a woman despite the male name on the title page, he found much to praise. Norman called the novel "remarkable," and noted "in spite of its occasional youthful lapses, the whole story is of fascinating interest, and, what is more, of great moral power."

After its publication, Schreiner moved back to her homeland and continued to pursue a writing career, putting her energies into nonfiction dealing with a variety of social concerns. Schreiner published several other novels, including *From Man to Man* and *Undine*. Although her later novels contained feminist themes similar to *African Farm* and found critical favor for their depiction of the exotic African landscape, they were deemed, on the whole, inferior to Schreiner's first published work of fiction.

Woman and Labour *Woman and Labour* is considered Schreiner's most important piece of writing and social statement. The book attacks the economic and personal oppression of working women and was hailed throughout the Western world as a persuasive, timely document. In *Woman and Labour* she used scientific observation to argue that gender roles are "neither universal nor innate." Rather, she believed, future eras would find men and women living side by side as "comrades and co-workers." In *Olive Schreiner: Her Friends and Times*, D. L. Hobman called *Woman and Labour* "one of the noblest books which have ever appeared in defense of feminism."

Responses to Literature

1. Critics have claimed that Schreiner is more of an activist than a writer. Using examples from some of her works, write a short essay explaining why you agree or disagree.

2. Compare Schreiner's writings about South Africa with more modern writers from the same region, such as J. M. Coetzee and Alan Paton. In a paper, address the topic and include the answers to these questions: Who seems to know more about the landscape? How can you tell?

3. Research the Boer War and create an oral presentation explaining Schreiner's involvement.

4. *Woman and Labour* and Woolf's *A Room of One's Own* have similar themes, but Woolf's is usually the more well regarded of the two. With a group of your classmates who are familiar with Woolf and Schreiner, discuss why that might be true.

BIBLIOGRAPHY

Books

Barash, Carol, ed. *An Olive Schreiner Reader: Writings on Women and South Africa*. London: Pandora, 1987.

First, Ruth, and Ann Scott. *Olive Schreiner*. New York: Schocken, 1980.

Periodicals

Norman, Henry. "Theories and Practice of Modern Fiction." *Fortnightly Review* (December 1, 1883): 870–86.

Web Sites

"Olive Schreiner: Biographical Overview." Emory University. Accessed July 2, 2008, from http://www.emory.edu/ENGLISH/Bahri/Schreiner.html.

"Olive Schreiner (1855–1920)." Drew University. Accessed July 2, 2008, from http://www.depts.drew.edu/wmst/corecourses/wmst111/timeline_bios/OSchreiner.htm.

"Olive Schreiner." Spartacus Educational. Accessed July 2, 2008, from http://www.spartacus.schoolnet.co.uk/TUschreiner.htm.

"Olive Schreiner." Washington State University. Accessed July 2, 2008, from http://www.wsu.edu:8080/~dee/Schreiner.html.

◈ Bruno Schulz

BORN: *1892, Drohobycz, Galicia, Austria-Hungary*

DIED: *1942, Drohobycz, Poland (now Ukraine)*

NATIONALITY: *Polish*

GENRE: *Fiction, nonfiction*

MAJOR WORKS:
The Street of Crocodiles (1934)
Sanatorium Under the Sign of the Hourglass (1937)

Overview

Schulz is considered one of twentieth-century Poland's greatest writers, though he was hardly prolific. His reputation rests on a small body of extant work: the short-story collections *Sklepy cynamonowe* (*The Street of Crocodiles*) and *Sanatorium pod klepsydra* (*Sanatorium Under the Sign of the Hourglass*). An amalgam of autobiography, fantasy, and philosophy, Schulz's stories are often compared to the dreamlike works of surrealism, symbolism, and expressionism. Such comparisons notwithstanding, Schulz was not a member of any of these schools, and his work represents a significant departure from the dominant tenets of each.

Works in Biographical and Historical Context

An Unhappy Teacher Longing to Write Schulz was born in Drohobycz, a provincial town that became part of Poland when that country regained independence from the Austro-Hungarian Empire in 1918. The youngest son of a Jewish textile merchant, Schulz studied architecture for three years at Lvov Polytechnikum. While he did not attain a degree at the Polytechnikum, his proficiency in graphics later earned him a teaching post at a high school in Drohobycz. According to his biographer, Jerzy Ficowski, Schulz loathed his job and devoted his spare time to writing and drawing.

Imagination Flowing in Letter Somewhat reclusive, Schulz rarely left his hometown and relied on correspondence for much of his communication with other writers and artists. Among his correspondents was Deborah Vogel, a poet who edited the literary journal *Cuszjtar*. In his letters to Vogel, Schulz included strange and fantastic narratives based on his childhood experiences. At Vogel's suggestion, Schulz shaped these stories into his first book, *The Street of Crocodiles*. Published in 1934, this volume impressed the Warsaw literati and won

LITERARY AND HISTORICAL CONTEMPORARIES

Schulz's famous contemporaries include:

Jorge Luis Borges (1899–1986): Famed Argentine author, internationally recognized as one of the most important Latin American writers and thinkers of the twentieth century.

Léopold Senghor (1906–2001): Senghor, a poet and cultural theorist of international repute, was even better known as Senegal's first (and longest-serving) president after independence from France, which he helped negotiate. Senghor remained in office from 1960 to 1980.

William Carlos Williams (1883–1963): One of the most celebrated American poets of all time, Williams was associated with both modernism and imagism, and was also a practicing physician for many years.

James Joyce (1882–1941): One of the most highly regarded literary figures of the twentieth century, this Irishman is best known for his famous short stories and novels; these include *Dubliners* (1914), *A Portrait of the Artist as a Young Man* (1916), *Ulysses* (1922), and *Finnegans Wake* (1939).

Dwight Eisenhower (1890–1969): Eisenhower was the thirty-fourth president of the United States, from 1953 to 1961; prior to his presidency, he presided over the Allied forces' defeat of the Axis powers in Europe during World War II.

Joseph Stalin (1878–1953): Ruthless dictator of the Soviet Union from 1922 until his death in 1953, Stalin was responsible for the murder of millions of his citizens as well as for the rapid industrialization of Russia and other member-states of the Soviet Union.

a golden laurel from the Polish Academy of Letters. Schulz published only one more book in his lifetime, *Sanatorium Under the Sign of the Hourglass*, although he had been working on a novel titled *Mesjaz* (*The Messiah*) when he was fatally shot by a soldier in Nazi-occupied Drohobycz in 1942. The manuscript is believed to have been lost or destroyed during World War II.

Works in Literary Context

In the thirty-two short stories that constitute his entire body of work, Schulz offered his readers an original presentation of a world whose character transcends politics, psychology, or philosophy. The vision of subtle spirituality that he created owes a great deal to a sublime imagination that reveals and evokes, through kaleidoscopic change and metaphoric language, hidden realms of reality. In addition to being a writer, Schulz was also an artist. His many drawings and sketches can thematically be divided into Drohobycz sketches, self-portraits, erotic scenes, and illustrations for his short stories. Though these works share certain elements with his fiction, the latter far surpasses them in pure imagination and originality.

Childhood and the Grotesque *The Street of Crocodiles* and *Sanatorium Under the Sign of the Hourglass* have been compared to the fiction of writers such as Franz Kafka and Marcel Proust. In their fiction, both Kafka and Schulz transform banal places, people, and events into highly symbolic and often grotesque narratives. For example, in *The Street of Crocodiles*, the narrator tells of his father's physical and mental deterioration through symbolic metamorphoses into a bird, a cockroach, and a crab. Many critics contend, too, that Schulz's writing resembles Proust's in its obsession with childhood and time. In his stories Schulz devotes much attention to the narrator's impressions of his past and to the process of memory itself.

Oneself in the Past and One's Dead in the Future Unlike *The Street of Crocodiles*, which focuses primarily on the narrator's peculiar father, *Sanatorium Under the Sign of the Hourglass* deals mostly with the experiences of the narrator himself, who resides in a quasi-magical world where time and space are malleable. In this world it is possible to move through both time and space as though neither existed fully independent of one's movement. In one episode, for instance, the narrator visits his dead father in a strange sanatorium, where the older man carries on a posthumous existence.

Of *Sanatorium Under the Sign of the Hourglass*, Emil Breiter observes that "[Schulz] tears the mask off the world by depriving it of the principle of causality, both temporal and spatial. In the apparent chaos that rules in 'supernumerary time' or in illusory space, the writer preserves such discipline in reasoning, shaping, and observation that one would think he existed in the clearest of realms, one perfectly ordered and free from contradictions." This "tearing the mask off the world," however, should not be mistaken for a refusal of some reality principle. Rather, Schulz is tracing out what it might mean to understand the world not simply as a function of some external and eternal set of natural laws, but also as something that comes into being for us depending on where we stand.

Works in Critical Context

Bruno Schulz is widely considered one of twentieth-century Poland's greatest prose stylists, though his body of work was small indeed. The two volumes of short stories he published have generated and played host to a broad range of criticism from essayists around the world. In the *Boston Review*, Benjamin Paloff writes, "Schulz's stories, phantasmagoric portraits of small-town life during the disintegration of the Austro-Hungarian empire, are told in a lush, lyrical prose that is widely credited with reinvigorating the Polish literary language of the 1930s." Further, Schulz's biographer Jerzy Ficowski writes in his definitive study, *Regions of the Great Heresy*, "In a small provincial town, Bruno Schulz, a modest drawing teacher, undertook the lonely creation of a new world. He created a personal and disquieting bible: two collections of stories in which the object of worship is the secret essence of things which transcend their own limitations—the magic of creation." In short, Schulz was profoundly concerned with reality, but it was reality's essence—creation and invention themselves—not its external appearance, that concerned him. And what could be more at the heart of reality than, as Schulz himself put it in the story "The Book," "this sense of things beyond name whose first taste on the tip of the tongue exceeds the capacity of our admiration"?

Responses to Literature

1. Why do so many authors, poets, dramatists, and others work so hard to offer visions of the world that are not "reality" as we know it but that readers will nonetheless find plausible? Why do you think readers identify with these visions? Structure your answer as an essay responding to the structure and elements of fiction in one or more of Schulz's stories, analyzing both Schulz's rationale for his craft and your own response to it.

2. One theme that frequently arises in Schulz's work is the relationship of a child with his or her father. Compare and contrast three of Schulz's short stories with regard to the way they treat relationships with parents. What overall trends do you see in Schulz's treatment of this theme?

3. Research the short story as a genre, considering at least two prominent definitions. Compare and contrast two of Schulz's short stories with regard to what a short story "should be" or "really is." In what ways does Schulz's work confirm and/or challenge the definitions with which you are working? Are there ways in which his writing asks you to rethink these definitions? If so, how would you redefine the short story in a way that accounts for his work?

4. Consider the processes of disintegration that Schulz describes in his short stories. What trends do you see in his descriptions? Look closely at word choice and sentence structure, at the elements of language that Schulz mobilizes to evoke a fuller sense of loss and disarray. Do you also see opposing tendencies in the same stories? What do these stories communicate, overall, with respect to the themes of loss and disintegration?

BIBLIOGRAPHY

Books

Banks, Brian R. *Muse & Messiah: The Life, Imagination and Legacy of Bruno Schulz.* Cornwall, U.K.: Exposure Publishing, 2006.

Brown, Russell E. *Myth and Relatives: Seven Essays on Bruno Schulz.* Munich: Verlag Otto Sagner, 1991.

Ficowski, Jerzy. *Regions of the Great Heresy: Bruno Schulz, a Biographical Portrait.* New York: W. W. Norton, 2004.

Ficowski, Jerzy, ed. *The Drawings of Bruno Schulz.* Evanston, Ill.: Northwestern University Press, 1990.

Goslicki-Baur, Elisabeth. *Die Prosa von Bruno Schulz.* Bern: Herbert Lang/Frankfurt: Peter Lang, 1975.

Kitowska-Lysiak, Malgorzata, ed. *Bruno Schulz. In Memoriam.* Lublin, Poland: Wydawnictwo Fis, 1992.

Lewis, Henri. *Bruno Schulz ou Les strategies messianiques.* Paris: La Table Ronde, 1989.

Stala, Krysztof. *On the Margins of Reality: The Paradoxes of Representation in Bruno Schulz's Fiction.* Stockholm: Almqvist & Wiksell International, 1993.

Wyskiel, Wojciech. *Inna twarz Hioba: Problematyka alienacyjna w dziele Brunona Schulza.* Kraków: Wydawnictwo Literackie, 1980.

COMMON HUMAN EXPERIENCE

Schulz was an author who treated normal reality as fantastical. This practice situates his work within the broad-reaching genre of magic realism. Here are a few other texts that are magic realist in orientation, being set in the world we know but asking us to believe that it follows a set of rules different from those we are used to:

The Tin Drum (1959), a novel by Günter Grass. This German author's postwar novel about Oskar Matzerath—ostensibly an autobiography written from memory while its narrator (though not its actual author) is in a mental hospital—traces the life of a boy who not only remembers his own birth but who also deliberately stopped growing at the age of three and whose screams shatter glass.

Paradise (1998), a novel by Toni Morrison. This novel explores the history and tensions of the fictional town of Ruby, Oklahoma, an all-black town near which a women's commune has recently been established in an old convent. In following the lives and deaths of the women from this convent, Morrison makes use of several reality-bending elements of magic realism.

The Satanic Verses (1988), a novel by Salman Rushdie. This much-maligned novel earned Rushdie a fatwa, or edict of death, from the Ayatollah Khomeini, the leader of Iran at the time of the book' publication. The novel centers on two Indian Muslim actors who survive the midair explosion of a hijacked airplane, and afterwards transform: one into an angel, and one into the devil.

Walter Scott

BORN: *1771, Edinburgh, Scotland*

DIED: *1832, Abbotsford, Scotland*

NATIONALITY: *Scottish*

GENRE: *Fiction, poetry*

MAJOR WORKS:
The Lady of the Lake (1810)
Waverley; or, 'Tis Sixty Years Since (1814)
Ivanhoe (1820)

Overview

Modern scholars consider Scottish author Sir Walter Scott both the inventor of the historical novel and the first best-selling novelist. In addition to elevating the novel to a status equal to that of poetry, Scott single-handedly created the genre of historical fiction, vividly bringing to life both Scottish and English history.

Works in Biographical and Historical Context

Childhood Illness Scott was born in Edinburgh, Scotland, on August 15, 1771, into a prosperous middle-class family. His father, also named Walter, was a lawyer with strong ties to the Scottish Border country,

Sir Walter Scott *Scott, Sir Walter, photograph. AP Images.*

the area on the border of Scotland and England. His mother was Anne Rutherford Scott, daughter of a professor of medicine.

When he was eighteen months old, Scott contracted polio (an infectious virus that can cause paralysis in the arms and legs due to lesions to the central nervous system), which left his right leg permanently crippled. Despite his illness, Scott was an active child, and his parents often sent him to the countryside to stay with his paternal grandfather, hoping the fresh air and country living would improve Scott's health. Interested in Scottish history and literature during his childhood, Scott also developed an appreciation for the natural scenery that became such a defining characteristic of his writing.

Embraced Scottish Culture Scott enrolled in Edinburgh High School in 1778, and five years later entered Edinburgh University, where he studied history and law. In 1786, he was apprenticed to his father's legal firm and became a lawyer in 1792. During his apprenticeship, Scott traveled a good deal in the Scottish Border country and Highlands, gathering folk ballads and enjoying the oral tradition of simple farmers and shepherds.

In 1797, Scott married Charlotte Carpenter, with whom he had two daughters and two sons. Scott read widely in politics and history, and soon he was composing his own versions of traditional oral ballads. In 1798 he was appointed sheriff of Selkirkshire, Scotland, in the Border country. Shortly thereafter, the Act of Union of Great Britain and Ireland was passed. Thus, in 1800, the United Kingdom, which included Scotland, England, Wales, and Ireland, formally came into being. Scotland, like the rest of the United Kingdom, was ruled by King George III of the House of Hanover at this time.

Poetic Success In *Minstrelsy of the Scottish Border* (1802), his first publication, Scott's interests as a poet, an antiquarian, and a Scottish cultural nationalist came together for the first time. This work contained the Scottish ballads he had collected over the years, many of which had never before appeared in print. Encouraged both by praise from friends and by the popularity of this collection, Scott wrote the highly successful narrative poem *The Lay of the Last Minstrel* (1805), a work Scott intended to illustrate the customs and manners of inhabitants on both sides of the Scottish-English border during medieval times.

Around this time, Scott quit practicing law full time and entered into a longtime relationship with the printer James Ballantyne, purchasing a third share in the business that would publish many of his works throughout the years. Scott followed the success of *The Lay of the Last Minstrel* with a series of highly popular poems featuring Scottish backgrounds and themes. *Marmion: A Tale of Flodden Field* (1808), for example, tells of a famous—and disastrous—Scottish battle against the English. In 1810, Scott published his best-known long poem, *The Lady of the Lake*, set in the Scottish Highlands.

The Waverly Novels The triumph of the first two cantos of Lord Byron's poem *Childe Harold* in 1812 convinced Scott that he could not compete with the younger poet. By the time Scott's next work, *Rokeby*, appeared in 1813, readers were beginning to lose interest in his poetry. Anxious to keep his audience and income, Scott decided to revise and complete a fragment of a novel that he had begun ten years before about the Jacobite revolution in Scotland, an attempt to restore the old Stuart line to the Scottish and English thrones. Published in 1814, *Waverley; or, 'Tis Sixty Years Since* quickly became the most successful work of its kind ever to appear, and the novel brought huge profits to Scott and his publisher.

Over the next seventeen years, Scott wrote more than two dozen novels and stories in a series now known as the Waverly Novels. Because he never worked out his plots ahead of time, rarely revised his manuscripts, and followed strict work habits, Scott was able to maintain an impressively prolific pace. Through the speech, manners, and customs of past ages, most of the Waverly Novels describe the lives of ordinary individuals who become involved in historical events. This body of work is often divided into three groups: the "Scotch Novels," including *Old Mortality* (1816), which deal with Scottish culture and history; the novels that focus on medieval history in England and Europe, such as *Ivanhoe* (1820); and those that are concerned with the Tudor-Stuart era in England, including *Woodstock* (1826).

Because writing novels was considered less respectable than writing poetry during this time, Scott published the Waverly Novels anonymously. Even when the success of this series increased general public appreciation for novelists, Scott chose to remain anonymous—most likely a result of his perception that the mystery surrounding the novels contributed to their sales. The Waverly Novels were published as "by the Author of *Waverly*," and the author was often referred to simply as the Great Unknown. Although the Waverly Novels were published anonymously, many readers and critics alike knew Scott's identity, and he became not only the most popular writer in contemporary English literature, but also a highly esteemed personality throughout Europe. In 1818, Scott was made a baronet and thereafter was known as Sir Walter Scott.

Personal Tragedies In 1826, a dual tragedy struck. His wife, Charlotte, died in May of that year, followed by Scott's financial ruin when the Ballantyne printing company went bankrupt. His debt was well over one hundred thousand pounds, an enormous sum. The following year, so that he could begin putting his affairs in order, Scott publicly acknowledged authorship of the Waverley Novels and turned with renewed urgency to his writing. Eventually, the debt was paid, but at a terrible cost to the author's health. Despite suffering a stroke in 1830, Scott continued to write and travel. Everywhere he trav-

eled, he was received as a celebrity, one of the first authors to enjoy international fame. During his travels, however, he was forced to return home after another stroke, and he died on September 21, 1832.

Works in Literary Context

Influenced by History Scott's reading of the workds of Edmund Spenser and Torquato Tasso and Thomas Percy's *Reliques of Ancient English Poetry* (1765) did much to shape his later poetry, as did his many expeditions to the countryside, where he spent time collecting ballads, local legends, and folklore. Scott was greatly influenced by the history and life of people who lived in his native Scotland.

Novel Incorporations Scott worked a number of ballads, songs, and other lyrics into his novels. Gothic writers such as Ann Radcliffe and Matthew Lewis had revived the convention of interspersing lyric poems in prose narratives that was characteristic of earlier English

COMMON HUMAN EXPERIENCE

Scott essentially invented the genre of historical fiction, a genre that still flourishes today. Here are some more recent works of historical fiction:

Gudrun's Tapestry (2003), a novel by Joan Schweighardt. Set in the fifth century, this story vividly brings to life Attila the Hun and an ancient Norse saga.

I, Mona Lisa (2006), a novel by Jeanne Kalogridis. The author creates the life of a young woman in fifteenth-century Florence, Italy, who is the model for Leonardo da Vinci's famous painting.

Joshua's Bible (2003), a novel by Shelly Leanne. This novel follows a young African American man in the 1930s who goes to South Africa as a missionary and confronts the early days of apartheid.

Night of Flames (2007), a novel by Douglas W. Jacobson. In this novel, a married couple is separated while fleeing Nazi-occupied Poland during World War II.

Snow Flower and the Secret Fan (2006), a novel by Lisa See. This novel, set in nineteenth-century China, examines women's roles in rural China.

The Sugar Cane Curtain (2000), a novel by Zilia L. Laje. This novel explores the Cuban Revolution and Fidel Castro's rise to power in Cuba.

romances such as Sir Philip Sidney's *Arcadia* (1590, 1593) and Thomas Lodge's *Rosalynde* (1590). Scott used this device to much greater effect than his Gothic predecessors did. His early mastery of song and ballad forms enabled him to establish atmosphere and character, and his use of lyrics to comment on or foreshadow the action of the novels is often quite subtle and effective.

Influence Twentieth-century critics have emphasized Scott's important role in English literary history, as well as his considerable impact on nineteenth-century European literature. Literary historians have traced his influence on the masterpieces of novelists as diverse as Charles Dickens, Gustave Flaubert, Honoré de Balzac, and William Makepeace Thackeray. Scholars have also explored Scott's significant contribution—through his invention and development of the historical novel—to the history of ideas, specifically with respect to the modern concept of historical perspective.

Works in Critical Context

Influence on Historical Perspective The novelty of Scott's writing style, as well as his compelling subject matter, captivated his early audience. Most early reviewers of his poetry and novels noted the superiority

of his works, citing their originality, vivid portrayal of history, and lively characters. Throughout the nineteenth century, Scott's reputation among readers and critics alike had progressively declined to the point that by the turn of the century, many conceded that Scott was no longer a major literary figure. Many contemporary critics observed such flaws as careless plotting, prolixity, and bad grammar, especially in his shorter fiction, but the critical tide turned in the mid-twentieth century. Modern scholars have acknowledged Scott's seminal influence on the development of the European novel genre, particularly with regard to historical perspective and the realization of the effects of social change on the lives of ordinary people.

Waverly; or, 'Tis Sixty Years Since The first in the Waverly Novels series, *Waverley* (1814), proved a popular sensation when first published and quickly became the most successful work of its kind ever to appear. Contemporary critical reaction, though also positive, did cite certain deficiencies in the work, including careless construction and prolixity. Yet most early reviewers quickly acknowledged the strengths of the novel, noting its originality, vivid portrayal of history, and lively characters.

Like most of Scott's novels, *Waverley* has fallen out of favor, although it continues to attract the attention of scholars interested in the view of history it offers. In the late 1960s, Robert C. Gordon wrote in *Under Which King? A Study of the Scottish Waverly Novels,* "*Waverly,* then is one of the most distinguished innovations in literary history. It is also a splendid work in its own right. Scott found his solution to the problems of dealing with Jacobitism in the story of an immature, vain yet fundamentally proper young hero who becomes a warrior."

Other studies have been greatly influenced by the criticism of Georg Lukàcs in *The Historical Novel.* In this work, Lukàcs examined Scott as a dialectical historian, claiming that he "endeavors to portray the struggles and antagonisms of history by means of characters who, in their psychology and destiny, always represent social trends and historical forces." Numerous critics have taken up Lukàcs's idea and applied this thinking to Edward Waverley as he represents a significant moment of cultural transition in Scottish and English history.

Responses to Literature

1. In an essay, address the following questions: Do you think that novels are worth reading even if they are not considered "great literature"? When you read something, do you think about how well it is written, or do you simply enjoy the story? Who should define what "good" literature and music are—the critics or ordinary people? Why?

2. Since 1999, Scotland has had its own governing body, although it is still part of Great Britain. There is a movement toward Scotland's breaking its union with England and establishing complete independence. Research the independence movement and write an essay that analyzes the pros and cons of Scottish independence.

3. Historical novels and movies can make history come alive in a way that textbooks often cannot. Choose a period or movement that you have studied in school, and find a novel or movie about it. Read the novel or watch the movie and write a short essay analyzing it. Did it engage you or make you think differently? Did it contain historical inaccuracies in order to enhance dramatic effect?

4. Research the history of the state you live in. When was it established, and what were the conflicts in its early days? Do any of those conflicts continue today? Choose one event from your state's history, and write a short story patterned after the historical fiction of Scott. Develop your characters in such a way that captures the language, clothing, and settings of the past.

BIBLIOGRAPHY

Books

Brown, David. *Walter Scott and the Historical Imagination.* New York: Routledge & Kegan Paul, 1979.

Chandler, Alice. *A Dream of Order: The Medieval Ideal in Nineteenth-Century Literature.* Lincoln: University of Nebraska Press, 1970.

Devlin, D. D. *The Author of Waverley: A Critical Study of Walter Scott.* London: Macmillan, 1971.

Hart, Francis R. *Scott's Novels: The Plotting of Historic Survival.* Charlottesville: University Press of Virginia, 1966.

Johnson, Edgar. *Sir Walter Scott: The Great Unknown.* New York: Macmillan, 1970.

Kerr, James. *Fiction Against History: Scott as Storyteller.* Cambridge: Cambridge University Press, 1989.

Kroeber, Karl. *Romantic Narrative Art.* Madison: University of Wisconsin Press, 1960.

Shaw, Harry E. *The Forms of Historical Fiction: Sir Walter Scott and His Successors.* Ithaca, N.Y.: Cornell University Press, 1983.

Periodicals

Smith, D. Nichol. "The Poetry of Sir Walter Scott." *University of Edinburgh Journal* 15 (1951): 63–80.

Web Sites

Edinburgh University Library. The Walter Scott Digital Archive. Retrieved March 15, 2008, from http://www.walterscott.lib.ed.ac.uk.

Eugène Scribe

BORN: *1791, Paris, France*

DIED: *1861, Paris, France*

NATIONALITY: *French*

GENRE: *Fiction, drama*

MAJOR WORKS:

A Night at the National Guard (1815)

The School for Politicians; or, Non-Committal (1833)

The Glass of Water (1840)

Adrienne Lecouvreur (1849)

The Ladies' Battle (1851)

Overview

Eugène Scribe was one of the most prolific and popular French dramatists of the nineteenth century. Although his works are seldom produced today, Scribe is remembered for his mastery of the "well-made" play, which profoundly influenced the works of his contemporaries and successors. Scribe is known for plays that feature elaborate plots full of clever twists and light, witty dialogue. In addition, he wrote music and librettos to accompany his own stage plays and the operas of the time.

Eugène Scribe   *Scribe, Eugène, engraving.*

Works in Biographical and Historical Context

Early Prodigy Augustin Eugène Scribe was born in Paris on December 24, 1791. At this time, France was undergoing a period of social and political upheaval; the ten year French Revolution (1789–1799), which began shortly before Scribe's birth, transformed the government according to the principles of the Enlightenment, paving the way for changes in the literary arena. Scribe's father, a silk merchant, died when Eugène was an infant but left enough for his widow to raise their son without financial worries. She was able to send him to good schools, and he was a brilliant student at the Collège Sainte-Barbe, where he finished with a first prize in his last year. He received his prize under the dome of the Académie Française and, coincidentally, from the hands of Vincent-Antoine Arnault, whose seat at the Académie Scribe eventually inherited.

Rejecting Law for Theater Following his university education, Scribe's mother placed him with a prominent attorney, expecting him to demonstrate his talents in the field of law, but the young Scribe had developed a passion for the theater, and neither his mother's nor his employer's efforts could keep him away from it. When his mother died in 1807, his inheritance provided him an adequate living, and he devoted himself fully to the theater. He soon graduated from merely watching plays to writing them in collaboration with his former classmate, Germain Delavigne, among others.

Early Failures, Eventual Successes The first of Scribe and Delavigne's plays to be staged, on January 13, 1810, was *The Accidental Suitor; or, Opportunity Makes the Thief*, which did not make it through its first performance. Over the next five years more plays followed, none of which were successes. After several failures Delavigne gave up, but Scribe struggled on, and eventually his persistence was rewarded. In November 1815, he achieved his first hit with *A Night at the National Guard*, which introduced themes (such as virtue versus vice) that he would pursue for the rest of his career.

Prolific Career Although *A Night at the National Guard* was followed by several failures, it did not take long for the successes to mount as Scribe's prolific pen churned out more than a dozen works a year. Many were written with collaborators, which was a frequent practice at the time, and Scribe was always generous with his colleagues, sharing both credit and profits even though in many cases he did more than his share of the work.

Théâtre du Gymnase The opening of the new Théâtre du Gymnase in 1820 added to the prominence of Scribe. He provided its first play and was bound to the theater by a long-term contract. Over the next decade he wrote more than a hundred plays for the Théâtre du Gymnase, which did not keep him from filling other theaters with more than forty more. His production included not only vaudevilles but also full-length dramas for the Théâtre-Français and librettos for the Opéra-Comique and the Opéra. He showed that he could be serious as well as humorous and that he understood the special needs of the musical genres, which made him much in demand as a librettist.

Important Contributions Scribe's popularity made him an invaluable member of the Sociétédes Auteurs et Compositeurs Dramatiques, which he helped found in 1827. Writers had little leverage in dealing with theater managers and often had to settle for nominal payments for their work even if it went on to make a fortune for the theater. The new organization was able to establish fairer practices that set minimum payments and allowed those in great demand, such as Scribe, to negotiate upward from the base payments.

Académie Française In 1834, Scribe entered the Académie Française, replacing Arnault in the seat that had once belonged to Jean Racine. The next year he used the English court for a character study on the love of power in *The Ambitious* (1835) and a few years later chose the same locale for what is probably his best-known play, *The Glass of Water* (1840).

Late Marriage and Slowed Production Scribe remained single until he was forty-eight, when he married Madame Biollay, the widow of a wine merchant. It appears that she managed to do what his mother could not—get him to think at least occasionally about something other than the theater. His productivity after his marriage decreased significantly. It was the ideal bourgeois marriage that he favored so consistently in his plays—comfortable and harmonious. Scribe did continue to work, however, up until his death, which claimed him without warning on February 20, 1861, as he rode home in his carriage after a meeting. He was sixty-nine years old. Thousands turned out to watch his funeral cortège pass.

Works in Literary Context

A "Well-Made" Style Scribe was influential as the author who perfected the well-made play: he took forms and devices from the theater of earlier periods, like the recommendations made in Aristotle's *Poetics* for example, and combined them in inventive and systematic ways that formed a new type of play adaptable to various styles and genres. This new form, with its clarity, logic, and intriguing combination of inevitability and surprise, seldom failed to please the public.

The main plot, and the real subject of the play, might involve events and themes from history, politics, or various social issues of the day, but the focus of the play was action rather than philosophy. In many of Scribe's plays the structure centers around a single character whose actions and decisions vitally affect the lives of the other characters. Often this character makes a decision and then changes it several times, provoking appropriate reactions from the other characters before the final decision brings about the play's resolution, or denouement.

Whatever the basic structure, Scribe obviously believed that the audience wanted the action to keep moving. Each scene makes a definite contribution to the development of the plot. Lyrical interludes and development of character beyond what is needed for the plot or for engaging the interest of the audience are considered unnecessary; they interrupt the flow of the action, so they are kept to a minimum, if not eliminated entirely.

Another major element of the construction of the well-made play is the arrangement of the entrances and exits and the onstage combinations that result. The scenes are usually tightly linked together, and each scene leads into the next; Scribe makes sure that each scene has a combination of characters that will permit the action to move forward according to a plan.

Scribe often linked a love interest to the principal plot. Most of his plays, however, have at least one subplot (and sometimes as many as seven), usually solidly connected to the main plot. In *The Glass of Water* (1840), for example, the love plot of Masham and Abigail and the struggle of Bolingbroke to overthrow the duchess become interdependent when the first three characters join forces. The subplot may be minor or nearly as important as the main plot, and it may stretch from beginning to the end of the play or just occupy a part of it, but it must be satisfactorily resolved before the final curtain. There can be no loose ends in a well-made play.

Human Virtue and Vice as Theme Scribe chose a wide variety of subjects for his plays. Many are linked to historical events in various times and places, including England, Russia, France, and even the United States during the American Revolution. They are only in a limited sense historical plays, for they tend to emphasize private lives against a historical backdrop rather than to portray political history for its own sake.

The values Scribe expresses consistently include the standard virtues and values that are generally called bourgeois. He opposes the old aristocratic prejudices against earning a living and favors individual merit above class origin. He shows the consequences of gambling, adultery, and a variety of character weaknesses. His characters speak constantly of money, reflecting its importance in society, but he repeatedly shows those who are excessively concerned about it in an unfavorable light, especially those who sacrifice their happiness, or that of others, to it. *Marrying for Money* (1827), for instance, puts primary emphasis on a theme that appears as a secondary consideration in many of his plays—the role of money in marriage. Scribe's most frequently represented form of happiness is a good marriage, one in

which there is enough money for a modicum of comfort and a genuine affection between the partners.

He was widely imitated by playwrights as different as Henrik Ibsen, Bernard Shaw, Émile Augier, and Georges Feydeau, to name but a few, many of whom denied their debt to him and joined his detractors, who had almost from the beginning loudly proclaimed his supposed faults. Such sustained criticism and a vogue for new forms led to his eventual eclipse. A few of his plays have been produced in modern times, but today few among the theatergoing public even know his name although the techniques he used so masterfully continue to permeate the theater and made their way into the cinema and eventually into television.

Works in Critical Context

When Scribe took the seat at the Académie Française in 1894, his election was by no means universally acclaimed. Many critics, especially those associated with the Romantic movement, had long decried his "lack of style," as Théophile Gautier put it. They placed primary emphasis on the literary value of dramatic works, and they forgave him neither his preference for realistic dialogue nor the commercial success he enjoyed and that was denied more "literary" authors. Scribe, following his usual practice when attacked, did not bother to respond.

Although many critics and playwrights recognized Scribe's mastery of dramatic construction and technique, few made more than a cursory attempt to explain it. Such an omission may be the result of disdain, since for some

COMMON HUMAN EXPERIENCE

Here are a few works by writers who, like Scribe, focused on the consequences of greed, selfishness, ambition, and other vices in their work:

Othello (c. 1603), a play by William Shakespeare. In this classic tragedy, ambition is combined with jealousy and greed to destroy a marriage, a political relationship, and a life.

The Miser (1668), a play by Molière. In this comic drama, grown children seek to get away from their miserly father.

Wuthering Heights (1847), a novel by Emily Brontë. In this classic novel, the two main characters have grown up together, love each other deeply, and are torn apart by the choices one makes based on selfishness and a sense of superiority.

Forbidden Love: A Harrowing True Story of Love and Revenge in Jordan (2003), a novel by Norma Khouri. In this book an Arabic Muslim woman must face the dire personal and cultural consequences of falling in love with a Catholic man.

---

the phrase "well-made play" indicated inferior, lowbrow culture. But it may also have been with some amount of envy that his critics derided the playwright. Scribe was the first French playwright to make a fortune solely by writing plays. He was proud to acknowledge the source of his income and went so far as to have inscribed over the gate of his country estate: "The theater funded this rustic retreat. Thanks, traveler! I may owe it to you."

The Glass of Water *The Glass of Water* played a key role in the career of a man who was both, as literary critic Philip G. Hill puts it, "hailed and acclaimed during his lifetime as a playwright wildly popular with the public" and "vilified and derided since his death, blamed for all the shortcomings of the playwrights who came after him." "Neither position," Hill concludes, "is completely fair." What Scribe accomplished, in *The Glass of Water* perhaps above all, was "the structuring of theatrically effective plots out of nearly any subject matter that came to hand, so that the 'well-made play' became almost a formula." From another perspective, scholar Stephen S. Stanton notes that "the reason the social dramatists adopted Scribe's technique was that he had evolved a very tricky, though essentially mechanical, method of dealing with lightly social and moral themes, so as to make them seem amusing to a jaded and blasé society." Stanton also observes that at times *The Glass of Water*, "for all its dependence on a hand prop and its skilful timing, seems more credible [than other, more 'literary'

dramas] and not just another variation of a standard farce plot."

Responses to Literature

1. Eugène Scribe is credited with creating the theatre genre known as the well-made play. Discuss the elements that make this kind of play and match the list of criteria against one of Scribe's works. What are Scribe's important techniques of action, characterization, and plot?

2. The term "well-made play" had negative connotations by the mid-nineteenth century. Yet several writers of the time and at the end of the 1800s refused to give up the convention. Study a play by Anton Chekov, Henrik Ibsen, August Strindberg, or Émile Zola and, using the list of criteria for the well-made play, try to identify the elements that survived criticism. Defend your findings with examples from the text.

3. *Libretto* is Italian for "little book," and is a text created for the production of, usually, an opera. Scribe was considered both a playwright and a librettist. Giuseppe Verdi and Jacques Offenbach were famous librettists. Investigate the history of the libretto. With an idea of the necessary components needed in a script for an opera, write a modern libretto: Choose a favorite short story or scene from a novel; decide on the best music to use; and add some action and dialogue set to music. Consider the reasons for your choices. For instance, why would a certain song fit with a moment in the opera? How would the best parts of the prose text be played out musically on stage? How can you cater to your audience as carefully as Scribe did?

4. Citing specific examples from the text, compare and contrast the conflicts in *The Glass of Water* and *Adrienne Lecouvreur*. Comment on these tensions with regard to aspects of the well-made play.

BIBLIOGRAPHY

Books

Gautier, Théophile. *The History of Dramatic Art in France for Twenty-five Years.* Paris: Magnin, Blanchard, 1858–1859.

Gillespie, Patti P. *The Well-Made Plays of Eugène Scribe.* Ann Arbor, Mich.: University Microfilms, 1971.

Koon, Helen, and Richard Switzer. *Eugène Scribe.* Boston: Twayne, 1980.

Stanton, Stephen Sadler. *English Drama and the Well-Made Play, 1815–1915.* Ann Arbor, Mich.: University Microfilms, 1958.

Periodicals

Cardwell, Walter Douglas, Jr. "The Role of Stage Properties in the Plays of Eugène Scribe."

Nineteenth-Century French Studies 16 (Spring/
Summer 1988): 290–309.

Matthews, J. Brander. "Pleasant Land of Scribia," *Yale
Review* 8 (1919): 836–44.

Stanton, Stephen Sadler. "Shaw's Debt to Scribe."
PMLA 76 (December 1961): 575–85.

Web Sites

1911 Encyclopedia. "Augustin Eugène Scribe."
Retrieved March 31, 2008, from http://
www.1911encyclopedia.org/Augustin_Eugene_
Scribe.

Project Gutenberg. "Scribe, Eugène, 1791–1861."
Retrieved March 31, 2008, from http://
www.gutenberg.org/browse/authors/s#a4444.

Turney, Wayne S. *Eugène Scribe (1791–1861) & the
"Well-made Play"*. Retrieved March 31, 2008, from
http://www.wayneturney.20m.com/scribe.htm.

◈ George Seferis

BORN: *1900, Smyrna, Asia Minor*

DIED: *1971, Athens, Greece*

NATIONALITY: *Greek*

GENRE: *Poetry, nonfiction*

MAJOR WORKS:

Turning Point (1931)

The Cistern (1932)

Tale of Legends (1935)

Logbook III (1955)

Three Hidden Poems (1966)

Overview

Winner of the Nobel Prize in Literature in 1963, George
Seferis is one of the most important poets and literary
critics of Greece; his views on the Greek demotic, or
common, folk tradition and literary canon determined
the course of modern Greek letters for the better part
of the twentieth century.

Works in Biographical and Historical Context

Son of a Law Professor   George Seferis, pen name of
Giorgos Seferiadis, was born on March 13, 1900, in
Smyrna (now Izmir), Asia Minor (now Turkey), the son
of Stelios and Despo Seferiadis. The family left Smyrna in
1914 for Athens, where Stelios Seferiadis taught law at
the University of Athens.

*Successful Experiments with Poetics While Greece
Was in Turmoil*   After Seferis finished his secondary
schooling in Athens, he pursued a law degree in Paris
from 1918 to 1924, briefly visiting London from 1924 to
1925. Spending the formative years from the ages of

eighteen to twenty-five abroad, he remained attentive to
the literary movements of the day, especially those of
symbolism and surrealism. Meanwhile, Greece was torn
apart by political struggles. After World War I (1914–
1918), the centuries-old Ottoman Empire (which controlled much of eastern Europe, the Middle East, and
northern Africa), began to collapse. This left a power
vacuum in the areas that are now Greece and Turkey.
Ethnic Greeks and ethnic Turks fought each other to win
territory. The Greeks got half-hearted support from Britain other allies, who were drained and weary after World
War I. The Turkish got the upper hand in the Greco-
Turkish war, and the Greek population fled Asia Minor
(now part of Turkey). After chasing them across the
country, the Turks had hundreds of thousands of refugees cornered in the port city of Smyrna. Despite orders
from the Turkish leaders not to harm noncombatants, the
Turkish army massacred the Greeks and burned the city
to the ground while British ships in the port refused to
help or even take in the refugees. The event looms large
in Greek history.

In 1931, with the publication of his first poetry
collection, *Turning Point*, Seferis embarked on his career
as a poet. In this work and in his later poetry collections—*The Cistern* (1932), *The Mythical Story* (1935),
Logbooks I–III (1940), *The Thrush* (1947), and *Three
Secret Poems* (1966)—he solidified his status as one of
the most revered national poets of Greece. Seferis's
experimentation with symbolist and modernist poetics
and his exclusive use of demotic, or common, Greek as
the language of choice earned him a privileged place in
the collective body of work produced by his generation of
poets, known in Greek literary criticism as "the Generation of the 1930s."

Advancing Literary Criticism   Along with others
of the "Generation of the 1930s," Seferis also published
his literary criticism extensively in some of the most
important literary journals in Greece. He is credited with
advancing the genre to a new level of rigorousness and
sophistication, the influence of which was felt for the
better part of the twentieth century. Seferis was also an
accomplished translator, publishing his translation of T.
S. Eliot's poetry in *The Waste Land and Other Poems*
(1936) as well as *Antigraphes* (1965), a volume of translations of poets primarily of the symbolist and modernist
traditions, such as William Butler Yeats, Paul Valéry, D.
H. Lawrence, Ezra Pound, Marianne Moore, André
Gide, and W. H. Auden.

Astute Political Writings   By virtue of the various
diplomatic positions he had held in the Greek Ministry of
Foreign Affairs during his lengthy career from 1926 to
1962, Seferis was an astute observer of Greece's most
tragic national crises, including the terrible aftermath of
the Greco-Turkish War. The Albanian campaign of 1940
and 1941 was immediately followed by the Nazi occupation of Greece from 1941 to 1943. The ensuing Greek

LITERARY AND HISTORICAL CONTEMPORARIES

Seferis's famous contemporaries include:

Louis "Satchmo" Armstrong (1901–1971): American jazz trumpeter, he was an innovative and therefore primary influence in the advancement of jazz music.

Nikos Kazantzakis (1883–1957): Greek novelist best known for *The Last Temptation of Christ* (1951) and *Zorba the Greek* (1946).

Luis Buñuel (1900–1983): Spanish filmmaker who worked mainly in Mexico and France. Buñuel is considered one of the most important directors in the history of cinema.

Margaret Mitchell (1900–1949): American author who won the 1937 Pulitzer Prize for her novel *Gone with the Wind*.

T. S. Eliot (1888–1965): English-American poet, dramatist, and literary critic, he was instrumental in advancing literary theory and contributed one of the most definitive and representative works in history with *The Waste Land* (1922).

civil war from 1946 to 1949 was followed by the Cyprus conflict during the 1950s. Reactions to these crises abound in Seferis's private, political, and autobiographical journals, such as his *Political Journals and Manuscript Sept. '41.*

Political Crisis Reflected in Poetry Seferis's poetry also reflected the crises. In the aftermath of the destruction of Smyrna and the displacement of more than a million refugees into Greece, Greek society was burdened by a great sense of defeat and loss. The twenty-four poems that make up the collection *The Mythical Story* (1935) were written in the context of this psychological defeatism. Although Seferis does not explicitly refer to the evacuation of Smyrna, his birthplace, fleeting images in the poem recall scenes from this tragic episode in recent history that had become embedded in Greek popular memory. In *Logbook II* (1944), written in the period of World War II (during which Seferis was in exile) and thereafter, he presents a cluster of poems that thoughtfully deal with the theme of the destructiveness and futility of war.

The Nobel Prize and Other Honors Seferis won the Nobel Prize in 1963, the first Greek national to win any of the five annual prizes since the Swedish Academy began issuing the awards in 1901. Seferis received several honorary doctoral degrees from Cambridge (1960), Oxford (1964), the Aristotle University of Thessaloniki (1964), and Princeton University (1965). Seferis also

become an honorary foreign member of the American Academy of Arts and Sciences and was appointed honorary fellow of the Modern Language Association in 1966. He was invited to become Charles Eliot Norton Professor of Poetry at Harvard for the academic year 1969–1970. Although he was honored by the invitation, he declined because he was uncomfortable with the idea of lecturing at Harvard at a time when exercising the freedom of expression had been prohibited in Greece. At the time, Greece was under the control of a repressive military junta.

After he returned to Greece, because of mounting public pressure, Seferis issued his first public statement condemning the junta in what had hitherto been two years marked by the regime's repressive measures, including widespread censorship, political detentions, and torture. Seferis's statement was made on March 29, 1969, on the BBC and distributed to every newspaper in Athens. Defying martial law, he called for an end to the dictatorship. He regarded the widespread curbing of liberties a national "humiliation" and concluded that "We have all learned that in dictatorial regimes the beginning may seem easy, yet tragedy lurks, inexorably in the end."

George Seferis, however, did not live to see the end of the junta. He died in Athens, after extensive hospitalization, on September 20, 1971. His funeral in Athens drew a vast crowd and was linked to the protest movement against the dictatorial regime of his native Greece. The junta fell from power in 1974.

Works in Literary Context

In his early years abroad, Seferis was exposed to the work of many influential writers of the late nineteenth and early twentieth centuries, such as Charles Baudelaire, Arthur Rimbaud, Stéphane Mallarmé, Paul Valéry, and T. S. Eliot. In early collections like *Turning Point* (1931), Seferis also presents a diction that pays homage to his literary predecessors: Homer, seventeenth-century Cretan Renaissance poet Vincentzos Kornaros, and nineteenth-century poet Ioannis Makryannis. It is Makryannis's *Memoirs* that Seferis went on to hold in his lectures and literary criticism of the 1940s as an exemplary model of demotic Greek folk tradition. It is in his themes and style, however, that Seferis returns to being a symbolist taking much influence from modernist poets like Eliot.

Themes of Recovery of the Antique Past The idea of the need for a recovery of antiquity permeates Seferis's poems. It is both the textual tradition (the study of history) and the preserving of collective consciousness (group awareness) of history that concern Seferis. His poems "The King of Asine" from the collection *Logbook I* (1940) and "Mycenae" from the collection *Gymnopaidia* (1935) best illustrate his interests. "The King of Asine," for example, is based upon an obscure textual reference in Homer's *Iliad* and features the contemporary poet in search of the lost king, walking among ruins at an archaeological site. The poet attempts to interpret these broken fragments, to give meaning in his present to the archaeological ruins of the past.

Seferis recalls how the understanding of the ancient past underlying the discourse of European Hellenism since the nineteenth century was founded upon the reading of fragments. In this case, he deciphers stone fragments to contemplate the existence of those who had once lived there. But those ancient peoples remain remote and inaccessible now. The stones instill in him a void, and he concludes that only through nostalgia can the past revive: "nostalgia," as Seferis puts it, "for the weight of a living existence" brings the fragments back to life and renders them meaningful to modern consciousness.

Preoccupation with History and Myth Seferis's preoccupation with history and myth in his poetry and his translation and explication of Eliot's work in his literary criticism of the 1930s and 1940s prompted many critics of his day to proclaim the so-called influence of Eliot on Seferis. His early poems, for instance, convey a use of literary devices that were often closely associated with Eliot's *The Waste Land* (1922). Imagery of broken stones and fragments and arid landscapes were interpreted as metaphors for the spiritual emptiness and emotional vacuity of the narrators of the poems.

Modern Symbolist Style Seferis's early poetry shows his affinity for symbolism. Though he remained critical of the avant-garde artistic movements that relied heavily on symbolism, which he viewed as "facile poetry," what particularly distinguishes his style is his use of symbols. Throughout his work there are both readily decipherable ones ("stones," "statues," "landscape") and obscure ones intelligible only to himself ("swans," "angelic and black light"). Scholars and critics considered this trademark practice to be associated with the symbolist movement in European and Anglo-American literary and artistic circles.

In its adherence to such principles, symbolist poetry, just as many other modernist texts, lent itself to multiple interpretations. These elements were most closely considered part of a "pure poetry." They were also closely associated with the ever-changing definitions of symbolism, as represented in the work of contemporaries. These connections linked Seferis's experimentation with symbolist practice to Valéry, to Yeats, and again to Eliot.

Works in Critical Context

When Seferis won the Nobel Prize in 1963, the critical appreciation of his poetry concerning his nation and its past and present was clear: in awarding this prize, the academy was paying "tribute to the Greece of today, whose rich literature has had to wait, perhaps too long, for the Nobel laurels." Much of Seferis's work demon-

strates how deserving he was of this praise for his "tributes" to Greece, including, for example, "Mycenae."

"Mycenae" In this poem from the collection *Gymnopaidia*, Seferis acknowledges the continuing relevance of the model of Aeschylean justice. The narrator, presumably a modern-day Orestes, refers to the stones at the ancient archaeological site in Mycenae and conveys their overwhelming impact on him, "Whoever lifts these heavy stones sinks / I lifted these stones for as long as I could / I loved these stones for as long as I could." The "stones" in these lines have been interpreted by critics over the years to signify the burden of the ancient past on modern Greek consciousness. The consciousness (of the speaker) in "Mycenae" looks upon antiquity as being inextricably linked to modernity. That is its fate. Yet, it remains a past that is enigmatic and virtually unidentifiable.

At the Nobel Prize Awards banquet in his presentation speech, the permanent secretary of the academy, Anders Österling spoke to the key symbols that distinguish Seferis's poetry by saying that the poet had astutely interpreted "the mystery of the stones, of the dead fragments of marble and of the silent, smiling statues." And echoing the reception of critics and citizens alike Österling added, "Seferis's poetic production is not large, but because of the uniqueness of its thought and style and the beauty of its language, it has become a lasting symbol of all that is indestructible in the Hellenic affirmation of life."

Responses to Literature

1. Seferis made a connection with history by observing the ruins of his ancient Greece and considering how they represented the past. Find an object at your school, home, or local museum that is from the distant past. Using all of your senses (first make sure you have freedom to touch the item), except maybe taste, describe the object. Then decide what you believe this object "represents" from the past.

2. Seferis was considered a symbolist poet at numerous periods in his writing life. Before researching further, consider one important object in your life (or consider what one single tattoo you would get if you could). Why did you choose this object or image? What did it make you think of? What feelings come from the object/image for you? What does your choice say about who you are? That is, how does your choice represent your personality? You may even wish to research a symbolism Web site or a dream meaning Web site to see what someone else thinks the item says about you.

3. Research the symbolist movement. What was the philosophy of the symbolists? How were you a symbolist when you completed one of the above tasks? How is Seferis a symbolist? What items does he use in his poetry and what are the associations connected to these objects?

BIBLIOGRAPHY

Books

Dimiroulis, Dimitris. *The Poet as Nation: Aestheticism and Ideology in G. Seferis.* Athens: Plethron, 1999.

Leontis, Artemis. *Topographies of Hellenism: Mapping the Homeland.* Ithaca, N.Y.: Cornell University Press, 1995.

McHale, Brian. *Postmodernist Fiction.* New York & London: Methuen, 1987.

Österling, Anders, Permanent Secretary of the Swedish Academy. *1963 Nobel Prize in Literature Presentation Speech.* The Nobel Foundation, 1963.

Thaniel, George. *Seferis and Friends (Some of George Seferis' Friends in the English-Speaking World),* edited by Ed Phinney. Stratford, Ont.: Mercury, 1994.

Tziovas, Dimitris. *The Transformation of Nationism and the Ideologeme of Greekness.* Athens: Odysseas, 1989.

Periodicals

Keeley, Edmund. "T. S. Eliot and the Poetry of George Seferis." *Comparative Literature* 8, no. 3 (1956): 214–26.

Loring Danforth. "The Ideological Context of the Search for Continuities in Greek Culture." *Journal of Modern Greek Studies* 2 (1984): 53–85.

Martha Klironomos. "Ancient anamnesis, National mneme in the Poetry of Giorgos Seferis." *Journal of Modern Greek Studies* 20, no. 2 (October 2002): 215–39.

Web sites

Greece Poetry International Web. *George Seferis (Turkey, 1900).* Retrieved March 18, 2008, from http://greece.poetryinternationalweb.org/piw_cms/cms/cms_module/index.php?obj_id=2453.

Nobel Prize Foundation. *Georgos Seferis Nobel Prize Banquet Speech.* Retrieved March 18, 2008, from http://nobelprize.org/nobel_prizes/literature/laureates/1963/seferis-speech.html.

◈ Jaroslav Seifert

BORN: *1901, Prague, Austro-Hungary*

DIED: *1986, Prague, Czechoslovakia*

NATIONALITY: *Czech*

GENRE: *Poetry, nonfiction, essay*

MAJOR WORKS:

Halley's Comet (1967)
Casting of Bells (1967)
The Plague Column (1970)

Jaroslav Seifert   Seifert, Jaroslav, photograph. AP Images.

Overview

The winner of the 1984 Nobel Prize in Literature, Seifert is widely considered to be the Czech national poet as well as one of the foremost Czech literary figures of the twentieth century. Respected for his courage and integrity in the face of the political repressions of both the Nazi and the Communist eras, Seifert was a prolific author, publishing more than thirty volumes of poetry over a span of sixty years. His verse, thought to embody the spirit of the Czech people, is infused with Czech history, literature, and culture and frequently pays homage to Seifert's hometown, the Czech capital city of Prague.

Works in Biographical and Historical Context

A Former Communist Resists the Nazis Seifert, son of a working-class family, published his first volume of poems in 1921 and, together with other young intellectuals, joined the newly formed Czechoslovakian Communist Party. In 1929, when that party's leadership changed its course to reflect developments in the Soviet Union—most notably the rise to power of Joseph Stalin—seven of the foremost writers among its members, including Seifert, protested publicly and were expelled. After his break with the Communists, Seifert worked as a literary editor, mostly on social democrat periodicals, and published one collection of poems after another. During the Munich crisis of 1938—when the great powers of Europe essentially gave Hitler free rein in "reclaiming" the Sudetenland, a largely German-speaking portion of Czechoslovakia—and the subsequent catastrophes that shattered the country, leaving its people dominated by Nazi Germany, Seifert became a spokesman for Czechoslovakian nationalism and penned many poems urging resistance.

Disloyalty and Treachery—or an Independent Mind? During the immediate post–World War II period, Seifert directed an eclectic review, the *Bouquet*, but this was shut down in 1948 when the Communists seized power. The new authoritarian government silenced Seifert and many other writers for failing to promote the slogans of social realism. A series of poems by Seifert in 1950 honoring his native village and rural novelist Bozena Nemcova, a greatly admired Czech novelist and female rebel of the classic period of Czech literature, earned him the denunciation of official critics as "disloyal," "bourgeois," "escapist," and "a traitor to his class." Seifert then turned to writing children's literature, a genre to which his direct, simple style was well suited. One of these efforts, *Maminka*, has become a classic of Czech literature, epitomizing, according to Alfred French in *Czech Writers and Politics, 1945–1969*, "a whole trend of literature away from the monumental to the humble; from public themes to private; from the

pseudoreality of political slogans to the known reality of Czech home life which was the product of its past." This turn to the private, in a way, prefigured the "apolitical politics" that would characterize the resistance to authoritarian rule that developed with the Charter 77 group in 1977 and thereafter.

The Dean of Czech Letters In 1956, when the Soviet regime in Czechoslovakia tightened controls on artistic freedom, Seifert spoke out at a writers' association meeting on behalf of imprisoned and silenced writers. His speech had little immediate effect beyond infuriating the establishment sufficiently to suspend publication of his new works, but the poet was from that time on generally regarded as the dean of Czech letters, a man from the old days whose contemporaries were almost all dead, who could always be counted on to speak the truth.

Seifert reemerged in the mid-1960s at the forefront of the drive among Czech writers to support the liberalization and de-Sovietization of the Communist regime, a national movement known as the Prague Spring. The liberalization of the Prague Spring, however, was cut short by a Warsaw Pact invasion of Czechoslovakia in August 1968, assuring that Soviet rule would continue until the bloodless revolution of 1989. The following October, the National Writers Union elected Seifert president to replace the exiled Eduard Goldstucker, but the country's leaders dissolved the union in 1970. Seifert refused to join a new government-backed writers union and was one of the first to sign the Charter 77 human rights manifesto. Consequently, the poet was again out of favor, and for a decade the Czech authorities published no new work of his.

His new writings were published mainly privately or abroad, the best known of which was *The Plague*

COMMON HUMAN EXPERIENCE

Even though Seifert experienced many problems in his native Czechoslovakia, including a fair bit of political disfavor, his entire body of work demonstrates his love for his country. He frequently invokes the characters, places, and traditions of Czechoslovakia in order to enliven his poetry and to honor his heritage. Here are a few other examples of art that expresses or addresses national feeling:

This Is the Army (1943), a musical play directed by Michael Curtiz. This American musical was designed to boost morale during the long and difficult World War II years. Future president of the United States Ronald Reagan was one of the stars of the film.

"This Land Is Your Land" (1940), a folksong by Woody Guthrie. This song by the famed American folksinger celebrates the beauty of the American landscape and the sense of community he feels in sharing it with his compatriots.

Jingo (1997), a novel by Terry Pratchett. The title of this novel, about a war between two countries over a newly formed island, refers to "jingoism," or belligerent patriotism.

Column, published in Czech in 1977 by the émigré publishing house Index in Cologne, West Germany, and later translated into English. A single, long poem, it celebrates the monument erected by the people of Prague soon after the end of the Thirty Years' War in thanks for deliverance from the plague.

The Nobel Prize   In view of Seifert's great popularity and the occasion of his eightieth birthday, Czech officials relented and allowed the publication of an edition of *The Plague Column* in 1981. A year later, they also allowed Seifert's memoirs, *All the Beauties of the World*, to be released. Two years after that, in 1984, Seifert was awarded the Nobel Prize in Literature. In fact, during the last years of his life, Seifert enjoyed a unique position among his fellow writers: He had been a dissident and published abroad, yet he was, at the end of his long career, acceptable to the Prague regime. "He is not liked by the state, but they cannot silence him because he is so famous," exiled Czech poet Pavel Kohout told United Press International on the day of the Swedish Academy's announcement of the 1984 Nobel Prize winner, adding, "He's really a voice of the people." Seifert died in relative seclusion in 1986, three years before the monumental shift in Czechoslovakia and other Eastern bloc countries that has been termed the "Revolution of 1989"—a shift that signaled the end of Soviet hegemony and, indeed, the beginning of the end of the Soviet Union itself.

Works in Literary Context

Seifert's career as a poet ranged from an intensely lyrical period when he began writing in the 1920s, to a surrealistic phase in the 1930s, to vehement patriotism during the Nazi occupation, and, finally, to a meditative, philosophical stage toward the end of his life. But throughout, his themes remained constant: celebration of his homeland and his native Prague, a deep concern for the suffering of others, and a sensuous delight in the beauty of the physical world and the love of women. Critics credit his appeal as a poet to his work's utter simplicity and unpretentiousness and its haunting and lyrical qualities.

From Proletarian Poetry to Pure Poetry and Beyond   As a young man, Seifert passed through the then-dominant phase of "proletarian" poetry, as revealed in his first two collections, *The City in Tears* and *Nothing but Love*; these were celebrations of the common person and the bright future of socialism. He also embraced the succeeding "pure poetry" phase, with its emphasis on exotic and playful imagery, as evidenced by *On Radio Waves* and *The Nightingale Sings Badly*. Seifert's poetic maturity reputedly began with the cycle of poems *The Carrier Pigeon* and peaked with *Jablko z klina*, a collection in which the clever manner and fireworks of earlier works had been abandoned for a new style, one notable for its sincerity and directness and for its cultivation of natural, unaffected images rendered in fresh, at times almost colloquial, language. Love, including its sensual aspects, a frequent theme in Seifert's earlier collections, is his main subject in *An Apple from the Lap* and continues to dominate his next collection, *The Hands of Venus*.

In the years leading up to and following the Prague Spring, Seifert published the trilogy that is perhaps his best-known work: *Halley's Comet*, *Casting of Bells*, and *The Plague Column*. These poems evoked themes that had called to Seifert from the beginning of his poetic career; yet, within the new poetic environment of free verse and an abstinence from ornament, Seifert's lyric takes on a stronger ethical challenge and a more meditative tenor than it had before. As a result, the trilogy represents the strongest, most effective, and most critically acclaimed work of Seifert's long and prestigious career.

Patriotism   The national catastrophe at Munich in 1938 and the Nazi occupation that followed brought out Seifert's deep patriotism, reflected in some of his most acclaimed collections. These include *Put Out the Lights*, which expresses the poet's anxiety after the betrayal of Czechoslovakia at Munich, *Dressed in Light*, a poetic tribute to Prague written by Seifert during the Nazi occupation of Czechoslovakia, and *The Helmet of Clay*, several cycles of patriotic verses published after the war, celebrating in particular the Prague uprising against the remnants of the occupying Nazi army in May of 1945. In *The Helmet of Clay*, a tremendously popular collection that is generally credited with establishing Seifert as a national poet, he pits the brief violence and the eerie excitement of improvised barricades against the startling beauty of the lilacs, the acacias, and the chestnuts in bloom.

Works in Critical Context

Many commentators have found it difficult to understand the implications of Seifert's work in its translated form. Critics note that what Seifert called his poems' "inner rhythms"—as well as the many ethnic nuances and allusions—have not been captured adequately by translators. Nevertheless, his poetry has been widely praised, and is described in his Nobel Prize citation as work that, "endowed with freshness, sensuality, and rich inventiveness, provides a liberating image of the indomitable spirit and versatility of man."

With his patriotic poems, writes fellow Czech poet Josef Skvorecky in the *New Republic*, "full of both linguistic beauty and encoded messages—clear to the Czechs, impenetrable to the Nazi censor, the poet boosted the morale of the nation." These were poems that, in the words of *Listener* contributor Karel Janovicky, "plucked the secret strings of the nation's soul while the Nazi censor looked on bewildered."

Halley's Comet, Casting of Bells, and The Plague Column
Seifert's stylistic innovation in the impressive and imposing collections *Halley's Comet*, *Casting of Bells*, and *The Plague Column* showed, as critics have noted, that, though he was installed as a national icon, he was by no means a fixed, static entity but a flexible poet with artistic currency. The poetry of this trilogy was haunted by the dual and dueling themes of the wages and rewards of being human: death, war, and loss on the one side, and the vital and immortal power of poetry, love, and sensuality on the other. Prague—the city of nostalgia and trauma—was the background against which these forces were examined. Like earlier readers of Seifert's trilogy, more recent critics have tended to respond at least in part to Seifert's tremendous political integrity. Zdenek Salzmann, for instance, describes Seifert's role in Czechoslovakia, expressed in these volumes, as "a symbol of courage and political incorruptibility." Meanwhile, critics such as Dana Lowey have lamented the "damaging translations" that have resulted in "misunderstandings, inaccuracies, and downright misrepresentations of Seifert's art." Coming in for particular criticism in this regard is an early rendering of *Casting of Bells* by translators Paul Jagasich and Tom O'Grady.

Responses to Literature

1. Read *The Plague Column*. How does Seifert both use and examine Czech history and culture in his poetry? Analyze specific passages in your response.

2. Seifert's poetry has been praised for its simple, straightforward style, but it has also been said that Seifert is sometimes difficult to understand for non-Czech readers. Read *Casting of Bells*. Evaluate Seifert's style in terms of the seemingly contradictory assessment that his poetry is both extremely accessible and yet difficult to understand. Do you think it is more important for a writer to reflect the culture in which he or she works or to appeal to readers on a more universal level? Why?

3. Using the Internet and the library, research patriotism. Then, read a couple of examples of patriotic literature. In a short essay, examine the following question: How does your school's fight song compare to patriotism and the patriotic literature you have read, in terms of its expressions of love and devotion for a place and the people who inhabit it? What are the potential problems posed by such patriotism?

4. Using the Internet and the library, research the treatment of other writers in Czechoslovakia during the heyday of Communism and Nazism. How does Seifert's treatment compare with these other writers' treatment?

BIBLIOGRAPHY

Books

French, Alfred. *Czech Writers and Politics, 1945–1969.* New York: Columbia University Press, 1982.
———. *The Poets of Prague.* New York: Oxford University Press, 1969.
Harkins, William E. *Anthology of Czech Literature.* New York: Columbia University Press, 1953.
Skvorecky, Josef. *Cross Currents: A Yearbook of Central European Culture.* Ann Arbor: University of Michigan Press, 1985.

Periodicals

Hájek, Igor. "All the Beauty of the World—or What's Left of It." *Scottish Slavonic Review* (1984).
Pisa, A. M. "Jaroslav Seifert." *Cin* (1931).

Seneca

BORN: *4 BCE, Corduba (now Córdoba), Spain*

DIED: *65 CE, Rome*

NATIONALITY: *Roman*

GENRE: *Nonfiction, drama, poetry*

MAJOR WORKS:

Medea (composition date unknown)

Thyestes (composition date unknown)

On Favors (63 CE)

Natural Questions (63 CE)

Moral Epistles (64 CE)

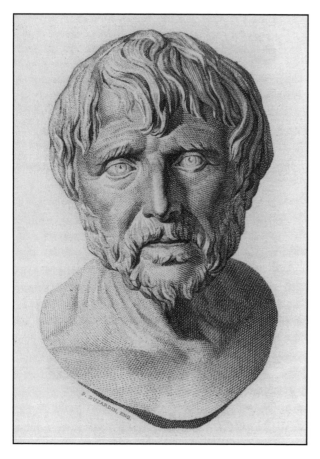

Seneca   *Archive Photos / Getty Images*

Overview

Seneca (known as Seneca "the Younger") is the principal Stoic philosopher, essayist, and tragedian of imperial Rome. A prolific and versatile writer, Seneca was a respected man of letters who also fully and actively participated in the politics of his time. Serving as tutor and advisor to the young emperor Nero, Seneca helped to direct Nero's political policies between the years 54 and 62 CE, ensuring a greater measure of tolerance and justice in Rome. Seneca's tragedies—alternately lauded for his powerful portrayals of extreme circumstances and mental states and criticized for his presentation of lurid onstage violence—left a permanent mark on English drama and are considered his most enduring contribution to literature.

Works in Biographical and Historical Context

Early Studies, Travel to Egypt, and Tuberculosis

Lucius Annaeus Seneca was born in 4 BCE, or shortly before, in Corduba (modern Córdova) in southern Spain, the second son of Seneca the Elder, a famous rhetorician and teacher. Brought to Rome by his maternal aunt when he was a small child, Seneca embarked on the study of grammar and rhetoric, eventually turning to philosophy. During that period, he traveled to Egypt, where his aunt and uncle were living, while his uncle served as provincial governor. Seneca experienced a serious illness during this stay, and scholars agree that he probably suffered from ill health for most of his life due to a tubercular condition.

Exile, Return, and Rise to Power

When he returned to Rome in 31 CE after a long convalescence in Egypt, he held the government post of quaestor (magistrate) and was eventually admitted to the Roman Senate. He rose to fame as both an orator and an author. His popularity and stature, as biographers speculate, aroused the jealousy of the emperor Caligula. He survived the brief rule of Caligula (37–41 CE) only to be exiled to Corsica in the first year of Claudius's reign (41 CE). The charge was adultery with Caligula's sister, Julia Livilla, brought by the new empress, Claudius's young wife, Messalina.

Seneca's exile came at a time of great personal distress—both his father and his son had recently died. For much of these eight tedious years, Seneca devoted his time to literary compositions, including his treatise *On Anger* (41 CE). By this time, his Stoic philosophy was well developed. Stoics regarded emotions as unhealthy effects of the unnatural condition they called "vice." In his elaborate exposition, Seneca defines anger as "the burning desire to avenge a wrong," and represents it as the most hideous of all the emotions. He then offers prescriptions on how to prevent and extinguish anger.

In 48 CE, Messalina was executed. The following year, Seneca, through the agency of Agrippina, Claudius's new wife, was allowed to return to Rome in order to work as tutor to her son Nero and to assume the office of praetor (a high ranking magistrate and army commander). His literary and philosophical reputation was now well established, and this appointment as Nero's tutor placed Seneca again at the center of the Roman world. When Agrippina poisoned her emperor-husband, and Nero ascended the throne in 54 CE, Seneca suddenly wielded immense power and influence.

Political Power

For the first eight years of Nero's reign, Seneca and the commander of the praetorian guard, Afranius Burrus, acted as his chief ministers and political counselors, shaping and substantially controlling his policies. Historians assert that during these years Seneca's influence on Nero was a tempering one, for he encouraged the young ruler to work toward a more enlightened and socially beneficent state. They also note, however, that Seneca must have bowed to many of Nero's wishes in order to preserve his position in the court and that he may have aided, or helped to cover up, Nero's murder of his mother, Agrippina, in 59 CE.

Between Seneca's return from exile in 49 CE and his effective retirement in 62 CE, he wrote most of his philosophical dialogues. These works espouse Stoic positions on ethical issues: They advocate virtue, endurance, and self-sufficiency; they condemn evil, emotions, and the false values of wealth and power; they praise reason, wisdom, and poverty; they show contempt for the fear of death. To this period too are dated *On Mercy* (55–56 CE), written as advice to Nero, and *Pumpkinification* (54 CE), a sharp satire deriding the deification of Claudius, designed to reflect well on the image of the new potentate.

As Nero's rule progressed, Seneca became increasingly subject to criticism for the gap between his Stoic exhortations and Nero's tyrannical tendencies, which included the murder of his stepbrother, Britannicus, in full view of the imperial court. Seneca also drew attacks for hypocrisy; his praise of poverty did not prevent him from amassing a huge fortune through his position in the court. His treatise *On the Happy Life* (c. 58 CE), in which wealth is justified as a potential instrument of virtue, was probably written as a personal apologia.

Seneca's Moral Epistles   One of Seneca's longer philosophical works, *On Favors* (c. 61 CE), illuminates Roman social and moral codes by examining, in detail, the complexities surrounding individual acts of kindness. Its composition late in Seneca's political career—as the monstrous acts of the former pupil he no longer controlled began to breach Roman codes—is but one of many ironies defining Seneca's life.

Following the death of Burrus in 62 CE, Seneca retired from public life. His last works include a scientific volume on *Natural Questions* (c. 62 CE), and the letters addressed his friend Lucilius, known as the *Moral Epistles* (c. 62–65 CE). The latter became Seneca's most popular prose work from antiquity to the present day, and its popularity is easy to understand. The fictive pose of correspondence enables Seneca to cover an enormous range and variety of subject matter, addressed in an informal manner that strikes readers as authentic and sincere. The epistles have been called the forebears of the modern discursive essay.

In 65 CE, Seneca was accused of participating in an unsuccessful conspiracy against Nero. The emperor ordered him to commit suicide, and Seneca obeyed, dying in a highly theatrical manner with self-conscious allusions to the death of Socrates and to his own place in history. His final act, judged a heroic one, was recorded by Tacitus in his *Annals*.

Senecan Drama   A good portion of Seneca's body of writing survives to the present day; among his lost works are writings on science, geography, and philosophy, as well as all of his speeches. In addition to his prose, he is today remembered for his contribution to the Roman stage. At least seven complete tragedies can be assigned to Seneca. Two others may be his, but their authorship is disputed; one more, *Phoenissae*, exists in fragments, suggesting that it was never finished. Scholars surmise that the tragedies were written between 45 and 55 CE.

Most of his plays, such as *Medea* and *Oedipus*, are based on existing works by the Greek dramatists Euripi-

des and Sophocles, respectively; however, they differ from their Greek models in two main respects: their style is highly rhetorical, filled with sophisticated wordplay and verbal argumentation, and their atmosphere is gloomy and larded with portents of horror.

Seneca's tragedies reflect more vividly than the philosophical works the cultural and moral turbulence of early imperial Rome. Born during the reign of Augustus and committing suicide three years before Nero's similar fate, Seneca was encompassed by the social and moral convolutions of his era. Power resided essentially in one man, who could be (as Caligula was) violent and cruel. In Rome, and especially at the court itself, nothing and no one was secure. Political and personal freedoms were nullified. The themes of Seneca's tragedies—vengeance, madness, passions, murder, incest, and hideous death—were the stuff of his life experience. The most frequently cited example of Senecan gore is from *Thyestes*, where Atreus exacts vengeance on his brother, who seduced the former's wife, by serving him a meal made of his own children. Over and over again in these plays, passion leads to madness and chaos, and the natural universe responds by giving way to disorder and preternatural happenings.

Works in Literary Context

The scholarly consensus is that as a thinker, Seneca was not very original; his teachers were disciples of the Roman Stoic philosopher Quintus Sextius, and Seneca rarely strayed from their beliefs. As for his literary endeavors, the soundness of Seneca's education gave him a wide variety of models on which to base them: the epics of Homer; Greek poets and dramatists, as well as his fellow Romans Horace, Virgil, and Ovid; the early Stoics, Plato, Aristotle, and the entire spectrum of Hellenistic philosophy; and Roman rhetoricians from Cicero to Caesar. The copious references to other texts in his dramas reflect his absorption of these literary traditions.

COMMON HUMAN EXPERIENCE

Seneca's tragedies are an integral part of a theatrical tradition that encompasses the entirety of Western history, from ancient Greece to the present day. Here are some examples of great stage tragedies:

The Trojan Women (415 BCE), a play by Euripides. This tragedy follows the characters of Helen, Cassandra, Hecuba, and Clytemnestra after the sacking of Troy.

The Jew of Malta (1589), a play by Christopher Marlowe. The protagonist of this revenge tragedy, Barabas the Jew, was the model for Shylock in Shakespeare's *Merchant of Venice*.

Coriolanus (1623), a play by William Shakespeare. Shakespeare deftly explores the choice between democracy and autocracy in this bloody tragedy, set in Rome during the fifth century BCE

Phedre (1677), a play by Jean Racine. This masterpiece of the French stage depicts a story from Greek mythology, Phaedra's unrequited love for her stepson Hippolytus.

Textuality and Theatricality Senecan tragedy engages in a constant counterpoint with the dramatic and poetic tradition. This intertextuality underscores one of the recurrent themes of Senecan tragedy, the recycling of the past as the present. The world of early imperial Rome was indeed dominated by the forms of its own past—political, social, religious, and legal—and by the playing out of conventional rituals and roles. Inevitably, in this theatrical world, Senecan tragedy frequently draws attention to its own theatricality. Medea requires Jason as an audience to give meaning to her own murderous play; the Trojan dead are summoned as "spectators" to Cassandra's recited play in *Agamemnon*. The recurrent focus on action as spectacle, and behavior as role-playing, show Seneca's interest in drawing attention to the conventions and artifice of the stage.

Rhetoric Part of what made imperial Rome theatrical was its love of rhetoric, and Seneca's tragedies, like his philosophical dialogues, are highly rhetorical. Seneca is a master of both expansive declamation and the compressed or "pointed" style of discourse. Seneca's tragedies and prose works are the product of a sensibility informed by rhetoric, at a time when rhetoric was the controlling principle of both education and literary composition. Contemporary audiences responded fully to all kinds of dialectical and verbal ingenuity. Senecan tragedy is rhetorical, as Elizabethan tragedy is rhetorical; both are the product and index of an age.

Influence on Elizabethans Seneca's works were approved by the early Christian Church and studied by medieval writers such as Francesco Petrarch, Geoffrey Chaucer, and Dante Alighieri. Even more than his prose and philosophical writings, Seneca's tragedies influenced European, and especially Elizabethan, literature in a profound manner. The introduction of Seneca to English audiences—through a performance of the *Troades* at Cambridge University in 1551—marked an important event in the history of English drama. Many later playwrights, including such luminaries as Ben Jonson, Christopher Marlowe, and William Shakespeare, eagerly modeled their works on Seneca's style and themes. Scholars list the tragedies of Seneca among the most significant influences on the Elizabethan theater, noting that many stock characters and situations derive directly from Seneca's plays. On the continent, Seneca served as a model for seventeenth-century playwrights Pierre Corneille and Jean Baptiste Racine.

Works in Critical Context

Seneca is admired for the elegant presentation of ideas in his prose and for the powerful influence he exerted on Elizabethan and later drama. Critics have praised the prose style of his essays, letters, and treatises as one of the foremost examples of the "pointed," or epigrammatic, style of the Latin Silver Age, noting its didactic yet accessible tone and skillful use of colorful figures of speech.

Moral Epistles: A Hit for Two Thousand Years Seneca has remained a popular literary figure for nearly two millennia. The early Christian writers admired his philosophical writings, finding in them many similarities to Christianity and judging Seneca the most Christian of the pagan authors. In the Middle Ages, his works figured very prominently, along with Cicero's, among the main educational texts used. His essays and epigrams, incorporated into commonplace books and termed "Seneks," served as an important tool for teaching morality. His epistles were a major influence on Montaigne, regarded as the founder of the modern essay form. His drama, through its profound impact on Elizabethan theatre, has remained influential to the present day.

Seneca was defended in the eighteenth century by Jean-Jacques Rousseau and Denis Diderot. Writing in 1893, critic John W. Cunliffe wrote extensively of Seneca's influence on Elizabethan tragedy, labeling him "the most modern of the ancients." Twenty-first-century critics continue to debate the issues that have been at the center of Seneca studies since his own time. Some grant him the status of a major thinker, while others see his philosophical concepts as superficial. Dialogue continues on the question of whether Seneca's dramas were intended to be performed or simply declaimed to an audience. The relationship between the tragedies and the philosophical works, particularly the degree to which the plays express a Stoic perspective, continues to be a subject of debate. Some contemporary scholars have closely scrutinized Seneca's historical context; others have become interested in his handling of character portrayal and psychology. For instance, in his discussion of grief in his book *Everything Has Two Handles* (2008), Tufts University psychologist Ronald Pie judges Seneca's works from this modern perspective. He writes, "Seneca was hard-nosed but not completely insensitive when it came to grief and mourning," and goes on to state that "many psychologists and psychiatrists would disagree with Seneca" on some of his views.

Responses to Literature

1. Analyze the qualities of dialogue and rhetoric in one of Seneca's tragedies. How does Seneca's rhetorical style affect the way you understand the play?

2. Studying one of Seneca's philosophical dialogues; discuss how the author uses the text to accomplish underlying political motives. Why do you think Seneca's work was favored by the Church and used as a teaching tool during the Middle Ages?

3. Respond to the philosophical content in Seneca's prose or letters. What is your attitude toward Stoicism? Can you trace any modern group of thinkers or artists that adopt a Stoic attitude? How are their modern ideas alike or different from Seneca's?

4. Choose one of Shakespeare's well-known tragedies—perhaps *Othello*, *Hamlet*, or *King Lear*—and compare it to a play written by Seneca. What do the works have in common in terms of style and theme? Can you identify why the Elizabethans were drawn to Seneca's works?

BIBLIOGRAPHY

Books

Beacham, Richard C. *The Roman Theatre and Its Audience*. Cambridge, Mass.: Harvard University Press, 1992.

Bieber, Margarete. *The History of the Greek and Roman Theater*. Princeton, N.J.: Princeton University Press, 1961.

Boyle, A. J. *Tragic Seneca: An Essay in the Theatrical Tradition*. London: Routledge, 1997.

Braden, Gordon. *Renaissance Tragedy and the Senecan Tradition: Anger's Privilege*. New Haven, Conn.: Yale University Press, 1985.

Costa, C. D. N., ed. *Seneca*. London: Routledge & Kegan Paul, 1974.

Griffin, Miriam T. *Seneca: A Philosopher in Politics*. Oxford: Oxford University Press, 1976.

Henry, Denis, and Elisabeth Henry. *The Mask of Power: Seneca's Tragedies and Imperial Rome*. Warminster, U.K.: Aris & Phillips, 1985.

Miola, Robert S. *Shakespeare and Classical Tragedy: The Influence of Seneca*. Oxford: Oxford University Press, 1992.

Rosenmeyer, Thomas G. *Senecan Drama and Stoic Cosmology*. Berkeley and Los Angeles: University of California Press, 1989.

Periodicals

Fitch, John G. "Sense-pauses and Relative Dating in Seneca, Sophocles and Shakespeare." *American Journal of Philology* 102 (1981): 289–307.

Tarrant, R. J. "Senecan Drama and Its Antecedents." *Harvard Studies in Classical Philology* 82 (1978): 213–63.

⊠ Léopold Sédar Senghor

BORN: *1906, Joal, Senegal (French West Africa)*

DIED: *2001, Normandy, France*

NATIONALITY: *Senegalese, French*

GENRE: *Poetry, nonfiction*

MAJOR WORKS:
Songs of Shadow (1945)
Black Hosts (1948)
Ethiopiques (1956)
Nocturnes (1961)

Overview

Léopold Sédar Senghor served as president of the Republic of Senegal for twenty years following its independence from France in 1960. This popular statesman was also an accomplished poet and essayist whose work, written in French, affirms the rich traditions of his African heritage. Along with Aimé Césaire, he is best known for developing "negritude," a wide-ranging movement that influenced black culture worldwide. As the chief proponent of negritude, Senghor is credited with contributing to Africa's progress toward independence from colonial rule, and he is considered one of the most important African thinkers of the twentieth century. His career represents the successful fusion of apparent opposites: politics and poetics, intellectual and folk traditions, and African and European culture.

Works in Biographical and Historical Context

Education and Negritude Senghor was born October 9, 1906, in the predominantly Islamic province of Joal, in what was then French West Africa. Raised as a Roman Catholic, he attended French missionary schools in preparation for the priesthood. At the age of twenty, he abandoned religious studies for a European education at a French secondary school in Dakar. Upon his

Léopold Senghor   *Senghor, Léopold, photograph. The Library of Congress.*

graduation in 1928, he earned a scholarship to study at the Sorbonne in France.

Senghor received an elite education amid the intellectual scene of Paris. He met the West Indian writers Aimé Césaire and Leon Gontran Damas, who introduced him to African American literature of the Harlem Renaissance. Senghor came to recognize the impact of African expression on modern European art, especially in music and the visual arts. With Césaire and Damas, Senghor launched *The Black Student*, a cultural journal.

In the early 1930s, Senghor, Césaire, and Damas began to speak of "negritude," a term coined by Césaire to give a positive connotation to a word often used as a racial slur. Senghor credits Jamaican poet and novelist Claude McKay with having supplied the values promoted by the new movement: to seek out the roots of the black experience and to rehabilitate black culture in the eyes of the world. For Senghor, negritude exalted the intuitive and artistic nature of the African psyche, qualities that white Europeans masked with reason and intellect.

Senghor became the first black African to graduate from the Sorbonne with a grammar aggregation, the highest degree granted in French education, and he began teaching in Parisian schools. As fascism and racial prejudice swept through Europe in the 1930s, Senghor

angrily rejected European culture, but he soon softened his position.

Poetry in Wartime   The poems Senghor wrote in the late 1930s were published after World War II in the collection *Songs of Shadow*. Although largely traditional in structure and meter, these pieces evoke the intricate rhythmic patterns of songs from Senghor's native village. These poems express Senghor's nostalgia for Africa, his feelings of exile and cultural alienation, and his native culture's sense of dignity. The poems also lament the destruction of African culture under colonial rule.

When Germany invaded Poland in September 1939, Senghor was immediately drafted to protect France as an infantryman at the German border. France fell to the German assault in June 1940, the same month Senghor was captured and taken prisoner. He spent two years in the Nazi camps and wrote some of his finest poems during that time. These poems later formed the core of Senghor's second published collection, *Black Hosts*.

Black Hosts explores the poet's sense of unity with blacks as an exploited race, and especially with other blacks fighting for Europe, such as those from the United States and the West Indies. The poems "Prayer for the Tirailleurs of Senegal" and "Despair of a Free Volunteer" celebrate the humility and endurance of Senegalese soldiers, whose battlefield experiences Senghor equates with the sufferings of their ancestors under colonialism.

Overlapping Political and Literary Careers
After his release in 1942, Senghor resumed teaching in suburban Paris and joined the Resistance movement. He became dean of linguistics at the National School of Overseas France. After the war, he was elected as a Senegalese representative in the French National Assembly. He founded the Senegalese Democratic Bloc (BDS) in 1948. With a socialist platform and a strong base among the peasants, this party rose to dominance in Senegalese politics. Senghor was reelected to the assembly in 1951, and again in 1956. That year, he became the mayor of the Senegalese city of Thies.

During this time, Senghor continued his literary pursuits as well. In 1947, he cofounded the literary journal *African Presence*, which became a powerful vehicle for black writing worldwide. The following year, he edited a book with a powerful introduction by French intellectual Jean-Paul Sartre that became a manifesto of the negritude movement: an anthology of French-language poetry from the black diaspora—a scattering of people with a common origin or background.

A collection of poems Senghor had been working on since 1948 was published as *Ethiopiques* in 1956. These poems reflect Senghor's growing political involvement and his struggle to reconcile European and African allegiances. One long poem in *Ethiopiques*, "Chaka," is a dramatic adaptation of Thomas Mofolo's historical novel about a Zulu warrior king of the nineteenth century. In reality, Chaka was a ruthless killer and a tyrant; Senghor, however, is less interested in the leader's exploits than in his state of mind.

The Poet-President As Algeria battled French forces for independence in the late 1950s, the colonies of French West Africa also pressed for freedom from their colonial rulers. Senghor advocated a path toward national or federal governments for African states. Although he helped bring several territories together into the Mali Federation in 1959, this structure did not last long. Senegal became an independent republic in 1960, and Senghor was elected its first president.

During Senghor's years in power, Senegal enjoyed relative political stability. Senghor survived an attempted coup d'état staged in 1962 by his rival, prime minister Mamador Dia, and afterward Senegal rewrote its constitution to give the president more power. He was reelected in 1968 and 1973, and resigned in 1980, before the end of his fifth term. No previous African president had voluntarily left office.

After 1960 Senghor mainly wrote political prose, especially that promoting African democratic socialism. He wrote a series of five books on political theory under the omnibus title *Liberty*. Poems Senghor wrote before his election as president of Senegal were published in 1961 as *Nocturnes*. This collection discusses the nature of poetry and the role of the poet in contemporary society. *Nocturnes* also reprints in its entirety Senghor's previously published volume *Songs for Naett*, a series of lyrical love poems written to a woman who represents the African landscape. In 1964, Senghor's most significant verse became available in English translation.

Later Career After retiring from Senegalese politics, Senghor divided his time between Paris, Normandy, and Dakar. He continued writing poetry, and he penned a memoir, *What I Believe: Negritude, Frenchness, and Universal Civilization* (1988). He died in Normandy in 2001.

Works in Literary Context

During his years as a student, first in French West Africa and later in Paris, Senghor read widely in the canon of French literature. Some authors whose influence is apparent in Senghor's poetry include Arthur Rimbaud, the surrealist André Breton, the Catholic poet Paul Claudel, and Saint-John Perse, winner of the 1960 Nobel Prize for Literature. Not coincidentally, both Claudel and Perse were professional diplomats whose work reflects an immersion in the social currents of the world beyond European shores.

However, it was Senghor's exposure to the African American writers of the Harlem Renaissance—writers such as Langston Hughes, Claude McKay, W. E. B. DuBois, and Zora Neale Hurston—that helped him find his voice as a modern African. In Paris, Senghor was exposed to political movements such as socialism and

---

LITERARY AND HISTORICAL CONTEMPORARIES

Senghor's famous contemporaries include:

Jean-Paul Sartre (1905–1980): A French author and philosopher known for his existentialist works.
Albert Camus (1913–1960): A French-Algerian existentialist author and philosopher. Camus was the first African-born winner of the Nobel Prize for Literature.
Pablo Neruda (1904–1973): Chilean poet and diplomat who won a Nobel Prize for Literature.
Richard Wright (1908–1960): African American novelist and essayist who immigrated to Paris.
James Baldwin (1924–1987): African American novelist, essayist, and activist who immigrated to Paris.
Julius Nyerere (1922–1999): The first president of Tanzania (1964–1985).
Charles de Gaulle (1890–1970): A French military leader during World War II, de Gaulle served as president of France from 1959 to 1969.

---

humanism, ideologies that are apparent throughout his literary and political work.

Voice of His People Senghor has said that his poetry bears a kinship to folk poetry, yet his work is also very clearly the result of a modern, cosmopolitan sensibility. No tradition of modernist African poetry—certainly not in French—existed when Senghor began his career. He drew on his African heritage and European education to forge something new. Under the French colonial policy of assimilation, Senghor's advanced French education placed him in a position of potential leadership among his people. Senghor's poetry and his development of the theory of negritude represent cultural and intellectual leadership, which led to his political achievements.

Other men of letters have entered the political arena, such as the Czech playwright Vaclàv Havel and the Peruvian novelist Mario Vargas Llosa. Senghor's career is exceptional in that the poet and the politician are nearly impossible to separate. Even in his early work, there is little distinction between the personal and public aspects of his expression. Poems that explore the tension between the Africa of his youth and his later experience in the colonial center reveal a deep awareness of the broader forces involved. Quite easily, a reader can discern that the poet aspires to speak for his people as a whole. This type of representation, even in work with no explicitly political content, became more palpable in Senghor's poetry as his political profile grew.

Negritude and Black Consciousness Aside from his achievements as president of Senegal, Senghor's most

COMMON HUMAN EXPERIENCE

Senghor's most well known book is probably the *Anthology of the New Black and Malagasy Poetry in French*, which became a touchstone of the negritude phenomenon. Here are other landmark literary anthologies that brought attention to emerging social movements:

> *The New Negro* (1925), an anthology edited by Alain Locke. Known as the Harlem Renaissance, the flowering of African American art and literature in the 1920s is brilliantly displayed in this collection.
>
> *Black Fire: An Anthology of Afro American Writing* (1968), an anthology edited by Amiri Baraka and Larry Neal. This anthology of essays, poems, and short stories captures the aesthetic component of the Black Power movement of the 1960s.
>
> *Sisterhood Is Powerful* (1970), an anthology edited by Robin Morgan. This anthology is one of the first widely available publications from the Second Wave of the women's movement.
>
> *This Bridge Called My Back* (1981), an anthology edited by Cherrie Moraga and Gloria Anzaldua. Moraga and Anzaldua have selected an influential collection of writing "by radical women of color."

enduring contribution is probably the theory of negritude with which he is associated. Launched as a creative response to French colonialism, negritude provided a basis for proclaiming a cultural commonality throughout the African diaspora. Under the mantle of negritude, new generations of black artists in Africa, Europe, and the Americas transcended the limitations that European traditions and norms had placed on their expression. Influenced itself by the creative fervor of the Harlem Renaissance, negritude is an important precursor to Afrocentricity and other movements in black culture.

Works in Critical Context

For all its influence, the theory of negritude, as articulated by Senghor, has attracted considerable criticism. Some intellectuals have condemned its emphasis on skin color as the single basis of cultural distinctions. Many take issue with its simplistic, somewhat stereotypical formulations, such as the claim that European reasoning is analytical and African reasoning is intuitive. Examining Senghor's theoretical prose, some critics detect an unspoken acceptance of certain assumptions of European superiority.

Biographers and commentators on Senghor, such as Sebastian Okechuwu Mezu, have noted the close connection of his poetic and political identities, often assessing the former through the lens of the latter. As for Senghor's literary style, it has been characterized as serenely and resonantly rhetorical. While the lush sensuality of his verse has many admirers, there are those who view his efforts to reconcile African and Western cultural idioms as only partly successful. Some scholars detect a lack of dramatic tension in Senghor's poetry. Instead of conforming to European styles of narrative verse, his is a poetry of affirmation rather than explanation, declaration rather than argumentation, and celebration rather than observation.

Many critics, such as his principal English translators, John Reed and Clive Wake, compare Senghor to the nineteenth-century American poet Walt Whitman. Using intensely rhythmic free verse, each of these writers looked deep within themselves to capture and communicate the experience of a people giving birth to a new nation.

Responses to Literature

1. Research the French colonial policy of assimilation, in which colonial subjects were encouraged to abandon their native languages and adopt French culture and customs. How does the life of Senghor represent the impact of this policy?

2. Reading *Songs of Shadow* and *Black Hosts*, what hints and evidence do you find that their author would assume a position of political leadership?

3. Compare and contrast the poetry of Léopold Sédar Senghor and Walt Whitman.

4. Read the essay "Black Orpheus" written by Jean-Paul Sartre to introduce *Anthology of the New Black and Malagasy Poetry in French*, the book of black poetry that Senghor edited. Citing Sartre's essay, explain the relationship between postwar French intellectual culture and the negritude movement.

5. Assessing Senghor's controversial poem "Chaka" from *Ethiopiques*, determine how the poem reflects its author's attitudes toward the acquisition and use of political power. Keep in mind that the real Chaka was a ruthless killer and tyrant. To what extent do you think Senghor depended on Thomas Mofolo's historical novel about a Zulu warrior king of the nineteenth century?

BIBLIOGRAPHY

Books

Blair, Dorothy S. *African Literature in French.* Cambridge: Cambridge University Press, 1976.

Collins, Grace. *Man of Destiny: Leopold Sedar Senghor of Senegal.* Mt. Airty, Md.: Sights, 1997.

Crowder, Michael. *Senegal: A Study in French Assimilation Policy.* Oxford: Oxford University Press, 1962.

Hymans, Jacques Louis. *Leopold Sedar Senghor: An Intellectual Biography.* Edinburgh, U.K.: Edinburgh University Press, 1971.

Kluback, William. *Leopold Sedar Senghor: From Politics to Poetry*. New York: Peter Lang, 1997.

Mezu, Sebastian Okechuwu. *The Poetry of Leopold Sedar Senghor*. Madison, N.J.: Fairleigh Dickinson University Press, 1973.

Spleth, Janice, ed. *Critical Perspectives on Leopold Sedar Senghor*. Washington, D.C.: Three Continents, 1991.

Vaillant, Janet G., and Brenda Randolph. *A Trumpet for His People: Leopold Sedar Senghor of Senegal*. Mt. Airty, Md.: Sights, 1996.

William Shakespeare

BORN: *1564, Stratford-upon-Avon, England*

DIED: *1616, Stratford-upon-Avon, England*

NATIONALITY: *British, English*

GENRE: *Poetry, drama*

MAJOR WORKS:

Romeo and Juliet (1595–1596)

Sonnets (1590s)

Hamlet (1600–1601)

King Lear (1605)

The Tempest (1611)

William Shakespeare *Shakespeare, William, illustration. The Library of Congress.*

Overview

William Shakespeare drew upon elements of classical literature to create distinctly English forms of poetry and drama. His work was hardly limited to strict classical idioms, however; he successfully utilized a much broader range of literary sources than any of his contemporaries. Moreover, his extraordinary linguistic abilities—his gift for complex poetic imagery, mixed metaphor, and brilliant puns—combined with a penetrating insight into human nature, are widely recognized as the makings of a unique literary genius. Over the centuries Shakespeare's works have obtained an unparalleled critical significance and exerted an unprecedented influence on the development of world literature.

Works in Biographical and Historical Context

Family and Early Life William Shakespeare was probably born on April 23, 1564, though the precise date of his birth is uncertain. He was the eldest of the five children of John Shakespeare, a tradesman, and Mary Arden Shakespeare, the daughter of a gentleman farmer. It is thought that Shakespeare attended the local grammar school, where the main course of instruction was in Latin. There is no evidence that he attended college.

In 1582, he married Ann Hathaway of Stratford; they would have three children together. Shakespeare's life from this date until 1592, when he became known as a dramatist, is not well documented.

Early Work Shakespeare's first plays, the three parts of the Henry VI history cycle, were presented in 1589–1591. He also wrote a pair of narrative poems directly modeled after Ovid's *Metamorphoses*: *Venus and Adonis* (1593) and *The Rape of Lucrece* (1594). These works, which acknowledged the contemporary fashion for poems written with mythological themes, were immensely successful, and established Shakespeare as a poet of the first rank.

Success as Actor and Playwright Shakespeare further enhanced his reputation as a professional actor and playwright when he joined the Lord Chamberlain's Men, a well-regarded acting company formed in 1594. The success of the Lord Chamberlain's Men is largely attributable to the fact that after joining the group in 1594, Shakespeare wrote for no other company. In 1603, shortly after his accession to the throne, James I granted the Lord Chamberlain's Men a royal patent, and the company's name was changed to the King's Men to reflect the king's direct patronage.

Surviving records of Shakespeare's business transactions indicate that he benefited financially from his long career in the theater. By 1610, with his fortune made and his reputation as the leading English dramatist unchallenged, he appears to have largely retired to Stratford-upon-Avon. Shakespeare died on April 23, 1616. He was buried in the chancel of Trinity Church in Stratford.

Publication History The publication history of Shakespeare's plays is extremely complex and the subject of much scholarly debate. The earliest collected edition of his dramas, known as the First Folio, was compiled by two fellow actors and published posthumously in 1623. The First Folio, which classifies the dramas into distinct genres of comedy, history, and tragedy, contains thirty-six of the thirty-seven plays now believed to be written by Shakespeare. Of the works included, thirteen had never before been published.

Shakespeare's Comedies The "early" comedies, as the name implies, are among the first works Shakespeare wrote. The plays in this group, such as *The Comedy of Errors* (1592–1594), *The Taming of the Shrew* (1593–1594), and *Love's Labour's Lost* (1594–1595), generally adhere closely to established comedic forms. The "romantic" comedies, including *A Midsummer Night's Dream* (1595–1596), *The Merchant of Venice* (1596–1597), *As You Like It* (1599), and *Twelfth Night* (1601–1602), display a consistency in style and subject matter and focus on themes of courtship and marriage. As a group, the "romantic" comedies comprise his most popular and critically praised comedies.

Shakespeare's "dark" comedies, including *All's Well That Ends Well* (1602–1603) and *Measure for Measure* (1604), are characterized by marked seriousness in theme, somberness in tone, and strange, shifting narrative perspectives. This group, which also includes *The Tempest* (1611), is characterized by an emphasis on themes of separation and loss. These plays typically include a wandering journey that ultimately results in a reunion amid a spirit of forgiveness and reconciliation.

Shakespeare's History Plays The most immediate "source" of the English history play in Shakespeare's time appears to have been the heightened sense of national destiny that came in the wake of the British Royal Navy's seemingly God-sent victory over the Spanish Armada in 1588. Eight of the ten history plays collectively trace the English monarchy from the fourteenth century to the sixteenth century. They are commonly grouped in two tetralogies: The first contains the three parts of *Henry VI* and *Richard III* (1592–1593); the second, depicting chronologically earlier events but written later in Shakespeare's career, includes *Richard II* (1595), the two parts of *Henry IV* (1596–1598), and *Henry V* (1599). This last work presents the king as the triumphant leader of his people in a glorious battle against the French. Within the history plays Shakespeare demonstrated his capacity for investing plot with extraordinary dramatic tension, and demonstrated his flair for original characterization through the use of subtle, ironic language.

Shakespeare's Tragedies Shakespeare's tragedies, like his comedies, are commonly divided into separate though related categories, the "Roman" tragedies and the "great" tragedies. The Roman plays drew their inspiration from histories of classical antiquity. The major tragedies of this type, *Julius Caesar* (1599) and *Antony and Cleopatra* (1606–1607), explore the themes of political intrigue and personal revenge and are distinguished by their clear, poetic discourse and ironic representation of historical incidents.

The four great tragedies are *Hamlet* (1600–1601), regarded by many critics as Shakespeare's finest work, *King Lear* (1605), *Macbeth* (1606), which explores the issue of regicide, and *Othello* (1604), a story of domestic intrigue set in the Venetian Republic. In these works Shakespeare characteristically presents the fall of the heroes in terms that suggest a parallel collapse of all human values or a disordering of the universe itself.

Although frequently judged by critics to be of a lesser rank than the great tragedies, *Romeo and Juliet* (1595–1596) remains one of the most frequently performed of Shakespeare's dramas.

Shakespeare's Sonnets The *Sonnets* are also considered a central work in the Shakespeare canon. Shakespeare's sonnets are arranged in a narrative order. They consist of a series of metaphorical dialogues between the poet and two distinct personalities: Sonnets 18 to 126 are addressed to a fair young man, or "Friend," and are concerned with the themes of beauty, friendship, and immortality; Sonnets 127 to 154 are addressed to a "Dark Lady" who is described as sensual, coarse and promiscuous. Their brilliant versification and subtle analysis of human emotion are together regarded as the work of a unique poetic genius. Consequently, scholars often place the *Sonnets* on an equal level with Shakespeare's dramas.

Works in Literary Context

Dramatic Influences Shakespeare's approach to drama was eclectic. He appropriated stylistic elements from Roman classicism (specifically comedy as defined by Plautus and Terence and tragedy by Seneca), medieval morality plays, French popular farce, and Italian drama such as the improvised comedic forms of the commedia dell'arte. Shakespeare's use of these sources was not purely imitative, however; he experimented with traditional forms in an original way. Of the three genres, the comedies reveal the closest affinity to the themes of Italian Renaissance literature. If Shakespeare's earliest efforts in the dramatization of history derived from his response to the political climate of his day, his first experiments in comedy seem to have evolved from his reading in school and from his familiarity with the plays of such predecessors on the English stage as John Lyly, George Peele, Robert Greene, and Thomas Nashe.

King Lear is structurally without parallel in the Shakespearean canon. Written in the tradition of the Old Testament book of Job, which focuses on proving the presence of spiritual grace in the presence of evil, *King Lear* has been thought by many to evoke more existential terror than all of Shakespeare's other tragedies combined. The experiences of Lear can be seen as comparable to that of another long-suffering king, the protagonist in Sophocles' *Oedipus at Colonus*.

Historical Epic   Tracing the monarchy in his history plays gave Shakespeare a theme of epic proportions, similar to the subject matter in ancient Greece and Rome that had inspired such classical authors as Homer and Virgil in narrative genres and Aeschylus, Sophocles, Euripides, and Seneca in dramatic genres. It accorded with the biblical treatment of human destiny that Shakespeare's age had inherited from earlier generations, an approach to historical interpretation that had been embedded in such didactic entertainments as the morality play (allegorizing the sin, suffering, repentance, and salvation of a typical member of mankind) and the mystery play (broadening the cycle to a dramatization of the whole of human history according to the Bible). As with the earlier English history plays, *Richard II* and the three *Henry* plays that followed derived in large measure from the 1587 second edition of Raphael Holinshed's *Chronicles of England, Scotland, and Ireland*. In all probability, they were also influenced by, and possibly even inspired by, the 1595 publication of Samuel Daniel's *Civil Wars*.

The Sonnet Form   Like the dramas, the sonnets are patterned after a literary model widely imitated in Shakespeare's age: the sonnets of Petrarch. The sonnet sequence was a highly self-conscious form. The sonnet speaker was an example—partly to be repudiated, partly to be admired, partly to be emulated—whose eloquence permitted him to articulate the stages of some emotional or personal crisis. Shakespeare's speaker, however much he may recall King David of the biblical Psalms, Ovid, Horace, or Petrarch, is steeped in the English tradition. Readers in 1609 would have noticed similarities between Shakespeare and poets such as Sir Philip Sidney, Samuel Daniel, Edmund Spenser, Thomas Watson, and Michael Drayton.

Works in Critical Context

The Tragedies   The four great tragedies display the greatest intensity of tragic pathos of all Shakespeare's dramas. Scholars have suggested that such vividly portrayed upheavals reflect a generalized anxiety among Shakespeare's contemporaries that underlying social, political, and religious tensions would upset the hierarchical order of the Elizabethan world.

Romeo and Juliet was the subject of little scholarship or critical attention in the decades after Shakespeare's

---

LITERARY AND HISTORICAL CONTEMPORARIES

Shakespeare's famous contemporaries include:

Queen Elizabeth (1533–1603): Known as the Virgin Queen because she never married, this queen of England and Ireland gave her country a long and stable reign.

Christopher Marlowe (1564–1593): English playwright, translator, and poet; known for his blank verse, he is considered the chief Elizabethan playwright before Shakespeare.

Ben Jonson (1572–1637): English playwright, actor, and poet; known for his satirical works, such as *Volpone*.

Francis Drake (1540–1595): English politician, pirate, and navigator; influential in the defeat of the Spanish Armada.

Galileo Galilei (1564–1642): Italian astronomer and physicist who was forced by the Inquisition to recant some of his knowledge of science, such as that the Earth revolves around the sun, as it went against a literal interpretation of the Bible.

---

death. Diarist Samuel Pepys wrote of his experience viewing a production of the play on March 1, 1662: "Thence my wife and I by coach, first to see my little picture that is a drawing, and thence to the Opera, and there saw 'Romeo and Juliet,' the first time it was ever acted; but it is a play of itself the worst that ever I heard in my life, and the worst acted that ever I saw these people do, and I am resolved to go no more to see the first time of acting, for they were all of them out more or less." The play has been criticized for its dependence on coincidence and on causes external to the protagonists for the conditions that bring about the tragic outcome—an emphasis implicit in the play's repeated references to fortune and the stars. Critics have also encountered difficulty in their attempts to reconcile the purity of Romeo and Juliet's devotion to each other with the play's equal insistence that their relationship is a form of idolatry, ultimately leading both lovers to acts of desperation that audiences in Shakespeare's time would have considered far more consequential than do most modern audiences. But it is not for its revenge elements that most of us remember *Romeo and Juliet*, but for the lyricism with which Shakespeare portrays the beauty and idealism of love at first sight.

The Sonnets   John Benson's *Poems: Written by Wil. Shake-speare. Gent* (1640) was part of an attempt to "canonize" Shakespeare, collecting verses into a volume that could be sold as a companion to the plays. However, this met with little success; the fashion for sonnets was

COMMON HUMAN EXPERIENCE

William Shakespeare's plays have appealed to audience throughout the centuries and are still influential and relevant today. Here are some contemporary adaptations of his works:

The Merchant of Venice (2004), a movie directed by Michael Radford. This close adaptation of Shakespeare's play stars Al Pacino as Shylock, portraying the character as a tragic hero rather than a villain.

Shakespeare in Love (1998), a movie directed by John Madden. Winning multiple Academy Awards and making no claim to historical accuracy, this film follows Will Shakespeare as he falls in love with Viola, a noblewoman who longs to act.

10 Things I Hate About You (1999), a movie directed by Gil Junger. This movie adapts *The Taming of the Shrew*, setting it in an American high school.

West Side Story (1961), a movie directed by Robert Wise and Jerome Robbins. Considered a Broadway classic, this musical translates *Romeo and Juliet* into the story of doomed love between members of rival New York City gangs.

long over. For the next century and a half, they were regularly excluded from editions of Shakespeare. After 1780, however, Edmond Malone published a critical edition of the *Sonnets* based on Thorpe's quarto, and included a detailed introduction and commentary. Ten years later he included them in his great edition of the *Plays and Poems*; thus, the sonnets became "literature" in the heyday of the romantic poets and the new vogue for literary biography. Thereafter, they were assumed to be highly personal writings.

Responses to Literature

1. Many people believe that Shakespeare's sonnets are thinly veiled autobiographical writings. Does it matter to you if a poem or song reflects the artist's own life? Why or why not? Why would an author use this method of writing?

2. William Shakespeare's plays were highly popular in his day and critically praised. Are there any filmmakers or directors today with a similar reputation? Do you think they will remain equally popular as time goes by?

3. Shakespeare's history plays, in which he traced the lives of the British monarchy, were inspired by current political events. Pretend that you are going to write a play about some part of American history, based on recent events. Write two or three paragraphs outlining what your play would be about, using specifics, and what prompted your choice.

4. Shakespeare based some of his plays on classical myths. Choose a myth of your own by researching online or in your library, and rewrite it in contemporary terms.

5. Because Shakespeare came from an ordinary background, some critics do not believe that he wrote the plays he is known for. Research both sides of the argument at the Shakespeare Authorship Roundtable (www.shakespeareauthorship.org/) and How We Know That Shakespeare Wrote Shakespeare (http://shakespeareauthorship.com/howdowe.html). Write an essay comparing and contrasting the arguments for each side. Which do you find most convincing?

BIBLIOGRAPHY

Books

Andrews, John F. *William Shakespeare: His World, His Work, His Influence*. New York: Scribner, 1985.

Champion, Larry S. *The Essential Shakespeare: An Annotated Bibliography of Major Modern Studies*. New York: G. K. Hall, 1986.

Fineman, Joel. *Shakespeare's Perjured Eye: The Invention of Poetic Subjectivity in the Sonnets*. Berkeley: University of California Press, 1986.

Kay, Dennis. *William Shakespeare: His Life, Works, and Era*. New York: Morrow, 1992.

Prior, Moody E. *The Drama of Power: Studies in Shakespeare's History Plays*. Evanston, Ill.: Northwestern University Press, 1973.

Schoenbaum, S. *William Shakespeare: Records and Images*. London: Oxford University Press, 1981.

Whitaker, Virgil K. *The Mirror up to Nature: The Technique of Shakespeare's Tragedies*. San Marino, Calif.: Huntington Library, 1965.

Young, David. *Something of Great Constancy: The Art of "A Midsummer Night's Dream"*. New Haven, Conn.: Yale University Press, 1966.

Periodicals

Berger, Harry. "Miraculous Harp: A Reading of Shakespeare's *Tempest*." *Shakespeare Studies* 5 (1969): 253–83.

Bowers, Fredson. "Hamlet as Minister and Scourge." *PMLA* 70 (September 1955): 740–49.

Castaldo, Annalisa. "A Text of Shreds and Patches: Shakespeare and Popular Culture." *West Virginia Shakespeare And Renaissance Association Selected Papers (SRASP)* 20, 1997.

Coghill, Nevill. "The Basis of Shakespearian Comedy: A Study in Medieval Affinities." *Essays & Studies* 3 (1950): 1–28.

Hardison, Jr., O. B. "Myth and History in *King Lear*." *Shakespeare Quarterly* 26 (Summer 1975): 227–42.

Levin, Harry. "The Primacy of Shakespeare." *Shakespeare Quarterly* 26 (Spring 1975): 99–112.

Web sites

Absolute Shakespeare. *Absolute Shakespeare*. Retrieved May 25, 2008, from http://absoluteshakespeare.com/.

Bernini Communications. *Open Source Shakespeare*. Retrieved May 25, 2008, from http://www.opensourceshakespeare.org/.

Gray, Terry A. *Mr. William Shakespeare and the Internet*. Retrieved May 25, 2008, from http://shakespeare.palomar.edu/. Last updated on May 22, 2008.

Shakespeare Resource Center. *Shakespeare Resource Center*. Retrieved May 25, 2008, from http://www.bardweb.net/. Last updated on May 22, 2008.

George Bernard Shaw

BORN: *1856, Dublin, Ireland*

DIED: *1950, Ayot St. Lawrence, England*

NATIONALITY: *British*

GENRE: *Drama, fiction, nonfiction*

MAJOR WORKS:

Mrs. Warren's Profession (1893)

Man and Superman (1901–1902)

The Doctor's Dilemma (1906)

Pygmalion (1912)

The Intelligent Woman's Guide to Capitalism and Socialism (1928)

Overview

The British playwright, critic, and pamphleteer George Bernard Shaw produced more than fifty-two plays, three volumes of music and drama criticism, and one major volume of socialist commentary. Shaw is generally

George Bernard Shaw *Shaw, George Bernard, photograph. AP Images.*

considered the greatest dramatist to write in the English language since William Shakespeare. Following the example of Henrik Ibsen, he succeeded in revolutionizing the English stage, disposing of the romantic conventions and devices of the "well-made" play, and instituting a theater of ideas grounded in realism. During his lifetime, he was equally famous as an iconoclastic and outspoken public figure. Essentially a shy man, Shaw created the public persona of G. B. S.: showman, satirist, pundit, and intellectual jester, who challenged established political and social beliefs.

Works in Biographical and Historical Context

A Young Socialist Born in Dublin, Ireland, on July 16, 1856, George Bernard Shaw was largely an academic failure in school. Part of his nonacademic training was handled by his mother, a music teacher, and Shaw grew up with an excellent ear and good musical taste. After school, he sought to make something of himself in business, but, in March 1876, gave up on this career and joined his mother and two sisters in London, where they conducted a music school. Shaw spent the next nine years supported by his parents, reading constantly and widely, writing music and drama reviews for newspapers, and occasionally singing for hire at London society parties.

During this time Shaw also wrote five novels, some of them reflecting the socialist politics that he had become committed to in London. *Immaturity*, the first, remained unpublished, and the other four, after a series of rejections from London publishers, appeared in radical periodicals. At the age of twenty-eight, Shaw joined the socialist Fabian Society, and he served on the executive committee for the next twenty-seven years. The Fabian Society was a socialist movement comprised largely of British intellectuals and had the aim of bringing about a socialist state by degrees rather than by revolution, as was advocated by contemporaries such as Russians Leon Trotsky and Vladimir Lenin (the architects of the Russian Revolution of 1917). *Fabian Essays* (1887), edited by Shaw, emphasized the importance of economics and class structure; for him, economics was "the basis of society." Shaw's politics also inform *Common Sense About the War* (1914), a criticism of the British government and its policies during the early part of World War I. *The Intelligent Woman's Guide to Capitalism and Socialism* (1928), which came much later, supplied a complete summary of his political position and remains a major volume of socialist commentary to this day.

True-to-Life Drama and Prodigious Productivity Shaw wrote drama between 1892 and 1947, when he completed *Buoyant Billions* at the age of ninety-one. In 1893, preoccupied by the current issues of women's rights centered on the suffrage movement (granting women the right to vote), Shaw wrote *The Philanderers*.

He also wrote in 1893 his most famous play, *Mrs Warren's Profession*, which was not produced until 1902 because of British censorship. It remains a powerful play in the history of literature about the rights of women. Shaw's dramas are opposed to the mechanical comic plots of conventional dramas and also against the nineteenth-century tendency to idealize Shakespeare and drama in general. Like the Norwegian playwright Henrik Ibsen, whom he helped to promote in England, Shaw preferred a more true-to-life drama that substituted realism and political engagement for sentimentality and nostalgia.

Starting in 1901, Shaw's political and literary theories propelled him into a remarkable period of productivity. *Man and Superman* (1901–1903) and *Major Barbara* (1905) are both "dramas of ideas," posing challenging questions about poverty and capitalism. *Androcles and the Lion* (1911) takes on religion, *John Bull's Other Island* (1904) deals with the political relations between England and Ireland, and *Heartbreak House* (1913–1916) analyzes the domestic effects of World War I. Sometimes Shaw's plays carry long prefaces that are not directly related to the drama itself, exploring such topics as marriage, parenthood, education, and poverty; these essays form an important part of his ouevre. It was for his drama in particular, though, that Shaw was awarded the Nobel Prize for literature in 1925.

Written during a timespan that included both World Wars (1914–1918 and 1939–1945) and began the separation of the world into a communist East and a capitalist West, Shaw's plays express a complex range of impulses, ambitions, and beliefs. Reflecting on his life and his work, he explained at seventy:

> Whether it be that I was born mad or a little too sane, my kingdom was not of this world: I was at home only in the realm of my imagination, and at ease only with the mighty dead. Therefore I had to become an actor, and create for myself a fantastic personality fit and apt for dealing with men, and adaptable to the various parts I had to play as an author, journalist, orator, politician, committee man, man of the world, and so forth. In all this I succeeded later on only too well.

Shaw's death in 1950 in England was a loss not only for literature, but also for the working class for which he had done battle over so many years.

Works in Literary Context

Shaw was in many ways the product of Victorian England, although in other ways he helped to make the transition away from its literature into that of Modernism. The Victorian period, named for the long-reigning Queen Victoria (1837–1901), was a time of great literary creativity that resists easy categorization. Nevertheless, the parts of it that influenced Shaw were its tendencies toward realism, its confident championing of self-reliance and inner strength, its moral earnestness, its advocacy of charity and social reform, and its patriotic British nationalism. The authors who perhaps best embody all of these things would be the novelist Charles Dickens, the poet Alfred, Lord Tennyson, and the critic Matthew Arnold.

Naturalist Ideals Shaw took from Victorianism its moral earnestness and commitment to social reform, but he left behind its nationalism and its confidence that core British values would steer a sure path to a brighter future at home and around the world. Shaw felt that the Victorian version of "realism" was too idealized—it turned a blind eye to controversial issues, it glorified heroes for the wrong things, and it packaged life too neatly into "well-made" stories with predictable structures and sentimental conclusions. Shaw is more in line with the "naturalism" movement which began in late nineteenth-century France, culminating in the novels of Guy de Maupassant (1850–1893) and Émile Zola (1840–1902) and aiming to represent a "slice of life" marked by a detached, objective description of society with careful accuracy of detail and historical background. People who had been neglected in earlier literature, such as housewives, the poor, or criminals, were given priority. Whereas naturalist writers often showed individual freewill to be ineffective against the powerful forces of history, society, or biology, however, Shaw strongly believed that creative adaptability, powered by the strength of human willpower, is the "life force" that ensures our evolution as a species.

Evolution The idea of "evolution" was highly charged in Shaw's day. Charles Darwin had published *The Origin of Species* in 1859, detailing the evidence for his conclusion that species (including man) evolved from lower-order animals through a process of natural selection and random mutations. The idea that God might not be the sole guiding hand in creation, especially the creation of mankind, scandalized the nineteenth century and still reverberates today. Shaw was an early supporter of Darwinian evolution, applying the ideas to socialism, women's rights, and other reformist political ideas. Literature and other arts, he strongly felt, could play a part in mankind's evolution to a higher state.

Socialist Ideals The other figure that scandalized the late nineteenth century, and whose influence also reverberates today, was Karl Marx (1818–1883). Marx was German, but he developed his socialist theory after observing the lives of factory workers in the north of England. Marx wrote that economics is the engine of history, and the unfairness of a capitalist society—where business owners are motivated to pay workers as little as possible, and workers do not own the products of their own labor—can only be changed by revolution. Marx's ideas were quickly assimilated into literature and literary criticism, and Shaw consistently applied socialist ideas in his plays, prefaces, and essays. Shaw's socialism shared with Marxism its commitment to social change via economics but remained committed to political reforms within the system and not by revolution from outside it.

LITERARY AND HISTORICAL CONTEMPORARIES

Shaw's famous contemporaries include:

Henrik Ibsen (1828–1906): Norway's most famous playwright helped to establish, along with Shaw, an entirely new way of approaching drama. Gone was the "well-made play" with an orderly plot and conventional moral; in its place were highly symbolic, character-driven plays that dealt with controversial issues and current events.

Friedrich Nietzsche (1844–1900): Perhaps the most influential philosopher of the late twentieth century, German philosopher Nietzsche rejected anything irrational and supernatural, including religion, saying that it leads us away from coping with the realities of earthly life.

Theodore Dreiser (1871–1945): A Chicago novelist who was a leader in American naturalism, a movement that tried to study characters in fiction in the same objective way scientists study their subjects.

Gustave Klimt (1862–1918): An Austrian painter involved in the art nouveau movement, creating decorative murals, paintings, and posters with naturalistic figures appearing within elaborately ornamented backgrounds.

Fritz Lang (1890–1976): An innovative filmmaker born in Austria but who worked in the United States, successfully making the transition from silent to sound motion pictures. His expressive films often deal with the psychology of crime and death, and they set a high standard for the emotional depth and artistic potential for early cinema.

That said, Shaw did not shy away from celebrating the effects of revolution. After a visit to the USSR (Union of Soviet Socialist Republics) in the 1930s, when he met long-time Soviet dictator Joseph Stalin, he returned to England convinced that the Soviet Union was leading the world to a brighter future. This conviction, held by many leftist artists and intellectuals of the time—most of whom saw the Soviet experiment as a truly socialist project, rather than the façade for authoritarianism that it ultimately became—was unshaken by evidence of Stalin's "pogroms," or slaughter of countless of his own citizens in order to achieve "state security."

From Ibsen to the Postmodern Stage The playwright who had the most influence on Shaw was the Norwegian writer Henrik Ibsen, who wrote realistic and intellectual dramas about pressing social issues that had never before been discussed on the stage. Shaw details his debt to Ibsen, in the context of Shaw's own socialism, in *The Quintessence of Ibsenism* (1891, rev. 1913).

COMMON HUMAN EXPERIENCE

Shaw wrote often about women's rights, most famously in his play *Mrs Warren's Profession* (1893). Influenced by Ibsen's *A Doll's House* (1879) and *Hedda Gabler* (1890), Shaw demonstrated how the few options available for women to lead a life of culture and refinement come at a very high cost. He also rebelled against the trend in nineteenth-century dramas and novels that emphasized plot over character. His dramas were sometimes criticized for being too "talky," finding their dramatic tension not so much in story or romance as in debate and discussion of important ideas. Here are some other works that focus on ideas and on female independence:

> *My Fair Lady* (1956), a novel by Alan Jay Lerner and musical by Frederick Loewe. This enormously popular stage musical, made into an equally popular movie in 1964, set the record for the longest theatrical run in history up to its time. Based upon Shaw's play *Pygmalion* (1913), the cultured professor Henry Higgins takes on the lower-class flower girl Eliza Doolittle as an experiment in linguistics—he teaches her how to speak with a proper British accent, and she learns how to become, not just imitate, a proper lady.

> *Their Eyes Were Watching God* (1937), a novel by Zora Neale Hurston. Hurston was a leader in the Harlem Renaissance, an explosion of artistic creativity in the African American community during the 1920s–1930s. This realistic novel shows the struggles of a poor black woman in the south as she gains, loses, and regains a life of love, fulfillment, respect, and freedom.

> *Travesties* (1974), a play by Tom Stoppard. Here, Stoppard imagines what would happen if the intellectual dynamos of 1917 were to all be in the same room together talking about whatever passed through their iconoclastic minds: Vladimir Lenin (Russian leader), James Joyce (novelist), and Tristan Tzara (Dada artist). Weaving through the sparkling dialog and some zany plot twists borrowed from Oscar Wilde's *The Importance of Being Earnest*, Stoppard addresses important questions about the function of politics in art and the role of the artist in society.

> *Hamlet, Prince of Denmark* (c. 1601), a play by William Shakespeare. While certainly not sacrificing anything in terms of plot and action, this single most influential play in the history of theater was the first to make extensive and integral use of the "dramatic monologue," or speech made directly to the audience that reflects a character's inner thoughts. Through the use of this technique, Shakespeare made *Hamlet* the first play primarily about thinking as such.

Immediately after Shaw's time, his influence on drama was eclipsed by the more symbolic, avant-garde, and impressionistic (although no less politically challenging) work of Bertolt Brecht (1898–1956) and Samuel Beckett (1906–1989). In recent years, however, "postmodern" British and American stages have seen a great deal of "Shavian" drama, which are plays that contain intellectual discussion, are based more upon character than plot, and engage the audience with important social issues. It is easy to imagine Shaw applauding heartily for two of the most ambitious and important plays in the last several decades, Tony Kushner's two-part "Angels in America" (dealing with AIDS) and Tom Stoppard's trilogy "The Coast of Utopia" (dealing with the Russian Revolution).

Works in Critical Context

It has been easy for critics to point out that despite his allegiance to realism, Shaw's characters sometimes seem more like intellectual concepts rather than real people, especially when compared to the characters in Ibsen or August Strindberg (1849–1912). Other critics locate this as one of Shaw's strengths: that ideas come alive at the center of his dramas.

Saint Joan Shaw's early plays were very popular, but when he began questioning England's participation in World War I, he was suspected of being a German sympathizer and his support quickly evaporated. Shaw kept writing about the war, however, and as World War II was starting he only increased his attacks on capitalist democracy and was again suspected of aiding the enemy. His reputation benefited from *Saint Joan* in 1923, a play about the martyr Joan of Arc that suggested criticism of England's cruel treatment of Ireland, propelling him toward the Nobel Prize in Literature in 1925.

Pygmalion After the wars, Shaw's criticisms began to seem more like prophesies, and his critical standing and popularity improved. The huge success of *My Fair Lady*, a musical adaptation of Shaw's play *Pygmalion*, also helped to renew affection for Shaw's work. Some critics denounced Shaw's plays for their preachiness and unsympathetic characters, while others applauded his efforts to raise the tone of British drama, while his depiction of independent women characters found an attentive audience with feminist critics starting in the 1960s. Contemporary observer Sunder Katwala describes Shaw as "a persistent pioneer of both feminism and racial equality," and notes, "Shaw's genius cannot be doubted. Nor his astonishing range, from his major contribution to music criticism to his being the only Nobel laureate to also bag an Oscar."

Shaw is now seen as one of the most significant British dramatists of the modern era, and at least until the 1970s with the rise of Tom Stoppard, he is often recognized as the greatest British dramatist since Shakespeare. Perhaps, though, he is most important for the example he sets of what it can mean to "speak truth to power." Biographer and commentator Michael Holroyd remarks on the particular need we have for Shaw in a world obsessed with fear, writing, "In such a climate of terrified legislation, we have need of Bernard Shaw—need of his stimulating incorrectitudes, need of his ability to show where dishonour truly lies and of his power to ridicule such absurdities out of court."

Responses to Literature

1. Is a "drama of ideas" a contradiction in terms? What assumptions are you making about each term as you come up with your answer?

2. Situate Shaw's artistic achievement with respect to the other great dramatists of the twentieth century. In what ways did his work contribute to and/or work against the Modernist asthetic that developed in literature during his heyday?

3. Some of the films and television series that have received the most critical praise over the last decade have been ones that address controversial topics and give a human dimension to some of the urgent political and social issues of today. Do you think that Shaw's strongest legacy today may not be in the theater at all, but in film and television? How have the issues changed from Shaw's day to ours?

4. Read one of the plays, such as *Mrs Warren's Profession,* to which Shaw added a long preface discussing problems he wanted to see reformed. What do you think of this practice? Are the prefaces unnecessary distractions, or do you find that they help to set up interpretations of the play that you may not have had otherwise?

BIBLIOGRAPHY

Books

Bentley, Eric. *Shaw on Music.* New York: Applause Books, 1995.

Evans, T. F. *Shaw: The Critical Heritage.* Boston, Mass.: Routledge & Kegan Paul, 1976.

Henderson, Archibald. *Bernard Shaw: Playboy and Prophet.* New York: Appleton, 1932.

Holroyd, Michael. *Bernard Shaw: The One-Volume Definitive Edition.* New York: W. W. Norton, 2005.

Innes, Christopher, ed. *The Cambridge Companion to George Bernard Shaw.* Cambridge, U.K.: Cambridge University Press, 1998.

Meisel, Martin. *Shaw and the Nineteenth-Century Theater.* Princeton, N.J.: Princeton University Press, 1963.

Ohmann, Richard M. *Shaw: The Style and the Man.* Middletown, Conn.: Wesleyan University Press, 1962.

Strauss, Erich. *Bernard Shaw: Art and Socialism.* London: Victor Gollancz, 1942.

Weintraub, Stanley. *Journey to Heartbreak: The Crucible Years of Bernard Shaw, 1914–1918.* New York: Weybright & Talley, 1971.

Periodicals

Albert, Sidney P. "Bernard Shaw: The Artist as Philosopher." *Journal of Aesthetics and Art Criticism* 14 (1956): 419–38.

Holroyd, Michael. "Send for Shaw, not Shakespeare." *Times Literary Supplement* July 19, 2006.

Katwala, Sunder. "Artist of the Impossible." *(UK) Guardian* July 26, 2006.

Web sites

The Shaw Society. Retrieved March 16, 2008, from http://www.shawsociety.org.uk

Holroyd, Michael. "Send for Shaw, Not Shakespeare." *Times Literary Supplement:* July 19, 2006. Retrieved March 16, 2008, from http://tls.timesonline.co.uk/article/0,,25338-2277082,00.html

Mary Wollstonecraft Shelley

BORN: *1797, London*

DIED: *1851, London*

NATIONALITY: *British*

GENRE: *Fiction, poetry, nonfiction*

MAJOR WORKS:

Frankenstein; or, The Modern Prometheus (1818)

The Last Man (1826)

Lives of the Most Important Literary and Scientific Men of Italy, Spain, and Portugal (1835–1837)

Overview

British author Mary Wollstonecraft Shelley was a skilled editor and critic, an influential travel writer, a literary historian, and a dabbler in verse as well as short stories. By the age of nineteen, Shelley had created the greatest and what many believe to be the first science fiction novel in history: *Frankenstein; or, The Modern Prometheus* (1818). This one novel has risen above the gothic and horror genres to gain recognition as a work of psychological and philosophical depth. Although she wrote several other novels, along with respected nonfiction pieces, Shelley's legacy lives on through *Frankenstein.*

Works in Biographical and Historical Context

Unhappy Childhood   Born in London on August 30, 1797, Shelley was the daughter of two great intellectual rebels of the 1790s: Mary Wollstonecraft, an early feminist who wrote the renowned *Vindication of the Rights of*

Mary Wollstonecraft Shelley   *Shelley, Mary Wollstonecraft, illustration.*
Source unknown.

Women (1792), and William Godwin, a novelist and political philosopher. Ten days after Shelley was born, her mother died from complications related to her birth, leaving Godwin to care for Shelley and Fanny Imlay, Wollstonecraft's three-year old-daughter from a previous relationship. Although her father was not particularly affectionate or attentive, Shelley did not grow up alone.

After Godwin remarried in 1801, Mary gained more siblings. Her stepmother, Mary Jane Clairmont, favored her own two children and the son she and Godwin shared over Wollstonecraft's daughters. Mary's childhood was not happy. At one point, she was sent to live with family friends in Scotland for two years, probably because of conflict between her and her stepmother. Although Shelley received no formal education—which was somewhat common for British girls at this time—she found consolation in intellectual pursuits, especially books.

Married Percy Bysshe Shelley Shelley's father hosted many of the prominent intellectuals and writers of the day, including poets Samuel Taylor Coleridge and Percy

Bysshe Shelley. Percy met Mary when she was fourteen. However, they were not romantically interested in one another until two years later. At this time, Percy Shelley was married, his wife pregnant with their second child. Nevertheless, he and Shelley felt that matters of the heart were more significant than legal ties, and the couple ran away together in July 1814, a month before Shelley's seventeenth birthday.

Love and Loss The couple spent the subsequent years traveling in Switzerland, Germany, and Italy even though Percy Shelley's father, a wealthy baronet, discontinued his son's substantial allowance after Percy Shelley abandoned his family. (Until 1858, a divorce could only be obtained by an act of Parliament, an expensive and formidable task.) These years were marked by personal tragedy as well. Their first child died eleven days after she was born, and Fanny, Shelley's half-sister, and Harriet, Percy's wife, both committed suicide in 1816.

Ghost Stories The couple spent most of the summer of 1816 in Geneva, Switzerland, with Lord Byron, a poet, and John Polidori, a writer and physician. That year was an auspicious one; because of the weather, 1816 became known as "the year without a summer." Probably because of the effects of several major volcanic eruptions that caused an extreme buildup of atmospheric dust, there was essentially no extended summer that year in much of the northern United States, parts of Canada, and northern Europe as well as other parts of the world. Temperatures shifted between typical summer warmth and near freezing within short amounts of time. Because of the atypical summer, most crops were lost and the areas hardest hit suffered from food shortages. In Switzerland, for example, there was widespread famine that led to food riots and the government's declaring a national emergency.

During a June snowstorm in Geneva, the group read aloud a collection of German ghost stories that inspired Byron to challenge the others to write their own ghost stories. While Percy Shelley wrote an inconsequential story, Byron wrote a fragment of a story, and Polidori began "The Vampyre" (1819), what some view as the first modern vampire tale. Shelley, inspired by a vivid nightmare, began writing *Frankenstein*.

Married Life In part because they sought custody of Percy Shelley's two children, Percy and Mary married in London in December 1816. Still, custody was denied. After two more of the couple's own children died before the age of three, Mary Shelley fell into a deep depression until the 1819 birth of their only surviving child, a son, Percy Florence. Despite marital problems caused by Shelley's depression and her husband's involvement with other women, including his sister-in-law Claire Clairmont, both Shelleys were prolific writers and were dedicated to their studies of European literature and Greek, Latin, and Italian language, art, and music. Intelligent and remarkably gifted, Shelley completed *Frankenstein; or, The Modern Prometheus* at the age of nineteen.

Percy Shelley's Death The Shelleys settled near Lenci, Italy, on the Gulf of Spezzia. Sailing to meet fellow poet Leigh Hunt in 1822, Percy Shelley drowned during a storm. Grief-stricken, Shelley remained in Italy for a year and then returned permanently to England with her son, where she struggled to support the two of them. When Percy Shelley's father offered her a small stipend on the condition that she keep the Shelley name out of print, she published her works anonymously. Besides writing four novels in the years after Percy's death, she contributed a series of biographical and critical essays to *Chamber's Cabinet Cyclopedia*, in addition to submitting occasional short stories—pieces she considered hackwork—to literary journals.

As Shelley's son got older, her father-in-law increased the boy's allowance, providing the resources for mother and son to journey to Italy and Germany, travels Shelley describes in *Rambles in Germany and Italy in 1840, 1842, and 1843* (1844). She spent the last years of her life focused on editing her late husband's work and writing his biography. In 1848, Shelley began showing symptoms of the brain tumor that would eventually kill her, and by the time of her death in London on February 1, 1851, she was almost completely paralyzed. She died without completing Percy's biography, which had become her most treasured project.

Works in Literary Context

Gothic and Biblical Influences Through the years, Shelley's influences have been well documented by scholars. Without a doubt, the Gothic tradition of the late eighteenth and early nineteenth centuries played a role in Shelley's creation of *Frankenstein*. Other sources of inspiration included the myth of Prometheus, the Bible, and the works of Johann Wolfgang von Goethe, along with discoveries regarding electricity, chemistry, and anatomy made during Shelley's lifetime. Especially evident in Shelley's work is her familiarity with John Milton's biblical epic *Paradise Lost* (1667).

Science Fiction In the genre of science fiction, *Frankenstein* is viewed as an archetype, its premise commonly used by authors intent on illustrating how destructive the relentless pursuit of scientific knowledge can be. The foundation of Shelley's story is simple and familiar: A scientist rejects accepted theories and turns instead to his own research, which leads to deadly consequences. However, in many ways *Frankenstein* is unlike much science fiction published since.

In style and structure, it is much closer to its eighteenth-century predecessors: an epistolary novel told in increasingly tightening circles or frames and interspersed with poetry (including that of Shelley's husband). It also differs from much science fiction in its use of Gothic

conventions. While Shelley departed from many of the characteristics of the mode, with its haunted castles and threatened maidens, she nonetheless successfully conveys a Gothic atmosphere, which, in its sense of the strange and the irrational, stands in sharp contrast both to Enlightenment rationality and to the scientific objectivity of modern science fiction.

The novel is about a driven doctor, Victor Frankenstein, and his desire to bypass God and create human life in the laboratory. Like a character in ancient Greek tragedy whose fatal flaw is hubris, or excessive pride, Frankenstein is punished for his arrogance by the very forces he has unleashed upon the world. The principal reason scholars have identified *Frankenstein* as an influential work of science fiction is the result of Victor Frankenstein's reliance on natural or scientific means to create his man. Ultimately, nature becomes a mechanized force with the ability to create and destroy.

COMMON HUMAN EXPERIENCE

Shelley, like other Romantic writers, often wrote of isolated individuals in a fallen world. The theme of being alone after the destruction of the world is one that writers have explored for centuries, as shown by the works listed below:

Robinson Crusoe (1719), a novel by Daniel Defoe. Shipwrecked off the coast of Trinidad, Crusoe develops the survival skills necessary for living alone on an island.

I Am Legend (2007), a film directed by Francis Lawrence. Robert Neville, a military scientist who thinks he may be the lone survivor after a man-made virus infects the world, works to discover a cure while living in a city inhabited by bloodthirsty victims of the virus.

A Gift upon the Shore (2000), a novel by M. K. Wren. Surrounded by complete devastation from a nuclear holocaust and its aftermath, two women dedicate their lives to collecting and preserving the great books of Western culture.

Alas, Babylon (1959), a novel by Pat Frank. With tensions between the United States and the Soviet Union at an all-time high, Frank published his novel about the survival tactics of a small Florida town after all the major cities in Florida are destroyed in a nuclear war.

Shelley's Legacy Few literary works have had such a profound impact on the genres of fantasy and horror, the development of science fiction, and the Western world's conception of both. Inspiring plays, an opera, movie and television adaptations, numerous sequels, and countless imitators, *Frankenstein* has taken on a life of its own. In fact, Shelley's novel often surprises those modern readers whose knowledge of the story is limited to movie versions that are not faithful to the story itself.

Works in Critical Context

Literary Value With *Frankenstein* dominating critical discussions of her writing, Shelley's other fictional works have received little attention. Critics generally agree that her five later novels are characterized by awkward plotting and verbosity; all the same, most of them have some element of literary value. For instance, scholars consider *The Last Man*, Shelley's best-known work after *Frankenstein*, to be an early prototype of science fiction, with its description of the destruction of the human race in the twenty-first century. Thought by many to be autobiographical, the novels *Lodore* (1835) and *Falkner* (1837) have been studied for clues to the lives of the Shelleys and their circle of literary friends. In regard to Shelley's nonfiction, critics admire the intelligent, insight-

ful essays she wrote for *Chamber's Cabinet Cyclopedia*, as well as her enlightening notes on Percy Shelley's poetry.

Frankenstein Having been adapted for a variety of media, the *Frankenstein* myth has become part of modern culture. However, when *Frankenstein* was first published, critics typically looked upon the novel as another addition to Gothic fiction, a genre unworthy of serious literary analysis. Early Victorian critics held the same viewpoint, though later scholars began to appreciate the psychological depth beneath the horror in *Frankenstein*. Critics have also focused on the prometheanism in the novel, an aspect that Shelley herself highlighted in the book's subtitle. This line of inquiry, which continues to engage critics, likens Dr. Frankenstein to the Greek mythic figure who wreaks his own destruction through abuse of power. Since then, generations of critics have delved into the novel, discovering the complexities overlooked by early scholars.

Modern critics agree that Shelley's depiction of a godless world in which science and technology have gone awry continues to be a powerful metaphor for the modern age. The monster, who is often the focus of criticism, has been interpreted as representing issues ranging from the alienation of modern humanity to the oppression of women. On the other hand, his maker must confront his sin against the moral and social order. George Levine, for example, comments on the novel's conflict between individual desire and social responsibility: "*Frankenstein* spells out both the horror of going ahead and the emptiness of return. In particular, it spells out the price of heroism."

In describing Frankenstein's efforts to bring his creature to life by scientific rather than supernatural means, Shelley fuses Gothic atmosphere with philosophical allegory. Critic Bonnie R. Neumann points out the fact that *Frankenstein* illustrates a common theological theme, the "initiation—or fall—from . . . innocent, happy illusions . . . into the reality of [life] with its knowledge of loneliness, pain, and death." Farsighted and relevant, *Frankenstein* has presented to the world Victor Frankenstein, a scientist whose name has become synonymous with the reckless use of science and technology—and its potential for catastrophe.

Responses to Literature

1. As the monster in *Frankenstein* develops, he learns to speak and read and eventually comes to understand how he was created. Most film versions of *Frankenstein* depict the monster as mute or vocally incoherent. How do the monster's verbal skills and powers of persuasion in the novel evoke a different reaction toward his existence? Compare and contrast the monster from the novel to the monster in film versions in a paper.

2. In a critical essay, analyze the importance of narrative shifts in *Frankenstein*. Explain the differences in foreshadowing in the narratives of Victor, the monster, and Walton. How does the novel's shift in narrative perspective add to or detract from the overall message of the novel?

3. Although written by the daughter of a famous feminist, *Frankenstein* is noticeably lacking in strong female characters. As you read the novel, take notes about the following female characters: Justine, Elizabeth, and Caroline Beaufort. Discuss the role of women in *Frankenstein*. Do Victor and the monster have differing views of women? Why do you think Shelley chose to create weak female characters? Create a presentation of your findings.

4. From her mother's legacy to her scandalous elopement with a married man to her famous husband's death, Shelley's personal life has often overshadowed her literary work. Research what the critics say about Shelley's personal life and write a related essay. Why do you believe critics and general readers alike are so attracted to details unrelated to actual textual analysis?

BIBLIOGRAPHY

Books

Bloom, Harold, ed. *Mary Shelley: Modern Critical Views*. New York: Chelsea House, 1985.

Gerson, Noel B. *Daughter of Earth and Water: A Biography of Mary Wollstonecraft Shelley*. New York: Morrow, 1973.

Harris, Janet. *The Woman Who Created Frankenstein: A Portrait of Mary Shelley*. New York: Harper, 1979.

Levine, George, and U. C. Knoepflmacher, eds. *The Endurance of Frankenstein*. Berkeley: University of California Press, 1979.

Miller, Calvin Craig. *Spirit Like a Storm: The Story of Mary Shelley*. Greensboro, N.C.: Morgan Reynolds, 1996.

Neumann, Bonnie R. *The Lonely Muse: A Critical Biography of Mary Wollstonecraft Shelley*. New York: Edwin Mellen, 1979.

Smith, Johanna M. *Mary Shelley*. Boston: Twayne, 1996.

Sunstein, Emily W. *Mary Shelley: Romance and Reality*. London: Little, Brown, 1989.

◈ Percy Bysshe Shelley

BORN: *1792, near Horsham, Sussex, England*

DIED: *1822, off the coast of Livorno, Italy*

NATIONALITY: *British*

GENRE: *Poetry*

MAJOR WORKS:

The Revolt of Islam (1818)

The Cenci (1819)

Prometheus Unbound (1820)

Adonais (1821)

A Defence of Poetry (1840)

Overview

Percy Shelley was a poet, literary theorist, translator, political thinker, pamphleteer, and social activist. An extensive reader and bold experimenter, he was a major English Romantic poet. His foremost works, including *The Revolt of Islam* (1818), *Prometheus Unbound* (1820), *Adonais* (1821), and *The Triumph of Life* (1824), are recognized as leading expressions of radical thought written during the Romantic age, while his odes and shorter lyrics are often considered among the greatest in the English language. In addition, his essay *A Defence of Poetry* (1840) is highly valued as a statement of the role of the poet in society.

Works in Biographical and Historical Context

The Elder Son of a Noble Family Born on August 4, 1792, Percy Bysshe Shelley was the son of Timothy and Elizabeth Shelley. As the eldest son, Percy stood in line not only to inherit his grandfather's considerable estate but also to sit in Parliament one day.

Percy Shelley   *Shelley, Percy B., photograph. AP Images.*

While in school at Eton, Shelley began two pursuits that he would continue with intense fervor throughout his life: writing and love, the two often blending together so that the love became the subject matter for the writing. Although Shelley began writing poems while at Eton, some of which were published in 1810 in *Original Poetry; by Victor and Cazire* and some of which were not published until the 1960s as *The Esdaile Notebook*, his first publication was the gothic novel, *Zastrozzi* (1810).

Oxford When Shelley went to University College, Oxford in 1810, he was already a published and reviewed writer and a voracious reader with intellectual interests far beyond the rather narrow scope of the prescribed curriculum. Timothy Shelley, proud of his son and wanting to indulge his apparently harmless interests in literature, could not have foreseen where it might lead when he took Shelley to the booksellers Slatter and Munday and instructed them as follows: "My son here has a literary turn; he is already an author, and do pray indulge him in his printing freaks."

Shortly after entering Oxford Shelley met another freshman, Thomas Jefferson Hogg. The two young men immediately became fast friends, each stimulating the imagination and intellect of the other in their animated discussions of philosophy, literature, science, magic, religion, and politics. In his biography of Shelley, Hogg recalled the time they spent in Shelley's rooms, reading, and discussing, arguing, with Shelley performing scientific experiments.

Ousted for "Atheism" During his brief stay at Oxford, Shelley wrote a prose pamphlet, *The Necessity of Atheism* (1811), which was to have a disastrous effect on his relationship with his family and a dramatic effect on his life. Indeed, Shelley's decision to publish *The Necessity of Atheism* and send copies of it to the conservative Oxford dons, seemed more calculated to antagonize and flaunt authority than to persuade by rational argument. Actually the title of the pamphlet is more inflammatory than the argument, which centers upon "the nature of belief," a position Shelley derived from the skeptical philosophies of John Locke and David Hume. Nevertheless, the Oxford authorities acted swiftly and decisively, expelling both Shelley and his cohort Hogg in March of 1811. The two could probably have been reinstated with the intervention of Shelley's father, but they would have had to disavow the pamphlet and declare themselves Christians. Shelley's father insisted upon the additional demand that they should not see each other for a stipulated period of time. The result was a complete break between Shelley and his father, which led to financial distress for Shelley until he came of age two years later.

Harriet and Mary After his expulsion from Oxford, Shelley courted Harriet Westbrook, an attractive young woman of sixteen. Toward the end of 1811 the couple eloped to Scotland. The three years they spent together were marked by financial difficulties and frequent moves to avoid creditors. Despite these pressures, Shelley was actively involved in political and social reform in Ireland and Wales, writing radical pamphlets in which he set forth his views on liberty, equality, and justice. He and Harriet enthusiastically distributed these tracts among the working classes, but with little effect.

The year 1814 was a pivotal one in Shelley's personal life. Although their marriage was faltering, he remarried Harriet in England to ensure the legality of their union and the legitimacy of their children. Weeks later, however, he fell in love with Mary Godwin, the sixteen-year-old daughter of the radical English philosopher William Godwin and his first wife, the feminist author Mary Wollstonecraft. Shelley and Mary ran away together and, accompanied by Mary's stepsister, Jane (Claire) Clairmont, spent six weeks in Europe. On their return, Shelley entered into a financial agreement with his family that ensured him a regular income. When Harriet declined to join his household as a "sister," he provided for her and their two children, but continued to live with Mary.

Byron and the "Satanic School" In the summer of 1816, Shelley, Mary, and Claire traveled to Lake Geneva to meet with Lord Byron, with whom Claire had begun an affair. Though Byron's interest in Claire was fleeting, he developed an enduring friendship with Shelley that proved an important influence on the works of both men. Shortly after Shelley's return to England in the fall, Harriet drowned herself in Hyde Park. Shelley thereupon legalized his relationship with Mary and sought custody of his children, but the Westbrook family successfully blocked him in a lengthy lawsuit. Citing his poem *Queen Mab* (1813), in which he denounced established society and religion in favor of free love and atheism, the Westbrooks convinced the court that Shelley was morally unfit for guardianship. Although Shelley was distressed by his separation from his daughter and infant son, he enjoyed the stimulating society of Leigh Hunt, Thomas Love Peacock, John Keats, and other literary figures during his residence at Marlow in 1817.

Death and Posthumous Success The following year, however, motivated by ill health and financial worries, Shelley relocated his family in Italy. Shelley hastened to renew his relationship with Byron, who was also living in Italy, and the two poets became the nucleus of a circle of expatriates that became known as the "Satanic School" because of their defiance of English social and religious conventions and promotion of radical ideas in their works. The years in Italy were productive for Shelley, despite the deaths of his two children with Mary and the increasing disharmony of their marriage.

In 1819 and 1820 Shelley wrote two of his most ambitious works, the verse dramas *Prometheus Unbound* and *The Cenci*. *Prometheus Unbound*, on its surface a reimagining of a lost, ancient Greek play by Aeschylus, is also a statement of Shelley's revolutionary political ideas. In Shelley's version of the play—which was meant to be read, not performed—the leader of the Greek gods, Zeus, is overthrown and the Titan Prometheus, who had been condemned to eternal punishment for providing humanity with fire, is set free. Shelley based the tragedy of *The Cenci* on the history of a sixteenth-century Italian noble family. The evil Count Cenci rapes his daughter, Beatrice; she determines to murder him, seeing no other means of escape from continued violation, and is executed for parricide, or the killing of a close relative.

One of Shelley's best-known works, *Adonais*, an elegy on the death of fellow poet John Keats, was written in 1821. Drawing on the formal tradition of elegiac verse, Shelley laments Keats's early death and, while rejecting the Christian view of resurrection, describes his return to the eternal beauty of the universe.

Death and Posthumous Success Shortly before his thirtieth birthday in 1822, Shelley and his companion, Edward Williams, drowned when their boat capsized in a squall off the coast of Lerici. Shelley's body, identified by the works of Keats and Sophocles in his pockets, was cremated on the beach in a ceremony conducted by his friends Byron, Hunt, and Edward John Trelawny. His ashes, except for his heart, which Byron plucked from the fire, were buried in the Protestant cemetery in Rome.

Mary Shelley took on the challenge of editing and annotating Shelley's unpublished manuscripts after his death. Her 1840 collection included Shelley's greatest prose work, *A Defence of Poetry*. Writing in response to *The Four Ages of Poetry* (1820), an essay by his friend Peacock, Shelley details his belief in the moral importance of poetry, calling poets "the unacknowledged legislators of the world." In addition to several other philosophical essays and translations from the Greek, Shelley's posthumous works include the highly personal odes addressed to Edward Williams's wife, Jane. "To Jane: The Invitation," "To Jane: The Recollection," and "With a Guitar: To Jane" are considered some of his best love poems. At once a celebration of his friends' happy union and an intimate record of his own attraction to Jane, these lyrics are admired for their delicacy and refined style.

Works in Literary Context

Much of Shelley's writing reflects the events and concerns of his life. His passionate beliefs in reform, the equality of the sexes, and the powers of love and imagination are frequently expressed in his poetry, and they caused much controversy among his conservative contemporaries.

Controversial Subject Matter Shelley's first mature work, *Queen Mab*, was printed in 1813, but not distributed due to its inflammatory subject matter. It was not until 1816, with the appearance of *Alastor; or, The Spirit of Solitude, and Other Poems*, that he earned recognition as a serious poet. In *Alastor*, a visionary and sometimes autobiographical poem, Shelley describes the experiences

of the Poet who, rejecting human sympathy and domestic life, is pursued by the demon Solitude.

Shelley also used a visionary approach in his next lengthy work, *Laon and Cythna; or, The Revolution of the Golden City* (1818), written in friendly competition with Keats. An imaginative account of a bloodless revolution led by a brother and sister, the poem deals with the positive power of love, the complexities of good and evil, and ultimately, spiritual victory through martyrdom. *Laon and Cythna* was immediately suppressed by the printer because of its controversial content, and Shelley subsequently revised the work as *The Revolt of Islam*, minimizing its elements of incest and political revolution. Even the author's attempts at more popular work met with disapproval: Although Shelley hoped for success on the English stage with his play *The Cenci*, his controversial treatment of the subject of incest outraged critics, preventing the play from being produced.

Lyrical Poetry and the Core of Shelley's Themes Throughout his career Shelley wrote numerous short lyrics that have proved to be among his most popular works. Characterized by a simple, personal tone, his minor poems frequently touch on themes central to his more ambitious works: The "Hymn to Intellectual

COMMON HUMAN EXPERIENCE

Shelley was the prototypical sensitive, misunderstood poet, whose musings on nature and beauty have been much imitated in the centuries since his death, particularly among the Romantic and transcendentalist poets he helped inspire.

Leaves of Grass (1855), a poetry collection by Walt Whitman. Revised in several editions over the poet's lifetime, the poems contained in this collection for the most part celebrate nature, the role of humans in it, and the sensual experiences of the material world.

The Poems of Emily Dickinson (1999), a collection by Emily Dickinson. Although she only published a dozen poems during her lifetime, Dickinson wrote over eighteen hundred, many of which touch upon a recurring theme of the beauty and serenity of gardens and flowers.

Nature (1836), an essay by Ralph Waldo Emerson. This work formed the cornerstone of transcendentalism; in it, Emerson asserts that Nature is not a thing to be learned, but a primal force that is understood at a primal level by all of us.

Beauty" and "Mont Blanc" focus on his belief in an animating spirit, while "Ode to the West Wind" examines opposing forces in nature. In other lyrics, including "Lines Written Among the Euganean Hills," "Stanzas Written in Dejection, Near Naples," and "Lines Written in the Bay of Lerici," Shelley explores his own experiences and emotions. Political themes also inspired several of his most famous short poems, among them "Ode to Liberty," "Sonnet: England in 1819," and *The Masque of Anarchy* (composed 1819; published 1832).

Works in Critical Context

The history of Shelley's critical reputation has been characterized by radical shifts. During his lifetime he was generally regarded as a misguided or even depraved genius; critics frequently praised portions of his poetry in passing and deplored at length his atheism and unorthodox philosophy. In addition, because of their limited publication and the scant critical attention given his works, he found only a small audience. Those few critics who voiced their admiration of his talents, particularly Hunt, who defended him vigorously in the *Examiner*, were ironically responsible for further inhibiting his success by causing him to be associated in the public mind with the despised "Cockney School" of poets belittled by John Gibson Lockhart and others in *Blackwood's Magazine*. Nevertheless, Shelley was known and admired by his great contemporaries: Byron, Keats, William Wordsworth, Samuel Taylor Coleridge, and Robert Southey regarded his works with varying degrees of sympathy and approval.

Legacy After his death, Shelley's reputation was greatly influenced by the efforts of his widow and friends to portray him as an angelic visionary. Biographies by Trelawny, Peacock, and Hogg, though frequently self-serving, inaccurate, and sensationalized, succeeded in directing interest toward Shelley's life and character and away from the controversial beliefs expressed in his works. Critics in the second half of the nineteenth century for the most part ignored Shelley's radical politics, celebrating instead the spiritual and aesthetic qualities of his poetry. In the Victorian age he was highly regarded as the poet of ideal love, and the Victorian notion of the poet as a sensitive, misunderstood genius was largely modeled after Shelley.

Shelley's works, however, fell into disfavor around the turn of the century. Many critics, influenced by Matthew Arnold's assessment of Shelley as an "ineffectual angel," objected to his seemingly vague imagery, nebulous philosophy, careless technique, and, most of all, his apparent intellectual and emotional immaturity. In the late 1930s Shelley's reputation began to revive: As scholars came to recognize the complexity of his philosophical idealism, serious study was devoted to the doctrines that informed his thought. Since that time, Shelley scholarship has covered a wide array of topics, including his style, philosophy, and major themes. In examining his style, commentators have generally focused on his imagery, use of language, and technical achievements. His doctrines of free love and sexual equality have also attracted commentary on the poet as an early proponent of feminism. Recent criticism of Shelley's works is generally marked by increasing respect for his abilities as a poet and his surprisingly modern philosophy.

Prometheus Unbound Shelley knew that *Prometheus Unbound* would never be popular, but he thought that it might have a beneficial influence on some already enlightened intellects. In letters to his publisher Charles Ollier, Shelley proclaimed that although this was his "favorite poem," he did not expect it to sell more than twenty copies and instructed Ollier to send copies to Keats and Byron, among others. The reviewers were predictably harsh in their condemnation of the poem's moral and political principles, with the reviewer for the *Literary Gazette and Journal of the Belles Lettres* quipping that "no one can ever think [*Prometheus*] worth binding," but there was also praise, with words such as "beauty" and "genius" used in various reviews.

The Cenci In his hope that the play would be read widely and staged, Shelley again misjudged the predominance of conservatism in the literary world of pre-Victorian England. The taboo theme of incest, the horror of parricide, the "blasphemous" treatment of religion, the implicit attack on the family and all patriarchal institutions, and Shelley's own dangerous reputation—all broke the rules of British society and ensured *The Cenci* would be condemned by all but a few reviewers and friends, such as Leigh Hunt, to whom the play is dedicated. One reviewer's response in the *British Review* is typical: "The ties of father and daughter...ought not to be profaned as they are in this poem." The play was staged only once in the nineteenth century, by the Shelley Society in 1886.

Responses to Literature

1. Many feel that Shelley's dramatic power was informed in large part by his wild and reckless lifestyle. Do you think artists must "live on the edge" in order to produce works of dramatic power? Why or why not? How do you think Shelley's work would differ if he had led a more conventional lifestyle?

2. Shelley's reputation in his own time suffered from his lifestyle choices. How has his reputation changed since his death? Do you think artists' lifestyles still have an effect on how we judge their work? Try to think of a modern example of a famous artist—such as an author or an actor—who is judged by lifestyle choices as much as by his or her body of work.

3. Compare and contrast Shelley's "A Dirge" with his contemporary John Keats's "When I Have Fears That I May Cease to Be." How do the two poems address the subjects of life, death, and loss?

4. Shelley wrote an "Address to the West Wind." Read the poem, then write the West Wind's response. What type of letter would the Wind write? Would it be formal or informal?

BIBLIOGRAPHY

Books

Allsup, James O. *The Magic Circle: A Study of Shelley's Concept of Love*. Port Washington, N.Y.: Kennikat Press, 1976.

Blank, Kim, ed. *The New Shelley: Later Twentieth-Century Views*. New York: St. Martin's, 1991.

Brown, Nathaniel. *Sexuality and Feminism in Shelley*. Cambridge, Mass.: Harvard University Press, 1979.

Engelberg, Karsten Klejs. *The Making of the Shelley Myth: An Annotated Bibliography of the Criticism of Percy Bysshe Shelley 1822–1860*. London and Westport, Conn.: Mansell/Meckler, 1988.

Greenfield, John R. "Percy Bysshe Shelley." *DISCovering Authors*. Online ed. Detroit: Gale, 2003.

"Ode to the West Wind." *Poetry for Students*. Ed. Marie Rose Napierkowski and Mary K. Ruby. Vol. 2. Detroit: Gale, 1998.

O'Neill, Michael. *Percy Bysshe Shelley: A Literary Life*. New York: St. Martin's, 1990.

"Shelley, Percy Bysshe (1792–1822)." *DISCovering Authors*. Online ed. Detroit: Gale, 2003.

"Study Questions: A Dirge." *Exploring Poetry*. Online ed. Detroit: Gale, 2003.

"Study Questions for Percy Bysshe Shelley." *DISCovering Authors*. Online ed. Detroit: Gale, 2003.

Trelawny, Edward John. *Recollections of the Last Days of Shelley and Byron*. London: Edward Moxon, 1858.

Wilson, Milton. *Shelley's Later Poetry: A Study in His Prophetic Imagination*. New York: Columbia University Press, 1959.

◈ Richard Brinsley Sheridan

BORN: *1751, Dublin, Ireland*

DIED: *1816, London, England*

NATIONALITY: *Irish*

GENRE: *Drama*

MAJOR WORKS:

The Rivals (1775)

The School for Scandal (1777)

The Critic (1779)

Richard Brinsley Sheridan *Sheridan, Richard Brinsley, photograph. The Library of Congress.*

Overview

Irish author Richard Brinsley Sheridan was both a dramatist and a statesman. He is best known for his contribution to the revival of the English Restoration comedy of manners, which depicts the amorous intrigues of wealthy society. His most popular comedies, *The Rivals* (1775) and *The School for Scandal* (1777), display his talent for sparkling dialogue and farce. Like other writers of the genre, Sheridan satirized society, though his dramas reflect gentle morality and sentimentality.

Works in Biographical and Historical Context

Born into Literary Family Sheridan was born in October of 1751 in Dublin, Ireland, the son of a prominent actor and a noted author. His mother, Frances Chamberlaine Sheridan, wrote one fairly successful play and one respected novel. She died while he was an adolescent. His father, Thomas Sheridan, was a playwright, actor, theater manager, orator, and also a scholar of English elocution who published a dictionary. Sheridan's paternal grandfather, Thomas Sheridan, spent many intimate years with Irish author Jonathan Swift, who wrote *Gulliver's Travels* (1726).

Drama and Marriage When Sheridan was eight, the family moved to London, where he attended the prestigious boarding school, the Harrow School. Though he disliked school, he proved to be an excellent student and began writing poetry at an early age. After composing dramatic sketches with friends, Sheridan considered becoming a playwright. His father, however, intended him to study law, and he began an informal program of legal studies after leaving the Harrow School in 1768.

When the family moved to Bath in 1770, Sheridan met Elizabeth Linley, an outstanding singer and famed beauty, with whom he eloped three years later. Shortly after their marriage, Sheridan abandoned his legal studies in order to devote himself to writing. Soon, Sheridan found himself living in London during the 1773–1774 season without an income and with a child on the way. Sheridan would not permit his wife to sing for money, even though she could command as much as fifteen hundred pounds for a series of concerts.

While Sheridan was not yet successful writing dramas, the theater had widespread popularity in this period in Great Britain. Theater appealed to the upper, middle, and even lower classes. Upper gallery seats could be purchased for as little as one shilling, allowing for the poor to attend on occasion. The repertoire performed in this period reflected all genres, including comedies, melodramas, farces, tragedies, and dramas.

First Success as Playwright Success for Sheridan began with *The Rivals* in 1775. Initially, the performance of the play failed because of miscasting and the play's excessive length. Undaunted by the poor reception, Sher-

idan recast several roles, abbreviated sections of the play, and reopened it ten days later to a unanimously positive response. The success of *The Rivals* derived from the use of one of comedy's oldest devices: the satirizing of manners.

The favorable reception of *The Rivals* led immediately to other opportunities for Sheridan. At Covent Garden on May 2, 1775, his two-act farce *St. Patrick's Day; or, The Scheming Lieutenant* appeared and earned for itself a minor place in the afterpiece repertoire. The farce contains many of the elements of *The Rivals*: idiosyncratic but essentially good-natured characters, scenes of disguise and of revelation, quick, verbal strokes, and a farcical starring role rich in numerous assumed disguises for the principal male actor.

Continued Popularity In *The Duenna*, first performed at Covent Garden on November 21, 1775, Sheridan once more rose beyond competence to brilliance. *The Duenna* played an unprecedented seventy-five nights that first season and was praised by audiences and critics alike.

Sheridan earned a small fortune in this first year and a half of dramatic penmanship and directing. When famed actor and director David Garrick retired as part-owner of the Drury Lane Theatre, Sheridan, in concert with his father-in-law, Thomas Linley Sr., and wealthy physician James Ford, purchased Garrick's share. In the following two years, Sheridan revived a number of Restoration comedies, and wrote and produced his most successful comedy, *The School for Scandal*, which debuted on May 8, 1777.

End of Playwriting Career In 1779, Sheridan produced his last successful work, *The Critic; or, Tragedy Rehearsed*. His last play was *Pizarro* (1799). A historical drama, *Pizarro* met with popular acclaim but was soon forgotten. Critics today consider it a disappointing conclusion to Sheridan's theatrical career.

Political Career In 1780, Sheridan made a career change. He was elected to the House of Commons, where he excelled as an orator. His speeches are considered brilliant masterpieces of persuasion and verbal command. At the time, Great Britain was facing challenges to its empire and supremacy. The ongoing American Revolution, which did not completely end until 1783, resulted in the loss of many of Britain's North American colonies. However, Britain soon began settling Australia and New Zealand, adding again to its colonial empire. At home, the Act of Union of Great Britain and Ireland resulted in the formal creation of the United Kingdom in 1800.

During his time in Parliament, however, Sheridan's interest in politics kept him from his theatrical endeavors, and his management of Drury Lane became haphazard. In an attempt to beautify the aging theater, he rebuilt the interior, but it burned down shortly thereafter. Left without resources, Sheridan was unable to finance another parliamentary campaign. His last years were spent in poverty and disgrace.

Sheridan died in London on July 7, 1816, in the sixty-fifth year of his life. Though Sheridan expired in poverty, he was mourned widely and was buried at Westminster Abbey, in the Poets' Corner.

Works in Literary Context

Scandal as Theme A product of his time, Sheridan's plays showed the influence of William Shakespeare's plays (consciously or unconsciously). It is also believed that Sheridan was greatly influenced by his contemporary William Congreve and Sir John Vanbrugh as well as the comedies of the David Garrick era. Sheridan also reacted to the tenor of his times by including in his plays a tolerance of human nature that he believes will support social good rather than individual self-interest. Sheridan's originality was to dramatize the agents of scandal and slander more vividly than any purely decorative comic wits or would-be wits had been represented since the time of Congreve.

Influence Plays like *The Rivals* and *The School for Scandal* were believed to be principally responsible for an English revival of comedy, though some later scholars disagreed. *The School for Scandal* in particular affected British playwrights who followed. Through his partial interest in Drury Lane—though he was a distracted manager for much of his tenure—Sheridan was also able to play an influential role in the course of British theater.

Works in Critical Context

Frequently Performed Sheridan wrote and produced three plays that have been performed more frequently than the works of any other playwright between Shakespeare and Shaw. *The Rivals*, *The School for Scandal*, and *The Critic* entered the performing repertoire immediately upon their first appearance in the 1770s, and one or more of them is still performed every year. Since their debut, both *The Rivals* and *The School for Scandal* have been popular with critics and audiences alike. Modern critics have focused on Sheridan's skilled use of dialogue and manipulation of character in his major dramas.

The Rivals Tom Moore, Sheridan's biographer and first systematic critic, wrote, "The characters of *The Rivals*...are not such as occur very commonly in the world; and, instead of producing striking effects with natural and obvious materials, which is the great art and difficulty of a painter of human life, [Sheridan] has here overcharged most of his persons with whims and absurdities, for which the circumstances they are engaged in afford but a very disproportionate vent." Subsequent critics have attributed the comedy's greatness to its exuberant play with language and with language's power to obfuscate reality, but this language emanates from, as

well as serves to form, distinctly drawn, wonderfully absurd characters. One of Sheridan's recent critics argues persuasively that the twenty-three-year-old playwright, who denied plagiarism in the preface to the first edition of *The Rivals*, depended heavily upon Shakespeare.

The School for Scandal Few disputed the artistry of *The School for Scandal* in its time. It has been presented on stage to paying audiences every year since its premiere. Henry James and George Bernard Shaw, a century after its first appearance, found fault with its sentimentality. But a century after James and Shaw, critics have rediscovered Sheridan's greatest play and found it worthy of serious attention.

With *The School for Scandal*, Sheridan answered the expectations many had for his management of Drury Lane after Garrick. There were detractors, including his father, Thomas Sheridan, who remarked: "Talk about the merit of Sheridan's comedy, there's nothing to it. He had but to dip in his own heart and find there the characters both of Joseph and Charles." Most critics welcomed Sheridan's greatest comedy and hoped the playwright would produce more of them.

Responses to Literature

1. List the types of humor in *The Rivals* and *The School for Scandal*. Create a presentation of your lists using examples from the plays.

2. In a short essay, analyze Sheridan's view of love and marriage as revealed in his plays.

COMMON HUMAN EXPERIENCE

Sheridan was adept as using the "reversal of fortune" plot line to comic effect. Here are some other works that contain the reversal-of-fortune plot, sometimes known as peripeteia:

Great Expectations (1860–1861), a novel by Charles Dickens. Things change for the poor orphan Pip when he learns of a large fortune coming his way.

The Little Princess (1905), a novel by Frances Hodgson Burnett. A young girl whose father has died in the jungle grows up in poverty, until one day she realizes she is the lost heir to a vast fortune.

Reversal of Fortune (1990), a film by Barbet Schroeder. In this movie based on the true events surrounding husband and wife Claus and Sunny von Bülow, a large fortune is to be gained if a lawyer can wrangle the appeal.

Trading Places (1983), a film directed by John Landis. In this Academy Award–nominated comedy, two wealthy brothers make a bet on whether or not a poor man will be affected by instant wealth.

3. How did Sheridan's involvement in the theater community affect his plays? See *The Critic* in particular. Write an essay about your conclusions.

4. In a group discussion, highlight the different classes in Sheridan's plays. Which class does he seem to understand and empathize with the most?

5. Sheridan's Mrs. Malaprop is responsible for a literary term. Discuss in an essay why audiences find Mrs. Malaprop amusing. Then research *malapropism* and find your own examples of such usage.

BIBLIOGRAPHY

Books

Davidson, Peter, ed. *Sheridan: Comedies.* London: Macmillan, 1986.

Loftis, John. *Sheridan and the Drama of Georgian England.* Cambridge, Mass.: Harvard University Press, 1977.

Moore, Thomas. *Memoirs of the Life of the Right Honourable Richard Brinsley Sheridan.* London: Longman, Hurst, Rees, Orme, Brown & Green, 1825.

Sichel, Walter. *Sheridan.* London: Constable, 1909.

Periodicals

Auburn, Mark S. "The Pleasures of Sheridan's *The Rivals*: A Critical Study in the Light of Stage History." *Modern Philology* 72 (February 1975): 256–71.

Durant, Jack D. "The Moral Focus of *The School for Scandal.*" *South Atlantic Bulletin* 31 (November 1972): 44–53.

Jackson, J. R. De J. "The Importance of Witty Dialogue in *The School for Scandal.*" *Modern Language Notes* 76 (November 1961): 601–607.

James, Henry. "*The School for Scandal* at the Boston Museum." *Atlantic Monthly* 34 (December 1874): 754–57.

Jason, Philip K. "A Twentieth-Century Response to *The Critic.*" *Theatre Survey* 15 (May 1974): 51–58.

Leff, Leonard J. "The Disguise Motif in Sheridan's *The School for Scandal.*" *Educational Theatre Journal* 22 (December 1970): 350–60.

Shaw, George Bernard. "The Second Dating of Sheridan." *Saturday Review* 81 (1896): 648–50.

Mikhail Sholokhov

BORN: *1905, Kruzhlino, Russia*

DIED: *1984, Veshenskaya, Rostov-on-Don, Soviet Union*

NATIONALITY: *Russian*

GENRE: *Fiction*

MAJOR WORKS:
The Quiet Don (1928)
Virgin Soil Upturned (1932)
"The Fate of a Man" (1957)

Overview

Russian author Mikhail Sholokhov is one of a few Soviets who wrote fiction for the Communist Party. *The Quiet Don* (1928), a four-book epic about life in a Cossack village from 1912 to 1922, and *Virgin Soil Upturned* (1932), his story of collective farming, were part of the curriculum in all Soviet schools. Sholokhov's body of work is not large, but his works have been translated into more than forty languages and have sold millions of copies.

Works in Biographical and Historical Context

Cossack No More Sholokhov was born Mikhail Stefanovich Kuznetsov on May 11, 1905, on a farm near the River Don in Russia. This region was dominated by the Cossacks, a privileged group of people who were required to serve in the Russian Army. Neither of Sholokhov's parents were Cossacks, but he was registered as a Cossack at his birth, due to his mother's marriage to an elderly officer who was not Sholokhov's father. After the old man died in 1912 and Sholokhov's father and mother were officially married, Mikhail lost his Cossack status.

Mikhail Sholokhov   *Imagno / Getty Images*

Effects of Revolution   Sholokhov attended a quality regional school in the town of Boguchar, Voronezh Province, but he was forced to leave because of the German invasion in 1918 near the end of World War I. Russia fought in the conflict on the side of France, Great Britain, and the United States against Germany, Turkey, and Austria-Hungary. Unlike its allies, Russia's battles against Germany often ended in defeat and Russia lost considerable territory to Germany when a peace treaty was created between the two countries.

During World War I, Tsar Nicholas II and his autocratic rule became increasingly unpopular. Though he allowed elected Dumas (legislatures) beginning in 1906, Nicholas and his ministers had firm control of the government. This situation came to a head in 1917 and 1918 as several groups vied for control of the country, including the Tsar, until he abdicated in November 1917; the Mensheviks (socialists); the Bolsheviks, led by Vladimir Lenin; and several other groups. The resulting civil war saw Lenin and the Bolsheviks gain control of the government, though the conflict lasted until the early 1920s as Lenin and his followers fought to retain control of Russia.

In the civil war that followed the Bolshevik revolution, Sholokhov's family lived in territories controlled by the White Russian armies, which were fighting the Soviet Red Army. Sholokhov witnessed the brutal conflict and later described it in realistic detail in *The Quiet Don*.

Early Affinity for Communism   At the age of fourteen, Sholokhov was forced to make a decision that influenced the rest of his life. He joined the Communists (as the Bolsheviks came to be called) and went to work for the Revolutionary Committee. For a time, he served as a machine gunner with a Red Army supply detachment and volunteered to fight in a special forces unit. He also took part in the cultural life of the Don region, helping produce a daily newspaper and organize the local theater. Captured and interrogated in 1920, Sholokhov was spared from execution.

Once the fighting had stopped and Soviet power was established, Sholokhov went to Moscow to continue his education. He worked at various jobs from 1922 to 1924 before he turned to writing. Sholokhov published his first work in 1923 and wrote stories that later appeared in the book *Tales from the Don* (1926).

In Moscow, he befriended numerous writers and became a member of the Russian Association of Proletarian Writers, an arm of the Bolshevik Party. Unable to make ends meet in Moscow, however, Sholokhov and his wife returned to the Don region, where he lived until his

LITERARY AND HISTORICAL CONTEMPORARIES

Sholokhov's famous contemporaries include:

Boris Pasternak (1890–1960): Author of *Doctor Zhivago* (1957), this Russian novelist and poet won the Nobel Prize for Literature in 1958.

Mikhail Zoshchenko (1895–1958): Zoshchenko was a popular Soviet novelist and satirist whose books include *Nervous People* (1927).

George Orwell (1903–1950): This English novelist and essayist is the author of the political classics *Animal Farm* (1945) and *1984* (1949), depicting the consequences of totalitarianism.

Evelyn Waugh (1903–1966): Many novels by this English satirical novelist parody British aristocracy and high society, including *Decline and Fall* (1928) and *Brideshead Revisited* (1945).

Sergei Eisenstein (1898–1948): Eisenstein was a Soviet film director famous for his use of montage in silent cinema. His films include *Strike* (1925) and *October* (1927).

Leonid Brezhnev (1906–1982): From 1964 until 1982, Brezhnev was general secretary of the Communist Party, the leader of the Soviet Union.

death. He knew by then that his literary subject would be the people and places he had known since birth.

Wrote The Quiet Don By the end of 1926, Sholokhov had two short-story collections in print and was gaining recognition for his writing. Working on his first novel in 1927, he realized that it needed more of a historical context for the average reader to understand it. Consequently, he began a description of the Don Cossacks prior to World War I, and this work became the starting point for *The Quiet Don*. Depicting Cossack life up to the Bolshevik Revolution, the first two segments of the epic were published serially in the journal *October* in 1928.

Reviewers and readers responded positively, but publication ceased after Communist officials objected that the book was insufficiently proletarian in outlook. When Joseph Stalin (who gained power in the Soviet Union in 1928, four years after the death of Lenin and after defeating other top Communist officials for the post) and the Communist Party endorsed the work in 1930, Sholokhov applied for party membership. After Sholokhov was accepted into the party, he proudly described himself as a Communist first, a writer second.

Completed Epic An English translation of the first two books of Sholokhov's epic, *And Quiet Flows the Don*, appeared in 1930. The author ran into censorship

problems with the third book, which describes the actual events of the 1919 uprising. According to the most cited version of events, Stalin ordered that publication proceed following a meeting with Sholokhov and leading Soviet author Maxim Gorky. Part seven of *The Quiet Don* was serialized in 1937 and 1938. Stalin held up the final installment, insisting that the hero convert to Communism by the end. Sholokhov objected and surprisingly won the standoff. Part eight was published, its ending unchanged, in 1940.

A Survivor Because Stalin believed that the Soviet Union had to be able to feed itself, he mandated the transformation of Soviet agriculture from individual farms into a system of large collective farms. With Stalin's help, Sholokhov published the first book of his novel *Virgin Soil Upturned*, a powerful yet objective account of Soviet collective farming. At risk of being named an enemy of the Party, Sholokhov courageously pointed out both benefits and detriments of collective agriculture, presenting the stories of dispossessed Cossacks and peasants. Still, he remained a party loyalist and believed that collectivization would ultimately benefit Russia.

Sholokhov became a member of the Supreme Soviet in 1936 and an elected delegate to all Communist Party Congresses from 1936 to 1984. Sholokhov's service to the Soviet state earned him many accolades. He was among the first recipients of the Stalin Prize, shortly before the Nazi invasion of Russia in June 1941 during World War II. He quickly enlisted in the army as a war correspondent. In 1943, *Pravda*, the official state newspaper, began featuring chapters from Sholokhov's patriotic novel, *They Fought for Their Country*. Although new chapters appeared over the course of Sholokhov's postwar career, the novel was never completed, most likely because his role in political affairs greatly reduced his literary productivity.

A Communist Nobel Prize While some renowned Soviet literary figures became targets of vilification, Sholokhov's position in the party grew stronger. He served publicly as a government spokesperson, even while his own writing was embroiled in censorship battles. He was forced to revise *The Quiet Don* drastically; amended versions appeared in 1952 and 1953. After Stalin's death in 1953, the original text was mostly restored.

Sholokhov was awarded the Nobel Prize for Literature in 1965, despite being a controversial figure. He was a loyal Communist who fervently accused other writers of treason, while maintaining that literary freedom in the Soviet Union was unrestricted. Western intellectuals condemned him as an agent of the totalitarian state. In the 1970s, the expelled Soviet dissident Aleksandr Solzhenitsyn charged that Sholokhov had plagiarized *The Quiet Don*, reviving allegations dating back to the 1920s. Despite official commissions and even scientific investigations confirming Sholokhov's authorship, the issue was not fully resolved at the time of his death in 1984 and is still debated today.

Works in Literary Context

Sholokhov formed his ideological and artistic identities at an early age. During his school years in Boguchar, he lived in the home of a priest, who introduced him to such important writers as Aleksandr Ertel, a nineteenth-century master of the colloquial Russian language; Maxim Gorky, who later became known as the father of Soviet socialist realism; and the Ukrainian-Russian writer Vladimir Korolenko. Sholokhov's writing reflects these influences, as well as that of Aleksandr Serafimovich, a Don Cossack who became his mentor and sponsor. The subject matter and epic sweep of *The Quiet Don* resembles that of Serafimovich's novel *The Iron Flood* (1924). Some critics have also likened Sholokov's novels to those of Leo Tolstoy.

Regional Interest Sholokhov's feeling for the history, geography, and culture of his particular region around Rostov-on-Don is evident from his earliest stories. Lyrical landscape passages and abundant Cossack folklore give his work a sense of locality that is rare in Russian literature. In the *New Republic*, Malcolm Cowley observed that in addition to his passion for the land, Sholokhov "also has a sense of people that is somewhat commoner in Russian fiction, though rare enough in the literature of any country. He writes about them as if he had always known and loved them and wanted the outside world to understand just why they acted as they did."

Socialist Realism Sholokhov's artistic success within Soviet society has much to do with his application of the conventions of socialist realism, the required genre of all literature under Stalin. *The Quiet Don* demonstrates the principle of historical inevitability, in which people must either adapt to or be destroyed by historical forces. Sholokhov championed socialist realism, claiming in his Nobel Prize acceptance speech that "it expresses a philosophy of life that accepts neither a turning away from the world nor a flight from reality." At the same time, Sholokhov resisted efforts to alter the political ideas in his work and did not shy away from objectively describing the problems and even tragedies that accompanied the Soviet revolution. In his best work, political doctrine is artfully fused with the requirements of his narrative. At other times, rigid adherence to the party line is seen as compromising his work's literary merit.

Works in Critical Context

The Best and the Worst In the Soviet Union, the Communist Party's efforts at social control meant that literature and all the arts took place in a highly politicized cultural context. The early reception of Sholokhov's epic demonstrates this. Since Sholokhov was not yet a party

member, he was open to political attack. The more orthodox Communist critics branded Sholokhov a peasant writer who did not sufficiently highlight the plight of proletarians. They questioned why he took the perspective of the defeated White Army and not the victorious Bolsheviks.

In 1928, Sholokhov's authorship officially came under question. Sholokhov had to submit his notes and drafts to the offices of *Pravda* to prove the texts were his. The official response silenced critics but did not put suspicions to rest.

Ever since the 1991 collapse of the Soviet Union, Sholokhov's name has remained mired in controversy. Public opinion is divided between his attackers and defenders. For some, he is an emblem of everything that was vile and destructive in the old Soviet system. A more diplomatic assessment, voiced by critic David Hugh Stewart, is that Sholokhov represents both the best and the worst aspects of Soviet literature.

The Quiet Don Sholokhov's *The Quiet Don* is at the center of much of the controversy over his legacy. Solzhenitsyn as well as many Soviet literary experts like Herman Ermolaev and R. A. Medvedev, believe the book was plagiarized to greater or lesser degrees. Solzhenitsyn wrote in the *Times Literary Supplement*, "From the time when it first began to appear in 1928 *The Quiet Don* has posed a whole series of riddles which have not been satisfactorily answered even today.... A twenty-three-year-old beginner had created a work out of material which went far beyond his own experience of life and his level of education." Away from this controversy, critics acknowledged that this novel had merit. Ernest J. Simmons of the *New York Times Book Review* concluded, "He reached artistic heights only in his great novel *The Quiet Don....* Gregor Melekhov, perhaps the most fully realized and sympathetically portrayed tragic figure in Soviet fiction, remains in the end a complete individualist, alien to the Bolshevik cause that ultimately destroys him."

Responses to Literature

1. Why do you think Stalin relented and allowed Sholokhov to publish part eight of *The Quiet Don* without revising the work so that the hero converted to Communism by the end? When you consider the fact that writers and artists were often executed for challenging the Communist regime, what is more important: ignoring the censorship of socialist realism and remaining true to one's art, or complying with the edicts of such tyrannical rulers as Stalin? Write a paper that outlines your conclusions.

2. Sholokhov's Communist critics objected that the author wrote *The Quiet Don* from the perspective of the White Russians rather than the Bolsheviks. What does the work gain or lose as a result of Sholokhov's decision? What might have happened—critically, socially, politically—if Sholokhov had written from the Bolshevik point of view? Create a presentation of your findings.

3. Aside from an allegiance to Communism, what specific social or political values does Sholokhov champion in his prose? What distinctions can you make by assessing Sholokhov's work on purely literary terms, leaving aside political considerations? Write an essay that outlines your views.

4. Research the collectivization of Soviet agriculture under Stalin for a presentation. Does *Virgin Soil Upturned* fairly portray the impact of this Soviet policy? Do you agree with socialized farming? Explain your answers.

BIBLIOGRAPHY

Books

Ermolaev, Herman. *Mikhail Sholokhov and His Art.* Princeton, N.J.: Princeton University Press, 1982.

Klimenko, Michael. *The World of Young Sholokhov: Vision of Violence.* North Quincy, Mass.: Christopher, 1972.

Muchnic, Helen. *Russian Writers: Notes and Essays.* New York: Random House, 1971.

Slonim, Marc. *Soviet Russian Literature: Writers and Problems, 1917–1977.* London: Oxford University Press, 1977.

Stevens, H. C. *Mikhail Sholokhov and the Novels of the Don Cycle.* New York: Knopf, 1960.

Stewart, David Hugh. *Mikhail Sholokhov: A Critical Introduction.* Ann Arbor: University of Michigan Press, 1967.

Struve, Gleb. *Russian Literature under Lenin and Stalin, 1917–1953.* London: Routledge and Kegan Paul, 1972.

Periodicals

Salisbury, Harrison E. "Khrushchev Bid to Sholokhov Follows a Dispute over Novel." *New York Times,* September 1, 1959, 1, 6.

Simmons, Ernest J. "Muddy Flows the Don." *New York Times Book Review,* August 20, 1967, 28–29.

Solzhenitsyn, Alexander. "Sholokhov and the Riddle of *The Quiet Don.*" *Times Literary Supplement,* October 4, 1974, 1056.

■ Zhou Shuren

SEE *Lu Xun*

▣ Nevil Shute

BORN: *1899, Ealing, England*

DIED: *1960, Melbourne, Australia*

NATIONALITY: *British and Australian*

GENRE: *Novels*

MAJOR WORKS:

What Happened to the Corbetts (1939)

A Town Like Alice (1950)

In the Wet (1953)

On the Beach (1957)

Overview

Nevil Shute lived, in some ways, as two very different people: Nevil Shute Norway, the successful airplane engineer and business entrepreneur, and Nevil Shute, the author of escapist adventure novels and science fiction. He was careful to keep the two separate, writing under a shortened version of his full name, fearing that his reputation as a best-selling novelist would undermine his credibility as an engineer whom people would trust with their lives in his airplanes. By the end of his unusual and successful career, however, he had made significant and enduring contributions to both aeronautical design and popular fiction—a claim that few others, if any, can make.

Works in Biographical and Historical Context

A Taste for Adventure Nevil Shute Norway was born on January 17, 1899, in Ealing, west of London.

Nevil Shute   *Central Press / Getty Images*

and he was determined to keep at it. He later spoke of his early work as not being particularly good, but Shute's novels come from the perspective of someone who found writing to be mostly a relaxing and amusing pastime to do after work. The many novels Shute wrote between 1924 and 1930 are often easy-to-read adventure stories about pilots, as Shute often flew a small plane himself during this time. Some of them did address serious issues, however, such as *So Disdained* (1928), which expressed his concern for pilots who, after serving in World War I, were now poorly paid. The American edition was published as *The Mysterious Aviator*.

Wartime Efforts and Inspiration   After 1938, Shute's novels began to show the political tensions of the period. When the war began, Shute was highly critical of America's refusal to come to the aid of Great Britain and its European allies. *Pied Piper*, about an elderly British lawyer who rescues refugee children from France just before the German invasion, was one of the books Shute aimed at American readers, hoping that the United States would end its isolation.

After the war, Shute traveled to Burma to briefly work for the ministry of information, and he returned to England and his full-time writing career in 1945. *The Chequer Board* (1947) grew out of his time in Burma. In 1947 Shute traveled by car around the United States, seeking a firsthand glimpse into the real America so he could better describe it in several of his novels (written with an eye toward the American movie industry).

Futuristic Visions   In 1950 Shute and his family moved permanently to Australia. During this period, in spite of his stammer, Shute began to lecture on professional writing. Among the topics he discussed were the elements he believed fiction readers want: information, romance, heroism, and a happy ending—even if it involves death. As Julian Smith points out, Shute's next novel, *In the Wet* (1953), supplied those four things, plus a fifth element—relevance to current events, in particular the coronation of Queen Elizabeth II. Moreover, *In the Wet* includes a vision of the 1980s, in which Australia is the center of a thriving British Empire free of socialism.

The 1950s saw the rise of the Cold War between the United States and the Soviet Union, and with it the constant threat of nuclear annihilation. In his best-known work, *On the Beach*, Shute takes up his most ambitious subject yet: the destruction of the world in a nuclear holocaust. The novel tells how in 1962 a nuclear war begins with the bombing of Tel Aviv and ends thirty-seven days later, presumably in total devastation. Southern Australia is the last part of the world to be affected by the spreading deadly radioactivity. The novel depicts the things people focus on in their final weeks and days—alcohol, auto racing, church attendance, vegetable gardens, and suicide drugs. *On the Beach* was not the first novel to address this topic, but Shute's treatment of the subject was noteworthy, both for the vividness of his

He spoke with a stutter, a problem he never completely overcame. His father became the head of the postal service in Ireland, and in 1912 the family moved to Dublin. Shute served in the medical corps during the Easter Rebellion in Ireland, during which Irish rebels supporting independence from England occupied some key government offices; in the ensuing conflict, Shute's father's post office was burned. He enlisted in the infantry just before World War I ended.

Shute began work as an engineer at the de Havilland Aircraft Company in 1922, where he learned to fly. While at de Havilland, Shute bought a typewriter, perhaps encouraged by the writing activities of his family: His grandmother had been a writer of children's books, his father had published travel books, and his mother edited a volume of correspondence about the family's experiences in the Irish rebellion. All of these genres influenced his later novels—the simple adventure narratives owe a debt to adolescent fiction, travel and life abroad is represented throughout Shute's novels, and the experiences of determined individuals confronting violence and the threat of death appear in many of Shute's stories.

An Amusing Pastime   In 1923 and 1924 Shute's first two novels were rejected by publishers, but he had learned that he enjoyed writing and could do it quickly,

LITERARY AND HISTORICAL CONTEMPORARIES

Shute's famous contemporaries include:

Amelia Earhart (1897–1937): Famed pilot and the first woman to fly solo across the Atlantic Ocean. During an attempt to fly around the world in 1937, her plane disappeared over the Pacific near Hawaii. It has never been found.

Edgar Rice Burroughs (1875–1950): Author of over seventy novels, most of them fantasy adventures or science fiction. His best known work, *Tarzan of the Apes*, has been adapted in countless sequels, films, and television shows.

Harry S. Truman (1884–1972): The thirty-third president of the United States. Just four months into his administration, he ordered the atomic bombings of Hiroshima and Nagasaki, Japan, which effectively ended World War II.

Howard Hughes (1905–1976): An eccentric, brilliant, and enormously innovative multimillionaire who designed and built several experimental aircraft and broke many speed records, later moving to commercial aircraft and founding Trans-American Airlines.

Glenn Miller (1904–1944): One of the best-selling musicians of the World War II era. He joined the army in 1942 so he could lead a band to entertain the troops and raise morale. His plane disappeared over France in 1944 and was never found.

depiction of the war's human consequences and for the remarkable popularity of the book. It was made into a star-studded movie in 1959, although Shute was unhappy with certain changes made to the story and characters.

Shute finished only two novels in his last four years, returning to subjects that had sustained him throughout his long career: *The Rainbow and the Rose* (1958), about a pilot reviewing the life of his mentor, and *Trustee from the Toolroom* (1960), which opens in Shute's birthplace of West Ealing, and is about an accomplished engineer. His work on the latter was impaired somewhat by a stroke he suffered in December of 1958. He began a new novel that was to metaphorically depict the Second Coming of Christ in the southern Australian wilderness, and he was working on it when he died on January 12, 1960.

Works in Literary Context

Shute did not write "literary" novels, so academic critics and Shute have largely ignored one another. According to Julian Smith, the leading authority on Shute and his works, "If Nevil Shute ever influenced another writer or the course of English literature, there is no evidence to that effect." Still, Shute was very much a product of his times. Best sellers can often reveal aspects of popular culture that wider literary trends cannot—for example, while literary authors of the world-wars era such as Virginia Woolf and Graham Greene were exploring complex characters and lyrical prose styles, Shute was content to just tell good stories that let people escape from their troubled times for a few hours. "His prose was never exciting, nor was it ever dull," writes Smith. "It was simply as functional as the aircraft he built in his engineering days."

Aviation   As a pilot and aeronautical engineer himself, it is not surprising that many of Shute's characters are pilots, and the majority of his tales deal with flying in some respect. For example, his first several novels are all adventures centered on pilots. The main character of *In the Wet* is a member of the Royal Australian Air Force, while the narrator of *No Highway* is an aeronautics engineer. The main character of *Round the Bend* is an engineer and pilot who becomes something of a religious leader.

Pulp Fiction Conventions   The trends in popular fiction of the 1930s–1950s tended toward heroic adventure stories, westerns, mysteries, and (from the 1950s onward) science fiction. These novels, and the short stories that filled the sensationalistic magazines of the era, are often called "pulp fiction" after the cheap wood-pulp paper on which they were printed. While Shute did not write westerns, he did set some of his novels in the Australian outback and in the American Rockies. He did not write mysteries, but his novel *Requiem for a Wren* (1955) does tell the story of a young lawyer investigating the supposed suicide of a parlor maid. What Shute does share with the pulp fiction tradition is an attraction to stories of noble middle-class heroes winning success through hard work and commitment, grand adventures to exotic locations, and futuristic tales of impending disasters.

Human and Societal Ideals   The future, for Shute, was a setting that allowed him to consider how the world could be a better or worse place as a result of moral and political decisions that we make today. For example, while it is true that *On the Beach* is about a nuclear holocaust, it is mostly about the ways in which the best aspects of human nature—especially tolerance for other races and religious beliefs—are a key part of mankind's redemption from our primitive instincts for violence and revenge. Similarly, *In the Wet* explores a unique idea for maintaining the spirit of democratic ideals: a government that allows its citizens to earn more than one vote by meeting certain conditions, such as achieving higher education or raising a family without divorcing.

Works in Critical Context

Shute did not attract much literary attention while he was alive, but after he died, critics began to assess the role he had been playing in popular culture. There were relatively few serious book reviews of his works as they came out, but when he died in 1960, there was a flurry of respectful obituaries such as the one in *Time* magazine that concluded that "later years may find [his novels] a remarkably reliable portrait of mid-20th century man and his concerns." Edmund Fuller wrote in the *Saturday Review*: "Nevil Shute will be missed. He was one of our most prolific and diversified storytellers. His twenty novels varied widely in tone and pace, as well as in scene, and time, ranging from his own Australia, where he lowered the curtain on the human race, to England and America, and from a little into the future back to the Vikings."

Shute did attract the attention of several important literary figures. George Orwell appreciated *Landfall: A Channel Story* (1940), saying that it brought out "the essential peculiarity of war, the mixture of heroism and meanness." C. P. Snow wrote in 1970 that Shute was a rare bridge between two very different cultures, engineers and general readers.

In recent years more has been written about Shute, including a book-length study by Julian Smith in 1976. The most attention is given to *On the Beach* because of its treatment of nuclear war and role in the history of British science fiction. Other recent critics are more interested in Shute's later novels and their portrayal of Australia and South Asian locales.

Responses to Literature

1. Is someone who is able to design a good airplane likely to be able to design a good novel, too? Are there basic thinking skills common to all construction, whether it be something mechanical or something literary? What assumptions are you making about engineers and novelists as you form your answer?

2. In the 1940s and 1950s, it was unusual for novels to emphasize how personal and political actions at home can have far-reaching influences all the way around the world. How does Shute deal with this theme in his novels? Is this theme more or less relevant today, in the age of the Internet and instant communications?

3. Research some of the government propaganda about nuclear war created during the Cold War of the 1950s and 1960s. (The film *The Atomic Café* is a good place to start.) Does Shute's treatment of nuclear holocaust in *On the Beach* seem more or less extreme to you when seen in this wider cultural context?

4. Read one of the books by Shute that was adapted into a film, and then watch the film. How faithful is the movie to the book? What was added or left out, and to what effect? What did the critics, and Shute himself, have to say about the movie?

COMMON HUMAN EXPERIENCE

The prospect of nuclear war, and the possible total annihilation of the human species that could very easily come with it, have cast a haunting shadow over the twentieth and twenty-first centuries. Here are some works that consider the aftermath of nuclear attacks, both fictional and nonfictional:

Hiroshima (1946), a nonfiction work by John Hersey. At 8:15 AM on August 6, 1945, nearly one hundred thousand people in this Japanese city died suddenly in an attack like no other. The book chronicles the lives of six ordinary survivors, tracing their will to survive, lifetime plights, illnesses, and fears.

A Canticle for Leibowitz (1960), a novel by Walter M. Miller Jr. This science fiction classic and Hugo Award winner is set in a monastery in the aftermath of an apocalyptic nuclear war.

The Day After (1983), a made-for-television movie directed by Nicholas Meyer. The broadcast of this movie was a huge television event at the time. It gives a small-town perspective on the possible aftermath of a nuclear war.

The Great Fire (2003), a novel by Shirley Hazzard. The "great fire" of the title is the bombing of Hiroshima. The novel by National Book Award winner Hazzard centers on a British soldier in Japan after the Allied victory to study the effects of the bomb on the country.

If You Love this Planet (1982), a documentary directed by Terre Nash. This short film won an Academy Award for its illustration of the potential medical and social results of a nuclear war.

BIBLIOGRAPHY

Books

Bennett, Jack. "Beyond Britain: Nevil Shute's Asian Outlook." In *Perceiving Other Worlds*. Ed. by Edwin Thumboo. Singapore: Times Academy, 1991.

———. "Nevil Shute: Exile by Choice." In *A Sense of Exile: Essays in the Literature of the Asia-Pacific Region*. Edited by Bruce Bennett and Susan Miller. Nedlands, Western Australia: Centre for Studies in Australian Literature, 1988.

Higdon, David Leon. "'Into the Vast Unknown': Directions in the Post-Holocaust Novel." In *War and Peace: Perspectives in the Nuclear Age*. Edited by Ulrich Goebel. Studies in Comparative Literature 18. Lubbock: Texas Technical University Press, 1988.

Smith, Julian. *Nevil Shute*. English Author Series, 190. Boston: Twayne, 1976.

———. *Nevil Shute: A Biography*. Kerhonkson, N.Y.: Paper Tiger, 2002.

Periodicals

Erisman, Fred. "Nevil Shute and the Closed Frontier." *Western American Literature* 21, no. 3 (November 1986): 207–17.

Martin, David. "The Mind That Conceived *On the Beach*." *Meanjin* 19 (1960): 193–200.

Smith, Julian. "On the Beach at Amchitka: The Conversion of Nevil Shute." *South Atlantic Quarterly* 72 (1973): 22–28.

"The Two Lives of Nevil Shute," *Time*, January 25, 1960, 94.

◈ Sir Philip Sidney

BORN: *1554, Kent, England*

DIED: *1586, Zutphen, the Netherlands*

NATIONALITY: *British*

GENRE: *Poetry, fiction, criticism*

MAJOR WORKS:

The Countess of Pembroke's Arcadia (1590)

Astrophel and Stella (1591)

The New Countess of Pembroke's Arcadia (revision) (1593)

An Apologie for Poetry (1595)

Sir Philip Sidney   *Sidney, Sir Philip, lithograph by Phillibrown after a painting by A. More, photograph. The Library of Congress.*

Overview

The English poet, diplomat, and soldier Sir Philip Sidney realized more dramatically than any other figure of the English Renaissance the ideal of the perfect courtier and the universal gentleman. Sidney saw writing as an important part of a complete gentleman's portfolio of accomplishments, an idea that remains influential in education to this day. Through his arguments in *An Apologie for Poetry* and in his own practice, Sidney demonstrated the value of literature during the Renaissance.

Works in Biographical and Historical Context

Early Signs of Promise   The son of a noble and well-connected family, Philip Sidney was born at Penshurst, his father's estate in Kent. His formal education began with his entrance into the Shrewsbury School in 1564. In 1568 he moved on to Christ Church, Oxford. Sidney's correspondence and school records indicate that as a youth he already showed clear signs of brilliance but that he was of sober temperament and uncertain health. Leaving Oxford without a degree—common for noblemen—Sidney completed his education with a three-year tour (1572–1575) of France, Germany, Austria, Poland, and Italy.

Entering a Life of Aristocracy: Travel and Diplomacy   On his return to England, Sidney entered quickly into the life of the aristocracy, dividing his time between the London house of his uncle, the powerful Earl of Leicester, and the country home of his sister, the Countess of Pembroke. Late in 1576 he paid a visit to his father, then Lord Deputy of Ireland, and observed political and social conditions in Ireland firsthand. Upon returning to England he addressed to the queen his "Discourse on Irish Affairs," defending his father's administration from the many criticisms leveled against it. In 1577 Sidney was sent on a diplomatic mission to Germany, during which he enthusiastically but unsuccessfully attempted to reconcile the quarreling Protestant factions and organize a unified resistance against the Catholic nations.

Literary Contact   Sidney's interests and relationships were not restricted to the worlds of the court and diplomacy, however. He enjoyed frequent contacts with a variety of literary men, notably Fulke Greville, Edward Dyer, and Edmund Spenser. Works probably written during this period include his *Lady of May* (1578), an elaborate entertainment performed in honor of Queen Elizabeth I, a large part of his sonnet sequence *Astrophel and Stella* (the names mean "star lover" and "star") (1591), and the first draft of his prose romance, the *Arcadia* (1590). His *Apologie for Poetry* (1595) was most likely composed shortly after the publication of Stephen Gosson's *School of Abuse* (1579), an attack on the theater that had been dedicated to Sidney without his knowledge or approval.

Dissatisfaction at Court   Meanwhile, Sidney's situation at court was not entirely satisfactory. He had for some years been regarded as a young man of promise and importance, but he was still without any steady paid position. Sidney had for some time known and admired the "Stella" of his sonnets, Penelope Devereux, the daughter of the Earl of Essex, but she married someone else in 1581. Two years later Sidney married the daughter of Sir Francis Walsingham and was knighted the same year.

Death in the Battle of Zutphen   Sidney had been a leader of the strong Puritan faction promoting English involvement in the wars of the Protestant Dutch against their Catholic Spanish rulers. This conflict, known as the Dutch Revolt or Eighty Years' War initially began as a fight for Dutch independence. In 1585, after Elizabeth I finally acceded to this faction's demands and sent an army to the Netherlands, Sidney was named governor of Flushing, one of the towns that the Dutch had ceded to the queen in return for her support. For several months he fought and commanded troops at the side of his uncle, the Earl of Leicester, in Flanders. At the battle of Zutphen on September 22, 1586, he was fatally wounded. A biography written by his friend Greville tells how Sidney was vulnerable because he had generously lent a part of his protective armor to a fellow knight.

Works in Literary Context

The Romance and the Pastoral   *Arcadia* has examples of many dominant genres of the day, and taken as a whole, it becomes an innovative genre of its own. It is mostly a romance, a long prose fiction that is a prototype of the modern novel. Romance, however, makes no attempt to maintain the connections to real life or the illusions of reality that novels generally try to keep. Romances build upon the medieval stories of King Arthur and his questing knights—by Sidney's day the dragons and wizards are gone, but the heroism, atmosphere of magic, and passionate love stories remain. Sidney frames his romance in the context of a pastoral, a highly idealized vision of country life populated by lovelorn and elegant shepherds and disdainful shepherdesses. Woven throughout are songs, poems, a highly complex intrigue plot that we see in some Renaissance dramas, and a high-flown baroque writing style, making *Arcadia* quite different from anything that had appeared before or would appear after it. It was popular throughout the 1600s and provided ample material for dramatists, although later generations often found it unbearable: William Hazlitt called it "one of the greatest monuments of the abuse of intellectual power upon record."

The Sonnet Sequence   Sidney's was the first English sonnet sequence—a series of sonnets, each of which can

stand on its own but when arranged in order tell a loose story of the progress of an affair. Sonnet sequences immediately became a fashion throughout the Renaissance. The sonnets in *Astrophel and Stella*, first printed in 1591, expressed varying moods and intensities of passionate love in smooth, confident, and flexible verse. Sidney was influenced, as were all Renaissance sonneteers, by the emotionally wrought Italian poetry of Francesco Petrarch (1304–1374).

Literary Criticism   Sidney's *Apologie for Poetry* (1595) was the first major critical essay during the Renaissance, an era when England was first starting to become self-conscious of its literary tradition. Sidney condensed the classical defense of "poetry" (by which he meant all forms of creative writing), and he insisted

COMMON HUMAN EXPERIENCE

The sonnet sequence is a demanding genre. Sonnets themselves are highly compressed poems, each following a set structure in both the meter and the ordering of ideas in fourteen lines. Each sonnet needs to be substantially different from all the others, able to make sense on its own but tell part of a story when arranged in a sequence. Sonnet sequences are less like coherent novels than an emotional scrapbook of a passionate, usually unrequited love affair. Below are some other notable examples of sonnet sequences.

Song Book (c. 1374), a sonnet sequence by Francesco Petrarch. Petrarch, who wrote his verse in Italian, is considered by many to be the father of the sonnet sequence. A large section of this collection amounts to a sonnet sequence concerning his love of a woman named Laura.

Pamphilia to Amphilanthus (1621), a sonnet sequence by Lady Mary Wroth. Wroth was a relative of Sidney's, and this sequence of forty-eight sonnets was the only significant set composed by a woman during the Renaissance.

The House of Life (1870), a sonnet sequence by Dante Gabriel Rossetti. Rossetti said this set of 101 sonnets was about life, death, and the ideals of art and beauty, but many other readers see the poems biographically as representing Rossetti's complex emotions over the death of his wife and his unrequited passion for the wife of a friend.

Fungi from Yuggoth (1930–1947), a sonnet sequence by H. P. Lovecraft. This work contains unusual themes for a sonnet sequence: it is a tale of science fiction and horror. In it, the narrator discovers a book that allows him to travel to distant planets, where he meets unusual races of creatures.

on the ethical value of art, which aims to lure men to "see the form of goodness, which seen they cannot but love ere themselves be aware, as if they took a medicine of cherries." It establishes the idea, now the familiar creed to millions of English literature majors, that imaginative literature is worth studying because it "teaches while it delights." Sidney goes so far as to argue that this is why poetry is a more worthwhile subject of study than philosophy (too dry) and history (where sometimes the villains have to win). Literature alone is free to alter reality to show us all varieties of virtue; at the same time it makes learning persuasive by making the lessons delightful and memorable. Even apart from its bold ideas, the *Apologie* is seen as a classic work of literature itself for its masterly rhetorical control. Two hundred years later, one of the other great literary critics of English literature, Samuel

Johnson, would borrow heavily from its ideas to place William Shakespeare once and for all into the ranks of the world's great dramatists.

Works in Critical Context

Idealized Portrait As soon as Sidney died, biographers began the process of mythologizing him as an English hero. Edmund Spenser began calling him "Astrophel," after the lover in Sidney's sonnet sequence. Fulke Greville wrote a highly laudatory biography in 1610 that used several dubious stories to heighten Sidney's reputation. Throughout the rest of the seventeenth century, Sidney's influence was very strong both as a writer and as a personal role model. Material from *Arcadia* regularly appeared in Renaissance dramas, and the sonnet sequence became a literary fad.

Cherished by nostalgic Victorians in the nineteenth century, the idealized portrait of Sidney the gentleman-warrior, a fulfillment of mythic aspirations, continued to obscure his merits as a poet and theorist well into the twentieth century. Nineteenth-century critic Edmund Goose cautioned against inflating Sidney's merits as an author: "Sidney is most interesting as a radiating centre of sympathy, intelligence, brightness. . . . As a great author, surely, we must never venture to regard him."

Apologie for Poetry In the eighteenth century, literary tastes swung away from the highly decorative prose style of *Arcadia*, although Sidney's poetry was still much admired. Most influential was his *Apologie for Poetry*, however. Samuel Johnson's "Preface to Shakespeare" repeats some of Sidney's points about the classical "unities." Sidney's and Johnson's eras both shared a high regard for the literature of classical Greece and Rome, and one of their literary values was that dramas should stay consistent and unified in their setting, action, and the parallel timing between the events of the plot and the time it takes to perform the play. Sidney claimed that imaginative literature has no need to follow these restrictions, and Johnson agreed, using them to make a widely influential claim about Shakespeare's superiority to all other playwrights, including Sophocles.

Today, while Sidney is perhaps the least studied of all the major Renaissance writers (and all of them are dwarfed by the attention given to Shakespeare), much excellent scholarship has been undertaken to separate the actual life of the man from the legend created after his death. While a less distinguished, experienced, favored, and rational Sidney has emerged, he is for many a more authentic and compelling figure.

Responses to Literature

1. Where do you see *sprezzatura*—the "easy grace" of doing difficult things with apparent ease—reflected in the style and/or content of the *Apologie for Poetry*?

2. Summarize the "plot" of the sonnet sequence *Astrophel and Stella*. What are the strengths and weaknesses of the story's being as sketchy as it is? Do you think it is helpful, or unnecessary, to know the events of Sidney's courtship of Penelope Devereux as you read the sonnets?

3. The characters in *Arcadia*, even the shepherds, speak in a convoluted, exaggerated, and high-flown literary style. How can we, or should we, take this at all seriously? Is *Arcadia* just too "out there" for modern tastes, or do you feel that its fantasies can make it more appealing today than it has been in a long time?

BIBLIOGRAPHY

Books

Boas, Frederick S. *Sir Philip Sidney, Representative Elizabethan: His Life and Writings.* London: Staples, 1955.

Buxton, John. *Sir Philip Sidney and the English Renaissance.* 2nd ed. New York: St. Martin's, 1987.

Connell, Dorothy. *Sir Philip Sidney: The Maker's Mind.* Oxford: Clarendon, 1977.

Davis, Walter R. *A Map of* Arcadia: *Sidney's Romance in Its Tradition.* New Haven, Conn.: Yale University Press, 1965.

Duncan-Jones, Katherine. *Sir Philip Sidney: Courtier Poet.* New Haven, Conn.: Yale University Press, 1991.

Greville, Fulke. *The Life of Sir Philip Sidney.* Edited by Nowell Smith. Oxford: Clarendon, 1907.

Hager, Alan. *Dazzling Images: The Masks of Sir Philip Sidney.* Newark: University of Delaware Press, 1991.

Hamilton, A. C. *Sir Philip Sidney: A Study of His Life and Works.* Cambridge: Cambridge University Press, 1977.

Kay, Dennis, ed. *Sir Philip Sidney: An Anthology of Modern Criticism.* Oxford: Clarendon, 1987.

Van Dorsten, Jan, Dominic Baker-Smith, and Arthur F. Kinney, eds. *Sir Philip Sidney: 1586 and the Creation of a Legend.* Leiden, the Netherlands: Leiden University Press, 1986.

Periodicals

Greenblatt, Stephen. "Sidney's *Arcadia* and the Mixed Mode." *Studies in Philology* 70 (July 1973): 269–78.

Hamilton, A. C. "Sidney's *Arcadia* as Prose Fiction: Its Relation to Its Sources." *English Literary Renaissance* 2 (Winter 1972): 29–60.

———. "Sidney's *Astrophel and Stella* as a Sonnet Sequence." *English Literary History* 36 (March 1969): 59–87.

Web Sites

Sir Philip Sidney. Retrieved April 6, 2007, from http://www.luminarium.org/renlit/sidney.htm. Last updated on April 6, 2008.

Sir Philip Sidney's *Apology for Poetry.* Retrieved April 6, 2007, from http://www.wam.umd.edu/~mlhall/PhilipSidney.html. Last updated on February 24, 2007.

❖ Alan Sillitoe

BORN: *1928, Nottingham, England*

NATIONALITY: *British*

GENRE: *Fiction, poetry*

MAJOR WORKS:

Saturday Night and Sunday Morning (1958)

The Loneliness of the Long Distance Runner (1959)

The Open Door (1989)

Overview

British writer Alan Sillitoe is often classed as one of the "Angry Young Men" of 1950s England, a group of novelists and playwrights whose stark portrayals of working class people served as sharp social criticism. Sillitoe is best known for the novel *Saturday Night and Sunday Morning* (1958) and the short story collection *The Loneliness of the Long Distance Runner* (1959).

Works in Biographical and Historical Context

A Hard-Knock Childhood in Nottingham Sillitoe's fiction is frequently based on his personal life. The son of a functionally illiterate man, Sillitoe was raised in

Alan Sillitoe *Granville Davies / Writer Pictures / drr.net*

LITERARY AND HISTORICAL CONTEMPORARIES

Sillitoe's famous contemporaries include:

Fidel Castro (1926–): The Cuban revolutionary and Communist who was head of state from the Cuban revolution in 1959 to his retirement in 2008. Castigated by various U.S. administrations as a terrible dictator, Castro was a key player in the Cuban missile crisis, in which the world came as close to all-out nuclear war as it ever has, as well as in the modernization of his country's health-care and employment systems.

Jawaharlal Nehru (1889–1964): A key leader in the Indian independence movement and close associate to Mohandas Gandhi, Nehru became India's first prime minister after independence from British rule was secured in 1947.

Albert Finney (1936–): Eminent British actor who first achieved fame for his starring role in the 1960 film adaptation of *Saturday Night and Sunday Morning*.

John Osborne (1929–1994): British playwright famous for the 1956 work *Look Back in Anger*. Like Sillitoe, he was considered one of the "Angry Young Men" of the 1950s.

John F. Kennedy (1917–1963): Kennedy's brief presidency was an eventful one, including the Bay of Pigs invasion, the Cuban missile crisis, the beginning of America's military involvement in Vietnam, the beginning of the space program, and the civil rights movement. Highly popular and charismatic, his term was cut short by an assassin in 1963, a turning point in American history.

Nottingham, England, where unemployment was widespread prior to World War II. To help ease his family's financial burden, Sillitoe left school at age fourteen to work in a bicycle plant, then escaped the tedium of factory work by joining the Royal Air Force four years later, in 1946. He served as a wireless radio operator in Malaya (then controlled by the British) just after World War II, contracting tuberculosis while there and thus participating in the long tradition of British colonists and soldiery who have come down with pernicious diseases while stationed in the tropics. Two years after completing his military service, and much travel later, Sillitoe married American poet Ruth Fainlight and relocated to France, where he found the necessary detachment to write about the social injustices of his own country.

A Life Told in Novels   Sillitoe's best-known characters, the Seatons, mirror his own family and are instilled with the resilient spirit Sillitoe acquired during his harsh childhood. *Saturday Night and Sunday Morning* (1958) follows the life and loves of Arthur Seaton, a bored young factory

worker whose life is composed of good wages, sexual adventures, and wild weekends at the neighborhood pub.

The title story of *The Loneliness of the Long Distance Runner* (1959), a collection for which Sillitoe received the Hawthornden Prize, is set in a boys' reformatory, and revolves around a cross-country race that becomes a battle between subjection and independence. Both "The Loneliness of the Long Distance Runner" and *Saturday Night and Sunday Morning* were adapted for film. Although critics first identified Arthur Seaton as Sillitoe's fictional counterpart, the author actually expressed an affinity with Brian Seaton, Arthur's older brother.

Southeast Asian Experiences Find Expression Written during the early moments leading up to the Vietnam War, the novel *Key to the Door* (1961), looks at Britain's own history in Southeast Asia. It concentrates on soldier-protagonist Brian's military experiences in Malaya, where he is gripped with uncertainty about the war (World War II) and repelled by England's political system. This protagonist also appears in several short stories. In 1989, Sillitoe published *The Open Door*, a continuation of Brian's story written as a stream-of-consciousness narrative. The work is largely autobiographical.

Sillitoe lives and writes still in London, England. He recently published a memoir account of his travels in Russia, *Gadfly in Russia* (2007).

Works in Literary Context

Regionalism and the Spirit of the Outsider On a thematic level, Sillitoe seems to draw inspiration from both the old and the new. As is true of many contemporary writers, he often centers his stories on an individual isolated from society, studying what the *Guardian*'s Roy Perrot calls "the spirit of the outsider, the dissenter, the man apart." But instead of limiting himself strictly to the psychological confines of this one person and allowing the rest of the world to remain somewhat shadowy, Sillitoe places his rebellious outsider in a gritty, distinctive milieu—Nottingham, an English industrial town (and the author's birthplace) where, as Charles Champlin explains in the *Los Angeles Times*, "the lower-middle and working classes rub, where breaking even looks like victory, and London is a long way South." This strong regionalism, reminiscent of the regionalism common in nineteenth-century British fiction, is one of the most striking features of Sillitoe's writing.

The Jungle and Brutality In all Sillitoe's fiction, the world is seen as a jungle, yet the nature of the jungle changes. In the earliest fiction, like *Saturday Night and Sunday Morning* and "The Loneliness of the Long Distance Runner," society and the exterior world are jungles in which the protagonist, himself neutral, must survive through a combination of luck and shrewd skill. But, starting with *Key to the Door* (1961), the jungle is both the exterior worlds of Nottingham and Malaya and the questions, uncertainties, false starts, and violence within the protagonist himself.

The theme of brutality, in Sillitoe's world, is also treated in its rationalized and institutionalized version, the military. Although many of the working-class characters deride the military and none is patriotic, Sillitoe demonstrates, particularly in the novel *The Widower's Son* (1976), the use of the military career as the conscious focus for working out all the stresses of the individual and social jungles within modern man.

Works in Critical Context
The Loneliness of the Long Distance Runner and Beyond

Upon the publication of his first two major works, critics associated Sillitoe with the Angry Young Men, a group of writers whose literary output reflected the social consciousness of post–World War II England. Reviewers contended that both books powerfully evoke the country's prosperous yet bitter postwar atmosphere, and many commentators have characterized the title story of *The Loneliness of the Long Distance Runner* as a masterpiece of short fiction. Critics also commended Sillitoe's humorous, perceptive portrait of his protagonist in *The Open Door*. Brian Morton notes, "*The Open Door* is an extraordinary, almost symphonic development of deceptively familiar materials, and confirms [Sillitoe's] standing as one of Britain's most powerful and sophisticated fiction writers." The conclusion of *Her Victory* (1982), however, in which Pam returns pregnant and subservient to Tom, elicited negative critical reaction. Several reviewers considered *Her Victory* to be a chauvinistic treatment of the feminist movement, impugning the lack of emotional growth in an "emancipated" character. Although his later collections of short fiction have not achieved the enormous success of *The Loneliness of the Long Distance Runner*, Sillitoe's short stories are usually considered superior to his longer works of fiction. Eric Moon argues, "The background of Sillitoe's stories is generally as unrelieved as that of his novels, but in the stories he is more able to vary his pace and his attitudes. He often reveals humor and a greater compassion, and sometimes he achieves a curiously convincing blending of his usual realism and passion with a lyrical romanticism."

Angry Young Man or Throwback? What reviewers cannot agree upon in their evaluations of Sillitoe's work is whether he writes in the tradition of an earlier age (notably the American proletarian novelists of the 1930s) or in the tradition of certain British authors of the 1950s and 1960s whose bitter attacks on the political and social establishment earned them the name Angry Young Men. Stanley Kauffmann, for one, feels Sillitoe is a victim of the cultural "timelag" that exists between the United States and England and is therefore merely rediscovering the themes that once preoccupied American writers such as John Steinbeck, Erskine Caldwell, Theodore Dreiser,

and John Dos Passos. Saul Maloff shares this view, commenting: "Sillitoe is a throwback.... His protagonists are profoundly rooted in their class, and draw such strengths as they possess—or come finally to possess—from that identification." This, he adds, makes Sillitoe very different from other postwar writers. "[He] is a historical surprise. In the utterly changed circumstances of the fifties and sixties, he has partially validated as art the 'proletarian novel' of the thirties; and standing eccentrically against the current driven by his defter contemporaries, he has made possible a working-class novel."

John W. Aldridge suggests that part of Sillitoe's inspiration may date back even earlier than the 1930s. States the critic: "Sillitoe stands as a comforting reminder to the English that the grand old roistering 'low life' tradition of [Henry] Fielding and [Charles] Dickens may have lost its sting, but is not yet dead.... Although [the author] does have his grievances, he seems basically content to keep the working man in his place, and as a writer he evidently wants to remain a working man." Aldridge indicates, however, that other writers "did all that he has done first and better than he.... There is little virtue in repeating the discoveries or the mistakes of one's predecessors, or in trying to make literature out of a cultural lag that merely social reform and the payment of some money can rectify."

On the other hand, some critics see nothing but youthful anger in Sillitoe's writings. Commenting in the

New York Times Book Review, Malcolm Bradbury notes that "if the heroes of some...English novels are angry young men, Mr. Sillitoe is raging." Although John R. Clark of the *Saturday Review* also sees Sillitoe as an Angry Young Man, he feels that "his anger and fictions have altered with time. In [his] early work there was something single-minded and intense in the actions and scenes, particularly in the shorter novels." On the other hand, "Later novels reveal a broader social and political horizon. Sillitoe's characters not only privately rebel but become dedicated to larger 'movements.'"

Responses to Literature

1. In your opinion, is Sillitoe's early work a "throw-back" to the work of American authors of the 1930s like John Steinbeck, or a part of the new existentialist Angry Young Man movement? What evidence can you provide from Sillitoe's writing to support your position?

2. Discuss how madness and freedom are interrelated in Sillitoe's stories. Do you think Sillitoe believes madness is necessary to achieve freedom?

3. Sillitoe has been accused of antifeminist character-ization in *Her Victory*. Do you think this accusation is accurate? Why or why not? What evidence from the text can you use to support your interpretation?

4. Analyze the question of identity in Sillitoe's love stories.

BIBLIOGRAPHY

Books

Atherton, Stanley S. *Alan Sillitoe: A Critical Assessment.* London: W.H. Allen/Virgin Books, 1979.

Hanson, Gillian Mary. *Understanding Alan Sillitoe.* Columbia: University of South Carolina Press, 1997.

Hitchcock, Peter. *Working-Class Fiction in Theory and Practice: A Reading of Alan Sillitoe.* Rochester: University of Rochester Press, 1989.

Rusz, Renata. *Keyword: Anger.* Saarbruecken, Germany: VDM Verlag, 2008.

Sawkins, John. *The Long Apprenticeship: Alienation in the Early Work of Alan Sillitoe.* New York, Berlin, Oxford: Peter Lang Publishing, 2001.

◈ Georges Simenon

BORN: *1903, Liège, Belgium*

DIED: *1989, Lausanne, Switzerland*

NATIONALITY: *Belgian, French*

GENRE: *Fiction*

MAJOR WORKS:

Intimate Memoirs (1984)

Maigret and the Tavern by the Seine (1990)

Georges Simenon   *Simenon, Georges, 1986, photograph. AP Images.*

Overview

With over five hundred titles to his credit and translations of his work into more than forty languages, Belgian novelist Georges Simenon, who wrote in French, is prob-ably best known for his series of detective novels featuring French police inspector Jules Maigret. Through this pro-tagonist, Simenon introduced to detective fiction the exploration of character as the primary means for solving a crime. Simenon's non-Maigret novels, also highly regarded, feature characters who are compelled to com-mit crimes due to some kind of psychological crisis. The detail of atmosphere his writing possesses sets him apart from his European contemporaries.

Works in Biographical and Historical Context

Early Callings   Georges Simenon was born in Liège, Belgium, on February 13, 1903, to insurance accountant Désiré and homemaker Henriette Simenon. A bright pupil, he was determined to become a writer. When his father died, Simenon's schooling was cut short, and he was apprenticed to a pastry chef to learn a trade. Simenon abandoned his apprenticeship after one year, and at the age of seventeen he began his career as a writer by taking a newspaper job with the *Liège Gazette* as an assistant night police reporter. It was also at the age of seventeen that he published his first novel, *Au pont des arches* (*Aboard the Ark*, 1921), under the pen name Georges Sim.

Prolific Output Between 1921 and 1934 he wrote nearly two hundred novels, which he published under more than a dozen pseudonyms. Simenon moved to Paris in 1924, and in 1930 he began the famous Maigret series of detective novels, which he published under his own name.

For many critics, however, Simenon's best novels are those that lie outside the Maigret series. In the 1930s he wrote many other thrillers, a notable example being *The Man Who Watched the Trains Go By* (*L'Homme qui regardait passer les trains*, 1938). *Pedigree*, written during the war years and published in 1948, is a largely autobiographical novel that presents a powerful and convincing picture of the life of a boy and his parents in Liège from 1903 to 1918. Subsequently, Simenon wrote novels in which the psychological analysis of the leading character, exceptional in some way, forms the center of interest. Examples include *The Heart of a Man* (*Les Volets verts*, 1950), which portrays the closing stages in the life of a great actor, and *The Little Saint* (*Le Petit Saint*, 1965) about the formative years in the life of a great artist.

Simenon's desire to be known as an earnest novelist was tempered by his lack of self-confidence as a writer and his distrust of the intellectual community. He therefore formed "a theory of the 'semi-literary' novel, or, more earthily, 'semi-alimentary,'" according to one critic, who continued, "The theory was that he wrote pulps to make money, was aiming at 'straight' novels but felt insecure about 'high' literature, and took up the detective story as a midway step." In an article titled "Simenon on Simenon" for the *Times Literary Supplement*, Simenon illuminated the man behind the writer who believed that humility was the grandest virtue one could hope to possess. "Simenon," he wrote about himself, "is truly a modest man. He knows his own limitations and does not make for himself the claims that have sometimes been made for him by some of his more florid admirers. He describes himself as a craftsman, has a healthy distrust of intellectuals . . . of literary occasions and intellectual conversations, feels ill at ease at social functions, and is quite unambitious in conventional terms: recognition, decorations, and so on. He can, it is true, well afford to be."

Final Output Simenon retired from writing fiction in 1974 after producing a range of novels, short stories, diaries, and other works. In 1978, the author suffered the greatest tragedy in his life when his daughter, Marie-Georges, committed suicide in her apartment. Devastated by his loss, Simenon felt the need to write about it. The result was his lengthy *Intimate Memoirs* (*Memoires intimes*, 1981), an exhausting book for the writer to compose. It was his last work.

Although he described himself as a craftsman, Simenon's popular Maigret novels, as well as his more serious works, came to be admired by distinguished French crit-

---

LITERARY AND HISTORICAL CONTEMPORARIES

Simenon's famous contemporaries include:

Ella Josephine Baker (1903–1946): Baker was a leading African American civil rights activist who worked behind the scenes alongside Dr. Martin Luther King and several others.

Agatha Christie (1890–1976): A popular mystery/detective writer with record-breaking book sales, she was dubbed "Queen of Crime" in the twentieth century.

Sir Winston Churchill (1874–1975): Twice prime minister of the United Kingdom, this statesman and acclaimed orator was also a Nobel Prize–winning author.

Ernest Hemingway (1899–1961): He is best known as the famous expatriate writer whose name is synonymous with the Great American Novel.

Dashiell Hammett (1894–1961): Hammett wrote *The Maltese Falcon* (1930), which introduced the famous detective Sam Spade.

---

ics. Nobel laureate André Gide called him "perhaps the greatest and most genuine novelist of today's French literature." Simenon died in Lausanne, Switzerland, in 1989.

Works in Literary Context

Plain Style Simenon is above all a storyteller. His style is deliberately simple, as he aims at a kind of "universal vocabulary." He builds compelling action and atmosphere through careful, subtle touches, and his readers are immediately gripped by their desire to know what happens next. Simenon's themes are particularly focused on the inner workings of the human mind. Commenting on the astonishing range of characters that move through his world, Simenon said, "Some people collect stamps; I collect human beings." In this respect he excludes politics, religion, history, and metaphysics from his books and instead concentrates on psychology and on the minor, yet often extraordinary, details of human existence.

Maigret Because of the dozens of novels in which he appears, as well as the many films and television adaptations starring his character, Inspector Maigret, of police headquarters in Paris, has become almost as well known as Arthur Conan Doyle's Sherlock Holmes. Though recognizable to fans, Maigret is unlike any other fictional detective. A man with simple tastes who is sensible and tolerant but not brilliant, Maigret puzzles his way to the solution of his cases by intuition, as opposed to deductive reasoning or by relying on stereotypical clues such as

COMMON HUMAN EXPERIENCE

Maigret is one of the most famous fictional detectives in world literature. Other famous fictional detectives appear in these works:

A Study in Scarlet (1887), a novel by Arthur Conan Doyle. Legendary detective Sherlock Holmes makes his first appearance in this novel.

Murder Must Advertise (1933), a novel by Dorothy L. Sayers. In this murder mystery, Lord Peter Whimsey tracks down the murderer of the copywriter Victor Dean.

The Maltese Falcon (1930), a novel by Dashiell Hammett. Hard-boiled detective Sam Spade appears in this novel about the fate of a mysterious black bird.

A is for Alibi (1982), a novel by Sue Grafton. The first of the Kinsey Millhone Alphabet Mysteries, this novel picks up where Sam Spade left off.

fingerprints or lab reports. An element of immeasurable importance in Maigret's investigations is his extraordinary patience; sometimes he spends weeks simply observing the scene of a crime. He attempts to understand the victim and suspect completely by immersing himself in their lifestyles and by examining the psychological reasons that provoked the crime. This added psychological dimension enhances the reader's typical interest in learning the solution to a mystery. A surprising trait for a detective to have is compassion for the criminal; Maigret often feels sorry after he catches the perpetrator he has sought.

Unconventional Detective Stories In the same way that Inspector Maigret is unlike most famous fictional sleuths, Simenon's crafting of the stories themselves differs from the traditional form of the mystery and detective genre. Anthony Boucher observed that Simenon's work in this area departed "from the well-shaped plot and the devious gimmick (though he could be very good at these when he chose) to lay stress on the ambience and milieu of the crime and on the ambivalent duel... between the murderer and Maigret." Devotees of mystery and detective fiction agree that the Maigret stories do not strictly adhere to the conventional features of the field. In the introduction to their *Catalogue of Crime*, Jacques Barzun and W. H. Taylor stated that "anyone who says, 'I can't bear detective stories, but I love Simenon' is saying that he prefers the art" of Simenon's mysteries, a quality which is atypical of the detective genre. Because the usual Simenon novel "is often of the highest order" artistically, Barzun and Taylor contend that "it is not detective fiction. True, Maigret, like any

other policeman, wants to get his man, and he knows where to wait for him—he has had previous information. But what he contributes is the patience of a god. And what his readers enjoy is his boredom, fatigue, wet feet, and hunger."

Works in Critical Context

Attesting to the uniqueness of Simenon's mystery fiction in general and his Maigret series in particular, novelist and critic Julian Symons wrote in his *Mortal Consequences: A History—from the Detective Story to the Crime Novel*, "The Maigret stories stand quite on their own in crime fiction, bearing little relation to most of the other work done in the field. (Simenon is not much interested in crime stories and has read few of them)....There are no great feats of... [logical reasoning or deduction] in them and the problems they present are human as much as they are criminal."

Serious Novels Although Simenon "attempted to persuade critics and publishers that he should be taken seriously as an author of...serious novels," observed *Dictionary of Literary Biography* contributor Catharine Savage Brosman, "sales figures suggest that the Maigret series and a few other books in the same vein have the most appeal, and his fame continues to rest principally on them." Brosman later explained, "His serious novels do not offer wisdom or illumination, and, despite the strong characterization, the reader does not enter into their world....In the detective mode, however, his work sets the standard, rather than following it."

Delicate and Refined Readers André Gide, an admirer and long-time critical correspondent of Simenon asserted that there is a "profound psychological and ethical interest "in all of Simenon's books," not just the serious novels. Gide stated, "This is what attracts and holds me in him. He writes for 'the vast public,' to be sure, but delicate and refined readers find something for them too as soon as they begin to take him seriously. He makes one reflect; and this is close to being the height of art."

Responses to Literature

1. Research the psychological profiles of at least three infamous criminals from the past fifty years. Do you notice any characteristics these people have in common? Pretend you are an attorney defending one of these criminals. How would you argue his/her case from a psychological perspective? Write an opening statement for the trial.

2. Make a "Wanted" poster for the suspects in two or more of Simenon's novels. Use character descriptions from the texts to visually portray the suspects. You may draw the characters on posterboard; take photos of people you know or cut out pictures from magazines of people who fit the descriptions; or

create a poster using the computer program of your choice. Underneath each picture, include a short paragraph describing both the physical characteristics of the characters and the characters' alleged roles in the crimes for which she or he has been accused.

BIBLIOGRAPHY

Books

Assouline, Pierre. *Simenon: A Biography.* New York: Knopf, 1997.

Barzun, Jacques, and Wendell Hertig Taylor. *A Catalogue of Crime: Being a Reader's Guide to the Literature of Mystery, Detection, and Related Genres.* New York: Harper, 1989.

Becker, Lucille Frackman. *Georges Simenon.* Boston: Twayne, 1977.

Bertrand, Alain. *Maigret.* Brussels, Belgium: Labor, 1994.

Dictionary of Literary Biography. Vol. 72 of *French Novelists, 1930–1960.* Detroit: Gale, 1988.

Gide, Andre. *The Journals of Andre Gide.* Vol. 4: 1938–1949. New York: Knopf, 1951.

Symons, Julian. *Mortal Consequences: A History—from the Detective Story to the Crime Novel.* New York: Harper, 1972.

Periodicals

Simenon, Georges. *Times Literary Supplement,* December 14, 1940; November 25, 1960; July 29, 1983; August 12, 1988.

Web Sites

Books and Writers. Georges (Joseph Christian) Simenon (1903–1989). Retrieved February 14, 2008, from http://www.kirjasto.sci.fi/simenon.htm.

Trussel, Steve. "Simenon and His Maigret". Retrieved February 17, 2008, from http://www.trussel.com/f_maig.htm. Last updated on February 16, 2008.

Claude Simon

BORN: *1913, Tananarive (now Antananarivo), Madagascar*

DIED: *2005, Paris, France*

NATIONALITY: *French*

GENRE: *Fiction*

MAJOR WORKS:

The Wind (1957)

The Flanders Road (1960)

The Palace (1962)

Histoire (1967)

The Invitation (1987)

Claude Simon   *Simon, Claude, photograph. © Jerry Bauer. Reproduced by permission.*

Overview

Claude Simon is commonly identified as one of the first of the French New Novelists. Like Alain Robbe-Grillet, Nathalie Sarraute, Michel Butor, and others connected with the New Novel movement that emerged after World War II, Simon does not attempt to impose artistic order on the chaos of human experience. Instead, his works reflect the fragmented nature of reality. In his major novels, including *The Wind* and *The Flanders Road*, Simon dispenses with conventional narrative structures and concentrates on the essential processes of language, memory, and perception. The destructive effects of war, as well as the ravages of time itself, are themes repeated throughout his work.

Works in Biographical and Historical Context

Born in Madagascar, Raised in France On October 10, 1913, Claude Eugene Henri Simon, son of Louis and Suzanne Denamiel Simon, was born in Tananarive (now Antananarivo), Madagascar, then a French possession where his father was an army officer. Because Simon was only six months old when he left Africa to

LITERARY AND HISTORICAL CONTEMPORARIES

Simon's famous contemporaries include:

Georges Clemenceau (1841–1929): Prime minster of France and promoter of the Treaty of Versailles, the truce that ended World War I but contributed to the development of World War II.

Marcel Proust (1871–1922): French writer most known for his *Remembrance of Things Past*, an autobiographical book that focused on what some might call the mundane details of everyday life.

William Faulkner (1897–1962): American novelist who often used a complex, disjointed literary style to emphasize Southern hypocrisy.

Alain Robbe-Grillet (1922–2008): French writer and filmmaker responsible for the "new novel" movement.

return to the ancestral home of his mother's family in the south of France, it is not surprising that his novels contain little in the way of exotic colonial experiences other than evocations of the fragmentary scenes on postcards that Simon's own father, like the father in *Histoire*, sent back to France from his travels. Soon after Simon returned to France, however, his father volunteered to serve as a cavalry officer in World War I and was killed in one of the early battles of the conflict. Though Simon would spend many summers of his youth visiting with his father's relatives, he would be raised primarily by his mother and her family, explaining perhaps why the theme of the maternal plays such a large role in his works.

After his father's death Simon was brought up in the ancient family residence under the supervision of his maternal uncle, the model for Uncle Charles in several of his novels. For most of his life, Simon spent part of the year living in Salses, situated in Roussillon between Perpignan and Les Corbieres, in close proximity to the location of his maternal family's vineyards and ancient home. Many biographical details connected with that location are relevant to his novels.

Art and War Simon's secondary studies took place in Perpignan and then at the prestigious College Stanislas in Paris. He successfully completed his baccalaureate studies in Paris with the final year of study being devoted not to philosophy, as he has often pointed out when questioned by critics on philosophical matters, but to mathematics. In response to family pressures, he began studies for a naval career at the Lycée Saint-Louis, but his lack of interest was manifest from the start, and he was dismissed shortly. His family then agreed to allow him to study painting, which he did for a time in Paris with Andre Lhote, a master of constructions that Simon character-

ized as carefully designed but overly cerebral and lacking in a sense of color. Those studies were eventually abandoned because of what Simon described as a lack of "plastic talent."

Simon's involvement in major historical events left a profound mark on his work. After having served as a cavalryman in the Thirty-first Dragoons at Luneville in 1934–1935, he joined up as a volunteer in the Spanish civil war on the Republican side, acting for a time as a gunrunner. His participation was centered in Barcelona, the location of the Hotel Colon described in *The Palace* and other works. He then served again as a cavalryman in the French army in 1939–1940, barely escaping death in May 1940 during the battle of the Meuse. Captured at Solre-le-Chateau near Avesnes and sent to a German prison camp in Saxony, he managed to be transferred to a prisoner-of-war camp in France, from which he escaped in November 1940. He then spent the remainder of the war years participating in the resistance movement in Perpignan, in contact with Raoul Dufy and others. He painted during the day, while pursuing his literary career in the evenings. By 1941 he had completed not only *The Cheater*, which was not published until 1946, but also other works that he later destroyed.

A Microscopic Illness Another decisive influence in Simon's life came in the postwar years when he was bedridden for months with tuberculosis, a highly contagious and potentially deadly disease that usually affects the lungs. While ill, he was unable to do anything but look out the window: Vision and memory were all he had. Simon claimed that this confinement was a turning point that enabled him to appreciate fully the simple, nonintellectual pleasures of such favorite objects as stones, which he kept on his desk. It was then that he fully developed his enduring fascination with matter seen through a microscope. Working steadily and peacefully, removed from the bustle of Parisian intellectual life, Simon gave simple but stirring expression to man's day-to-day experience.

Simon was awarded the Nobel Prize in Literature in 1985, and continued writing until his death in 2005. During one speech, when asked why he wrote, he said simply: "Because I was not capable of doing anything else."

Works in Literary Context

Cubist Words Simon, who studied art in his youth, claimed to have adapted the methods of proto-cubist painter Paul Cézanne for his own literary experiments. Indeed, critics frequently point out the influence of visual aesthetics, such as those borrowed from painting or cinema, in his novels. Simon disregarded linear plot in favor of evocative descriptions full of sensory details. His later novels take Simon's exercises in literary cubism even further, as Simon adopted a new method of composition.

Working from separate visual images, Simon wove a series of associations between them, to form a unified narrative. In order to organize these complex word tapestries, Simon reportedly uses colored pencils, color-coding each narrative strand as he wrote.

Horses Perhaps paying homage to his father's career as a cavalry officer, the descriptions in *The Flanders Road* and several other novels focus on the key motif of horses. Air and water, whose fragmented forms merge with hoof-beats, are symbolic of the human perception of time during war. Horses on a racing field, decorated with bright colors such as coral, evoke Corinne. The cavalry-men return on four occasions to a spot where a dead horse lies decaying, its physical deterioration symbolizing the same invisible change as the growth of the grass in *The Grass.* Simon described the pattern formed by the repeated descriptions of the dead horse as a cloverleaf drawn by beginning at a certain point and, without lifting pencil from paper, returning to it three times.

Works in Critical Context

The critical reception of Simon's works over the decades has passed through various stages. Though considered one of the most important New Novelists in France, Claude Simon has been slow to gain recognition in the United States. Because at first glance Simon's writing "seems incoherent, merely a series of disconnected fragments, a lyrical but meaningless collection of images," observed Morton P. Levitt, "even a reasonably conscientious reader is apt to be confused by what appears to be, in the worst modern tradition, a narrative experiment without meaning or substance."

Histoire Superficially, *Histoire* (1967) is "the history of the narrator's story of his family as it is captured on the page by reminiscences of intimately evocative material possessions: the ancestral home, bits of furniture, family portraits, faded album photos and postal cards," stated the *Virginia Quarterly Review.* But Georges Schlocker noted that "the essence of the book lies in the confrontation of its characters with passing time and in the states of mind resulting therefrom." "The past often invades the present without the usual typographical warnings of a new sentence or paragraph," Leo Bersani observed, "and the mixture is made even more confusing by the fact that the whole novel is written in past tenses. The 'he' referred to in one line may not be the same person as the 'he' mentioned in the next line."

Responses to Literature

1. Simon's style has often been compared to those of William Faulkner and Marcel Proust. Choose one of these writers and read either one of their stories or an excerpt from their novels. Do you see similarities or differences? Has Simon used or developed their techniques?

2. Look up the word "minutiae" and think about why small objects and items resonate through Simon's

---

COMMON HUMAN EXPERIENCE

Though creative and innovative, Simon wrote primarily auto-biographical novels, relying on incidents from his life to give his work honesty and originality. Here are some other works based primarily on real life events and experiences:

The Sun Also Rises (1926), a novel by Ernest Hemingway. The main character of this novel is an injured war veteran who journeys to Spain with several friends, all of whom are emotionally lost or damaged in different ways.

On the Road (1957), a novel by Jack Kerouac. This novel chronicles a cross-country road trip where the characters are thinly disguised versions of the major figures of the Beat Generation.

The Bell Jar (1963), a novel by Sylvia Plath. Based on her real-life experience with depression, this book was Plath's only novel.

Ham on Rye (1982), a novel by Charles Bukowski. From the name of the protagonist—Henry Chinaski—to the events based in Los Angeles, this novel is highly true to the life of its author.

---

work. How do characters react to these objects? Why does Simon focus on the physical world instead of the spiritual world?

3. Simon's work can be divided into three periods. What do you think defines these periods? How do the themes of the works in these periods relate to the historical events of the times?

4. Do you think Simon writes effectively about war? Why or why not? Does he make distinctions between the experiences of World War I and those of World War II? If so, what are they? How do they affect the characters in his novels?

5. Simon has resisted the idea that he is one of the New Novelists. Research this literary movement and the beliefs of those involved with it. Why did Simon deny association with these writers? Do you think he can be categorized with the movement regardless?

BIBLIOGRAPHY

Books

Brewer, Maria Minich. *Claude Simon: Narrativities without Narrative.* Lincoln: University of Nebraska Press, 1995.

Britton, Celia. *Claude Simon: Writing the Visible.* London: Cambridge University Press, 1987.

Duffy, Jean H. *Reading between the Lines: Claude Simon and the Visual Arts.* Liverpool, U.K.: Liverpool University Press, 1998.

Duncan, Alistair. *Claude Simon: Adventures in Words.* Manchester, U.K.: Manchester University Press, 1994.

Fletcher, John. *Claude Simon and Fiction Now.* London: Calder & Boyars, 1975.

Gould, Karen, and Randi Birn, eds. *Orion Blinded: Essays on Claude Simon.* Lewisburg, Pa.: Bucknell University Press, 1981.

Jimenez-Fajardo, Salvador. *Claude Simon.* London: Twayne, 1975.

Kadish, Doris Y. *Practices of the New Novel in Claude Simon's "L'Herbe" and "La Route des Flandres."* York: York Press, 1979.

Loubere, J. A. E. *The Novels of Claude Simon.* Ithaca, N.Y.: Cornell University Press, 1975.

Troiano, Maureen DiLonardo. *New Physics and the Modern French Novel: An Investigation of Interdisciplinary Discourse.* New York: Lang, 1995.

◈ Edith Sitwell

BORN: *1887, Scarborough, England*

DIED: *1964, London, England*

NATIONALITY: *English*

GENRE: *Poetry*

MAJOR WORKS:

The Mother, and Other Poems (1915)

Gold Coast Customs (1929)

The Song of the Cold (1948)

The Outcasts (1962)

The Queens of the Hive (1962)

Overview

An eccentric, controversial figure in English literature, Edith Sitwell was best known for avant-garde verse emphasizing the sound and rhythm of poetry. With her brothers she created a literary circle whose satirical, experimental poetry signaled the demise of Victorianism and the onset of modernism. Despite the fact that early contemporaries condemned Sitwell's poetry as pretentious, inaccessible, and devoid of substance, she later received critical accolades when she moved away from strict experimentalism toward verse that explored universal human experiences through religious, mythical, and natural imagery. While Sitwell's position in English letters remains controversial, her poetry is increasingly valued for its spontaneous vitality and moral vision.

Works in Biographical and Historical Context

A Pampered Upbringing   Edith Sitwell was born in Scarborough, England, on September 7, 1887, into a family of landed gentry. She was the daughter of Sir George and Lady Ida Sitwell, an unhappily married cou-

Dame Edith Sitwell   *Baron / Getty Images*

ple who disliked their daughter's awkward physical appearance and willful manner. Educated by governesses, she resented the fact that she was not given what she considered a proper education. She was close to her younger brothers, Osbert and Sacheverell.

Making Connections   Sitwell experienced her first major transition in 1914 when, at the age of twenty-seven, she moved to London to share a flat with Helen Rootham, her former governess, and gained prominence as the sharp-witted editor of *Wheels*, an annual anthology of verse she and her brothers founded. She published her first book of poems, *The Mother, and Other Poems* in 1915. Two years after she published her first book of poems, Sitwell gave her first reading in December 1917. Sitwell's interest in spoken poetry reached its full expression in the sequence of poems titled *Façade* (1922).

During the 1920s, the period of her greatest creative activity, Sitwell lived in a flat with Rootham in Bayswater, London. She and her brothers participated in the literary life of the capital. Their friends included T. S. Eliot and Aldous Huxley, although there was a break with Huxley in 1922, following the publication of a story by him that included a very unkind portrait of Osbert. Sitwell was an admirer of Eliot's work, but she was also concerned by the fact that his poem *The Waste Land* (1922) got far better reviews and far more critical attention than her books. Although an acquaintance of Virginia Woolf's, she was never more than on the fringes of the Bloomsbury Group (English intellectuals who met for discussion in the Bloomsbury area of London from the early 1900s until the 1930s). Sitwell thought the group too close knit for her rather independent tastes; even so, there were affinities between the Sitwells and Woolf's associates, including their strong opposition to war.

Sitwell lived mostly in Paris with Helen Rootham from 1932 until Rootham's death in 1938. In Paris she met, through Gertrude Stein, the great love of her life, the surrealist painter Pavel Tchelitchew. Since Tchelitchew was homosexual, the love remained unfulfilled, and Sitwell often felt betrayed by him. Nonetheless, she remained a constant friend and supporter over many years as she attempted to find buyers for Tchelitchew's paintings.

In 1948 Edith and Osbert Sitwell undertook a lecture tour of the United States that lasted almost six months. It was highly successful and contributed greatly to her reputation in America. She made a new recording of *Façade*, and she was the guest of honor at a party given by the Gotham Book Mart, attended by Marianne Moore, Randall Jarrell, Elizabeth Bishop, Gore Vidal, Tennessee Williams, and W. H. Auden, among other notable writers. The success of this tour led to a second one in 1950, which included a visit to Hollywood, where she read from *Macbeth*. Her interest in Shakespeare had grown considerably during the late 1940s, and several of the plays, particularly *King Lear*, had a marked influence on her work. Her interest in the Elizabethan period included a fascination with Elizabeth I, which gave rise to her book *Fanfare for Elizabeth* (1946) and the ill-fated plans for a Hollywood film based on it, to be directed by George Cukor.

Kudos and Catholicism Largely unrecognized or scorned during her earlier years, Sitwell was lavished with honors in her last years. In 1951 she received an honorary doctorate in letters from Oxford. Three years later, she was made a Dame Commander of the Order of the British Empire by the queen. Her seventieth birthday was celebrated by a luncheon given by the *Sunday Times*, her seventy-fifth by a concert at the Royal Festival Hall, which included a performance of *Façade*. From the time she discovered the poetry of Wilfred Owen as an editor at *Wheel*, Sitwell was an avid supporter of young artists. In the 1950s, Robert Lowell, Allen Ginsberg, and James Purdy were among her favorites.

In the meantime, Sitwell's religious beliefs had intensified, and she converted to Roman Catholicism in 1955. The church provided consolation for her during her last years of ill health, and Sitwell received the last rites of the church before her death in London on December 11, 1964.

Works in Literary Context

In the introduction to *The Canticle of the Rose* (1949), Sitwell wrote: "At the time I began to write, a change in

the direction, imagery and rhythms in poetry had become necessary, owing to the rhythmical flaccidity, the verbal deadness, the dead and expected patterns, of some of the poetry immediately preceding us." Her early work was often experimental in creating melody and used striking conceits, new rhythms, and confusing private allusions. As her technique evolved, she came to use sound patterns as an element in the construction of philosophic poems that reflect on her period in time and on the human condition.

Antiwar Poems While her anti-World War II poems—such as "Still Falls the Rain," based on the air raids on England at the beginning of the war, and "Three Poems of the Atomic Age," based on the bombing of Hiroshima—would make her a legend of the literary period, they were initially dismissed because of her unorthodox manner of presenting them. These early poems intermingle startling images of demonic, mechanical, and natural worlds to present an elaborately distorted picture of a world gone mad. They also reflect the richness of color and sensuality that had stirred her as a child and influenced her poetry throughout her life. Finally, these poems exhibit an extraordinary sense of rhythm which, with other experiments in sound, proved to be Sitwell's most marked and controversial gift to contemporary poetry.

Singing Poetry Public readings became important for establishing Sitwell's reputation, and much of her early poetry owes its character to the presumption that it

COMMON HUMAN EXPERIENCE

The manner in which Sitwell chose to present her works was so genuinely avant-garde that in 1923 the audience at the first public theatrical presentation of *Façade* thought itself the victim of a hoax. Here are a few works by other writers who have also succeeded in delivering unique and innovative poetry:

I Love Artists (2006), poems by Mei-mei Berssenbrugge. Berssenbrugge's poetry incorporates the New York school of poetry, phenomenology, visual arts, sensual science, and more.

The Dancers Inherit the Party and Glasgow Beasts (1997), poems by Ian Hamilton Finlay. Finlay's poetry is tactile and joins type, line, and sculpture for an experience of the senses.

The Book of Disquiet (2002), poems by Fernando Pessoa. Metaphysical poetry is conveyed through the writer's many heteronyms, or words that appear the same in written form but sound different when pronounced aloud and have different meanings.

Tender Buttons (1914), an experimental text by Gertrude Stein. Stein's experiments with language manipulation made her a pioneer in style and method.

would be read aloud. It was Sitwell more than anyone else who realized the importance of sound and texture in modern poetry, and she introduced a poetry designed to take full advantage of the flexible rhythms of the spoken voice. She did not invent the idea of reciting poetry set to music, but her performances of *Façade* gave it its most distinguished form. Sitwell's interest in modern art was considerable, and *Façade* should be considered an integral part of the international movement that embraced poetry, painting, and dance. Half of the poems that eventually found a place in *Façade* were composed earlier, while the others were written specifically for music by William Walton.

The poems were recited through a Sengerphone, a large megaphone with a mouthpiece. Since the Sengerphone and the reciter were concealed behind a curtain, the spoken voice achieved simultaneous clarity and impersonality. Sitwell considered the poems abstract; to her they were patterns in sound. She saw them as explorations of the qualities of rhythm, in which meaning was secondary. Sitwell was also exploring the possible application of the means of one medium to another. While this practice had already become frequent in the poetry of the French symbolists and their successors, nothing quite like it had been seen in English verse. The poems were not sung but read, thereby emphasizing the inherently rhythmic quality of spoken verse. Sitwell explored the possibil-

ities of rhyme, alliteration, assonance, and what she termed "colour."

Influences on Art Sitwell's manner of dress—flowing gowns, turbans, amulets, and silver nail polish—generated as much attention as her unconventional poetry, and she became a sought-after subject of painters and photographers. Her influence among artists has continued into the twenty-first century. For example, she has appeared in literary and musical compositions by Kingsley Amis, Saul Bellow, and Andrew Lloyd Webber. The Grateful Dead's Robert Hunter drew from Sitwell's "Polka" when writing the song "China Cat Sunflower" and the punk-pop-rock British band Shakespeare's Sister borrowed from Sitwell's "Hornpipe" for their song "I Don't Care." Clearly, Sitwell's lasting influence has justified her career, that of a poet who had as many early detractors as she now has devotees.

Works in Critical Context

Sitwell's Work as a Whole The *Times* of London stated of Sitwell in 1955 that "she writes for the sake of sound, of color, and from an awareness of God and regard for man." Sitwell believed that "poetry is the deification of reality, and one of its purposes is to show that the dimensions of man are, as Sir Arthur Eddington said, 'half way between those of an atom and a star.'" Admiring critic John Lehmann, author of *Edith Sitwell and a Nest of Tigers: The Sitwells in Their Times*, admitted that "her tendency has always been rather to overwork her symbolism; by a certain overfluid quality in her imagination to make the use of the symbols sometimes appear confused and indiscriminate." This elaborate quality has its admirers, however. In *Poetry in Our Time*, Babette Deutsch wrote: "Like the medieval hangings that kept the cold away from secular kings and princes of the Church, the finest of [Dame Edith's] poems have a luxurious beauty that serves to grace the bareness, to diminish the chill of this bare, cold age." Writing in the *Times* of London, Geoffrey Elborn commented that Sitwell's best work was written in the 1920s. "These . . . [poems were] written with a highly individual use of language still unsurpassed for its peculiar, inimitable artifice. Far from being trivial, these early poems by one 'a little outside life' should now find a greater acceptance in an era more concerned with Sitwell's concepts than her own age, earning her the deserved and secure reputation for which she herself so earnestly but recklessly fought."

Gold Coast Customs Sitwell's body of work contains rare political poetry in an equally rare format and style for the period in which she wrote. One such example is *Gold Coast Customs*, the culmination of Sitwell's development toward a position as a poet of social commentary. Marxist critic Jack Lindsay noted that *Gold Coast Customs* represented "the deepest—almost the only—political poetry" of the age in England. Technically, for many critics, *Gold*

Coast Customs is a major accomplishment. It interweaves the funeral customs of the African Ashantee nation with contemporary society life of London—Sitwell's contemporary figure, Lady Bamburgher, is a symbol of the moral and social corruption that lies beneath the surface of fashionable life. It illustrates an almost complete abandonment of a straightforward narrative; instead, it is structured around a series of contrasts. The poem's strong beat and clear voice give a striking portrayal of historical patterns of decay and betrayal. In keeping with other works of Sitwell's that are accompanied by religious imagery of rebirth at a time when religious faith in poetry had become unpopular, *Gold Coast Customs* concludes with a vision of transformation and salvation.

Criticism through the Years Sitwell's career has undergone a great deal of reevaluation through the years. In light of her eccentric personality and literary friendships, several critics continue to agree with F. R. Leavis's early estimation that Sitwell belongs "to the history of publicity rather than poetry." However, others regard her as a formidable figure whose career traces the development of English poetry from the immediate post–World War I period of brightness and jazzy rhythms through the political involvements of the 1930s and the return to spiritual values after World War II. Dilys Powell asserted, "The fact remains that she was one of the writers who bridged the gap between the sterile years of the early war and the post-war years of excited experiment; that she helped keep interest in poetry alive when it was near extinction." She should be remembered as the angry chronicler of social injustice, and as a poet who has found forms adequate to the atomic age and its horrors.

Responses to Literature

1. Imagine you are in charge of setting the stage for a Sitwell poetry performance. What props would you include to enhance the meaning of her work? Create a visual representation of what the stage would look like. You may draw, paint, make a collage, use computer programs, photograph people or objects, etc.

2. Research writers in the twentieth century who converted to Catholicism as adults. What can you infer both from their writing and from events of the 1900s that might have led to their conversion?

3. Read some of Osbert Sitwell's poetry. How does his work compare/contrast with that of his sister?

BIBLIOGRAPHY

Books

Brophy, James. *Edith Sitwell: The Symbolist Order*. Carbondale: Southern Illinois University Press, 1968.

Glendinning, Victoria. *Edith Sitwell: A Unicorn among Lions*. London: Weidenfeld & Nicolson, 1981.

Villa, José Garcia, ed. *A Celebration for Edith Sitwell*. New York: New Directions, 1948; Freeport, New York: Books for Libraries Press, 1972.

Web Sites

Edith Sitwell: A Nearly Forgotten Poetess. Retrieved February 14, 2008, from http://165.29.91.7/classes/humanities/britlit/97–98/sitwell/Sitwell.htm.

The Lied and Art Song Text Page (Emily Ezust, ed.). *Author: Edith Sitwell (1887–1964), Texts Set to Music*. Retrieved February 14, 2008, from http://www.recmusic.org/lieder/s/sitwell.

Josef Skvorecky

BORN: *1924, Nachod, Czechoslovakia*

NATIONALITY: *Canadian, Czech*

GENRE: *Fiction, poetry*

MAJOR WORKS:

The Cowards (1958)

The Engineer of Human Souls: An Entertainment of the Old Themes of Life, Women, Fate, Dreams, the Working Class, Secret Agents, Love, and Death (1977)

Dvorak in Love (1991)

When Eve Was Naked (2002)

Overview

Josef Václav Skvorecky, who writes and publishes primarily in Czech, has resided in Canada since he fled Czechoslovakia after the 1968 Soviet invasion. Although he initially gained notoriety in his native country for his first published novel, *The Cowards*, which was condemned by government officials, Skvorecky remained virtually unknown outside Czech-speaking communities until the 1984 English publication of *The Engineer of Human Souls: An Entertainment of the Old Themes of Life, Women, Fate, Dreams, the Working Class, Secret Agents, Love, and Death*. Writing in several genres, including the novel, the detective story, and the essay, Skvorecky questions all notions of ideology and emphasizes literature's significance to the development of cultural history and liberal thought.

Works in Biographical and Historical Context

A Life of Resistance: From Early Mistrust to Adult Rebellion Skvorecky was born and raised in Nachod, a small town on the northeastern border of the Bohemian province. During his forty-four years in Czechoslovakia, Skvorecky lived through the Nazi occupation, the postwar era of Stalinist communism, and the Soviet invasion of 1968, after which he immigrated to

Josef Skvorecky   *Sean Gallup / Getty Images*

increasing use of censorship and intimidation, Skvorecky, along with many other writers, became actively involved in the Prague literary underground.

Suppression of The Cowards   Although Skvorecky wrote *The Cowards* shortly after Czechoslovakia's Communist Party gained control of the country in 1948, he did not submit the novel for publication until 1958 for fear that party members would object to its presumably bourgeois elements. Satirically describing the events that transpire during eight days in a small Czechoslovakian village in May of 1945, *The Cowards* is told from the viewpoint of Danny Smiricky, a young saxophone player who watches conservatives and liberals scramble for power as a new political era begins. Garnering widespread attention in Czechoslovakia because of its irreverent examination of Marxist ideology and its seemingly sympathetic attitudes toward Western music and literature, this work was quickly condemned by government officials for ignoring the tenets of socialist realism.

All copies of *The Cowards* were seized from Czechoslovakian bookstores, but, ironically, the book attained underground cult status as a result. After the publication and the subsequent suppression of *The Cowards* Skvorecky lost his post as deputy editor in chief of *Svetová literatura* and survived for almost five years in official disfavor in his earlier position as a book editor. Skvorecky was not taken off the list of banned authors until 1963. He translated American fiction into Czech and wrote detective stories, first under the name of his collaborator, the poet and translator Jan Zábrana. For the rest of his literary career he remained faithful to detective literature.

Effectively Exiled   Skvorecky's literary reputation was rising in the second half of the 1960s: His writing was praised; his short stories and scripts were made into successful movies (in which he even played cameo roles); he had a regular jazz-music radio program; and in 1966 Gallimard published *La Légende d'Emoke* in French. Together with many well-known authors, who had by that time become public figures in Czechoslovakia, Skvorecky took an active part in the Prague Spring of 1968, a movement that attempted to democratize the Czechoslovak Communist regime—although his own political thinking had always been more radical than the reformism that prevailed at that time. The Warsaw Pact invasion of Czechoslovakia on August 21, 1968, cut short the high hopes of the reformers, and Skvorecky and his wife left their native country for Canada on January 31, 1969. On the North American continent, Skvorecky spent some time at Cornell University and the University of California at Berkeley, but in the end he settled in Toronto, where he became writer-in-residence at the University of Toronto and later joined the Department of English as a full-time member. He continued to write and publish, with *Dvorak in Love* appearing in 1991—just as the Soviet Union was dissolving and the

Canada. As an adolescent, Skvorecky attended the local grammar school, a traditional institution that emphasized such classical subjects as Latin and mathematics. During the Nazi annexation, most subjects, especially geography and history, were taught in German so as to indoctrinate Czechoslovakian youth into Nazi social theory. Skvorecky explains: "It was the Nazis who introduced the term 'ideology' into our vocabulary; can anyone wonder why ever since I have mistrusted that word and all the varying contents it signified?"

Although he passed his college entrance examinations, Skvorecky, along with all other able-bodied Czech men and women, was mobilized by the Nazis to serve in the armament industry. Working fourteen-hour shifts alongside students, businessmen, and lawyers, Skvorecky was exposed to a wide array of experiences and opinions that were expressed in the privacy of the factory washroom: "The discussions were profound, lively, and on many subjects; sometimes the shitting room resembled a philosophy seminar." After World War II, Skvorecky enrolled at Charles University in Prague. Following one semester at the University Medical Facility, Skvorecky decided to study English and philosophy, receiving his doctoral degree in 1951. Due to the government's

Iron Curtain falling (and two years after the bloodless revolution that had brought democracy and an era of constitution-building to Czechoslovakia). He continues to teach in Toronto today, and his recent volume of short stories, *When Eve Was Naked* (2002), has garnered high accolades from critics.

Works in Literary Context

Using such elements as nostalgia, irony, and sentimentality, Skvorecky explores themes of displacement, the misrepresentation of history, and the relationship between art and reality in a manner that reveals the joy and despair in individual lives. Recognized for his vivacious, melodic narrative style and his extensive use of colloquial dialogue, Skvorecky frequently examines the harshness of life under authoritarian regimes and the fanaticism he associates with political dogma. Skvorecky has particularly found himself drawn to so-called popular fiction or "genre" fiction, writing many detective stories and, later, working on historical fiction.

Detective Stories and the Nature of Truth Shortly after the success of *The Cowards*, Skvorecky began to question the role of the writer in society and, therefore, the quality and purpose of his own work. After reading numerous detective stories and realizing that this genre "may not be much of an art, but it is a hell of a craft," Skvorecky began to write crime fiction. Skvorecky also discovered that, in addition to its providing him with financial stability, "this debased genre may be useful.... I realized I could tell quite serious things through [it]." The stories in *The Mournful Demeanor of Lieutenant Boruvka* feature a morose civil police lieutenant as their title character and are comically ironic; the protagonist is reluctant to fire a gun and tends to solve crimes through accident and coincidence rather than logic. As Stewart Lindh observed:

> A reader can choose to treat these narratives as parodies of mystery stories, but lurking at the side of every story is the following question: How can a detective find truth in a society concealing it? He can't. This, too, is perhaps part of Lt. Boruvka's gloom. He lives in a society that itself is guilty of a monstrous crime: the murder of truth.

Historical Fiction In addition to writing extensively in the detective story genre, Skvorecky also dabbled in historical fiction, a genre in which an author takes a moment or person from history and creates fictional characters and events to surround it. *Dvořák in Love: A Light-Hearted Dream*, for instance, is a historical novel about the Czechoslovakian composer Antonín Dvořák, who directed the National Conservatory of Music in New York City from 1892 to 1895. Although another piece of historical fiction, *The Miracle Game: A Political Whodunnit*, was originally published in Czech in 1972, the novel did not appear in English translation until 1990. Set in Communist Czechoslovakia, this work

is based on an actual incident in which Communist government officials purportedly tried to discredit Catholicism.

Works in Critical Context

To say that critical response to Skvorecky's work has always been strong—either positive or negative—would be an understatement. Skvorecky's first novel, *The Cowards*, caused a flurry of excitement that led to "firings in the publishing house, ragings in the official press, and a general purge that extended eventually throughout the arts," according to Neal Ascherson in the *New York Review of Books*. The book was banned by Czech officials one month after publication, marking "the start of an incredible campaign of vilification against the author," a *Times Literary Supplement* reviewer reports. Skvorecky subsequently included a "cheeky and impenitent Introduction," Ascherson notes, in the novel's 1963 second edition. "In spite of all the suppression," the *Times Literary Supplement* critic explains, "*The Cowards* became a milestone in Czech literature and Joseph Skvorecky one of the country's most popular writers."

The Cowards Ascherson explains why *The Cowards* caused so much controversy: "It is not at all the sort of mirror official Czechoslovakia would wish to glance in. A recurring theme is...pity for the Germans, defeated and bewildered....The Russians strike [the main character] as alluring primitives (his use of the word 'Mongolian' about them caused much of the scandal in 1958)." The *Times Literary Supplement* writer adds, "The novel turned out to be anti-Party and anti-God at the same time; everybody felt himself a victim of the author's satire." The narrator, twenty-year-old Danny Smiricky, and his friends—members of a jazz band—observe the flux of power, human nature, and death around them

COMMON HUMAN EXPERIENCE

Skvorecky is known for putting his own twist on the detective novel genre. Some other works that play on detective novel conventions include:

> *The Yiddish Policemen's Union* (2006), a novel by Michael Chabon. Pulitzer Prize winner Chabon here sets a detective novel in an imagined world in which U.S. president Franklin D. Roosevelt had established a temporary Jewish homeland in Alaska.
>
> "The Garden of the Forking Paths" (1941), a short story by Jorge Luis Borges. Postmodernist master Borges here delivers a "deconstruction" of the classic detective novel.
>
> *The Club Dumas* (1993), a novel by Arturo Perez-Reverte. Spanish author Perez-Reverte creates a mystery novel in which the characters seem to be re-creations of figures from the fiction of Alexandre Dumas.
>
> *Gun, with Occasional Music* (1994), a novel by Jonathan Lethem. Lethem blends science fiction and the hard-boiled detective genre in this novel set in a not-so-distant dystopian future.

while devoting their thoughts and energies to women and music. "These are, by definition, no heroes," states Stuart Hood in the *Listener.* "They find themselves caught up in a farce which turns into horror from one minute to the next." The group may dream of making a bold move for their country, but, as Charles Dollen notes in *Best Sellers,* "they never make anything but music." All the same, Skvorecky often employs jazz "in its familiar historical and international role as a symbol (and a breeding-ground) of anti-authoritarian attitudes," according to Russell Davies, writing in the *Times Literary Supplement.*

The Engineer of Human Souls *The Engineer of Human Souls,* winner of the 1985 Governor General's Literary Award, remains Skvorecky's best-known work in English-speaking countries. The novel reintroduces protagonist Danny Smiricky who, reflecting Skvorecky's own fate, is now a professor of literature at the University of Toronto. Interweaving Smiricky's experiences with those of his students and members of the Czech community in Toronto and with letters from dissidents and émigrés, Skvorecky conveys impressions about both the injustices of totalitarian states and the naïveté of Western political values. Though literature is the unifying motif in *The Engineer of Human Souls,* jazz music appears as a metaphor for individualistic, antiestablishment attitudes. While some commentators castigated Skvorecky for his frequent shifts between past and present, others considered the

book a convincing and potent means by which to examine the cyclical nature of history. James Lasdun explains, "[Unfettered] by the demands of a linear plot, Skvorecky is free to jump back and forth in time, grouping disparate incidents for the sake of the patterns they reveal in human affairs."

Responses to Literature

1. Read *The Engineer of Human Souls.* In this text, Skvorecky is said to have made keen observations about both Czech and Western culture. What role do Skvorecky' stylistic choices play in making these observations more or less accessible and potent?

2. Read *The Cowards.* Then, using the Internet and the library, research what really happened to prisoners of war after the end of World War II. In a short essay, compare the history you discover on the topic to the fictional reality Skvorecky presents. In what ways does Skvorecky's fiction seek also to evoke something true?

3. Skvorecky has written in the "historical fiction" genre. Pick a character or event from history. Then, imagine how you might go about writing a fictional story based on that person or event. Which elements do you think would most likely be made up? Which would be based on reality?

4. Skvorecky is not the first and will not be the last author to be pushed into exile for his writings. What is it about the word in literature that makes it so threatening to figures of authority? What power, in fact, do words have? Ground your answer in a detailed analysis of passages from Skvorecky's writings.

BIBLIOGRAPHY

Books

Galligan, Edward L. *The Truth of Uncertainty: Beyond Ideology in Science and Literature.* Columbia: University of Missouri Press, 1998.

Porter, Robert. *An Introduction to Twentieth-Century Czech Fiction: Comedies of Defiance.* Portland, Ore.: Sussex Academic, 2001.

Solecki, Sam. *Prague Blues: The Fiction of Josef Skvorecky.* ECW, 1990.

——, ed. *The Achievement of Josef Skvorecky.* University of Toronto Press, 1994.

Trensky, Paul I. *The Fiction of Josef Skvorecky.* New York: St. Martin's, 1991.

Periodicals

Zekulin, Gleb. "The Intellectuals' Dilemma: The Hero in the Modern Czech Novel." *Canadian Slavonic Papers* (1972).

Christopher Smart

BORN: *1722, Shipbourne, Kent, England*

DIED: *1771, London, England*

NATIONALITY: *Welsh, British*

GENRE: *Poetry*

MAJOR WORKS:

On the Omniscience of the Supreme Being: A Poetical Essay (1752)

Hymn to the Supreme Being, on Recovery from a Dangerous Fit of Illness (1756)

A Song to David (1763)

Jubilate Agno (1939)

Overview

Known primarily for his 1763 *A Song to David* and the posthumously discovered poem *Jubilate Agno* (discovered in 1939), Christopher Smart is regarded as one of the most influential—and eccentric—writers of the eighteenth century. Although he suffered mental instability and frequent poverty throughout his life, Smart produced poems marked by narrative innovation and spiritual fervor. He is often characterized as a proto-Romantic; his combination of visionary power, Christian ardor, and lyrical virtuosity, however, was unappreciated in his own

Christopher Smart   *Smart, Christopher, photograph of a painting.*

age. Beginning with Robert Browning in the nineteenth century, poets rather than critics have been the warmest and most perceptive admirers of the poetry of Christopher Smart. In a 1975 radio broadcast in Australia, Peter Porter spoke of Smart as "the purest case of man's vision prevailing over the spirit of his times."

Works in Biographical and Historical Context

School and City Life   Christopher Smart was born on April 11, 1722, at Shipbourne in Kent, the youngest of three children of Peter and Winifred Griffiths Smart. His father was a steward for a large estate, and as a boy, Smart spent long hours outdoors observing nature. On his father's side, Smart belonged to an established family from the north country of England; he was extremely proud, however, of his mother's Welsh lineage and its folklore.

After distinguishing himself in classical studies as a youth, Smart attended Pembroke Hall, Cambridge, at the age of seventeen, with the help of an annual allowance from the duchess of Cleveland (Henrietta Fitzroy). As an undergraduate, he earned acclaim both for his classical learning and his abilities as a poet. In 1742 he was awarded the coveted Craven scholarship. He graduated the following year, celebrating the occasion with an ode. Two years later, he was elected to a fellowship at Pembroke.

By 1744 he had begun to frequent London; soon he was spending more time in town than in college, competing for recognition as a poet, enjoying the pleasures of the city, and running up tailor's bills. At Cambridge, he showed little inclination to settle down to the tranquil seclusion of college life. Nevertheless, during this period Smart's first original publication appeared: Smart enhanced the second edition of his Latin version of Alexander Pope's ode with his own "Ode for Musick on St. Cecilia's Day."

Smart's career at Cambridge effectively ended in 1749 when he was granted a leave of absence from college and moved to London, though he retained his fellowship until his subsequent marriage to Anna Maria Carnan, stepdaughter of the publisher John Newbery. Initially, the marriage seems to have been happy. His daughters, Marianne and Elizabeth, were born in 1753 and 1754, respectively. Despite his rich family and social life, he never lost sight of his serious ambitions as a poet in these busy years from 1749 to 1756.

The Onset of Illness   Smart continued throughout the early 1750s to pour out a stream of poems: songs, epigrams, epitaphs, fables, complimentary addresses, verse epistles, and one full-dress satire, *The Hilliad* (1753). His writings for the periodical *The Universal Visiter* began with the January 1756 issue, but Smart's contributions were soon cut short: twice since leaving

LITERARY AND HISTORICAL CONTEMPORARIES

Smart's famous contemporaries include:

Alexander Pope (1688–1744): British satirist famous for his translations of Homer and his mock-epic poem *The Rape of the Lock*.
Henry Fielding (1707–1754): English author most famous for his novel *Tom Jones*.
Samuel Johnson (1709–1784): Witty English critic and dictionary writer.
William Blake (1757–1827): Mystical poet and pre-Romantic writer.

Cambridge he had suffered bouts of dangerous illness, and in 1756 he had an attack of such severity that his family feared he would die. Some historians argue that these bouts were mental breakdowns, but such evidence as there is points rather to an acute and recurrent fever of some kind, no doubt accompanied by delirium. Whatever the cause, the third and gravest of the attacks was, by his own account, a turning point in Smart's life, which he commemorated with *Hymn to the Supreme Being, on Recovery from a Dangerous Fit of Illness* (1756). The poem describes the course of his illness in terms of a spiritual crisis. At the height of his sufferings, he relates, reason, sense, and religious faith all failed him.

Less than a year later, Smart was admitted to the curable ward of St. Luke's Hospital for Lunatics on Windmill Hill in London. What Smart described in his hymn was a classical conversion experience; the cause of his insanity has been much debated, but contemporary evidence is clear on one point: The form it took was religious mania, with a compulsion to pray in public. Samuel Johnson's brisk and charitable comments on the subject were: "My poor friend Smart shewed the disturbance of his mind, by falling upon his knees, and saying his prayers in the street, or in any other unusual place." In the light of modern psychiatric theory, Sir Russell Brain diagnosed Smart's condition as manic-depressive—a verdict that has not subsequently been challenged.

Despite all the suffering he endured, the "well-nigh sev'n years" (as he counted it) of his incarceration brought forth an astonishing quantity of brilliant and original poetry. Between 1757 and 1763, he wrote *A Song to David*; most if not all of *A Translation of the Psalms of David* and "Hymns and Spiritual Songs for the Fasts and Festivals of the Church of England" (published together in 1765); and the lengthy manuscript of *Jubilate Agno*, the surviving fragments of which, amounting to more than seventeen hundred verses, represent only about a third of what he actually wrote.

Financial and Legal Troubles This period was soured, however, by quarrels with his critics and self-imposed alienation from his family. Within three years of Smart's release from the madhouse he was again in danger of imprisonment, this time for debt. In December 1765 he was arrested and was never again wholly out of trouble over money, in spite of diligent efforts on the part of his friends to secure employment or support for him. The last five years of Smart's life were spent in increasing poverty and need: Most of his surviving letters after 1766 are concerned with money troubles. When Newbery died in 1767, provisions in his will ensured that none of the money left to Anna Maria Smart should be "subject or liable to the debts power or control of her present husband"; and in 1769 Smart was disappointed in the hope of benefiting from the Durham estate of his cousin, Francis Smart.

By the time *Hymns, for the Amusement of Children* reached the printers, Smart was in prison. He was arrested for debt in April 1770 and committed to the King's Bench Prison, where he remained until his death a year later. Even in jail, Smart's affectionate disposition earned him friends among his fellow prisoners. Smart died on May 20, 1771, after a short illness.

By the time of his death, Smart's reputation as a poet had suffered a drastic eclipse. From being the pride of Cambridge he sank in estimation into "poor Smart the mad poet," as Thomas Percy described him in an October 17, 1786, letter. But a turning point came with the discovery in 1939 of *Jubilate Agno*, the work which, even more than *A Song to David*, has captured the interest of poets including Allen Ginsberg, Alec Hope, Jeremy Reed, and Wendy Cope—many of whom have paid him the tribute of imitation and parody.

Works in Literary Context

Praise and Prophecy *Jubilate Agno*, even in its fragmentary form, is Smart's "prophetic book": an evangelical and philosophical manifesto, personal diary, and commonplace book all in one, as well as a remarkable experiment in poetic form. The sections were probably intended to be related in the same fashion as the Anglican liturgy. The *Let* verses—so named because they each begin with the word "let"—are invocatory and mostly impersonal, calling on the universal choir of creation to glorify the Lord; the *For* verses (each beginning with the word "for") add comments, reflections, topical references, and details of Smart's private life and feelings. At the same time, each series of verses is sequentially ordered or linked, thus yielding a complex pattern (not consistently maintained) of vertical and horizontal connections.

The poem is primarily intended as a work of praise and thanksgiving, in accord with Smart's belief in the primacy of gratitude: "For there is no invention but the gift of God, and no grace but the grace of gratitude," he declares. He envisages himself, the poet, as "the Lord's News-Writer—

the scribe-evangelist," spreading the Word and adventuring in the name of the Lord to combat the evil influence of atheistic philosophy and scientific materialism by renewing the spirit of Christian worship in England.

... And Cats In Smart's belief, as Marcus Walsh observes in *Christopher Smart: Selected Poems* (1979), "every creature worships God simply by being itself, through its peculiar actions and properties.... The well-known lines on Smart's cat Jeoffry, far from exemplifying a childlike naivety of vision, are an elaborate demonstration of how each closely observed act may be taken as part of the cat's divine ritual of praise."

Works in Critical Context

Overall Reception In 1936 William Butler Yeats singled out *A Song to David* in the introduction to the *Oxford Book of Modern Verse* as the inaugural poem of the romantic period, in which man, "passive before a mechanized nature," began to beat against the door of his prison. Even without knowledge of *Jubilate Agno*, Yeats recognized that *A Song to David* was more than a religious poem of unusual scale and splendor; as Browning also recognized, it was a reaffirmation of spiritual realities in an age of scientific materialism, of the conjunction of nature and super-nature in an age of natural theology.

A Song to David In its own time, *A Song to David* was received with more perplexity than either admiration or hostility: "a very curious composition, being a strange mixture of dun obscure and glowing genius at times," wrote James Boswell on July 30, 1763 to a friend, Sir David Dalrymple. *The Critical Review* (April 1763) hinted at the impropriety of "a Protestant's offering up either hymns or prayers to the dead," conceding, however, that "great rapture and devotion is discernable in this extatic song" and concluding that it was "a fine piece of ruins." Contemporary readers regarded as regrettable what modern critics have seen as daring originality.

Jubilate Agno When *Jubilate Agno* was first published in William Force Stead's edition under the title *Rejoice in the Lamb*, it was understandably regarded mainly as a fascinating curiosity, at best the incoherent outpourings of a mad genius, although showing remarkable gifts of observation and expression and flashes of spiritual insight. Elizabeth Scott-Montagu, who reviewed Stead's edition in *Nineteenth Century* (June 1939), was exceptional among early critics in her recognition of a powerful and consistent vision behind the seemingly insane disorder of the work. Donald Greene, however, was the first to recognize the far-reaching and subversive implications of Smart's philosophical and scientific ideas, claiming him as "the earliest of the outright rebels against Newtonian and Lockean 'rationalism'" and arguing that his criticism of Newtonianism was as radical as William Blake's and conducted with "rather more philosophic precision."

COMMON HUMAN EXPERIENCE

Smart's poetry mainly focused on the word of God according to the Bible. Here are some other works, like *A Song to David* and *Jubilate Agno*, that have a pronounced ideological agenda:

Secrets of the Self (1915), poetry by Allama Iqbal. This collection, written by one of Pakistan's most famous poets, explores the relationship of Muhammad and the individual Indian Muslim.

Dulce Et Decorum Est (1920), a poem by Wilfred Owen. This poem, written by a soldier who later died in action, questions the nobility of war and suggests that fighting is not so honorable after all.

Reds (1981), a film by Warren Beatty. This movie, based on real events, sympathetically centers around John Reed, a Communist and chronicler of the Russian Revolution.

The Satanic Verses (1988), a novel by Salman Rushdie. This novel, which includes a nontraditional view of the life of Muhammad, is so controversial that Rushdie still receives death threats for its publication.

Responses to Literature

1. Compare some of William Blake's poems to Smart's. Why do you think Blake is usually regarded as the better poet?

2. Smart wrote at a time when the Protestant Church of England was falling out of favor. Do you think his poems may have restored people's faith?

3. Some say that Smart's religious zeal is a result of a brain anomaly. Can you find any evidence of this in *Hymn to a Supreme Being*? Does it matter?

4. Think about something you believe strongly in, and write a dramatic, enthusiastic poem about your topic. Do you feel a sense of relief afterward?

BIBLIOGRAPHY

Books

Ainsworth, Edward G. and Charles E. Noyes. *Christopher Smart, a Biographical and Critical Study.* Columbia: University of Missouri, 1943.

Boswell, James. *Boswell's Life of Samuel Johnson, Together with Boswell's Journal of a Tour to the Hebrides and Johnson's Dairy of a Journey into North Wales*, 6 volumes, Ed. George Birkbeck Hill, Rev. L. F. Powell. Oxford: Clarendon Press, 1934–1964.

Claridge, Gordon, Ruth Pryor, and Gwen Watkins. "The Powers of Night: Christopher Smart," in their *Sounds from the Bell Jar: Ten Psychotic Authors.* London: Macmillan, 1990, pp. 71–87.

Devlin, Christopher. *Poor Kit Smart*. London: HartDavis, 1961.

Toynbee, Paget, and Leonard Whibley, eds. *Correspondence of Thomas Gray*, revised by H. W. Starr, 3 volumes. Oxford: Clarendon Press, 1971.

Periodicals

Adams, Francis D. "*Jubilate Agno* and the 'Theme of Gratitude.'" *Papers on Language and Literature* 3 (Summer 1967): 195–209.

Gedalof, Allan J. "The Rise and Fall of Smart's David." *Philological Quarterly* 60 (Summer 1981): 369–86.

Saltz, Robert D. "Reason and Madness: Christopher Smart's Poetic Development." *Southern Humanities Review* 4 (Winter 1970): 57–68.

Williamson, Karina. "Christopher Smart's Hymns and Spiritual Songs," *Philological Quarterly* 38 (October 1959): 413–24.

Alexander McCall Smith

BORN: *1948, Bulawayo, Rhodesia*

NATIONALITY: *Scottish*

GENRE: *Fiction*

MAJOR WORKS:

The No. 1 Ladies' Detective Agency (1998)

Portuguese Irregular Verbs (2003)

The Sunday Philosophy Club (2004)

44 Scotland Street (2005)

Overview

The diverse accomplishments of Alexander McCall Smith include a distinguished career as a legal scholar and more recent fame as a best-selling novelist. A professor of medical law at Edinburgh University, Smith has published many works on medical ethics and criminal law. For example, he has written about the duty to rescue and the impact of medical advances on parental rights. Smith also had in print numerous books of fiction for children and short-story collections before he published a series of detective stories set in Botswana. The first installment, *The No. 1 Ladies' Detective Agency* (1998), became a best-selling novel in the United States after it was popularized by word of mouth. Readers and critics have been charmed by the stories, which are more about relationships, customs, and informal justice than sleuthing.

Works in Biographical and Historical Context

Growing Up in Africa   Smith was born on August 24, 1948, in Bulawayo, Rhodesia (later known as Zimbabwe), where his father worked as a public prosecutor in what was then a British colony. His mother wrote a number of unpublished manuscripts. The youngest of

Alexander McCall Smith   *McCall Smith, Alexander, photograph. Juda Ngwenya / Reuters / Landov.*

four children, Smith spent the whole of his childhood in Bulawayo and attended the Christian Brothers College there. He left Africa when he was seventeen years old to continue his education in Scotland.

Law and Teaching   After completing his education, Smith began teaching law at Queens University in Belfast, Northern Ireland. He then went back to Africa—first to Swaziland to teach and then, by 1980, to Botswana. He assisted in creating Botswana's first law school, taught law at the University of Botswana, and wrote a criminal code for Botswana. Many years later, he would publish *The Criminal Law of Botswana* (1992). The book interested critics with its discussion of how the country's criminal law is unlike others in southern Africa and how it resembles the Queensland Criminal Code of 1899.

Smith eventually returned to Scotland, where he became a professor in medical law at the University of Edinburgh. Over the years, he wrote a number of significant articles and books about law and related questions in medical ethics. In 1983, he cowrote with Ken Mason *Law and Medical Ethics* which was updated every few years. In 1987, he coauthored *Butterworths Medico-Legal*

Encyclopedia with John Kenyon Mason. One interesting title was *Forensic Aspects of Sleep* which considered, among other topics, the legal culpability of those who committed an alleged crime while sleepwalking.

As Smith's reputation as an expert in medical legal ethics grew, he was granted many prestigious positions. He did several year-long professorships abroad, including a stint at the law school at Southern Methodist University in Dallas, Texas. He also served as the deputy chairman of the Human Genetics Commission for the British government. In addition, Smith served as Great Britain's representative on the bioethics commission for the United Nations Educational, Scientific, and Cultural Organization (UNESCO). He regularly traveled around the globe in his UNESCO position, helping answer questions about issues such as how to manage DNA databases and protect the information therein.

Serial Writing   By the late 1990s, Smith branched out into adult fiction. After a visit to Botswana, he was inspired to write the 1998 novel *The No. 1 Ladies' Detective Agency*. Following *The No. 1 Ladies' Detective Agency*, Smith wrote five more books featuring Precious Ramotswe and other central characters. While the success of the series was satisfying for Smith, he began writing other series of fiction for adults. The protagonist of the *Sunday Philosophy Club* series is Isabel Dalhousie, a moral philosopher who faces various ethical dilemmas that arise in each book. This more "traditional" mystery series was generally praised, and the British Broadcasting Corporation bought the rights to turn it into a television series.

Intellectual concerns were the center of another series written by Smith that was published in the early 2000s. Originally written in 1997 and self-published at that time, *Portuguese Irregular Verbs* was a collection of short stories focused on the odd world of three German professors and their inability to function in everyday life. Poking fun at academics, Smith wrote the book after being inspired by a German professor he met at a conference in the 1980s. The original work was passed around among these intellectuals who appreciated the joke, and the author wrote two more books with the same characters and in the same lighthearted manner.

The prolific Smith had other ideas for series, starting with *Fatty O'Leary's Dinner Party* (2004) and another less traditional series, *44 Scotland Street*. The *Scotsman* commissioned Smith to write *44 Scotland Street* as a serialized novel to be published five days a week for six months in 2004. This approach was highly stylized, yet at the same time was modernized, using reader input to steer the direction of the narrative.

Smith's book contracts required him to produce a certain number of books a year, and despite his prolific writing abilities, Smith needed time to focus on his writing. In early 2004, Smith decided to take an unpaid leave of absence from teaching for the next three years. Also in

2004, he resigned as vice chairman of the Human Genetics Commission and relinquished his duties with UNESCO.

Currently, Smith lives in Edinburgh with his wife Elizabeth, who is a doctor, and his two daughters. He is the cofounder of an amateur orchestra called "The Really Terrible Orchestra," in which he plays the bassoon.

Works in Literary Context

While Smith has been likened to the British comic author P. G. Wodehouse, creator of the Jeeves and Wooster series of novels, he cites as a chief literary influence the late but eminent Indian novelist R. K. Narayan. More important influences, though, are people and their environments, especially those of non-Western cultures. Much of his fiction, especially *The No. 1 Ladies' Detective Agency*, contains powerful descriptions of both the countryside of Africa and the kinship of its people because it has remained so much a part of him throughout his life.

Children's Books   Smith's books for children reflect both Western and non-Western cultural influences and are mostly written for beginning readers. One example showing Smith's African background is "The White Hippo," a story set in Gambia about the unsuccessful efforts of villagers who want to protect an albino hippo from a white man claiming to be a photographer. The twenty-seven stories in *Children of Wax: African Folk Tales* (1991) are more suited for older children and storytellers. Smith collected the tales from old and young members of the Ndebele people of Zimbabwe. Featuring shape-changing animals and supernatural powers, they nevertheless contain realistic portrayals of hardship and danger. The stories often serve to condemn bad behaviors such as greed and unfounded

COMMON HUMAN EXPERIENCE

Smith has a particular gift for creating detective fiction laced with humor. Here are some other works that combine mystery and humor:

The Thin Man (1933), a novel by Dashiell Hammett. Hammett, original master of the hard-boiled detective genre, introduces the witty married couple of Nick and Nora Charles in this novel, which inspired several "Thin Man" films.

The Mousetrap (1952), a play by Agatha Christie. This is the longest running play in theatrical history by the best-selling mystery writer of all time.

Lean Mean Thirteen (2007), a novel by Janet Evanovich. The latest volume in the Stephanie Plum "number series" finds bounty hunter Stephanie and her sidekick Lula in search of what has happened to Stephanie's ex-husband.

Deathtrap (1978), a play by Ira Levin. Levin's play was the longest running comedy-thriller in Broadway history. It was adapted into a 1982 film starring Michael Caine and Christopher Reeve.

trust and show that justice does not always follow wrongdoing.

Adult Fiction The collection *Heavenly Date and Other Stories* (1995) is comprised of original stories by Smith that are international in scope. Among them, "Intimate Accounts" is set in a fictional world, "Bulawayo" happens in Southern Rhodesia, and others take place in Zurich, Switzerland; Lisbon, Portugal; and Northern Queensland, Australia. The dark and funny pieces relate all kinds of strange dates, meetings, and exchanges between men and women.

An African Woman's Perspective? Critics and readers alike have noted that Smith entered uncharted territory with *The No. 1 Ladies' Detective Agency*. In fact, some readers have found it hard to believe that a white Scottish man could understand African women so well. With more than 1 million copies in the series having been sold, readers have apparently accepted Smith's gift of perspective. He has made Africa and its people accessible around the world. In a statement explaining the novel's setting, Smith said, "In Botswana, ties of kinship, no matter how attenuated by distance or time, linked one person to another, weaving across the country a human blanket of love and community." According to Allison Block in *Booklist*, "It is those ties and that sense of community that continue to make this series so appealing to both genre and nongenre readers."

Works in Critical Context

The Importance of Kindness Although a few critics have dismissed his works as too gentle and unassuming, Smith has consistently believed in his work. He told Sarah Lyall of the *New York Times*, "There is a role for books that say to people that life is potentially amusing and that there are possibilities of goodness and kindness—that kindness needn't be dull, that it can also be elevating and moving."

The No. 1 Ladies' Detective Agency Precious (Mma) Ramotswe, and Smith's novels about her, have charmed reviewers, who have found the novels fresh, amusing, and affecting. In *BookLoons*, G. Hall described the first installment as "truly unique," explaining that "the best part of the book is, in fact, not the mysteries but the stories of Precious and her father." Mahinder Kingra of the *Baltimore City Paper* judged that in this "deceptively frivolous" novel there is "as honest and sympathetic a portrait of contemporary African life as [Nigerian writer Chinua] Achebe's." Kingra commented that the book is "one of those rare, unassuming novels that seems to contain all of life within its pages, and affirms life in telling its story." Christine Jeffords noted on the Best Reviews Web site that Smith "succeeds in giving his story a lilting, lyrical flavor that makes the reader feel almost as if she is listening to a story being spun by a native tale-teller." Comments on the first three novels by Anthony Daniels in the *Spectator* credit Smith with an admirably simple writing style and the remarkable feat of "creating fictional characters who are decent, goodhearted but not in the least bit dull." In addition, the critic said that "for all their apparent simplicity, the Precious Ramotswe books are highly sophisticated."

When Alida Becker reviewed the first three books for the *New York Times*, dubbing Mma Ramotswe the "Miss Marple of Botswana," it dramatically increased public awareness of the series. As Becker noted, film rights for the series had already been sold to Anthony Minghella, director of *The English Patient*. Writing in the *Wall Street Journal*, Matthew Gurewitsch found *The No. 1 Ladies' Detective Agency* to be no less than "one of the most entrancing literary treats of many a year."

Nonfiction Works Most of Smith's legal scholarship treats subjects relating to medical and criminal law issues. He served as coeditor for and contributor to *Family Rights: Family Law and Medical Advances* (1990), which contains seven essays about the legal and ethical implications of new medical capabilities that affect the creation of life as well as the extension of life. The essays consider the impact of laws on a family's ability to make their own medical decisions. Reviewers of *Family Rights: Family Law and Medical Advances* described the book as an in-depth treatment suitable for both specialists and general readers. In the *Sydney Law Review*, Belinda Bennett recommended it as "a very readable collection" that avoids jargon and explains the necessary medical and scientific terminology. Jenny L. Urwin wrote in the *Journal of Medical Ethics* that it provides "interesting and thoughtful analysis" on a previously neglected subject. The book's "interdisciplinary and comparative flavour" was noted in *Family Law* by Andrew Bainham, who also wrote, "The scholarship in this volume is, for the most part, as original as it is provocative and the two most impressive contributions are by the editors themselves." Writing for *Nature*, Andrew Grubb commented on the context of Smith's essay, saying, "Faced with this largely interventionist judicial attitude, it is left to Sandy McCall Smith to challenge its basis and to sound a note of caution."

Responses to Literature

1. In *The No. 1 Ladies' Detective Agency*, how does Smith depict his female protagonist and other female characters? How does he depict the men in the novel? What are the female views of the males in the book? Given the title and the gender treatments, would you say this is a "woman's" book? Why or why not?

2. Using your library and the Internet, find out more about the history of Rhodesia, now called Zimbabwe. Write a paper describing British involvement in Rhodesia, the development of the independent country of Zimbabwe, and recent events in Zimbabwe.

BIBLIOGRAPHY

Web sites

Random House. *Reader Group Guide: The No. 1 Ladies' Detective Agency*. Retrieved February 14, 2008, from http://www.randomhouse.com/features/mccallsmith/books_ladies_rgg.html.

McCall Smith, Alexander. Official Website. Retrieved February 14, 2008, from http://www.alexandermccallsmith.co.uk/Pages/Home.aspx.

◈ Mario Soldati

BORN: *1906, Turin, Italy*

DIED: *1999, Lerici, Italy*

NATIONALITY: *Italian*

GENRE: *Fiction, nonfiction, drama*

MAJOR WORKS:

America First Love (1935)

The Commander Comes to Dine (1950)

The Confession (1955)

The Real Silvestri (1960)

Mario Soldati   *Slim Aarons / Hulton Archive / Getty Images*

Overview

Mario Soldati achieved success in various genres. As an essayist, he was engaging and provocative; he is best known as the author of *America First Love*, a collection of essays that has been reprinted six times since it was first published in 1935. As host of a television series that ran for two years, *Voyage in the Po Valley in Search of Genuine Wines*, (1955–1956), he became one of Italy's most popular figures. When his other television series, *In Search of Genuine Food*, ended in 1959, he had the fame of a movie star. Soldati was also active in the motion picture industry as a director and critic, as well as a screenplay writer. His most successful movie was *Little Old-Fashioned World*. He wrote twelve novels, three of which were awarded major literary prizes. Six were best sellers. Soldati investigated the self in relation to inherited values and scrutinized good and evil, honesty and dishonesty, and truth and fraud to reveal the invalidity of absolute judgments.

Works in Biographical and Historical Context

Influenced by Jesuits and Art   Soldati was born in Turin on November 17, 1906, into an old and prosperous

LITERARY AND HISTORICAL CONTEMPORARIES

Soldati's famous contemporaries include:

Jorge Luis Borges (1899–1986): Argentine master of the tangled, surreal short story.
Federico Fellini (1920–1993): Italian director known for his experimental, avant-garde films, including *Satyricon* and *8½*.
Italo Calvino (1923–1985): Italy's most translated fiction writer.
Sophia Loren (1934–): Famous Italian actress and international icon.

family that had been known in the city since the eighteenth century. He was educated at the Jesuit Istituto Sociale, the most fashionable private school in Turin at the time. When he expressed a desire to join the order of the Jesuits, he was told to contemplate the decision for a year—which was, as it turned out, time enough for him to change his mind. Although many of his characters rebel against the religious morality imparted by the Jesuits, Soldati spoke fondly of their moral integrity and intellectual rigor and remained grateful for their introducing him to Greek, Roman, and French culture. More important is the impression that his Jesuit teachers left on Soldati: The relentless probing in which he engaged in his works suggests the Jesuits' style of argumentation, epitomized by their motto "Grant little; deny often; distinguish always."

Soldati earned a degree in art history at the University of Turin in 1927 and continued his studies at the Institute for Advanced Study in Art History in Rome. He published his first volume of short stories, *Salmace*, in 1929. That same year he left for the United States, having won a fellowship in art history at Columbia University. While there, he also served as an instructor. Unable to obtain a regular university teaching appointment, he returned to Italy in January 1931. In May of that year he married a former student, Marion Rieckelman. They had three children, but the marriage ended in 1934. Soldati visited the United States in 1932 and 1933; his experiences on these trips are related in his *America First Love*. In 1941, Soldati began a relationship with Giuliana Kellermann. They married and had three children. From 1946 to 1960, Soldati lived in Rome. In 1960, he and his family moved to Milan.

Success with Thrillers In 1937, Soldati published his first novel, a psychological thriller titled *The Truth About the Motta Case*, as a serial in the literary magazine *Omnibus*; it appeared in book form in 1941. The mystery of

Motta's disappearance seems to unfold in the usual fashion of the whodunit, but the novel suddenly enters a world of fantasy, magic, and horror: The missing lawyer is living in the sea with an enormous, Felliniesque (as if from a Federico Fellini film of fantasy images) siren queen.

Seventeen years later, Soldati completed a second, more complex novel, *The Capri Letters*. It received the Strega Prize and became one of the first post–World War II best sellers in Italy, though many critics found the work's intricacies, tricks, and surprises rather excessive.

Creating Across Genres During the 1930s, Soldati began scripting scenarios for several of the most distinguished Italian directors, like Alessandro Blasetti and Mario Camerini. He then graduated to direction, serving as codirector with F. Ozep. However, after the success of his later 1930s fiction, he turned increasingly to fiction writing, publishing works like *The Motta Affair*. But Soldati did maintain his contacts with the film industry. As a film director he proved to be particularly good at handling adaptations of literary texts, especially those with a nostalgic bent. In the 1950s and 1960s, Soldati became very active in television and continued to pursue his writing and film career until his death in Italy in 1999.

Works in Literary Context

Surreality of Language In Soldati's work, an intriguing mixture of the real and the surreal, the banal and the fantastic, the mundane and the bizarre, the pleasant and the horrific tantalizes the reader. This dynamic, stylistic layering explains why writer Italo Calvino, himself the creator of invisible cities and nonexistent knights, would express his appreciation of *Lo smeraldo* (*The Emerald*, 1974) on the dust jacket, but even the realist Pier Paolo Pasolini admired the work's language, lack of "viscosita" (viscosity), and its "assoluta leggerezza" (absolute lightness).

Writing the Self Much of Soldati's writing appears to have a strong autobiographical dimension, as demonstrated in his early nonfiction work such as *America First Love*, as well as in a much later novel, *The American Bride* (1977). The former, rooted in the observations of his postgraduate years in the United States, sifts myth and reality through European conceptions of the American way of life. *The American Bride*, one of his last novels, reexplores some of the issues of cultural difference he had examined from various perspectives in a number of stories and is a sensitive account of irresolvable tensions and misunderstandings in a marital relationship. Themes rooted in childhood and adolescent experience, more particularly the personal and moral implications of a sexually repressive education, inform some of his best work. Translation of such experience into fictional terms is seen in *The Jesuit Friend* (1943) and *The Confession*.

Love and Lies Many of Soldati's works are concerned with self-deception in relationships. The tightly written novella *The Real Silvestri* juxtaposes the views held of a mutual friend by a middle-class lawyer and an attractive working-class woman. For the latter, Silvestri is a cheat and blackmailer, while the former remembers him only as the very model of kindness, consideration, and personal honesty. Gradually, the lawyer appreciates how impossibly idealized the memory of his friend was, but comes to understand and feel for him all the more by accepting his human flaws.

Although his plots can exploit the bizarre and the extraordinary, Soldati chronicles the human ordinariness in the romantic deceptions and misunderstandings of friendship, marriage, and other love relationships. Additionally, a strong element of the erotic permeates his work, the more powerful for never being overt or exploitative. This romantic, even titillating dimension, reinforced by the sure sense of the storyteller, helped to win him a wide readership in Italy and abroad.

Works in Critical Context

Overall Reception Dubbed "one of the most gifted of all living Italian storytellers"in the *Times Literary Supplement*, Soldati, in his films as well as his writings, reveals a special talent for description and narrative. His writing did not appear in English translation until the publication of *Dinner with the Commendatore* in the early 1950s. The three stories in that book, wrote Charles J. Rolo of the *New York Times Book Review*, "are somewhat reminiscent of the long short stories of Somerset Maugham. While Soldati's plots are not, perhaps, as arresting as Maugham's, he deals more subtly with the mysteries of the human heart and mind.... This is storytelling in the great tradition."

The Real Silvestri *The Real Silvestri* divided the critics. A few accused the author of artificiality: Carlo Bo, in his review for *La stampa*, felt compelled "to solve a difficult problem of a literary nature: up to what point is the writer sincere with himself; where does the game begin?" Emilio Cecchi, however, was among those who thought that this novel was one of Soldati's most authentic works and that Aurora was one of his most genuine characters.

The Real Silvestri attacks fundamental problems of character, as a man learns from his dead friend's mistress about his friend's real personality. Notes Helene Cantarella in the *New York Times Book Review*, "This incisive study of adult personalities, with its skillful insights into the complexities and bitter ironies of adult emotional life, is the work of a mature mind. In its unusual amalgam of wry, sophisticated humor, brittle analysis, and elementary human compassion, it is Soldati at his best." Alice Ellen Mayhew of *Commonweal* observed that *The Real Silvestri*, like Soldati's other work, "suggests the trained,

---

---

methodical, quick-clever eye of the cinema artist.... His style is naturalistic: the camera/narrator moves listlessly about among the characters.... It is the problem, as well as the method, of *The Real Silvestri*, to discover the real motives of the characters.... [but] Soldati's method breaks down in posturing and mannerism.... The voices drone, the camera wanders, becomes silly and vague, the pictures blur off into placid idiocy."

The American Bride Having lived and worked in the United States, Soldati had a special interest in encounters between American and Italian cultures and sensibilities. In his 1977 novel *The American Bride*, he writes about an Italian professor married to an American woman and about the professor's affair with his wife's Italian American friend. Anthony Thwaite of the *U.K. Observer* called *The American Bride* "a disappointment from one of the most senior and most respected Italian novelists." Thwaite found the book lacked a "thorough sense of a particular world," and he objected to what he called "a good deal of wooden authorial signalling ... and limp gestures toward emotion." But Fantazzi, writing in *World Literature Today*, praised Soldati's "subtle if not always profound psychology and ... cruel analysis of the fine distinction between sincerity and pretense."

Responses to Literature

1. Read one of Soldati's essays and then watch a film that Soldati directed. Write a brief, informal essay discussing how you see Soldati's style of writing reflected in his directing style. Compare the essay with the film. Do they have a similar tone? Setting? Perspective?

2. With a classmate, discuss how Soldati distorts the traditional mystery in *The Truth About the Motta Case.*

3. Soldati often writes about romantic relationships with candor. Make a poster on which you chart a comparison between some of the marriages and relationships in *The American Bride* and *The Real Silvestri.* Be prepared to explain your findings to the class.

4. Using resources in your library or on the Internet, research magic realism. Write a report about the genre, using selections from Soldati as supporting examples.

5. Think about a Soldati book you are assigned and write an essay on how Soldati's studies in visual art manifest in his writing and directing. Use examples from the text to support your idea.

BIBLIOGRAPHY

Books

Bassani, Giorgio, *Le parole preparate.* Turin: Einaudi, 1966, pp. 127–33, 189–201.

Heiney, Donald, *America in Modern Italian Literature.* New Brunswick, N.J.: Rutgers University Press, 1964, pp. 29–34, 187–201.

Siciliano, Enzo, *Autobiografia letteraria.* Milan: Garzanti, 1970, pp. 356–60.

Periodicals

Banti, Anna, "Soldati," *Paragone,* 8 (August 1957): 94–96.

Cecchi, Emilio, "La narrativa di Mario Soldati," in *Letteratura italiana del Novecento,* vol. 2 (Milan: Mondadori, 1972): 992–999.

Garboli, Cesare, "La Fortuna critica di Soldati," in *Opere.* (Milan: Rizzoli, 1991): 883–920.

de Tommaso, Piero, "Mario Soldati," in *Letteratura italiana, I contemporanei,* volume 3. (Milan: Marzorati, 1969): 495–513.

Verdino, S., "Nel mondo di Soldati," *Nuova corrente: Rivista di letteratura,* 106 (July–December 1990): 215–48.

Aleksandr Solzhenitsyn

BORN: *1918, Kislovodsk, Russia*

DIED: *2008, Moscow, Russia*

NATIONALITY: *Russian*

GENRE: *Fiction, nonfiction*

MAJOR WORKS:

One Day in the Life of Ivan Denisovich (1962)

The First Circle (1968)

Cancer Ward (1968)

The Gulag Archipelago, 1918–56: An Experiment in Literary Investigation (1973)

Aleksandr Solzhenitsyn *Solzhenitsyn, Alexander, photograph. AP Images.*

Overview

As the first opponent of Soviet communism inside Russia whose views became widely known, Aleksandr Solzhenitsyn is a hero to numerous people around the world. Throughout a life packed with drama, Solzhenitsyn remained a political personality and historian vitally engaged with the central issues of his era. A survivor of eleven years of Soviet prisons, forced-labor camps, and exile, he was one of the most visible Soviet dissidents influential in exposing human-rights violations in the Soviet Union. He inspired many to voice their own dissent, advocate for free speech, and circulate clandestine literature. Like his predecessors Leo Tolstoy and Fyodor Dostoyevsky, Solzhenitsyn focused predominantly on Russia, yet he addressed concerns that resonate far beyond any national boundaries.

Works in Biographical and Historical Context

Raised in Squalor by a Single Mother Aleksandr Isayevich Solzhenitsyn was born in 1918 in Kislovodsk, Russia. Solzhenitsyn never knew his father, who died in a hunting accident before Solzhenitsyn was born.

Solzhenitsyn's mother was denied sufficient employment by the Soviet government, and the family lived in squalor. Solzhenitsyn had some sense of his literary ambition by the age of nine, and before he was eighteen he resolved to write a major novel about the Russian Revolution of 1917, which led to the overthrow of the previous czarist Russian government and ultimately to the formation of the Soviet Union. After earning degrees in linguistics, mathematics, and physics, Solzhenitsyn began teaching physics in 1941.

Military Imprisonment and Exile With the Nazi invasion of the Soviet Union during World War II, Solzhenitsyn was drafted into the Red Army to help repel the German forces. In 1945, while serving as the commander of a Soviet army artillery battery, counter-intelligence agents discovered letters in which Solzhenitsyn had criticized Stalinism, the sometimes brutal system of government practiced by Soviet ruler and dictator Joseph Stalin. Found guilty of conspiring against the state, he was confined for more than a decade in numerous institutions, including a labor camp in Kazakhstan, and Marfino Prison, a *sharashka*, or government-run prison and research institute. It was while in Moscow's Lubyanka prison that he read otherwise unobtainable works by such authors as Yevgeny Zamyatin, the great Soviet prose writer of the 1920s, and American novelist John Dos Passos, whose expressionist style later influenced Solzhenitsyn's own writing. On March 5, 1953, the day Stalin died, he was released from prison and exiled to central Asia. There, Solzhenitsyn taught mathematics and physics in a secondary school and began writing poems and plays as well as taking notes for a novel. During this time he was also diagnosed with cancer, which nearly led to his death; his experiences during treatment inspired his later novel *Cancer Ward* (1968).

Freed from exile in 1956, Solzhenitsyn returned to central Russia, where friends encouraged him to submit his writings to the Russian periodical *Novy Mir*, which published *One Day in the Life of Ivan Denisovich* (*Odin den' Ivana Denisovicha*) in 1962. Appearing during a period of openness fostered by Soviet leader Nikita Khrushchev, the novel proved a considerable success. However, with the fall of Khrushchev and the rise of much less tolerant regimes, Solzhenitsyn quickly fell from official favor and was closely monitored by security forces. When he was awarded the Nobel Prize in Literature in 1970, he was unable to attend the award ceremony because the Soviet government would not guarantee his reentry into Russia. The French publication of *The Gulag Archipelago* (*Arkhipelag Gulag*) in 1973—a sweeping history of forced labor camps in the Soviet Union—led to his arrest, and in 1974 he was expelled from his homeland and eventually settled in the United States. In May 1994, after twenty years of exile in Vermont, Solzhenit-

LITERARY AND HISTORICAL CONTEMPORARIES

Solzhenitsyn's famous contemporaries include:

Andrei Sakharov (1921–1989): Russia's leading physicist, Sakharov battled nuclear war and communist dictatorship.

Joseph Brodsky (1940–1996): Expelled from the Soviet Union in 1972, this Russian-born poet won the Nobel Prize in Literature in 1987.

Nelson Mandela (1918–): Mandela served as president of South Africa (1994–1999) after twenty-seven years in prison for leading the antiapartheid movement.

Vaclav Havel (1936–): A Czech playwright and former anticommunist dissident, Havel served as president of Czechoslovakia (1989–1992) and the Czech Republic (1993–2003).

Isaac Asimov (1920–1992): The Russian-born Asimov was a legendary science fiction writer in the United States.

syn and his wife Natalia returned to live in Russia. Though in frail health, Solzhenitsyn continued to work until his death from heart failure in 2008.

Works in Literary Context

Socialist Realism Socialist realism was the official artistic doctrine approved by Stalin in 1934. It dictated that the creative artist should serve society by being realistic, optimistic, and heroic. Creativity and freedom of expression were more than discouraged; they were illegal, forcing Solzhenitsyn to disguise his political and social messages in many of his best-known works.

Set in Stalinist Russia, *One Day in the Life of Ivan Denisovich* (1962), the first published Soviet work of its kind, focuses on a simple prisoner who wants only to serve out his sentence with a certain integrity. In the novel, Solzhenitsyn strove to reverse the usual procedure of socialist realism, which imposed thoughts and feelings on its readers. Therefore, he rendered his tale in an ironic, understated, elliptical manner intended to elicit spontaneous feelings unrelated to official propaganda.

Paradoxes An appraisal of Solzhenitsyn's life and work must address irresolvable paradoxes—he acquired fame as a protest writer, but at heart he was an aesthete. His moral and spiritual authority came from the way he has bore witness to twentieth-century totalitarianism, but his dislike of publicity and his reclusiveness made him an anachronism. Solzhenitsyn's work needs to be discussed in relation to the tradition from which it came, for he responds to socialist realism, which was proclaimed in

COMMON HUMAN EXPERIENCE

One Day in the Life of Ivan Denisovich opened the eyes of the international community to the brutalities of the Soviet prison system. The novel takes its place in a literary tradition of factual and fictional works depicting incarceration, including the following:

> *The House of the Dead* (1862), a novel by Fyodor Dostoyevsky. This novel is based on Dostoevsky's four years in a Siberian prison camp.
>
> *The Ballad of Reading Gaol* (1898), a poem by Oscar Wilde. Wilde's poem is a meditation on suffering and the injustice of capital punishment, written after Wilde's incarceration for "gross indecency."
>
> *Memoirs from the Women's Prison* (1994), a memoir by Nawal el Saadawi. In a highly literary memoir, a doctor, author, and women's rights advocate recounts nightmarish experiences amongst political prisoners in Egypt.
>
> *I Refuse to Die: My Journey for Freedom* (2002), a memoir by Koigi wa Wamwere. A Kenyan human rights activist recalls thirteen years of imprisonment under President Daniel Arap Moi.

1932 as the only acceptable form of art in the Soviet Union. Because the literature of socialist realism resembles many Western best sellers in its accessible style, positive heroes, and happy endings, it cut off Russian literature from its rich heritage of the nineteenth and early twentieth centuries.

In his own way, Solzhenitsyn engaged in an ongoing attempt to restore wholeness to Russian society by reconnecting the pre- and postrevolutionary periods. He wrote to make sense of the evolution of twentieth-century Russia in terms of the lives and works of the nineteenth-century Russian classics. Accordingly, he knew intimately the works of Russian masters such as Aleksandr Pushkin, Nikolai Gogol, Yury Lermontov, Ivan Turgenev, Leo Tolstoy, Fyodor Dostoyevsky, and Anton Chekhov. Solzhenitsyn's efforts were rewarded in 1970 when he received the Nobel Prize in Literature for what the Nobel committee termed "the ethical force with which he has pursued the indispensable traditions of Russian literature."

Works in Critical Context

As a writer and a public figure, Solzhenitsyn has evoked strong reactions, from crude abuse to enthusiastic admiration. Critical responses to Solzhenitsyn have consistently depended on the commentator's ideological sympathies in regard to Soviet communism. During the Cold War era in which Solzhenitsyn's most important works appeared in the West, he was praised for the courage of his stance toward Soviet authorities. More rarely have critics probed substantially into the philosophical and moral dimensions of his message.

One Day in the Life of Ivan Denisovich Written in sparse, plain prose, *One Day in the Life of Ivan Denisovich* tells of one prisoner's typical activities. "Ivan Denisovich," affirmed Shirley J. Paolini in *Reference Guide to Short Fiction*, "represents the common individual incarcerated in a Soviet camp for an insignificant crime; his energies are devoted entirely to survival under brutal conditions." Lauren Livingston, writing in the *English Review*, summarized *One Day in the Life of Ivan Denisovich* as a "haunting read," and Gleb Zekulin, writing in *Soviet Studies*, recommended it as "a mine of information." Still another enthusiast, Vladimir J. Rus, wrote in *Canadian Slavonic Papers* that "Solzhenitsyn has given the world a moving picture of... a genuine joy in one's own existence, even when so limited in time, space, and one's own consciousness." Abraham Rothberg's *Aleksandr Solzhenitsyn: The Major Novels* acknowledges that in *One Day in the Life of Ivan Denisovich*, Solzhenitsyn "explored new terrain in the use of language, exploiting a combination of prison slang, peasant and pornographic slang," and Christopher Moody, in *Solzhenitsyn*, deemed the story an "eloquent protest." Similarly, Robert L. Yarup observed in the *Explicator* that the novel concerns "man's irrepressible instinct for freedom."

"Matryona's House" *One Day in the Life of Ivan Denisovich* proved an immense success with Soviet readers, and Solzhenitsyn followed it in *Novy Mir* with short stories, including "Matryona's House," in which a former prisoner befriends an aging peasant woman who serves as his landlady. Andrej Kodjak, in his study *Alexander Solzhenitsyn*, noted that "Solzhenitsyn draws on his own experience to create the narrator, Ignatich." John Clardy, in a *Cimarron Review* essay, expressed particular praise for Solzhenitsyn's handling of characterization in "Matryona's House," declaring that "Matryona, like Tolstoy's Anna Karenina, stands out in our minds as a real personality." Leonid Rzhevsky, meanwhile, quoted another reader, in *Solzhenitsyn: Creator and Heroic Deed*, who considered Matryona "the most brilliant image of the peasant woman in all of the Russian literature I have read." Still another critic, Stephen S. Lottridge, wrote in *Russian Literature Triquarterly* that "Matryona's House" relates "the trials and loss endured by an innocent and righteous person," while Robert Louis Jackson, in a piece featured in *Solzhenitsyn: A Collection of Critical Essays*, summarized the tale as "significant art." Sheryl A. Spitz, meanwhile, described the short work in a *Russian Review* essay as "the story of one individual's moral maturation."

The First Circle *The First Circle* was described by an essayist in *Encyclopedia of World Biography* as "harshly satiric." In the novel, according to David M. Halperin in an essay included in *Aleksandr Solzhenitsyn: Critical Essays and Documentary Materials*, Solzhenitsyn "examines both the omnipresence of lying as a demonstrable feature of Soviet society and as a metaphysical, demonic device." Furthermore, Solzhenitsyn, in his characterization of Stalin, emphasized that the dictator, however monstrous and however powerful, was nonetheless human. "In his portrait of Stalin in *The First Circle*," wrote Paul N. Siegel in *Clio*, "Solzhenitsyn, in cutting the towering figure of the Stalin of Stalinist myth-making down to size, showed him to be a human being at ironic variance with the image."

Responses to Literature

1. Do you agree with Solzhenitsyn's decision to return to the country that both exiled and imprisoned him? What are the most important factors for an expatriate to consider before returning home?

2. Why do you think Solzhenitsyn was able to conduct the extensive research that enabled him to produce *The Gulag Archipelago*, while concealing the project from authorities?

3. Read George Orwell's *Animal Farm*. If you could include Solzhenitsyn as a character in the novel, what or who would he be? How would you show his role and actions in your characterization?

BIBLIOGRAPHY

Books

Barker, Francis. *Solzhenitsyn: Politics and Form*. New York: Holmes and Meier, 1977.

Bloom, Harold, ed. *Aleksandr Solzhenitsyn, Modern Critical Views*. Philadelphia, Pa.: Chelsea House, 2001.

Burg, David and George Feifer. *Solzhenitsyn: A Biography*. New York: Stein and Day, 1972.

Dunlop, John B., Richard Haugh, and Alexis Klimoff, eds. *Aleksandr Solzhenitsyn: Critical Essays and Documentary Materials*. New York and London: Collier-Macmillan, 1975.

Ericson, Edward E., Jr. *Solzhenitsyn and the Modern World*. Washington, D.C.: Regnery Gateway, 1993.

Feuer, Kathryn, ed. *Solzhenitsyn: A Collection of Critical Essays*. Englewood Cliffs, N.J.: Prentice-Hall, 1976.

Labedz, Leopold, ed. *Solzhenitsyn: A Documentary Record*. Bloomington: Indiana University Press, 1973.

Mahoney, Daniel J. *Aleksandr Solzhenitsyn: The Ascent from Ideology*. Lanham, Md.: Rowman & Littlefield, 2001.

Pearce, Joseph. *Solzhenitsyn: A Soul in Exile*. Grand Rapids, Mich.: Baker, 2001.

Scammell, Michael. *Solzhenitsyn: A Biography*. New York: Norton, 1984.

Thomas, D. M. *Alexander Solzhenitsyn: A Century in His Life*. New York: St. Martin's Press, 1998.

⊠ Sophocles

BORN: *c. 496* BCE, *near Athens, Greece*

DIED: *c. 406* BCE, *Athens, Greece*

NATIONALITY: *Greek*

GENRE: *Poetry, drama*

MAJOR WORKS:
Antigone (442 BCE)
Oedipus Rex (c. 425 BCE)
Electra (c. 425–410 BCE)
Philoctetes (409 BCE)
Oedipus at Colonus (401 BCE)

Overview

During the fifth century BCE, the Golden Age of Athens, new forms of art and literature were being developed with extraordinary speed and energy. Classical Greek author Sophocles, along with Aeschylus and Euripides, was a primary innovator of the new genre of tragedy, shaping stage conventions that have become central to dramatic art. Sophocles' ability to blend irony and poetry with effective dramatic technique has earned him a reputation as the greatest playwright of world literature.

Sophocles   *Mansell / Time Life Pictures / Getty Images*

Works in Biographical and Historical Context

Early Artistic Ability Sophocles' date of birth is believed to be 497 BCE or 496 BCE . His father was a wealthy businessman named Sophillus. As such, Sophocles enjoyed a Greek education that included art and music. His musical ability presented him with a solo part that he sang in the victory paean after the battle of Salamis in 480 BCE). (This naval battle between Greek city-states and Persia took place in the strait between Piraeus and Salamis Island. The Greeks won handily, preventing Persia from conquering the Peloponnese.)

Prize Winner at the Greater Dionysia When Sophocles completed his education, he competed in the dramatic festival the Greater Dionysia, held every spring for five days. During the time of the festival, all business stopped in Athens, and everyone was invited to participate, even prisoners, who were freed to participate. At the festival of 468 BCE, Sophocles defeated Aeschylus, winning first prize. Sophocles went on to win first prize more than twenty times, never receiving anything below second prize, a unique feat among Greek dramatists.

Elite Athenian As a member of the Athenian elite at a time when Athens enjoyed extraordinary cultural and political supremacy, Sophocles held important political positions. He held the post of treasurer (Hellenotamias) in either 443 or 442 BCE, and served as general along with Pericles (a prominent Athenian general, statesman, and orator) in the war to suppress a revolution in Samos from 441 to 439 BCE. (Samos had been occupied by Athenians in 441 BCE.) Sophocles was also made a member of the Athenian senate. In addition to his political appointments, Sophocles showed his devotion to traditional religion by serving as a priest of the healing deity Amynos.

Debatable Dates It is estimated that Sophocles wrote some 123 plays. Titles and fragments of ninety exist, but only seven tragedies survive in their entirety. Of these seven, there is a only one that is firmly dated, *Philoctetes*, in 409 BCE. *Oedipus at Colonus* is known to have been Sophocles' last creation because it was produced posthumously in 401 BCE. There are grounds for placing *Antigone* close to 441 BCE. The date of *Women of Trachis*, a play whose authenticity has been doubted by a few in the past, is now generally put at sometime before *Antigone*.

Ajax is also deemed to be relatively early: 450 BCE. The date of *Oedipus Rex* has been endlessly discussed without an agreement being reached; stylistically it seems not far from *Electra*, whose placing on the chronological table is uncertain as to whether it precedes or follows Euripides' *Electra*, written in 413 BCE. It appears, then, that of the seven surviving plays, the ones deemed to be "early" belong to a time when the poet was already in his fifties; and some of his finest choral writing, in *Oedipus at Colonus*, belongs to a man of ninety.

Sophocles died c. 406 BCE, in Athens, Greece, though the details surrounding his death are vague.

Works in Literary Context

Among Sophocles known influences were Greek mythology as interpreted and shaped by poets such as Homer as well as Aeschylus—the author of such plays as *The Persians* (472 BCE)—who was twenty-eight years older than Sophocles but also Sophocles' rival during his early years as a writer. Like Aeschylus, Sophocles was affected by the flowering of Athenian culture and the related intellectual life. In addition, the military conflicts with the Persians and with Sparta influenced the work of Sophocles.

Technical Innovations The extraordinary dramatic and poetic power of Sophocles' tragedies stems, in part, from certain technical innovations that he introduced into the Athenian theater. Unlike Aeschylus, whose dramatic trilogies provide plot continuity and share characters, Sophocles focuses on individual tragedies. By limiting his narrative scope, he achieved a more concentrated emotional intensity and action. In addition, Sophocles enhanced the usually bare Greek stage with *skenographia*, or scene painting, and more expressive masks, thereby bringing greater realism to each scene.

Perhaps Sophocles' most important innovation was the introduction of the use of a third actor. Traditionally, two actors (all roles were played by male actors), along with the chorus, participated in the *epeisodia*, or episodes, of the play. The addition of the third actor enabled Sophocles to construct a more complex dialogue, thereby keeping the focus on the characters rather than on the chorus. He increased the chorus from twelve to fifteen members and, while limiting its participation in the action, composed some of his most beautiful poetry for it. Many commentators have praised the imaginative form, striking imagery, and emotional power of Sophocles' choral songs, with particular attention to their poetical and philosophical content.

Sophocles' dramatic style is often described as a divine union of strength and control. In measured, simple, and piercingly direct language, Sophocles' dramas move swiftly, logically, and inexorably toward their seemingly inevitable conclusions. The most painful human situations—utter personal humiliation, the accidental murder of a loved one, a cataclysmic reversal of one's station in life—are presented in a manner that implies compassion for the suffering individual but also places personal misfortune in a universal, cosmic context.

Free Will The hallmark of Sophocles' style is his gift for portraying exceptional characters under stress. His dramas are built around a strong-willed, highly principled character who encounters a seemingly insurmountable ethical or moral difficulty. For Sophocles, the center of interest was the individual human being who will not compromise even when he or she clearly perceives the advantages that compromise would bring. Sophocles creates characters of heroic proportions, yet these heroic qualities often lead to disaster. By creating characters who refuse to compromise, Sophocles sows the seeds of a person's own destruction. At the same time, such a character is plainly the kind that he admires and for whom he seems to invite admiration by others. In this respect, his emphasis is on human free will. The hero has only to change his mind, to adapt to circumstances, and catastrophe will be averted.

Prophecy There is another counter-theme running through six of the seven tragedies: the theme of oracular predictions and the inevitability of their fulfillment. Though the extent of their participation in human affairs remains unclear, the gods are respected and feared in the world of Sophocles' plays. Oracles are consulted and heeded. This tension between human free will and divine predestination presents problems of interpretation. Artistically the interest revolves around a person's own free decision, but the development of the plot leaves no doubt as to the outcome.

Influences Sophocles is regarded as the pinnacle of Greek dramatic art and one of the greatest dramatists in Western literature. The stage conventions that he helped initiate have become central to dramatic art, and he is acknowledged as one of the shapers of the genre. Sophocles' plays and innovations have also profoundly influenced the development of European literature.

Works in Critical Context

Sophocles is considered one of the greatest dramatists in Western literature. His surviving tragedies attest to his consummate craftsmanship in plot construction, characterization, and versification. In fact, critics acknowledge

COMMON HUMAN EXPERIENCE

Sophocles's plays sometimes feature a "deus ex machina" (literally, "god from the machine"), an improbable and sudden solution to the conflict at hand. Though literary critics frown on the deus ex machina as an easy way out of a plotting problem, it has been used countless times in literature and film. A few other works that employ this device:

Alcestis (438 BCE), a play by Euripides. In this play, the title character, who has sentenced herself to death, is revived at the last minute by the hero Heracles.
The Winter's Tale (1623), a play by William Shakespeare. At the end of this play, a statue magically comes to life and reveals itself as the previously dead character Hermione.
The War of the Worlds (1898), a novel by H. G. Wells. The terrible alien invasion in this novel ends abruptly when the Martians all catch a cold and die.
Donnie Darko (2001), a film by Richard Kelly. In this movie, the title character's problems appear to be solved when a plane crashes into his bedroom.

him as one of the shapers of dramatic art. His reputation as a dramatist has been secure ever since his own time. Sophocles' technical skill as a dramatist, unforgettable characters, and haunting, perfectly plotted plays, have secured his standing in world literature.

Oedipus Rex Of all Sophocles' plays, *Oedipus Rex*—a tragedy denied first prize either because it was ahead of its time or because of the vagaries of the Athenian voting system at the dramatic festival—is at once his least typical play and the one that has left the deepest imprint. Perhaps the most famous play ever written, *Oedipus Rex* describes the tragic events that lead Oedipus to murder his father and marry his mother, unaware of their true identities. In *Poetics* (c. 335 BCE), Aristotle plainly regarded the play as the greatest masterpiece of the genre, claiming it was a model tragedy, containing Sophoclean elements such as reversal and discovery.

However, when put under the microscope, critics have noted that *Oedipus Rex* is teeming with every kind of illogicality and inconsistency. Some of these problems were mercilessly pointed out by Voltaire in the preface to his own *Oedipe* (1718). Oedipus begins with a city stricken by a plague, but as the play progresses the plague is forgotten, and the emphasis shifts completely from the question "Who killed Laius, King of Thebes?" to "Who is Oedipus and what is his relationship with the last royal house?"

Despite such problems, *Oedipus Rex* has received considerable attention in modern times, partly due to the father of modern psychiatry, Sigmund Freud. Freud was tremendously moved by the play and popularized the notion of the Oedipus Complex. While critics still agree that the play is a gripping exploration of the role of the gods in a man's life and a warning to man to avoid becoming too proud, some critics have focused their attention on the play's themes, the playwright's use of irony, the function of the chorus, and the Freudian interpretation, among other issues.

Writing about *Oedipus Rex* in 1953, F. J. H. Letters wrote in *The Life and Work of Sophocles*, "The *Oedipus tyrannus (King Oedipus)* is the best-known and best-built of classical tragedies. Yet in its treatment of inherent improbabilities...it is also the best illustration of the difference between ancient and modern views as to the limits of dramatic license. Sophocles' originality shows itself less in the making than in the shaping of the plot."

Responses to Literature

1. Using a Venn diagram, compare and contrast Electra with her sister Chrysothemis and their actions and motivations in the play *Electra*.

2. In a group discussion, explain the roles of fate and free will in Sophocles' plays.

3. Write a brief report explaining why you think *Oedipus Rex* is considered Sophocles' masterpiece.

4. Research Sigmund Freud's Oedipus and Electra complexes. Are these terms fair to Sophocles' characters? Write an essay about your conclusions.

5. In small groups, create alternative ways in which you could solve Antigone's problems without using a deus ex machina.

BIBLIOGRAPHY

Books

Bowra, C. M. *Sophoclean Tragedy.* Oxford: Oxford University Press, 1944.

Dawe, R. D., ed. *Sophocles, the Classical Heritage.* New York: Garland, 1996.

Jebb, R. C. *Oedipus Tyrannus.* 3rd ed. Cambridge: Cambridge University Press, 1893.

———. *Trachiniae.* Cambridge: Cambridge University Press, 1892.

Kirkwood, G. M., *A Study of Sophoclean Drama.* Ithaca, N.Y.: Cornell University Press, 1958.

Knox, B. M. W. *The Heroic Temper: Studies in Sophoclean Tragedy.* Berkeley: University of California Press, 1964.

Lesky, Albin. *Greek Tragic Poetry.* New Haven, Conn.: Yale University Press, 1983.

Letters, F. J. H. "The *Oedipus Tyrannus.*" In *The Life and Work of Sophocles.* London: Sheed and Ward, 1953.

Waldock, A. J. A. *Sophocles, the Dramatist.* Cambridge: Cambridge University Press, 1951.

Winnington-Ingram, R. P. *Sophocles: An Interpretation.* Cambridge: Cambridge University Press, 1980.

◈ Wole Soyinka

BORN: *1934, Abeokuta, Nigeria*

NATIONALITY: *Nigerian*

GENRE: *Fiction, poetry, drama*

MAJOR WORKS:

The Lion and the Jewel (1963)

The Interpreters (1965)

The Man Died: Prison Notes of Wole Soyinka (1972)

Death and the King's Horseman (1975)

Aké: The Years of Childhood (1981)

Overview

Wole Soyinka's plays, novels, and poetry record twentieth-century Africa's political turmoil and its struggle to reconcile tradition with modernization. With a style that combines the European dramatic form with traditional folk-drama in the Yoruba tongue, a Niger-Congo language family, Soyinka presents both satire and spectacle

Wole Soyinka   *Soyinka, Wole, 2006, photograph. AP Images.*

on the stage. The first black African writer to be awarded the Nobel Prize in Literature, Soyinka is also well-known as a political activist in Nigeria.

Works in Biographical and Historical Context

British Colonial Upbringing in Nigeria Akinwande Oluwole Soyinka was born in Abeokuta, in the British colony of Western Nigeria, on July 13, 1934, to Samuel Ayodele, headmaster for the village school established by the British, and Grace Eniola Soyinka, a Christian convert. His grandfather introduced him to the 401 gods of Yoruba and to other West African tribal folklore.

After high school and a brief period as a clerk in Lagos, Soyinka attended the University College in Nigeria. He published several poems and short stories before leaving Africa in 1954 to attend the University of Leeds in England, where *The Invention*, his first play, was produced in 1957. At Leeds, Soyinka expanded his awareness of Western literary and theatrical traditions. He was awarded a BA in 1957, started work on a master's degree, and moved to London, all the while continuing to be involved in the theater.

Critiquing Western Modernization Soyinka returned to Nigeria in 1960, shortly after independence from colonial rule under the United Kingdom had been declared. He began to research Yoruba folklore and drama in depth and incorporated elements of both into his play *A Dance of the Forests* (1960), commissioned as part of Nigeria's independence celebrations. In the play, Soyinka warned the newly independent Nigerians that the end of colonial rule did not mean an end to their country's problems. Among Soyinka's best-known works is the play *The Lion and the Jewel* (1963), which mocks the unquestioning embrace of Western modernization. Its 1966–1967 London production established Soyinka as a significant English-language dramatist.

In 1962 Soyinka began as a university lecturer at University College in Ife, Nigeria. Disgusted by the weakness shown by college authorities in the face of political pressure, he resigned the following year. During 1965, Soyinka became a senior lecturer in English at the University of Lagos. He allowed his genius for satire full rein in *The Republican* (1963), *The (New) Republican* (1964), and *Before the Blackout* (1965), attacking a variety of targets, exposing clearly identifiable individuals to ridicule, and commenting on the state of Nigeria since independence.

Political Critiques Lead to Imprisonment Soyinka was well established as Nigeria's premier playwright when he published his first novel, *The Interpreters* (1965). The novel allowed Soyinka to expand on themes in his plays and to present a sweeping view of Nigerian life immediately following independence. Essentially plotless, *The Interpreters* is loosely structured around the informal discussions among five young Nigerian intellectuals.

Solitary Confinement The year 1965 also marked Soyinka's first arrest by the Nigerian police. He was accused of using a gun to force a radio announcer to broadcast incorrect election results. No evidence was ever produced, however, and Soyinka was released from jail after three months, only to be arrested two years later during Nigeria's civil war. After the Nigerian region of Biafra had declared itself an independent republic in 1967, Soyinka traveled to Biafra to establish a peace commission of leading intellectuals from both sides. When he returned home, the Nigerian police accused him of helping the Biafrans to buy jet fighters. This time, Soyinka was imprisoned for more than two years, even though he was never formally charged with any crime. In solitary confinement during most of his detention, Soyinka was denied reading and writing materials, but he managed to manufacture his own ink and began writing a prison diary on toilet paper, cigarette packages, and in between the lines of a few books he had secretly obtained. Published as *The Man Died: Prison Notes of Wole Soyinka* (1972), Soyinka's diary should be regarded not as a factual account of his prison experience but as a creative response to detention.

Release from Prison and Self-Exile in Europe Soyinka was released in 1969 and, in an act of self-exile, left Nigeria soon after and did not return until 1975. He spent most of 1972 in Europe and delivered a series of lectures at Churchill College and Cambridge University during 1973–1974. Subsequently published as *Myth, Literature and the African World* (1978), the lectures combine criticism of specific texts with discussions that reveal the extent of Soyinka's knowledge of literary and theatrical traditions.

Returning Home Soyinka returned to Nigeria in 1975, and in 1976 became a professor at the University of Ife. The Nigeria to which Soyinka had returned was a country where the rich had become richer and the poor had become even poorer than before. This polarization in wealth was due, in part, to the oil boom of the 1970s; while revenues from sales of Nigeria's oil were significant, most of the money fell into the hands of corrupt politicians. In reaction to conditions in Nigeria, Soyinka wrote *Death and the King's Horseman* (1975), a work that explores the complexities of situations, ambiguities, and uncertainties in human relations. The work was not well received in Nigeria.

Work in the U.S. Yields More Publications During the 1980s, Soyinka held visiting professorships at American universities and continued to write and direct. He published *Aké: The Years of Childhood* (1981), followed almost ten years later by *Isara: A Voyage around "Essay"* (1990), which explores the world in which his father grew up. In between these two works, *A Play of Giants* (1984) was published and performed. This drama

LITERARY AND HISTORICAL CONTEMPORARIES

Soyinka's famous contemporaries include:

Sani Abacha (1943–1998): President of Nigeria from 1993 to 1998, Abacha banned political activity, suppressed the press, and was named the fourth most corrupt world leader in recent history by the anticorruption coalition Transparency International.

Idi Amin (mid-1920s–2003): Hundreds of thousands of people were killed during the brutal rule of Amin, who seized power in a military coup and became president of Uganda from 1971 to 1979.

Yuri Gagarin (1934–1968): In 1961, this Soviet cosmonaut became the first person in space and the first person to orbit the Earth.

Jayakanthan (1934–): Jayakanthan is an Indian novelist and playwright from the Tamil Nadu region whose works question middle-class beliefs and conventions.

Ken Saro-Wiwa (1941–1995): This Nigerian author and activist led a campaign against environmental damage caused by multinational oil companies; he was executed after a sham trial under Achaba's rule, provoking international outrage.

is partly a specific campaign against Ugandan dictator Idi Amin and partly the presentation of a more general concern about the lack of responsible leadership in Africa.

Humble Acceptance of International Recognition In recognition of his achievements as a widely produced playwright, Soyinka was elected president of the International Theatre Institute in 1986. That same year, he was awarded the Nobel Prize in Literature for being "a writer who in a wide cultural perspective and with poetic overtones fashions the drama of existence." Soyinka stated that the prize was not an award for himself "but to all the others who laid the basis and were the source from which I could draw. It is the African world which can now be recognized."

Political Questions Drive Ongoing Work A collection of Soyinka's essays, *Art, Dialogue and Outrage* (1988), and a volume of poetry, *Mandela's Earth* (1988), followed. In 1996's *The Open Sore of a Continent: A Personal Narrative of the Nigerian Crisis* (1996), Soyinka examines Nigeria's dictatorship. A compilation of essays originally delivered as lectures at Harvard University, *The Open Sore* questions corrupt government, ideas of nationalism, and international intervention.

In 1998, Soyinka ended a four-year self-imposed exile from Nigeria. His exile can be traced back to 1993, when a democratically elected government was to

have assumed power. Instead, General Ibrahim Babangida, who had ruled the nation for eight years, prohibited the publication of the voting results and installed his deputy, General Sani Abacha, as head of the Nigerian state. Soyinka, along with other pro-democracy activists, was charged with treason for his criticism of the military regime. Faced with a death sentence, Soyinka went into exile in 1994, during which time he traveled and lectured in Europe and the United States. Following the death of Abacha, who held control for five years, the new government, led by General Abdulsalem Abubakar, released numerous political prisoners and promised to hold civilian elections. Soyinka's return to his homeland renewed hope for a democratic Nigerian state. Like other acts of aggression against Soyinka by the leaders of his country, this incident failed to deter him from writing. He published a poetry collection *Outsiders* (1999), a play of political satire "King Baabu" (2001), and another poetry collection *Samarkand and Other Markets I Have Known* (2002).

After a relatively calm period of several years, however, Soyinka once again plunged into political activism as the leader of a grassroots group called "Citizens Forum." He was tear-gassed and arrested in May of 2004 while protesting then-Nigerian President Olusegun Obasanjo's attempt to amend the constitution to allow him to run for a third term. In 2006, Random House published Soyinka's memoirs, titled "You Must Set Forth at Dawn." In April of 2007, two weeks after the country's presidential elections, Soyinka advocated for the election's cancellation, citing on-going violence and corruption. Today, he continues to take a strong stance against political corruption in Nigeria and abroad.

Works in Literary Context

Significant influences on Soyinka's writing, include, among others, Irish author J. M. Synge, traditional African theatre, and the mythology of his tribe, the Yoruba. Some reviewers link Soyinka's writing style, particularly that used in *The Interpreters*, to that of novelists James Joyce and William Faulkner. Others dislike the formless quality of the novel, but critic Eustace Palmer asserts in *The Growth of the African Novel* (1979), "If there are reservations about the novel's structure, there can be none about the thoroughness of the satire at society's expense."

Synthesizing Traditions In his plays, Soyinka has consciously combined African—particularly Yoruba—forms with the European tradition of dialogue drama. For instance, *Opera Wonyosi* (1981) uses Bertoldt Brecht's *Threepenny Opera* (1928) as the basis for an attack on the vices of Nigeria and Africa. The Nigerian version of the story is patterned after Brecht's play, and therefore, to some extent, after English Renaissance playwright John Gay's *Beggar's Opera* (1728). Because Soyinka adds new characters and sequences, he gives the work a distinctively African and Nigerian flavor.

As Palmer observes, works including Soyinka's *Interpreters* notably influenced the African fiction that followed it, shifting the focus "from historical, cultural and sociological analysis to penetrating social comment and social satire."s

Works in Critical Context

Soyinka's work is frequently described as demanding but rewarding reading. Although his plays are widely praised, they are seldom performed, especially outside of Africa. Their dancing and speech, reminiscent of the classical Greek chorus, are unfamiliar and difficult for non-African actors to master. However, when the Swedish Academy awarded Soyinka the Nobel Prize in Literature in 1986, its members singled out *Death and the King's Horseman* and *A Dance of the Forests* as "evidence that Soyinka is 'one of the finest poetical playwrights that have written in English,'" reports Stanley Meisler. Thomas Hayes summarizes Soyinka's importance: "His drama and fiction have challenged the West to broaden its aesthetic and accept African standards of art and literature. His personal and political life have challenged Africa to embrace the truly democratic values of the African tribe and reject the tyranny of power practiced on the continent by its colonizers and by many of its modern rulers."

The Man Died: Prison Notes of Wole Soyinka
The Man Died is "the most important work that has been written about the Biafran war," believes Charles Larson. "*The Man Died* is not so much the story of Wole Soyinka's own temporary death during the Nigerian Civil War but a personified account of Nigeria's fall from sanity, documented by one of the country's leading intellectuals," Larson asserts. Gerald Weales suggests that the political content of *The Man Died* is less fascinating than "the notes that deal with prison life.... They are vehicles to carry the author's shifting states of mind, to convey the real subject matter of the book; the author's attempt to survive as a man, and as a mind." Larson, however, underlines the book's political impact, noting that, ironically, "Soyinka, who was placed in solitary confinement so that he wouldn't embarrass the government, was writing work after work." A *Times Literary Supplement* reviewer characterizes *The Man Died* as "a damning indictment of what Mr. Soyinka sees as the iniquities of wartime Nigeria and the criminal tyranny of its administration in peacetime."

Aké: The Years of Childhood Soyinka's account of his first ten years stands as "a classic of childhood memoirs wherever and whenever produced," states James Olney. "This is the ideal circle of autobiography at its best. It is what makes *Aké*, amidst its other virtues, the best introduction available to the work of one of the liveliest, most exciting writers in the world today." John Leonard writes, "Most of *Aké* charms; that was Mr. Soyinka's intention. The last fifty pages, however, inspire and confound; they are transcendent."

COMMON HUMAN EXPERIENCE

Much of Wole Soyinka's work attacks corrupt societies and regimes. Here are several other works that examine public corruption and its effects:

Imelda, Steel Butterfly of the Philippines (1988), a biography by Katherine W. Ellison. This work tells the story of Imelda Marcos, former First Lady of the Philippines, who, accused of racketeering and fraud in 1990, was acquitted of thirty-two counts of money laundering in 2008.

The Last King of Scotland (2006), a movie directed by Kevin Macdonald. Forrest Whitaker won an Academy Award for his portrayal of Ugandan dictator Idi Amin in this movie, which is based on the novel of the same name by Giles Foden.

A Russian Diary: A Journalist's Final Account of Life, Corruption, and Death in Putin's Russia (2007), a published diary by Anna Politkovskaya. This work documents eighteen months of increasing power and corruption within Russian president Vladimir Putin's government; the author was murdered in 2006.

Enron: The Smartest Guys in the Room (2005), a film directed by Alex Gibney. This critically acclaimed documentary details the collapse of the energy giant Enron, a corporate scandal in which investors and employees lost everything while company executives walked away with millions.

Responses to Literature

1. Read part of A. R. Ammons's long poem *Tape for the Turn of the Year* (1965), which he typed on long, narrow paper. How does the paper's shape affect the work? Discuss writing media in the context of Soyinka's *The Man Died*. How do you think the work would be different if Soyinka had been given access to books and paper while in prison?

2. Discuss Soyinka's blend of European and African cultural elements in his work.

3. Citing specific examples from the text, analyze examples of fantasy and satire in *A Dance of the Forests*.

4. Discuss the style and format of *The Interpreters*. Describe your emotional reaction(s) to the text.

BIBLIOGRAPHY

Books

Adeniran, Tunde. *The Politics of Wole Soyinka*. Ibadan, Nigeria: Fountain, 1994.

Chinweizu, Onwuchekwa Jemie, and Ihechukwu Madubuike. *Toward the Decolonization of African*

Literature. London: Routledge & Kegan Paul, 1985.

Gakwandi, Shatto Arthur. *The Novel and Contemporary Experience in Africa*. New York: Africana, 1977.

Goodwin, Ken. *Understanding African Poetry: A Study of Ten African Poets*. London: Heinemann, 1982.

Larson, Charles R. *The Emergence of African Fiction*. Bloomington: Indiana University Press, 1971.

Wilkinson, Jane. *Talking with African Writers*. London: Currey, 1992.

Wright, Derek. *Wole Soyinka Revisited*. New York: Twayne, 1993.

Periodicals

Borreca, Art. "Idi Amin Was the Supreme Actor." *Theater* 16 (Spring 1985): 32–37.

Gates, Henry Louis, Jr. "An Interview with Wole Soyinka." *Black World* 24 (August 1975): 30–48.

Muriel Spark

BORN: *1918, Edinburgh, Scotland*

DIED: *2006, Florence, Italy*

NATIONALITY: *Scottish*

GENRE: *Fiction, nonfiction, poetry*

MAJOR WORKS:

The Ballad of Peckham Rye (1960)

The Bachelors (1960)

The Prime of Miss Jean Brodie (1961)

The Mandelbaum Gate (1965)

Muriel Spark *Evening Standard / Hulton Archive / Getty Images*

Overview

Dame Muriel Spark found her writing voice late in life, yet within a short time established herself as a competent biographer, literary critic, and poet, and made her name as a fiction author with great universal appeal. In almost fifty years, Spark produced almost fifty volumes of writing, including several award-winning masterworks.

Works in Biographical and Historical Context

Edinburgh Youth Muriel Sarah Camberg was born in Edinburgh, Scotland, on February 1, 1918, to a Jewish English father and an Anglican mother. She was educated at James Gillespie's High School for Girls, and from 1934 to 1935 studied commercial correspondence and writing at Heriot-Watt College. After teaching English for a short time, she took a job as a secretary in a department store.

Seven-Year Marriage She married Sidney Oswald Spark in September of 1937 and soon followed her husband to Rhodesia (now Zimbabwe), where she stayed for seven years. The Sparks' son, Robin, was born in July

1938, but the family would not last. Muriel determined her husband was a manic depressive, especially based on his tendency toward violent outbursts, and in 1940 left him and her son. Returning to the United Kingdom, Spark worked in the Political Intelligence Department of the British Foreign Office during World War II. Though she left Robin behind with his father, and though Robin returned to the United Kingdom with his father and was then raised by his maternal grandparents in Scotland, Spark consistently sent money to support him and would do so for the next forty years, helping him as he struggled as an artist in his own right.

After a period as general secretary of the Poetry Society from 1947 to 1949, serving as the editor of *Poetry Review* in 1949, and founding the short-lived literary magazine *Forum*, Spark worked as a part-time editor for Peter Owen Ltd. By this time, she had already achieved some recognition as a critic, biographer, and poet when she made her first attempt at fiction, the short story "The Seraph and the Zambesi." She entered the story in a 1951 Christmas writing contest sponsored by the *London Observer* and not only won top honors but attracted a great deal of attention for the piece's unconventional treatment of the Christmas theme. Several other stories set in Africa and England followed, and Spark's successes in fiction soon began to overshadow those in criticism and poetry.

Religious Conversion   While working in the areas of nonfiction, Spark had begun to undergo a crisis of faith. During this time of great individual evaluation, she received financial and psychological assistance from Graham Greene, also a Roman Catholic convert, and was eventually converted herself, a move that had significant influence on her novels. Spark published *The Comforters* in 1957 and followed that with *Robinson* in 1958, the same year she authored her first short-story collection, *The Go-Away Bird and Other Stories*. In this same period she began writing radio plays, with *The Party Through the Wall* in 1957, *The Interview* in 1958, and *The Dry River Bed* in 1959.

Literary Success   It was in 1959 that Spark had her first major success, *Memento Mori*. She followed this with *The Ballad of Peckham Rye* in 1960, *The Bachelors* (1960), and *Voices at Play* (1961). Spark also published the novel generally regarded as her masterwork, *The Prime of Miss Jean Brodie* (1961), which subsequently was made into a play, a film, and a six-part television adaptation.

In 1962, Spark's sole venture into theater, *Doctors of Philosophy*, was presented in London and was not a resounding success. She returned to fiction and over the next decade wrote eight more works, novels and short stories, among them such successful titles as *The Mandelbaum Gate* (1965), which was awarded both the Yorkshire Post Book of the Year award in 1965, and the James Tait Black Memorial Prize in 1966.

Continued Success   With five awards to her name already, in 1973 Sharp published *The Abbess of Crewe*, a work alive with paradox. A well-received book, it too went on to be filmed in 1976 under the title *Nasty Habits*. Then came seven more novels and two short-story collections, along with three more book awards as well as the honor Officier de l'Ordre des Arts et des Lettres, which France bestowed upon Spark in 1988. Also in 1988, however, was an event that got as much publicity as her work. Spark had for many years had a difficult relationship with her estranged son. That year, however, Robin declared that because he was Jewish he wished to petition for his late maternal grandmother to be recognized as Jewish, as well. A devout Catholic for over three decades, Spark responded by calling her son a publicity seeker, only making this latest attempt to further his typically weak career as an artist.

Partly to correct critical misunderstandings and inaccuracies about her life, as well as to put together the facts about her life and her fiction, in 1993 Spark published *Curriculum Vitae: Autobiography*. She then returned to the novel form in 1997 with *Reality and Dreams*. Her twentieth novel, it explored the boundaries and connections between realities and dreams. She continued with

---

LITERARY AND HISTORICAL CONTEMPORARIES

Spark's famous contemporaries include:

Iris Murdoch (1919–1999): Irish novelist famous for such works as *Under the Net* (1954) and *The Green Knight* (1993).

Tadahiko Hayashi (1918–1990): Japanese photographer best known for his portraiture and documentary work on a wide range of subjects, from postwar Japan to Miss Universe contender trips through America.

Chaim Herzog (1918–1997): Soldier of the British Army and the Israel Defense Forces who served as the sixth president of Israel from 1983 to 1993.

John Updike (1932–): Award-winning novelist, essayist, and literary critic often appreciated for his in-depth chronicling of American psychological, social, and political cultures.

---

the novel form in 2000 with *Aiding and Abetting*. In 2001, a limited edition of twenty-six copies of *A Hundred and Eleven Years Without a Chauffeur* was published by Colophon Press, each copy signed and inscribed with a passage and a letter of the alphabet by Spark. Spark's final novel was *The Finishing School* (2004).

Final Word   In April 2006, the eighty-eight-year-old author, who had been made Dame Muriel Spark by the Order of the British Empire in 1993, died in Florence, Italy. When she had moved to Rome from New York City in the late sixties, Spark met artist and sculptor Penelope Jardine. In the early seventies, the two moved into a farmhouse in Tuscany, where they lived together—amid the rumors—until Spark's death. In her will, filed in an Italian court, Spark left her entire estate worth several million to Jardine.

Works in Literary Context

Emphasis on Character Relationships   In much of Spark's work, her storylines are mischief-filled "fun-house plots, full of trapdoors, abrupt apparitions, and smartly clicking secret panels," as fellow author John Updike described them in a *New Yorker* article. These plots involve the often bizarre behavior of people belonging to a small, select group: elderly men and women linked by long-standing personal relationships in *Memento Mori*; unmarried male and female residents of the same London district in *The Bachelors*; and students and teachers at a Scottish girls' school in *The Prime of Miss Jean Brodie*.

In terms of setting, the author usually chooses to locate her modern morality tales in upper-class urban

COMMON HUMAN EXPERIENCE

Here are a few works by writers who have also succeeded in exploring, in an often humorous way, important human themes of identity, class, religion, and personal philosophy:

Brideshead Revisited (1945), a novel by Evelyn Waugh. Waugh portrays the twilight of the British aristocracy in this melancholy novel.

Manservant and Maidservant (1947), a novel by Ivy Compton-Burnett. In this novel, English author Compton-Burnett pokes fun at the "master" of a British household and his underlings.

Saturday Night and Sunday Morning (1960), a film directed by Karel Reisz. This film, based on the 1958 novel by Alan Sillitoe, details the lives of some young members of the working class in Nottingham, England.

The World of Malgudi (2000), a collection of short novels by R. K. Narayan. In this collection of four short novels, the author examines modern Indian life from a variety of perspectives.

areas of England or Italy, and in the tradition of the intellectual novelist, avoids florid descriptions of the physical world, preferring instead to concentrate on dialogue, on "the play of ideas and experiences upon the mind, and the interplay of minds upon each other," writes scholar Joseph Hynes. The "action" in these stories springs from the elaborate ties—of blood, marriage, friendship—Spark concocts these between the members of each group, and her characterizations are quick, sharp, and concise.

Moral Wisdom Spark's themes do not seem to reflect her strong religious and moral preoccupations. They are instead, as the Catholic Book Club defined them when granting her the 2001 Campion Award, "universal to the human condition—good and evil, honor and duplicity, self-aggrandizement and self-pity and courage amid poverty." Such themes are carried by characters who embody what critic George Stade called "traditional moral wisdom" (in the case of Miss Jean Brodie) as they experience what critic *Washington Post Book World*'s Nina King and others pointed out as "the mysteries of evil and suffering, destiny and predestination, guilt and intention" (in the case of Margaret in *Symposium*, 1990). All this Spark masterfully delivered in what Nina King also called an "exquisitely balanced tone [that] proves that the richest comedy is that which explores the darkest themes."

Influences Spark's crisis of faith in the early fifties was strongly influenced by the writings of Newman, the nineteenth-century Anglican clergyman who became a convert to Roman Catholicism and eventually a cardinal in

that faith. Her conversion was also moved along by the financial and moral support from author Graham Greene, also a Roman Catholic convert. As she struggled the first three years to sort out the aesthetic, psychological, and religious questions raised by her conversion to Catholicism and her attempt at writing longer fiction, her efforts led to much speculation. Many scholars and critics have approached her work by focusing on the extent to which her Catholicism influenced her writing. Just as many more have considered her writing, especially her earlier work, in terms of how it has impacted readers and writers to follow, with her combined new faith and theory of the novel and the novelist as godlike creation authored by a godlike, omniscient and omnipotent being.

Works in Critical Context

Critical opinion has been generally kind, if not generous, to Spark's work for four decades. Literary scholar Duncan Fallowell spoke for many when he observed, "She is the master, and sometimes mistress, of an attractive, cynical worldliness which is not shallow." Critic Rebecca Abrams of the *New Statesman* concluded that the "trademark" of all Spark's fiction, both novels and short stories, "is its lightness, the way it seems almost to shrug its shoulders at the people and lives it so piercingly brings to life." Yet, as critic Barbara Grizzuti Harrison of the *New York Times Book Review* reminded readers, Spark is at heart "a profoundly serious comic writer whose wit advances, never undermines or diminishes her ideas."

Symposium The 1990 best-seller *Symposium* centers on Margaret Demien, a character whose wealthy mother-in-law dies while Margaret is away at a dinner party. Appearing to all as virtuous at first, Margaret openly expresses a more sinister intent. She is also connected to other mysterious deaths, so that when the guests receive news of the older woman's death, Margaret is a suspect. Peter Parker commented in the *Listener*, "This is a marvelous premise for a novel, and, as one would expect, Spark makes the most of opportunities for dark comedy." As Parker continues to explain, "The book's epigraphs...supply hints both of the book's resolution and of Spark's fictional method." The epigraphs also provide clues about the five couples at the dinner party, that in some way represent the varieties of love Plato defined.

Responses to Literature

1. Focus on a favorite Spark character. Consider how he or she copes, survives, and lives through a particular experience. Imagine how that character would advise you if you had to deal with a similar issue. Describe the scenario and present the advice in first person, as the direct voice of the character you have selected.

2. Spark was one of several British writers who became devout Christians well into adulthood. Evelyn

Waugh, C. S. Lewis, and T. S. Eliot also turned to Christianity later in life. Using your library and the Internet, find out more about these writers. Do you think they have anything in common with Spark? Why do you think religion came to play an important part in their lives?

3. *The Prime of Miss Jean Brodie* is set in an all-girls school. While single-sex education was common before the mid-twentieth century, it came under fire as inherently sexist in the 1960s and subsequent decades. Recently, however, some educators and parent groups have renewed their support for single-sex schools. Using your library and the Internet, find out more about the controversy surrounding single-sex education. Write a brief paper outlining your position on the issue.

BIBLIOGRAPHY

Books

Fallowell, Duncan. *20th Century Characters*. New York: Vintage Press, 1994.

Hynes, Joseph, ed. *Critical Essays on Muriel Spark*. New York: G. K. Hall, 1992.

Spark, Muriel. *Curriculum Vitae: An Autobiography*. Boston: Houghton Mifflin, 1993.

Sproxton, Judy. *The Women of Muriel Spark*. New York: St. Martin's Press, 1992.

Stade, George, ed. *European Writers: The Twentieth Century Volume 12 George Seferis to Yannis Ristos*. New York: Charles Scribner's Sons, 1990.

Web sites

Young, Dr. Alan R. *Class Web Page by English 1106D0: Muriel Spark, The Prime of Miss Jean Brodie*. Retrieved February 14, 2008, from http://plato.acadiau.ca/courses/engl/young/e1106ce/Spark/spark.htm.

National Library of Scotland. *Muriel Spark Archive*. Retrieved February 14, 2008, from http://www.nls.uk/murielspark/index.html.

Stephen Spender

BORN: *1909, London*

DIED: *1995, London*

NATIONALITY: *British*

GENRE: *Poetry, nonfiction, drama, fiction*

MAJOR WORKS:

Poems (1933)

Vienna (1934)

The Still Centre (1939)

World within World (1951)

The Struggle of the Modern (1963)

Stephen Spender   *Spender, Stephen, photograph. © Jerry Bauer. Reproduced by permission.*

Overview

Stephen Spender is best known as a member of the generation of British poets who came to prominence in the 1930s known as the Oxford Poets. Like others in the group, Spender wrote with a social and political consciousness, reflecting such turbulent events as the Great Depression, the Spanish Civil War, the rise of fascism, and World War II. After the Second World War, Spender produced less poetry and concentrated on critical and autobiographical writing, editing, and lecturing at universities in England and the United States.

Works in Biographical and Historical Context

Early Loss of Parents   Stephen Harold Spender was born February 28, 1909, in London, to Harold Spender, a liberal political journalist, and his wife, Violet Hilda, an invalid who painted and wrote poetry. Both parents died while Spender was still an adolescent. The Spender family was of mixed German, Jewish, and English origin. Spender did not discover his Jewish ancestry until he was sixteen. The discovery confirmed his lifelong sense of himself as an outsider.

From Oxford to Weimar Germany After transferring from a boarding school to University College School in Hampstead, Spender went to University College at Oxford. At Oxford in the late 1920s, Spender felt isolated, despite developing a close friendship with W. H. Auden. Spender printed his first volume of poetry, *Nine Experiments: Being Poems Written at the Age of Eighteen* (1928), on his own handpress. He later destroyed copies of his early efforts, but several of the poems he wrote between 1928 and 1930 would appear in his volume *Poems* published in 1933.

In the summer of 1930, before his senior year, Spender left Oxford without a degree and followed fellow writer Christopher Isherwood to Germany. Sexual liberation, artistic rebellion, and social unrest were prevalent in the last years of the Weimar Republic. (After the end of World War I, the defeated Germany was forced to give up its colonies and territories won in the Franco-Prussian War, nearly totally disarm, and pay reparations. Germany also became a republic, governed under the liberal Weimar constitution. Though Germany was a liberal country in this period, it also faced serious economic and social dislocations and, by the early 1930s, an economic depression.) There, Spender began writing a novel—*The Temple*, which would not be published until 1988—about a young Englishman in Germany, enjoying his youth, but concerned about the rising Nazi movement.

Rise of Hitler Affects Poems In 1933, Adolf Hitler and his National Socialist (Nazi) Party came to power. A fascist, Hitler converted the republic into a dictatorship, consolidated Germany's position at home and abroad, and began a military expansion. Like many young English intellectuals, Spender watched with horror the onset of fascism in both Berlin and Vienna. Spender's first important volume, *Poems*, was published in 1933. This collection exemplifies the social and political concerns of the time and triggered Spender's career. He became recognized as a major poet and literary celebrity. The following year, Spender produced *Vienna* (1934), a long poem that blends details of the fascist suppression of socialist insurgency in Austria with his own personal conflicts.

Spender and the 1930s The generation that grew up between the two world wars was acutely aware of the rupture World War I had created in European life. Seeing the established world crumbling around them, the writers of the period sought to create a new reality to replace a mindset that appeared obsolete. Spender, an ardent idealist, briefly joined the Communist Party, thinking it represented a viable alternative to fascism. When the Spanish Civil War broke out, Spender went to assist the International Brigades that had formed to fight the fascist forces of General Francisco Franco in that country. As a pacifist, however, he did not partake in the armed struggle, which ended with Franco firmly in power. In 1937, Spender coedited a volume of "poems for Spain."

Spender also wrote outside of poetry in his most prolific decade, the 1930s. His first book of prose was *The Destructive Element* (1935), a work of literary criticism on such authors as Henry James, W. B. Yeats, T. S. Eliot, James Joyce, and D. H. Lawrence. A book of short stories, *The Burning Cactus* (1936), is reminiscent of Lawrence in its intense, suppressed emotion. He also authored a five-act, antifascist verse drama, *Trial of a Judge* (1938). His only full-length novel, *The Backward Son* (1940), is a thinly disguised autobiographical account of English boarding school life, which he hated.

His poetry continued to be significant as well. *The Still Centre* (1939) is based on Spender's experiences in Spain and records his growing detachment from communism. The Spanish Civil War poems resemble the World War I poetry of Wilfred Owen in their rejection of the heroic idea of war. *The Still Centre* is a key volume in Spender's poetic career because, in its pages, Spender turns from public, political verse back to his private, personal attempt to convey the "felt truth" of reality.

From Poetry to Prose In 1939, Spender and Cyril Connolly became coeditors of a literary magazine, *Horizon*. Barred from military service for health reasons during World War II (which broke out when Germany invaded Poland in 1939, compelling both Britain and France to declare war), Spender served in the London Auxiliary Fire Service. He published two poetry collections during the war. Poetry occupied a lesser place in his postwar career, as he turned increasingly to literary criticism, political and historical works, translations, and autobiography. During the 1950s and 1960s, he held visiting professorships at several prestigious American and English universities and traveled the world as a cultural ambassador with the United Nations' cultural organization UNESCO. From 1970 to 1977, he was an English professor at University College, London.

Postwar Life Spender contributed to *The God That Failed* (1949), an essay collection by disillusioned ex-Communists, including Arthur Koestler, André Gide, and Richard Wright. Spender and Irving Kristol cofounded a transatlantic, anticommunist periodical called *Encounter* in 1953. He resigned after fourteen years as an editor when he discovered that the publication was covertly funded by the U.S. Central Intelligence Agency.

Spender wrote several volumes of criticism in his later career, including *The Creative Element* (1953), a companion piece to his earlier *The Destructive Element*. In *The Struggle of the Modern* (1963), Spender portrays literary modernism as an endeavor to reconcile the past and the present, and heal the divide between art and life. He also produced several volumes of autobiography, journals, and collected letters, most notably the 1951 memoir *World within World*, a valuable document of literary and cultural history that re-creates the social and political atmosphere of the 1930s. This book exemplifies the commitment to honesty and candor of an author who claimed that all of his art is essentially autobiographical. At its publication, the book created a stir for Spender's frank disclosure of a homosexual relationship he had before his first marriage in 1936.

Accused Author of Plagiarism Spender continued to write poems and nonfiction throughout his life, though his poems were published more sporadically. Later collections include *The Generous Days* (1969). In 1994, a year before his death, Spender sued American author David Leavitt for plagiarism, alleging that Leavitt had modeled his novel *While England Sleeps* on events from Spender's life. Leavitt made editorial changes and the case was settled. Spender died in London on July 16, 1995.

Works in Literary Context

Spender's poetics reflect three major influences. The first is the Romantic poets; Spender's ethereal lyricism and youthful idealism made him something of a twentieth-century Percy Bysshe Shelley. A second influence comes from the modernists of the generation preceding his, such as Rainer Maria Rilke, W. B. Yeats, and, especially, D. H. Lawrence. Lastly, his Oxford cohorts, primarily Auden and Isherwood, shaped his understanding of the poet's role in commenting on society.

The so-called "Auden generation" reacted against the chilly esotericism of T. S. Eliot, insisting that poetry should be clear, accessible, and engaged with the issues of the day. Yet Spender's career exemplifies the split between personal and political life his generation felt. Even while they were transforming British letters with their brazenly political verse, at some level Spender and his colleagues felt divided between the artistic muse and the urge to confront fascism. The struggle to connect outer and inner reality is, in fact, Spender's overarching theme.

The "Pylon Poets" Spender's name is invariably associated with that of W. H. Auden, perhaps the most famous poet of the thirties, whose renown surpassed Spender's. The two poets were dissimilar in many ways, but they burst upon the literary scene at the same time and earned the collective name of the "pylon poets." The term refers specifically to "The Pylons," a poem by Spender, which many critics described as typical of the Auden generation: images of the ugliest features of the urban-industrial landscape reflecting political and social concerns. This felt obligation constrained the spontaneous lyricism of Spender's early verse.

Style Critics have called the Auden group politically radical, yet formally conservative. Spender was slow to break free of formal poetic conventions. He preferred truncated, sonnetlike structures. Yet as he developed, he used less rhyme or meter and drifted toward free verse. The sound of his poems is distinctive, although he uses

few seductive aural techniques, such as alliteration, assonance, full or near rhyme, or regular rhythms. The imagery, though painterly, often lacks concreteness. One weakness of his poetry is a tendency toward rhetorical abstraction.

Inner and Outer The autobiographical impulse is obvious in Spender's poetry. Its obsessive theme is an introspective search for a valid, sustaining faith, a coherent approach to uniting the self with the world, the personal with the political. In *The Destructive Element*, Spender argues that the prose of Lawrence successfully balances the inner and outer worlds. Spender sought to emulate Lawrence in his poetry. This search for a united, integrated self is notable in *The Still Centre*, especially in the poem "Darkness and Light." The poem reflects the ambivalence and conflict between opposites that has so bedeviled Spender's life; they are reconciled within the poem, but not in life.

Influence As a leading poet of the twentieth century, Spender influenced poets that followed him, especially through the idealism that runs through his poems. As a lionized writer, a respected critic, an important player in cultural politics, and a university lecturer, he was much read, observed, respected, and emulated by practicing

COMMON HUMAN EXPERIENCE

Spender's political poetry reflects the social upheaval of the 1930s, as do these other key literary works from that decade.

Brave New World (1932), a novel by Aldous Huxley. The dystopian classic is about a society happily tranquilized by government-issued drugs.

The U.S.A. Trilogy (1930, 1932, 1936), novels by John Dos Passos. These three experimental novels reflect a pessimistic view of American life in the early twentieth century.

Nausea (1938), a novel by Jean-Paul Sartre. In this philosophical work, the overwhelming nausea experienced by the protagonist is a clue to the nature of existence.

Homage to Catalonia (1938), a nonfiction book by George Orwell. A first-person account of the Spanish Civil War was written by one of England's leading political journalists and a well-known novelist in his own right.

"September 1, 1939" (1939), a poem by W. H. Auden. This poem was written upon the outbreak of World War II. The poet later disavowed this work, with its famous exhortation, "We must love one another or die."

poets. Dylan Thomas found licenses for his subjectivity in Spender's exploration of the "I." Spender also encouraged and helped Thomas. Philip Larkin, Charles Tomlinson, Ted Hughes, and Seamus Heaney were also believed to be affected by Spender's work. Some critics believed that his autobiography and criticism had more influence on later authors as they revealed what it was like to be a poet in Britain in the 1930s.

Works in Critical Context

Spender's verse is admired for its lyrical transcendence and powerful imagery. However, some deride his poetry for its excessive idealism. The acclaim he earned as a young man, and the romantic image he developed in the 1930s, cast a shadow over the remainder of his career—as did the far greater acclaim that went to his friend Auden. After his first success with the 1933 *Poems*, Spender showed promise of becoming one of the century's greatest poets. Some critics, surveying his career as a whole, contend that he is an overrated poet who failed to realize his potential.

Spender published some below-average volumes of poetry, and response to his critical prose has been decidedly mixed. Critic V. S. Pritchett observes that Spender's "insights are better than his arguments and he is best when he proceeds, as we would expect a poet to do, by vision." Critics have taken more kindly to his autobiographical prose, especially to *World within World*. The

relentless, public self-examination found in his body of work is, for some, his greatest contribution to twentieth-century letters.

Critics note that Spender's poetic and political attitudes, developed in the 1930s, continued to influence the poet throughout his life. Over time, Spender became increasingly identified with that decade, as it became clear that none of his subsequent writing would surpass the vividness of his early work. By the end of the 1950s, his work had fallen out of fashion. The common perception of Spender was that he was a figure from the past. His postwar drift from political radicalism to mainstream liberalism, and his years as an international spokesman for free speech, gradually mellowed his reputation. After the passage of still more time, Spender now appears as a symbol of the decade he helped to define.

The Generous Days One of Spender's last collections of poetry, *The Generous Days* was his first in two decades when it was published in 1969. Critics gave the collection mixed reviews. In *Books and Bookmen*, Derek Stanford wrote "there are some half dozen pieces so right, or true, or personally authentic (the criterion of being *well-written* is not one we think of applying to Spender) that the book is justified by their existence." Other critics, like Roy Fuller in *London Magazine*, found more to like in the poems. Fuller wrote, "The tenderness of feeling for family life, the eye for nature and the rooting out of the precise word to express it, the poetic explosion—all these *are* to be found and sustain the book's interest."

Responses to Literature

1. In an essay, address the following question: What similarities do you identify between Spender's poetry and that of Percy Bysshe Shelley, with whom he is sometimes compared?

2. Citing two or more of Spender's works, explore in a paper how Spender addresses the theme of integrating the self with the wider world.

3. In a chart, list the images and allusions in *Vienna* and discuss how the poet sees the world.

4. Research the role of antifascist volunteers in the Spanish Civil War. In a paper, contrast the account of the war with the war images in Spender's poems and discuss how the poet views the broad significance of the fight.

5. In a paper, write about the relationship between personal and political expression in poetry, providing a careful reading of one or several of Spender's early poems.

BIBLIOGRAPHY

Books

Connors, J. J. *Poets and Politics: A Study of the Careers of C. Day Lewis, Stephen Spender and W. H. Auden in the 1930s.* New Haven, Conn.: Yale University Press, 1967.

Fraser, George S. *Vision and Rhetoric.* London: Faber & Faber, 1959.

Hoskins, Katharine B. *Today the Struggle: Literature and Politics in England during the Spanish Civil War.* Austin: University of Texas Press, 1969.

Hynes, Samuel. *The Auden Generation: Literature and Politics in England in the 1930s.* London: Bodley Head, 1976.

Isherwood, Christopher. *Christopher and His Kind, 1929–1939.* New York: Farrar, Straus & Giroux, 1976.

Kulkarni, H. B. *Stephen Spender: Poet in Crisis.* Glasgow, Scotland: Blackie, 1970.

Maxwell, D. E. S. *Poets of the Thirties.* London: Routledge and Kegan Paul, 1969.

Press, John. *A Map of Modern English Verse.* London: Oxford University Press, 1969.

Scarfe, Francis. *Auden and After: The Liberation of Poetry, 1930–1941.* London: Routledge, 1942.

Sutherland, John. *Stephen Spender: The Authorized Biography.* London: Viking, 2004.

Weatherhead, A. K. *Stephen Spender and the Thirties.* Lewisburg, Pa.: Bucknell University Press, 1975.

Periodicals

Fuller, Roy. "Ungenerous Measure." *London Magazine,* February/March 1972: 145–46.

Stanford, Derek. Review of *The Generous Days. Books and Bookmen,* January 1972: 64–65.

Edmund Spenser   *Spenser, Edmund, drawing.*

of the English language, and perhaps the single most important poet of the of the sixteenth century.

▣ Edmund Spenser

BORN: *c.1552, London*

DIED: *1599, London*

NATIONALITY: *English*

GENRE: *Poetry*

MAJOR WORKS:

The Shepheardes Calender (1579)

The Faerie Queene (1590, 1596)

"Amoretti" and "Epithalamion" (1595)

Prothalamion (1596)

A View of the Present State of Ireland (1633)

Overview

English poet Edmund Spenser was a man of his times, and his work reflects the religious, humanistic, and nationalistic ideals of Elizabethan England. His contributions to English literature—in the form of an enlarged poetic vocabulary, a flexible verse style, and a rich fusing of the philosophic and literary currents of the English Renaissance—make him one of the most influential poets

Works in Biographical and Historical Context

Educated at Cambridge   Spenser, born in London in or about 1552, was the son of a poor tailor. His early schooling took place at the Merchant Tailors' Free School, where he received an education considered quite progressive by the standards of the day. He studied a humanist curriculum that included the study of English language and literature—an unusual innovation at the time. Spenser excelled in the study of languages in school and in 1569 went to Cambridge University. He studied Italian, French, Latin, and Greek; he read widely in classical and modern literature, and he wrote some Latin verse.

Position of Influence   After completing his studies, Spenser went to the district of Lancashire where he increased his familiarity with local dialects. Shortly after leaving the university, Spenser also spent time in the service of the highly influential Earl of Leicester (Robert Dudley), who was regarded as the head of the Puritan faction of the government. By this time, Elizabeth I was England's ruler, and the earl was her favorite for many years. With the power he wielded at court, the Leicester-led Puritan party desired war with Spain. Puritans wanted to remain with the dominant Church of England—formed by Elizabeth's father, Henry VIII, after breaking with the Roman Catholic Church—but wanted it to be further reformed and distanced from its Catholic roots.

Spenser may have traveled as an envoy for Leicester to Ireland, Spain, France, and Italy. By 1579, he was back in London, and he was much involved in discussions about English language and literature. Probably at this time Spenser made the acquaintance of Sir Philip Sidney, the poet and courtier.

Published First Work Spenser's first published work was *The Shepheardes Calender* (1579), which he dedicated to Sidney. This poem, consisting of twelve pastoral eclogues (or conversations between highly idealized shepherds), is full of references to the various political and religious problems of this complex period in British history as various Protestant factions as well as remaining Catholics fought for power and influence. Spenser's time in London was also full of other literary projects, and he was already at work on what would become his greatest achievement, *The Faerie Queene* (1590, 1596).

Meanwhile, he was also studying law and hoping to secure a position in the civil or diplomatic service. His efforts were rewarded in 1580, when, through the influence of the Earl of Leicester, he was named secretary to Lord Grey, the new Lord Deputy of Ireland. Spenser accompanied Grey to Dublin, and Ireland was to remain Spenser's home for the rest of his life. At this time, the whole of Ireland was controlled by Great Britain. Under the rule of Queen Mary I, Elizabeth's elder sister, the British began wholesale confiscations of Irish land and large plantations of English colonists were formed. This practice continued under Elizabeth and several of her successors.

Completed Part of The Faerie Queen By 1589, three of the seven cantos of *The Faerie Queene* were complete. When Sir Walter Raleigh visited the poet that year, he was so impressed with the poet's work that he took Spenser with him back to England, where the cantos were published with an elaborate dedication to Queen Elizabeth (the "Faerie Queene" of the title). Spenser's ambition was to write the great English epic. His plan was to compose twelve cantos, each concerned with one of the twelve moral virtues as classified by Greek philosopher Aristotle. Each of these virtues was to be embodied by a knight. Thus, the poem would combine elements of a chivalric romance, a handbook of manners and morals, and an epic poem about the history and character of a nation. The poem can also be read in its historical context as an allegory about the struggle between the Protestant traditions of England and the many threats posed by England's Roman Catholic neighbors.

The publication of the first three cantos of *The Faerie Queene* met with much acclaim, but in courtly circles

Spenser was a still an insignificant figure without an official profession. In 1591, he returned to Ireland, famous but disappointed. His mood at the time may have been expressed by the title of a collection of minor poems he prepared at the time, *Complaints: Sundry Small Poems of the World's Vanity* (1591).

Poems Inspired by Marriage Back in Ireland, Spenser wrote the greater part of *Colin Clouts come home againe* (1595), an idealized poetic autobiography dedicated to Raleigh. It is another allegorical pastoral that recounts Spenser's reception in London and his impressions (mostly negative) of courtly life. Meanwhile, Spenser was courting Elizabeth Boyle, an Anglo-Irish woman of a well-connected family. They were married on June 11, 1594.

His sonnet sequence "Amoretti" and his "Epithalamion" (both 1595) together form an imaginatively enhanced poetic chronicle of his courtship and marriage. Some of the "Amoretti" sonnets were probably written earlier, but Spenser intended this collection to represent the fluctuations and the emotions of his love for his wife. The "Epithalamion" is generally acknowledged to rank among the greatest love poems in English. The poem is ingeniously constructed with twenty-four stanzas to represent the twenty-four hours of the wedding day, with many other more subtle parallels.

Named Sheriff of Cork In 1595, Spenser returned to London and stayed for more than a year. He published three more cantos of *The Faerie Queene* and several other works, including his *View of the Present State of Ireland* (1633), a prose tract in which he defended the policies of his earlier patron, Lord Grey, in dealing with rebellious Irish subjects and reforming their government. Spenser eventually did receive his long-awaited government position when he was named sheriff of the Irish county of Cork in 1598. He had hardly taken control of that office when a local political revolt broke out. Spenser's home was burned, and he was forced to flee Cork with his family, which now included four young children.

In December, the provincial governor of Ireland sent Spenser as a messenger to Queen Elizabeth. He arrived in the capital at the end of 1598, weakened by the hardships of the preceding months. Spenser presented his messages to the queen, together with a personal statement of his position on the Irish situation. Soon after his arrival he became ill and died on January 16, 1599.

Works in Literary Context

Spenser was a product of the Renaissance (a word that means "rebirth"), an outburst of artistic and intellectual activity that began around the late fifteenth century, and greatly influenced by its ideas and ideals. One of the results of a confluence of money, reform, exploration, and a revived spirit to *carpe diem* ("seize the day") at this time was a cultural movement known as humanism. Humanism shifted the emphasis from the afterlife to *this* life. The focus was on man in the world, engaged in his civic duty and doing many things well, from poetry to warfare (the "Renaissance Man" ideal).

Humanism Spenser was one of the earliest English Renaissance poets to explore humanist ideas for everything they could contribute to English language and poetry. He was close with the greatest humanists of Elizabeth's court, including the courtier/poet Philip Sidney and the explorer Walter Raleigh. But Spenser was the first to attempt to pull various strands of humanist thought together into a single poem that would combine the best of the past with the controversies and challenges of the present, capturing it all in an epic structure that would assure its permanence for the future.

The Faerie Queene borrows from classical philosophy a vision of love and beauty that operates in parallel harmony on both the human and divine levels. It also shares the classical values of a disciplined analysis of morals and personal responsibility. What Spenser brings to *The Faerie Queene* from his own time is a strong Protestant sensibility, making all of his heroes embody good Calvinist or Anglican traits and his villains represent the lies of Roman Catholicism. *The Faerie Queene* is therefore a perfect example of the fusion of classical and Christian ideals that is central to Renaissance humanism.

Poetic Language *The Faerie Queene* and *The Shepheardes Calender* are interesting humanist texts because of their distinctive use of poetic language. Spenser was a student of classical and European languages, and his study was unusual for also including the history of the English language. It had long been assumed that literature written for the ages must be written in Latin, and that if English were to be used, it should certainly avoid unrefined regional dialects that only a limited number of people would understand.

Spenser believed that the English language and the structures of folksongs were capable of poetry on the highest level, and he took a nationalistic pride in the achievement of such medieval poets as Geoffrey Chaucer and John Gower. He felt that English (including its regional dialects) had the ability to dignify great poetry, just as great poetry can in turn dignify the evolving language. The unusual and archaic spellings of Spenser's works may seem awkward to modern readers, but in Spenser's day, they were a bold, scholarly, and even patriotic assertion of the poetic capabilities of English speech—especially when used for the most dignified classical form of them all, the epic.

Influence In his own time, Spenser exerted an influence on English culture that rivaled that of any poet in the language. Such contemporaries as Michael Drayton, Samuel Daniel, and Thomas Lodge were beginning to imitate *The Faerie Queene* and *The Shepheardes Calender*, and Spenser's influence continued to grow among writers of the seventeenth century such as Ben Jonson and John

LITERARY AND HISTORICAL CONTEMPORARIES

Spenser's famous contemporaries include:

John Webster (c. 1580–1625): An English dramatist, Webster was popular for his tragedies about bloody revenge stories. While plays such as *The White Devil* (1612) and *The Duchess of Malfi* (1613) are not nearly as sophisticated as Shakespeare's tragedies, they are often seen as comparable in their energy and poetic lyricism.

Tomás Luis de Victoria (c. 1548–1611): A Spanish composer who was quite important in his time in Spain. He was also a priest, and his religious music captures much of the evocative mysticism of the Spanish Catholic church.

William Shakespeare (1564–1616): An English playwright who is widely recognized as one of the greatest poets and dramatists in English literature. Shakespeare was enormously innovative, fusing existing stories and historical materials into plays that remain unsurpassed in the originality of their construction and their emotional impact. His plays include *Romeo and Juliet* (1595) and *Julius Caesar* (1599).

James I (1566–1625): James was the king of England from 1603 to 1625. He was the king of Scotland when Elizabeth I, the queen of England, died without an heir in 1603. His insistence on the "divine right of kings," or the right of the king to base his personal authority on the will of God, helped to bring about the English Civil War.

Tintoretto (1518–1594), pseudonym of Jacopo Robusti. Tintoretto was one of the most prolific and influential portrait artists in Renaissance Venice. He is famous for his innovations in perspective that give a new dynamism to his paintings of New Testament scenes, including *Crucifixion* (1565) shown from a side angle and *Last Supper* (1592–1594) seen from an upper-diagonal angle.

Milton. Even more striking, however, is the response of writers in the eighteenth century, during which time scores of poets produced literally hundreds of imitations, adaptations, and continuations of Spenser's works. No other English poet except Milton can claim a greater following among the writers of that period.

By the nineteenth century the flood of imitations in England had narrowed, but it had also grown deeper. Along with Chaucer, Shakespeare, and Milton, Spenser stood as one of the great English sources of inspiration for the Romantic age, providing in *The Faerie Queene* the quasi-medieval setting, the romance form, the structural patterns, the archaic language, and the mingling of the

COMMON HUMAN EXPERIENCE

Spenser made extensive use of allegory, the technique of using abstract ideas and values as named characters. Allegory is an ancient technique that is just as suitable for religious instruction as for biting satire. Here are some other works that use allegory:

A Tale of a Tub (1704), a prose parody by Jonathan Swift. This allegory satirizes the splits in the Christian Church by representing the main divisions as three brothers: Peter (Catholicism), Jack (Puritans), and Martin (the Anglicans/Lutherans). They fight over a coat that their father left them—symbolic of the Bible that God gives mankind—until it is left in tatters that none of them can use.

Everyman (c. late fifteenth century), a play by an unknown author. This is a "morality play," a form of allegorical drama authorized by the Catholic Church to teach Bible stories and moral lessons to common people. In this perfect example of the genre, the title character, Everyman, receives a summons from Death, but Good Deeds is the only one of his friends—the others include Fellowship, Kindred, Worldly Goods, Beauty—who can go along with him to the final meeting.

"Young Goodman Brown" (1835), a short story by Nathaniel Hawthorne. In this allegory, set in Puritan New England, a young man has his faith tested during a late-night walk in the woods.

natural with the supernatural that became the very stuff of Romanticism. Every one of the major Romantic poets was a serious reader of Spenser's works. In England, prose writers such as Sir Walter Scott, Charles Lamb, and George MacDonald were deeply touched by Spenser's work, and in America, where religious sympathies were perhaps closer to Spenser's own devout brand of Protestantism, Nathaniel Hawthorne and Herman Melville turned to *The Faerie Queene* for its moral allegory.

Works in Critical Context

From the sixteenth century to the present day, Spenser's work has maintained a place of distinction in English literature. His masterpiece, *The Faerie Queene*, was very favorably received upon its publication and has remained popular ever since. While *The Shepheardes Calender* was also enthusiastically praised by early critics, its popularity waned by the twentieth century, and it is now considered a minor work. Nonetheless, Spenser's importance and his impact on the development of English poetry has been judged incalculable. While twenty-first-century critics generally agree with this judgment, much of the more recent criticism of his work has concentrated on its allegorical aspects and on Spenser's role as a stylistic innovator.

The Faerie Queene *The Faerie Queene* is a work that elicits strong reactions, both positive and negative. Its length and complexity have daunted many readers. Ben Jonson, who once remarked about *The Faerie Queene* that "Spencers stanzas pleased him not, nor the matter," nevertheless listed him among the great writers in the language. Francis Thompson has stated flatly that *The Faerie Queene* "is in truth a poem no man can read through save as duty, and in a series of arduous campaigns (so to speak)."

Other critics had more favorable reactions to *The Faerie Queene*. Most critics have focused on the lushness of the poem as its most admirable aspect. In 1910, Edward Dowden described the poem as "a labyrinth of beauty, a forest of old romance in which it is possible to lose oneself more irrecoverably amid the tangled luxury of loveliness than elsewhere in English poetry."

Responses to Literature

1. Write an essay in which you address these questions: What are the values of heroism seen in the knights of *The Faerie Queene*? How have they been modified from the medieval sources for a Renaissance audience?

2. Does *The Shepheards Calender* reflect humanist values, or is the pastoral too idealized and nostalgic a form to contain such progressive ideas? Answer in the form of a an essay.

3. How does structure reinforce meaning in the "Epithalamion"? How are the years, months, days, and hours represented in the form of the stanzas and in the form of the poem overall? Create a presentation with your conclusions.

4. Spenser used archaic and unusual spellings of words in his works to good effect. Can you think of a contemporary writer that plays with spelling, grammar, or form to the same effect? Research a writer that does this and find out why. Could they, like Spenser, be making a statement about language and speech? How so? Be specific in your analysis in your paper.

BIBLIOGRAPHY

Books

Berger, Harry, Jr., ed. *Spenser: A Collection of Critical Essays*. Englewood Cliffs, N.J.: Prentice Hall, 1968.

Bernard, John D. *Ceremonies of Innocence: Pastoralism in the Poetry of Edmund Spenser*. Cambridge: Cambridge University Press, 1989.

Bloom, Harold, Ed. *Modern Critical Views: Edmund Spenser*. New York: Chelsea House, 1986.

Bradshaw, Brendan, Andrew Hadfield, and Willy Maley, eds. *Representing Ireland: Literature and the Origins of Conflict, 1534–1660*. Cambridge: Cambridge University Press, 1993.

Cavanagh, Sheila T. *Wanton Eyes and Chaste Desires: Female Sexuality in "The Faerie Queene"*. Bloomington: Indiana University Press, 1994.

Frushell, Richard C., and Bernard J. Vondersmith, eds. *Contemporary Thought on Edmund Spenser*. Carbondale: Southern Illinois University Press, 1975.

Hamilton, A. C., ed. *Essential Articles for the Study of Edmund Spenser*. Hamden, Conn.: Archon, 1972.

Hamilton, Donald Cheney, W. F. Blissett, David A. Richardson, and William W. Barker, eds. *The Spenser Encyclopedia*. Toronto: University of Toronto Press, 1990.

Hieatt, A. Kent. *Short Time's Endless Monument: The Symbolism of the Numbers in Edmund Spenser's "Epithalamion."* New York: Columbia University Press, 1960.

Hume, Anthea. *Edmund Spenser: Protestant Poet*. Cambridge: Cambridge University Press, 1984.

Johnson, Lynn Staley. *"The Shepheardes Calender": An Introduction* . University Park: Pennsylvania State University Press, 1990.

Judson, Alexander C. *The Life of Edmund Spenser*. Baltimore: Johns Hopkins University Press, 1945.

Lewis, C. S. *The Allegory of Love*. Oxford: Clarendon, 1936.

Web Sites

Luminarium. "Edmund Spenser (1552–1599)." Retrieved March 26, 2008, from http://www.luminarium.org/renlit/spenser.htm

◈ Gertrude Stein

BORN: *1874, Pennsylvania*

DIED: *1946, France*

NATIONALITY: *American*

GENRE: *Poetry, drama, fiction, nonfiction*

MAJOR WORKS:

Three Lives (1909)

Tender Buttons (1914)

Geography and Plays (1922)

The Autobiography of Alice B. Toklas (1933)

The Mother of Us All (1947)

Overview

A controversial figure during her lifetime, Stein is now regarded as a major literary modernist and one of the most influential writers of the twentieth century. Working against the naturalistic conventions of nineteenth-century fiction, she developed an abstract manner of

Gertrude Stein   *Stein, Gertrude, 1942, photograph. AP Images.*

expression that was a counterpart in language to the work of the postimpressionists and cubists in the visual arts. Stein wrote prolifically in many genres, composing novels, poetry, plays, and literary portraits. Her radical approach to these forms was admired and emulated by other writers of her era and has served as a key inspiration for such postmodernist writers as the French New Novelists.

Works in Biographical and Historical Context

Childhood in California The youngest daughter of a wealthy Jewish family, Stein spent most of her childhood in Oakland, California. Biographers describe her mother as a weak, ineffectual woman and her father as an irrational tyrant; a few have inferred that this family situation is the origin of Stein's lifelong aversion to patriarchal cultural values. Lacking a satisfactory relationship with her parents, she grew very close to her brother Leo.

The Influence of William James When Leo went to Harvard in 1892, Stein enrolled in the all-female Harvard Annex—soon to become Radcliffe College— the following year. Radcliffe, and in particular her favorite professor there, the psychologist William James, proved a decisive influence on her intellectual development. Many of James's teachings, including his theories of perception and personality types, would inspire her own theories of literary aesthetics.

LITERARY AND HISTORICAL CONTEMPORARIES

Stein's famous contemporaries include:

Ernest Hemingway (1899–1961): American expatriate writer who prompted Stein to remark upon the "Lost Generation."

Pablo Picasso (1881–1973): Famous Spanish artist responsible for cubism and a good friend of Stein.

Alfred Stieglitz (1864–1946): One of the first to make photography a respectable art form, Stieglitz is also famous for his marriage to artist Georgia O'Keeffe.

Guillaume Apollinaire (1880–1918): French writer and friend of Stein; one of the founders of the surrealist movement.

William James (1842–1910): Brother of novelist Henry James; famous American philosopher, psychologist, and doctor; mentor to Gertrude Stein.

Decision to Pursue Psychology With James's encouragement, Stein decided to become a psychologist and began medical studies at Johns Hopkins University as part of her training. In 1902, however, after several years of study, she grew disaffected with medicine and left the university without completing her degree. In the months that followed, Stein devoted herself to the study of literary classics. Inspired by her reading, particularly the works of Gustave Flaubert and Henry James, she began to write her first novels.

Violating Formal Conventions: The Modernist Movement In 1903, after travels in Europe and Africa, Stein and Leo settled in Paris, where they began to collect work by the new modernist painters and became personally acquainted with many of them, including Paul Cézanne, Henri Matisse, and Pablo Picasso. The Steins's apartment became a salon where numerous artists and literary figures, such as Guillaume Apollinaire, Marie Laurencin, and Max Jacob, met regularly. Stein particularly enjoyed the company of Picasso, who in 1906 painted a portrait of her that would become one of his best-known works, and she greatly admired his artistic style, as well as that of such other painters as Cézanne and Juan Gris, who experimented in their works with ways of conveying a more profound and truthful vision of reality than that allowed by the naturalistic techniques of the nineteenth century. This revolution in the visual arts encouraged Stein to formulate a literary aesthetic that would, similarly, violate existing formal conventions in order to allow the reader to experience language and ideas in provocative new ways.

A Lifelong Partnership with Alice B. Toklas Leo, however, who was not as enthusiastic about mod-

ernist painting, responded to his sister's work with scorn, causing her anxiety and self-doubt. Stein found a much more appreciative audience in her friend Alice B. Toklas, a young woman from California who was staying in Paris. In 1909 Stein invited Toklas to live with her, and the women developed a close and affectionate relationship that Stein referred to as a marriage; they remained together for the rest of their lives. Toklas was not only Stein's devoted friend and lover but a vital part of her literary work, helping her to prepare manuscripts and providing her with much-needed encouragement. Because commercial publishers initially rejected her work, Stein was forced to subsidize the printing of her first books. However, many of her distinguished and influential friends, most notably art patron Mabel Dodge, critic Carl Van Vechten, and poet Edith Sitwell, admired and promoted her writings, and by the outbreak of World War I she was regarded as a central figure in the modernist movement.

Volunteering in World War I Stein and Toklas were sent to Alsace to help provide relief for civilians during World War I. Prior to the war, Alsace was controlled by the German Empire but in 1918, after the Treaty of Versailles was signed, the region reverted to France. So dedicated to the volunteer effort were Stein and Toklas that they sold their last Matisse painting, the once controversial *Woman with a Hat*, in order to take the assignment. At the end of the war, the French recognized their services with the Médaille de la Réconnaissance Française.

Lectures at Oxford and Cambridge In 1925, after Stein's unsuccessful attempt to have Hogarth Press publish *The Making of Americans*, Edith Sitwell, realizing that Stein needed more publicity, arranged for Stein to lecture at Oxford and Cambridge in 1926. By 1930, Stein and Toklas were living a pleasantly domestic life of gardening, preserving, and baking cakes in their summer residence at Bilignin. Basket, the white poodle they had acquired in 1928, had made a dog lover of Stein. "I am I because my little dog knows me," she would write in 1935: one's identity was the self that others knew.

Death from Inoperable Cancer On July 19, 1946, Gertrude Stein collapsed on her way to stay at the country house of a friend. She was immediately rushed to the American Hospital at Neuilly, where she was diagnosed with inoperable cancer, but against medical discretion, she ordered the doctors to operate. On July 23 she made her will, then settled in to wait, heavily sedated and in considerable pain, for the operation, scheduled for July 27. She died on the operating table while still under anesthesia. "What is the answer?" she asked Toklas just before her death. Toklas remained silent. "In that case what is the question?" Stein added. Toklas herself died on March 7, 1967, and is buried next to Stein in Père-Lachaise Cemetery in Paris.

Works in Literary Context

In her innovative uses of language Stein has bridged the gap between conventionalism and experimentalism. A writer who strove to revitalize communication and rescue it from hackneyed clichés, she sought an instinctive use and understanding of language. For Stein language was the only tool capable of advancing social harmony and personal integrity and of negotiating the affiliation between thought and word. Stein's writings were influenced by the work of psychologist William James and Gustave Flaubert, the paintings of Paul Cézanne, and her relationship with her life partner, Alice B. Toklas.

Redefining Rhythm and Rhyme In his introduction to Gertrude Stein's *Four in America* (1947), Thornton Wilder observed:

> She knew that she was a difficult and an idiosyncratic author. She pursued her aims, however, with such conviction and intensity that occasionally she forgot that the results could be difficult to others. At such times the achievements she had made in writing, in "telling what she knew" (her most frequent formalization of the aim of writing) had to her the character of self-evident beauty and clarity. A friend, to whom she showed recently completed examples of her poetry, was frequently driven to reply sadly: "But you forget that I don't understand examples of your extreme styles." To this she would reply with a mixture of bewilderment, distress, and exasperation: "But what's the difficulty? Just read the words on the paper. They're in English. Just read them. Be simple and you'll understand these things."

Pieces such as the rhythmic and evocative "Susie Asado" (in *Geography and Plays*), Marjorie Perloff has pointed out, must be read as multiple interlocking and open-ended systems in which each element and system is as important as any other. In "Susie Asado" such systems include the sound patterns of flamenco-dance rhythms, the series of sensual suggestions in phrases such as "the wets," the pun on "sweet tea" or "slips slips hers," and the suggestion of a tea ceremony in a garden—"told tray," "sash," "rare bit of trees," and the Japanese sound of the name Susie Asado.

Stein's radical approach to literature was admired and emulated by other writers of her era, including Ernest Hemingway, Thornton Wilder, and Sherwood Anderson and has served as a key inspiration for such postmodernist writers as the French New Novelists and William H. Gass.

Works in Critical Context

Always a writer's writer, Stein's influence is still growing. The persistent activity of her artistic vision makes her a major writer of this century, comparable in the magnitude of her perception and achievement to her contemporaries Ezra Pound and James Joyce. During Stein's lifetime, however, her innovative writing, often the butt of reviewers' parodies, received little recognition or understanding.

The Autobiography of Alice B. Toklas With *The Autobiography of Alice B. Toklas*, Stein proved to her critics that she was capable of writing a relatively conventional, commercially successful work. While most reviewers were charmed by the autobiography's wit and engaging conversational style, not all were pleased. A group of Stein's friends from the art world, including Tristan Tzara and Henri Matisse, published "Testimony against Gertrude Stein," in which they condemned the *Autobiography* as a shallow, distorted portrayal of their lives and work. "Miss Stein understood nothing of what went on around her," protested painter Georges Braque. Stein nevertheless followed the popular success of the *Autobiography* with other memoirs.

Stanzas in Meditation "It came to Gertrude Stein," critic Donald Sutherland points out, that "after all grammar and rhetoric are in themselves actualizations of ideas." In *Stanzas in Meditation*, he adds, "Stein solved the problem of keeping ideas in their primary life, that is of making them events in a subjective continuum of writing … about ideas about writing." Sutherland places the poem with Pound's *Cantos* and T. S. Eliot's *Four Quartets* in the "tradition of the long, rambling, discursive poem whose interest and energy are primarily in the movement of the poet's mind writing."

Responses to Literature

1. Read the poem "Susie Asado." Can you find evidence of Japanese influence? Provide examples.
2. Why do you think most of Stein's plays are called "landscape plays"?

3. Using your library and/or the Internet, research the cubist and surrealist art movements. What are the main characteristics of each? Do you think Stein's early work reflects more of a cubist style or a surrealist style? Why?

4. *The Autobiography of Alice B. Toklas* is essentially Stein's own autobiography, written from the point of view of her partner. How does she describe herself as a character in her own memoir? Why do you think she chose to write the book from the point of view of Toklas instead of herself?

BIBLIOGRAPHY

Books

De Koven, Marianne. *A Different Language: Gertrude Stein's Experimental Writing*. Madison: University of Wisconsin Press, 1983.

Haas, Robert Bartlett, and Donald Clifford Gallup, comps. *A Catalogue of the Published and Unpublished Writings of Gertrude Stein*. New Haven, Conn.: Yale University Press, 1941.

Hoffman, Michael. *The Development of Abstractionism in the Writings of Gertrude Stein*. Philadelphia: University of Pennsylvania Press, 1965.

Luhan, Mabel Dodge. *European Experiences*. Volume 2 of *Intimate Memories*. New York: Harcourt, Brace, 1935.

Sutherland, Donald. *Gertrude Stein: A Biography of Her Work*. New Haven, Conn.: Yale University Press, 1951.

Toklas, Alice B. *What Is Remembered*. New York: Holt, Rinehart & Winston, 1964.

Periodicals

Gass, William H. "Gertrude Stein: Her Escape from Protective Language." *Accent* 18 (Autumn 1958): 233–44.

Perloff, Marjorie. "Poetry as Word-System: The Art of Gertrude Stein." *American Poetry Review* 8 (September/October 1979): 33–43.

Williams, William Carlos. "The Work of Gertrude Stein." *Pagany* 1 (Winter 1930).

Stendhal

BORN: *1783, Grenoble, France*

DIED: *1842, Paris, France*

NATIONALITY: *French*

GENRE: *Nonfiction, fiction*

MAJOR WORKS:

On Love (1822)

Armance (1827)

The Red and the Black (1830)

Stendhal   *Imagno / Getty Images*

Overview

Among the four most important novelists of nineteenth-century France, Stendhal is noteworthy for the intensity of conscience and feeling in his characters and for beginning his publication of fictional works later in life than did Honoré de Balzac, Gustave Flaubert, and Émile Zola. These two facts may have a common cause. Stendhal was usually preoccupied with self-image, and as a result he was by turns timid or brazen, sensitive or cynical, evasive or forthright, never sure of how he was being perceived by others. These aspects of his personality appear in the portraits of his heroes and in his narrative technique, but they may also account for his waiting until age forty-four to publish his first novel. Having filled hundreds of pages in his diaries, and with nonfiction works already in print, he finally had the confidence to risk public scrutiny of a totally creative work. His sense of the craft of fiction developed quickly after the appearance of his novel *Armance* (1827), and his later novels have an important place in the development of literary realism. Stendhal's techniques of handling point of view and psychological portraiture are distinctive and have been much admired by critics and writers alike.

Works in Biographical and Historical Context

A Turbulent Childhood and the Death of His Mother Stendhal was born Marie-Henri Beyle on

January 23, 1783, in Grenoble to Joseph-Chérubin Beyle, a lawyer, and his wife, Caroline-Adélaide-Henriette. He was the first child in the family to survive, a previous Marie-Henri having died a few days after birth the year before. Later siblings included Pauline, to whom the young Stendhal was very close, and Zénaide, for whom he professed dislike. Letters written to Pauline after Stendhal had left Grenoble at age sixteen are an important part of his collected correspondence. His mother died in 1790, when he was seven. Thanks to reminiscences in Stendhal's autobiographical works, much is known about his childhood memories. In a famous passage from *Vie de Henry Brulard*, he claims that, before his mother's death, he loved her ardently and desired to cover her body with kisses. In a contrast that has provoked much Freudian criticism, Stendhal never had a good relationship with his father, whom he described as authoritarian, hypocritically conventional, and bourgeois.

French Revolution, Paris, and the Napoleonic Wars During the years of the French Revolution (1789–1799), Stendhal, captivated by rhetoric of liberation from tyranny, followed the events enthusiastically. Though the revolution, aiming as it did at the overthrow of the monarchy and the establishment of a more democratic political system (it succeeded in the former and failed quite thoroughly in the latter), spent the greater part of its energy in Paris, it extended far enough into the countryside for Stendhal's father's royalist sentiments to earn him several months of incarceration. The newly created public school in Grenoble, l'École centrale (Central School), afforded Stendhal much interaction with peers (he undertook a duel using pistols with one schoolmate), and the opportunity to excel at mathematics, which he saw as his ticket out of Grenoble. Indeed, in November of 1799 he arrived in Paris, where he was supposed to sit for the entrance exam given by l'École polytechnique. He did not take the exam, however, and instead benefited from the patronage of a powerful cousin, Pierre Daru, who obtained for him a position as clerk in a government office.

Stendhal longed to write plays and become the Molière of his time, but for the present he was being paid to write official letters for Daru's signature. A few months later Daru sent him, commissioned as a second lieutenant, across the Saint Bernard pass into northern Italy, where Napoléon Bonaparte's Italian campaign was in progress. Having read voraciously during his childhood, Stendhal identified with the heroes of romances by Ludovico Ariosto and Torquato Tasso as he endured the perils and rigors of a soldier's lot on the way to Milan. He was enchanted by the solder's life, and the vivid memories of this experience would find their place in the composition of *The Charterhouse of Parma* nearly forty years later.

Accusations of Plagiarism and the Start of a Literary Career In 1814, Stendhal's first book appeared, bearing the unwieldy title *The Life of Haydn, in a Series of Letters written at Vienna, followed by the Life of Mozart, with Observations on Metastasio, and on the present State of Music in France and Italy, 1817*, and fancifully attributed to a pseudonymous Louis-Alexandre-César Bombet. Sales were less than brisk, and three hundred unsold copies were republished in 1817 with a new binding and a much shorter title, by which the work is known today: *Lives of Haydn, Mozart, and Metastasio*. The pseudonym was all the more appropriate in that Stendhal's book had borrowed to the point of plagiarism from other sources, principally from Giuseppe Carpani's *Le Haydine* (1812). Carpani discovered the theft and complained in the French press, but the matter was never taken seriously. Comparison of Stendhal's text with Carpani's reveals much translation and adaptation but also considerable originality in style, scope, and critical judgment. Having subsidized the printing himself, Stendhal lost money on the venture but found his calling.

French Romanticism From 1821 to 1830, Stendhal lived in Paris, frequenting the salons of Marie-Joseph, Marquis de Lafayette, Destutt de Tracy, Cabanis, Etienne Delécluze, and others. He interacted with the major figures of the Restoration—the return to the throne of the House of Bourbon accompanying Napoléon's fall from power—particularly those with a liberal orientation, and acquired the reputation of being a witty (and sometimes irritating) conversationalist. His friendship with Prosper Mérimée, who published a portrait of Stendhal titled *H. B.* (1850), dates from these years. He met other Romantic writers in the salons and contributed to their movement a pamphlet, *Racine and Shakespeare*, first published in 1823, then revised and enlarged in 1825.

Because of his attachment to the liberal ideals of the Enlightenment, Stendhal stood apart from the early French Romantics, who had a nostalgia for the traditional values of legitimate monarchy and church, which had been stigmatized and even outlawed during the turbulent revolutionary and Napoleonic years. Indeed, the 1823 version of his pamphlet does not seem to have attracted wide attention. But French Romanticism was already in the process of becoming more liberal, as it contended against the reestablished French establishment's condemnation of the movement. The 1825 version of *Racine and Shakespeare* enjoyed a good measure of success and influence, including a favorable review in the liberal *Globe* in London, which had been founded only the year before. Stendhal would later parlay this minor success into further critical publications and, ultimately, the novel *The Red and the Black* (1830), for which he is best known.

An Unrecognized Masterpiece The arrival of *The Red and the Black* on the literary scene of Paris, however, went largely unheeded. Stendhal himself wrote with some resignation that he published for "the Happy Few," although later authors (such as Honoré de Balzac were

LITERARY AND HISTORICAL CONTEMPORARIES

Stendhal's famous contemporaries include:

Washington Irving (1773–1859): An American author most famous for his stories "Rip Van Winkle" and "The Legend of Sleepy Hollow."

Charles Lamb (1775–1834): An English essayist also responsible for making Shakespeare accessible to children in his book *Tales from Shakespeare*.

Charles Nodier (1780–1844): A French author who wrote during the same period as Stendhal but whose work involved gothic themes, including vampires.

Benoit Fourneyron (1802–1867): The French engineer who designed the first usable water turbine, a device that captures energy from moving water.

William Fox Talbot (1800–1877): An English inventor, and a pioneer of the photographic process.

Charles Darwin (1809–1882): An English naturalist responsible for defining and defending his theory of natural selection as a mechanism for evolution.

outraged by the tepidity of the reception of this and other works), and he took up a post as consul to the papal state of Civitavecchia in 1931. For the next ten years, he held this post, publishing a wide variety of fiction and non-fiction texts, until an apoplectic fit forced him—in 1841—to request leave to recover in Paris. The following year, another such fit struck him as he was walking down the street, and he died at the age of seventy-eight in his Paris apartment. Publishing his first novel only at the age of forty-four, and unheralded in his lifetime, Stendhal has since been recognized as one of the greatest literary figures France—indeed, the world—has ever produced.

Works in Literary Context

Stendhal's fiction is marked primarily by its emphasis on "realism." Unlike the wild narratives of novels such as *Don Quixote*, Stendhal's fiction tries to represent the world as it is, catching both the small and large details of his characters' lives in order to paint them as realistically as possible. As literature would continue to develop over the next century and, indeed, to this day, the tendency to represent fictional worlds realistically has continued. Novelists as divergent in subject and theme as Mark Twain and Toni Morrison have written in the realist tradition for which Stendhal was at least partially responsible.

Realism Like most of his previous works, *The Red and the Black* relied in part on borrowed material and sprang from the account of a crime that Stendhal had read in the *Journal of Criminal Cases*. A blacksmith's son

named Antoine Berthet had been sentenced to death after shooting a woman—with whom he may have had a romantic history—in a church during Mass. Stendhal's Julien Sorel differs from the real-life Berthet in important ways, but their stories have similar outlines. Given that Stendhal works from actual accounts of real-world events, it is no wonder that this novel, like much of his work, emphasizes "realism," a technique in which an author tries to portray his characters and worlds as realistically as possible—as opposed to fantasy literature, such as science fiction, in which considerations of "the way things really are" is minimal.

Stendhal's narrator touts his realist aesthetic in some direct statements in *The Red and the Black*, the most famous of which defines the novel as a mere reflector of reality: "Why, sir, a novel is a mirror that is carried along a highway." In other interventions as well, the narrator pretends to apologize for elements of the story that might in some way be objectionable, but that must be reported because they are part of the story's declared historical reality. Such protestations of "reality," which accompanied the emergence of the novel as a distinct genre, may call attention to the artifice that underlies the invented narration, but do so without compromising fictional illusion—an important development in the history of literature. The importance of realism in the novel is further emphasized by Stendhal's subtitle at the beginning of book one, "Chronicle of 1830," despite the absence in the work of any mention of the crucial revolution of 1830 and the end of the Bourbon regime in France.

Works in Critical Context

During his lifetime Stendhal's works enjoyed much less popular success than those of contemporaries whose work has not endured, but his works were well known to the cultured elite. Consequently he had a certain reputation in Paris salons but did not derive a substantial income from his writing. Stendhal reflected that it was less desirable to have a wide following among his contemporaries than to appeal to readers in 1880 or 1935, and curiously, his choice of dates proved somewhat prophetic. Zola, in an essay first published in 1880, discussed Stendhal as one of his precursors (along with Balzac and Flaubert), and in 1882 an article by the novelist Paul Bourget, along with the influence of Hippolyte Taine's continuing enthusiasm, consolidated Stendhal's reputation in the French literary canon. By 1935 a growing critical industry of "Stendhaliens" had published a wealth of texts on and by their author. In his own time, however, Stendhal had to rely on work as a journalist, a specialist in military supply, and as French consul abroad to supplement income from publications and his father's estate.

Armance In part to distract himself from dejection after the end of a love affair, Stendhal wrote his first novel, *Armance*, in 1827. Stendhal took the premise of his novel from another author's book. Henri de Latouche had published an anonymous novel, *Olivier*, in 1826; this in turn was based on an unpublished story of the same title by Claire de Durfort, Duchesse de Duras. The reading public and Stendhal's friends, however, had a largely negative reaction to *Armance*, and the eight hundred to one thousand copies of the first printing found so few buyers that in 1828 the remainders were rebound and announced as a second edition. Indeed, despite his prodigious output, Stendhal frequently misjudged the appeal of his work to the reading public. Although he often picked scandalous and timely subjects, plucked from gossip circles, he could never quite make a lasting connection with critics of his time. Perhaps this was due, to the novel's gender-bending literary trickery, on which some recent criticism has focused. Maryline Lukacher, for instance, suggests that "in *Armance*, the title is deceitful and enigmatic, since it does not correspond to what it is supposed to describe. Under the cover of a woman's name, Stendhal is effectively telling the story of a man."

The Red and the Black   By far Stendhal's most popular and most frequently read work today is *The Red and the Black*. Responses to the novel have come from a wide variety of directions, including everything from psychoanalysis to philosophy of science, political science to theater studies. John Vignaux Smyth surveys this criticism, noting that "'Red' and 'Black' are often identified by critics with the poles of honesty and hypocrisy," and arguing, "The venerable comparison of fiction and truth to clothes and body takes us beyond fiction-as-representation to fiction as a relation between concealment and revelation." Meanwhile, writing from the perspective of psychoanalytically informed feminism, Julia Kristeva writes that Stendhal's women, here and elsewhere, "have the strength of destiny, the power of ancient divinities."

Responses to Literature

1. Read *The Red and the Black*. In your opinion, how successful is Stendhal's portrayal of "reality"—how real is his realism? In your response, consider his portrayal not only of physical details—descriptions of places and objects—but also his portrayal of human nature. Collect your thoughts in a short essay in which you analyze specific examples from the text to support your thinking.

2. Read, watch, or listen to a work that is "based on a true story." The examples from the "Common Human Experience" sidebar might provide some possibilities. Then, using the Internet and the library, research the real events upon which this story is based. In a short essay, discuss the choices the artist made in shaping the final text—which details were kept, and which were lost? What details seem to have been distorted for artistic effect?

3. Choose an event that is currently being talked about frequently in the news or in your circle of friends.

COMMON HUMAN EXPERIENCE

Stendhal looked to real-life events for the plots of his novels *The Red and the Black* and *Armance*. He was not the first artist to look to real life for inspiration for his fictional work. To a certain extent, the practice dates back to Homer's *Iliad*, which was believed by the ancient Greeks to have taken place in the distant past. The film, novel, and song that is "based on a true story" or "inspired by real events" is now a staple of the entertainment industry. Here are a few examples:

Catch a Fire (2006), a film directed by Philip Noyce. After Patrick Chamusso is falsely accused of an act of terrorism and after the South African government beats him and intimidates his wife, he vows revenge.

Into the Wild (1996), a speculative biography by Jon Krakauer. In this text, Krakauer recounts the short life of Christopher McCandless, who, at the age of twenty-two, left behind his affluent family to live off the land, though he wound up dying in the Alaskan wilderness only two years later.

"Hurricane" (1975), a song by Bob Dylan. In this song, Dylan describes the imprisonment of Rubin Carter, who had been framed by crooked cops and lawyers for multiple counts of murder.

Then, create a short story or film that is based on this event. Review Stendhal's fiction, particularly *Armance* and *The Red and the Black*, as examples if necessary.

4. In modern times, plagiarism of another author's work is not only frowned upon but a violation of copyright law. In the time of Shakespeare, however, the kind of plagiarism Stendhal committed was not considered a serious crime. Using the Internet and the library, research the history of plagiarism and its perceived inappropriateness. In a short essay, present an overview of this history and make an evaluation of what you've discovered. Do modern copyright laws provide suitable protection for writers? Do these laws restrict freedom of expression in some ways?

BIBLIOGRAPHY

Books

Adams, Robert M. *Stendhal: Notes on a Novelist*. New York: Noonday, 1959.

Alter, Robert. *A Lion for Love: A Critical Biography of Stendhal*. New York: Basic Books, 1979.

Auerbach, Erich. *Mimesis: The Representation of Reality in Western Literature*. Princeton, N.J.: Princeton University Press, 1953.

Brombert, Victor. *The Romantic Prison: The French Tradition.* Princeton, N.J.: Princeton University Press, 1978.

Erdman, David V., ed. *The Romantic Movement: A Selective and Critical Bibliography.* West Cornwall, Conn.: Locust Hill, 1988.

Josephson, Matthew. *Stendhal, or the Pursuit of Happiness.* Garden City, N.Y.: Doubleday, 1946.

May, Gita. *Stendhal and the Age of Napoleon.* New York: Columbia University Press, 1977.

Talbot, Emile. *Stendhal and Romantic Esthetics.* Lexington, Ky.: French Forum, 1985.

Wood, Michael. *Stendhal.* Ithaca, N.Y.: Cornell University Press, 1971.

◼ Laurence Sterne

BORN: *1713, Clonmel, Ireland*

DIED: *1768, London, England*

NATIONALITY: *Irish, British*

GENRE: *Fiction*

MAJOR WORKS:

The Life and Opinions of Tristram Shandy, Gentleman (1759–1767)

A Sentimental Journey through France and Italy (1768)

Laurence Sterne   Sterne, Laurence, painting. The Library of Congress.

Overview

Laurence Sterne's enduring reputation as an author rests upon two works, *The Life and Opinions of Tristram Shandy, Gentleman* (1760–1767) and *A Sentimental Journey through France and Italy* (1768), both of which were written and published during the last nine years of his life. During that time he was the recipient of excessive praise and the target of scathing criticism, heralded as a second François Rabelais, Miguel de Cervantes, or Jonathan Swift, but also condemned as an immoral hypocrite. Controversy continues about the precise nature of Sterne's contribution to English literature, but few scholars would deny him a place among the most important of eighteenth-century writers. It is Sterne more than any other author of that century whose work has seemed, time and again, of special interest to modern fiction writers as they experiment with realism, psychology, and "metacommentary" as the organizing principles of narrative.

Works in Biographical and Historical Context

Penniless Youth Sterne was born in Clonmel, in County Tipperary, Ireland. His English father made a poor living as a soldier in the army; his mother, a woman of Irish and French ancestry, was of a lower class than her husband, who apparently married her to settle a debt

with her father. Sterne spent much of his childhood moving with his family from one army barracks to another throughout England and Ireland, and his recollections of the military surroundings in which he grew up formed the basis for the characters of Uncle Toby and Corporal Trim in Tristram Shandy. In 1723, Sterne began attending a school in Halifax, Yorkshire, but when his father died penniless in 1731, he was forced to discontinue his education and live with relatives in Elvington, Yorkshire. Two years later his cousin arranged for him to enter Jesus College, Cambridge, as a sizar, which allowed Sterne to defray his university expenses by working as a servant to other students. At Cambridge he met John Hall-Stevenson, a rich and reckless young man whose home—Skelton Castle, renamed "Crazy Castle"—has figured prominently in the Sterne legend as the site of boisterous drinking parties and of a library containing a notable collection of curiosa and erotic literature.

Life in the Church After receiving his bachelor's degree from Cambridge, Sterne was influenced by his uncle Jacques, a prominent churchman active in Whig politics, to enter the clergy. Sterne's decision to follow an ecclesiastic career resulted from his need to earn a living rather than from any sense of spiritual calling. He was ordained a deacon in 1736, a priest in 1738, and afterward received various appointments in Yorkshire. In

1741 Sterne was married to Elizabeth Lumley, who is described by Sterne's biographers as an unpleasant woman whose instability—she eventually became insane—was not improved by her husband's incessant philandering. Despite his lack of faithfulness, however, Sterne was not the cruel husband and parent once portrayed by his detractors. After his marriage was effectively dissolved in separation, which was actually initiated by Elizabeth rather than Sterne, he continued to provide for his wife and daughter.

From the time of his marriage until the publication of *Tristram Shandy* in 1759, Sterne lived for the most part the life of an average Yorkshire clergyman, although some of his activities—his extramarital affairs, his frequenting the society of Hall-Stevenson's "Demoniacs" at Crazy Castle, his lawful but self-serving acquisition of his parishioners' property, and his casual attitude toward the theological doctrines of his church—would by subsequent generations be considered extraordinary conduct, however common it was in Sterne's time. Prior to the composition of his masterpiece, Sterne's only works were the sermons in which he preached an abstract rather than specifically Christian morality, articles of political propaganda written at the instigation of his uncle Jacques, and *A Political Romance* (1759), a satirical allegory concerned with local church politics that indicates some of the humor and narrative flair of Sterne's major work.

Literary Celebrity Sterne was forty-six when the initial volumes of *Tristram Shandy* were published, and his fictional alter-ego Tristram vowed to produce two additional volumes each year for the remainder of his life. Although the novel received mixed reviews, readers of the time elevated both the book and its author to a phenomenal status of celebrity. A short while after the publication of *Tristram Shandy*, Sterne happened to be in London and found himself the center of a following that included aristocrats, members of fashionable society, and leading figures in the arts. His lively, amusing manner made him well liked, and his attendance at social affairs was eagerly sought. However, upon the discovery that the author of *Tristram Shandy* was a clergyman, Sterne was attacked in the English press, which complained that the slyly erotic and scatological humor of Sterne's novel was unacceptable coming from a man of the cloth. Nevertheless, with the appearance of subsequent volumes of his novel, Sterne retained much of his popularity, not only in England but throughout the rest of Europe as well. The social successes of London were repeated when Sterne visited Paris in 1762. A second visit to continental Europe in 1765 served as the material for *A Sentimental Journey*, a work which in its extreme subjectivity, emotionalism, and narrative verve is as striking a contrast to the literary travelogue as *Tristram Shandy* is to the realistic novel. During his remaining years, Sterne continued to compose installments of *Tristram Shandy* and wrote *The Journal to Eliza* (1904), a self-conscious record of his

LITERARY AND HISTORICAL CONTEMPORARIES

Sterne's famous contemporaries include:

Voltaire (1694–1778): Born François-Marie Arouet, but better known by his pen name, Voltaire was one of the leading writers of the French Enlightenment. His thoughts on civil liberties, freedom of religion, and the ills of society were to prove highly influential on the leaders of both the French and American revolutions.

George Washington (1732–1799): The first president of the United States, Washington led the Continental Army during the American Revolution and is often described as the Father of His Country.

Frederick II of Prussia (1712–1786): Dubbed Frederick the Great for his spectacular military victories during the Seven Years' War, Frederick began the ascendancy of Prussia as a major power in Europe.

Adam Smith (1723–1790): Smith's views on economics, expressed in his book *The Wealth of Nations*, published in 1776, have formed the foundation of modern economic theory. His ideas on competition and self-interest promoting a healthy economy have long been used to defend free trade and capitalism.

Robert Burns (1759–1796): A writer known as "Scotland's favourite son," Burns's poetry was written in Scots dialect as often as in English. He was both a cultural icon and inspiration to later Romantic poets and liberal thinkers.

Mary Wollstonecraft (1759–1797): British philosopher and feminist, her *A Vindication of the Rights of Women* argued that women were not naturally inferior to men, as was widely believed at the time.

romance with a woman named Eliza Draper. Having suffered poor health since his youth, Sterne died of tuberculosis in London a few weeks after the publication of *A Sentimental Journey*.

Works in Literary Context

The Black Sheep of Eighteenth Century Literature *Tristram Shandy* is an unusual work by the literary standards of any period, but it particularly stands out in the century that saw the birth and early development of the realistic novel. While such novels as Daniel Defoe's *Moll Flanders*, Samuel Richardson's *Pamela*, and Henry Fielding's *Tom Jones* display their authors' attempts to make prose fiction a means for depicting contemporary life, Sterne demonstrates in *Tristram Shandy* aspirations of an entirely different kind. His characters, although profoundly human, are also profoundly odd and do not have the significant connections with their society held by

COMMON HUMAN EXPERIENCE

The bildungsroman traces the growth and development of a single character, often from youth to old age. *Tristram Shandy* is just one classic bildungsroman story; here are some others.

> *Pamela* (1740), a novel by Samuel Richardson. The first epistolary novel—that is, a novel told through a series of letters—this tale follows a young maid who resists her master's advances until he agrees to marry her. The success of the book led to many more such epistolary tales throughout the eighteenth and nineteenth centuries.
>
> *Tom Jones* (1749), by Henry Fielding. After writing two parodies of *Pamela*, Fielding tried his hand at novel-writing (at the time a new form of storytelling); the resulting tale, which follows a boy in his growth to a successful young man, stands as one of the classics of eighteenth-century literature.
>
> *The Catcher in the Rye* (1951), a novel by J. D. Salinger. This controversial tale of teenage discontent is an account by Holden Caulfield of life following his expulsion from a prep school at the age of sixteen.
>
> *Into the Wild* (1996), a nonfiction work by Jon Krakauer. This book is an ultimately tragic account of a free-spirited, nature-loving young man who leaves his life and family behind in search of his own identity.
>
> *Harry Potter and the Sorcerer's Stone* (2001), a film by Chris Columbus. Based on the first book of the best-selling Harry Potter series of novels by J. K. Rowling, this introductory tale follows young Harry as he begins his adventures at Hogwarts School of Witchcraft and Wizardry.

characters in the great realistic novels of the time; his style is one of cultivated spontaneity and unpredictability, a series of digressions as opposed to the progressive movement of events common in the works of Sterne's contemporaries; and, perhaps most conspicuously, his narrator is concerned with relating his "Life and Opinions" rather than the more usual "Life and Adventures" of the eighteenth-century bildungsroman (coming-of-age tale), making the novel largely a plotless discourse on an encyclopedic array of subjects.

Unsentimental Journey Sterne's other major work, *A Sentimental Journey*, is a nonfiction memoir that conveys much the same sensibility as the fictional *Tristram Shandy*. An account of Sterne's travels in France and Italy, this memoir has as its central concern the subjective side of the author's experiences rather than the objective rendering of people and places, which is the more usual concern of the travel writer. V. S. Pritchett has written

that "Sterne displays the egotist's universe: life is a personal dream," an observation that is illustrated by the minute and self-conscious attention that Sterne pays to his own feelings in *A Sentimental Journey*. Sterne's preoccupation with feelings, especially those of tender pathos, led to his establishing the word "sentiment" as it is presently understood, giving connotations of heightened, somewhat artificial emotion to a term which previously had denoted "thought" and "moral reflection." The deliberate courting and elaborate description of feeling in *A Sentimental Journey* also appears in Sterne's letters and his *Journal to Eliza*, provoking a major controversy in criticism of Sterne—the sincerity or pretense of both his personal writings and those written for a reading audience. As the issue of sincerity by its nature is restricted to the realm of individual opinion, critics have tended to praise or condemn Sterne to the extent that they believe in the truth of the feelings he describes. Modern critics have generally treated the question of Sterne's sincerity as a more subtle and complex matter than had been previously realized, attributing to him a facility for taking an ironic view of his most intense feelings or, as in Ernest Nevin Dilworth's *The Unsentimental Journey of Lawrence Sterne*, finding in his work a satirical mockery of sentiment.

Works in Critical Context

Perhaps the most important factor contributing to the controversies surrounding Sterne's work is his provocative and persuasive humor. Some critics have seen this quality of Sterne's writing as an end in itself, a viewpoint represented by Wilbur L. Cross, who contends that Sterne "was a humorist pure and simple, and nothing else." Other critics, including those of the English Romantic movement and most modern commentators, perceive more profound motives underlying these works, with a number of recent studies contending that Sterne's humor derives from an acute awareness of the ultimate evil and suffering of human existence and that each farcical antic is an allusion to a grim truth. Whether or not it is justified to place Sterne in the philosophical company of modernists who blend comedy and despair in their works, critics are now largely in agreement that Sterne is an exceptional case of an eighteenth-century writer whose works are particularly sympathetic with the concerns and temperament of twentieth-century readers.

The Life and Opinions of Tristram Shandy, Gentleman *Tristram Shandy*'s uniqueness brought about its wide success during the 1760s, and the novel's universal appeal has enabled the work to overcome the disparagement of such important eighteenth-century authors as Samuel Johnson—whose comment on Sterne's novel was that "nothing odd will do long"—and to survive the outright loathing of such nineteenth-century figures as William Makepeace Thackeray.

William Kenrick wrote of the work and the author in 1759, "His characters are striking and singular, his observations shrewd and pertinent; and, making a few exceptions, his humour is easy and genuine." By contrast, author Horace Walpole, writing in 1760, called the book "a very insipid and tedious performance" and stated, "It makes one smile two or three times at the beginning, but in recompense makes one yawn for two hours." Critic Edmund Burke pointed out one defining aspect of the novel that has been the subject of much critical discussion over the centuries: "The author perpetually digresses; or rather having no determined end in view, he runs from object to object, as they happen to strike a very lively and very irregular imagination. These digressions so frequently repeated, instead of relieving the reader, become at length tiresome."

As additional volumes of the ongoing work were published, more critics echoed the sentiment of Burke. Owen Ruffhead, reviewing the third and fourth volumes in 1761—and who, like many at the time, assumed Tristram Shandy to be the actual author of the work—directed his criticisms directly at the author: "We must tax you with what you will dread above the most terrible of all imputations—nothing less than *dullness*. Yes, indeed, Mr. Tristram, you are dull, *very dull.* . . . Your characters are no longer striking and singular. . . . The novelty and extravagance of your manner pleased at first; but Discretion, Shandy, would have taught you, that a continued affectation of extravagance, soon becomes insipid." Despite this critical backlash, Sterne's most famous work remained the subject of favorable scholarship throughout the nineteenth century, with prominent figures such as Samuel Taylor Coleridge and William Hazlitt complimenting many elements of the books.

Influence Unlike many authors whose works are discussed in relative isolation from their lives, Sterne is closely identified with his narrator, Tristram Shandy. Especially in the eighteenth and nineteenth centuries, Sterne was often judged by the narrator's opinions and liberties of taste; inverting this approach, an appraisal of Sterne's work became inseparable from an appraisal of his life, either to demonstrate a reprehensible similarity between the two or a paradoxical contrast. The issue of the often salacious humor in *Tristram Shandy* pervaded Victorian commentary, both positive and negative, on Sterne's work. In the twentieth century, critics have emphasized the remarkable likenesses between the narrative techniques in *Tristram Shandy* and the formal experimentation of modern literature, particularly in Sterne's unorthodox punctuation, his use of nonverbal devices like drawings, his disregard for sequence, and his self-conscious dwelling on his manner of composition. Despite the evidence presented by John Ferriar and others that Sterne borrowed heavily and blatantly from a number of sources, including Robert Burton's *Anatomy of Melancholy* and Rabelais's *Gargantua and Pantagruel*, few critics have questioned the success with which he adapted these borrowings to his own purposes and transformed old materials into one of the most original and important works in literature.

Responses to Literature

1. Many critics have argued that the method of storytelling in *Tristram Shandy* is more akin to current novels rather than those of the eighteenth century. Do you think this is true? Pick two to three recent experimental novels and compare their format and narrative strategies with that of *Tristram Shandy*.

2. Describe Sterne's interest in travel and unusual settings, customs, and people. Contrast this to other eighteenth-century writers, such as Jonathan Swift or Voltaire, who utilized unusual settings and people in their stories. How do the writers' works differ?

3. In 2005, filmmaker Michael Winterbottom directed the film *Tristram Shandy: A Cock and Bull Story*, but remarked that Sterne's story was "utterly unfilmable." Watch Winterbottom's film and try to decipher the problems he faced in adapting the novel to film. Where does he succeed and where does he fail? Come up with a strategy of how you would have adapted the film, including ideas for dialogue, scenes, and actors and actresses you would cast.

4. Do you feel that the digressive action in *Tristram Shandy* dominates the story, or is there an overarching plot that the digressions ultimately serve? In your opinion, is an overarching plot a defining characteristic of a novel? Why or why not?

BIBLIOGRAPHY

Books

Cash, Arthur H. *Laurence Sterne: The Early and Middle Years*. London: Methuen, 1975.

———. *Laurence Sterne: The Later Years*. London: Methuen, 1986.

———, and John M. Stedmond, eds. *The Winged Skull: Papers from the Laurence Sterne Bicentenary Conference*. Kent, Ohio: Kent State University Press, 1971.

Hartley, Lodwick. *Laurence Sterne: An Annotated Bibliography, 1965–1977*. Boston: G. K. Hall, 1978.

Moglen, Helene. *The Philosophical Irony of Laurence Sterne*. Gainesville: University Presses of Florida, 1975.

New, Melvyn. *Laurence Sterne as Satirist: A Reading of* Tristam Shandy. Gainesville: University of Florida Press, 1969.

Stedmond, John M. *The Comic Art of Laurence Sterne: Convention and Innovation in* Tristam Shandy *and* A Sentimental Journey. Toronto: University of Toronto Press, 1967.

◈ Robert Louis Stevenson

BORN: *1850, Edinburgh, Scotland*

DIED: *1894, Vailima, Samoa*

NATIONALITY: *British*

GENRE: *Fiction, nonfiction*

MAJOR WORKS:

New Arabian Nights (1882)

Treasure Island (1883)

Strange Case of Dr. Jekyll and Mr. Hyde (1886)

Kidnapped (1886)

In the South Seas (1896)

Overview

The life of Robert Louis Stevenson was regarded by his public, his friends, and his biographers to be as thrilling as the adventures in the stories he wrote. Stevenson began his career primarily as an essayist and travel writer, though he soon moved on to short fiction, and after the publication of *Treasure Island* in 1883, the novel was his preferred form. He wrote memorable poetry and forgettable plays, but it was short fiction, particularly his famous *Strange Case of Dr. Jekyll and Mr. Hyde* (1886), that gained him a large adult readership.

Robert Louis Stevenson *Hulton Archive / Getty Images*

Works in Biographical and Historical Context

A Sickly Childhood in Edinburgh Robert Louis Stevenson was born to Thomas and Margaret Isabella Balfour Stevenson in Edinburgh on November 13, 1850. From birth he was sickly, and throughout much of his childhood he was attended by his faithful nurse, Alison Cunningham, known as Cummy in the family circle. She told him morbid stories, read aloud to him Victorian penny-serial novels, Bible stories, and the Psalms, and drilled the catechism into him—all with his parents' approval. Robert's father Thomas Stevenson was quite a storyteller himself, and his wife doted on their only child, sitting in admiration while her precocious son expounded on religious doctrine. Stevenson later reacted against the morbidity of his religious education and to the stiffness of his family's middle-class values, but that rebellion would come only after he entered Edinburgh University.

An Indifferent Student Sets Out to Write In November 1867 Stevenson entered Edinburgh University, where he pursued his studies indifferently until 1872. Instead of concentrating on academic work, he busied himself in learning how to write, imitating the styles of William Hazlitt, Sir Thomas Browne, Daniel Defoe, Charles Lamp, and Michel de Montaigne. By the time he was twenty-one, he had contributed several papers to the short-lived *Edinburgh University Magazine*, the best of which was a fanciful bit of fluff entitled "The Philosophy of Umbrellas." Edinburgh University was a place for him to play the truant more than the student. His only consistent course of study seemed to have been of bohemia: Stevenson adopted a wide-brimmed hat, a cravat, and a boy's coat that earned him the nickname of Velvet Jacket, while he indulged a taste for haunting the byways of Old Town and becoming acquainted with its denizens.

On a trip to a French artists' colony in July 1876 with his cousin Bob, Stevenson met Fanny Van de Grift Osbourne, a married woman, an American, and ten years Stevenson's senior. The two were taken with one another, and Osbourne said she would be getting a divorce from her husband.

Impetuous Transatlantic Pursuit of a Married Woman In August 1879, Stevenson received a cablegram from Fanny Osbourne, who by that time had rejoined her husband in California. With the impetuosity of one of his own fictional characters, Stevenson set off for America to find her. On August 18, he landed, sick, nearly penniless, in New York. He was most likely suffering from tuberculosis (the disease was commonly called "consumption" at the time, and it was often misdiagnosed), which was incurable. From there he took an overland train journey in miserable conditions to California, where he nearly died. After meeting with Fanny

Osbourne in Monterey, and no doubt depressed at the uncertainty of her divorce, he went camping in the Santa Lucia mountains, where he lay sick for two nights until two frontiersmen found him and nursed him back to health. Still unwell, Stevenson moved to Monterey in December 1879 and thence to San Francisco, where he was ever near to death, continually fighting off his illness (people with tuberculosis often had periods of relative wellness interspersed with bouts of sickness). When Stevenson had left Scotland so abruptly, this had temporarily estranged him from his parents. They were also upset about his relationship with a married woman. However, hearing of their son's dire circumstances, they cabled him enough money to save him from poverty. Fanny Osbourne obtained her divorce from her husband, and she and Stevenson were married on May 19, 1880, in San Francisco.

Tuberculosis, Travel, and Writing While in Bed

In the next seven years, 1880 to 1887, Stevenson did not flourish as far as his health was concerned, but his literary output was prodigious. Writing was one of the few activities he could do while confined to bed because of hemorrhaging lungs (a common tuberculosis symptom). During this period, he wrote some of his most enduring fiction, notably *Treasure Island* (1883), *Kidnapped* (1886), *Strange Case of Dr. Jekyll and Mr. Hyde* (1886), and *The Black Arrow* (1888). He was also busy writing essays and collaborating on plays with W. E. Henley, the poet, essayist, and editor who championed Stevenson in London literary circles and who became the model for Long John Silver in *Treasure Island*.

This was also a period of much traveling. His and Fanny's various temporary residences in England, Switzerland, and southern France had more to do with his probable tuberculosis than with his love for travel. The main accepted treatment for tuberculosis at the time was the seeking of "healthy air," although doctors disagreed about what made air healthy. Switzerland was a popular destination for tuberculosis patients because of its clear mountain air. It was at Braemar in Scotland that *Treasure Island* was begun, sparked by a map that Stevenson had drawn for the entertainment of his twelve-year-old stepson Lloyd Osbourne. Stevenson had quickly imagined a pirate adventure story to accompany the drawing, and a friend arranged for it to be serialized in the boys' magazine *Young Folks*, where it appeared from October 1881 to January 1882. By the end of the 1880s, it had become one of the most popular and widely read books of the period.

Bound for the South Seas

In 1888, Stevenson made a drastic decision. In a letter to his friend Baxter in May of 1888, he wrote that he would be taking a South Seas cruise, one that he expected to heal him emotionally as well as physically: "I have found a yacht, and we are going the full pitch for seven months. If I cannot get my health back . . . 'tis madness; but of course, there is the

hope, and I will play big." Sea air was also considered beneficial to people suffering from tuberculosis.

South Pacific Journey and a Home in Samoa

The Stevenson party—including Stevenson, his wife, his stepson, and his mother—chartered the yacht *Casco* and sailed southwest from San Francisco to the Marquesas Islands, the Paumotus, and the Society Islands, and thence northward from Tahiti to the Hawaiian Islands by December of 1888. They camped awhile in Honolulu, giving Stevenson time to visit the Molokai leper settlement and to finish his novel *The Master of Ballantrae* (1889). In June 1889 they set out southwest from Honolulu for the Gilbert Islands aboard the schooner *Equator*. From there in December 1889 the Stevensons traveled to the island of Upolu in Samoa. By that time Stevenson realized that he was too ill to return to Scotland, despite his friends' urgings and his own homesickness; each time that he ventured far from the equator he fell sick. In October of 1890, the Stevenson party returned to Samoa to settle, after a third cruise that had taken them to Australia, the Gilberts, the Marshalls, and some of the more remote islands in the South Seas. The

COMMON HUMAN EXPERIENCE

Stevenson's later novels and stories examine moral dilemmas presented in an atmosphere imbued with mystery and horror. They include certain recurring themes, such as those of the divided self and the nature of evil. Here are some other works that deal with the theme of the divided self:

The Invisible Man (1897), a novel by H. G. Wells. This novel centers around a scientist who discovers a formula for invisibility but becomes mentally unstable as he copes with the problems of his condition while attempting to become visible again.

Seize the Day (1956), a novella by Saul Bellow. This novella chronicles a day in the life of Tommy Wilhelm, born Wilky Adler, a character who embodies the notion of the divided self.

Psycho (1960), a film directed by Alfred Hitchcock. This suspense/horror film explores the moral dimensions of crime and murder.

Samoan islands had been claimed by Great Britain, Germany, and the United States, by this time, and Stevenson developed a lively disdain for their colonial presences—in many cases taking much more the part of the Samoans, whom he saw as unjustly governed in slapdash fashion by slovenly rulers.

Death at the Height of His Power While he lived in the Pacific, Stevenson kept up his usual impressive literary output, but in the last two years of his life his letters to his friends in Great Britain increasingly revealed a longing for Scotland and the frustration he felt at the thought of never seeing his homeland again. To S. R. Crockett he wrote, "I shall never see Auld Reekie. I shall never set my foot again upon the heather. Here I am until I die, and here will I be buried. The word is out and the doom written." It may have been this preoccupation with Scotland and its history that made *Weir of Hermiston* so powerful a tale. With its theme of filial rebellion, and its evocation of Scotland's topography, language, and legends, it is a masterly fragment and the most Scottish of all his works. *Records of a Family of Engineers*, a biographical work that recounts his grandfather's engineering feats, reveals, too, that Stevenson was trying to find a bridge back to his own family and finally coming to terms with his earlier rejection of the engineering profession. In *Records of a Family of Engineers* he depicts his grandfather as a scientist-artist, linking his own growing objectivity in his style of writing to the technical yet imaginative work of his forebears. Increasingly Stevenson's art embraced more of the everyday world and drew on his experiences in the South Seas for its strength.

When he died of a stroke on December 3, 1894, in his house at Vailima, Samoa, he was at the height of his creative powers.

Works in Literary Context

In "A Penny Plain and Two-pence Coloured" (1884), Stevenson recounts how the seeds of his own craft were sown in childhood when he purchased Skelt's Juvenile Drama—a toy set of uncolored or crudely colored cardboard characters (hence the title of Stevenson's essay) who were the principal actors in a usually melodramatic adventure. Stevenson maintained that his art, his life, and his mode of creation were all in some part derived from the highly exaggerated and romantic world he had inherited from Skelt. Indeed, he saw himself as the literary descendant of British Romantic author Sir Walter Scott. The best storytelling, he felt, had the ability to whisk readers away from themselves and their circumstances.

Daydreams and Nightmares, but Without Escapism Although much of Stevenson's fiction was aimed at entertainment, his later novels and stories cannot be easily categorized as escapist. In one sense, *Strange Case of Dr. Jekyll and Mr. Hyde* can be taken as a satire of the times in which a respectable and educated man is forced so to repress his animal nature as to turn it into an uncontrollably violent beast. Yet there is much in the tale that does not allow such an interpretation to go unqualified. There is a wildness in Hyde that does not really lend itself to possible accommodations to a moral world, even one more liberal and permissive than that of the 1880s. Furthermore, as it progresses the story seems preoccupied less with social and moral alternatives than with the inevitable progress into vice. Part of the appeal of the tale is, as the title suggests, its strangeness. It has its own obsessive logic and momentum that sweep the reader along. Thus, though various morals can be drawn from it (warnings against intellectual pride, hypocrisy, and indifference to the power of the evil within), the continuing attraction of *Strange Case of Dr. Jekyll and Mr. Hyde* is perhaps the exact reverse of that of *Treasure Island*: One is an almost perfect literary rendition of a child's daydream of endless possibilities, the other of an adult's nightmare of disintegration. In both cases, whether gleefully or frightfully ensconced in the realm of the fantastic, Stevenson's work is if not precisely escapist then at least elsewhere-directed.

Works in Critical Context

Pinnacle to Nadir, and Back: A Treasure Not Just for Children At the time of his death in Samoa in 1894, Robert Louis Stevenson was regarded by many critics and a large reading public as the most important writer in the English-speaking world. "Surely another age will wonder over this curiosity of letters," wrote Sir Arthur Quiller-Couch at the time, "that for five years the needle of literary endeavor in Great Britain has quivered toward a little island in the South Pacific, as to its magnetic pole." Critics as demanding as Henry James and Gerard Manley Hopkins agreed on Stevenson's importance. This idealized portrait was attacked in the 1920s and 1930s by modernist writers who labeled his prose as imitative and pretentious and who made much of Stevenson's college-day follies. In the 1950s and 1960s, however, his work was reconsidered and finally taken seriously by the academic community. Outside of academia, *Treasure Island* and *Strange Case of Dr. Jekyll and Mr. Hyde* continue to be widely read over a century after they were first published, and show promise of remaining popular for centuries to come. As such, they have influenced generations of writers, including Ernest Hemingway, who noted that Stevenson's *Treasure Island* was one of his favorite books as a child. In this vein, R. H. W. Dillard has remarked, "When future scholars manage to see past their blind spot concerning the influence of children's books on adult literature and come to look for (apart from the usual suspects) the sources of the best twentieth-century prose, they may well find to be more important than they currently imagine."

Responses to Literature

1. *Treasure Island* tops the list of children's classics, and many famous authors have noted that the book was one of their favorites in their youth. It has been adapted for film numerous times, and its characters are generally familiar even to those who have never read the book. Read *Treasure Island*, then write a paper examining whether or not the youth of today would find the story and the style as gripping as readers of the past. Why or why not?

2. Stevenson's life was given nearly as much attention as his writings. Do you think a writer's life should be a focus of the audience's attention, or should readers and critics look only at the words and stories instead? Have you found that learning about authors' lives adds to or takes away from your understanding and appreciation of their works?

3. Stevenson's Dr. Jekyll character has been used in many movies since the book was published. What is the attraction of this character? Is it simply an entertaining notion, or does Dr. Jekyll have an enduring appeal because his story tells us something deeper about our modern selves?

4. Many of Stevenson's writings chronicled his travels and personal adventures. Today, blogging is a widely used forum for this same kind of writing, and bloggers have the advantage of being able to publish their works instantly, often from faraway places. Does the immediacy of blogging add to or take away from this form of writing? Do blogs today have the same quality of writing and insight as the travel writings of authors like Stevenson?

BIBLIOGRAPHY

Books

Balfour, Graham. *The Life of Robert Louis Stevenson.* New York: Scribners, 1901.

Calder, Jenni. *RLS: A Life Study.* London: Hamilton, 1980.

Chesterton, G. K. *Robert Louis Stevenson.* London: Hodder & Stoughton, 1927.

Daiches, David. *Robert Louis Stevenson.* Norfolk, Conn.: New Directions, 1947.

Dillard, R. H. W. "Introduction," in *Treasure Island.* New York: Signet Classics, 1998.

Eigner, Edwin M. *Robert Louis Stevenson and Romantic Tradition.* Princeton, N.J.: Princeton University Press, 1966.

Ferguson, De Lancey, and Marshall Waingrow, eds. *R. L. S.: Stevenson's Letters to Charles Baxter.* New Haven, Conn.: Yale University Press, 1956.

Furnas, J. C. *Voyage to Windward: The Life of Robert Louis Stevenson.* New York: Sloane, 1951.

Hammerton, J.A., ed. *Stevensoniana.* Edinburgh: Grant, 1910.

Kiely, Robert. *Robert Louis Stevenson and the Fiction of Adventure.* Cambridge, Mass.: Harvard University Press, 1965.

Prideaux, W. F. *A Bibliography of the Works of Robert Louis Stevenson*, revised edition, ed. and supp. Mrs. Luther S. Livingston. London: Hollings, 1918.

Smith, Janet Adam, ed. *Henry James and Robert Louis Stevenson: A Record of Friendship and Criticism.* London: Rupert Hart-Davis, 1948.

———. *Robert Louis Stevenson.* London: Duckworth, 1947.

Swearingen, Roger G. *The Prose Writings of Robert Louis Stevenson: A Guide.* Hamden, Conn.: Archon, 1980.

❖ Bram Stoker

BORN: *1847, Clontarf, Ireland*

DIED: *1912, London, England*

NATIONALITY: *Irish*

GENRE: *Fiction, Nonfiction*

MAJOR WORKS:
Dracula (1897)
The Lair of the White Worm (1911)

Overview

Irish writer Bram Stoker wrote several novels in different genres, but he is typically, if not exclusively, best known for his Gothic horror novel *Dracula* (1897). Stoker scholars often agree that with *Dracula*, Stoker not only created one of the most identifiable figures in popular culture but set the standards for all horror-mystery books that followed.

Bram Stoker   *Stoker, Bram, 1906, photograph. AP Images.*

Works in Biographical and Historical Context

Childhood in Ireland Marked by Illness   Bram Stoker was the third of seven children born to Abraham Stoker Sr. and Charlotte Thornley Stoker on or about November 8, 1847, in Clontarf, a village just north of Dublin Bay. In rural Ireland, this was the time of the potato famine in which around a million Irish people died of starvation and another million or more immigrated to the United States, Canada, and Australia to escape the horrors in their home country. The Stokers, however, were solidly middle class, with the father a civil servant, working as a chief secretary at Dublin Castle, the administrative center of the country. The mother was two decades younger than her husband and a rugged west-of-Ireland woman who had survived the cholera epidemic of 1832 in her native Sligo. She was a social activist who fought for the rights of impoverished women and was a formidable presence for her children. Charlotte was especially important to Bram, a sickly child who was often bedridden during his first seven years. While Bram enjoyed his father's well-stocked library, he also listened avidly to the gruesome tales his mother spun to entertain him—perhaps the seeds of his own future horror stories.

Civil Service Career and Work in the Theater Stoker began writing ghost stories in his childhood, predicting that someday he would be famous for his literary efforts. As a student at Trinity College he excelled in athletics and earned honors in mathematics. Upon graduation, he worked as a civil servant. For ten years in the Irish Civil Service, Stoker kept this unfulfilling position but one which left energy for his literary pursuits, including writing drama reviews for the *Dublin Mail*, a newspaper co-owned by his fellow horror writer, Sheridan Le Fanu. Stoker's drama criticism led him to meet with actor Henry Irving, whom he much admired. The friendship was mutual, and Irving hired Stoker as his personal manager as well as secretary, and even director of his Lyceum Theatre in London, positions he held until Irving's death in 1905. It was about this time, too, that he fell in love with his nineteen-year-old neighbor, the stunning Florence Balcombe. The two soon married, on December 4, 1878.

Inspiration for Dracula   While working at the theater, Stoker entertained a wide variety of people, including the Hungarian adventurer and professor Arminius Vambery, who would relate stories of vampires in Eastern Europe. Shortly after this meeting, Stoker began researching vampirism. He would later claim that *Dracula* came to him in a nightmare following a particularly indulgent crab dinner, but scholars also believe that Stoker likely knew of several existing vampire stories: "Carmilla" (1872) by Sheridan Le Fanu, "Le Horla" (1887) by Guy de Maupassant, and *The Vampyre* (1819), a novel by Dr. William Polidori. For four years, Stoker did extensive research and labored over his vampire novel. The book was published in 1897, and was a smashing success. Unlike any other vampire in popular artistic culture, Count Dracula became an international icon. Critics have speculated that the foreign, exotic villain with his evil, dirty habits played on British concerns about the growing number of Eastern European immigrants in England at the end of the nineteenth century. Many Jews of Eastern European origin fled persecution in their home countries in the late nineteenth and early twentieth centuries. They resettled in large numbers in England and the United States, where they often faced prejudice from those who feared their unfamiliar culture.

After Dracula   None of Stoker's later books matched the popularity of *Dracula*. His final novel, *The Lair of the White Worm* (1911), however, has received some critical attention in the decades since its publication, though not perhaps the kind of attention Stoker would have hoped for. As critics Daniel Farson and Philip Dematteis once noted, "Hilarious throughout, without one line of intentional humor, it could still become a cult classic." A campy 1988 film adaptation of the novel by Ken Russell seemed to bear out that prophecy.

Stoker was already seriously ill when writing *The Lair of the White Worm* and died on April 20, 1912.

Works in Literary Context

Little critical importance is attached to most of Stoker's work, but *Dracula* is considered a landmark of horror fiction. Some critics have even dubbed it the first true horror novel.

Influences Stoker was inspired by those he admired, and his realistic writing took influence from the period in which he lived, but many of his horror influences originated when he was young and very ill. His enforced bedridden state clearly made an impression on the course Stoker's life would take. During the long months and years of his illness, Stoker's mother would entertain her young son with macabre tales from her own youth, such as the story of the army sergeant who had apparently died of the plague. When the undertaker attempted to bury the man, he found the corpse's legs were too long for the coffin. Determined to chop the legs off at the knee to ease the fit, the undertaker took an axe to the legs, but at the first hit, the sergeant suddenly revived. Such tales informed much of Stoker's youth and his later horror works.

Epistolary Novel Stoker's most successful work, *Dracula*, was written during the literary period when the novel was not yet fully defined nor developed. Nineteenth-century authors were writing episodic works, publishing weekly chapters in the local newspapers (now known as serialized novels), and introducing the novel's story and characters by way of collections of letters or journal entries written by the characters themselves or a narrator. This form, called the epistolary form, was used by Aphra Behn, a woman now considered to be one of the first novelists of the seventeenth century. It was also characteristic of eighteenth-century writers such as publisher and author Samuel Richardson and French philosopher and writer Jean-Jacques Rousseau and was further refined by Wilkie Collins in the nineteenth century. *Dracula* is written this way—as an epistolary novel made up of journal entries, a ship's log, newspaper articles, letters, and phonograph recordings that tell of Count Dracula's attempt to settle in England and of his ultimate demise at the hands of a team of Englishmen. It is a style of writing that, with the Gothic elements of the novel, allowed Stoker to contrast his characters' actions with their own explanations of their acts.

Horror Fiction Horror fiction is distinguished from Gothic fiction or novels about supernatural occurrences by its aim: to frighten or unsettle the audience. American author Washington Irving's short story "The Legend of Sleepy Hollow" (1820) is an early example. It features a monstrous headless horseman that pursues the hero.

Monsters such as vampires, werewolves, and zombies all arise out of human fears of the blurring of boundaries between life and death, human and animal. Stoker subtly brought many other fears into action in *Dracula*. For example, some scholars have pointed that there is a suggestion of an interracial relationship between Mina and the Count, something that would have been taboo to Stoker's contemporaries. Later masters of horror fiction include Stephen King (author of *The Shining*, 1977, and many books) and Dean Koontz (author of *Demon Seed* and many other books).

Works in Critical Context

Although most of Stoker's novels were fairly well received when they appeared, they are dated by their stereotyped characters and romanticized Gothic plots and are rarely read today. Even the earliest reviews frequently decry the stiff characterization and tendency to melodrama that flaw Stoker's writing. Critics, however, have universally praised his beautifully precise descriptions of various settings. Stoker's short stories, while sharing the faults of his novels, have fared better with modern readers. Anthologists frequently include Stoker's stories in collections of horror fiction. "Dracula's Guest," originally intended as a prefatory chapter to *Dracula*, is one of the best known.

Dracula Initially, *Dracula* was interpreted as a straightforward horror novel, with early critics noting the "unnecessary number of hideous incidents" that could "shock and disgust" readers. One critic even advised keeping the novel away from children and nervous adults. Yet the Gothic horror novel was widely read and appreciated. A large part of the novel's initial success was due not to its Gothicism but to how, as Daniel Farson points out, "to the Victorian reader it must have seemed daringly modern." An early reviewer of *Dracula* in the *Spectator* even commented that "the up-to-dateness of the book—the phonograph diaries, typewriters, and so on—hardly fits in with the mediaeval methods which ultimately secure the victory for Count Dracula's foes."

Further criticism points to the sensual or sexual appeal of the work. In 1916, critic Dorothy Scarborough wrote that "Bram Stoker furnished us with several interesting specimens of supernatural life always tangled with other uncanny motives." In 1931, scholar Ernest Jones drew attention to the theory that these "other uncanny motives" involve repressed sexuality. And besides approaching the book from several angles—folkloric, political, feminist, medical, and religious—modern critics have continued to view *Dracula* from a Freudian psychosexual standpoint. Having fallen prey to Count Dracula, heroines Lucy and Mina change from pure and near-sexless to aggressively sensual. Were Stoker alive today, suggests Brian Murray, "the publicly prudish Stoker—who once wrote an essay calling for the censorship of works that exploit 'sex impulses'—would probably be shocked to read much of the recent criticism of *Dracula*."

Responses to Literature

1. Consider the differing roles of men and women in nineteenth-century England. How were women expected to behave in the company of men? What was expected of them socially as well? How were men expected to behave? Where do the men and women in *Dracula* break with convention? How does their behavior in the novel affect the plot and dialogue?

2. Using your library and the Internet, find out more about the pseudo-science of eugenics. Write a paper in which you explore whether Stoker was influenced by eugenics in his descriptions of various classes and races of people in *Dracula*.

3. Why is society fascinated with horror stories? In your mind, what is this fascination based on? Can you find a passage in *Dracula* that may have been particularly horrifying at the time, but to a contemporary audience, might really seem almost silly? What defines "horror" today? Name a horror writer today that is successful and discuss why that is so. What is his appeal?

BIBLIOGRAPHY

Books

Carter, Margaret L. *Dracula: The Vampire and the Critics*. Washington, D.C.: UPI Research Press, 1988.

Dictionary of Literary Biography, Gale, vol. 36: *British Novelists, 1890–1929: Modernists*, 1985, p. 247–60; vol. 70: *British Mystery Writers, 1860–1919*, 1988, p. 284–89.

Farson, Daniel. *The Man Who Wrote Dracula: A Biography of Bram Stoker*. New York: St. Martin's Press, 1975.

Jones, Ernest. *On the Nightmare*. New York: St. Martin's Press, 1976.

Scarborough, Dorothy. *The Supernatural in Modern English Fiction*. London: Kessinger Publishing, LLC, 1917.

Senf, Carol A. *The Critical Response to Bram Stoker*. Westport, Conn.: Greenwood Press, 1993.

Web sites

Librivox. Audio. *Dracula by Bram Stoker*. Retrieved February 14, 2008, from http://librivox.org/dracula–by–bram–stoker. Catalogued on May 10, 2006.

The Literature Network. *Bram Stoker*. Retrieved February 14, 2008, from http://www.online–literature.com/stoker.

McAlduff, P.S. *Bram Stoker*. Retrieved February 14, from http://www.geocities.com/psmcalduff.

▨ Tom Stoppard

BORN: *1937, Zlin, Czechoslovakia*

NATIONALITY: *English*

GENRE: *Drama*

MAJOR WORKS:

Rosencrantz and Guildenstern Are Dead (1966)

Tom Stoppard   *Stoppard, Tom, photograph.* © *by Jerry Bauer.*
Reproduced by permission.

Jumpers (1972)
Travesties (1974)
Shakespeare in Love (1998)
The Coast of Utopia (2002)

Overview

One of England's most important playwrights, Tom Stoppard has gained a wide international audience. His plays revolutionized modern theater with their uniquely comic combinations of verbal intricacy, complex structure, and philosophical themes.

Works in Biographical and Historical Context

Born into Conflict Thomas Straussler (Stoppard) was born on July 3, 1937, in Zlin, Czechoslovakia, to Eugene, a doctor, and Martha Straussler. In 1939, troops from Nazi Germany invaded the country; according to Nazi racial laws, there was "Jewish blood" in the family, so Stoppard's father was transferred to the island of Singapore in Southeast Asia in 1939, taking the family with him. When the Japanese invaded Singapore in 1942, the

women and children were taken to India. Dr. Straussler stayed behind as a British Army volunteer and was killed as a captive in a Japanese prison camp.

From School to Journalism In Darjeeling, India, Thomas attended an American boarding school. In 1945, his mother married Kenneth Stoppard, a British Army major, and both of her sons took his name. When the family moved to England, Stoppard continued his education at a preparatory school in Yorkshire until the age of seventeen, when he felt that he had had enough schooling. Stoppard became first a reporter and then a critic for the *Western Daily Press* of Bristol from 1954 to 1958. He left the *Daily Press* and worked as a reporter for the *Evening World*, also in Bristol, from 1958 to 1960. Stoppard then worked as a freelance reporter from 1960 to 1963. During these years, he experimented with writing short stories and short plays. In 1962 he moved to London in order to be closer to the center of the publishing and theatrical worlds in the United Kingdom.

Radio Plays Stoppard's first radio plays for the British Broadcasting Company (BBC) were aired in 1964, with two more following in 1965—the same year he met and married his first wife, nurse Josie Ingle. His first television play appeared the next year, as did his only novel and the stage play that established his reputation as a playwright, *Rosencrantz and Guildenstern Are Dead*. The play takes two minor characters from William Shakespeare's *Hamlet* and shows the world of the Danish prince from a different perspective. More than an oblique look at a dramatic classic, it is an examination of existentialist philosophy—the belief that human beings are both free and responsible for their actions and that this responsibility is the source of their feelings of dread and anguish—with protagonists who learn that they are to die and must accept their fate. The play earned Stoppard his first Tony Award in 1966.

Television Plays That same year, Stoppard produced *Tango*, based on a work by Slawomir Mrozek, followed by two more television plays in 1967. The year 1968 saw another television play and two short works for the theater. By 1970, after Stoppard returned to the BBC with two more radio plays, two more television plays, and another stage piece, he began to make connections in the world of alternative theater. He became acquainted with Ed Berman from New York City's off-off-Broadway, who was attempting to establish an alternative theater in London. Stoppard composed a single play for performance in 1971 at the Almost Free Theater, a feeble double bill in 1975, and *Night and Day*, which prompted lengthy discussion in 1978.

In 1972, the same year Stoppard met and married Miriam Stern, he presented *Jumpers*, his second major work, which begins with circus acts and evolves into religious and moral philosophy. As philosophical ideas began to eclipse characters in his drama, critics began to

LITERARY AND HISTORICAL CONTEMPORARIES

Stoppard's famous contemporaries include:

Vladimir Bukovsky (1942–): Russian author and activist. Bukovsky is most noted for being a former Soviet political dissident.

Václav Havel (1936–): Czech writer and dramatist who was the ninth and final president of Czechoslovakia and the first president of the Czech Republic.

Mick Jagger (1943–): An English rock musician who performs as the front man for one of the world's most successful bands, the Rolling Stones.

Peter O'Toole (1932–): An award-winning Irish actor often remembered for his iconic performance in *Lawrence of Arabia*.

Edward Albee (1928–): An American playwright associated with the theater of the absurd, which explores domestic frustration and anguish.

André Previn (1930–), a German-born American award-winning pianist, composer, and conductor.

get restless. While Stoppard was making a name for himself with intellectual debates over ethics, morality, censorship, and other modern problems, critics were shifting in their seats.

Major Stage Plays After a collaborative effort with Clive Exton two years later, Stoppard produced his third major work, *Travesties*. The play is based on the premise that Vladimir Lenin, James Joyce, and Tristan Tzara all lived in Zurich, Switzerland, during World War I. Stoppard illuminates the purpose and significance of art by fostering the interaction of the three men's theories: Lenin's Marxism, Joyce's modernism, and Tzara's Dadaism. *Travesties* won Stoppard his second Tony Award in 1976.

A year later, Stoppard presented *Every Good Boy Deserves Favour*, a tour de force premiered by the Royal Shakespeare Company and the hundred-piece London Symphony Orchestra conducted by André Previn at the Royal Festival Hall. Brought to the United States, it was presented at the Metropolitan Opera House in New York with an eighty-one-piece orchestra. Concerning a dissident in an Iron Curtain country who has been placed in a mental institution, the play's attack on the totalitarian state was the author's strongest political statement up to that time. He was named a commander of the British Empire that same year.

The year 1979 brought three more plays, and by 1982, Stoppard was delivering his fourth major work. *The Real Thing* won Stoppard another Tony Award in 1984, but again critical opinion was divided: Some

reviews touted Stoppard's continued combination of humor and complexity, while other critics, such as Robert Brustein, discounted the work as just "another clever exercise in the Mayfair mode, where all of the characters... share the same wit, artifice and ornamental diction."

Multiple Successes Throughout the 1980s and 1990s, Stoppard enjoyed a series of successes, including the Emmy Award–nominated television play *Squaring the Circle* (1984); the Academy Award–nominated screenplay *Brazil* (1985); and the Academy Award–winning screenplay *Shakespeare in Love*. He was knighted in 1997 and elevated to the Order of Merit in 2000. Also in 2000, Stoppard's play *The Real Thing* was performed in a limited engagement at the Albery Theatre, London, before opening on Broadway at the Ethel Barrymore Theatre. It won a Tony Award for Best Revival of a Play.

In 2006, Stoppard's significantly revised trilogy of plays, *The Coast of Utopia*, opened at its U.S. premiere in New York City. It is also heavily rumored that the successful playwright was on-site to assist with the dialogue in George Lucas's *Indiana Jones and the Last Crusade* (1989) and *Star Wars Episode III: Revenge of the Sith* (2005), as well as in Tim Burton's *Sleepy Hollow* (1999). On June 3, 2006, Stoppard's *Rock 'n' Roll* premiered at the Royal Court Theatre in London. As with Stoppard's former successes, the play received mixed reviews for its controversial treatment of anticommunist, leftist, and artistic dissent. The rock music-driven drama opened in February 2007 at Prague's National Theatre and in November 2007 at the Bernard B. Jacobs Theatre in New York, where it was scheduled to run until March 2008.

Works in Literary Context

Complexity Describing Stoppard's style, critic and scholar Enoch Brater notes in *Essays on Contemporary British Drama* how Stoppard presents "a funny play" in which he "makes coherent, in terms of theatre, a fairly complicated intellectual argument." Brater also adds, "That the argument is worth making, that it is constantly developing and sharpening its focus, and that it always seeks to engage an audience in a continuing dialogue, are the special characteristics of Stoppard's dramatic achievement. They are also the features which dignify and ultimately transform the comic tradition to which his work belongs." Brater has summarized the complexity of language, ideas, and technique as they are so skillfully combined with humor.

Entertainments "Writing entertainments," Stoppard told interviewer Mel Gussow, is what he considers he has been doing all along. Stoppard does, however, understand that his humor is complicated by intellectual ideas that sometimes displace the characters. Between fun plays like *The Real Inspector Hound* and "plays of ideas like *Jumpers*," he told Gussow, "the confusion arises because

I treat plays of ideas in just about the same knockabout way as I treat the entertainments." Still, he reasoned to *Washington Post* interviewer Joseph McLellan, "The stuff I write tends to work itself out in comedy terms most of the time."

Humor in Problematic Truth   Whatever the degree of comedy or seriousness in Stoppard's approach, scholar and critic Benedict Nightingale of the *New York Times* concludes that Stoppard is consistent in the themes he examines: "All along he's confronted dauntingly large subjects, all along he's asked dauntingly intricate questions about them, and all along he's sought to touch the laugh glands as well as the intellect." Because of the contrasting light tone and cerebral weightiness of his plays, however, others have made specific efforts to define Stoppard's thematic concerns as he presents them within his plays. His ideas encompass such concepts as "the nature of perception, art, illusion and reality, the relativity of meaning, and the problematic status of truth," scholar Anne Wright observes in a *Dictionary of Literary Biography* article, with "recurring themes includ[ing] chance, choice, freedom, identity, memory, time, and death." Stoppard, however, has offered a simpler interpretation. Speaking to Tom Prideaux of *Look*, the enigmatic playwright said, "One writes about human beings under stress—whether it is about losing one's trousers or being nailed to the cross."

Influences   Stoppard has been said to show—and sometimes admits to showing—influences from Henry James, James Joyce, and A. E. Housman, as well as absurdists such as Polish writer Václav Havel and Irish minimalist writer Samuel Beckett. Stoppard also takes inspiration from the works of existentialist philosophers, such as Albert Camus and Jean-Paul Sartre, primarily since existentialism is a fundamental part of the Theater of the Absurd. Because of Stoppard's unique and unmatched approach to blending such schools of thought and such wit with traditional theatrical conventions, the full measure of the impact Stoppard has had on others is yet to be seen.

Works in Critical Context

Against Classification   Because Stoppard's work demonstrates a union of the intellectual to convey ideas with the emotional to express dark humor, several critics have made efforts to classify his works as either philosophical or humorous. Stoppard, however, diplomatically discourages efforts at classification. As he told *Newsweek*'s Jack Kroll, "Theater is an event, not a text. I respond to spectacle. Ambushing the audience is what theater is all about."

A Serious Comic Writer   This "ambush," the way he shrewdly infuses his plays with sophisticated concepts, is what keeps the critics talking. As *Washington Post* writer Michael Billington described, Stoppard "can take

COMMON HUMAN EXPERIENCE

Stoppard is celebrated for his linguistically playful and experimental style. Other works known for their linguistic virtuosity include:

Endgame (1957), a play by Samuel Beckett. In this one-act play, the action is minimal and the dialogue is absurdly unique.

The Importance of Being Earnest (1895), a play by Oscar Wilde. In this comedy of manners, the dialogue is stark and explosive with irony, sarcasm, and social puns.

Lolita (1955), a novel by Vladimir Nabokov. Nabokov's novel is renowned for its wordplay and innovative form.

a complex idea, deck it out in fancy dress and send it skipping and gamboling in front of large numbers of people," for the playwright has "a matchless ability to weave into a serious debate boffo laughs and knockdown zingers." Stoppard scholar Joan Fitzpatrick Dean concurred, saying, "Like the best comic dramatists, his gift for language and physical comedy fuses with an active perception of the excesses, eccentricities, and foibles of man."

Critic Enoch Brater summarized the essence of Tom Stoppard, saying, "Stoppard is that peculiar anomaly—a serious comic writer born in an age of tragicomedy and a renewed interest in theatrical realism. Such deviation from dramatic norms . . . marks his original signature on the contemporary English stage," for his 'high comedy of ideas' is a refreshing exception to the rule." Among the plays that best demonstrate this is *Rosencrantz and Guildenstern Are Dead*.

Rosencrantz and Guildenstern Are Dead   "Stoppard's virtuosity was immediately apparent" in his first major dramatic work, *Rosencrantz and Guildenstern Are Dead*, *New York Times* critic Mel Gussow asserted. The play revisits Shakespeare's *Hamlet* through the eyes of the two players whose task of delivering Hamlet's death sentence prompts their own execution instead. Vaguely aware of the scheming at Elsinore and their own irrelevance to it, Rosencrantz and Guildenstern meander through the drama playing games of language and chance until they cease to exist. "In focusing on Shakespeare's minor characters Stoppard does not fill out their lives but rather extends their thinness," writer Anne Wright observed. By turning *Hamlet* "inside out" in this way, the play is "simultaneously frivolous in conception but dead serious in execution," Brater added, and it addresses issues of existentialism reminiscent of Samuel Beckett's drama *Waiting for Godot*. The result, Brater concluded, "is not only a relaxed view of *Hamlet*, but a new kind of comic writing halfway between parody and travesty."

Especially notable is the play's innovative use of language and Shakespeare's actual text. *Rosencrantz and Guildenstern Are Dead* interweaves references to Hamlet with actual lines of the bard's verse. Stoppard packs the drama with "intricate word plays, colliding contradictions and verbal and visual puns," describes Gussow. This "stylistic counterpoint of Shakespeare's poetry and rhetoric with the colloquial idiom of the linguistic games and music-hall patterns" proves very effective, Wright commented. "Stoppard's lines pant with inner panic," a *Time* reviewer noted, as the title characters, according to *Village Voice*'s Michael Smith, ultimately "talk themselves out of existence." The play became one of Stoppard's most popular and acclaimed works: Twenty years after its premiere, Gussow contended, it "remains an acrobatic display of linguistic pyrotechnics as well as a provocative existential comedy about life in limbo." Jack Kroll of *Newsweek* concluded that *Rosencrantz and Guildenstern* established "the characteristic Stoppard effect."

Responses to Literature

1. Stoppard's *The Coast of Utopia* features the character Mikhail Bakunin, a real-life anarchist in prerevolutionary Russia. Find out more about Bakunin's philosophy by reading his *God and the State*, an unfinished work penned around 1871.

2. Stoppard reimagines the action of *Hamlet* from the point of view of Rosencrantz and Guildenstern. Pick another character from Hamlet—perhaps Ophelia, Gertrude, Horatio, or Polonius. Imagine the story from their point of view. Write a narrative in the voice of the character you pick describing the action of the play.

3. Make a list of puns and word play in *Rosencrantz and Guildenstern Are Dead*. How do these elements contribute to character development? What can you tell about each character by the language, puns, and humor he displays?

BIBLIOGRAPHY

Books

Barnes, Clive. *50 Best Plays of the American Theatre*. New York: Crown Publishers, 1969.

Bock, Hedwig, and Albert Wertheim, eds. *Essays on Contemporary British Drama*. Munich: Hüber, 1981.

British Dramatists since World War II. Volume 13 of *Dictionary of Literary Biography*. Detroit: Gale, 1982.

Brustein, Robert. *The Third Theatre*. New York: Knopf, 1969.

Dean, Joan Fitzpatrick. *Tom Stoppard: Comedy as a Moral Matrix*. Columbia: University of Missouri Press, 1981.

Dictionary of Literary Biography Yearbook: 1985. Detroit: Gale, 1985.

Gussow, Mel. *Conversations with Stoppard*. London: Nick Hern, 1995.

Hunter, Jim. *Tom Stoppard: A Faber Critical Guide*. London: Faber & Faber, 2000.

Kelly, Katherine E. *The Cambridge Companion to Tom Stoppard*. New York: Cambridge University Press, 2001.

Periodicals

Billington, Michael and Joseph McLellan. *Washington Post* (May 11, 1969; June 25, 1969; July 9, 1969; August 29, 1978; November 26, 1978; January 12, 1984; May 23, 1985).

Gussow, Mel, and Benedict Nightingale. *New York Times* (November 27, 1994); (April 9, 1995): H5.

Kroll, Jack. *Newsweek* (April 3, 1995): 64–65; (February 8, 1999): 58.

Prideaux, Tom. *Look* (December 26, 1967); (February 9, 1968).

Smith, Michael. *Village Voice* (May 4, 1967); (October 26, 1967); (May 2, 1974).

Time (October 27, 1967); (August 9, 1968); (March 11, 1974); (May 6, 1974); (June 20, 1983); (August 24, 1992): 69; (July 19, 1993): 60.

Web sites

Levity.com. *Tom Stoppard (1937–)*. Retrieved February 14, 2008, from http://www.levity.com/corduroy/stoppard.htm.

Malaspina Great Books. *Modern Theatre: Tom Stoppard*. Retrieved February 14, 2008, from http://www.mala.bc.ca/~MCNEIL/stoppard.htm.

▨ Alfonsina Storni

BORN: *1892, Sala Capriasca, Switzerland*

DIED: *1938, Mar del Plata, Argentina*

NATIONALITY: *Argentine*

GENRE: *Poetry, nonfiction*

MAJOR WORKS:
The Disquietude of the Rosebush (1916)
Irremediably (1919)
Ocre (1925)
World of Seven Wells (1934)

Overview

Argentine author Alfonsina Storni is one of Latin America's most widely read poets. She gained early fame through the publication of her first books of poetry, family cafe and then as a seamstress with her mother and older sister throughout childhood and adolescence.

After her father's death in 1906, she began to work in a hat factory in Rosario to help make ends meet. Early on, she demonstrated her ability to engage in multiple activities while at the same time developing her literary and theatrical interests. At fifteen, she joined a traveling theater company and spent three years with them. In 1909 she entered a two-year teacher-training program in Coronda, ending her formal education in 1911 at nineteen years of age. She then took a teaching job at an elementary school in Rosario. Throughout most of her adult life, Storni continued to combine teaching and an active writing career.

Single Motherhood and Work Storni's life took a dramatic turn after her first year of full-time teaching. In Rosario, she became pregnant by a married man with high standing in the community. She made the move to Buenos Aires when she was expecting a child and, as an unmarried woman, needed to escape the reduced social and professional circles of the provinces where her condition as an unmarried mother would make a teaching position impossible. At the time, Argentina was becoming a modern nation and attracting thousands of European immigrants each year who were looking for a better life. Between 1851 and 1910, Buenos Aires' population expanded from 90,000 to 1.3 million people. The city became known as the "Paris of South America."

Her son, Alejandro Alfonso Storni, was born there in 1912. In Buenos Aires, she worked at office and factory jobs for three years while writing *The Disquietude of the Rosebush* (1916). Despite the financial hardships of these early years, Storni moved quickly into the writing world and as early as 1913 began to publish in the popular magazine *Faces and Masks*.

By 1920, Storni began to work as a regular contributor to the *Nation*, one of the two major newspapers of the period. Her articles concerned almost all areas of women's experience: working women and their occupations, the relationship of women to national and cultural traditions, the role of the church, single mothers, female poverty, migration to the city, and fashion. Many of her contributions were published under the pseudonym "Tao Lao." These pieces were often impressionistic observations with highly personalized judgments. In a kind of urban adaptation of the travelogue, they recorded vignettes of daily life in Buenos Aires in a chatty tone with frequent asides to the reader.

Alfonsina Storni (right)   *© Eduardo Longoni / Corbis*

partly through their explicitly confessional nature, but also because of her defiant posture regarding the status of women. Although primarily a lyric poet, she often revealed a quick turn of humor. Her dramatic suicide in 1938 added to her legendary status as a writer and public figure, and in subsequent decades both her poetry and her personal story have acquired almost mythic status.

Works in Biographical and Historical Context

An Early Multitasker Born in Sala Capriasca, Switzerland, on May 29, 1892, Storni was the daughter of Alfonso and Paula Martigoni Storni. Her father was a beer manufacturer. She immigrated at four years of age to the provinces of Argentina, first to San Juan, then to the province of Santa Fe, finally settling in Buenos Aires in 1912. In many ways, her personal history is symbolic of a new class of literary and professional women who emerged from modest beginnings and gained access to opportunities through the public education system in Argentina. In addition to her studies, she worked in the

Poetry Storni's lasting fame is as a poet, and she wrote and published poetry during this period. Much of her poetry reads like an inventory of the concerns of women, particularly nonconformist women, with its anger at male expectations, the seeming impossibility of equality in love, and the dissatisfaction at the traditional roles imposed on women. One of her most enduring types of poems is the pattern of a female persona addressing a male "tú" (you), often by a series of rhetorical questions.

LITERARY AND HISTORICAL CONTEMPORARIES

Storni's famous contemporaries include:

Horacio Quiroga (1878–1937): This Argentinian writer and friend of Storni influenced the "magical realism" literary trend that became popular in Latin America. His poetry collections include *Cuentos de amor, de locura, y de muerte* (1917).

J. Paul Getty (1892–1976): This American businessman founded the Getty Oil Company. He wrote a memoir, *My Life and Fortunes* (1963).

Margaret Sanger (1879–1966): This American activist for women's rights founded what eventually became Planned Parenthood.

J. R. R. Tolkien (1892–1973): This British writer is best known for the fantasy fiction novels *The Hobbit, or There and Back Again* (1937) and *The Lord of the Rings* (1954–1955) trilogy.

Gabriela Mistral (1889–1957): A Chilean poet and fellow feminist, Mistral is often linked to Storni because of their similar careers. Mistral won the Nobel Prize in Literature in 1945. Her poetry collections include *Desolación*.

This pattern, often verging on stereotype, engages a wide variety of readers in echoing many of the joys and frustrations of erotic love and sentimental attachments within family and social structures. Undoubtedly, the most celebrated poem of this nature is "You Want Me White" from *El dulce daño* (1918), in which a woman insolently responds to male demands for female purity.

After Storni dabbled in playwriting for some years, in 1934 she published *World of Seven Wells*, which marked a significant change in her poetry. On the formal level, she leaves behind meter and rhyme and develops another style based on often idiosyncratic rhythms. Changed too are the topics she treats. The world viewed here is primarily the universe of the body, and the close-up visual focus, along with the altered rhythms, distance this poetry from the autobiographical vein of her earlier poetry.

Diagnosed with Cancer In 1935, Storni was diagnosed with breast cancer and underwent surgery to have one breast removed. The next few years were marked by her struggle with cancer, a struggle that emerges in her poetry as a confrontation with the physicality of the world, a distancing from a personal focus. The illness and decline of the writer Horacio Quiroga, for whom Storni had felt great passion and affection, was a serious blow. Despite his fame as a writer, when Quiroga committed suicide in 1937, he was in such reduced economic circumstances that there were not enough funds for his burial.

As she became increasingly aware of her own mortality because of her cancer, Storni struggled to finish her most important works. Late in 1937, she turned in the manuscript of her last book (*Mask and Clover*) and in 1938 prepared an anthology of her poetry (*Antologia poetica*). In 1938, she was invited to Montevideo, Uruguay, to participate in a program with the Uruguayan poet Juana de Ibarbourou, and in late October of the same year, she made a trip to the seaside city of Mar del Plata. On October 25, 1938, she mailed to the major newspaper a farewell poem to her friends and readers, "I Am Going to Sleep." She then walked into the sea and drowned.

Works in Literary Context

Although Storni never consciously allied herself with any literary school, her early collections of poetry contain elements of Romanticism and reflect traces of the Hispanic modernist movement of Rubén Darío. Her early works focus on the themes of love, passion, and the suffering they often bring. In contrast, her last two collections marked the final stage in her poetic development and reflect the influence of the avant-garde movement, particularly that of Federico García Lorca, whom she described in "Retrato de García Lorca." Storni's break with traditional forms and the less subjective tone in her last two volumes can be seen because of her incorporation of techniques that had marked the poetry of the 1920s, especially with the ultraísta movement led by Jorge Luis Borges.

Sentiment Primarily autobiographical, Storni's early poetry revolves around lyrical and sentimental themes, portraying the misunderstood, rebellious poet standing alone against the world. Her first collection, *The Disquietude of the Rosebush*, reflects the restlessness and emotional conflict that persisted throughout her life. Storni later renounced this volume, and critics generally agree that it is her least significant work. Storni's next collections, *El dulce daño* (1918), *Irremediablemente* (1919), and *Languidez* (1920), express her disillusionment with love and her desire to renounce physical passion.

Much of the outrage and suffering evident in these verses resulted from her frustrations with contemporary stereotypes of women. In "You Want Me White," for example, she indicts the Spanish American male for wanting women to be pure. Storni strove to articulate the collective concerns of women in these collections and pleaded for a more balanced and intellectual relationship between the sexes. Her fifth collection, *Ocre* (1925), demonstrates her increasing maturity as a poet and exhibits a new conciseness of style. Relying more on metaphors instead of similes, she steps outside herself to observe life more analytically. In contrast to the bitter resentment of her early confessional verse, these more cerebral, cynical, and ironic poems demonstrate her increasingly caustic attitude toward men.

Alienation and Death The poems of *Mundo de siete pozos* (1934) depict a fragmented reality consisting of moods and dreams, surrealistic imagery, and abstract language. Abandoning the literary conventions of her previous collections, Storni used free verse to communicate her predominant themes, urban alienation and death, which she often associated with images of the sea. For *Mascarilla y trébol* (1938), published posthumously, she created a new, unrhymed verse form that she called the "anti-sonnet." Here, Storni completely abandoned the preoccupation with love and passion that had characterized her earlier collections and instead devoted herself wholly to the craft of poetry. Exceptionally abstract and obscure, these poems, according to Storni, were "the individual results of moments of near loss of consciousness." Combining images of the physical world, particularly the sea, with scenes from dreams, Storni expressed intense grief and explored the magical and metaphysical significance of such geometric forms as the circle.

Influence Storni and Uruguayan poet Delmira Agustini are the two major figures credited with changing the nature of female eroticism in poetry in Spanish. They influenced many female poets who worked in this genre in succeeding generations as well as other feminist poets in general.

Works in Critical Context

During her lifetime, Storni was one of the most prominent female poets in Latin America, yet her works remained controversial due to their feminist themes and open expression of female passion. While Storni is included among the ranks of leading Latin American women writers, her work stands out as the most courageously and openly critical of male-dominated society. Critical response to her body of poetry has developed through two distinct phases. Her early works were popular with the reading public, while receiving mixed critical response, due to her feminist stance. Her later works were met with waning popularity as well as harsh criticism for their experimental forms and obscure meanings. Critics in the late twentieth century viewed her later work, most notably *Mascarilla y trébol*, as her most mature and important contribution to Latin American literature.

The Disquietude of the Rosebush This collection established Storni as a new voice in Argentine culture. Shortly after publication, she became the first woman in the country to join a literary circle, from which she obtained critical comment and encouragement. Storni's unconventional views, however, along with her status as an unmarried mother, sometimes resulted in critical censure of her work. Irritated at her frank, often resentful attacks on female stereotypes and on those who propagated them, some of her contemporary critics attributed her feminist ideas to personal dissatisfaction and dismissed her arguments for parity between the sexes as merely the complaints of an unhappy woman. Later in her career, Storni herself renounced the book in an interview quoted in Sonia Jones's *Alfonsina Storni*: "My first book . . . today frankly embarrasses me. I would love to be

---

COMMON HUMAN EXPERIENCE

Storni's later poems deal extensively with imagery devoted to the sea in which she eventually drowned herself. In these poems, the sea is symbolically presented as an overwhelming natural force. Here are some other works that center around a preoccupation with the sea:

The Old Man and the Sea (1952), a novella by Ernest Hemingway. This short book tells the story of an old Cuban fisherman's fight with a huge marlin.

Moby-Dick (1851), a novel by Herman Melville. It is the story of one man's hunt for a legendary whale told by the pensive, wandering sailor Ishmael.

Farewell to the Sea (1987), poems by Reinaldo Arenas. In this collection, Arenas extensively describes the shores of a Cuban beach. Like Storni, Arenas wrote a letter to the public and committed suicide after finding himself in ill health.

Omeros (1990), an epic poem by Derek Walcott. Walcott retells the *Odyssey* but sets the epic in the Caribbean, on the island of Santa Lucia.

---

able to destroy every single copy of that book until there was not a single trace of it left."

World of Seven Wells After a trip to Europe in 1934, Storni published *World of Seven Wells*. In this, her sixth poetical work, Storni made a nearly total break from the subjective lyricism and inner conflict that characterizes most of her previous poetry. Centering instead on the external world, the free verse and traditional sonnets display Storni's increased attention to imagery. Several critics considered Storni's new cerebral, ironic tone as an indication of a growing despair and preoccupation with death. Citing the volume's proliferation of sea imagery, for example, Sidonia Carmen Rosenbaum noted in her *Modern Women Poets of Spanish America: The Precursors* that

> never a poetess of joy and laughter, [Storni] sinks still deeper into the bitter waters of sadness and hopelessness. . . . If in other books she spoke of the sea, it seemed to be in a somewhat casual manner. Not so here where the sea and the thought of finding peace in its icy, turbulent depths, become almost an obsession.

Responses to Literature

1. In a paper, discuss which type of setting Storni most effectively describes: small or large. Look to *Ocre* for examples.

2. In Storni's earlier works, she often negatively emphasizes sexual passion and love. Can you find evidence that her views on male-female relationships

are not always negative? Write an essay that outlines your findings.

3. Create a presentation that addresses the following questions: How did Storni's journalistic writings add to her poetry? How did they detract from it?

4. Make a list of descriptions of the sea that Storni uses in her later poems. What do you think the sea symbolizes for her? Discuss your conclusions in a small group.

BIBLIOGRAPHY

Books

Dauster, Frank. "Success and the Latin American Writer." In *Contemporary Women Authors of Latin America: Introductory Essays*, edited by Doris Meyer and Margarite Fernandez Olmos. New York: Brooklyn College Press, 1983.

Delgado, Josefina. *Alfonsina Storni: Una biografía esencial*. Buenos Aires: Planeta, 1990.

Imbert, Enrique Anderson. "1910–1925." In *Spanish American Literature*, translated by John B. Falconieri. Detroit: Wayne State University Press, 1963.

Jones, Sonia. *Alfonsina Storni*. Boston: Twayne, 1979.

Kirkpatrick, Gwen. "Alfonsina Storni as 'Tao Lao': Journalism's Roving Eye and Poetry's Confessional Eye." In *Reinterpreting the Spanish American Essay: Women Writers of the Nineteenth and Twentieth Centuries*, edited by Doris Meyer. Austin: University of Texas Press, 1995.

Phillips, Rachel. *Alfonsina Storni: From Poetess to Poet*. London: Tamesis, 1975.

Rosenbaum, Sidonia Carmen. *Modern Women Poets of Spanish America: The Precursors; Delmira Agustini, Gabriel Mistral, Alfonsina Storni, Juana de Ibarbourou*. New York: Hispanic Institute in the United States, 1945.

Sarlo, Beatriz. *Una modernidad periférica: Buenos Aires, 1920 y 1930*. Buenos Aires: Ediciones Nueva Visión, 1999.

Soto-Smith, Mark I. *El arte de Alfonsina Storni*. Bogotá, Colombia: Tercer Mundo, 1986.

▨ August Strindberg

BORN: *1849, Stockholm, Sweden*

DIED: *1912, Stockholm, Sweden*

NATIONALITY: *Swedish*

GENRE: *Drama, fiction, nonfiction*

MAJOR WORKS:

Master Olof (1881)

The Father (1887)

Miss Julie (1888)

Inferno (1897)

To Damascus (1898–1904)

August Strindberg *Hulton Archive / Getty Images*

Overview

August Strindberg is considered one of the most important Swedish writers of the modern era. His drama *Miss Julie* (1888) has proven to be a classic, and several of his later plays, such as *The Dream Play* (1907) and the trilogy *To Damascus* (1898–1904), are recognized as forerunners of expressionism and the theater of the absurd. His psychologically astute plays, exposing the hidden roots of human conflicts, strongly influenced twentieth-century European literature.

Works in Biographical and Historical Context

A Distressing Childhood in Stockholm Johan August Strindberg was born in Stockholm on January 22, 1849. His father was a steamship agent; his mother, Nora, had at one time been a waitress in a tavern and later became the housekeeper of her future husband. In his autobiographical novel *The Son of a Servant* (1886), Strindberg underlines the class difference between his parents as one source of the conflict in his nature and worldview. The Strindbergs were devout Christians, and their family life was patriarchal. As a boy Strindberg was unhappy. His mother died when he was thirteen, and less than a year later, his father married the children's governess—a woman thirty years younger than his father. Strindberg's lifelong mental anguish can be attributed in part to his unhappy childhood.

Failing Chemistry and Turning to the Stage

An average student, Strindberg graduated high school in 1867 and enrolled in the University of Uppsala to study medicine. He failed his qualifying examination in chemistry, and left academia without a degree. His interest turned to the theater, but here, too, he failed to qualify; after an unsuccessful acting audition, he started writing plays. He completed his first three in 1869, at the age of twenty. In the summer of 1872 Strindberg completed *Master Olof* (1881), the first of his many historical dramas and his first important literary work. It concerns the sixteenth-century religious reformer Olaus Petri, a disciple of Martin Luther who helped free the Church of Sweden from Rome's domination. He wrote several versions of the play, in prose and verse, before it was staged in Stockholm in 1881.

During his early career, Strindberg supported himself partly as a journalist and translator. In 1874, he found more permanent employment as an assistant librarian. In the spring of 1875 he met his future wife, Siri von Essen. She was married to a baron, but her husband had amorous interests outside his marriage. Strindberg encouraged her aspirations to a theatrical career, and the two fell in love. Siri divorced her husband amicably, debuted as an actress in 1877, and married Strindberg that December.

Controversy and Exile

Strindberg's breakthrough as a prose writer—and the breakthrough of realism in modern Swedish literature—came with *The Red Room* (1879), a collection of satirical short stories about bohemian life in Stockholm. The title comes from a room at the popular Berns Salonger restaurant, where a coterie of young artists gathered regularly. The book was an overnight success, and put its author in the limelight. He followed this up with *Old Stockholm* (1880), a popular history of daily life in the city.

Commissioned in 1881 to write a major cultural history of Sweden, Strindberg produced a thousand-page volume that concentrated on the life of the common people, rather than the kings whose exploits traditionally fill the pages of history books. Criticized by professional scholars, Strindberg responded by publishing a scathing attack on Sweden's social and political establishment, *The New Kingdom* (1882). The book gave Strindberg new and powerful enemies, and its negative reception was probably the catalyst for Strindberg's decision to leave Sweden, which both ruined his marriage and was extremely productive for his work: he published more than twenty volumes of writing in the ensuing six years.

Strindberg soon provoked further controversy with his story collection *Married* (1884). In this work's preface, Strindberg brings up the so-called woman question—a hotly debated issue among the European intelligentsia at the time—and presents a program for gender equality that seems progressive even to many contemporary readers. The story "Virtue's Reward," which starkly depicts the social repression of adolescent sexuality, led Swedish authorities to confiscate the books and charge the author with blasphemy. Strindberg returned to Sweden to stand trial; he spoke eloquently in his own defense and was acquitted of all charges.

Lifelike Art or Artlike Life?

Strindberg's views on women soon darkened considerably, however; the second volume of *Married* (1886) is more bitter and resentful. The theme of male-female relationships seen as a battle of the sexes also surfaces in many Strindberg dramas, including some of his most celebrated ones. During this period, Strindberg became increasingly preoccupied by new discoveries in psychology. He now wanted to construct psychological case studies for the stage. The style he adopted for this venture was that of naturalism. His first great drama of psychic combat was *The Father* (1887), and he found the material for it in his own marriage: he suspected Siri of being unfaithful and questioned the paternity of his children. He transformed this anguish into a taut drama in which an unscrupulous wife provokes her husband to doubt his fatherhood, and drives him to a mental and physical collapse. Strindberg's marriage deteriorated rapidly after he wrote *The Father*, and the play was a great success, gaining Strindberg general European recognition (and leading some to question art's role as a vampiric force in Strindberg's life). The following year, he relayed the story of his marriage in *The Confessions of a Fool* (1888). This autobiographical novel has been called one of the great love stories in Swedish literature, though it contains a ruthless and even hateful depiction of his wife.

Surprisingly, just as his marriage was growing brittle, Strindberg began writing one of his sunniest novels, *The People of Hemso* (1887), about a farmhand who seduces a widow and tries to persuade her to marry him and sign over the farm. The novel has become a Swedish classic and mandatory reading for Swedish high school students.

In the summer of 1888, Strindberg composed his best-known drama, *Miss Julie*. The story is simple. During a midsummer night's celebration, a high-strung young noblewoman is seduced by her father's good-looking, social-climbing butler. Afterward she kills herself out of shame and desperation. Strindberg, the "son of a servant," undoubtedly drew upon his own marriage to an aristocratic woman for the play's undercurrent of class struggle.

Berlin and Paris

Strindberg moved to Berlin in 1892, and found there a following of artists and writers, as well as directors eager to stage his plays. He met his second wife there, a twenty-one-year-old journalist named Frida Uhl. The marriage lasted a year and a half; their parting became the opening scene of his pivotal novel, *Inferno* (1897). Strindberg then turned his hopes

LITERARY AND HISTORICAL CONTEMPORARIES

Strindberg's famous contemporaries include:

Henrik Ibsen (1828–1906): A Norwegian playwright and, along with Strindberg, one of the founders of modern drama.

Mark Twain (1835–1910): An American novelist and humorist and the author of *The Adventures of Huckleberry Finn*.

Émile Zola (1840–1902): A French novelist and playwright and a leading proponent of literary naturalism.

William James (1842–1910): An American psychologist and philosopher and the author of the influential textbook *Principles of Psychology*.

George Bernard Shaw (1856–1950): An Irish-English playwright and lifelong socialist who was awarded the Nobel Prize in Literature in 1925.

Selma Lagerlof (1858–1940): A Swedish novelist who in 1909 became the first woman awarded the Nobel Prize in Literature.

psychopathic king who proposed to Queen Elizabeth of England and was rejected.

Revolutions in Word and World Strindberg had previously attempted to open his own theater, without success. In 1907, he succeeded, founding the Intimate Theatre with a young producer named August Falk. For this stage, Strindberg wrote a series of "chamber plays"—plays composed like chamber music, with theme and development rather than plot and character. The chamber plays are usually set in a house that quickly assumes metaphorical significance: its respectable exterior hides the lies and deceits in the rooms within. The chamber plays culminate in the extraordinary *Ghost Sonata* (1908), with a peculiar blend of occult, fantastic, and surreal elements.

Alongside these plays that emphasize theme over plot, Strindberg also wrote a scathing, thinly fictionalized portrayal of several of his contemporaries titled *Black Banners* (1907). In 1910, inspired in part by the failed Russian Revolution of 1905, in which socialist workers and members of the military unsuccessfully sought to dismantle the Russian monarchy, he penned a series of polemics in a left-wing newspaper. These pieces, highly critical of the monarchy and the military, stirred up a lively national debate, later called the "Strindberg feud." Strindberg died of stomach cancer in May of 1912.

Works in Literary Context

August Strindberg's career was remarkable in the stages of its development. At every turn, he departed from literary conventions and customary dramatic norms. Many of his plays, particularly *Master Olof* and his later historical cycle, follow a Shakespearean model of stagecraft, but he absorbed numerous other artistic and philosophical influences along the way and innovated freely. As a young man, he studied the natural philosophy of Jean-Jacques Rousseau. By the mid-1880s, however, he had become an admirer of the German philosopher Friedrich Nietzsche.

Gendered Struggles of the Will Two aspects of Nietzsche's philosophy are readily apparent in Strindberg's writing: his conception of life as a succession of contests between stronger and weaker wills, and his emphasis on the refined superiority of the male intellect. If conflict is the driving force of Strindberg's mature plays, his principal theme is the battle of wills, especially as applied in the battle between the sexes for intellectual and psychological supremacy. Strindberg's attitude toward women was more ambivalent than negative. He was acutely aware of the problems facing women in the patriarchal societies of nineteenth-century Europe. Henrik Ibsen had fueled the debate in 1879 with his play *A Doll's House*, and Strindberg was one of many to respond to that important drama. Strindberg initially advocated an egalitarian relationship between the sexes. In his plays, though, female characters often appear as diabolical usurpers of man's "naturally" dominant role, cruelly shattering his psyche and draining his intellect.

to Paris, where he tried hard to market himself and had a victory with a Paris production of *The Father*.

In Paris, Strindberg underwent a spiritual crisis. Reading the works of Emanuel Swedenborg, the Swedish mystic, convinced him that he had gone through a hell on earth; that his sufferings were actually administered by a merciful higher power who intended to destroy his arrogance and make him a better person. This line of thinking is the essence of *Inferno*, which became one of Strindberg's best-known prose works.

A Return to Sweden Strindberg's new religious framework helped structure his "pilgrimage" trilogy, *To Damascus* (1898–1904). Invoking the New Testament story of Saul's conversion on the road to Damascus, Strindberg focused on a character called "the Stranger," who moves from despair to acceptance of the divine. After finishing *To Damascus* in 1898, Strindberg left Paris for good and returned to Sweden.

In the next five years, he wrote twenty-two plays, including one of his masterpieces, *The Dance of Death* (1900). Coming home after many years abroad, Strindberg negotiated the tensions of his return by composing a remarkable series of historical dramas. The eleven plays he wrote between 1899 and 1908, together with *Master Olof* from 1872, form a cycle dramatizing seven centuries of Swedish history. His model for this enormous project was Shakespeare. The best-known plays of the cycle portray leading Swedish figures such as *Gustav Vasa* (1899), the nation's founding father, and *Erik XIV* (1899), the

Naturalism Strindberg's efforts to portray psychic combat on stage went hand in glove with his conception of naturalism, an attempt to explore in literature the terrain of the new social sciences. In a preface to the published script of *Miss Julie*, Strindberg outlines the theatrical and philosophical principles of naturalistic drama: nothing should appear theatrical; there should be no intermissions, which might break the illusion of reality for the audience; characters are determined by their heredity and environment. This manifesto for naturalism is often considered as important for modern drama as *Miss Julie* itself. The play also adheres to the naturalist rule that a work of fiction should demonstrate a law of nature, in this case the Darwinian concept of the survival of the fittest. Strindberg's naturalism focuses on the "moment of struggle," the immediate conflict affecting his characters, and eliminates any extraneous incidents or dialogue, creating a spare, intense theatrical effect.

Forerunner of Modern Drama *To Damascus*, *The Dance of Death*, *The Dream Play*, and *The Ghost Sonata* employ dream symbolism to translate Strindberg's mystical visions into the language of drama. Highly abstracted characters appear and disappear in stylized settings; scenes and images change unexpectedly; and profound fears and ghastly fantasies materialize. By breaking with the realistic traditions of drama in his later career, Strindberg opened up new possibilities, prefiguring such major dramatic movements of the twentieth century as expressionism and exerting a powerful influence on dramatists such as Samuel Beckett, Eugene O'Neill, and Eugene Ionesco.

Works in Critical Context

During his lifetime, August Strindberg frequently courted controversy and deliberately outraged the establishment. It is no wonder that reaction to his creative work was often mixed. The first few years of his career were marked by his unconventional, grassroots approach to Swedish history; his outspoken assault on powerful leaders and institutions in *The New Kingdom*; and his 1884 blasphemy trial. Even the greatest triumphs of his naturalist period, *The Father* and *Miss Julie*, were clouded by personal scandal and controversy over his perspective on gender issues. His later plays, with their spooky effects and outlandish sensibility, bewildered his contemporaries still further. At the end of his iconoclastic life, the polemical "Strindberg feud" cast his legacy in the light of his role as social critic and political firebrand.

Despite or because of these recurrent controversies, Strindberg achieved lasting popularity in his home country. The whole city of Stockholm turned out to celebrate his sixtieth birthday in 1909. When he was passed over for the Nobel Prize in Literature that year—in favor of fellow Swede Selma Lagerlof, the first woman to receive the prize—a nationwide appeal went out to present Strindberg with a special award, including forty-five thousand crowns raised largely from small donations. At the

---

COMMON HUMAN EXPERIENCE

Strindberg was long a proponent of naturalism—a literary genre that attempts to represent human behavior with scientific detachment. Here are some well-known examples of the genre, which tends to be skeptical about the experience of freedom of choice, emphasizing instead hereditary, social, and evolutionary factors as determinants of human decisions.

Therese Raquin (1867), a novel by Émile Zola. Zola described this novel of adultery, murder, and guilt as akin to a scientific study of human temperaments.

Hedda Gabler (1890), a play by Henrik Ibsen. This landmark psychological play features one of the most highly regarded female roles in world theater.

Sister Carrie (1900), a novel by Theodore Dreiser. This classic American naturalist novel portrays the moral fall and material rise of a young woman in the big city.

The Lower Depths (1902), a play by Maksim Gorky. This work is a dark study in self-deception, first produced by the Moscow Arts Theatre and directed by the famous dramaturge Konstantin Stanislavsky.

Native Son (1940), a novel by Richard Wright. The first successful African American protest novel, *Native Son* portrays its protagonist's violence as an inevitable consequence of poverty and racial discrimination.

---

time of his death, Strindberg was a national treasure and a respected name among the European intelligentsia.

Miss Julie In the United States, Strindberg's best-known work is probably the gender play *Miss Julie*. His strongest champion in American theater was certainly Eugene O'Neill, who called him "the greatest genius of all modern dramatists," but he has also garnered much praise from other corners. Recent responses to *Miss Julie* have often focused on issues of gender and class, with neo-Marxist critics like Evert Sprinchorn arguing that "when Miss Julie kills herself, we understand that one social class is being replaced by another one." From the gender studies perspective, literary scholar Robert Gordon has observed that "for all its ambiguities *Miss Julie* is possibly the first nineteenth-century play by a male writer to have conceived the woman's role as subject of the drama, her point of view being as fully explored as the man's."

Responses to Literature

1. August Strindberg championed naturalism in his early career, and then later rejected it and pursued more expressionistic theatrics. Write about the uses and limits of naturalism in his plays, citing examples from his early and late work.

2. Explore the theories of the eighteenth-century mystic Emanuel Swedenborg, who influenced many famous writers. How do Strindberg's post-*Inferno* writings reflect Swedenborgian ideas?

3. Write about the theme of power as expressed in Strindberg's work. How do his characters acquire, display, and use power?

4. Many scholars have written about the bitter relations between men and women in Strindberg's dramas. Do you think his is a sexist point of view? Explain your position using detailed analysis of passages from Strindberg's writing.

5. How would you characterize Strindberg's beliefs about human nature?

BIBLIOGRAPHY

Books

Bellquist, John Eric. *Strindberg as a Modern Poet: A Critical and Comparative Study.* Berkeley and Los Angeles: University of California Press, 1986.

Carlson, Harry G. *Out of Inferno: Strindberg's Reawakening as an Artist.* Seattle: University of Washington Press, 1996.

Kvam, Kela, ed. *Strindberg's Post- Inferno Plays.* Copenhagen: Munksgaard/Rosinante, 1994.

McGill, Vivian. *August Strindberg: The Bedeviled Viking.* New York: Russell & Russell, 1965.

Meyer, Michael. *Strindberg: A Biography.* New York: Random House, 1985.

Mortensen, Brita, and Brian Downs. *Strindberg: An Introduction to His Life and Work.* Cambridge: Cambridge University Press, 1949.

Robinson, Michael. *Studies in Strindberg.* Norwich, U.K.: Norvik, 1998.

Robinson, Michael, and Sven Rossel, eds. *Strindberg and Expressionism.* Vienna: Praesens, 1999.

Steene, Brigitta. *Strindberg and History.* Stockholm: Almqvist and Wiksell, 1992.

Tornqvist, Egil. *Strindbergian Drama.* Stockholm: Almqvist and Wiksell, 1982.

Valency, Maurice. *The Flower and the Castle.* New York: Grosset and Dunlap, 1963.

Ward, John. *The Social and Religious Plays of Strindberg.* London: Athlone, 1980.

▣ Rosemary Sutcliff

BORN: *1920, Surrey, England*

DIED: *1992, Sussex, England*

NATIONALITY: *British*

GENRE: *Fiction*

MAJOR WORKS:

The Eagle of the Ninth (1954)

Rosemary Sutcliff   *Sutcliff, Rosemary, photograph by Mark Gerson. Reproduced by permission of Mark Gerson.*

Warrior Scarlet (1958)
The Lantern Bearers (1959)
The Mark of the Horse Lord (1965)

Overview

A Carnegie Medal–winning author, Sutcliff brought history to life through her heroes, the atmospheres she created, and the sense of continuity found in her works. Known primarily for her children's novels, she presented English history from the late Bronze Age through the coming of the Roman legions, the Dark Age invasions of the Angles and the Saxons, and the Norman Conquest, focusing on the experiences of young men and women who overcome the unrest of their times to find a measure of peace, despite their personal or physical limitations. Sutcliff also explored history through her many retellings of old legends or stories, such as those of King Arthur and the Knights of the Round Table and Beowulf. In these works, she presented well-known heroes, often adding a new dimension to their tales.

Works in Biographical and Historical Context

Budding Interest in War Themes   Rosemary Sutcliff was born in Surrey, England, in 1920. When Sutcliff was eleven years old, her father retired from the navy and the family settled in a somewhat isolated moorland house in north Devon. She contracted a debilitating form of arthritis called Still's disease as a child, but was nevertheless able to attend a normal school for a few years. Sutcliff's father returned to the navy at the onset of World War II, however, leaving mother and daughter alone again. Their isolation was broken when their house became a British Home Guard signals post, and Sutcliff's interest in battles and the military can be traced back to this time. The British Home Guard was a volunteer force composed of people who were ineligible for military service, who were assembled to protect Britain in case of a Nazi invasion.

Leaving school at the age of fourteen, Sutcliff began training as a painter of miniatures, a profession that was chosen for her because of her disability. Even though she had no inclination for the work, she made it through three years at Bideford Art School and became a professional.

Early Efforts at Writing Sutcliff made her fiction debut with *The Chronicles of Robin Hood* (1950), quickly followed up with and *The Queen Elizabeth Story* (1950). Within a few years, she found her literary voice with such novels as *Warrior Scarlet* and *The Lantern Bearers*.

A Consistent Career Perhaps the best of all Sutcliff's writing is found in two novels of the 1960s, *The Sword at Sunset* (1963), which tells of the life and death of the Celtic warlord Artos (Arthur) and his doomed fight against the Saxons, and *The Mark of the Horse Lord* (1965), where a freed gladiator impersonates a Scottish chieftain and inherits his Highlands kingdom. Both stories end in tragedy but contain an unforgettable blend of action, deep thinking, and striking landscapes.

The 1970s and 1980s saw a smaller amount of work by Sutcliff, but of high quality. *The Capricorn Bracelet* (1973), a collection of stories first used as radio broadcasts, covers three hundred years and six generations of Aquila descendants fighting for Rome in the Scottish Border country. *Blood Feud* (1977) is the story of the Anglo-Saxon Jestyn, captured by marauding Vikings, who journeys with them to Constantinople to fight for the Byzantine emperor. *Frontier Wolf* (1980) returns to Roman Britain, where Alexios Aquila commands a body of frontier scouts against Scottish tribesmen along Hadrian's Wall. Both novels are fine examples of Sutcliff's work.

A Perfect Mesh of History and Fiction In her autobiography, *Blue Remembered Hills* (1983), Sutcliff recalls her early life and her struggle against crippling arthritis. Sutcliff died on July 23, 1992.

Works in Literary Context

The isolation of Sutcliff's early life, her crippling illness, and the pain she experienced in a variety of relationships all influenced the trajectory her successful literary career would take. Inheriting the tradition of storytelling from

---

LITERARY AND HISTORICAL CONTEMPORARIES

Sutcliff's famous contemporaries include:

Mary Stewart (1916–): English novelist and children's author renowned for her historical fantasy series that focuses on the life of Merlin.

J. R. R. Tolkien (1892–1973): English writer who authored *The Hobbit* and the much-loved *Lord of the Rings* trilogy.

C. S. Lewis (1898–1963): Perhaps best known for his *Chronicles of Narnia* children's series, Lewis also wrote a number of philosophical and religious texts.

Queen Elizabeth II (1926–): Queen of England since the early 1950s, Elizabeth took the throne upon the death of George VI, her father; after Queen Victoria, she has reigned over the United Kingdom the longest of any monarch to date.

---

her mother, Sutcliff was exposed at a young age to both Celtic and Saxon legends; she later built upon her memory of these stories to write engaging works of historical fiction that continue to engage readers of all ages but particularly young adults.

Light vs. Dark Similar themes and images connect many of Sutcliff's books. Margaret Sherwood Libby, writing in the *New York Herald Tribune Book Review* about *The Lantern Bearers*, declared that "the plot, both interesting and plausible, has its significance heightened by the recurring symbolism of light in dark days." Margaret Meek, in *Rosemary Sutcliff*, recognized this theme of light and dark in all three of the books: "The conflict of the light and dark is the stuff of legend in all ages.... Sutcliff's artistry is a blend of this realization in her own terms and an instructive personal identification with problems which beset the young, problems of identity, of self-realization." For example, Aquila's lighting of the Rutupiae beacon becomes not only a personal symbol of his choice to remain in Britain but also a symbol of hope for those who fight on with him, a sign that the light of civilization will not die out forever.

Promises and Rings Another of the themes that run through Sutcliff's works is the great oath of loyalty, found in titles from *Warrior Scarlet* to *The Shield Ring*: "If we break faith... may the green earth open and swallow us, may the grey seas roll in and overwhelm us, may the sky of stars fall on us and crush us out of life for ever." The ritual of the spear that marks Drem's entrance into manhood in *Warrior Scarlet* is echoed many years later in a similar scene in *The Eagle of the Ninth*. Still another connection lies in the continuity of Aquila's family from

COMMON HUMAN EXPERIENCE

Sutcliff was one of many authors to draw on the legend of King Arthur for inspiration. Here are some other works that feature the mythic Arthur:.

The Once and Future King (1958), a novel by T. H. White. White focuses on Arthur's childhood and his relationship with the wizard Merlin in this popular version of the Arthurian legen.

The Mists of Avalon (1982), a novel by Marion Zimmer Bradley. Bradley presents an entirely fresh perspective on the tale of Arthur: she tells the story from the point of view of the women involved and places Arthur's struggles within the context of the dwindling power of paganism and the rising power of Christianity in England.

The Skystone (1992), a novel by Jack Whyte. The first book of *The Camulod Chronicles*, this novel details the beginning of King Arthur's England.

one generation to the next, symbolized by the massive golden ring, inset with a flawed emerald and carved with the figure of a dolphin, which is the emblem of Aquila's house. The ring reappears at intervals throughout Sutcliff's history: Marcus first sees it on a thong around the neck of an ancient warrior in the Scottish Highlands; it is a sign of recognition between Flavius and Justin when they first serve together in Britain; it comes to Aquila from his sister Flavia when he escapes from the Jutish camp; it comes to Owain more than a hundred years later from the hand of his dead father as he flees the battlefield; and it comes to Bjorn from his foster father, Haethcyn, six hundred years later still, when Bjorn marches with Aikin Jarlson's war band to fight the Normans, as a token that he has come into his father's estate.

While many of her adult books are now out of print, Sutcliff's children's stories continue to entertain young readers and influence writers such as Helen Hollick.

Works in Critical Context

"Most critics," contend May Hill Arbuthnot and Zena Sutherland in their *Children and Books*, "would say that at the present time the greatest writer of historical fiction for children and youth is unquestionably Rosemary Sutcliff." Despite this, Sutcliff's name is rarely mentioned among the great children's authors, nor is her life as discussed or investigated as are those of her more famous contemporaries.

The "Roman Britain" Trilogy Sutcliff's "Roman Britain" trilogy begins with *The Eagle of the Ninth*, which concerns a young Roman centurion and his first few years

spent in second-century Britain. *The Eagle of the Ninth* "is one of the few good stories" covering the period of Roman rule in Britain, maintains Ruth M. McEvoy in *Junior Libraries*. And a *Booklist* contributor concludes that the realistic background and characters make this a novel that "will reward appreciative readers."

The third book, *The Lantern Bearers*, "is the most closely woven novel of the trilogy," claims Margaret Meek in her book *Rosemary Sutcliff*. "The characterizations are vivid, varied and convincing," maintains Margaret Sherwood Libby in the *New York Herald Tribune Book Review*.

Warrior Scarlet With *Warrior Scarlet*, Sutcliff continued her tales of the making of Britain through two new young heroes. The story of the Bronze Age in England is told in *Warrior Scarlet* by focusing on a boy and his coming to manhood. "Sutcliff has widened her range to cover the hinterland of history," states Meek, "and realized, with the clarity we have come to expect, every aspect of the people of the Bronze Age, from hunting spears and cooking pots to king-making and burial customs, from childhood to old age. The book is coloured throughout with sunset bronze." *Warrior Scarlet*, according to a *Times Literary Supplement* reviewer, "is outstanding among children's books of any kind."

Sword at Sunset Like her novels for young adults, Sutcliff's adult novels also delve into history. *Sword at Sunset* is a retelling of the legend of King Arthur that blends "legend, historical scholarship and masterfully humane storytelling to illuminate the misty and romantic era that preceded the Dark Ages," remarks a *Chicago Tribune Books* reviewer. Sutcliff has placed Arthur outside the legends, imbuing him with more believability, according to Robert Payne in the *New York Times Book Review*. "This time," writes Payne, "he is a living presence who moves in a brilliantly lit and fantastic landscape only remotely connected with ancient England." Reflecting on the novel's craftsmanship, Payne concludes: "Sutcliff is a spellbinder. While we read, we believe everything she says. She has hammered out a style that rises and falls like the waves of the sea."

Responses to Literature

1. Why do you think Sutcliff is not mentioned as frequently as Tolkien or C. S. Lewis in discussions of young adult authors? Is it because her books are based more on history than on fantasy? In an essay, explain your thoughts on the author's relative obscurity.

2. How did Sutcliff's lifelong illness directly and indirectly influence her career as a writer?

3. Why do you think Sutcliff chose to retell the Arthurian legend, which has already been retold many times? What is the legend's allure? Do you think this allure is specific to England?

4. How are Sutcliff's adult novels different from her children's books? Compare the "Roman Britain" stories with *Sword at Sunset*.

BIBLIOGRAPHY

Books

Arbuthnot, May Hill, and Zena Sutherland. *Children and Books*. 4th ed. Glenview, Ill.: Scott, Foresman, 1972.

Egoff, Sheila A. *Thursday's Child: Trends and Patterns in Contemporary Children's Literature*. Chicago: American Library Association, 1981.

Meek, Margaret. *Rosemary Sutcliff*. New York: Walck, 1962.

Townsend, John Rowe. *A Sense of Story: Essays on Contemporary Writers for Children*. Philadelphia: Lippincott, 1971.

———. *Written for Children: An Outline of English Language Children's Literature*. Philadelphia: Lippincott, 1974.

Periodicals

Aiken, Joan. "Rosemary and Time." *Times Educational Supplement*, January 14, 1983, 24.

Evans, Ann. "The Real Thing." *Times Literary Supplement*, March 27, 1981, 341.

Libby, Margaret Sherwood. Review of *The Lantern Bearers*. *New York Herald Tribune Book World*, February 14, 1960, 11.

McEvoy, Ruth M. Review of *The Eagle of the Ninth*. *Junior Libraries*, January 1955, 33.

Jonathan Swift

BORN: *1667, Dublin, Ireland*

DIED: *1745, Dublin, Ireland*

NATIONALITY: *British*

GENRE: *Fiction, poetry*

MAJOR WORKS:

A Tale of a Tub (1704)

Gulliver's Travels (1726)

A Modest Proposal (1729)

Overview

Jonathan Swift is the foremost prose satirist in the English language. His greatest satire, *Gulliver's Travels* (1726), is alternately described as an attack on humanity and a clear-eyed assessment of human strengths and weaknesses. In addition to his work as a satirist, Swift was also an accomplished minor poet, a master of political journalism, a prominent political figure, and one of the most distinguished leaders of the Anglican church in Ireland. For these reasons he is considered one of the representative figures of his age.

Jonathan Swift   *Mansell / Time Life Pictures / Getty Images*

Works in Biographical and Historical Context

A Lonely Childhood Amid Political Turmoil
Swift's childhood was characterized by separation. His father died shortly before Swift's birth, and his mother left him in the care of a nurse for three years at a very young age. However, Swift was financially provided for, and he was educated in the best schools in Ireland. He was enrolled at Trinity College, Dublin when, in 1689, a wave of civil unrest erupted in the wake of the abdication of the Catholic King James II. Many Anglo-Irish escaped to the safety of England, including Swift.

The Temple Years   In England, Swift secured a position as secretary to Sir William Temple, a scholar and former member of Parliament engaged in writing his memoirs. Except for two trips to Ireland, Swift remained in Temple's employ and lived at his home, Moor Park, until Temple's death in 1699. During this period, Swift read widely, was introduced to many prominent individuals in Temple's circle, and began a career in the Anglican church, an ambition thwarted by Temple's inaction in obtaining Swift a promised preferment in the church. Around this time, he met Esther Johnson, stepdaughter of Temple's steward. "Stella," as Swift nicknamed her, became an intimate, lifelong confidante to Swift. Despite rumors to the contrary, their relationship remained platonic;

Swift's correspondence with her was later collected in *The Journal to Stella* (1963).

Toward the end of this period, Swift wrote his first great satires, *A Tale of a Tub* and *The Battle of the Books*. Both were completed by 1699 but were not published until 1704 under the title *A Tale of a Tub, Written for the Universal Improvement of Mankind, to which is Added an Account of a Battel between the Antient and Modern Books in St. James's Library*. Framed by a history of the Christian church, *A Tale* satirized contemporary literary and scholarly pedants as well as the dissenters and Roman Catholics who opposed the Anglican church, an institution to which Swift would be devoted during his entire career.

The Protestant control of England under Oliver Cromwell had resulted in an attempt by the government to impose the stringent, unpopular beliefs of Puritanism on the English populace. Swift detested such tyranny and sought to prevent it through his writings. *The Battle of the Books* was written in defense of Temple. A controversial debate was being waged over the respective merits of ancient versus modern learning, with Temple supporting the position that the literature of the Greek and Roman civilizations was far superior to any modern creations. Swift addressed Temple's detractors with an allegorical satire that depicted the victory of those who supported the ancient texts. Although inspired by topical controversies, both *A Tale* and *The Battle* are brilliant satires with many universal implications regarding the nature and follies of aesthetics, religious belief, scholasticism, and education.

Political Activism When Temple died in 1699, Swift was left without position or prospects. He returned to Ireland, where he occupied a series of church posts from 1699 to 1710. During this period he wrote an increasing number of satirical essays on behalf of the ruling Whig party, whose policies limiting the power of the crown and increasing that of Parliament, as well as restricting Roman Catholics from political office, Swift staunchly endorsed. In these pamphlets, Swift developed the device that marked much of his later satire: using a literary persona to express ironically absurd opinions. When the Whig administration fell in 1709, Swift shifted his support to the Tory government, which, while supporting a strong crown unlike the Whigs, adamantly supported the Anglican Church. For the next five years, Swift served as the chief Tory political writer, editing the journal *The Examiner* and composing political pamphlets, poetry, and prose. Swift's change of party has led some critics to characterize him as a cynical opportunist, but others contend that his conversion reflected more of a change in the parties' philosophies than in Swift's own views. Always one to place the interests of the church above party affiliation, he chose to serve the party that promoted those interests.

With the death of Queen Anne in 1714 and the accession of George I, the Tory party lost power to the Whigs, and Swift returned to Ireland in 1714 to become dean of St. Patrick's Cathedral. Except for brief visits to London, Swift spent the rest of his life in Ireland. For the first five years after his return, he refrained from political controversy. By 1720, however, he renewed his interest in the affairs of Ireland, producing a series of pamphlets attacking the economic dependence of Ireland upon England and criticizing the policies of Prime Minister Robert Walpole. His most well-known, *A Modest Proposal* (1729) is a bitter satire inspired by the plight of the masses of impoverished Irish. In it, Swift ironically suggests that a growing population and widespread starvation could both be alleviated if the poor began eating their children. Considered one of the greatest satirical essays in world literature, Swift's piece attacks complacency in the face of misery and the coldly rational schemes of social planners who fail to perceive the pain resulting from their action or inaction.

The "Travells" On August 14, 1725, Jonathan Swift wrote to his friend Charles Ford: "I have finished my Travells, and I am now transcribing them; they are admirable Things, and will wonderfully mend the World." *Gulliver's Travels* challenged his readers' smug assumptions about the superiority of their political and social institutions as well as their assurance that as rational animals they occupied a privileged position in the world. Universally considered Swift's greatest work of this period, *Gulliver's Travels* (published as *Travels into Several Remote Nations of the World, in Four Parts; by Lemuel Gulliver*), depicts one man's journeys to several strange and unusual lands. Written over a period of several years, some scholars believe that the novel had its origins during Swift's years as a political agitator, when he was part of a group of prominent Tory writers known as the Scriblerus Club. The group, which included Alexander Pope, John Gay, and John Arbuthnot, collaborated on several satires, including *The Scriblerus Papers*. They also planned a satire called *The Memoirs of Martinus Scriblerus*, which was to include several imaginary voyages. Many believe that *Gulliver's Travels* was inspired by this work. Although the novel was published anonymously, Swift's authorship was widely suspected. The book was an immediate success.

Life After Gulliver Swift remained active throughout the 1720s and 1730s as a political commentator, satirist, and, more importantly, as a poet. During this period, he wrote much of his best poetry, including *Verses on the Death of Dr. Swift*. The last years of Swift's life, from approximately 1736 until his death, have been the subject of much legend and misinformation. During the eighteenth and nineteenth centuries, critics and biographers mistakenly concluded that Swift was insane during the years before his death. However, throughout his life he had suffered from what is known as Meniere's

Syndrome, or labyrinthine vertigo, a disease of the inner ear that causes attacks of nausea, dizziness, temporary deafness, and extreme pain. He also suffered a paralytic stroke in 1740 that caused aphasia and loss of memory. Eventually, in 1742, he was declared incapable of caring for himself and placed in the custody of guardians. Swift died in 1745 and was buried beside Esther Johnson in St. Patrick's Cathedral.

Works in Literary Context

Satire or Cynicism? During the Enlightenment, eighteenth-century thinkers espoused an increasing faith in the rationality of human beings and in the capacity of reason to improve and even perfect the human condition. Swift categorically rejected these views; educated in the seventeenth century, he held to that period's emphasis on the imperfection of human beings resulting from the Fall of Man. Although Swift believed humans capable of reason, he also believed they rarely exercised this capacity. Thus, while he endorsed some measures of social reform, he argued for their implementation through means that acknowledged a need to control human corruptibility. Swift's departure from the prevailing thought of his time earned him censure in his lifetime, and for centuries afterwards, by critics who accused him of misanthropy and portrayed him as a bitter individual who hated humanity. However, his defenders, mostly twentieth-century critics, argued that his acerbic prose merely expressed his pain at the disparity between the world as it was and the world as it should have been. By portraying people in shocking extremes of baseness and monstrosity, they argue, he sought a better world. Swift defended his view of humankind by writing: "I have ever hated all Nations, professions, and Communityes and all my love is toward individuals...I hate and detest that animal called man, although I hartily love John, Peter, Thomas and so forth."

A Novel of Imaginary Voyages Of course *Gulliver's Travels* is satirical, but is it also a novel? "Probably not," Robert C. Elliot remarks, "although it is not easy to say (except by arbitrary stipulation) why it is not." Part of the problem in classifying *Gulliver's Travels* as a novel arises from Swift 's inclusion of large quantities of material which are neither purely narrative nor satirical, but are largely philosophical. Indeed, *Gulliver's Travels* has most often been described as an imaginary or "philosophic" voyage, a subgenre most clearly defined by William A. Eddy as "a didactic treatise in which the author's criticism of society is set forth in a parable form of an *Imaginary Voyage* made by one or more Europeans to a nonexistent or little known country...together with a description of the imaginary society visited."

Works in Critical Context

Between 1945 and 1985, nearly five hundred books and articles devoted their attention to Swift's most popular

LITERARY AND HISTORICAL CONTEMPORARIES

Swift's famous contemporaries include:

William Congreve (1670–1729): A poet and playwright, Congreve wrote some of the most popular English plays of the Restoration period, including *The Way of the World* (1700).

George I (1660–1727): When Queen Anne died childless in 1714, George, Prince-Elector of Hanover, was named King of Great Britain because of his Protestant faith— the other claimants were Catholics. The House of Hanover would rule Great Britain until the death of Queen Victoria in 1901.

Daniel Defoe (1661?–1731): Writer, journalist, and spy, Daniel Defoe is best remembered today for his novel *Robinson Crusoe*, one of the first, and still one of the most widely read, novels written in the English language.

Alexander Pope (1688–1744): The preeminent English poet of the eighteenth century, Pope is, according to *The Oxford Dictionary of Quotations*, the third most quoted writer in the English language, after Shakespeare and Alfred, Lord Tennyson. The movie *Eternal Sunshine of the Spotless Mind* derived its title from one of Pope's poems, for example.

George Frideric Handel (1685–1789): Perhaps the most well-known Baroque composer, Handel's most famous work is his *Messiah*, particularly the "Hallelujah" chorus. His work influenced later composers such as Mozart and Beethoven.

work, *Gulliver's Travels*. Even today, Swift scholars still do not know how to classify a work which has been regarded as a children's tale, a fantastic voyage, a moral allegory, and a novel.

Gulliver's Travels Gulliver's characterization has also been much debated. Early critics viewed him as Swift's mouthpiece and accepted everything Gulliver said as authorial opinion. Modern critics, however, recognize him as a distinct character whom Swift uses to subtler purposes. The most significant contemporary debate centers on Swift's intentions regarding the creation of Gulliver— whether he is meant to be a consistently realized character, a reliable narrator, or a satiric object whose opinions are the object of Swift's ridicule. This debate over the nature of Gulliver is important because critics seek to determine whether Gulliver is intended to be a man with definite character traits who undergoes a transformation, or an allegorical representative of humanity. In general, Gulliver is considered a flexible persona manipulated by Swift to present diverse views and satirical situations

COMMON HUMAN EXPERIENCE

Other works of literature considered to be exemplars of scathing satire include:

Adventures of Huckleberry Finn (1884), a novel by Mark Twain. Told through the eyes of an innocent abroad, Twain's greatest novel is an indictment of many entrenched ideas and prejudices, particularly racism.

Catch-22 (1961), a novel by Joseph Heller. Considered one of the greatest literary works of the twentieth century, this tale set during World War II turns nearly every moral and logical convention on its head: "the only way to survive such an insane system is to be insane oneself."

Babbitt (1922), a novel by Sinclair Lewis. Lewis's first novel, it quickly earned a place as a classic satire of American culture, particularly middle-class conformity.

and to indicate the complexity and unpredictability of human nature.

While Swift's earliest readers greeted *Gulliver's Travels* enthusiastically, later critics complained that the Voyage to the Houyhnhnms constituted a "real insult upon mankind." Edward Young spoke for many when he accused Swift of having "blasphemed a nature little lower than that of the angels." Victorian critics could only explain the corrosive satire of the Voyage to the Houyhnhnms by positing an author who was both misanthropic and mad. Sir Walter Scott, for example, traced Swift's "diatribe against human nature" to that "soured and disgusted state of Swift's mind, which doubtless was even then influenced by the first impressions of that incipient mental disease which in this case, was marked by universal misanthropy." Novelist William Thackeray Asked, "What had this man done? What secret remorse was rankling at his heart?" Thackeray's queries typify the desire of nineteenth- and early-twentieth-century biographers to explain Swift's satirical indignation by conjuring up a dark and largely imaginary past.

Responses to Literature

1. Using the Internet or a library, research how actual voyages of the so-called Age of Discovery (the sixteenth and seventeenth centuries) compare to Gulliver's journeys. In a report to the class, describe two or three tales you find of fantastical, far-away places described by real-life explorers.

2. Using the Internet or a library, research the conflict between the Irish and English during Swift's time. Write an essay describing how this conflict seems to motivate the Swift satire you have read. What is the historical significance of Swift's own Anglo-Irish heritage?

3. With a group of your classmates, research the philosophical theories of the great minds of the Age of Enlightenment, such as René Descarte, Thomas Hobbes, Gottfried Leibniz, and John Locke. Then, write a report for your class on how Gulliver's opinions in *Gulliver's Travels* reflect some of those ideas.

4. With a group of your classmates, discuss Swift's concept of absurdity among upper-class fashions and social mores. Use the most recent Swift text you have read as a group to support your opinions.

BIBLIOGRAPHY

Books

Lock, F. P. *The Politics of Gulliver's Travels.* Gloucestershire: Clarendon Press, 1980.

Nokes, David. *Jonathan Swift, A Hypocrite Reversed: A Critical Biography.* Oxford: Oxford University Press, 1985.

Pollak, Ellen. *The Poetics of Sexual Myth: Gender and Ideology in the Verse of Swift and Pope.* Chicago: University of Chicago Press, 1985.

Rawson, C. J. *Gulliver and the Gentle Reader.* London: Routledge & Kegan Paul, 1973.

Rosenheim, Edward, *Swift and the Satirist's Art.* Chicago: University of Chicago Press, 1963.

Tuveson, Ernest, ed. *Swift: A Collection of Critical Essays.* Englewood Cliffs, NJ: Prentice-Hall, 1964.

Voight, Milton, *Swift and the Twentieth Century.* Detroit, Mich.: Wayne State University Press, 1964.

Williams, Kathleen. *Jonathan Swift and the Age of Compromise.* Lawrence: University of Kansas Press, 1958.

Periodicals

Studies in English Literature 1500–1900 (Summer 1989).
Texas Studies in Language and Literature (Fall 1990).

Algernon Charles Swinburne

BORN: *1837, London, England*

DIED: *1909, Putney, England*

NATIONALITY: *British*

GENRE: *Poetry, drama, fiction, nonfiction*

MAJOR WORKS:

A Year's Letters (1862)

Atalanta in Calydon (1865)

Poems and Ballads (1866)

Overview

Swinburne was one of the most accomplished lyric poets of the Victorian era and was a preeminent symbol of

Algernon Charles Swinburne   *Hulton Archive / Getty Images*

work emphasized medieval subjects, elaborate religious symbolism, and a sensual pictorialism, and who cultivated an aura of mystery and melancholy in their lives as well as in their works. In 1860 Swinburne published two verse dramas in the volume *The Queen-Mother and Rosamond*, which was largely ignored.

He achieved his first literary success in 1865 with *Atalanta in Calydon*, which was written in the form of classical Greek tragedy. The following year the appearance of *Poems and Ballads* brought Swinburne instant notoriety. He became identified with the "indecent" themes and the precept of "art for art's sake" that characterized many of the poems in the volume. He subsequently wrote poetry of many different kinds, including the militantly republican *Song of Italy* (1867) and *Songs Before Sunrise* (1871) in support of the Risorgimento, the movement for Italian political unity. Although individual volumes of Swinburne's poetry were occasionally well received, in general his popularity and critical reputation declined following the initial sensation of *Poems and Ballads*.

A Most Peculiar Man   Swinburne's physical appearance, his personality, and the facts of his life have received much attention from biographers and from commentators exploring his works from a biographical standpoint. He was small, frail, and plagued by numerous peculiarities of physique and temperament, including an oversized head, nervous gestures, and seizures that may have been manifestations of a form of epilepsy. Throughout the 1860s and 1870s, he drank excessively, and until his forties, he suffered intermittent physical collapses that necessitated removal to his parents' home while he recovered. In 1879 Swinburne's friend and literary agent, Theodore Watts-Dunton, intervened, isolating Swinburne at a suburban home in Putney and gradually weaning him from alcohol as well as from certain companions and habits. Swinburne lived another thirty years with Watts-Dunton, whose friendship remains controversial. Watts-Dunton is credited with saving Swinburne's life and encouraging him to continue writing. Swinburne died in 1909 at age seventy-two.

Works in Literary Context

During Swinburne's lifetime, critics considered *Poems and Ballads* his finest as well as his most characteristic poetic achievement; subsequent poetry and work in other genres was often disregarded. Since the mid-twentieth century, however, commentators have been offering new assessments of Swinburne's entire career.

Scandalous Themes in the Victorian Era   Swinburne is regarded as a Victorian poet profoundly at odds with his age and as one of the most daring, innovative, and brilliant lyricists to ever write in English. Certainly, he shocked and outraged Victorian sensibility, introducing into the pious, stolid age a world of fierce atheism, strange passions, fiery paganism, and a magnificent new

rebellion against the conservative values of his time. The explicit and often pathological sexual themes of his most important collection of poetry, *Poems and Ballads* (1866), delighted some, shocked many, and became the dominant feature of Swinburne's image as both an artist and an individual.

Works in Biographical and Historical Context

Mystery, Melancholy, and Notoriety   Algernon Charles Swinburne was born into a wealthy Northumbrian family in 1837, the very year that marked the beginning of the Victorian era, during which Queen Victoria ruled England and its territories. Queen Victoria sat on the throne longer than any other British monarch, from 1837 until 1901. This period saw significant changes for both Britain and Europe as a whole, with advances in industrialization leading much of the population to jobs in factories instead of on farms as in the past. The era was also marked by a preoccupation with proper behavior in society and domestic life, which Swinburne famously rebelled against with his poetry.

Swinburne was educated at Eton and at Balliol College, Oxford, but did not complete a degree. While at Oxford, he met the brothers William Michael and Dante Gabriel Rossetti, as well as other members of the Pre-Raphaelite circle, a group of artists and writers whose

LITERARY AND HISTORICAL CONTEMPORARIES

Swinburne's famous contemporaries include:

George Meredith (1828–1909): English novelist and poet best known for his tragicomic novel *The Egoist* and for his role as a publisher's adviser, from which position he helped launch the careers of Thomas Hardy and many others.

Dante Gabriel Rossetti (1828–1882): An English poet, translator, and novelist of Italian descent. Also a cofounder of the realist Pre-Raphaelite Brotherhood and a significant painter in his own right.

Clorinda Matto de Turner (1853–1909): A Peruvian writer who spoke out strongly for the rights of indigenous people and whose own independence sparked the imagination of many during the era of independence movements in Latin America.

John Ruskin (1819–1900): An English art and social critic whose essays on art and architecture were extremely influential in both the Victorian and Edwardian periods.

David Livingstone (1813–1873): Scottish missionary and representative of British imperialism. Also the first European to see the Mosi-oa-Tunya waterfalls on the border between present-day Zambia and Zimbabwe; he promptly renamed them Victoria Falls in honor of the queen of England.

Emily Dickinson (1830–1886): One of the best-known American poets of all time, she published fewer than a dozen of the almost eighteen hundred poems she wrote during her quiet and private life.

lyrical voice the likes of which had never before been heard. His radical republicanism, a worship of the best instincts of man, pushed Victorian humanism well beyond the "respectable" limits of Matthew Arnold's writings. Additionally, his critical writings on art and literature greatly influenced the aesthetic climate of his age, and his extraordinary imitative facility made him a brilliant, unrivaled parodist. But most important, the expression of his eroticism in many poems about nature, particularly about the sea, wind, and sun, make him the Victorian period's greatest heir of the Romantic poets.

Lyricism   Another particularly important and conspicuous quality of Swinburne's work is an intense lyricism. Even early critics, who often took exception to his subject matter, commended his intricately extended and evocative imagery, delicate hand with meter, rich use of assonance and alliteration, and bold, complex rhythms. At the same time, the strong rhythms of his poems and his characteristic use of alliteration were sometimes carried to extremes, rendering his work highly susceptible to

parody. Some critics also regard his imagery as vague and imprecise and his rhymes as facile and uninspired. After establishing residence in Putney, Swinburne largely abandoned the themes of sexuality that had characterized much of his earlier poetry. Nature and landscape poetry began to dominate, as did poems about children. Many commentators maintain that the poetry written during the Putney years is inferior to Swinburne's earlier work, but others see examples of exceptional merit among his later works, citing in particular "By the North Sea," "Evening on the Broads," "A Nympholept," "The Lake of Gaube," and "Neap-Tide."

Historical Verse Drama   Swinburne was primarily a poet, with his prolific years from 1860 to 1862. During this time, in addition to a large body of lyrics, many of which were to appear in *Poems and Ballads*, Swinburne completed his tragedy *Chastelard* (not published until 1865), the first play in the eventually massive trilogy about Mary Queen of Scots that would include *Bothwell* (1874) and *Mary Stuart* (1881). Swinburne was drawn to the history of Mary Stuart both by his family's historic attachment to the Stuart cause and by his attraction to the character of Mary. Chastelard's bitter expression of his love for the queen pithily expresses Swinburne's main concern: "men must love you in life's spite; / For you will always kill them, man by man / Your lips will bite them dead; yea, though you would, / You shall not spare one; all will die of you." Swinburne's deep emotional involvement with the theme of painful, fatal love infuses his verse with passionate lyricism; *Bothwell* and *Mary Stuart* were well received on publication but are rarely read today.

Mythical Themes in Lyric Verse Drama   In 1865 and 1866, Swinburne became a literary lion and a literary scandal with the publication of *Atalanta in Calydon* and *Poems and Ballads*. *Atalanta in Calydon*, still justly regarded as one of Swinburne's supreme achievements, became a masterpiece partly because his choices of subject and form were perfectly adapted to his concerns and talents. The imitation of Aeschylean tragedy allowed him to exercise his superb lyrical gifts, the choice of the pagan Greek setting enabled him to express his antitheism convincingly, and the Meleager myth provided a vehicle with which to express his obsession with the fatal power of passion and of women. *Atalanta in Calydon* is a forceful attack on traditional Christianity, which Swinburne, like William Blake, saw as an instrument of moral repression that sets the ideals of the soul in conflict with the needs of the body. The message is summed up in the famous antitheistic chorus that denounces "The supreme evil, God," who "shapes the soul, and makes her a barren wife / To the earthly body and grievous growth of clay." *Atalanta in Calydon*, however, is not merely a play with a message; it also represents a rebirth of the powerful lyricism of Greek tragedy. Rejecting all belief in a beneficent scheme of things and even in the possibility of joy, it is Swinburne's most pessimistic major work, yet in its surging rhythms, in its fusion of the imagery of natural cycles, it achieves the intensity that John Keats saw as the essential quality of tragic art: the intensity that is "capable of making all disagreeables evaporate, from their being in close relationship with Beauty & Truth."

A Novelist   One of Swinburne's most significant prose works is the satiric epistolary novel of 1862, *A Year's Letters* (pseudonymously serialized in *Tatler* in 1877). *A Year's Letters* is a masterful, more or less autobiographical account of the aristocratic Victorian world that shaped Swinburne's character, "a world," writes Edmund Wilson in *The Novels of A. C. Swinburne* (1962), "in which the eager enjoyment of a glorious out-of-door life of riding and swimming and boating is combined with adultery, incest, enthusiastic flagellation and quiet homosexuality." This and other works were not significant merely for their sensational value, however. The subtle analysis of characters and relationships, the close portraits of an aristocratic way of life, the power of description, and the precise, beautifully cadenced prose of these works reveal Swinburne's genuine but often unrecognized talents as a novelist.

Literary Critic   Throughout his career, Swinburne also published literary criticism of great acuity. His familiarity with a wide range of world literatures contributed to a critical style rich in quotation, allusion, and comparison. He is particularly noted for discerning studies of Elizabethan dramatists and of many English and French poets and novelists. In response to criticism of his own works, Swinburne wrote essays, including *Notes on Poems and Reviews* (1866) and *Under the Microscope* (1872), that are celebrated for their wit and insight. Swinburne also left a second novel, *Lesbia Brandon*, unfinished at his death. Some critics have theorized that *Lesbia Brandon* was intended as thinly disguised autobiography; however, its fragmentary form resists conclusive interpretation.

Works in Critical Context

Intellectual Poet   Thanks to his sense of irony and gift for parody, Swinburne could do a better job making fun of himself than any of his critics, but this humor did not mean that he took himself or his work lightly. He wanted to be remembered not only as a great poet but also as a great poetic thinker. Along these lines, T. S. Eliot recognized that Swinburne's music and intellect cohere, in his finest moments, into a sort of single entity that "there is no reason to call anything but genius.... What he gives is not images and ideas and music, it is one thing with a curious mixture of suggestion of all three." Alfred, Lord Tennyson's famous remark that Swinburne was "a reed through which all things blow into music" expresses the enduring quality of Swinburne's achievement. The winds of primitive, savage passions—from love to the elemental forces of nature, the sea and sky, and on

---

COMMON HUMAN EXPERIENCE

Poems and Ballads and *A Year's Letters* are seen by many as obscene and offensive, though they are also acknowledged classics. Here are a few more examples of significant literary classics that were considered immoral when first published:

Aeropagitica (1644), a nonfiction work by John Milton. This treatise condemning censorship makes the case—coming from one of literature's most passionate defenders of Christian theology—that morality is only possible as a choice for those who have some minimal, albeit accidental, sense (even an imaginary sense) of immorality. It should be noted, however, that Milton was making the case for freedom of speech with the explicit goal of working toward a fuller understanding of the Christian god.

Tropic of Cancer (1961), a novel by Henry Miller. The publication of this novel led to a series of obscenity trials that tested American laws on pornography. The U.S. Supreme Court overruled state court findings of obscenity and declared the book a work of literature. The Modern Library named it the fiftieth-best book of the twentieth century.

Lady Chatterly's Lover (1928), a novel by D. H. Lawrence. This novel was originally to be called "Tenderness," and met with scandal on account of its explicit sex scenes, which included previously banned words. A portion of the outrage with which the novel's publication met may also have derived from the fact that the lovers were a working-class male and an aristocratic female. It is generally considered a classic of English literature.

---

to the "ruling song" of man—blew through Swinburne's remarkably open heart, and came forth in sophisticated yet joyously primitive song. Tennyson's comment does justice not only to Swinburne's unquestionable talent for lyrical beauty but also to his less-recognized gift for translating an unmediated experience of the universe into language, into verse.

"On the Cliffs"   One of Swinburne's finest poems, "On the Cliffs," was written at Holmwood in 1879, shortly after Watts-Dunton had rescued Swinburne from his rooms on Guildford Street. The poem approaches spiritual autobiography, which expresses the themes of *Poems and Ballads, Second Series* (1885) in a richly complex and precise syntax. The setting, as in "The Forsaken Garden" and later "By the North Sea," is a crumbling cliff that is being slowly eaten away by the sea—Swinburne's favorite image for his belief that all earthly life, even the Earth itself, is destined for oblivion. Some critics in the early twentieth century dismissed Swinburne's nature

poetry as ornamental and obscure, even verbose. They remarked, as noted in a Swinburne study by scholar David Riede, on the difficulty of Swinburne's "syntactical maze of modifying clauses and phrases" as well as his complicated literary allusion. Riede also suggests some critics dismissed Swinburne's "On the Cliffs" due to its meaning: the reader seems to always be in "continual doubt."

Bothwell In 1874 an anonymous reviewer in *Macmillan's Magazine*, writing on Swinburne's *Bothwell*, praised the dramatist's "strength and sweep of imagination" and suggested the play succeeds because Swinburne is "as much scholar as poet." The reviewer goes on to laud Swinburne's attention to history and his seriousness regarding the play's subject. George Saintsbury, in an 1874 issue of *The Academy*, also appreciated *Bothwell*, cheering its lyrical power and elevating its author to "the heights of the English Parnassus." Much more grounded in their analysis, twentieth-century critics like Curtis Dahl looked to *Bothwell* and the rest of Swinburne's trilogy on Mary, Queen of Scots as an autobiographical/biographical study. They believed the trilogy sheds new insight into how Swinburne saw himself at the time of publication.

Responses to Literature

1. Read *Atalanta in Calydon* with an eye to genre. Write an informal essay in which you explain whether you see the work as a play or a long piece of dramatic verse. Also, describe what you see as the difference between the two genres.

2. With a small group of your classmates, choose three poems with overlapping themes from *Poems and Ballads*. Consider the impact that they make when read together. Create a group presentation in which you explain what message they might communicate if read as parts of a whole, as opposed to individual poems. Engage the rest of your class in the following discussion: How does reading an entire collection of poems in their printed order differ from reading individual poems in that collection? Does the meaning change? Are different stories told?

3. In "By the North Sea" and other pieces, Swinburne paints linguistic pictures of bleak, desolate landscapes but often follows these dark pictures with hopeful or positive endings. Write a personal essay in which you imagine those poems as expressions of an internal landscape. Do you find the positive conclusions of "By the North Sea" emotionally convincing or compelling? Why or why not? How would you rewrite parts of the poem to make it say more about you and your life?

4. Swinburne is highly critical of organized religion throughout his body of work, especially in poems such as "Before a Crucifix," in which he parodies what he sees as a corrupt and greedy Church. Find another Swinburne poem that offers a similar view of religion. How do you think readers in his day responded to these works? Why?

BIBLIOGRAPHY

Books

Eliot, T. S. *The Sacred Wood.* London: Methuen, 1920.

Louis, Margot Kathleen. *Swinburne and His Gods: the Roots and Growth of an Agnostic Poetry.* Montreal: McGill-Queen's University Press, 1990.

Maxwell, Catherine. *The Female Sublime from Milton to Swinburne: Bearing Blindness.* Manchester, UK: Manchester University Press, 2001.

McGann, Jerome. *Swinburne: An Experiment in Criticism.* Chicago: University of Chicago Press, 1972.

McSweeney, Kerry. *Tennyson and Swinburne as Romantic Naturalists.* Toronto: University of Toronto Press, 1981.

Raymond, Meredith B. *Swinburne's Poetics: Theory and Practice.* The Hague: Mouton, 1971.

Riede, David G. *Swinburne: A Study of Romantic Mythmaking.* Charlottesville: University Press of Virginia, 1978.

Wilson, Edmund, ed. *The Novels of A. C. Swinburne.* New York: Farrar, Strauss, and Cudahay, 1962.

John Millington Synge

BORN: *1871, County Dublin, Ireland*

DIED: *1909, Dublin, Ireland*

NATIONALITY: *Irish*

GENRE: *Drama, fiction*

MAJOR WORKS:
In the Shadow of the Glen (1903)
Riders to the Sea (1904)
The Playboy of the Western World (1907)
Deirdre of the Sorrows (1910)

Overview

The author of *The Playboy of the Western World* (1907), Edmund John Millington Synge is considered the greatest dramatist of the Irish Literary Renaissance. In his unsentimental but compassionate portrayal of Irish peasants and his highly imaginative and poetic dialogue (patterned after the vernacular spoken by the rural population in the west of Ireland), Synge attempted to capture the essence of the Irish spirit, which he described in his preface to *The Playboy of the Western World* as "fiery and magnificent, and tender."

John Millington Synge *Synge, John Millington, drawing. Irish Tourist Board*

Works in Biographical and Historical Context

Reaction to Religious Upbringing Born in 1871 in Rathfarnham, a town near Dublin, into a middle-class Protestant family, Synge was raised by his devoutly religious mother after his father's death in 1872. Due to his poor health, he was educated at home by private tutors. Influenced by his reading of the works of Charles Darwin (who published the theory of evolution), Synge broke from his religious upbringing at the age of fourteen, and his ill feelings toward Christianity often arise in his plays. He studied Hebrew and Irish at Trinity College in Dublin and, after earning his bachelor's degree, he traveled extensively in Germany, France, and Italy, intent on a career in music.

Focused on Writing Eventually judging himself better suited to literary endeavors, he moved in 1895 to Paris, where he studied at the Sorbonne. The following year, he encountered two fellow expatriates, the political activist Maud Gonne and the poet and dramatist William Butler Yeats. Synge briefly joined Gonne's Irish League, an organization dedicated to liberating Ireland from English rule, but he quickly became disillusioned with the militant tactics she advocated. Ireland had been controlled by England for hundreds of years, and the Irish generally resented English policies that took their land

and denied them full legal rights. Over the years, especially in the late-nineteenth and early twentieth centuries, the Irish demanded home rule, if not independence, which gained them some reforms from the British government in this time period.

Yeats, the most prominent figure of the Irish Literary Renaissance, had a more lasting influence on Synge. (The Irish Literary Renaissance was a movement that sought to create a new literature out of the heritage, language, and folklore of the Irish people.) Yeats urged Synge to return to Ireland and to write about the peasants of the three small islands off the country's western coast, known collectively as the Aran Islands or, simply, Aran. The advice appealed to Synge, and he subsequently spent many summers on the islands observing the customs and dialect of the peasants. In their Anglo-Irish dialect, in their stories and legends, and in their spiritual beliefs—which he viewed as a hybrid of Christian teachings and the stronger, more exciting element of ancient paganism— Synge discovered the inspiration for most of his dramatic works.

The Dublin Years In 1903, Synge settled in Dublin, where the Irish National Theatre Society staged his first play, *In the Shadow of the Glen* (1903). Presenting the story of a suspicious husband who fakes his own death in order to determine whether his young wife is faithful, and who has his worst fears confirmed, the play shocked and revolted Irish audiences with its ironic depiction of marriage. However, it found popularity in the more liberal atmosphere of England. In 1905 Yeats and dramatist Lady Gregory produced Synge's *The Well of the Saints* at the new Abbey Theatre in Dublin. Containing Synge's most acerbic characterizations of Irish peasants in the sarcastic, feuding blind couple Martin and Mary Doul and in a saint of questionable virtue, the play greatly impressed Yeats with its colorful dialogue. Yet it, too, offended Dubliners.

The first production of *The Playboy of the Western World* incited a public outrage in 1907 when audiences took exception to its coarse language and what they considered an unflattering portrayal of the Irish peasantry. Attempts to disrupt performances of the drama were so hostile that police were called to the Abbey Theatre to protect the players. News of the so-called Playboy riots earned an international reputation for Synge, who defended the play against charges that no Irish citizen would behave as his characters did by insisting that the characterizations and the plot of the play were taken from actual events. Two years later, Synge died of Hodgkin's disease (a type of cancer affecting the lymphatic system), leaving *Deirdre of the Sorrows* (1910) complete but only partially revised.

Works in Literary Context

The stories, legends, folktales, customs, and speech Synge observed on the Aran Islands greatly influenced the

LITERARY AND HISTORICAL CONTEMPORARIES

Synge's famous contemporaries include:

William Butler Yeats (1865–1939): Often credited with driving the Irish Literary Revival, this Irish poet and dramatist is highly regarded as one of the most prominent literary figures of the twentieth century. His works include *The Tower* (1928) and *The Winding Stair and Other Poems* (1929).

Lady Augusta Gregory (1852–1932): This Irish dramatist and folklorist cofounded the Irish Literary Theater and the Abbey Theater. Her folk-influenced books include *A Book of Saints and Wonders* (1906).

Maud Gonne (1866–1953): A feminist and an actress, this Irish revolutionary captured the heart of William Butler Yeats. She published her autobiography in 1938, *A Servant of the Queen*.

Pablo Picasso (1881–1973): This famous Spanish artist cofounded the Cubist movement. His best known works include "Les Demoiselles d'Avignon" (1907) and "Guernica" (1937).

Joseph Conrad (1866–1953): This Polish author is considered by many to be one of the most remarkable novelists to write in the English language. His most studied work is *Heart of Darkness* (1899).

content and themes of his plays. His musical training and close study of art and natural history also serve as a foundation of his attempt to bring into harmony in his writing not only the sound, meaning, colour, and rhythm of language, but a harmony of nature, myth, and passion. Synge was also greatly influenced by his life experiences, and constantly strove to distill the essence of experience into his art.

Style to Theme in Riders to the Sea Synge is remembered primarily for his innovations as a linguistic stylist. While his dialogue, as he professed, was taken directly from the speech of Irish peasants, he used his aesthetic sensibilities to bring out the inherent poetic qualities of the Anglo-Irish dialect. As Yeats suggested, in response to objections that Synge's dialogue was not entirely "natural," "Perhaps no Irish countryman had ever that exact rhythm in his voice, but certainly if Mr. Synge had been born a countryman, he would have spoken like that." Synge's achievement, critics maintain, was the use of this style to complement the themes pervading his works: the possibilities and limitations of speech, the disparity between reality and illusion, and the painfulness of everyday existence.

Exhibiting all of these themes in a highly compressed format, *Riders to the Sea* is a one-act tragedy set inside an Aran cottage. The play presents vivid descriptions of the daily actions of the islanders and focuses on the danger of their custom of fishing in small boats, called curraghs. Synge renders the fatalism native to a region in which the people depend on the sea for their livelihoods and exist in constant fear of sudden and violent storms. In the course of the play, Maurya, who has already lost four of her six sons to drowning, discovers that her son Michael has also drowned. She protests in vain as her last remaining son, Bartley, subsequently sets forth on what will be another fatal expedition. She expresses her grief by keening, the ritual shrieking over a corpse, but ultimately assesses her situation in a characteristically simple and fatalistic pronouncement: "I've had a husband, and a husband's father, and six sons in this house—six fine men, though it was a hard birth I had with every one of them and they coming to the world—and some of them were found and some of them were not found, but they're gone now the lot of them."

Critics have compared *Riders to the Sea* to Greek tragedy due to its compactness of narrative and its symbolic structure, which mirrors the cyclical nature of human existence in the intertwined stories of the two deaths. Commentators also observe that the play contains numerous allusions to Greek and Irish myth, as well as the *Book of Revelations*. It is esteemed as Synge's most artful and poetic work, but the bleakness of its subject matter has prevented it from being widely produced.

Influence Synge was an important catalyst in the development of Irish drama, for in bringing Anglo-Irish dialect to the stage he greatly influenced his successors, among whom Sean O'Casey and Brendan Behan are notable examples. He remains one of the most revered figures in modern drama, and his plays had a great influenced on modern developments in the genre. In addition, his creation of a stylized language incorporating poetic imagery and vernacular speech patterns had a profound effect on such writers as William Butler Yeats and Samuel Beckett.

Works in Critical Context

Critics often gave mixed, if not hostile, reviews to Synge's plays when they were originally produced, though France and Germany quickly embraced him and his European-style of thinking. Criticism of the playwright and his work have moved away from the initial controversy to be seen as masterworks of twentieth-century theater. Time has only improved critical esteem of Synge. Critics focus much of their attention on the dialogue, themes, and sources for his plays.

Playboy of the Western World *Playboy of the Western World* is considered by some to be the finest play written in English during the twentieth century. Criticism of *The Playboy of the Western World* typically stresses the thematic opposition between reality and imagination in the drama, tracing Christy's development toward self-realization as an individual and as a poetic persona. The play's portrayal of his transformation is praised for suggesting a variety of mythological and biblical archetypes. For example, *Playboy* is often discussed in terms of the central themes and plot structures of the legends surrounding the hero Cuchulain from Irish mythology, and the drama's treatment of patricide is compared to that in Sophocles' tragedy *Oedipus Rex*.

Some commentators, emphasizing the rejection of Christy by his former admirers in the play's third act, have argued that Synge presents him as a Christ figure. However, comic and ironic elements in *Playboy* have caused critics to debate the degree of parody involved in Synge's approach to such prototypes. Christy, for example, is also considered a mock or secularized Christ in light of the drama's pagan themes and ironic use of religious allusions and expressions. *Playboy* has garnered much critical attention for eluding traditional classifications of comedy and tragedy, and is cited as an early example of the modern tragicomedy.

Synge's use of language in *Playboy* was also important from the first. Writing about the play in 1908, Louis Untermeyer in *Poet Lore*, noted "Wild poetry itself is in his utterance, for although Mr. Synge writes entirely in prose, his sentences are so steeped in similes of the skies that his very commonplaces are filled and colored with all the *nuances* of rhythm. The sunlight filters through his lines and the spell of scenic splendor is over all his work."

Responses to Literature

1. Account for the oppressive mood, atmosphere, and tableau settings of *Riders to the Sea* in a paper. How does this mood affect the actions and dialogue of the characters? Is Synge's depiction of the Aran Islands sympathetic? Hostile? Condescending?

2. Describe various types of humor and comedy in *The Playboy of the Western World* in an essay. Do these types of humor differ in class or along gender lines?

3. In an essay, discuss Synge's influence on the growth of the Abbey Theater. What made the Abbey Theater so important for its era, and for Irish national consciousness generally? Examine the history of the Abbey Theater alongside other culturally important theater groups and art collectives, such as the "Lost Generation" of American expatriates or the art circle surrounding Andy Warhol and the Velvet Underground. What role do such cultural collectives play in shifting national attitudes or social perspectives?

4. *The Playboy of the Western World* was considered so offensive at the time of its staging that it sparked riots. Choose two or three other twentieth-century dramas that have been denounced as obscene or offensive, and examine in a small group setting what it is that audiences have struggled so deeply with. Is there ever a good reason to ban or censor plays or works of art in general? What are the dangers of a refusal to engage with challenging or disturbing material?

COMMON HUMAN EXPERIENCE

Synge was particularly fascinated by the possibilities opened up and the limitations imposed by speech. Synge listened to the speech of the islanders, a musical, old-fashioned, Irish-flavored dialect of English. He conversed with them in Irish and English, listened to their stories, and learned the impact that the sounds of words could have apart from their meanings. Other works that explore dialectical language include:

Absalom, Absalom! (1936), a novel by William Faulkner. This tragedy of the American Deep South reveals, as do his other novels, a gift for capturing regional and racial vernacular.

Finnegans Wake (1939), a novel by James Joyce. This Irish novelist's sprawling final novel is best known for its obscure language and complexity. Joyce developed a basically new language that many commentators term *Wakese*—solely for the book. *Wakese* has a vocabulary of composite words drawn from sixty or seventy world languages to form puns or phrases meant to convey several layers of meaning at the same time.

Tender Buttons (1914), an experimental fiction book by Gertrude Stein. This book exemplifies the high modernist style. Basing her fiction in a technique of "automatic writing," she sought to access a deeper level of experience through language that was often jarring, alienating, or repetitive.

BIBLIOGRAPHY

Books

Bickley, Francis Lawrance. *J. M. Synge and the Irish Dramatic Movement*. Norwood, Pa.: Norwood Editions, 1975.

Greene, David H., and Edward M. Stephens. *J. M. Synge, 1871–1909*, rev. ed. New York: New York University Press, 1989.

Kiely, David M. *John Millington Synge: A Biography*. New York: St. Martin's Press, 1995.

Masefield, John. *John M. Synge: A Few Personal Recollections with Biographical Note*. Norwood, Pa.: Norwood Editions, 1978.

Mikhail, E. H. *J. M. Synge: Interviews and Recollections*. New York: Barnes & Noble, 1977.

Stephens, Edward M. *My Uncle John: Edward Stephens's life of J. M. Synge*. London: Oxford University Press, 1974.

Periodicals

Untermeyer, Louis. "J. M. Synge and the *Playboy of the Western World*." *Poet Lore*: vol. 19, no. 3: 364–67.

◈ Wislawa Szymborska

BORN: *1923, Prowent-Bnin, near Poznan, Poland*

NATIONALITY: *Polish*

GENRE: *Poetry, essays*

MAJOR WORKS:

Calling Out to the Yeti (1957)

Salt (1962)

Sounds, Feelings, Thoughts (1981)

People on a Bridge (1986)

View with a Grain of Sand (1995)

Overview

Winner of the 1996 Nobel Prize in Literature, Wislawa Szymborska is a private—some would say reclusive—widow. She has been described as "the [Wolfgang] Mozart of poetry...[with] something of the fury of [Ludwig van] Beethoven," and although she is perhaps Poland's most popular female writer and is valued as a national treasure there, she has only slowly made her way onto the radar of English-speaking readers.

Works in Biographical and Historical Context

Early Life in Krakow Wislawa Szymborska was born on July 2, 1923, in the small town of Bnin (which is now part of Kórnik). She spent her early childhood there, near the city of Poznan, the industrial and cultural center of the western part of Poland. Her father, Win-

Wislawa Szymborska   *Szymborska, Wislawa, photograph. AP Images.*

centy Szymborska, served as the steward of the Count Wladyslaw Zamoyski's family estate until taking a generous early retirement in the 1920s. In 1932, when Szymborska was eight, her family moved to the historic city of Krakow—as much the informal capital of southern Poland as Poznan is of its western reaches—to settle down for good. Since then, Szymborska's entire life, except for her infrequent and usually short travels, has been spent in Krakow.

From September 1935 until the outbreak of World War II in 1939, Szymborska attended Gimnazjum Siostr Urszulanek (Academy of the Sisters of the Ursuline Order), a prestigious parochial high school for girls in Krakow. When the Gimnazjum was shut down during the Nazi German occupation of the city, she attended underground classes, passing her final exams in the spring of 1941. During the war, she began to write short stories, of which she has remained critical. After the war Szymborska studied first Polish philology and then sociology at the Jagiellonian University in Krakow but never completed a degree.

The Postwar Years The war had a profound effect on Szymborska. Her poetic debut, "I'm Searching for a Word," appeared in a literary supplement to *Dziennik Polski* (The Polish Daily) in March 1945. The poem expresses the inadequacy of language in the face of the personal and collective experience of war. More broadly, many of her poems of this period, including "Remembering September, 1939," "Remembering January," "Leaving the Cinema," and "We Knew the World Backwards and Forwards," give voice to the desire to dispel the mirages of collective happiness that arise in the enthusiasm following the end of war. These poems and others of this period were published in newspapers and periodicals, and only a few of them were ever anthologized, generally much later.

In 1948 Szymborska assembled a collection of her poetry, which was to be titled simply *Poezje* (Poems), but the collection never found a publisher; its contents were deemed too "bourgeois" and "pessimistic," clashing with the socialist realist aesthetic that was beginning to take hold. Socialist realism was a movement promoted by the government of the Soviet Union as a way to ensure that all art contributed positively to society; to this end, the movement emphasized optimism and pride in communist ideals and cultural triumphs. The movement also worked against those artists who sought to question those in power or the current state of society. One of Szymborska's poems, "Sunday at School," even sparked a campaign against her, in which high school students were prodded to write letters of protest. She was accused of writing poetry that was inaccessible to the masses and too preoccupied with the horrors of war. A two-year poetic silence followed.

Krupnicza Also in 1948, at the age of twenty-four, Szymborska married Adam Wlodek, a minor poet and literary editor, and joined him at the writers' complex on Krupnicza Street in Krakow. (The marriage ended in divorce in 1954.) Krupnicza Street played an important role in the literary life of Poland in the postwar period. Following World War II, several dozen poets, writers, and translators shared close quarters and dined together at the Krupnicza complex, including Czeslaw Milosz, Jerzy Andrzejewski, poet Artur Miedzyrzecki, Maciej Slomczynski (Shakespeare translator and author of crime novels under the pen name Joe Alex), poets Konstanty Ildefons Galczynski and Anna Swieszczynska, and the foremost postwar scholar of Polish literature, Artur Sandauer. Some lived there for a short period of time, awaiting the rebuilding of Warsaw, but for Szymborska and others it was to be home for many years.

Szymborska worked as an assistant editor in publishing houses until 1953, when she became the editor of the poetry section of the Krakow-based weekly *Zycie Literackie* (Literary Life), a position she held until 1968. She remained on the board as a regular contributor until 1976.

A New Direction As time passed, Szymborska became disillusioned with communism as it was practiced in Poland and the Soviet Union. This point is evident in the contrast between the title of her first collection, *That's What We Live For* (1952), and that of her second, *Questions Put to Myself* (1954). In the semantic gap between these two titles is the first glimpse of the fully original voice that emerged with Szymborska's third collection, *Calling Out to Yeti* (1957). *Calling Out to Yeti* marks a turn in Szymborska's conception of the role of the poet: She distances herself from the demand to speak for others (the worker, the country, the party), electing to speak only in her own subjective voice. *Calling Out to Yeti* has been considered a transitional volume, one in which her basic themes begin to take shape.

Solidarity and Support During the 1970s, Polish protesters held mass anticommunism demonstrations. Although her sympathies were aroused by the growing political opposition, Szymborska remained hesitant to adopt the role of spokesperson for political causes, perhaps because she felt she had earlier misplaced her trust in the promise of socialism. For Szymborska, the 1970s were a relatively prolific period. She produced two volumes of poetry, both marked by a strong existentialist streak. Critics of the 1972 collection *Any Case* highlighted Szymborska's anti-Romanticism and praised her for her skepticism and humanism, sense of wonderment, and cool assessment of the limitations of human cognition, and pointed to her sensitivity and intellectual subtlety.

With the emergence of the Solidarity movement in 1980, the Society and similar initiatives found themselves briefly freed from earlier encumbrances. Szymborska began her affiliation with the newly formed Krakow journal *Pismo* (Writing), the editorial board of which included

---

LITERARY AND HISTORICAL CONTEMPORARIES

Szymborska's famous contemporaries include:

Václav Havel (1936–): Renowned playwright and author, Havel was both the last president of Czechoslovakia and the first president of the independent Czech Republic.

Lech Walesa (1943–): Walesa was the leader of Poland's primary resistance movement under authoritarian rule (Solidarity), winner of the Nobel Peace Prize in 1983, and first president of Soviet-free Poland (from 1990 to 1995).

Tom Wolfe (1931–): Cofounder of the New Journalism movement of the 1960s and 1970s (incorporating literary techniques into reporting), Wolfe is renowned for his fast-paced, technically brilliant nonfiction chronicles of contemporary society.

W. G. Sebald (1944–2001): Sebald has been hailed by many as the greatest German writer of the postwar period; his novels are known for their lucid but surreal shifts in perspective and style.

Leonid Brezhnev (1906–1982): After Joseph Stalin, Brezhnev was the longest-serving general secretary of the Communist Party of the Soviet Union. He was political leader of the authoritarian Union of Soviet Socialist Republics (USSR) from 1964 until his death in 1982.

---

many of her closest friends, among them fiction writer and poet Kornel Filipowicz, her longtime companion. Following the declaration of martial law on December 13, 1981, the composition of the editorial board of *Pismo* shrank as the government imposed demands on it, and Szymborska began to distance herself. Similarly, Szymborska terminated her thirty-year association with *Zycie Literackie* during this period. Under martial law, she chose to publish underground and in the émigré press under the pen name Stanczykowna, a feminized derivation of the name of a sixteenth-century court jester noted for his forthrightness.

Awards and Fame Although Szymborska's poems found their way into a few adventuresome literary periodicals during the 1980s, the political climate prevented her from publishing a volume of poetry until after the end of martial law, marking the longest hiatus between her collections. When it was published, *People on the Bridge* (1986) garnered her praise and several awards, including one from the Ministry of Culture, which she declined, and the Solidarity Prize, which she accepted.

Szymborska won her most prestigious award, the Nobel Prize in Literature, in 1996. Despite, or perhaps due to, giving the shortest acceptance speech in literary

COMMON HUMAN EXPERIENCE

More than perhaps any other poet of her generation, Szymborska has an eye for the small and the everyday. Here are a few other poets and authors whose reputation rests in part on their ability to see complexity in simplicity:

The Little Prince (1943), a children's story by Antoine de Saint Exupéry. The simplicity of this children's story lines up with a complex but unspoken philosophy of the world.

"The Red Wheelbarrow" (1923), a poem by William Carlos Williams. This poem is a quick sketch of a red wheelbarrow. It has captured the fancies of generations and has been seen as reflective of the imagist philosophy.

Death Comes for the Archbishop (1927), a novel by Willa Cather. This historical novel portrays two French priests setting out to establish a diocese in New Mexico.

Nobel history, she went from being an intensely private person to a public figure, vigorously pursued by the media. Since then, however, Szymborska has continued to be known for her quiet way of life and unwillingness to embrace the status of a celebrity. She shuns public gatherings, rarely travels abroad, hates being photographed or interviewed, and, except for her human rights and democratic reform activities, refuses to be involved in partisan politics. She is nevertheless quite involved in the cultural landscape of Krakow and maintains lively contacts with a small circle of friends. Her dislike of being in the limelight is by no means a sign of antisocial inclinations. Rather, it stems from her recognition that the larger part of a writers' public functioning is an empty ritual and an unnecessary waste of their inner resources.

Works in Literary Context

Skamander Szymborska's early work drew upon several literary movements, including the Polish avant-garde and the Skamandryci (Skamander formation). The Skamandryci was a group of interwar poets of diverse styles and literary lineages who shared a commitment to democratizing and expanding the range of poetry and poetic language, writing such "low" poetic forms as cabaret songs, nursery rhymes, and commercial slogans. Like the Skamander poets, Szymborska embraces colloquialism and is especially indebted to Julian Tuwim's poetics of the everyday.

Simple Details Szymborska emphasizes and examines the chance happenings of daily life and of personal relations in her poetry. "She is a master at recognizing the importance of the insignificant," explains James Beschta, continuing, "It is the innovative, playful use of language that dominates her style." Indeed, what sets Szymborska apart from her poetic peers is her insistence on speaking for no one but herself. She refuses to wear the cloak of the prophet and harbors no illusions about changing the world or even the local political landscape with her poetry. As a result, she writes with the liberation of a jester. Szymborska has drawn attention for her irreverence toward the lofty and self-important and for her exaltation of the lowly and seemingly trivial.

A Poet of Socialism? Szymborska's book debut came during the heyday of Stalinism. In 1952 she published her first collection of poetry, *What We Live For*, and was admitted to the Polish Writers' Union (ZLP) and the United Polish Workers Party (PZPR). With this involvement, she participated in the socialist-realist aesthetic that changed the course of Polish literature. As party pluralism was replaced by the authoritarian, single-party state, a new literature arose that served to illustrate ready-made slogans, culminating in formulaic propaganda. Szymborska was far from alone among her contemporaries in joining in the chorus of communist apologists, accepting the new codes of speech, and selecting topics fit for use as propaganda. Reflecting an enthusiasm for the socialist utopia, her first volume and its successor, *Questioning Oneself* (1954,), are dominated by politically engaged poetry. That is, they are filled with anti-Westernism, anti-imperialism, anticapitalism, and "struggle for peace."

Apolitically Political Poetry Szymborska later renounced her first two volumes of poetry as ignoble, however, criticizing herself for attempting to conform to the tenets of socialist realism. The Swedish Academy awarded her the Nobel Prize in 1996 on the basis of poems from her third collection, *Calling Out to the Yeti*, and thereafter. The Academy saw this collection as a reaction against Stalin, but Szymborska has challenged that interpretation of her work. "Of course, life crosses politics, but my poems are strictly not political," she noted in a rare interview. "They are more about people and life."

As a Polish poet gaining international prominence during the most frigid years of the cold war, she sought to write poems about people, about a common and simple humanity. This very emphasis on the human, however, has been identified as a part of an "apolitical politics" in Poland, Czechoslovakia, and other Eastern bloc countries. That is, in totalitarian political systems, where even the most mundane activities and everyday life itself are "for the Party," an insistence on humanness and connection *without* politics was itself a political statement.

Works in Critical Context

Wislawa Szymborska was thrust into the international spotlight in 1996 after receiving the Nobel Prize in Literature.

The reclusive and private Szymborska was described by the Swedish Academy as writing "poetry that with ironic precision allows the historical and biological context to come to light in fragments of human reality." Her poetry, in the words of *Los Angeles Times* critic Dean E. Murphy, is "seductively simple verse...[which has] captured the wit and wisdom of everyday life for the past half century."

Sounds, Feeings, Thoughts: Seventy Poems Although still not widely read outside her native Poland, Szymborska received critical acclaim for the first collection of her work to appear in English translation, *Sounds, Feelings, Thoughts: Seventy Poems.* "Of the poetic voices to come out of Poland after 1945, Wislawa Szymborska's is probably the most elusive as well as the most distinctive," writes Jaroslaw Anders in the *New York Review of Books.* Anders comments further: "*Sounds, Feelings, Thoughts* contains poems from [Szymborska's] five books written since 1957, comprising more or less half of what the poet herself considers her canon. Its publication is of interest not only because of Szymborska's importance as a poet, but also because her work demonstrates that the diversity of poetic modes in Poland is much greater than is usually perceived." Alice-Catherine Carls, in a review of *Sounds, Feelings, Thoughts* in *Library Journal,* calls the work "one of those rare books which put one in a state of 'grace.'" Robert Hudzik, also in *Library Journal,* claims: "This volume reveals a poet of startling originality and deep sympathy."

View with a Grain of Sand: Selected Poems The 1995 collection *View with a Grain of Sand: Selected Poems* was also praised by the critics, who lauded Szymborska's directness and distinctive voice. For the *Washington Post Book World,* Stephen Dobyns praises both the humor of Szymborska's work and the imaginative integrity of this translation by Stanislaw Baranczak and Clare Cavanagh. Celebrated proponent of the idea of "cultural literacy" Edward Hirsch agrees, arguing in the *New York Review of Books* that the volume reveals "the full force of [Szymborska's] fierce and unexpected wit." Louis McKee, in a *Library Journal* review, also praises the "wonderfully wicked" wit of Szymborska. Dobyns concludes his review by noting, "The poems are surprising, funny and deeply moving. Szymborska is a world-class poet, and this book will go far to make her known in the United States."

Responses to Literature

1. Choose four poems from *View with a Grain of Sand: Selected Poems* and discuss a common theme in these poems. Discuss why Szymborska opted to anthologize these poems together. Do the different poems reflect on one another in some ways?

2. Discuss Szymborska's representation of the unexpected within daily life. What sorts of details draw her attention? What are the advantages and disadvantages of taking on a perspective such as hers?

3. Find an example of a poem where Szymborska uses a small and apparently insignificant detail to reflect on a large and important issue. What are some of the effects of this technique?

4. In *The Century's Decline,* Szymborska writes, "The most pressing questions are naive ones." What do you think she means by this? What are some of the "naive" questions Szymborska poses in her poetry?

BIBLIOGRAPHY

Books

Gabrys, Malgorzata Joanna. "Transatlantic Dialogues: Poetry of Elizabeth Bishop and Wislawa Szymborska." PhD diss., Ohio State University, 2000.

Levine, Madeline G. *Contemporary Polish Poetry 1925–1975.* Boston: Twayne, 1981.

Neuger, Leonard and Rikard Wennerholm, eds. *Wislawa Szymborska—A Stockholm Conference, May 23–24, 2006* Stockholm: Kungl. Vitterhets Hisorieoch Antikvitets Akademien, 2006.

Periodicals

Badowska, Eva. "'My Poet's Junk': Wislawa Szymborska in Retrospect." *Parnassus: Poetry in Review* 28 (2004): 151–68.

Bojanska, Edyta M. "Wislawa Szymborska: Naturalist and Humanist." *Slavic and East European Journal* 41 (Summer 1997): 199–223.

Carpenter, Bogdana. "Wislawa Szymborska and the Importance of the Unimportant." *World Literature Today* 71 (1997): 8–12.

Kostkowska, Justyna. "'To Persistently Not Know Something Important': Feminist Science and the Poetry of Wislawa Szymborska." *Feminist Theory* 5, no. 2 (2004): 185–203.

T-V

◈ Rabindranath Tagore

BORN: *1861, Calcutta, India*

DIED: *1941, Calcutta, India*

NATIONALITY: *Indian*

GENRE: *Poetry, drama, fiction, nonfiction*

MAJOR WORKS:

Morning Songs (1883)

The Golden Boat (1894)

Gora (1910)

Gitanjali (1912)

The Home and the World (1916)

Overview

Rabindranath Tagore is India's most celebrated modern author. He received the Nobel Prize for Literature in 1913, the first non-European to be awarded this prize. Astonishingly prolific in practically every literary genre, he achieved his greatest renown as a lyric poet. His poetry is imbued with a deeply spiritual and devotional quality, while in his novels, plays, short stories, and essays, his social and moral concerns predominate.

Works in Biographical and Historical Context

Born into Literary Family in Calcutta Tagore was born into an upper-caste Hindu family in Calcutta on May 7, 1861. His grandfather, Dwarkanath Tagore, was a key figure in what is known as the Bengal renaissance in the mid-nineteenth century. Tagore's father, Debendranath, was a writer, religious leader, and practical businessman. Tagore was the fourteenth of his father's fifteen children and his father's favorite. From an early age, he embraced his father's love of poetry, music, and mysticism, as well as his reformist outlook.

Tagore was a precocious child who showed unmistakable poetic talent. As early as eight, he was urged by his brothers and cousins to express himself in poetry. This encouragement, which continued throughout his formative years, caused his talent to flourish. When Tagore was twelve, his father took him on a four-month journey to the Punjab and the Himalayas. This was Tagore's first contact with rural Bengal, which he later celebrated in his songs.

Public Recognition of Poetry After publishing his first poems at the age of thirteen, Tagore's first public recitation of his poetry came when he was fourteen at a Bengali cultural and nationalistic festival organized by his brothers. His acclaimed poem was about the greatness of India's past and the sorrow he felt for its state under British rule. India had been controlled by Great Britain in one form or another for some years. While the British had helped India develop economically and politically and expanded local self-rule, an Indian nationalist movement was growing in the late nineteenth century. This trend continued into the first decades of the twentieth, as well.

Tagore left India at age seventeen to continue his studies in England. During this time, he read extensively in English and other European literature, forming the universalist outlook he maintained throughout his life that included: a profound desire for freedom, both personal and national; an idea of the greatness of India's contribution to the world of the spirit; and poetry expressing both of these. His stay in England was brief, and when he returned home, he published the first of nearly sixty volumes of verse. He also wrote and acted in verse dramas and began to compose devotional songs for the *Brahmo Samaj*, the Hindu reformist sect his father promoted. In 1883, he married Mrinalini Devi. He was twenty-two years old, and she was ten. The couple had five children.

"The Lord of His Life" Tagore produced his first notable book of lyrics, *Evening Songs*, in 1882, followed by *Morning Songs* (1883). The latter work reflects Tagore's new mood initiated by a mystical experience he had while looking at the sunrise one day. His devotion to *Jivan devata* ("The Lord of His Life"), a new conception of God as humanity's intimate friend, lover, and beloved,

Rabindranath Tagore   *Tagore, Rabindranath, photograph. Source unknown.*

played an important role in his subsequent work. Several poems in the volume *Sharps and Flats* (1886) boldly celebrate the human body, reflecting his sense of all-pervading joy in the universe.

Creative Virility

In 1890, Tagore took charge of his family's far-flung estates, some of them in regions that are now part of Bangladesh. The daily contact with peasants and farmers aroused his empathy for the plight of India's poor. Coming in close touch with the people and geography of Bangladesh, Tagore was inspired to write his first major collection of verse, *The Golden Boat* (1894). The contemplative tone of his poetry gives his work the depth and serenity of his mature voice.

In the 1880s and 1890s, Tagore's creative output was tremendous, and his reputation steadily developed in his country as the author of poems, short stories, novels, plays, verse dramas, and essays. He moved through several phases at this time. If he began in the manner of the late Romantics, he soon became a writer of realistic fiction about everyday situations and people from all spheres of life. He frequently reinvented himself, creating new forms and introducing new genres and styles to Bengali literature—social realism, colloquial dialogue, light satire, and psychologically motivated plot development.

Music and Novels

Tagore was also known for his musical creations. His compositions started a new genre in Bengali music, known as *rabindrasangit* ("Tagore song"), an important part of Bengali culture. His music mingled elements of the folk music of boatmen and wandering religious with those of semiclassical love songs. He wrote more than two thousand songs in his lifetime, setting his poems, stories, and plays to music.

Tagore reached the peak of his fiction-writing career in 1910, when he published the novel *Gora*. This sociopolitical novel of ideas projects the author's concept of liberal nationalism based on international brotherhood. In the West, his best-known novel is *The Home and the World* (1916), which frankly expresses his conflicted sentiments regarding nationalist agitation in India.

Gitanjali and Worldwide Fame

Tagore's standing as the leading Bengali writer was confirmed in 1911, when he was given a public reception in Calcutta to celebrate his fiftieth birthday. As he was about to visit England for the third time, he fell ill, and his trip was delayed. Lacking energy to compose new writing, he began translating some of his recently published lyrics into free verse. He landed in England with a slender English manuscript of devotional poems from the volume *Gitanjali* (Song Offerings). In June 1912, Tagore read his translations to a select group of London literati, including W. B. Yeats and Ezra Pound. The response was overwhelming, and Tagore became a literary sensation. A limited edition of *Gitanjali*, with an introduction by Yeats, quickly sold out. A second edition became a best-seller.

Tagore sailed to the United States later in 1912. Pound, a tireless promoter of poetry, introduced Tagore to influential literary people in America. When Tagore returned to India in 1913, he left behind a distinguished group of European and American admirers. That year, he was awarded the Nobel Prize for Literature—the first such recognition of an Eastern writer. The prize gratified Tagore, but the sensation it created in Bengal also alarmed him. He would never again be out of the public eye.

Tagore as Public Figure

Between 1916 and 1934, Tagore made five visits to America and traveled to nearly every country in Europe and Asia, lecturing, promoting his educational ideas, and urging international cooperation. Wherever he went, he was greeted as a living symbol of India's cultural heritage. He was knighted by the British crown in 1915, but resigned his knighthood four years later after British troops fired into a crowd in the Punjab, killing four hundred people. He denounced the European nationalism and imperialism that had brought about the First World War. While the war was fought primarily in Europe and Africa, the Indian army was compelled to support Great Britain and provide troops for the conflict. Thousands of Indian soldiers died and were wounded during their service. In India, the call for self-rule only continued to grow.

Now a major figure in the movement for national emancipation, Tagore became close to leaders like Mohandas K. Gandhi. His relationship with Gandhi was tumultuous. He rejected Gandhi's strategy of economic self-sufficiency and derided "the cult of the spinning wheel." Instead, he favored education as the primary engine of national uplift. He founded the university called Visva-Bharati, at the site of his ashram (spiritual retreat) at Santiniketan. He also created an Institute for Rural Reconstruction, recruiting international assistance to create a model for popular education in poverty-stricken villages. Like Gandhi, Tagore fought against the Indian caste system and discrimination against the "untouchable" class.

In the second half of the 1930s, old age, failing health, and international turmoil put a stop to Tagore's travels. He suffered chronic pain and long bouts of illness in his final years. As he became conscious of his approaching death, Tagore wrote some of his finest poetry, continuing to experiment with technique and addressing issues of mortality. At his death on August 7, 1941, he had achieved what the contemporary Indian American writer Pico Iyer sees as a unique position: he had become "not just the world's leading symbol of India, but India's leading spokesman for the world."

Works in Literary Context

In terms of his literary inspiration, Tagore acknowledged three main sources: the Vaishnava poets of medieval Bengal and the Bengali folk literature; the classical Indian cultural and philosophical heritage; and European literature of the nineteenth century, particularly the English Romantic poets. Woven through all these influences is an acutely modern sensibility, in touch with the social and political currents of his era. Throughout his life, he refused to belittle Western contributions to culture, always seeking a fusion of East and West.

Innovations in Fiction The sheer volume of Tagore's contributions to every field of literature can obscure the innovative qualities of much of his work. For example, his two hundred short stories were the first in the Bengali language and represented a new genre in Indian prose. His stories depict the everyday lives of ordinary people, whether in rural settings or in Calcutta or in remote parts of India. The social reformer is evident in stories that target issues such as child marriage, dowries, or the tyranny of landlords.

Abundance of Poetic Themes The Western world has viewed Tagore primarily as a poet devoted almost exclusively to spiritual themes. However, that view does not reflect the variety nor the depth of his poetic voice. Sometimes the images he used were the old religious ones of the love between man and woman as representative of the love between humanity and God. Sometimes they were the earthy images of the boatmen of the vast rivers or the country marketplace. Sometimes they were drawn from the complex life of Calcutta. They were always images that touched something deep in the hearts and memories of the Bengali people. He excelled in everything from stately love poetry to nonsense rhymes,

LITERARY AND HISTORICAL CONTEMPORARIES

Tagore's famous contemporaries include:

George Bernard Shaw (1856–1950): Shaw, an Irish playwright, socialist, and Nobel Prize winner, revolutionized the English stage, disposing of the Romantic conventions and devices and instituting a theater of ideas grounded in realism. His plays include *Pygmalion* (1912).

W. B. Yeats (1865–1939): Yeats, an Irish poet and dramatist, befriended Tagore and championed his work. Yeats's poetry included *The Wanderings of Oisin* (1889).

André Gide (1869–1951): Gide is a French author known for relentless self-exploration and credited with introducing modern experimental techniques to the French novel. His novels include *The Immoralist* (1902).

Thomas Mann (1875–1955): This German novelist and essayist addressed aesthetic, philosophical, and social concerns in his writing, while combining elements of literary realism and symbolism. His novels included *The Magic Mountain* (1924).

Mohandas K. Gandhi (1869–1948): Tagore called Gandhi "Mahatma," or "Great Soul." This Indian political and spiritual leader is known for his nonviolent protests and passive resistance to British rule.

Albert Einstein (1879–1955): This German-born physicist and humanitarian was the most famous scientist of the twentieth century. His theory of relativity reconfigured notions of time, space, and matter that had been formulated by Isaac Newton.

from flights of fancy to realistic depictions of ordinary people and situations.

In his nearly sixty volumes of verse, Tagore also experimented with many poetic forms—lyrics, sonnets, odes, dramatic monologues, dialogue poems, long narrative works, and prose poems. Every volume of his poetry is distinctive, whether in form or content, and he kept developing until the end of his very long career.

One of the aspects of Tagore's genius is his use of the Bengali language, for his musician's ear caught natural rhythms and his free mind paid little attention to classical rules of poetry. The forms he created were new. Even in the poetry that he intended to be read rather than sung, rhythms, internal rhyme and alliteration, and a peculiar sonorousness almost make the poems sing themselves. These are things that cannot even be suggested in translation. The translations of Tagore's poetry available in English are hardly representative of his total work. *Gitanjali*, on which his reputation in the West is largely based, shows nothing of the humor, for example, or intellectual rigor of which he was capable. Tagore's published work is largely, though not completely, contained in twenty-six substantial volumes.

Influence   Tagore almost single-handedly transformed Bengali literature and enriched its culture. Bengalis continue to find in him an endless source of inspiration. His poems, plays, songs, and stories have become part of the lives of the people of the Indian subcontinent. He is not only the author of the Bangladeshi national anthem but the Indian one as well. Many leading literary figures in South America, such as Nobel Prize winners Gabriela Mistral, Pablo Neruda, and Octavio Paz, also acknowledge him as a major influence on their work.

Works in Critical Context

While some critics feel that Tagore's prodigious output is uneven in its artistic value, his very prolificacy is often considered a measure of his creative achievement. Critics of Tagore's work are nearly unanimous in designating him as one of the preeminent lyric poets of the twentieth century. While Tagore's novels are mostly conventional in style and plotting, dealing frequently with crossed romances and improbable coincidences of fate, they are considered effective in dramatizing the moral conflicts between tradition and modernity in colonial India.

Even among more sensitive critics, Tagore's cadences and stylistic choices appeared increasingly old-fashioned in the interwar period. Although Tagore was the first modern Indian writer to introduce psychological realism in his fiction, his novels appeared out of step with the bold innovations in the novel represented by artists such as James Joyce and Marcel Proust. The Nobel Prize made Tagore and his books instantly popular in the rest of the world. However, the Tagore craze was brief in England and the United States. On the European continent, his reputation held on somewhat longer. Both political and literary factors explain the decline in his standing. His rejection of his knighthood and criticism of British rule in India had rankled many in Britain.

However, as Tagore's critical reputation began to decline in the English-speaking West, he was welcomed with great enthusiasm in the Middle East, the Far East, and South America. With the passing of time, more of Tagore's writing has reached English-language readers, allowing a more complete picture of his achievements to emerge. Present-day critics worldwide are nearly unanimous in designating Tagore one of the preeminent twentieth-century authors, as well as an indispensable figure in the modern history of the Indian subcontinent.

Gitanjali   Outside his homeland, Tagore's reputation stemmed from his presentation of the *Gitanjali* translation in 1912. Artistically, *Gitanjali* came to be seen as Tagore's most characteristic work. Yeats, who publicly proclaimed his admiration for the poems, and Ezra Pound, who compared Tagore with Dante, set the tone for Tagore's reception in the West. In his, introduction to the 1912 London edition, Yeats explained, "I have carried the manuscript of these translations about me for days, reading it in railway trains, or on the tops of omnibuses and in restaurants.... These lyrics display in their thought a world I have dreamed of all my life long."

A *Times Literary Supplement* reviewer agreed with Yeats, commenting, "These poems are prophetic of the poetry that might be written in England if our poets could attain the same harmony of emotion and idea." Another critic noted of the poems in the collection, "*Gitanjali* has some of the finest descriptions of nature that Tagore has written."

Responses to Literature

1. Research Bengali literature and culture before the era of Tagore for a paper. How can you characterize Tagore's specific artistic influence on Bengali society?

2. Tagore said that his plays summon up "the play of feeling, not of action." What does this mean? Cite one or two of his plays to explain your answer in the form of an essay.

3. Based on *The Home and the World* and other works, summarize Tagore's attitudes toward Indian anticolonial activism. Create a presentation with your findings.

4. Read several poems from Tagore's youth, and some from his final years. In a small group, discuss some of the common elements. What do the poems tell you about the arc of his life?

5. Write an essay about the religious and spiritual perspectives expressed in Tagore's poetry.

BIBLIOGRAPHY

Books

Agarwala, R. S. *Aesthetic Consciousness of Tagore.* Calcutta: Abhishek Agarwal, 1996.

Atkinson, David W. *Gandhi and Tagore: Visionaries of Modern India.* Hong Kong: Asian Research Service, 1989.

Bhattacharya, Vivek Ranjan. *Tagore's Vision of a Global Family.* New Delhi: Enkay, 1987.

Chakrabarti, Mohit. *Rabindranath Tagore: A Quest.* New Delhi: Gyan, 1995.

Das Gupta, Uma. *Rabindranath Tagore: A Biography.* Delhi and Oxford: Oxford University Press, 2004.

Dutta, Krishna, and Andrew Robinson. *Rabindranath Tagore: The Myriad-Minded Man.* Calcutta: Rupa, 2000.

Hay, Stephen N. *Asian Ideas of East and West: Tagore and His Critics in Japan, China, and India.* Cambridge, Mass.: Harvard University Press, 1970.

Khanolakara, Gangadhara Devarava. *The Lute and the Plough: A Life of Rabindranath Tagore.* Bombay: Book Centre, 1963.

Mukherjee, Sujit. *Passage to America: The Reception of Rabindranath Tagore in the United States, 1912–1941.* Calcutta: Bookland, 1964.

Naravane, Vishwanath S. *Introduction to Rabindranath Tagore.* Delhi: Macmillan, 1970.

Pabby, D. K., and Alpana Neogy, eds. *Rabindranath Tagore's "The Home and the World": New Dimensions.* New Delhi: Asia Book Club, 2001.

Radhakrishnan, Sarvepalli. *The Philosophy of Rabindranath Tagore.* London: Macmillan, 1918.

Rhys, Ernest. *Rabindranath Tagore: A Biographical Study.* London: Macmillan, 1915.

Thompson, Edward J. *Rabindranath Tagore: Poet and Dramatist.* London: Oxford University Press, 1948.

Yeats, W.B. Introduction to *"Gitanjali" and "Fruit-Gathering,"* by Sir Rabindranath Tagore. New York: Macmillan, 1918.

▨ Alfred, Lord Tennyson

BORN: *1809, Somersby, Lincolnshire, England*

DIED: *1892, Aldworth, Surrey, England*

NATIONALITY: *British*

GENRE: *Poetry, drama*

MAJOR WORKS:

Poems (1842)

In Memoriam (1849)

"The Charge of the Light Brigade" (1854)

Maud (1855)

Idylls of the King (1874)

Overview

British author Alfred, Lord Tennyson is considered an icon of the Victorian period of English history and is regarded as one of the most accomplished lyric poets in the history of English verse. He was immensely popular in his lifetime, especially in the years following the publication of his lengthy elegiac poem *In Memoriam* (1850). While Tennyson was the foremost poet of his generation and the poetic voice of Victorian England, many critics have since found his poetry excessively emotive and moralistic, though he is universally acclaimed as a lyricist of unsurpassed skill.

Works in Biographical and Historical Context

Unhappy Childhood with an Unstable Father
The fourth of twelve children, Tennyson was born in Somersby, Lincolnshire, England, on August 6, 1809. His father, George Clayton Tennyson, was a rector who maintained his benefice grudgingly as a means of supporting himself and his family. The elder son of a wealthy

Alfred, Lord Tennyson *Lord Tennyson, Alfred, photograph. AP Images.*

landowner, he had obtained the rectory when his younger brother was designated as prospective heir to the family's estate. Tennyson's father had been essentially disinherited and reacted by indulging in drugs and alcohol, creating an unpleasant domestic atmosphere often made worse by his violent temper. It also believed that George Tennyson was mentally unstable, and each of his children also suffered to some extent from drug addiction or mental illness.

Biographers speculate that the general melancholy and morbidity expressed in much of Tennyson's verse is rooted in the unhappy environment at Somersby. He began writing poetry long before he was sent to school. All his life he used writing as a way of taking his mind off his troubles. One odd aspect of his method of composition was set in childhood as well. He would make up phrases or discrete lines as he walked, and store them in his memory until he had a proper setting for them.

Launched Writing Career

In 1827, when he was almost eighteen years old, Tennyson's first volume of poetry, *Poems by Two Brothers* was published. Later that year, Tennyson enrolled at Trinity College, Cambridge, where he won the chancellor's gold medal for his poem "Timbuctoo" in 1829. *Poems, Chiefly Lyrical*, published in 1830, was well received and marked the beginning of Tennyson's literary career. Another collection, *Poems*, appeared in 1832 but was less favorably reviewed, many critics praising Tennyson's artistry but objecting to what they considered an absence of intellectual substance.

The latter volume was published at the urging of Arthur Hallam, a brilliant Cambridge undergraduate who had become Tennyson's closest friend and was an ardent admirer of his poetry. Hallam's enthusiasm was welcomed by Tennyson, whose personal circumstances had led to a growing despondency. His father died in 1831, leaving Tennyson's family in debt and forcing his early departure from Trinity College. One of Tennyson's brothers suffered a mental breakdown and required institutionalization. Tennyson himself was morbidly fearful of falling victim to epilepsy or madness. Hallam's untimely death in 1833, which prompted the series of elegies later comprising *In Memoriam*, contributed greatly to Tennyson's despair.

Financial and Poetic Uncertainty

For nearly a decade after Hallam's death Tennyson published no further poetry. During this period, he became engaged to Emily Sellwood, but financial difficulties and Tennyson's persistent anxiety over the condition of his health resulted in their separation. As Tennyson struggled, Great Britain was also changing as Queen Victoria took the throne in 1837, beginning a long reign (which ended in 1901) and setting the tone for an important era in British history. During the Victorian age, the Industrial Revolution reached its peak and provided British colonial and military expansion during the nineteenth century. At home, there was a vast increase in the factory system, industrialization, and urbanization, changing the fabric of British society. Reform and social justice were also emphasized, as humanitarian legislation eliminated some long-standing abuses.

In this environment in 1842, yielding to a friend's insistence, Tennyson published his two-volume collection *Poems*, for which reviewers were virtually unanimous in expressing admiration. That same year, however, an unsuccessful financial venture cost Tennyson nearly everything he owned, causing him to succumb to a deep depression that required medical treatment. In 1845, he was granted a government pension in recognition of both his poetic achievement and his apparent need. Contributing to his financial stability, the first edition of his narrative poem *The Princess: A Medley*, published in 1847, sold out within two months. Tennyson resumed his courtship of Sellwood in 1849, and they were married the following year.

The timely success of *In Memoriam*, published in 1850, ensured Tennyson's appointment as poet laureate, succeeding William Wordsworth. The success of *In Memoriam* and his appointment as poet laureate assured Tennyson the opportunity to become the poetic voice of his generation, and in his ceremonial position he composed such poems as "Ode on the Death of the Duke of Wellington" and "The Charge of the Light Brigade", each of which is a celebration of heroism and public duty. *Idylls of the King* (1859), considered by Tennyson's contemporaries to be his masterpiece, and *Enoch Arden* (1864), which sold more than forty thousand copies upon publication, increased both his popularity and his wealth and earned him the designation "the people's poet."

Poet Laureate

Although the dramatic works written later in his career like *Queen Mary* (1875) and *The Foresters* (1892) were largely unsuccessful, Tennyson completed several additional collections of poems in the last decade of his life, all of which were well received. They included: *Ballads and Other Poems* (1880), *Tiresias, and Other Poems* (1885), and *Demeter, and Other Poems* (1889). In 1883 he accepted a peerage, the first poet to be so honored strictly on the basis of literary achievement. Ill for the last two years of his life, Tennyson died on October 6, 1892, at his home and was interred in Westminster Abbey.

Works in Literary Context

Tennyson's poetry had a number of influences, including Elizabethan songs, the traditional ballad, and the poetry of the Romantics who came before him. They included Percy Bysshe Shelley, Samuel Taylor Coleridge, and John Keats, as well as other authors like William Shakespeare, John Milton, and Sir Walter Scott. Traditional legends, classical mythology and poets, and fairy tales also informed some of his narrative subjects, such as "The Day-Dream." Tennyson had nearly a lifelong interest in the legends of King Arthur, which ultimately resulted in *Idylls of the King* (1889). Yet many critics believe that his most characteristic lyrics are unique and individual, marked by a Tennysonian "something" that had no precedent in English verse.

Idylls of the King and the British Empire   Tennyson's epic poem *Idylls of the King* followed the controversial *Maud* by examining the rise and fall of idealism in society. "I tried in my *Idylls*," Tennyson wrote, "to teach men the need of an ideal." F. E. L. Priestley has observed that Tennyson used the "Arthurian cycle as a medium for discussion of problems which [were] both contemporary and perennial," and concludes that the *Idylls* "represent one of Tennyson's most earnest and important efforts to deal with the major problems of his time." Tennyson was concerned with what he considered to be a growing tendency toward hedonism in society and an attendant rejection of spiritual values. *Idylls of the King* expresses his ideal of the British empire as an exemplar of moral and social order: the "Table Round / A glorious company" would "serve as a model for the mighty world." However, when individual acts of betrayal and corruption result from adultery committed by Arthur's wife and Lancelot, the ensuing disorder destroys the Round Table, symbolizing the effects of moral decay that were Tennyson's chief concern about the society of his day.

Theme of Death   In Tennyson's major work, *In Memoriam*, he expressed his personal grief over Hallam's death while examining more generally the nature of death and bereavement in relation to contemporary scientific issues, especially those involving evolution and the geologic dating of the earth's history, which brought into question traditional religious beliefs. Largely regarded as an affirmation of faith, *In Memoriam* was especially valued for its reflections on overcoming loss. Comprising 132 sections written over the course of nearly two decades, the poem progresses from despair to joy and concludes with a marriage celebration, symbolically expressing Tennyson's faith in the moral evolution of humanity and reflecting the nineteenth-century ideal of social progress.

Suicidal Bravery   In an earlier assessment of the narrative poem "The Charge of the Light Brigade" (1854) Christopher Ricks has argued that the poem is indirectly concerned with the idea of suicide, which pervades Tennyson's early poetry, but can also be discovered in his later works. In armed combat, self-extinction loses the stigma that traditionally attaches to it in Western society and is esteemed an honorable behavior instead. There is little doubt that military actions have sometimes been prompted by an urge for annihilation. Seen from this angle, the enthusiastic self-sacrifice of soldiers, loses its heroic note but gains a profoundly human significance that would have appealed to Tennyson. It is important to note in this connection that his description deviates at one point from the steadfast regularity that otherwise characterizes the advance. In the last stanza, lavish praise

---

LITERARY AND HISTORICAL CONTEMPORARIES

Tennyson's famous contemporaries include:

Julia Margaret Cameron (1815—1879): Cameron was a British photographer noted for taking pictures of Victorian celebrities, including Tennyson and his friends. She is also remembered for a cycle of photographs based on an Arthurian theme.

Prince Albert Edward (1841–1910): Prince Edward, who was Prince of Wales during Tennyson's lifetime, succeeded Queen Victoria to the throne in 1901. The Edwardian period in England saw many advances in technology and science and the reconstruction of the army between the Boer War and the outbreak of World War I.

Charles Dickens (1812–1870): British novelist Dickens was a prolific and beloved writer of the Victorian era and is best known for such novels as *Oliver Twist* (1838), *Bleak House* (1853), and *A Tale of Two Cities* (1859).

Oscar Wilde (1854–1900): A witty novelist, poet, and playwright, Wilde was known as the leader of the Decadent movement that dominated British literature at the end of the nineteenth century. His only novel was *The Picture of Dorian Gray* (1891), while his plays include *Lady Windemere's Fan* (1892) and *An Ideal Husband* (1895).

Florence Nightingale (1820–1910): Nightingale was a pioneer in the medical field who sought improved health care and conditions for the citizens of Great Britain. After serving as a nurse in the Crimean War, she launched a campaign for medical reform and started a nursing hospital in London.

---

is bestowed on the "wild charge" of the Light Brigade as if the poet had for once yielded to a secret conviction that the ride had a suicidal aspect.

The suicide motif arises from the argument advanced in the second stanza where the moment of awareness is expressly articulated. "Their's but to do and die": the steady progress of the collective body of troopers who pass lemminglike to their doom will raise associations that are more closely related to contemporary everyday life than to military engagement. The common man has become painfully aware of the infinite variety of administrative mishaps that devolve upon him in the shape of coercive patterns imposed from above. Legal restrictions, bureaucratic regulations, rigid codes of professional conduct, technocratic directions—the individual's existence is weighed down by constraints that we often know to be erroneous and yet are forced to comply with, since the rhythms of contemporary life depend on our enactment of predetermined roles.

COMMON HUMAN EXPERIENCE

Tennyson was just one of many authors to tackle the legends of King Arthur. Each work focuses on different aspects of the mythology, demonstrating the mutability and enduring popularity of the stories.

Le Morte d'Arthur (1485), a novel by Sir Thomas Malory. Perhaps the best-known version of the Arthurian saga, Malory drew upon a multitude of sources to construct the story of Arthur's life and reign, from the "sword in the stone" to Arthur's death at the hands of his son Mordred.

The Once and Future King (1958), a novel by T. H. White. In a modernized take on the Arthurian legends, the mythological figures are updated with real-life emotions, the events of a far-off time given contemporary relevance.

Acts of King Arthur and His Noble Knights (1976), a novel by John Steinbeck. This updated, "living" translation of Malory is by the noted American author, long an admirer of the Arthurian cycle.

A Connecticut Yankee in King Arthur's Court (1889), a novel by Mark Twain. A comedic take on King Arthur's Camelot, this novel features a time-traveling American who introduces modern concepts and inventions to his new medieval world.

The Mists of Avalon (1983), a novel by Marion Zimmer Bradley. The Arthurian cycle is retold from the perspective of the women, chiefly the Ladies of the Lake in this novel. The Knights of the Round Table and Arthur become the supporting characters, much as the women are in conventional tales.

Moreover, the predicament requires distinctly more than sheeplike obedience. Fortitude and active dedication are called for if the rigorous discipline of the modern state is to be maintained. Advancing or retreating with the steady measure of a pendulum, men may at all times be forced into situations that could terminate in personal annihilation. Modern society is still prepared to acknowledge the importance of unflinching loyalty on the part of the individual. Yet no purgatorial purification or spiritual reward, not even the certainty of lasting public esteem, could still be attained through acts of selfless devotion, and this is precisely the point where the "The Charge of the Light Brigade" falls short of illustrating the human condition in our time. Tennyson ended his poem on a note of praise, promising everlasting glory for the victims of an administrative blunder.

Influence As perhaps the leading poet of the Victorian era as well as the poet laureate of Great Britain, Tennyson was highly regarded in his lifetime as well as long after his death. Many Victorian readers were touched by his words, including Queen Victoria herself. University students were reading his verse, quoting it as a mark of sophistication. An extraordinary number of writers, both in Great Britain and the United States, count Tennyson as an influence, including T. S. Eliot, George Eliot, George Henry Lewes, and Walt Whitman.

Works in Critical Context

Today, Tennyson is considered one of the greatest poets in the English language. This critical reputation began in his lifetime when many of his poems were universally acclaimed. By the end of his lifetime, however, there were the beginnings of an anti-Victorian movement, as new styles of poetry and criticism emerged. Tennyson was so closely identified with his era that his critics began dismissing him with disillusionment for his Romantic stylistic and language choices, which were considered Victorian. Many early twentieth-century readers found his stylistic and subjective choices to be dated. By mid-century, Tennyson's importance was again recognized, and he continued to be appreciated into the twenty-first century. However, critics remain divided, as some critics consider him a minor poet of a minor historical period while others recognize his anticipation of twentieth century poetic movements.

Early Works Tennyson's first two significant collections, *Poems, Chiefly Lyrical* and *Poems*, were considered by many critics to be of high poetic merit but devoid of meaning or purpose beyond their pure artistry. In a review of the latter collection, philosopher John Stuart Mill urged Tennyson to "cultivate ... philosophy as well as poetry," expressing a sentiment not uncommon among Tennyson's early reviewers. The collection of *Poems* that appeared in 1842 included radically revised versions of his best poems from the earlier volumes, and addressed such themes as duty, self-discipline, and the complexities of religious faith, offering what critics considered to be a truer representation of human life than that of his early works.

Maud *Maud, and Other Poems* (1855) was the first collection Tennyson published as poet laureate, but it elicited a negative response. The title poem is a "monodrama" in which the changing consciousness of the narrator is traced through a series of tragedies that result in his insanity. Confined to an asylum, the protagonist is cured of his madness and asserts his love for humanity by serving his country in the Crimean War. Both author George Eliot and prime minister William Gladstone denounced the poem as morbid and obscure, and were among many who disapproved of Tennyson's apparent glorification of war, which he depicted as an ennobling enterprise essential to the cleansing and regeneration of a morally corrupt society. *Maud* has since been reevaluated by critics who find it Tennyson's most stylistically inventive poem, praising its violent rhythms and passionate language. Modern critics largely agree with Christopher

Ricks that *Maud* was for Tennyson an "exorcism"; as Ricks explains, "*Maud* was an intense and precarious attempt ... to encompass the bitter experiences of four decades of a life in which many of the formative influences had also been deformative." Thus madness, suicide, familial conflict, shattered love, death and loss, and untempered pursuit of wealth, all central sadnesses in Tennyson's life, are attacked openly and passionately in *Maud*, with war cultivating the spirit of sacrifice and loyalty that Tennyson felt essential to avert the self-destruction of a selfishly materialistic society.

Responses to Literature

1. What can you discern about Victorian values from reading Tennyson's "Ulysses"? In an essay, summarize the values laid out in the poem and how values have changed since the poem was written. What would an updated version of "Ulysses" be like?

2. In a presentation, explain the personal loss and resulting despair that motivated Tennyson's *In Memoriam*.

3. In "The Charge of the Light Brigade," Tennyson turned a military blunder into a tale of glory. In a group, discuss the following questions: What do you think is the significance of having the Light Brigade temporarily victorious in stanza 4? Does it add to the story's tension? Does it make these brave soldiers more admirable? How?

4. Read about the presidential administration of John F. Kennedy and write a paper that addresses the following questions: Why was it called "Camelot"? Find particular figures from the Arthurian myths that correspond to figures in U.S. politics. In particular, whom would you say is most like the Lady of Shalott?

BIBLIOGRAPHY

Books

Barreca, Regina, ed. *Sex and Death in Victorian Literature*. Bloomington: Indiana University Press, 1990.

Culler, A. Dwight. *The Poetry of Tennyson*. New Haven, Conn.: Yale University Press, 1977.

Kincaid, James R. *Tennyson's Major Poems: The Comic and Ironic Patterns*. New Haven, Conn.: Yale University Press, 1975.

Shannon, Edgar F., Jr. *Tennyson and the Reviewers: A Study of His Literary Reputation and the Influence of the Critics upon His Poetry, 1827–1851*. Cambridge, Mass.: Harvard University Press, 1952.

Tennyson, Charles, and Christine Fall. *Alfred Tennyson: An Annotated Bibliography*. Athens: University of Georgia Press, 1967.

Turner, Paul. *Tennyson*. London: Routledge & Kegan Paul, 1976.

❖ William Makepeace Thackeray

BORN: *1811, Calcutta, India*

DIED: *1863, London, England*

NATIONALITY: *British*

GENRE: *Fiction, poetry*

MAJOR WORKS:

The Yellowplush Correspondence (1838)

The Luck of Barry Lyndon (1844)

Vanity Fair: A Novel without a Hero (1848)

The History of Henry Esmond, Esq., a Colonel in the Service of Her Majesty Q. Anne (1852)

Roundabout Papers (1863)

Overview

British author William Makepeace Thackeray is best known for his satiric sketches and novels of upper- and middle-class English life and is credited with bringing a simpler style and greater realism to the English novel. *Vanity Fair: A Novel without a Hero* (1848), a panorama of early nineteenth-century English upper-middle-class society, is generally regarded as Thackeray's masterpiece. Although *Vanity Fair* has received more critical attention than any of his other works, many regard *The History of Henry Esmond, Esq., a Colonel in the Service of Her*

William Thackeray   *Thackeray, William, photograph. AP Images.*

Majesty Q. Anne (1852), a historical novel set in early eighteenth-century England, to be his most well-planned and carefully executed work.

Works in Biographical and Historical Context

Unhappy Childhood Spent in Boarding Schools
Thackeray was born in Calcutta, India, in 1811, where his father worked as a secretary for the British East India Company. At the time, India was under the colonial rule of the company, and, indirectly, Great Britain. The British East India Company was a trading company with political power that reaped high profits from such goods as salt, indigo, and coffee while modernizing India. After his father's death when Thackeray was six, however, Thackeray was sent to England, where he was cared for by relatives. His mother, who remarried and remained in India, did not return to England for four years. During these years Thackeray attended several boarding schools, where he was extremely unhappy. He later attended the prestigious Charterhouse School and then Trinity College, Cambridge, which he left before finishing his degree.

After reading law for a short time, Thackeray moved to Paris, where he studied art. Although he eventually abandoned the idea of making his living as a painter, Thackeray continued to sketch and paint throughout his life and illustrated many of his own works. While studying in Paris, he married a young Irishwoman named Isabella Shawe. Shortly after their marriage, they returned to London, where Thackeray began writing professionally, contributing to *Fraser's Magazine, New Monthly Magazine*, and later to *Punch*, to support himself and his new family after the fortune he inherited from his father was lost in an Indian bank failure in 1833. In 1839, the Thackerays' second daughter, Jane, died in infancy, and the next year, shortly after the birth of their third daughter, Harriet, Isabella Thackeray went mad, never regaining her sanity. Because she outlived him, Thackeray was unable to remarry and was thus deprived of the family life he so desired.

Published under Pen Names During the years before the success of *Vanity Fair* as he struggled to make a living, Thackeray wrote numerous reviews, essays, comic sketches, and burlesques under more than a dozen comic pseudonyms. Among the best known of his early nonfiction is *The Yellowplush Correspondence* (1838), a series of satiric sketches written in the guise of a cockney footman's memoirs published under the pen name Charles J. Yellowplush. The most successful of the early burlesques is the novella *Catherine* (1839–1840) published under the name Ikey Solomons, a parody of the crime story genre popular in Thackeray's day. This work is the strongest expression of Thackeray's contempt, discernible throughout his other works, for the prevalent literary convention of glorifying criminals.

The Luck of Barry Lyndon (1844), his first lengthy novel published under the name Fitz-Boodle, was strongly influenced by Henry Fielding's *The Life and Death of Jonathan Wild, the Great* (1743) and demonstrates his keen interest in eighteenth-century literary forms. *The Luck of Barry Lyndon*, which first revealed Thackeray's skill at depicting the language and manners of an earlier age, was also his first serious attack on social pretension. His increasing scorn for the shallow acquisitiveness of Victorian society is obvious in *The Book of Snobs* (1848), a collection of satiric character sketches, which first appeared as *The Snobs of England, by One of Themselves* in *Punch*. This series denounces the snobbery and greed bred by the changes in social attitudes and relationships brought about by the Industrial Revolution and the resulting redistribution of wealth and power. During the Victorian era, British society was undergoing other major transformations such as increased urbanization, population shifts, and a greater concern for reform and social justice in the face of unprecedented commercial and industrial prosperity.

Vanity Fair For *Vanity Fair*, his first signed work, Thackeray adopted the publication form of monthly periodical installments already made popular by Charles Dickens. This comprehensive satire of corruption in upper- and middle-class English society is set during the Waterloo crisis of 1815 (when Britain and a European coalition finally ended Napoléon's attempt to control Europe). The themes central to Thackeray's earlier writings are clarified and fully developed in *Vanity Fair*, in which he delivers his most scathing attack on the heartless pretension prevalent in nineteenth-century English life and concludes that self-interest is at the heart of human motivation.

Literary Success Finally successful and well known, Thackeray began suffering from a sudden decline in his health in the late 1840s, including what was believed to be a bout of typhoid in 1849. He also suffered from the emotional effects of a long, but unphysical, love affair with Jane Brookfield, the wife of his clergyman friend, Henry Brookfield. Thackeray came to realize that she had merely played with his affections and never intended to be unfaithful. Despite such troubles, Thackeray went on to write *The History of Pendennis: His Fortunes and Misfortunes, His Friends and His Greatest Enemy* (1849–1850), the first of three related novels based on his own experiences. *The History of Pendennis* chronicles the early life of Arthur Pendennis, who takes the role of the narrator in the sequels, which are titled *The Newcomes: Memoirs of a Most Respectable Family* (1854–1855) and *The Adventures of Philip on His Way through the World* (1862). All three novels are set in contemporary London and are narrated in the manner, according to Thackeray, of "a sort of confidential talk." Although their narrative technique is often considered diffuse and overly didactic, these novels are praised for their convincing characterization and vivid depiction of Victorian society.

Henry Esmond is Thackeray's only novel completely written before publication and issued in book form without first being serialized. Critics often cite these circumstances when praising the novel's careful organization and elegant style. Set during the reign of Queen Anne (1702–1714), Henry Esmond is written in imitation of early eighteenth-century English prose. The coarse, inconsiderate Lord Castlewood in the novel is a stab at Thackeray's former friend Brookfield. Although it offended some readers due to the incestuous overtones of Henry Esmond's marriage to Lady Castlewood, it is now regarded as one of the greatest nineteenth-century English historical novels. Its sequel, *The Virginians: A Tale of the Last Century* (1858–1859), is generally considered to be inferior.

Focused on Journalism In 1859, Thackeray became the first editor of and chief contributor to *Cornhill Magazine*. During his last years, he contributed numerous essays and several novels to the journal, including *Lovel the Widower* (1861) and *The Adventures of Philip on His Way through the World; Shewing Who Robbed Him, Who Helped Him, and Who Passed Him By* (1862). The essays collected in *The Roundabout Papers* (1863), however, are probably the most highly valued of these contributions. In these nostalgic, rambling pieces Thackeray wistfully recounts his childhood experiences, travels, and impressions of Victorian literature, politics, and society. He was in the midst of publishing *Denis Duval* (1864) in *Cornhill Magazine* when he died suddenly of an apoplectic stroke on Christmas Eve 1863.

Works in Literary Context

In his writings, Thackeray was greatly influenced by such writers as Miguel de Cervantes, Henry Fielding, Tobias Smollett, Fanny Burney, Sir Walter Scott, James Fenimore Cooper, and Alexandre Dumas. Honoré de Balzac, especially his *Cousine Bette* (1846) specifically inspired *Vanity Fair*. Beyond other authors, Thackerary was also influenced by the era in which he lived—the Victorian era—with all its contradictions and social conditions as well as the externals of everyday life, including personal connections, jobs, and marriages. Thackeray's need to question nineteenth-century ideals, as well as religion and moral choices, also informed his works.

"Novel without a Hero" Like many of his fellow Victorian novelists, Thackeray is noted for his ability to create memorable characters—for example, Major Gahagan, Charles Yellowplush, Becky Sharp, Major Pendennis, Henry and Beatrix Esmond, Colonel Newcome, and the roundabout commentator who addresses the reader in virtually all of Thackeray' works. In spite of giving such prominence to character delineation, Thackeray also came to develop an important new kind of novel, the "novel without a hero." Such a novel may have a chief figure, one who is neither a romantic hero nor a rogue hero but a flawed, recognizable human being like Arthur Pendennis or Philip Firmin. In the case of several of Thackeray's

LITERARY AND HISTORICAL CONTEMPORARIES

Thackeray's famous contemporaries include:

Anthony Trollope (1815–1882): A successful and prolific English Victorian author, Trollope was noted for his keen observations of social, cultural, and political issues of the day. His novels include *The Warden* (1855) and *The Last Chronicle of Barset* (1867).

Emily Brontë (1818–1848): One of a trio of literary sisters, Emily wrote only one novel—albeit one that was considered an instant classic: *Wuthering Heights* (1847)—before dying of tuberculosis at age thirty.

Jacob Grimm (1785–1863): As one half of the famous Brothers Grimm, Jacob was instrumental in conducting one of the first comprehensive surveys of folklore. Grimm was primarily a respected and influential figure in the study and history of the German language and wrote several authoritative works on the subject. His publications included *Deutsche Mythologie* (1835).

Honoré de Balzac (1799–1850): French novelist and playwright, whose *La Comédie humaine* (1799–1850), a one-hundred-volume collection of novels and stories, has exerted a strong influence over many famous authors, from Dickens to Proust to Kerouac.

Karl Marx (1818–1883): Called the "father of communism," Marx was both a political philosopher and activist. Although German by birth, Marx spent most of his adult life in London, where he refined his theories of class struggle and the emergence of a classless society. His books on the subject include *The Communist Manifesto* (1848).

Søren Kierkegaard (1813–1855): This Danish philosopher is best known for his probing questions on institutionalized religion, ethics, and faith. His publications include *Either/Or* (1843).

masterpieces, such as *Vanity Fair* (1847–1848) and *The Newcomes* (1853–1855), however, the center of interest is the complex network of relationships among the characters—an analog of society itself.

Class and Narrative Technique Thackeray's masterwork, *Vanity Fair*, includes the most comprehensive treatment of the concerns central to all of Thackeray's works—the divisive effects of greed, class, and social ambition—and epitomizes the sardonic wit and apt character sketching for which he is esteemed. This satiric novel revolves around the lives of two characters, the passive Amelia Sedley and the ambitious, conniving Becky Sharp. Thackeray's treatment of these characters has sparked endless debate, for although Becky is ostensibly the negative character, it is she who actively engages the reader's interest and

COMMON HUMAN EXPERIENCE

Thackeray's works often parody the pretensions of the upper classes. Other novels that also comment on the rich include:

Carry on, Jeeves (1925), a book of short stories by P. G. Wodehouse. These comic stories feature the bumbling British aristocrat Bertie Wooster and his levelheaded valet, Jeeves, who repeatedly extricates his employer from various amorous, legal, and familial difficulties.
Vile Bodies (1930), a novel by Evelyn Waugh. Known for his black satires, Waugh takes on young British socialites in this mordant novel.
The Philadelphia Story (1940), a film directed by George Cukor. This romantic comedy about a Philadelphia socialite planning for her wedding encourages viewers to reconsider their preconceptions about social class.

sympathy, while Amelia, though good-hearted, appears in the final analysis to be dull and ineffectual. Becky Sharp is often praised, in fact, as one of the most memorable antiheroines of the nineteenth century. The other major and minor characters are also noted for their lifelike complexity.

In addition, Thackeray first uses in *Vanity Fair* the narrative technique employed throughout his subsequent novels: the omniscient, didactic narrator who comments freely upon the motives and actions of the characters. Similarly, three related novels he published between 1849 and 1862 share an unusual narrative technique. *The History of Pendennis: His Fortunes and Misfortunes, His Friends and His Greatest Enemy* (1849–1850) is the first of three related novels based on Thackeray's own experiences. *The History of Pendennis* chronicles the early life of Arthur Pendennis, who takes the role of the narrator in the sequels, which are titled *The Newcomes: Memoirs of a Most Respectable Family* (1854–1855) and *The Adventures of Philip on His Way through the World* (1862). All three novels are set in contemporary London and are narrated in the manner, according to Thackeray, of "a sort of confidential talk." Although their narrative technique is often considered diffuse and overly didactic, these novels are praised for their convincing characterization and vivid depiction of Victorian society.

Influence While Dickens ultimately left a more prominent legacy than Thackeray, the latter's influence can still be felt in other works of Victorian literature that realistically examine society. Thackeray's journalistic work also affected many readers and writers in the nineteenth century and beyond. It is also believed that Thackeray's literary techniques also influenced such sweeping novels as Leo Tolstoy's *War and Peace* (1865–1869).

Works in Critical Context

During his life Thackeray's work was regarded as the great upper-class counterpart to Dickens's panorama of lower-class Victorian society. Indeed, because of his precise rendering of character types and his acuity in describing the social mores of his time, some critics have contended that he is Dickens's superior as a historical chronicler. However, Thackeray's reputation declined at the turn of the century. Early twentieth-century critics often found his vision of society limited and his characterization impeded by his deference to Victorian conventions. More recently there has been a resurgence of interest in Thackeray and numerous studies have appeared that afford his works a more sympathetic treatment. Thus, although Thackeray is no longer widely ranked as an equal of Dickens, his works continue to inspire a diverse body of critical interpretation, and he is generally recognized as one of the major writers of the mid-Victorian era.

Criticism of Thackeray's works primarily revolves around several issues, including his narrative technique and his use of satiric irony. Many early critics were particularly disturbed by Thackeray's apparent cynicism; some, including novelist Anthony Trollope, chided him for dwelling too exclusively on the negative traits of humanity. Others claimed that his satiric depiction of self-interested rogues served a useful moral purpose and was sufficiently balanced with sensitivity and compassion. In contrast, his twentieth-century detractors have been far more critical of the sentimentality that often creeps into his works.

Thackeray's omniscient narrative technique continues, however, to be the most controversial element in his fiction. While many claim that the authorial commentary is intrusive and interferes with dramatic unity, others believe that this method enhances Thackeray's work by creating a deliberate moral ambiguity that actively involves readers by forcing them to render their own judgments. Another area of interest for both critics and biographers is the possible autobiographical sources for Thackeray's works. Numerous studies have been published that examine the parallels between his private relationships and experiences and the characters and plots of his works. Critics often maintain that Thackeray's intense emotional involvement with characters based closely upon real-life models severely limited his artistic achievement.

Vanity Fair Critics believe that Thackeray's *Vanity Fair* represents a milestone in the development of fictional realism in England. The novel is widely regarded to be Thackeray's masterpiece and is considered to be as original and ambitious as any novel from the Victorian era. However, early critical reactions to the novel were mixed. A number of prominent authors expressed high praise for *Vanity Fair*, including Charlotte Brontë, who called the novel a "Herculean feat" and its author a "Titan" among Victorian writers. Some contemporary reviews objected to the work on moral grounds. Robert

Bell took exception to the "vicious and odious" qualities of the main characters.

In spite of the furor sparked by the book's supposed amorality and ruthlessness, most critics agreed that the novel represented a landmark of realistic fiction. John Forster wrote in the *Examiner*, "*Vanity Fair* must be admitted to be one of the most original works of real genius that has late been given to the world. . . . The very novelty of tone in the book impeded its first success; but it will be daily more justly appreciated; and will take a lasting place in our literature."

Beginning in the twentieth century, critical interpretation began to steer away from moral consideration of the novel and focus on Thackeray's stylistic innovations. Other critics began to recognize the possible strategies behind the work's structural imbalances, arguing that the lack of a clearly developed plot allowed the novel's themes to serve as a framework of the story. In more recent years, critics have returned to the moral considerations that preoccupied Thackeray's contemporaries.

Responses to Literature

1. Using Thackeray's novels as a base, research and explain the manners and customs of his time in a paper. How does Thackeray point out the peculiarities and foibles of members of Victorian society?

2. In a group, discuss the following questions: What impact do the Napoleonic Wars have on the characters in *Vanity Fair*? How closely are their lives touched by such monumental yet relatively far-off events?

3. Select a scenario in Thackeray's works in which a character manipulates or intimidates another. In an essay, express whether the method is physical force, political power, or social or educational superiority, and show how the submissive character is harmed.

4. Create a presentation that answers these questions: How are Thackeray's own life experiences reflected in the characters in *Vanity Fair*? Why do you think he chose to make the story "a novel without a hero"?

5. How is the society in which you live similar to the one depicted in *Vanity Fair*, and how is it different? Present your answer in any form you choose, such as an essay, short story, or poem.

BIBLIOGRAPHY

Books

Benjamin, Lewis Saul. *William Makepeace Thackeray: A Biography Including Hitherto Uncollected Letters and Speeches and a Bibliography of 1300 Items.* Washington, D.C.: Scholarly Press, 1968.

Colby, R. A. *Thackeray's Canvas of Humanity.* Columbus: Ohio State University Press, 1979.

Goldfarb, Sheldon. *William Makepeace Thackeray: An Annotated Bibliography, 1900–1975.* New York: Garland, 1977.

Hardy, Barbara. *The Exposure of Luxury: Radical Themes in Thackeray.* London: Owen, 1972.

Peters, Catherine. *Thackeray's Universe: Shifting Worlds of Imagination and Reality.* London: Faber & Faber, 1987.

Rawlins, Jack P. *Thackeray's Novels: A Fiction That Is True.* Berkeley: University of California Press, 1974.

Trollope, Anthony. *Thackeray.* London: Macmillan, 1879.

Wheatley, James M. *Patterns in Thackeray's Fiction.* Cambridge, Mass.: MIT Press, 1969.

Dylan Thomas

BORN: *1914, Swansea, Wales*

DIED: *1953, New York*

NATIONALITY: *British, Welsh*

GENRE: *Poetry, drama, fiction*

MAJOR WORKS:

Eighteen Poems (1934)

Deaths and Entrances (1946)

"Do Not Go Gentle into That Good Night" (1951)

Under Milk Wood (1954)

Dylan Thomas *Francis Reiss / Picture Post / Getty Images*

Overview

One of the most renowned authors of the twentieth century, Thomas is as well known for his life of excess as for his iconoclastic, critically acclaimed writings. Often focusing on such universal concerns as birth, death, love, and religion, Thomas's works remain distinctly personal through a blend of rich metaphorical language, sensuous imagery, and psychological detail.

Works in Biographical and Historical Context

Growing Up in Wales Born in a suburb of the port of Swansea, on the southern coast of Wales, Thomas was the second child and only son of middle-class parents. His father, an English teacher who had a great love for literature, encouraged similar devotion in his son, even going so far as to read the works of Shakespeare aloud to the infant Thomas in his cradle. Such efforts were rewarded when Thomas began writing verse at an early age. He was an otherwise undistinguished student, however, and left school at sixteen to work for the *South Wales Daily Post* in Swansea.

Thomas continued to compose verse while working at the *Post*. When he resigned from the paper early in 1933, poetry became his primary occupation. It was at this time that Thomas began to develop the serious drinking problem that plagued him throughout the remainder of his life and resulted in his death at the age of thirty-nine. His notebooks reveal that many of his most highly regarded poems were either written or drafted during this period and that he had also begun to experiment with short prose pieces. In May of 1933, his poem "And Death Shall Have No Dominion" was published in the *New English Weekly*, marking the first appearance of his work in a London journal, and in December of the following year his first poetry collection, *Eighteen Poems* (1934), was issued. Although this book attracted little attention, Thomas's second volume, *Twenty-five Poems* (1936), fared somewhat better, and as the decade progressed he gained increasing recognition for both his poetry and his prose.

Marriage and a Nomadic Life In the summer of 1937, Thomas married Caitlin Macnamara, an aspiring dancer of Irish descent whose reputation for unconventional behavior rivaled Thomas's own. For the next twelve years the couple led a nomadic existence, staying with friends, relatives, and a series of benefactors. The stories later collected in *Portrait of the Artist as a Young Dog* (1940) were written primarily during their stay in the Welsh coastal village of Laugharne in late 1938 and early 1939. Too frail for active military service, Thomas wrote scripts for propaganda films during World War II, at which time he also began to participate in radio dramas and readings for the BBC. His hometown of Swansea was targeted by German bombers during air raids in 1941, and a large urban portion of the town was completely destroyed. He later wrote about witnessing the

aftermath in the radio drama *Return Journey Home*. Thomas emerged from the war years a respected literary figure and popular performer; however, his gregarious social life and the excessive drinking it encouraged seriously interfered with his writing. Seeking an environment more conducive to poetic production, Thomas and Caitlin returned to Laugharne in 1949.

During the early 1950s, Thomas wrote several of his most poignant poems, including "Do Not Go Gentle into That Good Night" and "Lament." He also completed the radio drama *Under Milk Wood* (1954) and began work on an autobiographical novel, which was left unfinished at his death and published posthumously as *Adventures in the Skin Trade* (1955). Nevertheless, he feared that his creative powers were rapidly waning, and, partly in an attempt to avoid the pressures of writing, he embarked on a speaking tour of the United States in the spring of 1950. A highly charismatic speaker, Thomas charmed American audiences with his readings and shocked them with his often wild, irresponsible behavior.

Beyond Poetry Thomas focused on writing prose and screenplays during the last years of his life. Previous to this period, his most important prose appeared in the semi-autobiographical short stories, *Portrait of the Artist as a Young Dog*, which stylistically and thematically bear comparison to Joyce's *Dubliners* and *Portrait of the Artist as a Young Man*. The most significant prose piece to issue from Thomas's later period is the "play for voices," *Under Milk Wood*.

Thomas went to the United States on lecture tours four times, beginning in February 1951, leaving his home for the four and a half years before his death. In 1953, Thomas fell into a coma due to ailments complicated by alcohol and drug abuse. He died four days later, leaving behind a mound of debts that private contributions helped to pay.

Works in Literary Context

Passionate and intense, vivid and violent, Thomas wrote that he became a poet because "I had fallen in love with words." His sense of the richness and variety and flexibility of the English language shines through all of his work.

The theme of all of Thomas's poetry is the celebration of the divine purpose that he saw in all human and natural processes. The cycle of birth and flowering and death suffuses his poems. He celebrated life in the seas and fields and hills and towns of his native Wales. In some of his shorter poems, he sought to recapture a child's innocent vision of the world.

Words and Style Thomas set a new standard for many mid-twentieth-century poets through works that display his mastery of vivid imagery, involved word play, fractured syntax, and personal symbology. He was passionately dedicated to his "sullen art," and he was a competent, finished, and occasionally intricate craftsman. He made, for example, more than two hundred versions of "Fern Hill" before he was satisfied with it. Like James Joyce before him, Thomas was obsessed with words—with their sound and rhythm and especially with their possibilities for multiple meanings. His early poems are relatively obscure and complex in sense and simple and obvious in auditory patterns. His later poems, on the other hand, are simple in sense but complex in sounds.

Depictions of Wales One key element in Thomas's works is his depiction of his native Wales. His radio play *Under Milk Wood* is an example of this work, as a pageant of eccentric, outrageous, and charming Welsh villagers reminisce about the casual and crucial moments of their lives. This is also shown in *Return Journey Home*, where he describes the devastation of Swansea by German bombers during World War II.

Old Age and Death Thomas frequently utilizes the notion of the cycle of life by contrasting young and old or living with dying. This is shown in his most famous poem, "Do Not Go Gentle into That Good Night," where the narrator advises a dying person to fight back against the onset of death, with the emotion of rage being equated with life. It is also shown in his poem "Fern Hill," found in the aptly named collection *Deaths and Entrances*. In the poem, Thomas begins by relating the experiences of youth, and concludes with an aged narrator lamenting his coming death. Though Thomas generally depicts death and old age negatively, his poem "And Death Shall Have No Dominion" offers a hopeful view of life after and beyond death.

Works in Critical Context

From the outset of Thomas's career there has been much critical disagreement as to his poetic stature and importance. Many commentators regard Thomas's work as too narrow and unvarying; he essentially confines himself to the lyric expression of what Stephen Spender calls "certain primary, dithyrambic occasions," chiefly birth, love, and death. The influence of the seventeenth-century metaphysical poets is often cited in connection with Thomas's unorthodox religious imagery, while the influence of the Romantic poets is seen in his recurrent vision of a pristine beauty in childhood and nature.

Dylan Thomas's life, work, and stature among twentieth-century poets are all matters of controversy and speculation. An essentially shy and modest man when sober, Thomas called himself the "captain of the second eleven" on the team of modern poets, an uneasy, pivotal ranking between the clearly major and the clearly minor poets. Others, too, such as John Crowe Ransom, have found difficulty in formulating a final opinion of Thomas: Is he really only the best of the minor poets—those who achieve distinction within inherited modes and procedures—or is he the weak man, if that, among the major poets—those who absorb the tradition of ideas and forms that they then in some way radically change?

LITERARY AND HISTORICAL CONTEMPORARIES

Thomas's famous contemporaries include:

Igor Stravinsky (1882–1971): Stravinsky was a Russian composer famous for his music for the ballets *The Rite of Spring* (1913) and *The Firebird* (1910), and is widely considered to be one of the most influential composers of the twentieth century.

John Cage (1912–1992): Cage was an American avant-garde composer who was instrumental in the development of modern dance and electronic music.

John Berryman (1914–1972): Berryman was an American poet who was one of the founders of the confessional school of poetry.

Shirley Jackson (1916–1965): Jackson was a popular and influential American writer of novels and short stories best known for "The Lottery" (1948).

Jack Kerouac (1922–1969): Kerouac was an influential American poet and novelist who was part of the Beat generation; he is most famous for his semiautobiographical novel *On the Road* (1957).

Poetry Collections The critical reception that greeted *Eighteen Poems* was overwhelmingly positive; reviewers sensed in Thomas a highly unique yet traditional poetic voice. In many of these poems Thomas drew upon his childhood and adolescent experiences. Often described as incantatory, *Eighteen Poems* records Thomas's experimentations with vibrant imagery and with sound as "verbal music." Thomas's brilliant debut—and subsequent brief career and life—would later prompt comparisons to the short, dazzling, and ultimately tragic career of American poet Hart Crane, who drowned himself in 1932.

Twenty-five Poems contains many of the same themes as his first work. William York Tindall referred to Thomas's first two books as the poet's "womb-tomb" period because of his penchant to focus on the polarity of birth and death. Critics also noted that Thomas frequently questions or comments upon religion, using images and terminology from Christian mythology, history, and doctrine. "And Death Shall Have No Dominion" was considered by many critics to be a breakthrough work in Thomas's career. In it, the poet addresses the Christian ideas of life and death, ultimately defying death and celebrating the possibility of eternal life. Another acclaimed poem, "Altarwise by Owl-Light," is a sequence of ten sonnets discussing the crucifixion of Christ. Both poignant and comic, the sequence is generally regarded as one of Thomas's best works.

Under Milk Wood Critics have often noted similarities between Thomas and James Joyce. In *Under Milk Wood* and

COMMON HUMAN EXPERIENCE

Many of Thomas's poems incorporate autobiographical aspects. Other poems compare the poet to the natural world. Here are some other works constructed in a similar way:

"Death of a Naturalist" (1966), a poem by Seamus Heaney. This poem details the exploits and thoughts of a young boy collecting frogspawn in a flax-dam.

"The Drunken Boat" (1871), a poem by Arthur Rimbaud. This poem is well known for both its surreal, dazzling imagery and its symbolism.

The Golden Age (1895), stories by Kenneth Greene. This collection of stories represents children as having perception that is far superior to that of the unimaginative, pleasure-stifling adults.

Walden (1854), a nonfiction work by Henry David Thoreau. Thoreau spent two years living in a cabin in the Massachusetts woods in order to gain perspective on human society for this work.

Ulysses, respectively, each author captures the life of a whole society as it is reflected in a single day; for Joyce it is the urban life in Dublin, while for Thomas it is the Welsh village community of Llareggub. Criticism of *Under Milk Wood* generally concentrates on the play's lack of moral center. David Holbrook, who has written two books attacking Thomas, argues that his "place of love" is infantile, that his lyric boisterousness is really sniggering dirty-mindedness, and that we are finally invited to laugh cruelly at the characters. While there is some justice in this view, it recalls the moral sensibility that is appalled to discover that "Llareggub" is "Buggerall" spelled backward. Raymond Williams, on the other hand, seems to find genius in Thomas's mastery of an unrealistic but still convincing "pattern of voices"; Thomas, he implies, in transmuting the lives of a community into art, produced a play "not inconsiderable" in substance and superior to the verse drama of Christopher Fry or T. S. Eliot. William Ayres Arrowsmith expresses the same preference for Thomas's life-affirming, Dionysian vision over Eliot's "sterility."

Responses to Literature

1. Thomas was known for his inspired performances, his entertaining public personality, and his colorful personal life. As a class, discuss whether Thomas's poems would be as interesting on their own. How much did his personal mystique contribute to the positive reception of his works?

2. Read several of Thomas's poems from *Twenty-five Poems*. Choose one and write a brief analysis of the poem's rhythm and theme. Point out any evidence of mysticism or religion that you can find in the poem.

3. Critics and readers have noted that Thomas's prose and scripts draw heavily on the author's life. Attempt to re-create some of Thomas's life by identifying autobiographical details in his prose and poetry.

4. Thomas's reading tours in the United States in the early 1950s won him great acclaim. Write an essay tracing the impact of his trips to the United States on his later works.

BIBLIOGRAPHY

Books

Ackerman, John. *Dylan Thomas: His Life and Work*. Basingstoke, U.K.: Macmillan, 1990.

Brinnin, John Malcolm. *Dylan Thomas in America*. Boston: Atlantic/Little, Brown, 1955.

Davies, Walford. *Dylan Thomas*. Cardiff: University of Wales Press, 1990.

Gaston, Georg M. A. *Critical Essays on Dylan Thomas*. Boston: G. K. Hall, 1989.

Jones, Gwyn. *Background to Dylan Thomas, and Other Explorations*. Oxford: Oxford University Press, 1992.

Moynihan, William T. *The Craft and Art of Dylan Thomas*. Ithaca, N.Y.: Cornell University Press, 1966.

Peach, Linden. *The Prose Writing of Dylan Thomas*. Basingstoke: Macmillan, 1988.

Read, Bill. *The Days of Dylan Thomas*. London: Weidenfeld & Nicolson, 1964.

Rolph, J. Alexander. *Dylan Thomas: A Bibliography*. London: Dent, 1956.

Sinclair, Andrew. *Dylan Thomas: No Man More Magical*. New York: Holt, Rinehart & Winston, 1975.

Periodicals

Bruns, Gerald L. "Daedalus, Orpheus, and Dylan Thomas's Portrait of the Artist." *Renascence*, Spring 1973.

Davies, Richard A. "Dylan Thomas's Image of the 'Young Dog' in *Portrait*." *Anglo-Welsh Review*, Spring 1977.

French, Warren. "Two Portraits of the Artist: James Joyce's *Young Man*; Dylan Thomas's *Young Dog*." *University of Kansas City Review*, June 1967.

◈ J.R.R. Tolkien

BORN: *1916, Bloemfontein, South Africa*

DIED: *1995, Thirsk, England*

NATIONALITY: *English*

GENRE: *Fiction, nonfiction*

MAJOR WORKS:

The Hobbit, or There and Back Again (1936)

The Lord of the Rings (1954–1955)

The Silmarillion (1977)

J.R.R. Tolkien   *Tolkien, J.R.R., photograph. AP Images.*

Overview

A leading linguist of his day, Tolkien was an Oxford University professor who, along with colleagues C.S. Lewis and Charles Williams, helped revive popular interest in the medieval romance and the fantastic tale genre. Tolkien is best known for his novels of epic fantasy, the trilogy *The Lord of the Rings* (1954–1955). Beneath his charming, adventurous surface story of Middle Earth lies a sense of quiet anguish for a vanishing past and a precarious future. His continuing popularity evidences his ability to draw audiences into a fantasy world, at the same time drawing attention to the oppressive realities of modern life. Many critics claim that the success of Tolkien's trilogy has made possible the contemporary revival of "sword and sorcery" literature.

Works in Biographical and Historical Context

Orphaned Young, Educated at Oxford   John Ronald Reuel Tolkien was born the son of English-born parents in Bloemfontein, in the Orange Free State of South Africa, where his father worked as a bank manager. To escape the heat and dust of southern Africa and to better guard the delicate health of her sons, Tolkien's mother moved back to England with him and his brother when they were very

young. Within a year of this move, their father, Arthur Tolkien, died in Bloemfontein; a few years later, the boys' mother died as well. The boys lodged at several homes from 1905 until 1911, when Tolkien entered Exeter College, Oxford.

Tolkien married his longtime sweetheart, Edith Bratt, and served for a short time with the Lancashire Fusiliers, a British infantry regiment assigned to the Western front during World War I. World War I was a horrific conflict that cost millions of military and civilian lives across Europe: England alone suffered nearly 900,000 military deaths and about twice that many casualties. While in England recovering from an illness he developed on the front in 1917, Tolkien began writing "The Book of Lost Tales," which eventually became *The Silmarillion* (1977) and laid the groundwork for his stories about Middle Earth. After the end of the war, Tolkien returned to Oxford, where he joined the staff of the *Oxford English Dictionary* and began work as a freelance tutor.

The Coalbiters and the Inklings   In 1920 Tolkien was appointed Reader in English Language at Leeds University, where he collaborated with E.V. Gordon on an acclaimed translation of "Sir Gawain and the Green Knight," which was completed and published in 1925. (Some years later, Tolkien completed a second translation of this poem, which was published posthumously.) The following year, having returned to Oxford as Rawlinson and Bosworth Professor of Anglo-Saxon, Tolkien became friends with a coworker, C.S. Lewis, author of *The Chronicles of Narnia* (1950–1956). They shared an intense enthusiasm for the myths, sagas, and languages of northern Europe; and to better enhance those interests, both attended meetings of "The Coalbiters," an Oxford club founded by Tolkien where Icelandic sagas were read aloud. The influence of these and other Germanic tales can be seen clearly in Tolkien's fantasy fiction.

As a writer of imaginative literature, Tolkien is best known for *The Hobbit* (1936) and *The Lord of the Rings*, tales that were conceived during his years attending meetings of "The Inklings," an informal gathering of like-minded friends, initiated after the demise of The Coalbiters. The Inklings, which was formed during the late 1930s and lasted until the late 1940s, was a weekly meeting held in Lewis's sitting-room at Magdalen. At these meetings, works-in-progress were read aloud, discussed, and critiqued by the attendees, all interspersed with free-flowing conversation about literature and other topics. The nucleus of the group consisted of Tolkien, Lewis, and Lewis's friend, novelist Charles Williams, bound together by their belief in Christianity and their love of stories. Having heard Tolkien's first hobbit story read aloud at a meeting of the Inklings, Lewis urged Tolkien to publish *The Hobbit*, which appeared in 1937. Tolkien also read a major portion of *The Fellowship of the Ring* (1954) to the Inklings group before it disbanded in the late 1940s.

LITERARY AND HISTORICAL CONTEMPORARIES

Tolkien's famous contemporaries include:

Aldous Huxley (1894–1963): Huxley was an English poet, essayist, and novelist whose most popular work is *Brave New World* (1932).

Norman Rockwell (1894–1978): The work of this American artist and illustrator frequently featured on the cover of *The Saturday Evening Post*.

Winston Churchill (1874–1965): Churchill, who held the position of prime minister of the United Kingdom during World War II, was also a renowned author.

Virginia Woolf (1882–1941): This English novelist used "free indirect discourse," a style of writing in which an author attempts to describe the many avenues a person's thoughts follow, a deceptively difficult feat in literature.

Louis Armstrong (1901–1971): This American jazz musician's unique, strained vocals made "What a Wonderful World" a hit.

The Father of Fantasy Tolkien's *The Lord of the Rings* appeared in three volumes in England in 1954 and 1955, and soon thereafter in the United States. The books made him a cult figure in the United States, especially among high school and college students. Uncomfortable with this status, he and his wife lived quietly in Bournemouth for several years, until Edith's death in 1971. In the remaining two years of his life, Tolkien returned to Oxford, where he was made an honorary fellow of Merton College and awarded a doctorate of letters. He was at the height of his fame as a scholarly and imaginative writer when he died in 1973. Critical study of his fiction continues and has increased in the years since his death.

Works in Literary Context

The concise edition of the *Oxford English Dictionary* defines philology as "the study of literature in a wide sense, including grammar, literary criticism and interpretation, the relation of literature and written records to history, etc." The stories of Middle Earth made a quiet, unassuming teacher of linguistics—whose life in most ways was uneventful and modest—into an international celebrity. Tolkien wrote in the foreword to the Ballantine edition of *The Lord of the Rings* trilogy that his task in writing his fairy-stories is "primarily linguistic in inspiration."

Philology Tolkien was a philologist in the literal sense of the word: a lover of language. In his scholarly biography *The Inklings*, Humphrey Carpenter explained, "It was a deep love for the look and sound of words [that motivated Tol-

kien], springing from the days when his mother had given him his first Latin lesson." After learning Latin and Greek, Tolkien taught himself some Welsh, Old and Middle English, Old Norse, and Gothic, a language with no modern descendant—he wrote the only poem known to exist in that tongue. Later, he added Finnish to his list of languages; the Finnish epic *The Kalevala* had a great impact on his *Silmarillion*. The Finnish language itself, said Carpenter, formed the basis for "Quenya," the High-elven tongue of his stories.

Ancient Myths So much of the art of Tolkien's storytelling relies on ancient, archetypal patterns derived from Greek, Germanic, Celtic, and Old and Middle English models. Tolkien's expertise in these established forms reveals a passion he developed early in life for exploring lost cultures and the ancient roots of modern cultures. Though the mythologies of many cultures can be discerned in *The Lord of the Rings*, the Germanic and Norse sagas are particularly dominant.

Allegory of the Modern World? Because *The Lord of the Rings* was written during World War II, it has been analyzed as a fictionalized, allegorical account of those horrors—Sauron, for example, being the equivalent of Hitler, and so forth. Nonetheless, Tolkien explicitly rejected such an interpretation. In the foreword to the Ballantine edition of *The Lord of the Rings*, he stated, "As for any inner meaning or 'message,' it has in the intention of the author none. It is neither allegorical nor topical." He continued, "I cordially dislike allegory in all its manifestations, and have always done so since I grew old and wary enough to detect its presence. I much prefer history, true or feigned, with its varied applicability to the thought and experience of readers. I think that many confuse 'applicability' with 'allegory' but the one resides in the freedom of the reader, and the other in the purposed dominations of the author."

Works in Critical Context

Critical response to Tolkien immediately after the publication of his most well-known work, *The Lord of the Rings*, was divided. Many critics felt the trilogy was written for children and consequently was not worthy of the same kind of critical evaluation as other, more "adult" fiction.

Upon its release, many critics, were hostile toward *The Lord of the Rings* because the book did not fit current fashions of adult fiction. It was not a realistic contemporary novel, and in the words of Edmund Wilson, "It is essentially a children's book—a children's book which has somehow got out of hand." Such misunderstandings were anticipated by the three authors commissioned to write the jacket blurb, so they concentrated on comparable authors such as Thomas Malory and Ariosto and on genres such as science fiction and heroic romance.

What these early critics could not predict, however, was that *The Lord of the Rings* would reawaken an appetite for fantasy literature among readers and create a new genre: adult fantasy. Since its publication, those critics who appreciate Tolkien have worked to establish criteria by which Tolkien and other fantasists should be judged. Among them was Elizabeth Cook, who wrote in *The Ordinary and the Fabulous*, "The inherent greatness of myth and fairy tale is a poetic greatness. Childhood reading of symbolic and fantastic tales contributes something irreplaceable to any later experience of literature. ... The whole world of epic, romance, and allegory is open to a reader who has always taken fantasy for granted, and the way into it may be hard for one who never heard fairy tales as a child."

Legacy Tolkien's life's work, the creation of Middle Earth, "encompasses a reality that rivals Western man's own attempt at recording the composite, knowable history of his species," wrote Augustus M. Kolich in the *Dictionary of Literary Biography*. Kolich continued, "Not since Milton has any Englishman worked so successfully at creating a secondary world, derived from the real world, yet complete in its own terms with encyclopedic mythology; an imagined world that includes a vast gallery of strange beings: hobbits, elves, dwarfs, orcs, and, finally, the men of Westernesse." Throughout the years, Tolkien's works—especially *The Lord of the Rings*—have pleased countless readers and fascinated critics who recognize their literary depth.

Responses to Literature

1. Discuss the effect of using children and other characters small in stature as opponents of evil in *The Hobbit*. Once you have explored this topic, use your conclusions to write a short children's story featuring a young character fighting the forces of evil.

2. Tolkien claimed that *The Lord of the Rings* is not meant to be an allegory of the modern world, specifically World War II. After doing some research on World War II, write a short paper tracing similarities and differences between the vast struggle faced by Middle Earth and that faced by our world during World War II.

3. Using the Internet and the library, research "flat characters" and "round characters." Then, choose four characters from either *The Hobbit* or *The Lord of the Rings*. Based on your research, do you feel these characters are flat characters or round characters? Compare them to characters from at least one other novel and one film who are flat or round characters. How could the flat characters be made round? Support your argument in a brief essay.

COMMON HUMAN EXPERIENCE

The story of David and Goliath is perhaps the most popular story of an underdog, but Frodo's struggle against the dark forces of Middle Earth, to some, is an equally compelling tale of a surprise victor. As the popularity of each of these stories indicates, humans enjoy participating in the fight against seemingly superior powers. Here are some more popular underdog stories:

The Hunchback of Nôtre Dame (1831), a novel by Victor Hugo. Hugo's unlikely hero is Quasimodo, a hunchback who lives in Paris's famous cathedral.

Rocky (1976), a film directed by John Avildsen. This Academy Award winner is the story of an obscure boxer in Philadelphia who gets a shot at the world championship.

Harry Potter and the Sorcerer's Stone (2001), a novel by J.K. Rowling. Harry, an orphan raised by his cruel aunt and uncle, is transformed from a timid weakling to a powerful hero when he attends Hogwarts, a school for wizards.

BIBLIOGRAPHY

Books

Carpenter, Humphrey. *The Inklings: C.S. Lewis, J.R.R. Tolkien, Charles Williams and their Friends*. Boston: Houghton Mifflin, 1979.

Collins, David R. *J.R.R. Tolkien: Master of Fantasy*. Minneapolis, Minn.: Lerner, 1992.

Cook, Elizabeth. *The Ordinary and the Fabulous*. Cambridge: Cambridge University Press, 1969.

Helms, Randel. *Tolkien and the Silmarils*. Boston: Houghton Mifflin, 1981.

Johnson, Judith A. *J.R.R. Tolkien: Six Decades of Criticism*. Westport, Conn.: Greenwood Press, 1986.

Ready, William. *Understanding Tolkien and The Lord of the Rings*. New York: Warner Paperbacks, 1969.

Shippey, T.A. *The Road to Middle-earth*. Boston: Houghton Mifflin, 1983.

◫ Leo Tolstoy

BORN: *1828, Yasnaya Polyana, Russia*

DIED: *1910, Astapovo, Russia*

NATIONALITY: *Russian*

GENRE: *Fiction, nonfiction*

MAJOR WORKS:

Childhood (1852)

War and Peace (1869)

Anna Karenina (1877)

A Confession (1884)

The Death of Ivan Ilyich and Other Stories (1886)

Resurrection (1899)

Overview

Russian novelist and moral philosopher Leo Tolstoy was one of the great rebels of all time, a man who during a long and stormy life was at odds with the Church, government, literary tradition, and his own family. His novel *War and Peace* has been called the greatest novel of all time. Tolstoy's brooding concern for death made him one of the precursors of existentialism, yet the bustling spirit that animates his novels seems to convey more life than life itself.

Works in Biographical and Historical Context

Religious Aunt Leaves Strong Impression Leo (Lev Nikolayevich) Tolstoy was born on August 28, 1828, in the Tula Province of Russia, the youngest of four sons. His mother died when he was two years old, whereupon his father's distant cousin Tatyana Ergolsky took charge of the children. In 1837 Tolstoy's father died, and an aunt, Alexandra Osten-Saken, became legal guardian of the children. Her religious fervor was an important early influence on Tolstoy. When she died in 1840, the children were sent to Kazan to live with another sister of their father.

Tolstoy was educated at home by German and French tutors. Not a particularly apt pupil, he was good

Leo Tolstoy   *Tolstoy, Leo, 1897, photograph. The Library of Congress.*

at games. In 1843 he entered Kazan University to study Oriental languages, intent on a diplomatic career. Finding these studies too demanding, he switched two years later to study law. Despite the relative ease of this new pursuit, Tolstoy left in 1847 without taking his degree.

Army Life and Early Literary Career Nikolay, Tolstoy's eldest brother, while on furlough from military service, asked Tolstoy to join him in the south. Tolstoy agreed. After a meandering journey, he reached the mountains of the Caucasus, where he sought to join the army as a Junker, or gentleman-volunteer. He passed the necessary exams and was assigned to the 4th Battery of the 20th Artillery Brigade, serving on the Terek River against the rebellious mountaineers.

Tolstoy's border duty on a lonely Cossack outpost consisted of hunting, drinking, sleeping, chasing girls, and occasionally fighting. During the long lulls he first began to write. In 1852 he sent the autobiographical sketch "Childhood" to the leading journal of the day, the *Contemporary*. Nikolai Nekrasov, its editor, was ecstatic, and when it was published (under Tolstoy's initials), so was all of Russia. Tolstoy now began *The Cossacks* (1863), a thinly veiled account of his life in the outpost.

From November 1854 to August 1855 Tolstoy served in the battered fortress at Sevastopol. He had requested a transfer to this area, where one of the bloodiest battles of the Crimean War was in process. (The Crimean War of 1853–1856 was a clash between Russia and the allied forces of France, England, Sardinia, and the Ottoman Empire. The war was infamous for brutality and its many examples of military incompetence.) He later fictionalized his experience of the 4th Bastion, the hottest area in the conflict for a long while, in writing and revealed his distinctive Tolstoyan vision of war as a place of confusion, banality, and heroism. The first of the three "Sevastopol Tales" was the talk of Russia, attracting (for almost the last time in Tolstoy's career) the favorable attention of the czar.

School for Peasant Children In 1856 Tolstoy left the service (as a lieutenant) to look after his affairs in Yasnaya Polyana. He made his first trip abroad the following year. He did not like Western Europe, as his stories of this period show. He was becoming increasingly interested in education, however, and he talked with experts in this field wherever he went. In the summer he returned to Yasnaya Polyana and set up a school for peasant children. In 1860–1861 Tolstoy went abroad again, seeking to learn more about education; he also gambled heavily. During this trip he witnessed the death of his brother Nikolay in the south of France. More than all the grisly scenes of battle he had witnessed, this event brought home to Tolstoy the fact of death, the specter of which fascinated and terrified him throughout his long career.

Golden Years of Family Happiness and Professional Productivity In September 1862 Tolstoy wrote his aunt Alexandra, "I, aged, toothless fool that I am, have fallen in love." He was only thirty-four, but he was sixteen years older than Sofya Andreyevna Bers (or Behrs), whose mother had been one of Tolstoy's childhood friends. Daughter of a prominent Moscow doctor, Bers was handsome, intelligent, and, as the years would show, strong-willed. The first decade of their marriage brought Tolstoy the greatest happiness. Never before or after was his creative life so rich or his personal life so full. In June 1863 his wife had the first of their thirteen children.

Since 1861 Tolstoy had been trying to write a historical novel about the Decembrist uprising of 1825 (a failed revolt against the czar by about 3,000 soldiers). But the more he worked, the farther back in time he went. The work would become the vast *War and Peace*. The first portion of *War and Peace* was published in 1865 (in the *Russian Messenger*) as "The Year 1805." In 1868 three more chapters appeared; and in 1869 he completed the novel. Tolstoy had been somewhat neglected by critics in the preceding few years because he had not participated in the bitter literary politics of the time. But his new novel created a fantastic outpouring of popular and critical reaction.

From 1873 to 1877 Tolstoy worked on the second of his masterworks, *Anna Karenina* (1877), which also created a sensation upon its publication. The concluding section of the novel was written during another of Russia's seemingly endless wars with Turkey. The country was in patriotic turmoil. M.N. Katkov, editor of the journal in which *Anna Karenina* had been appearing serially, was afraid to print the final chapters, which contained an attack on war hysteria. Tolstoy, in a fury, took the text away from Katkov, and with the aid of N. Strakhov published a separate edition that enjoyed huge sales. Tolstoy's family continued to grow, and his royalties made him an extremely rich man.

Spiritual Crisis The ethical quest that began when Tolstoy was a child and that tormented him throughout his younger years now drove him to abandon all else in order to seek the ultimate meaning in life. At first he turned to the Russian Orthodox Church, visiting the Optina-Pustyn monastery in 1877. He found no answers there. When he began reading the Gospels, though, he found the key to his own moral system in Matthew: "Resist not evil." In 1879–1880 Tolstoy wrote his *A Confession* (1884) and his *Critique of Dogmatic Theology* (1891). From this point on his life was dominated by a burning desire to achieve social justice.

In the next few years a new publication was founded (the *Mediator*) in order to spread Tolstoy's word in tract and fiction, as well as to make good reading available to the poor. In six years almost twenty million copies were distributed. Tolstoy had long been under surveillance by the secret police, and in 1884 copies of *What I Believe* were seized from the printer.

Tolstoy's relations with his family were becoming increasingly strained. The more of a saint he became in

LITERARY AND HISTORICAL CONTEMPORARIES

Tolstoy's famous contemporaries include:

Alexander Pushkin (1799–1837): Russian Romantic poet known for his verse poem, *Eugene Onegin* (1833). Pushkin is also a distant cousin of Tolstoy's.

Ivan Turgenev (1818–1883): Aristocratic author of *Fathers and Sons* (1862) and lifelong friend of Tolstoy's.

Fyodor Dostoevsky (1821–1881): Another of the great Russian writers, and also one who dealt with issues of ethics and morals in his work.

Gustave Flaubert (1821–1880): French writer best known for his novel, *Madame Bovary* (1857).

Harriet Beecher Stowe (1811–1896): American abolitionist and novelist. Best known for writing *Uncle Tom's Cabin* (1852).

the eyes of the world, the more of a devil he seemed to his wife. He wanted to give his wealth away, but she would not hear of it. An unhappy compromise was reached in 1884, when Tolstoy assigned to his wife the copyright to all his works before 1881.

In 1886 Tolstoy worked on what is possibly his most powerful story, "The Death of Ivan Ilyich," and his drama of peasant life, *The Power of Darkness* (which could not be produced until 1895). In 1888, when he was sixty years old, his thirteenth child was born. In the same year he finished his sweeping indictment of carnal love, *The Kreutzer Sonata*.

Final Years Full of Personal Turmoil In 1892 Tolstoy's estate, valued at the equivalent of $1.5 million, was divided among his wife and his nine living children. Tolstoy's final years were filled with worldwide acclaim and great unhappiness, as he was caught in the strife between his convictions, his followers, and his family. Unable to endure the quarrels at home, he set out on his last journey in October 1910, accompanied by his physician and his youngest daughter, Alexandra. The trip proved too stressful and he died on November 9, 1910.

Works in Literary Context

An enormously important figure in Russian literature and culture, Tolstoy is famous not only for his novels, short stories, and plays but also for his moral authority. By the turn of the century, he had achieved worldwide recognition and prestige. The influence of his thought was felt not only by virtually all of Russia's leading cultural figures, but also beyond Russia's borders by contemporaries such as George Bernard Shaw, Mohandas Ghandi, William Dean Howells, and Romain Rolland. Tolstoyism has not

COMMON HUMAN EXPERIENCE

Tolstoy's most famous work, *War and Peace*, covers many characters over a long period in a time of war. Here are some other famous war epics:

> *The Iliad* (7th or 8th century B.C.), an epic poem by Homer. This epic poem details the siege of Troy by the Greeks.
> *Winds of War* (1971), a novel by Herman Wouk. Wouk's best-selling World War II epic became a popular mini-series in 1983.
> *Half of a Yellow Sun* (2006), a novel by Chimamanda Ngozi Adichie. This prize-winning novel follows the lives of three people caught up in the events surrounding Nigeria's civil war in the 1960s.

endured, however; the religious and moral movement he founded did not remain strong after his death in 1910. Rather, his literary masterpieces have survived, retaining their freshness and vitality for new generations of readers.

Didactic Fiction Though Tolstoy was a masterful stylist, his works are never meant purely for entertainment. Embedded in his novels are lessons, morals, that he strives to impart to the reader. This makes his work, especially *War and Peace*, part of the tradition of didactic literature, or literature that teaches. Tolstoy was always interested in theories of education. Even in his early years he felt a strong sense of responsibility as a writer, and even before his religious conversion in 1880 he wrote many simple, edifying stories for peasants and less sophisticated readers. He printed his theories in his own education journal, *Yasnaya Polyana*, which he founded in 1862. Tolstoy's writing style frequently made use of structural devices that have been associated with education. For example, he used repetition for emphasis, asked questions and then answered them, enumerated features or characteristics of phenomena he was analyzing, and appealed to logic in support of his views. His fictional writings can be seen broadly as instructional art. *War and Peace*, for instance, teaches about historical development, just as *Anna Karenina* teaches about the destructive power of passion. In his later fiction, the moral lessons of his works stand in even sharper outline, and his stories become more schematic.

Works in Critical Context

Tolstoy's novels *War and Peace* and *Anna Karenina* were warmly praised in his lifetime and continue to be regarded by critics as among the best examples of the novel as a genre.

War and Peace *War and Peace* is expansive in conception and execution, supporting a cast of more than six hundred characters who play out their roles against a historical backdrop provided by French leader Napoleon Bonaparte's military campaigns at the beginning of the nineteenth century. The novel's broad sweep, multiple perspectives, and lack of a clear generic identity has raised questions about its unity. Henry James and Percy Lubbock, for example, were critical of the novel's formlessness and lack of a center. Complaining that the work was truly two novels, not just one, Lubbock lamented the absence of a single point of view. Modern critics have responded to the problem of unity with various solutions. In "The Moral Vision: Tolstoy," Albert Cook, for example, found the novel's unity in its moral orientation; Edward Wasiolek, in *Tolstoy's Major Fiction*, found the structural principle in *War and Peace* to be the "interdiction of force in life," where force is understood as interference, violence, institutional intimidation, and psychological manipulation. This principle, he argued, underlies Tolstoy's entire creative activity.

One character in particular, Natasha Rostova, is universally praised, not only because she is so "full" a character, but also because she represents an ideal—the truly "natural person" Tolstoy strove to embody in his art. Another female character, Princess Marya Bolkonskaya, also occupies an important position. As he stated in *A History of Russian Literature*, D.S. Mirsky believed that it was with the women in this novel that Tolstoy really triumphed.

Anna Karenina *Anna Karenina* explores questions of love, sex, and marriage. For the depth of Tolstoy's treatment of these themes, it has achieved recognition as one of the great novels of world literature. Tolstoy's contemporary, Fyodor Dostoevsky, described the book as "flawless." Twentieth-century Russian writer and critic Vladimir Nabokov echoed Dostoevsky's sentiments, and even turned to Tolstoy's famous work in beginning his own novel about love and family life *Ada or Ardor: A Family Chronicle* (1969). Mirsky and others found in the novel's ending a reflection of Tolstoy's own growing spiritual perplexity, which culminated in his crisis and conversion to a new worldview. Tolstoy brought the novel to a conclusion with difficulty; the tragic atmosphere surrounding Anna's death is unsettling. As Mirsky commented, "the novel dies like a cry of anguish in the desert air."

Responses to Literature

1. Take a look at some of Tolstoy's educational writings. Would his ideas still work today? Can you think of any other suggestions to reform the educational system?

2. Tolstoy is said to have greatly influenced Mohandas Gandhi and Martin Luther King Jr. Take a look at some of their writings, perhaps "Letter from a Birmingham Jail" and find connections between the ideas of these later men and those expressed in Tolstoy's works.

3. After reading *Anna Karenina*, examine Gustave Flaubert's *Madame Bovary*. How are the title characters similar? How are they different?

4. Tolstoy was a bit of a mystic, and Russian culture over the years has been peppered with mystics such as Rasputin. What do you think accounts for these mystical and almost magical beliefs in an otherwise practical culture?

BIBLIOGRAPHY

Books

Benson, Ruth. *Women in Tolstoy: The Ideal and the Erotic.* Chicago: University of Illinois Press, 1973.

Bulgakov, Valentin. *The Last Year of Leo Tolstoy.* New York: Dial, 1971.

Christian, R.F. *Tolstoy: A Critical Introduction.* Cambridge: Cambridge University Press, 1969.

Davis, Helen Edna. *Tolstoy and Nietzsche.* New York: Macmillan, 1929.

Goldenweizer, A.B. *Talks with Tolstoy,* translated by S.S. Koteliansky and Virginia Woolf. New York: Horizon, 1949.

Gorky, Maxim. *Reminiscences of Tolstoy, Chekhov, and Andreev,* translated by S.S. Koteliansky and Leonard Woolf. New York: Viking, 1959.

Matlaw, Ralph, ed. *Tolstoy: A Collection of Critical Essays.* Upper Saddle River, N.J.: Prentice-Hall, 1967.

Mooney, Harry. *Tolstoy's Epic Vision: A Study of "War and Peace" and "Anna Karenina".* Tulsa, Okla: University of Tulsa Press, 1948.

Philipson, Morris. *The Count Who Wished He Were a Peasant.* New York: Random House, 1967.

Tolstoy, Alexandra. *The Real Tolstoy.* Morristown, N.J.: Henry S. Evans, 1968.

Tolstoy, Alexandra. *Tolstoy: A Life of My Father,* translated by Isabel F. Hapwood. New York: Harper, 1953.

Michel Tournier

BORN: *1924, Paris, France*

NATIONALITY: *French*

GENRE: *Fiction, nonfiction*

MAJOR WORKS:

Friday, or The Other Island (1967)

The Ogre (1970)

The Fetishist, and Other Stories (1978)

The Golden Droplet (1985)

Overview

Michel Édouard Tournier, one of the most popular novelists in France, writes provocative fiction that blends myth and symbolism with realistic depictions of characters and setting. Tournier is a radical social critic, challenging cultural notions of the social contract handed down through myth and showing characters who select alternative modes of relating to their environment. Like the works of Thomas Pynchon, John Barth, and Vladimir

Michel Tournier *Tournier, Michel, photograph. © Jerry Bauer. Reproduced by permission.*

Nabokov, Tournier's tales are densely packed with a complex network of symbols and allusions.

Works in Biographical and Historical Context

Influence of Germany and World War II Tournier was born on December 19, 1924, in Paris. His family was middle class. His father, Alphonse Tournier, founded and directed an organization that dealt with musical copyrights. Shortly after Tournier's birth, the family moved to the Parisian suburb of Saint-Germainen-Laye, where the author-to-be spent his childhood. When he was four years old, he underwent a painful tonsillectomy without anesthesia, which he later described as a kind of primitive initiation rite. Consequently, the theme of initiation figures prominently in many of his works. A sickly child, he excelled in theology and German studies.

Tournier's youth was indelibly marked by World War II. After attempts to appease the territorial ambitions of Adolf Hitler failed, the war began when Nazi Germany invaded Poland in 1939. Both Great Britain and France immediately declared war on Hitler and Germany. In the spring of 1940, France fell to Hitler's army and the country was occupied for much of the war.

The war years were particularly painful for Tournier, because he was raised in a household that had as much

LITERARY AND HISTORICAL CONTEMPORARIES

Tournier's famous contemporaries include:

Nelson Rockefeller (1908–1979): The vice president of the United States under President Gerald Ford, Rockefeller was a liberal Republican who had previously served as the governor of New York.

Margaret Thatcher (1925–): The first female British prime minister. Her tough, conservative leadership earned her the nickname the "Iron Lady."

Bobby Fischer (1943–2008): Often cited as one of the greatest chess players of all time, Fischer was a teenage prodigy who became the first American to win the World Chess Championship.

Steven Spielberg (1946–): A director, producer, and screenwriter, Spielberg's films have been the highest grossing of all time.

Ronald Reagan (1911–2004): Popular actor, governor of California, and two-term U.S. president.

Pablo Neruda (1904–1973): This Chilean writer is one of the most popular poets of the twentieth century and the winner of the Nobel Prize in Literature in 1971.

respect for genuine German culture as contempt for the Nazi parody of it. His family spoke German and often had spent summers in Germany. Although he was too young to serve actively in the war, living close to Paris provided him with opportunities to observe the varying reactions to the German occupation. He noted the pain and suffering of the French, but also in many cases, the French admiration for their German conquerors, as well as the frequently slavish adulation of Marshal Philippe Pétain and his puppet government at Vichy. After the war, Tournier was witness to the numerous distortions and fictionalizations that led to the creation of the myth of the "French Resistance."

Denied University Career Tournier's postwar studies led him to what was supposed to be a brief period at the German University of Tübingen. This visit wound up lasting four years (1946–1950), during which Tournier devoted himself to the study of philosophy. When he returned to Paris, it was to prepare for the difficult French examination called the *agrégation*. Tournier later recalled that, although he considered himself the finest philosopher of his generation, this opinion was not shared by his examiners, and he flunked the test. This setback effectively ended his hopes for a university career, and for a while he drifted in the exciting intellectual world of postwar Paris. He sat in on Claude Lévi-Strauss's anthropology lectures at the Musée de l'Homme. The influence of this experience is apparent in his first published novel, *Friday, or The Other Island* (1967).

Tournier held a number of media positions in France in the postwar period as well. He was a producer and director with the R.T.F. (Radiodiffusion-télévision française) from 1949 to 1954. In 1955, he joined Europe No. 1, a radio network, as a press attaché and announcer. (His short story "Tristan Vox," in the collection *The Fetishist, and Other Stories* (1978), displays his knowledge of the realities of the radio business, as well as the fantasies that can be engendered by the human voice.) Tournier left in 1958, when he joined the Parisian publishing house, Plon, as the director of literary services. During his decade-long tenure, he also did translations of German works, particularly the novels of Erich Maria Remarque.

Television Career Soon, television beckoned as well. From 1960 to 1965, Tournier hosted a series titled *The Black Box*, which concerned what was to become his principal hobby, photography. This interest led him to write many introductions to photographic collections. Tournier was also one of the founders of the annual Rencontres internationales de la photographie, which takes place in Arles. Photography figures in most of Tournier's fiction, and his ambivalent attitude toward the photographic image plays an important role in the novel *The Golden Droplet* (1985), as well as the short story "Veronica's Shrouds," which appears in *The Fetishist, and Other Stories* (1978).

Literary Success Every aspect of Tournier's varied career helped him to become a novelist, though it was philosophy education and his years as a translator that were particularly influential. While holding the media jobs, he figured out how to combine myth, philosophy, and fiction. He wrote three novels he deemed unworthy of publication, then completed *The Life and Strange Surprising Adventures of Robinson Crusoe* (1967), which inspired *Friday, or The Other Island*. Tournier was forty-three years old when he published *Friday* and began his meteoric career as a novelist. This book won him the prestigious Grand prix du roman de l'Académie française in 1967, and much acclaim. Tournier followed *Friday* with *The Ogre* (1970), an exploration of life in Nazi Germany, for which he received the Prix Goncourt. He was soon recognized as one of the most remarkable writers to appear on the postwar French literary scene and received international attention for his works. In 1972, he accepted an invitation to join the Académie Goncourt.

Focusing primarily on writing, Tournier continued to publish challenging novels intermittently in the 1970s through the early 2000s. He followed *The Ogre* with *Gemini* (1975) and *The Four Wise Men* (1982). The latter is a retelling of the biblical story of the Magi that finds the men resolving personal problems when they find the messiah in Bethlehem. Tournier also includes a fourth seeker of the Christ Child who misses the birth, spends the next thirty-three years in prison in another man's place, eats leftovers from the Last Supper, and is welcomed into heaven. The book received critical acclaim for its melding of religious and secular elements.

Simple Life After publishing the notorious novella *Gilles and Jeanne* (1983) and the novel *A Garden at Hammamet* (1985), Tournier put out the critically acclaimed *Golden Droplet* (1986), which looks at a quest for identity in a world where images are valued more than realities. Through the story of Idriss, a young Berber shepherd who goes to Paris, Tournier argues that the primary force of culture seems to be its ability to construct convincing illusions. Tournier challenged readers with his short-story collection *The Midnight Love Feast* (1991). The novel *Eleazar, Exodus to the West* (2002) finds Tournier returning to the Bible for inspiration. This time, he compared the journey of Moses across the desert with that of American immigrants heading west to California in search of a better life.

Tournier, a lifelong bachelor, has lived in a former rectory in the valley of the Chevreuse, for many years. Although he enjoys his considerable isolation, he also has been a frequent guest on French television talk shows, travels and lectures extensively in Europe and Africa, and gives talks to French schoolchildren. He has continued to publish other new works as well, including the observational diary *Journal extime* (2002).

Works in Literary Context

White Laughter In an effort to achieve his ends, Tournier makes use of two concepts that suffuse all of his writing, both of which are crucial for understanding his creative works. Both have bases in his philosophical studies, and both are replete with irony. They are *le rire blanc* ("white laughter") and the special meaning he gives to myth.

In *The Holy Spirit*, Tournier notes that the "white laughter denounces the fundamentally transitory, relative nature of everything human ...; the man who experiences white laughter has just seen the abyss open beneath him. He knows suddenly that nothing is important. He is filled with agony, yet at the same time delivered from all fear." White laughter reflects an awareness of life's utter meaninglessness. It is precisely this intuition that many of Tournier's major characters attempt to reject by their elaborate inventions of highly structured universes.

Myth An equally strong influence on Tournier's writing is myth. In his novels, he makes frequent use of a variety of myths, but principal among them is the myth of twinship he associates with Cain and Abel. These two figures represent types of opposing but complementary personalities. Cain is the sedentary, the person who fears the complex and unforeseen. He hopes to have his life unfold in a totally predictable manner within a clearly demarcated geographic space. Abel is the nomad, the individual who, at times despite himself, becomes a wanderer and is forced to confront some of life's complexities. It is tempting yet misleading to place Tournier's characters into one or the other category. For example, Robinson of *Friday* could easily be Abel and the slave Vendredi Cain. In *The Ogre*, the conveniently named

Abel Tiffauges would be an Abel figure, and his friend Nestor a Cain. The globe-trotting Jean in *Gemini* would be Abel and his brother Paul Cain. In spite of the neatness of this schema, it simply does not work. No single character is a Cain or an Abel; each has within himself the potential to be the other. The myth of twinship indicates for Tournier that the quest for self-fulfillment involves a struggle, not just with the beloved and despised other, but within the individual himself.

Influence As a leading modern French author, Tournier has influenced postmodern authors worldwide with his thematic, stylistic, and philosophical choices. Literary critics and fine-art students find such works as his collection of art criticism, *Le Tabor et le Sinaï Essais sur l'art contemporain* (1988), particularly useful.

Works in Critical Context

Since the publication of his first acclaimed novels, critics have acknowledged Tournier as an important figure in modern French literature. He has been praised for creating challenging works, but his novels have also been criticized for their pretentiousness and, on occasion, for their somewhat disturbing and even frightening themes. The controversial nature of his subjects has brought him much critical attention as well. As Bob Halliday comments in the *Washington Post Book World*, "In Europe, where Tournier is recognized as the major French novelist of the past 20 years ... his morally often uncomfortable works have aroused hot controversy and sold in the millions."

The Ogre Many critics, including Jean Amery in *Merkur*, gave *The Ogre* a hostile reception, calling it a glorification of neo-Nazi ideals. However, William Cloonan argues in the *Dictionary of Literary Biography* that this reading results from mistaking the main character, Tiffauges, as a spokesman for Tournier, who has deliberately presented his character in a negative light. It also ignores the fact that Tournier depicts Tiffauges as a man separated from recognizing the ultimate evil of his actions by elaborate self-delusions. Cloonan asserts that "Tournier is depicting a deeply confused person whose personality is at once a portrait and parody of the Nazi psyche," and an illustration of how important it is for individuals and nations to distinguish between fantasy and reality.

Other critics, too, have been baffled by the multiplicity of ideas and interpretations present in the story, yet they still regard reading it as a worthwhile literary experience. *Newsweek*'s Peter Prescott calls it a "fine novel" that is "more likely to be praised than read." "*The Ogre* is built in the way Bach built his fugues; themes and statements are introduced, inverted, tangled and marched past each other, all to be resolved in loud, majestic chords," described Prescott, adding, "and yet the symbols and correspondences of this story, which are far more complex than I have been able to indicate, would be insufficient to sustain it as fiction. Tournier's achievement rests in his remarkable blend of myth with realism.... [He] offers a succession of scenes ... which, as Abel says, not only decipher the essence of existence, but exalt it."

Responses to Literature

1. Tournier, like many French intellectuals of his age, was influenced by the philosophy of Claude Lévi-Strauss. In a paper, address these questions: What impact do you think Tournier's background in philosophy and the influence of Lévi-Strauss had on his writing? How does he interweave philosophy with his narratives?

2. In a group, discuss the following questions: What role do pairs play in Tournier's literature? What are his views of heterosexual pairings? How do these views compare with his take on homosexual relationships, or to the relationships between twins?

3. Create a presentation that addresses these questions: How does Tournier's depiction of the character Friday differ from the original *Robinson Crusoe* depiction by Defoe? What are some other modern interpretations of Friday? What different messages were the various authors (including Defoe) trying to convey with Friday? Why is Friday such a suitable character for transmitting an author's message?

4. In an essay, answer the following questions: How do you feel about the main character in *The Ogre*? Is it appropriate for an author to write from the perspective of such an unlikable character? How closely do you think Tournier identified with Tiffauges? Why?

BIBLIOGRAPHY
Books

Anderson, Christopher. *Michel Tournier's Children: Myth, Intertext, Initiation*. New York: Peter Lang, 1996.

Davis, Colin. *Michel Tournier: Philosophy and Fiction*. Oxford: Clarendon, 1988.

Roberts, Martin. *Michel Tournier: Bricolage and Cultural Mythology*. Saratoga, Calif.: ANMA Libri, 1994.

Georg Trakl

BORN: *1887, Salzburg, Austria*

DIED: *1914, Krakow, Poland*

NATIONALITY: *Austrian*

GENRE: *Drama, poetry*

MAJOR WORKS:

Gedichte (1913)

Sebastian Dreaming (1915)

Die Dichtungen (1918)

Georg Trakl *Imagno / Getty Images*

Overview

While the influence of Austrian author Georg Trakl's poetry has been widely discussed, his work is best known for its lyric qualities. His controlled uses of colors, sounds, and ciphers blend into brooding meditations that speak out against the doomed existence of man. Trakl's writing exhibits many of the techniques and themes employed by the imagists, surrealists, and impressionists, making his work difficult to classify. Many critics believe he was a modernist before his time, citing as evidence his lines that break free from traditional poetical modes in order to follow musical forms and expressions.

Works in Biographical and Historical Context

Emergent Schizophrenia Trakl, born in 1887 in Salzburg, was the son of affluent parents. Throughout his short life, he suffered from mental disturbances and persistent schizophrenia. Many critics have argued that his fragile mental state was exacerbated by his parents' unhappy marriage, his mother's opium habit, and the Catholic schooling he and his brothers and sisters received, although they grew up in a Protestant household. His condition, coupled with his drug and alcohol abuse, led Trakl quickly to his end. By age fifteen, Trakl was experimenting with chloroform and had begun drinking heavily. By 1906, he was forced to leave school prematurely. That year, he wrote two one-act verse tragedies, *All Souls Day* and *Fata Morgana*. The former was well-received by his Salzburg audience, while the other was a failure that temporarily blocked his creative impulses.

Both he and his sister Margaret, the sibling to whom he was the closest, found the paths of middle-class life unendurable compared to the ivory towers of their art. Their relationship, debatably incestuous, haunted him even as it nourished him. Her figure appears often in his work as "the sister," an alter ego, a beloved mirror-image or *doppelgänger*. Even though she married and was able to play the role of the bourgeois wife, she herself committed suicide a few years after Trakl did.

Access to Narcotics Soon after leaving the university, the patriot Trakl volunteered for a year in the Austro-Hungarian army and was assigned to the medical corps. After leaving the army and returning to work in Salzburg, Trakl began an apprenticeship in a pharmacy that, unfortunately, and ultimately, fed his future addiction to narcotics. From this point onward, events in his life are inextricably woven into his poetry. His increasing addiction to narcotics is reflected in his use of images, synaesthesia (experiencing one sense through another), and an inscrutable personal mythology. Likewise, his experiences during World War I also gave rise to a prolific period, but eventually proved too much for his fragile mental condition.

World War I After finding the working life unendurable, Trakl reenlisted in the army and was put on active duty. In 1912, while stationed in Innsbruck, he met

Ludwig von Ficker, editor of *Der Brenner*. Ficker became friend and mentor to Trakl for the remaining years of his short life, publishing the poet's work regularly in his literary journal. Trakl published his first collection of poetry in 1913, *Gedichte* (Poems).

While Trakl was still serving in the army, World War I broke out. The war began when the heir to the throne of Austria-Hungary, Archduke Franz Ferdinand, was assassinated by a terrorist in Sarajevo, Serbia, in June 1914. Austria-Hungary soon declared war on Serbia and its allies. Entangling alliances brought nearly every European country into the conflict. Austria-Hungary allied with Germany, Turkey, and, until 1915, Italy, against France, Russia, Great Britain, and, after 1917, the United States. In August 1914, Trakl went to Austrian-controlled Poland as a medic under the command of incompetent Austrian generals.

Mental Breakdown and Death After a bloody defeat at Grodek, which saw the Austrians lose control of the city, Trakl was left to care for ninety wounded throughout two days and two nights, without supplies or attending physicians. The battle at Grodek caused Trakl

COMMON HUMAN EXPERIENCE

Other poetic works that, like Trakl's, have focused on pain, death, and decay include:

"Another Elegy," a poem by Margaret Atwood. "Fine words, but why do I want / to tart up death?" Atwood is interested in the inevitability of death and the decay of the human body over time, and several of her poems, including "Another Elegy" address this theme.

"The Death of Raschi," a poem by Emma Lazarus. Best known for her sonnet "The New Colossus" ("Give me your tired, your poor . . .") that appears on the Statue of Liberty, Lazarus wrote about the Jewish experience and the sense of loss that it so often entailed in nineteenth-century Europe in "The Death of Raschi."

"Ode on a Grecian Urn," a poem by John Keats. Inspired by an exhibition of Greek artifacts, Keats wrote this enduring meditation on truth and beauty and their transcendence of time and decay.

to suffer a psychotic episode upon the unit's retreat. He threatened to shoot himself in front of his fellow officers but was disarmed and restrained.

In October, he was ordered to the hospital at Krakow for observation. Ficker hurried to Krakow to secure his release, because he knew that confinement would only cause Trakl's condition to deteriorate. Unable to secure the release, Ficker later received a letter from Trakl and a copy of "Grodek" and "Lament," Trakl's last two poems, the former considered to be one of his greatest lyrics. A week later, Trakl died of an overdose of cocaine. He had been working on his second collection, *Sebastian Dreaming*, which was published posthumously in 1915.

Works in Literary Context

Though he produced only a small amount of writing in his short life, Trakl is an important lyric poet in German literature of the early twentieth century. His work was influenced in part by the events around him, including World War I, as well as his own mental illness and substance addictions. He was exceedingly aware that his world, personal as well as external, was "breaking apart." This mood of suffering prevails in his poetry.

Imagism, Surrealism, and Symbolism Critics also associate his work with various modern artistic movements, and affinities with imagism have also been noted in Trakl's strikingly visual style. In addition, the dreamlike flow of images in his poems has indicated to some commentators a compositional method similar to the automatic writing of the surrealists, with whom Trakl also shared a preoccupa-

tion with violence, perversity, and death. Trakl's strongest literary affiliation, however, is with the French Symbolists of the nineteenth century, primarily Arthur Rimbaud, whose disordered and conflict-ridden genius is said to have incarnated in the Austrian poet.

Trakl was a dedicated perfectionist for whom the craft of poetry meant striving for absolute truth of expression, purity, and precision of language. His relatively small and cohesive oeuvre is remarkable for the extant number of variant versions of the poems. Though Arthur Rimbaud, Paul Verlaine, and Charles Baudelaire variously influenced his development, Trakl early established a pronounced personal style. This is distinguished by great linguistic concentration, recurrent patterns in diction and imagery, individual use of color symbolism, and a fine lyricism, which set him apart as a distinctive new voice in poetry. Like Friedrich Hölderlin, to whom he owes something of his elliptical conciseness and hymnic intensity, Trakl was essentially a visionary poet in whom the inner vision, the image-making faculty, takes precedence over the mimetic function of creative imagination.

Death and Decay In Trakl's work the melancholy and elegiac moods predominate, and his poetry heralds the calamity of World War I. The principal subject of this poetry is a darkened world of pain, death, and decay in which man is the passive suffering victim. The poet's self is repeatedly projected into mythopoetic personae who represent pure vessels of violated humanity, yet not without an ethereal strength and some redemptive significance. In Trakl's treatment, established religious imagery is fragmented, inverted, or distorted and projected into startling combinations that produce new resonances and meanings.

Works in Critical Context

Critics agree that though Trakl had been writing poetry from an early age, his best work dates from the final two years of his life, displaying a noticeable development from his efforts prior to 1912. Personal torment and an unrelieved sense of horror and disintegration dominated the earlier poems. Critical analysis of Trakl's work has revealed its disjointed, fragmentary nature, summarizing it as a collection of often-repeated symbols and motifs without consistent meaning. Later poems, however, are credited with a consistency of mood and attitude that unifies them into a cohesive, though nonrational, statement. In essence, they form the poet's protest against the corrupt, fallen condition of humankind.

Later Poems The tone of Trakl's later poems is more impersonal and ambiguous. In these works, Trakl transcends the extreme subjectivity of his former poetic self to universalize his existential vision. Some critics describe this new quality in Trakl's mature poems as a mythic objectivity, while confronting the paradox that this poet's world is essentially private, resembling that of a schizophrenic. Most critics also find that his later works were modern in nature, exhibiting an aggregate of rhythms, grammatical structures like musical scores, and poetic logic of colors, phrasings, and figures all his own. For example, Irene Morris noted in *German Life & Letters* that "Trakl's last poems are completely visionary in style and apocalyptic in content."

Responses to Literature

1. It is generally agreed that Trakl's poetry was at its best toward the end of his life, when he was suffering from drug addiction, depression, and schizophrenia. Do you feel Trakl's poetry benefited from these conditions, or in spite of them? Do you feel that works produced by the mentally ill should be evaluated by the same criteria as works produced by the non–mentally ill? Write an essay that addresses these questions

2. How does Trakl's poetry anticipate the horrors of World War I? Create a presentation that links his poetry to the war.

3. Trakl's poetry is often seen as transitional. In an essay, discuss the following questions: What elements can you identify as belonging to earlier Symbolist poetry? What elements of German expressionism can you identify?

4. Research German expressionism and other leading expressionist poets for a paper. How did Trakl influence the movement? How did other poets' works compare with Trakl's in subject matter and tone?

BIBLIOGRAPHY

Books

Cagey, T. J. *Manshape That Shone: An Interpretation of Trakl.* London: Blackwell, 1964.

Detsch, Richard. *Georg Trakl's Poetry: Toward a Union of Opposites.* University Park: Pennsylvania State University Press, 1983.

Leiva-Merikakis, Erasmo. *The Blossoming Thorn: Georg Trakl's Poetry of Atonement.* Lewisburg, Pa.: Bucknell University Press, 1987.

Williams, Eric B., ed. *The Dark Flutes of Fall: Critical Essays on Georg Trakl.* Columbia, S.C.: Camden House, 1991.

———. *The Mirror and the Word: Modernism, Literary Theory, and Georg Trakl.* Lincoln: University of Nebraska Press, 1993.

Periodicals

Morris, Irene. "Georg Trakl." *German Life & Letters* 2, no. 2 (January 1949): 122–37.

❖ Tomas Tranströmer

BORN: *1931, Stockholm, Sweden*

NATIONALITY: *Swedish*

GENRE: *Poetry*

MAJOR WORKS:

Seventeen Poems (1954)

Night Vision (1971)
Baltics (1971)
Truth Barriers (1978)
Grief Gondola No. 2 (1996)

Overview

Few poets have in their lifetimes been as abundantly translated or as willingly assimilated into other languages as the Swedish poet Tomas Tranströmer. His works can be read in practically every European language and in quite a few non-European languages as well. In his native Sweden, Tranströmer's reputation as a leading poet of his generation was assured almost from the publication of his first book in 1954. By the time he published his second book, his presence on the Swedish literary scene arguably marked a turning point in the history of the national literature.

Works in Biographical and Historical Context

A Grandfather Figure Tomas Tranströmer was born on April 15, 1931, in Stockholm, Sweden. Some

Tomas Tranströmer *© Bassouls Sophie / Corbis Sygma*

might say that he was the product of a broken home because his parents separated when he was three years old, and his father, Gösta Tranströmer, an editor and journalist, remained rather aloof thereafter. Yet the boy grew up in a remarkably harmonious and intellectual household. His mother, Helmy, taught primary school in an exclusive area on the other side of town, and her fair and caring approach as a teacher was legendary. The family's male caretaker—and Tranströmer's role model—was ship pilot Carl Helmer Westerberg, the boy's maternal grandfather. Tranströmer counts his time spent with Westerberg, whom the poet lovingly describes in the long poem *Baltics* (1974), among the most tender of his childhood memories.

World War II and School Years In the summer months the extended Westerberg-Tranströmer family typically stayed on Runmarö, an island located in the archipelago that separates Stockholm from the open sea. On the island, Tranströmer and his mother vacationed at Westerberg's two-story blue house, surrounded by similar houses inhabited by their cousins and siblings and friends. Tranströmer's childhood was not, however, merely idyllic, for World War II raged on the periphery of Sweden for six years, from the time that he was eight years old until he turned fourteen. During Sunday dinners the family listened avidly to the Allied news, and the young Tranströmer often wished he could demonstrate his family's anti-Nazi stance in a public way.

At Södra Latin, Tranströmer's high school, his classmates were an unusually clever and well-read group who participated in or wrote for formal and informal literary clubs, poetry competitions, and high-school magazines. After the grim war years of rationed food and isolation, as people recognized a need for culture and for beautiful objects, money became available for funding the production of lavish art books and small magazines and for encouraging these young literary talents. *While the Laurels Grow* was the high-school magazine in which Tranströmer's first works appeared. After his debut he coedited a poetry magazine, *Opening Note*, until 1957. The magazine introduced Swedish readers to the work of Greek, German, and French poets, and the teen had the opportunity to publish world poetry in translation.

Traveling Years In the early 1950s Tranströmer completed his obligatory military service and studied literature, psychology, philosophy, and the history of religion at the University of Stockholm. He also indulged his taste for travel and made trips to what in those days were out-of-the-way places, traveling with scarcely any luggage or money to Iceland, Morocco, Turkey, and Yugoslavia, among other locales. Witnessing the harsh conditions under which many people outside Sweden lived left a profound impression on him, as did his first encounter with communism in Yugoslavia.

Tranströmer's eight years of postsecondary school studying and traveling were nevertheless generally happy. He enjoyed friendships, new and old, and socialized with

intellectuals and artists, people with whom he shared interests in literature, modern classical music, and the arts. He also wrote poetry, played the piano, and read as much as he could—developing an enduring preference for surrealist poetry and a related taste for parapsychology. All the while he avidly collected experiences and broadened his range of interests, as the publication of his second volume of poetry, *Secrets on the Way* (1958), reflected. In 1958 Tranströmer took his first full-time job as a psychologist at the Psychotechnical Institute in Stockholm and also married Monica Bladh. When the couple traveled to Egypt, he recorded her reactions to the experience in poems published in *The Half-Finished Heaven* (1962).

Distanced from Poetic Shifts in Sweden In 1960 Tranströmer and his wife left Stockholm, and Tranströmer took on a job as psychologist in residence outside Linköping at Roxtuna, an institution for delinquent youth. In the beginning, the couple found the distance from Stockholm difficult at times, because they were away from friends, parties, gallery openings, and the theater. Nevertheless, poetry collections continued to appear at a steady rate, once every four years: *The Half-Finished Heaven* was published in 1962; *Resonances and Tracks* in 1966; and *Night Vision* in 1970.

A shift in poetics characterized Swedish literature from the mid-1960s to the mid-1970s, and expectations for lyric poetry altered radically. Swedish writers and poets coming of age in the 1960s began to feel that artistic form and aesthetic pleasure might be obstacles to empathy. The reason for the reevaluation of literature was the discovery of social problems and injustices overseas: graphic pictures of the suffering inflicted on the people of Vietnam and of the misery of the dispossessed in India and Africa were shown on the evening news. The bleakness of the situation in the world was being matched by engagement at home. Swedish writers and poets therefore saw artistic form as a hindrance, as for them it evoked indecency in the face of human suffering.

Tranströmer's verse was hardly designed to endear him to the politically committed, and eventually the differences between him and writers of the "new simplicity" appeared even more distinct. Ultimately, these irreducible differences found their way into Tranströmer's works, as he analyzed them in *Friends, You Drank Some Darkness* (1970) in such poems as "Going with the Current" and "About History."

Illness and Later Years Besides being a time of artistic reconsideration, the late 1960s and early 1970s were also years of serious illness in the Tranströmer family. During this period his mother passed away. As evidenced by its title, *Night Vision* (1971) includes poetry that reflects the poet's stress and pain. Yet, during those difficult years he was buoyed by his growing international reputation, by the steady increase of his readership in the United States, and his friendships with such champions of international poetry as American poet Robert Bly, whom Tranströmer has known since the 1960s.

When Tranströmer had a stroke in 1990, resulting in expressive aphasia, or the inability to talk, he again considered themes of illness and aging. The effects of the stroke had only temporary consequences, and in 1993 he published his memoir, *Memories Look at Me*, and saw the appearance in 1996 of another book of verse, *Grief Gondola No. 2*. Melancholy does not, however, completely overtake his works. There is also in his poetry a strong element of peace and reconciliation in the face of impending death: as Tranströmer wrote in *For the Living and the Dead* (1989), "We living nails hammered down in society! / One day we'll come loose from everything. / We'll feel the wind of death under our wings / and become milder and wilder than here."

Works in Literary Context

Modernist Influences Swedish critic Peter Hallberg wrote an essay analyzing the literary sources and influences in the poems "Song" and "Elegy" from *Seventeen Poems* in which he showed the debt that these early pieces owed to high modernism. These long, elaborate poems further show influences of esoteric material that ranges from Finnish folk literature to the parapsychology of J. W. Dunne, and from T. S. Eliot's *Four Quartets* (1944) to such nearly forgotten modernist texts as Jean-Paul de Dadelsen's *Jonas* (1962). "Song" and "Elegy" (as well as "Epilog") are considered Tranströmer's most modernist poems, though they also look to the forgotten Baroque tradition for models and inspiration.

Surrealist Style In interviews Tranströmer has said repeatedly that he wishes people would live their lives more intensely. He makes poetic efforts to wake up people and encourage them to do so. This is in line with the "*changer l'homme*" (change of mankind) tradition of Arthur Rimbaud, a tradition continued and developed by the French surrealists and also by the "deep image" poets in the United States.

Scholar and critic Urban Torhamn analyzed Tranströmer's poetic method and argued that the shock and power of his images derive from their unusual function in the poem: the metaphors do not aim at conveying information, nor are they a means of communicating by substitution. Rather, the poet uses metaphors as "explosions aiming at a total transformation of the experience of reality."

Tranströmer's early poetry often relies on surreal imagery. Involving dreams and the subconscious, he uses the poetic technique of linking images and things from different areas of experience. The poet takes from phenomena ordinarily viewed as widely disparate. This shocks readers, forcing them to make leaps of association and shifts of consciousness. In *Secrets on the Way* (1958), for instance, Tranströmer counterbalances the widely

LITERARY AND HISTORICAL CONTEMPORARIES

Tranströmer's famous contemporaries include:

Robert Bly (1926–): An American poet and activist who founded the Mythopoetic Men's Movement.
Ingmar Bergman (1918–2007): Swedish filmmaker who created classics of international cinema such as *The Seventh Seal* (1957) and *The Virgin Spring* (1960).
Max von Sydow (1929–): Actor famous for his collaborations with Ingmar Bergman as well as his roles in *The Greatest Story Ever Told* (1965) and *The Exorcist* (1973).
Ted Hughes (1930–1998): English poet and author famous for his marriage to Sylvia Plath and for his children's novel *The Iron Man*.

ranging imagination of the poems with a repeated crossing of the border between dreaming and wakefulness.

Works in Critical Context

In Sweden the critical response to Tranströmer's poetry has fluctuated between two extremes: for a decade or so after the appearance of *Seventeen Poems*, his work was much admired, while after 1966 he came under frequent attack for what was perceived as an outdated style. Nevertheless, several literary scholars have made serious attempts to regard his work from a critical angle, and insightful essays on his poetry have been published.

As early as 1954 a critic emphasized aspects of Tranströmer's poetry that included its exactitude and shocking leaps of association in conjunction with a matter-of-fact tone. These aspects were and still are experienced as a new departure and a clean break with Swedish modernism. Critic Göran Printz-Påhlson wrote in 1979, "The modernism professed by Tranströmer seemed . . . to be of a radically different nature from the dominant tendencies of the preceding decade, when Swedish modernism had come of age. . . . With its spare and ascetic style, graphic visualization and ultimately enigmatic content, it exhibited a clean break with what seemed fuzzy and blurred, sentimental or exhibitionistic in modernism." In 1999 Niklas Schiöler suggested that the distinctive quality of Tranströmer's verse can perhaps be best described as magic realism. Such an interpretation is verified in Tranströmer's "Grief Gondola No. 2."

Seventeen Poems Tranströmer's first collection, *Seventeen Poems*, received critical praise upon its publication in 1954. As Joanna Bankier describes in an essay for *Ironwood*, "There was a poise and a maturity in his first work that was compelling." Leif Sjöberg states of the work, "Its perfect employment of classical metrics, its

COMMON HUMAN EXPERIENCE

Here are a few works by poets and writers who have also considered themes of illness or struggle:

The Collected Stories of Katherine Mansfield (1945). Featured in this collection are themes of physical and mental illness expressed by a writer who suffered her share of the same, from depression to tuberculosis.

"The Jilting of Granny Weatherall" (1930), a short story by Katherine Anne Porter. In this story, Granny Weatherall's well-being is in the hands of family, who do all the talking and decision making for her.

Midnight's Children (1981), a novel by Salman Rushdie. This is the story of an Indian protagonist, born with 1,001 others on August 15, 1947, (India's Independence Day) amid political turmoil.

"The Yellow Wallpaper," (1892), a short story by Charlotte Perkins Gilman. This story, often viewed as an early feminist work, details the female narrator's descent into madness.

One Hundred Years of Solitude (1967), a novel by Gabriel García Márquez. In this work by the Father of Magic Realism, a family's generations of struggles are chronicled.

startling new discoveries in Swedish landscapes and seascapes, its amazing density of acute images (written in a mild modernism which is more suggestive of Éluard and Dylan Thomas than of Lindegren and Ekelöf) soon made Tomas Tranströmer the most imitated poet in Sweden."

Responses to Literature

1. Tranströmer's poetry is a mixture of modernism and surrealism. Find as many incidences of surrealism as you can in Tranströmer's work. For example, what is dreamlike about his writing? Discuss with others, and point out something the others in the group did not see, so you can collectively come up with your own understanding of surrealism.

2. The anthology *English and American Surrealist Poetry* includes Tranströmer as part of the "deep image" canon of translated poetry. Consider one of his poems and select all of the images you find striking. Make a list of these images. What senses does each image appeal to? Why does it move you?

3. Consider how many of these images can be considered to symbolize, or represent, a larger concept. Make note of any associations you have with the image. For instance, what do you think of when you

see the word *garden*? Go online to a symbolism dictionary and look up the imagery words you have collected. Do the symbolic meanings agree with your associations?

4. In a group, photocopy one of Tranströmer's poems—such as "Tracks"—and read it through together. Then, use scissors to cut the poem into pieces, one line of poetry per cut piece. Mix up the pieces (lines) and together with your groupmates decide how you will "rewrite" the poem by gluing the pieces in the new order your group chooses. When you are finished, read aloud your version. Why did your group decide to place lines in the positions they placed them? Why do you think Tranströmer decided to place lines in the positions he placed them? What messages do you think each poem version expresses, and how do they do that differently?

BIBLIOGRAPHY

Books

Bergsten, Staffan. *Den trösterika gåtan: Tio essäer om Tomas Tranströmers lyrik*. Stockholm: FIB:s Lyrikklubb, 1989.

Espmark, Kjell. *Resans formler: En studie i Tomas Tranströmers lyrik*. Stockholm: Norstedt, 1983.

Schiöler, Niklas. *Koncentrationens konst: Tomas Tranströmers senare poesi*. Stockholm: Bonnier, 1999.

"Tomas (Gösta) Tranströmer (1931–)." In *Contemporary Literary Criticism*, vol. 52, edited by Daniel G. Marowski, Roger Matuz, and Sean R. Pollock, 408–18. Detroit: Gale Research, 1989.

Tranströmer, Tomas. *Memories Look at Me*. Stockholm: Bonnier, 1993.

Periodicals

Lloyd, Roseann. "Swedish Psychology." *Borealis* (January/February, 2002): 34–35.

Printz-Påhlson, Göran. "Tranströmer and Tradition." *Ironwood*, special Tranströmer issue, 15 (Spring 1979).

Torhamn, Urban. "Tranströmer's Poetic Method." *Bonniers Litterära Magasin* no. 10 (1961): 799–80.

Web Sites

Poets.org. "Tomas Tranströmer." Retrieved March 18, 2008, from http://www.poets.org/poet.php/prmPID/1112.

Samizdat. Issue #3. "Haiku by Tomas Tranströmer." Retrieved March 18, 2008, from http://samizdateditions.com/issue3/transtromer1.html.

Tomas Tranströmer Official Website. Retrieved March 18, 2008, from http://www.tomastranstromer.com/.

Michel Tremblay

BORN: *1942, Montreal, Quebec, Canada*

NATIONALITY: *Canadian*

GENRE: *Drama, fiction*

MAJOR WORKS:
Stories for Late Night Drinkers (1966)
Les Belles-soeurs (1968)
Like Death Warmed Over (1970)
Hosanna (1973)
The Fat Woman Next Door Is Pregnant (1978)

Overview

Michel Tremblay is one of the first Canadian playwrights to have won international recognition. His plays have been translated into many languages and performed successfully on three continents. In Quebec, his work is frequently classified as "theatre of liberation" and given political significance due to his introduction of the Montreal working-class French *joual* (dialect) as a stage idiom, as well as to his merciless naturalism and the political parables that underlie many of his plays. Viewed from a

Michel Tremblay   *Tremblay, Michel, photograph by Yves Renaud. Agence Goodwin. Reproduced by permission.*

wider perspective, Tremblay's work is impressive particularly because of its memorable characters, sophisticated methods of dramatic composition, and the richness and complexity of its levels of meaning.

Works in Biographical and Historical Context

Humble Origins Tremblay was born in Montreal in 1942, the son of Armand and Rhéauna Rathier Tremblay. His father was an alcoholic printer and linotype operator, while his mother was an American who was part Cree Indian. Tremblay grew up in poverty in the eastside working-class neighborhood of Plateau Mont-Royal and the rue Fabre district. Raised primarily by five women in an extremely crowded house, Tremblay early developed a hostility toward family life. The oppressive conditions in this impoverished area, along with the glitzy nightlife of Montreal's Main district, later provided the backdrop for much of Tremblay's work. His maternal grandmother was uneducated but a voracious reader who shared her love of reading with her grandson.

Despite these inauspicious beginnings, Tremblay began writing when quite young. He was inspired to write in part because he realized by the age of twelve that he was homosexual and used writing to help him deal with his outsider status. He wrote a number of short stories with gay themes that were hidden by fantasy elements. By the time he attended the Catholic high school École de Saint-Stanislas, he was seen as a promising student who earned a scholarship to a collège classique (essentially, a prep school).

Unable to endure the elitist attitudes fostered at the school, Tremblay left after only two months to study graphic arts at the Institut des Arts Graphiques beginning in 1969 and become a linotype operator like his father. He worked there until 1966 but furthered his education by borrowing books from a friend who was taking courses at the school Tremblay had left. The influence of classical Greek drama appears throughout Tremblay's work. He continued to write and, by the time he was eighteen, had completed his first play, *Le train*. In 1964, the work won first prize in Radio Canada's Young Author Competition.

"Theatre of Liberation" After winning his 1964 prize, Tremblay published a collection of gay-oriented short stories, *Stories for Late-Night Drinkers*, in 1966. He drew on his Montreal background for a one-act play, *Five*, which also appeared in 1966. Two years later, Tremblay made Quebec theater history by writing *Les Belles-soeurs* (1968) in *joual*, or working-class Quebec dialect, instead of the classical French typically used in works for the stage. This decision signaled Tremblay's desire to supplant the province's traditional French culture with an independent Quebecois culture.

In the 1960s, there was a resurgence of French Canadian separatism, symbolized by a series of cultural

LITERARY AND HISTORICAL CONTEMPORARIES

Tremblay's famous contemporaries include:

Pierre Trudeau (1919–2000): Perhaps the most dominant political figure in twentieth-century Canadian politics, Trudeau served as prime minister from 1968 to 1979 and again from 1980 to 1984. Highly polarizing politically, he was noted for his outlandish personality, his jet-set lifestyle, and his iconoclasm.

Philip K. Dick (1928–1982): An influential American science fiction writer, Dick's dystopian, paranoia-infused stories often touch upon metaphysical or theological themes.

Dan Akroyd (1952–): A Canadian-born actor and comedian, Akroyd was one of the original cast members of *Saturday Night Live*. Since leaving the show, he has found success in movies and music.

René Lévesque (1922–1987): Founder of the political group Parti Québécois, Lévesque was an active advocate of Quebec's political independence, which he attempted to achieve through popular referendum. He served as premier of Quebec from 1976 to 1985.

Harry Turtledove (1949–): American historian-turned-novelist Turtledove has made a career for himself as author of a wide range of historical, fantasy, and science fiction novels.

agreements between France and Quebec. Tremblay's creative choice to use dialect can be seen as a reflection of the ongoing call for French Canadian autonomy as the author was a staunch supporter of the movement as well as independence for Quebec. He even refused to let *Les Belles-soeurs* be performed in English until the separatist Parti Québéois won elections in the province in 1976.

Thus, *Les Belles-soeurs* catapulted the young dramatist to fame and became an important contribution to what is known in Quebec as the "theatre of liberation." *Les Belles-soeurs* examines the deepest private thoughts and feelings of fifteen working-class housewives gathered at a party. Through stylized monologues and choral "odes" the characters reveal the banal and repetitive nature of their lives and their inability to achieve emotional or physical fulfillment. The play's overriding theme is the fundamental absurdity and meaninglessness of existence. Its popular success allowed Tremblay to devote himself to writing full time.

"Le Cycle des Belles-soeurs" After *Les Belles-soeurs*, Tremblay embarked on a cycle of eleven plays, set mostly in the Montreal east end locale of the playhouse. The remaining dramas in Tremblay's cycle, known as "Le Cycle des *Belles-soeurs*, focus on three distinct areas: daily family life in Montreal's rue Fabre neighborhood; the seamy underworld of transvestites, prostitutes, and homosexuals in the Main district; and the realm of pure fantasy. In such plays as *Like Death Warmed Over* (1970), *Forever Yours, Marie-Lou* (1971), and *Hello, There, Hello* (1974), Tremblay portrays the family as a detrimental institution that inevitably traumatizes individuals by fostering frustration, bitterness, ineffectual communication, and emotional sterility. Critics generally regard the family in Tremblay's plays as symbolic of Quebec itself.

In many of the plays in the cycle, individuals also try to escape from the despair of their environments by advancing toward new sexual or social realms. Two of the plays—*La Duchesse de Langeais* (1970) and *Hosanna* (1973)—feature gay characters, a new development in serious theater at the time. But Tremblay was living in the midst of a profound transformation in Quebec. He came out as a gay man during a 1975 television interview, but reported few instances of overt hostility or discrimination afterward.

Turned to Film and Novels During the 1970s, Tremblay began working in film, often with friend André Brassard. Their film *Françoise Durocher, Waitress* (1972) won three Genie Awards at the Toronto Film Festival. While the pair collaborated on two other films, Tremblay also translated and adapted various English-language plays for the Quebec market, including various works by Tennessee Williams, whose plays and subject matter have much in common with Tremblay's. While Tremblay continued to write dramas over the years, his most characteristic mode of production from the late 1970s onward was the novel.

Beginning with the novel *The Fat Woman Next Door Is Pregnant* (1978), Tremblay wrote a group of six novels set in his childhood neighborhood in Montreal and included strong autobiographical elements. Known as "Les Chroniques du Plateau Mont-Royal," the novels, which included *Thérèse and Pierrette and the Little Hanging Angel* (1980), *The Duchess and the Commoner* (1982), and *News of Edward* (1984), deal with the destructive effects of family life. Tremblay continued to write new novels into the early 2000s.

More Plays and Television Work While Tremblay wrote few plays in the 1980s through early 2000s, he did produce some of his best-known works in this time period. They included *The Real World* (1987), in which he looked back on and questioned his own artistic uses of the milieu in which he had grown up. Tremblay wrote about rural Quebec in the play *The Suspended House* (1990), a multigenerational saga. With his *For the Pleasure of Seeing Her Again* (1998), he honored his mother and the influence she had on his artistic personality. In the early 2000s, Tremblay moved into television by writing scripts for a series on French Canadian television, *The Open Heart*. This was the first series on Quebec television to explore an ongoing gay relationship.

Tremblay has remained a firm French Canadian separatist throughout much of his lifetime, but raised separatist eyebrows in 1999 when he accepted the Governor General's Award for Drama from the Canadian government. While this award was the highest literary honor given to authors, it came from what many French Canadian separatists consider their enemy. Tremblay again stirred up controversy in 2006 when he seemed to waver on the issue of Quebec separatism by criticizing the sovereignty movement for its focus on economic issues to the exclusion of cultural ones. Despite such statements, Tremblay has remained a resident of the province and a firm devotee to the idea of Quebec's independence.

Works in Literary Context

Tremblay combines a basically naturalistic view of the world with a variety of stylistic devices that reflect his chief models: Greek tragedy, Shakespearean monologue, and theater of the absurd. His originality lies, in part, in his method of composition. He conceives his plays in the manner of musical compositions, as "scores" for voices rather than as conventional dialogue. This method of composition gives his drama a poetic quality and puts the burden of visual interpretation of the text on the director. The musical quality of his plays is in no way hampered by his use of *joual* or of the somewhat less extreme *Quebecois* dialect. Also influenced by the tradition of psychosocial drama begun by Gratien Gélinas and Marcel Dubé, Tremblay has transcended the work of his predecessors, achieving a successful synthesis between realism and theatricalism in style, the regional and the universal in theme, naturalism and lyricism in dramatic idiom.

Family and the Underbelly Tremblay's dramatic world is firmly rooted in his own life experience in Montreal, in the rue Fabre neighborhood where he grew up and in the Main district off Sainte Catherine Street, known for its colorful night life. The first provides the setting for his analysis of "monstrous family" situations. The Main district provides the background for the cheap entertainers, whores, and transvestites who appear in Tremblay's work. In his attacks on the institution of the family, as well as in his fascination with marginal characters, Tremblay is within the mainstream of contemporary drama. His work takes on special significance in the context of Quebec's history and culture, however: the family plays may be seen as conscious efforts to counterbalance the traditional myths of the French-Canadian family created and encouraged by the Catholic Church; and his transvestite characters, beyond their symbolic significance for modern alienated man, carry heavily political overtones. For Tremblay, the transvestite best exemplifies life in Quebec since the conquest, with its foreign dominance, foreign models, and cultural colonialism.

COMMON HUMAN EXPERIENCE

Other works that, like Tremblay's, examine the detrimental effects of family life include:

Anna Karenina (1877), a novel by Leo Tolstoy. Often cited as the pinnacle of realistic fiction, Tolstoy's great novel begins with the immortal line, "Happy families are all alike; every unhappy family is unhappy in its own way."

Romeo and Juliet (1597), a stage play by William Shakespeare. The tragedy of the "star-cross'd lovers" is set in motion by the senseless feuding of their two families. It is only through the death of the title characters that the families realize they must finally end their enmity.

A Doll's House (1879), a stage play by Henrik Ibsen. Highly controversial in its day, this Norwegian play's scathing and harrowing portrayal of Victorian married life has made it Ibsen's most well known work.

Autobiography and Sexual Orientation Unlike most writers, whose early work reflects the experience of their childhood and early youth, Tremblay creates a world in which the autobiographical element unfolds progressively and by degrees as his universe expands. This is particularly true for the revelation of his sexual orientation. Although the homosexual element is present throughout his work, it first appears in a largely objective manner with the political symbolism of the transvestite figures of his early plays. The central transvestite figure reappears in the novels that make up "Les Chroniques du Plateau Mont-Royal." Finally, in the third phase of the author's work, Tremblay himself takes center stage, first as the thinly disguised Jean-Marc, the professor of French in the play *Remember Me* (1981) and the novel *The Heart Laid Bare* (1986), and at last openly in the stories of *The Movies* (1990), which tell how the boy Michel first discovers and faces his "abnormal" proclivities.

Influence Because Tremblay's works have been translated into more than twenty languages (including Spanish, Yiddish, and Polish), his influence can be seen worldwide on naturalistic authors as well as those who explore gay themes. Because of his importance in French Canadian society, his works also affected several generations of Quebecois writers as well. Prolific and versatile, Tremblay is seen as voicing the frustrations and aspirations of his native Quebec.

Works in Critical Context

Recognized as one of Canada's most important contemporary authors, Tremblay has risen to international prominence through his iconoclastic dramas about familial, political, linguistic, and identity problems that are unique to Quebec. Synthesizing local and universal themes and naturalist and symbolist styles, Tremblay has created a body of work that has prompted critic Geraldine Anthony to remark: "Tremblay's deep understanding of human nature and his mastery of dramatic technique are responsible for his position as one of the leading Canadian dramatists today." Similarly well-received are Tremblay's novels. Both critics and readers have generally praised his novels, especially *The Fat Woman Next Door Is Pregnant.*

Les Belles-soeurs *Les Belles-soeurs* is the first in what became an eleven-play cycle that, in its entirety, many critics regarded as Tremblay's finest achievement. John Ripley suggested that Quebec's "recent past, characterized by a desperate struggle to replace authoritarianism, negative identity, and destructiveness with self-respect, love, and transcendence, is nowhere better encapsulated than in the *Les Belles-soeurs* cycle." Ripley's sentiments were echoed by critic Renate Usmiani, who in his *Studies in Canadian Literature: Michel Tremblay* stated: "The most general underlying theme of all [Tremblay's] works is the universal desire of the human being to transcend his finite condition." More specifically, Usmiani proposed that the typical Tremblay character is either trying to escape from family life as represented by the rue Fabre, from the false world of the Main district, or from the limitations of self into a transcendent ecstasy.

Responses to Literature

1. Discuss Tremblay's contributions to Canadian theater in an essay. What political views does Tremblay support or oppose? How do his plays deal with the idea of a particular Quebecois identity?

2. Explain how Tremblay synthesizes regional and universal themes in his works in a presentation. Can his works be compared with those of other, non-Canadian playwrights? Which of Tremblay's themes are particular to Canada and which are universal?

3. In a paper, define *joual* and explain how Tremblay uses it in his works. Why does Tremblay choose to write in a dialect? How does this affect the audience?

4. Discuss in a group how Tremblay interweaves high and low culture in his works. How does he synthesize fantasy and reality?

BIBLIOGRAPHY

Books

Bélair, Michel. *Michel Tremblay.* Quebec City, Quebec: Presses de L'Université du Québec, 1972.

Usmiani, Renate. *Michel Tremblay: A Critical Study.* Toronto: Douglas & McIntyre, 1981.

⬨ Anthony Trollope

BORN: *1815, London, England*

DIED: *1882, Harting, Sussex, England*

NATIONALITY: *British*

GENRE: *Drama, fiction*

MAJOR WORKS:

Barchester Towers (1857)
Orley Farm (1862)
The Eustace Diamonds (1873)
The Way We Live Now (1875)

Overview

Anthony Trollope was one of the most prolific English writers of the nineteenth century, writing some forty-seven novels and many further volumes of travels, sketches, criticism, and short fiction. Although most critics consider him a major Victorian novelist, the precise nature of his achievement has often proved elusive. In spite of conflicting interpretations, commentators tend to agree that his realistic characterizations form the basis of his importance and appeal.

Anthony Trollope   *Hulton Archive / Getty Images*

Works in Biographical and Historical Context

A Poor Victorian Trollope lived nearly all of his adult life during a time known as the Victorian era. This era was named after Queen Victoria, who ruled England and its territories, including Ireland. Queen Victoria sat on the throne longer than any other British monarch, from 1837 until 1901. This period saw significant changes for both Britain and Europe as a whole, with advances in industrialization leading much of the population to jobs in factories instead of on farms as in the past. The era was also marked by a preoccupation with proper behavior in society and domestic life, common themes found in Trollope's works.

Anthony Trollope was born on April 24, 1815, in London. His father, Thomas Trollope, failed at law and farming before going bankrupt, and his mother, Frances, began what eventually became a lucrative writing career to support the family. Trollope's early years were marked by poverty and humiliation; he was under constant ridicule by his wealthier classmates at Harrow and Winchester. At the age of nineteen he found work as a junior clerk at the post office and seven years later was transferred to Ireland.

The Barsetshire Series Trollope's move to Ireland inaugurated a period of change: For the first time in his life he was successful in work, love, friendship, and financial matters. Trollope began writing, though his first novel, *The Macdermots of Ballycloran* (1847), received little critical attention. In the early 1850s Trollope's post office work absorbed all his energies. He was assigned to work out the routes for rural deliveries, first in a district in Ireland and then in a number of counties in England, particularly in the west. He did his work with zeal, riding over all the routes himself, determined to make it possible that a letter could be delivered to every remote residence in his district. It was while visiting the close of Salisbury Cathedral that he conceived the story of *The Warden*, the first in the series of novels about his invented county of Barsetshire that was to make him famous.

The Warden (1855), Trollope's fourth novel, was a moderate success. The story was followed by *Barchester Towers* (1857), the second novel in the series, which marked the public's recognition of a new major novelist. Many readers still regard it as the apogee of Trollope's achievement.

The other novels in the Barset series, with which Trollope was engaged intermittently over the next decade, were *Doctor Thorne* (1858), *Framley Parsonage* (1861), *The Small House at Allington* (1864), and *The Last Chronicle of Barset* (1867). Each of these novels is distinctive, with its own plot, new major characters, and a few recurring characters. All were set in the quiet cathedral city of Barchester with its surrounding town, villages, and ancestral estates of Barsetshire. *Framley Parsonage*, the fourth novel in the Barsetshire series, was Trollope's first work to appear in serial form, a method of magazine publication that promised a wide readership and greater critical response.

The Palliser Series Before he had written his last chronicle of Barset, Trollope had already launched into the first of a new series of interconnected novels, the Palliser, or political, novels. Young Plantagenet Palliser, a dedicated politician and the heir to the duke of Omnium, was first introduced as a minor character in *The Small House at Allington* in the Barset series. Where the clergy are the focus of interest in the Barset novels, politicians and their business are the concern of the Palliser novels; and the major scene of action shifts from the quiet though sufficiently busy rural county of Barsetshire to the more hectic bustle of the metropolis. Like the Barset novels, the Palliser novels all have separate plots and are complete in themselves, but characters introduced in one novel are apt to recur in subsequent ones.

Political Life Having returned to England in 1859, the pattern of Trollope's life seems to have changed in the late 1860s. He left the post office, worked as an editor, and attempted to pursue a career in politics. In 1868, he unsuccessfully ran for a seat in Parliament. Trollope called the years 1867 and 1868, the years of his resignation, editorship, second trip to America, and political campaign, "the busiest of my life." With the new decade he seemed to slow down a little. He continued to be busy, but he was perhaps less cheerful.

Declining Popularity The 1870s witnessed a decline in Trollope's popularity as his writing style and focus changed. Although they often include subjects similar to those in his earlier works, Trollope's later novels are more cynical and pessimistic in tone: *He Knew He Was Right* (1869) examines marriage and finds jealousy and corruption; *The Way We Live Now* (1875) studies society and uncovers financial and moral corruption. Critics objected to what they considered the sordid realism of these works, charging that Trollope ignored the novelist's responsibility of providing solutions to the social problems he depicted. In addition, because he was so prolific, Trollope was accused of commercialism.

Posthumous Self-Effacement During the 1870s, Trollope began to travel extensively and write travel books. He also found time to write literary criticism. Yet as he aged, he encountered trouble with asthma, deafness, and other ailments. During a friendly evening with his old friends, Trollope had a stroke. He lingered a few weeks, but died on December 6, 1882.

Trollope's prudent habit of keeping a manuscript or two on hand meant that the novels kept coming for a while, including *Mr. Scarborough's Family* (1883) and *The Landleaguers*, which he had not lived to finish, yet was published incomplete. His major posthumous publication, however, was *An Autobiography*, an engagingly frank account of his professional life and working habits that has continued to shock and delight his readers in almost equal measure.

LITERARY AND HISTORICAL CONTEMPORARIES

Trollope's famous contemporaries include:

Florence Nightingale (1820–1910): Called "The Lady with the Lamp" for her habit of caring for patients long into the night, Florence Nightingale became a public figure after her efforts to improve battlefield hospitals during the Crimean War. She was a lifelong advocate for nursing and patient care.

Lewis Carroll (1832–1898): The pen name of Charles Dodgson, Carroll was a master of the genre of literary nonsense, penning the surreal tales of *Alice's Adventures in Wonderland* and *Through the Looking Glass* and the poem "Jabberwocky."

Fyodor Dostoyevsky (1821–1881): One of the premier Russian novelists of the nineteenth century, Dostoyevsky focused on troubled psyches and is considered by many to be the father of existentialism.

William Gladstone (1809–1898): A lion of Victorian politics, Gladstone was Liberal prime minister on four occasions, repeatedly butting heads with both Queen Victoria and his Conservative rival, Benjamin Disraeli.

Cetshwayo (1826–1884): The last king of the Zulu nation, from 1872 to 1879, Cetshwayo was the grand-nephew of the legendary king Shaka.

Alexander II (1818–1881): From his ascension to the throne as leader of the Russian Empire in 1855 to his assassination in 1881, Alexander II led a program of systematic reforms, most notably the emancipation of the peasant class of serfs.

Works in Literary Context

Critics continue to dispute the nature of Trollope's achievement, and there is no general agreement on his rank among writers of fiction. Yet commentators universally applaud the quality of his characterizations. Many believe that Trollope was able to paint characters of such consistency, veracity, and depth because of his profound insight into and sympathy for his creations. Trollope himself considered the ability to live with one's characters essential and defined the main work of the novelist as "the creation of human beings in whose existence one is forced to believe."

Maidens and Women "There must be love in a novel," Trollope declared; and he became an acknowledged expert in handling a character's intricate vacillations between love and social constraints. It was for such portraits as that of Lucy Robarts that Henry James remembered Trollope as an author who celebrated the "simple maiden in her flower.... He is evidently always more or less in love with her."

There are several comparable features in Trollope's two major series, the Barset and the Palliser novels. A major character in each is a dominating woman who competes with her husband for power and then dies suddenly toward the end of the series. A noticeable change is in the presentation of the other female characters. Whereas in the Barset novels "the simple maiden in her flower" had predominated—such girls as Mary Thorne, Lucy Robarts, and Grace Crawley—in the Palliser novels the interest shifts from innocent girls to experienced women: Lady Laura Kennedy, who deserts her husband and declares her adulterous passion for another man; Madame Max Goesler, who, having married once for a settlement pursues a handsome young man for love and actually proposes to him; and Lady Glencora herself, who not only is much more sympathetically handled than Mrs. Proudie but also breaks the standard Trollope code by abandoning her first love and devoting herself to a second.

Densely Layered Novels *The Last Chronicle of Barset* is typical of Trollope's copious, variegated kind of novel. Its characters are numerous and diverse, and its world is composed of several plots and different settings. Although he wrote a number of relatively short novels in which a classic unity of action is clearly preserved, his greatest works are those in which the main plot is amplified by subplots and the themes are enlarged and qualified. "Though [the novelist's] story should be all one, yet it may have many parts," Trollope explained. "Though the plot itself may require but few characters, it may be so enlarged as to find its full development in many. There may be subsidiary plots, which shall all tend to the elucidation of the main story, and which will take their places as part of one and the same work."

Works in Critical Context

Trollope's enormous productivity has had much to do with a patronizing dismissal of his work by some critics and a rather apologetic attitude adopted even by his admirers. In a review of *Miss Mackenzie* the young Henry James admitted, "We have long entertained for Mr. Trollope a partiality of which we have yet been somewhat ashamed." It has been a recurring attitude. Even his major biographer, Michael Sadleir, writing in 1927, and his next major critic, Bradford A. Booth, have been tentative and cautious in their praise and have partly adopted the stance of apologists. Critics have found his elusive but undoubted quality difficult to analyze: "His work resists the kind of formal analysis to which we subject our better fiction," Booth admitted. His unambiguous style has not invited critical interpretation. Compared with George Eliot or George Meredith he has seemed lowbrow, and compared with Charles Dickens and Hardy his unemphatic social commentary has seemed mild.

Some critics, including several of his original reviewers, have found fault with Trollope's subsidiary plots and have wished them away. Recent criticism, however, has shown Trollope's impressive art in the orchestration of plot with subplot. In the article entitled "Trollope at Full Length," Gordon Ray demonstrates how Trollope "knew exactly how to assign each set of characters its proper part in the story, to time his shifts from one plot to another so as to obtain maximum emphasis, contrast, and change of pace, and to bring the whole to a smooth conclusion within the space allotted. Trollope, in fact, made himself a great master of the contrapuntal novel long before anyone had thought of the term."

The Barset Series   The Barsetshire series elicited several comments that were repeated throughout Trollope's lifetime. Above all, critics warmed to his characters and praised both Trollope's lively, readable style and his humorous portrayal of everyday life. They also noted his fidelity to the English character, particularly in his portraits of young girls, although some critics noted that he overused the plot scheme of a heroine vacillating between two suitors.

Trollope's early critics attributed a number of his faults, including careless construction, grammatical errors, and insubstantial story lines, to the fact that Trollope wrote quickly, and they blamed the exigencies of serial publication for his overly episodic and fragmentary plots. In addition, many commentators found Trollope's technique of allowing the narrator to constantly comment on the action and characters to be irrelevant and distracting.

Legacy   If it has taken time for critics to claim a place for Trollope among the greatest novelists, the readers have kept buying and reading his books. He has continued to be "obsessively readable," in C. P. Snow's phrase. He lost some readers during his lifetime and some more after his death; but after the 1890s reprints of his many novels have proved sound investments for many publishers. During the two world wars, Trollope and Barset were in enormous demand. In the 1970s his second series was adapted by the BBC as a highly successful television serial, *The Pallisers*. And increasingly in the two decades before the centenary of his death, the critics have ceased to be apologists. Trollope has been recognized as a major novelist.

Responses to Literature

1. Read several of Trollope's short stories. Discuss how Trollope presents Victorian life. What makes his characters different from those of other Victorian writers? Do you think his stories represent a realistic view? Find textual examples to support your position.

2. Using Trollope's autobiography as a source, analyze his objectivity in his introspective study of himself as an artist.

3. Contrast two characters from opposite ends of the social spectrum in one of Trollope's early novels, for example, *Barchester Towers*.

COMMON HUMAN EXPERIENCE

Trollope made a name for himself with the tales of the residents of an invented county that held recognizable elements from real locations despite its being fictional. Other works featuring famous fictional settings that bear a strong resemblance to real places include:

"The Dunwich Horror" (1929), a short story by H. P. Lovecraft. This pulp horror writer used Arkham County, a prototypical New England locale, as a setting for many of his stories. This, one of his best-known short stories, prominently features two of Arkham County's most famous locales: Miskatonic University and the town of Dunwich.

Far from the Madding Crowd (1874), a novel by Thomas Hardy. Hardy wrote a series of stories and poems set in the semifictional Wessex County; this was his fourth such story and first major success.

Gulliver's Travels (1726), a novel by Jonathan Swift. In this would-be travelogue, the locations visited by Gulliver—Lilliput, Brobdingnag, Laputa, and so forth—are allegorical countries, each representing a different aspect of human nature.

---

4. Compare Trollope to Charles Dickens. How did their literary styles differ? How were they similar? Which author do you feel is more emblematic of the Victorian period? Why?

BIBLIOGRAPHY

Books

Ap Roberts, Ruth. *The Moral Trollope*. Athens: Ohio University Press, 1971.

Dictionary of Literary Biography, Volume 21: Victorian Novelists Before 1885. A Bruccoli Clark Layman Book. Ed. Ira B. Nadel, University of British Columbia, and William E. Fredeman, University of British Columbia. Detroit: Gale Group, 1983.

Dictionary of Literary Biography, Volume 57: Victorian Prose Writers After 1867. A Bruccoli Clark Layman Book. Ed. William B. Thesing, University of South Carolina. Detroit: Gale Group, 1987.

Dictionary of Literary Biography, Volume 159: British Short-Fiction Writers, 1800–1880. A Bruccoli Clark Layman Book. Ed. John R. Greenfield, McKendree College. Detroit: Gale Group, 1996.

Halperin, John. *Trollope and Politics: A Study of the Pallisers and Others*. New York: Macmillan, 1977.

———. *Trollope Centenary Essays*. New York: St. Martin's, 1982.

Herbert, Christopher. *Trollope and Comic Pleasure.*
Chicago: University of Chicago Press, 1987.

Kendrick, Walter M. *The Novel-Machine: The Theory and
Fiction of Anthony Trollope.* Baltimore: Johns
Hopkins University Press, 1980.

McMaster, Juliet. *Trollope's Palliser Novels: Theme and
Pattern.* New York: Macmillan, 1978.

Morse, Deborah Denenholz. *Women in Trollope's Palliser
Novels.* Ann Arbor, Mich.: UMI Research Press, 1987.

Mullen, Richard. *Anthony Trollope: A Victorian in His
World.* London: Duckworth, 1990.

Nardin, Jane. *He Knew She Was Right: The Independent
Woman in the Novels of Anthony Trollope.*
Carbondale: Southern Illinois University Press,
1989.

Super, Robert H. *The Chronicler of Barsetshire: A Life of
Anthony Trollope.* Ann Arbor: University of
Michigan Press, 1988.

The Trollope Critics. Edited by H. John Hall. New York:
Macmillan, 1981.

Periodicals

Huntington Library Quarterly, volume 31, 1968.
Nineteenth Century Fiction, June 1949; September 1949.

▨ Leon Trotsky

BORN: *1879, Yanovka, Ukraine*

DIED: *1940, Mexico City*

NATIONALITY: *Russian*

GENRE: *Nonfiction*

MAJOR WORKS:

My Life (1930)

*The History of the Russian Revolution to Brest-
Litovsk* (1932)

The Revolution Betrayed (1937)

Overview

Leon Trotsky was a principal strategist of the Russian
revolution and a central leader in the founding of the
Soviet Union. He played an important role in the revolution that brought the communist Bolsheviks to power,
and he organized the Red Army during the ensuing civil
war. Trotsky was also a brilliant and influential author who
contributed thousands of essays, letters, and political tracts
to the literature of Marxism, as well as important works of
history, biography, and literary criticism. Trotsky was the
foremost critic of Joseph Stalin, the Soviet leader from
1924 to 1953, whose repressive policies resulted in the
deaths of millions of Soviet citizens. Exiled by Stalin,
Trotsky became—and remains—a figure of international
controversy.

Leon Trotsky   *Topical Press Agency / Getty Images*

Works in Biographical and Historical Context

Youthful Activism Trotsky was born Lev Davido-
vich Bronstein in the Ukrainian village of Yanovka in
1879 to a relatively prosperous Jewish farming family.
(The name on Bronstein's false passport—Trotsky—
would remain with him.) From the ages of nine to sixteen
he lived in Odessa with his mother's nephew, journalist
and publisher Mossoi Filipovich Spentzer, who oversaw
his education. The boy was strongly influenced by the
intellectual atmosphere of the Spentzer home, where
journalists and other writers frequently visited.

Trotsky was sent to the nearby seaport of Nikolaev
for his last academic year. There he met Russian socialists
for the first time and joined a radical discussion group.
One member of this group, Alexandra Sokolovskaya,
considered herself a Marxist, and Trotsky almost immediately opposed her ideology. He instead preferred the
populist view that education of the peasants was the best
way to achieve social progress.

Trotsky played a role in the formation of the Southern Russian Workers' Union, an underground group of
students and workers devoted to improving the lives of
the laboring class. Trotsky also wrote and printed leaflets
for the group, pointing out abuses in factories and in the

government. These leaflets provoked the ire of the authorities, and he and his companions were arrested as dissidents in 1898.

Trotsky was held in prison for the next two years and then sentenced to four years of exile in Siberia. While awaiting deportation, he first heard of Vladimir Lenin and his writings about Russian capitalism. Trotsky married Alexandra Sokolovskaya before leaving. During his exile, he studied works by such political theorists as Lenin and Karl Marx, and gradually his views became inclined toward Marxism. He wrote a steady stream of political essays and pamphlets for clandestine circulation among prisoners, and he began to develop a reputation.

Insurrection of 1905 Urged by his wife, Trotsky escaped from Siberia in 1902 using a fake passport. Leaders of the Russian underground movement directed him to London, where he joined the circle of exiled revolutionists, including Lenin and Julius Martov of the Russian Social Democratic Party. Trotsky was set to work writing for their newspaper, *Iskra* and within months was an established party leader.

The Social Democratic Party split the following year, divided on the question of whether to limit or expand party membership. In opposition to Lenin and his Bolsheviks, Trotsky found himself in the middle of the dispute, siding with Martov of the Menshevik faction in favor of a broad-based party. Trotsky wrote that Lenin's preference for concentration of power could eventually lead to dictatorship. History proved him correct—as Stalin's rise to power demonstrated—but his words mainly served to estrange him from Lenin. Ironically, Trotsky soon parted ways with the Mensheviks as well. Suspended between both factions, Trotsky discovered A. L. Helfand, a German-born Marxist theoretician, who wrote under the pen name of Parvus. Under his influence, Trotsky adopted the political theory that would later be associated with him, the notion of "permanent revolution."

In January 1905, government soldiers in St. Petersburg fired upon a group of citizens who had gathered to petition Czar Nicholas II for civil and political rights. Trotsky returned to Russia almost immediately and produced incendiary essays and pamphlets calling for insurrection. Demonstrations continued, culminating in a general strike that brought Russian industry and transportation to a standstill. This led to the formation of Russia's first elective body to represent the working class, the Council (or Soviet) of Workers' Deputies. Trotsky became a leader of the St. Petersburg Soviet, but by December its leaders were under arrest and martial law declared. The revolution was put on hold. Meanwhile, Trotsky was put on trial, and again exiled to Siberia. Again, he escaped.

Central Role in Bolshevik Revolution Trotsky spent most of the next decade in Vienna, Austria, editing the revolutionary newspaper *Pravda* and contributing political journalism to the European press. He refined his ideas of "permanent revolution," advocating a socialist revolution that would carry beyond Russia's borders. As Trotsky saw it, since Russia had not developed a powerful capitalist middle class, or bourgeoisie, the success of a revolution would depend on the lower class, or proletariat. Leadership of the state, Trotsky argued, should then pass immediately to the "dictatorship of the proletariat"—that is, the vanguard, or Communist elite. Furthermore, the survival of such a revolution would depend on economic support from abroad. The history of the Soviet revolution would bear out much of this theory; as historian Irving Howe has observed, "of all the Marxists it was Trotsky who best foresaw the course of events in Russia."

Threatened with internment by Austria as World War I broke out, Trotsky journeyed to Switzerland, France, and the United States. As the war progressed, Russia's domestic situation became increasingly unstable. In March 1917, the news arrived that the czar had been overthrown. By the time Trotsky arrived in Petrograd in early May, the country had fallen into political chaos. Trotsky quickly reconciled with Lenin and joined the Bolshevik Party, becoming its most eloquent orator. When Lenin, suspected of being a German spy, went into hiding, it was Trotsky who organized Bolshevik military regiments and spearheaded the bloodless takeover of the government, hereafter called the October Revolution.

In the Bolshevik government formed after the coup, Trotsky was offered the chairmanship of the ruling body, the Council of People's Commissars. He declined the post, offering instead to become press director for the new regime. Out of hiding, Lenin assumed the chairmanship and later persuaded Trotsky to serve as commissar for foreign affairs. In this capacity, he led the Soviet delegation to the Brest-Litovsk peace negotiations that ended Russia's participation in World War I. Soon afterward, civil war broke out in Russia between supporters and opponents of the Soviet regime. Trotsky became war commissar, assuming command of an exhausted and demoralized force of less than ten thousand soldiers. In what historian E. H. Carr calls his supreme achievement, Trotsky rebuilt the Red Army to over 5 million men, restored order and discipline, and by 1921, achieved victory over the anti-Bolshevik White Army, which had been armed by Britain, France, and the United States.

Exiled by Stalin As powerful an orator and capable a leader as Trotsky was, however, he was a blunt, arrogant man who made numerous enemies. When Lenin suffered a stroke in 1922, many believed Trotsky to be the best choice for his successor, but he had a small political base. His main opponent, Joseph Stalin, had better tactics and a stronger network of alliances. Stalin gradually gained control of the bureaucracy of the party and the Soviet state. He also reached out to Trotsky's enemies and effectively used Trotsky's own words, such as his previous attacks on Lenin, to discredit him. For his part, Trotsky made the error of declining to reply to many of Stalin's attacks. His dignified silence cost him even more political

LITERARY AND HISTORICAL CONTEMPORARIES

Trotsky's famous contemporaries include:

Vladimir Ilyich Lenin (1870–1924): Russian revolutionary and first leader of the Soviet Union.
Igor Stravinsky (1882–1971): Russian composer of classical works such as *The Firebird* (1910) and *The Rite of Spring* (1913).
Woodrow Wilson (1856–1924): U.S. president from 1913 until 1921.
Maxim Gorky (1868–1936): Russian author and proponent of socialist realism in literature.
James Joyce (1882–1941): Irish expatriate author who wrote modern classics such as *Finnegans Wake* (1939) and *Ulysses* (1922).

support. Between 1925 and 1927 he was forced to relinquish his political responsibilities. Trotsky, along with fifteen hundred other "Trotskyists," was expelled from the party in 1927 and exiled to central Asia in 1928.

Trotsky remained in exile until his death twelve years later, living at times in Turkey, France, Norway, and, finally, Mexico. He turned to literature, and wrote his most critically acclaimed books during this period, including *The History of the Russian Revolution to Brest-Litovsk* (*Von Oktober bis nach Brest-Litovsk*) (1932), *My Life* (*Moya zhizn*) (1930), and *The Revolution Betrayed* (1937). In this last work, Trotsky denounced Stalin's creation of a bureaucratic elite that sought to stifle opposition and extend its dominance.

During his final period of exile, Trotsky labored to create a Fourth International, a federation of socialist organizations dedicated to worldwide revolution; Stalin had taken over the Third (or Communist) International and made it an instrument of his own policies. However, the Fourth International never achieved a large membership. Stalin never let up his assault on Trotsky's reputation. In 1936, Trotsky was tried in absentia in the Soviet Union for treason, murder, conspiracy, and espionage. The Soviet courts convicted him, but a Western commission of independent scholars found him innocent of all charges. In 1940, a Stalinist assassin killed Trotsky in Mexico City.

Works in Literary Context

Political Leader vs. Author   Despite his renown as a political leader, Trotsky considered himself primarily an author. In fact, at many times in his life he remarked that the revolution was interfering with his literary work. Trotsky's combination of literary talent and political skill is particularly evident in his historical writings, most notably in *1905* and *The History of the Russian Revolution to Brest-Litovsk*. *1905*, Trotsky's first major work, was written early in his career and completed before the development of many of his important political ideas. Critics note that as a result, the work is free of the sweeping theoretical generalizations that characterize his later historical writings, although the influence of Marx and Lenin is evident.

Political Historian and Biographer   *The History of the Russian Revolution to Brest-Litovsk* is considered both Trotsky's masterpiece and the greatest Marxist history ever written. The work portrays on an epic scale the interaction of masses and individuals in the months between February and December of 1917. Trotsky maintained that "the most indubitable feature of a revolution is the direct intervention of the masses in historic events." Although the *History* is dominated by a Marxist perspective, the author's analysis emphasizes the dynamics of mass psychology along with economic factors.

Trotsky hurriedly composed a biography of Lenin after the leader's death in 1924, intending to complete a full-scale biography later. He completed only the first volume, entitled *The Young Lenin* (*Vie de Lenine, jeunesse*) (1936). This work has been widely praised for its sensitive and poetic portrayal of Lenin's childhood and youth. The opening chapters of Trotsky's autobiography, *My Life*, have been similarly praised for their vivid remembrance of childhood, earning favorable comparison to self-portraits by Leo Tolstoy and Maxim Gorky. The later chapters of the work, however, have been criticized for their concentration on political and public matters to the exclusion of Trotsky's inner and personal life. Trotsky himself noted that his *Diary in Exile* (1935), a journal kept during his exile in France and Norway, was dominated by political commentary and literary criticism. "And how could it actually be otherwise?" he wrote. "For politics and literature constitute the essence of my personal life."

Marxist Literary Critic   Trotsky's works of literary criticism also have considerable historical value. His most important work in this genre, *Literature and Revolution* (*Lituratura i revolyutsiya*) (1923), surveys prominent Russian authors and includes a controversial theoretical essay. Trotsky opposes "proletarian art," a concept championed after the revolution by artists and writers who believed that art and literature should reflect class consciousness and Marxist values. Trotsky maintained that "proletarian culture and art will never exist," arguing instead that the Russian Revolution "derives its historic significance and moral greatness from the fact that it lays the foundation for a classless society and for the first truly universal culture." His theories were strongly opposed by Soviet officials who sought to control intellectual life through regulation of the arts and by literary groups who sought official endorsement for their particular doctrines. In the years preceding Trotsky's exile to central Asia, his opponents cited these "anti-proletarian" views of art and culture as evidence that his thought was fundamentally counterrevolutionary. Among Western critics, however, *Literature and Revolution* is praised for its wit, originality, and insight, and is generally considered the definitive exposition of Marxist literary theory.

Works in Critical Context

Union of Thought and Action Although the controversy surrounding Trotsky has subsided somewhat since his death, few public figures of the century have inspired such intense emotions from both admirers and detractors. Decades after Stalin, Trotsky was still denounced in the Soviet Union as a heretic of Marxism. He was denounced as well by Western anticommunists who considered him a ruthless, or at best, misguided revolutionary fanatic. At the same time, many political leftists worldwide consider him among the most brilliant proponents of classical Marxist thought. Trotskyite political parties that campaign for worldwide revolution still exist in many countries. His achievements and his tragic life have inspired adulation by Western intellectuals who see in Trotsky the perfect union of thought and action.

Objectivity Critics are nearly unanimous in praising Trotsky's compelling prose style, especially in his *History of the Russian Revolution*. However, no consensus exists as to Trotsky's success in achieving the dispassion that historical scholarship requires. George Vernadsky, among others, calls the work "an impassioned invective against [Trotsky's] enemies" that is "undeniably permeated by ill-suppressed bias." Trotsky himself distinguished between "objectivity" and "impartiality," writing that he sought the former while disdaining the latter, and many critics agree that he succeeded in achieving intellectual honesty without sacrificing his commitment to a particular ideological perspective. According to Deutscher, "extreme partisanship and scrupulously sober observation go hand in hand" in the *History*.

The question of Trotsky's objectivity is even more central to his writings on Stalin. His scathing biography of Stalin, which denounces his personality and rise to power, is perhaps the most controversial of Trotsky's writings. Left unfinished at the time of Trotsky's death, the manuscript was pieced together from the author's notes by editor Charles Malamuth and submitted for publication in 1941. According to Bertram Wolfe, Malamuth's version differed enough on crucial issues from Trotsky's known views that the author's literary executors threatened legal proceedings to prevent its publication. This proved unnecessary, however, as the manuscript was voluntarily withheld by the publisher at the behest of the United States government, which was at that time allied with Stalin's Russia in World War II. Upon its appearance in 1946, the work was viciously received by many critics, who considered it a malicious and unjustified attack on Stalin and Stalinism motivated solely by personal vindictiveness. Such critics as Robert H. McNeal, on the other hand, assert that "it is rather to be wondered that the polemical reaction of a leader so naturally proud and combative as

Trotsky was so restrained, considering the provocation that Stalin gave him." Trotsky's intellectual integrity in this matter has some prominent defenders, but even those critics who consider the biography an accurate depiction of Stalin's personality and career agree that *Stalin* is largely unsuccessful as a work of literature.

Responses to Literature

1. What do you think Russia would have been like from 1940 to 1960—politics, economy, standard of living, art—if Stalin had been exiled in 1928 instead of Trotsky?

2. Evaluate Trotsky's theory of worldwide or "permanent" socialist revolution, in light of the rise and fall of Soviet communism in the twentieth century.

3. Research the cultural theory proposed by Trotsky in *Literature and Revolution*. How do his ideas shed light on the artistic genre of "socialist realism" that emerged from the Soviet Union?

BIBLIOGRAPHY

Books

Chamberlin, William Henry. *The Russian Revolution, 1917–1921*. New York: Macmillan, 1935.

Daniels, Robert V. *Red October: The Bolshevik Revolution of 1917*. New York: Charles Scribner's Sons, 1967.

Deutscher, Isaac. *The Prophet Outcast: Trotsky, 1929–1940*. London: Oxford University Press, 1963.

Dictionary of Russian Literature. Westport, Conn.: Greenwood Press, 1971.

Howe, Irving. *Leon Trotsky.* New York: Viking, 1978.

Knei-Paz, Baruch. *The Social and Political Thought of Leon Trotsky.* London: Oxford at the Clarendon Press, 1978.

Poggioli, Renato. *The Spirit of the Letter: Essays in European Literature.* Cambridge, Mass.: Harvard University Press, 1965.

Rowse, A. L. *The End of an Epoch: Reflections on Contemporary History.* London: Macmillan, 1947.

◈ Marina Tsvetaeva

BORN: *1892, Moscow, Russia*

DIED: *1941, Elabuga, Russia*

NATIONALITY: *Russian*

GENRE: *Poetry, fiction*

MAJOR WORKS:

Mileposts: Poems: Issue I (1916)

Mileposts: Poems: Issue II (1921)

"Downpour of Light" (1922)

Craft (1923)

After Russia (1928)

Overview

Along with Anna Akhmatova, Osip Mandelstam, and Boris Pasternak, Marina Tsvetaeva is included in Russia's "poetic quartet," a group of important authors whose works reflect the changing values in Russia during the early decades of the twentieth century. Tsvetaeva's central interest as a poet was language, and the stylistic innovations displayed in her work are considered a unique contribution to Russian literature.

Works in Biographical and Historical Context

A Childhood of Privilege and Poetry Marina Ivanova Tsvetaeva (also transliterated as Tsvetayeva, Cvetaeva, and Zwetaewa) was born in Moscow to art history professor Ivan Tsvetayev and concert pianist Mariya Meyn Tsvetayeva. Tsvetaeva grew up in Moscow in an upper-middle-class family distinguished for its artistic and scholarly pursuits. Her father was the founder of the Museum of Fine Arts, and her talented and accomplished mother encouraged Marina to follow a musical career. Attending schools in Switzerland, Germany, and at the Sorbonne in Paris, Tsvetaeva preferred writing poetry.

Two Books, Marriage, and Several Affairs In 1910, when Tsvetaeva was eighteen years of age, her first collection, *Evening Album*, was privately published. This volume received unexpected attention when it was reviewed by the prominent critic Max Voloshin and the poets Nikolay Gumilyov and Valery Bryusov, all of whom wrote favorably

Marina Tsvetaeva *The Granger Collection, New York. Reproduced by permission.*

of Tsvetaeva's work. In 1911, Tsvetaeva published a second collection of poetry, *The Magic Lantern*, and the following year was married to Sergey Efron. Throughout the marriage Tsvetaeva pursued romantic attachments with other poets, following a pattern of infatuation and disillusionment she had established in adolescence.

Russian Civil War During the Russian civil war, which lasted from 1918 to 1921, Tsvetaeva lived in poverty in Moscow while her husband fought in the Crimea as an officer of the czarist White Army. The Russian civil war was complicated by the presence of several opposing military factions, but had as its primary antagonists the Bolshevik, or Red, Army—which had a broad mandate following the 1917 Workers' Revolution—and the czarist White Army, desperately struggling to reestablish the old political order. Tsvetaeva wrote prolifically during this time, composing poetry, essays, memoirs, and dramas. But the anti-Bolshevik sentiments pervading many of these works prevented their publication. During a famine in 1919, the younger of her two children died of starvation, and in 1922 (the year after the Bolsheviks won the civil war and the year their leader, Vladimir Lenin, died), Tsvetaeva immigrated with her surviving child, Ariadna, to Germany. There—after five years of wartime separation—she rejoined Efron.

Adamant Pro-Soviet Stance While Tsvetaeva's family was living in Berlin, and later Prague, where her son, Georgy, was born in 1925, she began to publish the works she had written during the previous decade. These found favor with Russian critics and readers living in exile. Moving to Paris, Tsvetaeva continued to write poetry, but her changing politics brought her into disfavor. Tsvetaeva's reputation among other émigré writers began to deteriorate—largely because of her refusal to adopt the militant anti-Soviet posture of many émigrés, and her husband's pro-Soviet activities (Efron had at this point changed sides so completely as to have become a Communist agent).

Stalinist Terror, World War II, and Suicide Efron and daughter Ariadna returned to Russia in 1937. Tsvetaeva, who was being treated with indifference by Russian expatriates in Paris, followed in 1939 with son Georgy. At that time, artists and intellectuals, especially those with ties to the West, were at risk under the extremist policies of Joseph Stalin—which included paranoid and, even worse, deeply arbitrary torture and execution of suspected enemies of the state. The family was reunited only briefly in Moscow before Efron and Ariadna were both arrested and Efron was charged with anti-Soviet espionage.

When German troops attacked Moscow in 1941, breaking the Nonagression Pact that Stalin had secretly signed with German Nazi leader Adolf Hitler at the outset of World War II (1939–1945), Tsvetaeva and Georgy were evacuated to the village of Elabuga in the Tatar Republic. Despondent over the arrest and possible execution of her husband and daughter, denied the right to publish, and unable to support herself and her son, Tsvetaeva took her own life.

Works in Literary Context

Russian Influences Tsvetaeva's writings were significantly influenced by those of her contemporaries and by the events surrounding the Russian Revolution. Yet she remained largely independent of the numerous literary and political movements that flourished during this tumultuous era, perhaps because of the strength of the impressions left on her by her eclectic reading interests. *Evening Album* (1910), for example, bears the strong influence of the young Tsvetaeva's readings, which included much second-rate poetry and prose. In *Mileposts: Poems: Issue I* (1916), she is inspired by the architectural and religious heritage of Moscow, perhaps

LITERARY AND HISTORICAL CONTEMPORARIES

Tsvetaeva's famous contemporaries include:

Charles de Gaulle (1890–1970): A French general and the leader of the Free French Forces, he founded the French Fifth Republic and became its first president.

Vladimir Mayakovsky (1893–1930): A Russian poet and playwright, he is considered one of the forerunners of Russian Futurism.

Pablo Neruda (1904–1973): A Chilean poet and writer and political Communist; his 1971 receipt of the Nobel Prize in Literature caused much controversy.

Franklin Delano Roosevelt (1882–1945): An American politician and the thirty-second president of the United States, he was so popular with the people he was elected to the office for four terms.

Edith Stein (1891–1942): A Carmelite nun and German philosopher, she became a martyr of the Catholic Church upon losing her life at Auschwitz.

because of the work of Karolina Karlovna Pavlova, one of her favorite poets.

Tsvetaeva's numerous affairs, which often did not involve sex, were also apparent influences; she considered these essentially spiritual in nature, and they are credited with providing the highly charged emotion of her poetry, as well as inspiring poems dedicated to Osip Mandelstam, Aleksandr Blok, and Rainer Maria Rilke. Tsvetaeva's lyric dialogues with Blok, Mandelstam, and Akhmatova in *Mileposts* center on the themes of Russia, poetry, and love. While she based her poems predominantly upon personal experience, Tsvetaeva also explored with increased detachment such philosophical themes as the nature of time and space.

Russian Folk Style Tsvetaeva developed poetic traits early on that are largely preserved in her subsequent collections. Both volumes of *Mileposts* are marked by an extraordinary power and directness of language. The ideas of anxiety, restlessness, and elemental power are emphasized with language, as Tsvetaeva draws on common regional speech and refers to folksongs and Russian poetry of the eighteenth century. Her interest in language shows through the wordplay and linguistic experiments of her verse. Scholars have also noted the intensity and energy of verbs in her poems and her fondness for dark colors. On the level of imagery, archetypal and traditional symbolism prevail, for example, in her use of night, wind, open spaces, and birds.

In the early 1920s, Tsvetaeva experimented with narrative verse. She adapted traditional Russian folktales in *The King-Maiden* (1922) and *The Swain* (1924). In the volume

COMMON HUMAN EXPERIENCE

Here are a few works by writers who, like Tsvetaeva, also paid homage to their homelands, peoples, and fellow writers in folktales, poems, lyrics, and prose:

Folktales of Greece (1970), a collection edited by Georgios A. Megas. This collection includes such stories as "Almondseed and Almondella" and "Brother and Sister."

Popular Tales of the West Highlands (1890), a collection by John Francis Campbell. These tales hail from Scotland and include such titles as "The Tale of the Queen Who Sought a Drink from a Certain Well."

Vladimir Il'ich Lenin (1925), a tribute poem by Vladimir Mayakovsky. This three-thousand-line poem was a high-styled tribute to Lenin upon his death.

After Russia (1928) she fused her early romantic style with more regional diction. As the 1930s progressed, Tsvetaeva devoted more energy to prose than to poetry. In such memoirs as "Captive Spirit" and "My Pushkin" (both published in *Contemporary Annals* in 1934 and 1937, respectively), she recorded her impressions of friends and poets. In a prose style characterized by stream-of-consciousness narrative technique and poetic language, Tsvetaeva expressed her views on literary creation and criticism in such essays as "Art in the Light of Conscience" and "A Poet on Criticism" (both published in *Contemporary Annals* in 1932).

Works in Critical Context

After her death Marina Tsvetaeva and her work were virtually forgotten. For many years her name was unmentionable in the Soviet Union. Then her posthumous publications started to appear, and she soon gained recognition as one of the greatest Russian poets of all time. A veritable cult of Tsvetaeva developed in Russia and outside its borders. Today she is an internationally famous poet and the object of many scholarly studies that are on a par with criticism about Pasternak, Mandelstam, Akhmatova, or even classics of the Russian Golden Age. This reputation springs in part from Tsvetaeva's earlier poetry. *Craft* (1923), the last volume of poetry Tsvetaeva completed before her emigration, is praised for its metrical experiments and effective blending of folk language, archaisms, and biblical idioms. *After Russia* (1928) has been deemed by critics such as Simon Karlinsky "the most mature and perfect of her collections."

Demonstrating her literary merit further are both Tsvetaeva's mature verse and even her first verse work, *Evening Album*.

Evening Album (1910) Composed almost entirely before she was eighteen years old, *Evening Album* is considered a work of technical virtuosity. The volume's occasionally immature themes do not obscure Tsvetaeva's mastery of traditional Russian lyric forms. At the time of its publication it was noticed immediately by leading critics, who gave the book favorable reviews and emphasized its intimacy and freshness of tone. Valerii Iakovlevich Briusov, who, in his 1911 article "New Verse Collections" in *Russian Thought*, expressed some reservations concerning Tsvetaeva's domestic themes and commonplace ideas, nevertheless dubbed her an "undoubtedly talented" author capable of creating "the true poetry of the intimate life." Further reflecting the critical attitude at the time, Nikolai Sergeevich Gumilev wrote enthusiastically about Tsvetaeva's spontaneity and audacity, concluding in his 1911 article "Letters on Russian Poetry" in *Apollo*, "All the main laws of poetry have been instinctively guessed here, so that this book is not just a book of charming girlish confessions, but a book of excellent verse as well."

After her initial critical success and popularity, Tsvetaeva was largely neglected because of her experimental style and her refusal to assume either a pro- or anti-Soviet stance. Recent critics regard her work as among the most innovative and powerful Russian poetry of the twentieth century, with scholars such as Angela Livingstone writing, "An emotional but not a 'feminine' poet, she avoids all mellifluous sentimentality and instead loves, hates, lauds, castigates, laments, marvels, aspires ... with a kind of unflinching physicality, always pushing passions and stances to the point at which they will be fully revealed."

Responses to Literature

1. Tsvetaeva and her writing were influenced by the events of the Russian civil war, when the poet lived in poverty in Moscow while her husband fought in the Crimea as an officer of the czarist White Army. Research the Russian civil war. How did it specifically impact the civilians? How is this impact reflected in Tsvetaeva's work?

2. Tsvetaeva showed anti-Bolshevik sentiments in her poetry, plays, journals, and stories. This fact prevented publication of her writing for several years. Choose a poem by Tsvetaeva that you believe might have had such controversial political messages (you may need to research the Bolsheviks to understand this context). Explain why this poem may have been such a threat, using detailed analysis of passages from the poem to add depth to your position.

3. In her writing, Tsvetaeva has a commitment to folksongs, folk ditties, and Russian poetry of the eighteenth century. Research Russian folk tradition, mythology, or history to get a deeper sense of the people of Tsvetaeva's writings. How would you characterize the typical Russians of the time? Are they well-depicted in her work? What values do they have that

come through in the poet's writing? What do you learn about Russian tradition from Tsvetaeva's writing?

4. Tsvetaeva's work has been praised for its lyricism and "intuitive" grasp of what moves the human soul. Analyze the emotional effects produced by one of her poems that you find particularly striking; explain the different elements of poetry that she brings to bear in creating particular images for and inspiring particular feelings in a reader. Help your reader understand, ultimately, *how* the poem works.

BIBLIOGRAPHY

Books

Briusov, Valerii Iakovlevich. *Sredi stikhov 1894–1924: Manifesty, stat'i, retsenzii.* Compiled by Nikolai Alekseevich Bogomolov and Nikolai Vsevolodovich Kotrelev. Moscow: Sovetskii pisatel', 1990.

Gumilev, Nikolai Sergeevich. "Pis'ma o russkoi poezii." In *Sobranie sochinenii*, pp. 262, 293–294. Washington, D.C.: Victor Kamkin, 1968.

Karlinsky, Simon. *Marina Cvetaeva: Her Life and Art.* Berkeley: University of California Press, 1966.

———. *Marina Tsvetaeva: The Woman, Her World and Her Poetry.* Cambridge: Cambridge University Press, 1985.

Karlinsky, Simon, and Alfred Appel Jr., eds. *The Bitter Air of Exile: Russian Writers in the West, 1922–1972.* Berkeley: University of California Press, 1977.

Pasternak, Yevgeny, Yelena Pasternak, and Konstantin M. Azadovsky, eds. *Letters, Summer 1926: Boris Pasternak, Marina Tsvetaeva, Rainer Maria Rilke.* Translated by Margaret Wettlin and Walter Arndt. New York: Harcourt, 1985; reprinted, Oxford University Press, 1988.

Tsvetaeva, Marina, *Unpublished Letters.* Edited by Gleb Struve and Nikita Struve. Paris: YMCA-Press, 1972.

Periodicals

Burgin, Diana Lewis. "After the Ball Is Over: Sophia Parnok's Creative Relationship with Marina Tsvetaeva." *Russian Review* 47 (1988): 425–44.

Ciepiela, "Taking Monologism Seriously: Bakhtin and Tsvetaeva's 'The Pied Piper.'" *Slavic Review* 4 (1994): 1010–24.

Forrester, Sibelan. "Bells and Cupolas: The Formative Role of the Female Body in Marina Tsvetaeva's Poetry." *Slavic Review* 2 (1992): 232–46.

Gove, Antonina F. "The Feminine Stereotype and Beyond: Role Conflict and Resolution in the Poetics of Marina Tsvetaeva." *Slavic Review* 2 (1977): 231–55.

Hall, Bruce. "'The Wildest of Disharmonies': A Lacanian Reading of Tsvetaeva's 'Provoda' Cycle in the Context of Its Other Meanings." *Slavic and East European Journal* 1 (1996): 27–44.

Heldt, Barbara. "Two Poems by Marina Tsvetayeva from *After Russia*." *Modern Language Review* 3 (1982): 679–87.

Web Sites

Kneller, Andrey. *Translations of Marina Tsvetaeva: Selected Poems and Links.* Retrieved March 31, 2008, from http://home.comcast.net/~kneller/tsvetaeva.html.

Manevich, Vadim, and Olesya Petrova. *Heritage of Marina Tsvetayeva.* Retrieved March 31, 2008, from http://english.tsvetayeva.com/.

The World of Marina Tsvetaeva (in Russian). Retrieved March 31, 2008, from http://www.ipmce.su/~tsvet/.

Tu Fu

BORN: *712, Kung-hsien, Honan, China*

DIED: *770, T'an-chou, China*

NATIONALITY: *Chinese*

GENRE: *Poetry*

MAJOR WORKS:
"Eight Immortals of Drinking"
"Facing the Snow"
"Traveling North"
"A Song of Lo-Yu Park"

Tu Fu   *Chinese poet Tu Fu, photograph. The Art Archive / British Library / The Picture Desk, Inc.*

LITERARY AND HISTORICAL CONTEMPORARIES

Tu Fu's famous contemporaries include:

Charles Martel (688–741): Martel, also known as "the Hammer," was a towering figure in medieval European history: founder of the Carolingian dynasty, his tactical innovations led to a Frankish victory over the invading Moors at the Battle of Tours, the turning point that is regarded as the end of Muslim expansion in the West.

Jia Dan (730–805): Jia's writings on geography and trade routes have provided historians with detailed information on the Asian world of the eighth century. Commissioned by the emperor, Jia Dan oversaw the creation of a map of China and its neighbors that was thirty feet square.

Bede (672/673–735): Generally referred to as the Venerable Bede, this English monk was one of the most active scholars of the Dark Ages. His masterwork, *The Ecclesiastical History of the English People*, has led to his being called the Father of English History.

Harun al-Rashid (763–809): Beginning his reign around the time of Tu Fu's death, this Persian caliph's magnificent lifestyle is said to have inspired many of the tales in *The Book of One Thousand and One Nights*.

Li Po (701–762): Along with Tu Fu, Li Po is considered one of the two greatest poets in Chinese history. As renowned for his love of wine as for his imaginative Taoist verses, he is said to have died by drowning after drunkenly trying to embrace his own reflection in the moonlit Yangtze River.

Han Gan (706–783): Chinese painter renowned during his lifetime and for centuries after for his ability to paint horses.

Overview

Widely regarded as one of the greatest Chinese poets, Tu Fu is known for his contemplative verse that chronicled the political and social upheaval of mid-eighth-century China. Praised for his innovative use of traditional verse forms and his synthesis of a variety of elements drawn from previous Chinese literature, Tu Fu also drew imagery from his personal experiences to create compelling verse that served as an inspiration to succeeding generations.

Works in Biographical and Historical Context

Life and Work Tu Fu was born in Kung-hsien, Honan (also spelled Henan), a province of central China. His mother died when he was a child, and he was raised by an aunt in Loyang. In about 731, he began traveling through the Yangtze River and Yellow River regions, and approximately five years later he moved to Ch'ang-an, the capital, in order to secure an official post. Failing the imperial examination for public office, Tu Fu resumed traveling. In 744 he met the poet Li Po in Loyang. Tu Fu's friendship with Li Po served as material for some of his most famous poems, including "Eight Immortals of Drinking," which reflects on the carefree atmosphere of his time spent in Loyang. Tu Fu returned to Ch'ang-an in 746 to retake the examination for public office and failed again. He remained in Ch'ang-an until he acquired a minor post in the early 750s. While he attained some official recognition for his poetry during this period, his multiple failures of the literary examinations indicate that his work was not highly esteemed at court. When the An Lu-shan rebellion broke out in 755, Tu Fu was captured by the rebels, but later escaped and lived as a refugee until he was able to return to court in 757. He was soon banished from the capital as a result of his outspoken advice to the emperor. Tu Fu spent the next nine years wandering through various cities in Szechuan Province, at one point holding the position of military advisor in the governor's headquarters in Ch'eng-tu. This was his most prolific period, during which he wrote acclaimed poems about social issues. After his governor-appointed patron died in 765, Tu Fu began another trip along the Yangtze River that ended with his death at the age of fifty-eight.

Works in Literary Context

Alienation and Hardship Tu Fu's canon of more than fifteen hundred poems demonstrates a variety of verse forms and themes. Much of his work is characterized by a sometimes self-deprecating tone, particularly the later poems in which he chronicled the alienation he felt as an aging traveler. In "A Song of Lo-yu Park," he recalled the exuberance of an outdoor party, but ended the poem, "Nowhere to return after drinking, I am standing alone in the dusk, composing poems." A sense of loss and despair informs many of Tu Fu's poems from the post-rebellion period, including "Lament for Ch'ent'ao," "Lament for Ch'ing-fan," and "Facing the Snow," all sorrowful depictions of the destruction wrought by the rebellion and subsequent war. "Traveling North" is a melancholy description of Tu Fu's reunion with his family: "I am now facing my son after narrowly escaping from death. Let me forget for a while all the hardships of life." Many of Tu Fu's poems of social protest were written during the post-rebellion period and contrast the suffering of the impoverished villagers with the lavish life of the court.

Confucian Ideals, Warm Humanism Tu Fu is philosophically a Confucian earnestly accepting his duties to his family and to the state, and this perspective is reflected in his poems. Confucianism focuses primarily on the performing of good deeds as a way of expressing the divine. The ideal poet, as he conceives it, is the scholar who by virtue of knowing the realities, desires, and aspirations of human nature also knows how best to counsel and advise in matters of state. The poet is also the official, or, better, the ideal official is the ideal poet. In poetry he composes his "reminders" to the throne, intended as advice to the emperor. Politics is not to him a peculiar science, categorically apart from other branches of knowledge and understanding. In this respect also he is a true humanist.

Works in Critical Context

According to Stephen Owen, "Within the Chinese poetic tradition, Tu Fu is almost beyond judgment because, like Shakespeare in our own tradition, his literary accomplishment has itself become a major component in the historical formation of literary values." However, Tu Fu was not highly regarded during his lifetime; critics speculate that his contemporaries, accustomed to the rigid forms and styles of Chinese verse, were unable to appreciate his synthesis of traditional elements. However, his works were favorably reevaluated by Chinese poets and scholars several decades after his death, and since that time his enormous contributions to the development of Chinese literature have been meticulously researched.

Influence on Bashō Tu Fu's influence stretched beyond his native China. Matsuo Bashō, a seventeenth-century Japanese poet often credited with inventing the haiku form, displayed many thematic similarities to Tu Fu. Bashō borrowed various elements of imagery from Tu Fu. Several of them are found in his prose writings of the period preceding his maturity. Others are found in the poetry he composed as he was perfecting his style. The attraction that Tu Fu held for Bashō was admitted by him at the time he published a collection of haiku titled *Empty Chestnuts.* In the preface of this collection, written when Bashō was forty years old, he acknowledged the influence of Tu Fu, as well as that of other poets, by saying in regard to his own verses, "the spirits of Li Po and Tu Fu revive and Han Shan's Zennism prevails, while Saigyo's tranquility and elegance are newly explored." Although his self-styled affinity with these four renowned poets might not be appreciated by others, and the ordinary man might regard his poems as "empty chestnuts" (*minashiguri*) not worth picking up, the poems in *Empty Chestnuts* presented to Bashō the possibility of a new taste and the exploration of a new poetical realm.

The continuing influence of Tu Fu on Bashō appears repeatedly in the poetry written by him in the years following the publication of *Empty Chestnuts.* The poetic accounts of his travels throughout Japan and the verses he penned during periods of seclusion clearly attest to the inspiration he drew from the Chinese poet.

Modern Commentary Modern commentary often focuses on the implicit philosophy in Tu Fu's work. Critics also address the way in which Tu Fu explored in his poetry the social issues of his time. Burton Watson has

---

COMMON HUMAN EXPERIENCE

The T'ang Dynasty (618–907) was a fertile period for Chinese poetry. Study of the other major T'ang poets can provide a greater historical context for Tu Fu's place among his contemporaries.

The Selected Poems of Wang Wei (2006). A contemporary of Tu Fu, Wang Wei's poetry characterizes the then-emerging tenets of Ch'an (Zen) Buddhism: calm acceptance and close appreciation of nature.

The Mountain Poems of Meng Hao-jan (2000). A master of the landscape poem and another enthusiastic Ch'an poet, Meng Hao-jan is credited with starting the flowering of Tang poetry that would be carried on by the likes of Tu Fu.

The Selected Poems of Li Po (1998). Reputedly, Li Po could compose fully realized poems, in their finished form, extemporaneously. Over one thousand of his poems survive today, and he is still one of the most popular and widely read poets in China.

---

noted that "whereas most T'ang poets ... expressed their criticisms indirectly through the conventions of the yueh-fu style, borrowing the guise of the soldier or the peasant and setting the poem in some distant era of the past, Tu Fu boldly described in his own words the abuses and sufferings that he and his contemporaries encountered." The personal nature of Tu Fu's poetry has garnered critical admiration, particularly his poignant descriptions of his own experiences and his meticulous attention to detail in depicting everyday life during the T'ang dynasty.

Responses to Literature

1. Find some examples of historical events that Tu Fu relates in his poetry. Discuss how social upheaval and political instability influenced Tu Fu's poetry.

2. Read some of Tu Fu's reminders to the emperor. How do these reflect the author's Confucianism?

3. Li Po and Tu Fu, both acknowledged as China's greatest poets, were contemporaries. Discuss how Li Po influenced Tu Fu's poetry, and vice versa. Do you think they inspired each other to greater poetic heights, or is their work largely independent of the other's influence?

4. Select and examine the work of a modern poet who deals with a theme found in Tu Fu's work, such as alienation. How does the modern poet handle the theme differently than Tu Fu? How are the two poets similar in their handling of style and subject, if at all?

BIBLIOGRAPHY

Books

Davis, A. R. *Tu Fu*. New York: Twayne, 1971.
Hung, William. *Tu Fu: China's Greatest Poet*.
    Cambridge, Mass.: Harvard University Press, 1952.
Owen, Stephen. *Traditional Chinese Poetry and Poetics:
    Omen of the World*. Madison: University of
    Wisconsin Press, 1985.

Ivan Turgenev

BORN: *1818, Orel, Russia*

DIED: *1883, Paris, France*

NATIONALITY: *Russian*

GENRE: *Fiction*

MAJOR WORKS:
A Sportsman's Sketches (1852)
Fathers and Sons (1862)
Virgin Soil (1877)

Overview

The first Russian author to achieve widespread international fame, Ivan Turgenev was hailed as his country's premier

Ivan Turgenev   *Popperfoto / Getty Images*

novelist by nineteenth-century Westerners and is today linked with Fyodor Dostoyevsky and Leo Tolstoy as one of the triumvirate of great Russian novelists of that century. As a writer deeply concerned with the politics of his homeland, he vividly described the tumultuous political environment in Russia from the 1840s to the 1870s. Simultaneously, as a literary artist, he created works noted for their psychological truth, descriptive beauty, and haunting pathos.

Works in Biographical and Historical Context

A Daunting Household   Turgenev was born on October 28, 1818, in the city of Orel into a family of wealthy gentry. His father, by all accounts a charming but ineffectual cavalry officer, paid little attention to Turgenev, whose childhood on the family estate of Spasskoye was dominated by his eccentric and impulsive mother, Varvara Petrovna. Her treatment of her favorite son Ivan alternated between excessive affection and mental and physical cruelty; she ruled Spasskoye and its five thousand serfs with the same unpredictability. Biographers have cited his mother's influence to explain much about the development of Turgenev's personality—particularly his horror of violence and hatred of injustice—and his fiction, populated as it is by strong women and well-meaning but weak-willed men.

During Turgenev's early childhood, French was the primary language spoken in his household, as was customary among upper-class Russians. Although his mother later permitted the use of Russian, it is likely that Turgenev's first lessons in the vernacular came from the Spasskoye serfs. When Turgenev was nine, the family left the country for Moscow, where Ivan attended boarding schools before entering Moscow University in 1833. At the university, he earned the nickname "the American" for his interest in the United States and his democratic inclinations. In 1834, Turgenev transferred to the University of St. Petersburg. Upon graduation, he decided that the completion of his education required study abroad, so he went to Germany in 1838, enrolling at the University of Berlin. During the next several years, he studied philosophy, but he never finished his degree. Turgenev returned to Russia in 1841, but for the rest of his life he divided his time between his homeland and western Europe.

Early Career   Although Turgenev had begun writing poetry as a student in St. Petersburg and published his first verses in 1838, biographers generally cite the narrative poem *Parasha*, published in 1843, as the beginning of his literary career. This work attracted little attention from his contemporaries, however, and the friendships he made in the mid-1840s, including those with Pauline Viardot and Vissarion Belinsky, proved more important for his literary development—indeed, the rest of his life—than the poem. Viardot was a successful opera singer and a married woman when Turgenev met her in 1843. The precise nature of their relationship is uncertain. While Turgenev's letters to her seem to indicate a grand passion, at least on his side, there is no evidence that the two were ever lovers. At any rate, their relationship endured for the rest of Turgenev's life; he frequently followed Viardot to wherever her career took her and was on excellent terms with her husband and the rest of her family. Turgenev himself never married.

Turgenev's friendship with Belinsky, an extremely influential literary critic, also directed the course of his life. A political liberal and an ardent Westernizer, Belinsky sought to bring Russia's culture and political system nearer to that of Europe. Belinsky was closely associated with the radical periodical *Sovremennik* (*The Contemporary*), edited by Nikolay Nekrasov, and it was in this journal that Turgenev published his first prose work, the short story "Khor i Kalinych."

A Sportsman's Sketches Although Turgenev continued to write poetry and tried his hand at drama, he had found his niche and his audience in narrative prose. "Khor and Kalinych" was followed by a series of related pieces between the years 1847 and 1852, all first published in the *Contemporary* and later collected and published in book form in 1852 as *Zapiski okhotnika* (*A Sportsman's Sketches*). In these sketches, which range from brief slices of life to fully realized short stories, Turgenev adopted the persona of a hunter in the country, drawing on his experiences at Spasskoye and expressing his love for the land and people of rural Russia. The sensitive portraits of country peasants and landowners in *A Sportsman's Sketches* gently persuaded the reader not only that serfdom was unjust, but also that it damaged the character of the upper classes morally and spiritually. *A Sportsman's Sketches* is frequently compared to Harriet Beecher Stowe's contemporaneous antislavery novel *Uncle Tom's Cabin*, also published in 1852. Unlike the American novel, however, Turgenev's work is understated, his moral message implied rather than overt.

At their first publication, Turgenev's stories were enormously popular with almost everyone but government officials. In 1852, when he wrote an admiring obituary of Nikolai Gogol, whose socially conscious writing had inspired many in Turgenev's generation, Turgenev was arrested, supposedly for excessive approval of a suspect writer but more likely for his own social critique in *A Sportsman's Sketches*. After a month in jail, Turgenev was confined to Spasskoye, where he remained under house arrest for nearly two years. When the serfs were finally freed in 1861, there were many who credited *A Sportsman's Sketches* with having helped to effect their emancipation.

Turgenev's Novels Russia in the nineteenth century was a divided and politically troubled country, unsure of its future political course. Tension existed not only between conservatives and liberals but also between the radical liberals, who called for immediate change and economic communism—the sharing of all resources and wealth equally among citizens—and the moderate liberals, who

LITERARY AND HISTORICAL CONTEMPORARIES

Turgenev's famous contemporaries include:

Leo Tolstoy (1828–1910): Russian novelist, essayist, and philosopher who wrote the epic novel *War and Peace* (1869).

George Sand (1804–1876): Sand was a French Romantic writer who explored sexual identity and gender issues in her fiction.

Gustave Flaubert (1821–1880): French realist novelist Flaubert is best known for *Madame Bovary* (1857), the story of unhappy, adulterous Emma Bovary.

Alexander II (1818–1881): Emperor (czar) of the Russian Empire from 1855, Alexander II was assassinated in 1881.

Mark Twain (1835–1910): Renowned American author Twain penned *The Adventures of Huckleberry Finn* (1884), considered one of the masterworks of American fiction.

favored slow, peaceful reform and free enterprise. Turgenev managed to draw the hostility of nearly every Russian school of thought, from reactionary to revolutionary, with his next and most famous novel, *Fathers and Sons*. Bazarov, the protagonist of the book, is considered Turgenev's most successful and most ambiguous character—Turgenev himself confessed that he did not know whether he loved or hated his hero. Bazarov also provides an intriguing portrayal of a political type just then coming into existence in Russia: the nihilist, a person who rejects all conventional values. While Turgenev did not invent the term "nihilist" his depiction of Bazarov in *Fathers and Sons* brought it into general usage. Bazarov rejects every aspect of Russian political, social, and cultural life, believing in nothing but empirical science. *Fathers and Sons* was denounced on every side: blasted by conservatives as a favorable portrayal of a dangerous radical; attacked by liberals as a damning caricature of radicalism.

Depicting Russia from Abroad Distressed by the unfavorable reaction to *Fathers and Sons*, Turgenev spent more and more time abroad, residing in Baden, Germany, and Paris near his friend Pauline Viardot. He frequented social circles that included some of the most illustrious authors of his era. With the appearance of his next novel, *Smoke* (1867), critics charged that he was out of touch with his native land. This bitter work criticizes conservatives and radicals alike, portraying arrogance and ideological disdain for practicality in both camps.

During the next decade, Turgenev produced a relatively small body of novellas and short stories that are among his greatest works, including "First Love" (1870),

COMMON HUMAN EXPERIENCE

Turgenev's novel *Fathers and Sons* popularized the concept of "nihilism," or the rejection of all conventional values. Nihilism became an important undercurrent in modern literature, as the following works illustrate:

> *The Will to Power* (1901), a philosophical work by Friedrich Nietzsche. This work is a ruthless attack on the structures of morality from one of the most vital modern philosophers.
>
> *The Waste Land* (1922), a poem by T. S. Eliot. Despair and disillusionment are conveyed by the poem's image of a culture that is crumbling, not only from the impact of the Great War but also from its spiritual vacancy.
>
> *The Sun Also Rises* (1926), a novel by Ernest Hemingway. The unhappy characters in the novel, wounded both physically and emotionally by World War I, seemed to have lost their ability to believe in anything permanent.
>
> *Waiting for Godot* (1953), a play by Samuel Beckett. A founding work of the theater of the absurd, this drama reflects the pointlessness of the human condition.

"A King Lear of the Steppe" (1870), and "Torrents of Spring" (1872). These shorter pieces explore esoteric aspects of Russian life. After accusations of being a traitor who had rejected Russia, Turgenev created a gallery of striking Russian portraits such as "The Brigadier" (1868) and "An Unfortunate Woman" (1869).

Narodnik Movement By 1872, Turgenev had become interested in the *narodnik* movement that expressed the selfless desire of young Russians to repay the debt they felt they owed to the emancipated serfs. To describe this phenomenon to his countrymen, Turgenev returned to Spasskoye in 1876 and composed his last novel, *Virgin Soil* (1877). His hero and heroine, Aleksei Nezhdanov and Marianna Sinetskaia, attempt to put their radical principles into practice among the common people. Nezhdanov is another of Turgenev's ineffectual male protagonists, and his efforts fail tragically, leaving Marianna to join forces with the more practical-minded, Westernist factory owner, Vasilii Solomin. The accusations that Turgenev was out of touch with Russian reality vanished when the first mass *narodnik* trial was held in 1877.

Following the publication of *Virgin Soil*, Turgenev, now virtually self-exiled from his homeland, no longer attempted to describe the Russian political scene. His remaining works—prose poems and stories—are described by critics as nostalgic, philosophical, and frequently pessimistic, and are often concerned with the occult. After a long and debilitating illness, Turgenev died in Bougival, near Paris, with Pauline Viardot at his side. His body was returned to Russia by train. There, despite the unfavorable reception of his later works and the efforts of the Russian government to restrict memorial congregations, Turgenev was widely mourned by his compatriots.

Works in Literary Context

Ivan Turgenev was steeped in the literary traditions of western Europe as well as Russia. He even met several of his idols, including Gogol and Aleksandr Pushkin, as a student. Among his European influences were Goethe and Shakespeare, whose works he learned almost by heart.

A Master of Character The plots of Turgenev's novels are often slight. Instead, interest centers largely on the characters, who are both unique individuals and representatives of more universal qualities. Turgenev draws his characters with a psychological penetration; their minds and personalities are revealed through their own words and actions, not through direct exposition by the narrator. Turgenev was particularly adept at portraying women in love, and at creating an atmosphere of pathos, but not sentimentality, in his unhappy love stories. Fatalism and thwarted desires are hallmarks of the novelist's work. His characters are generally unable to control their destiny, either because of their own flaws or through arbitrary fate.

Lasting Influence Turgenev's sheer literary virtuosity—his skills with dialogue, character, descriptions of natural and social environments, and conveying ideas through image and illustration—earned him many admirers. Among the illustrious writers who claimed him as an influence were the French novelist Émile Zola and the American literary giants Henry James and Ernest Hemingway. At one point, Turgenev was a close friend of Tolstoy's, but their relationship was strained by ideology, as Tolstoy was a Russian patriot (or "Slavophile"), not a Westernist.

Works in Critical Context

Criticism Through the Years Turgenev's novels got an uneven critical reception at the time of their appearance. Because of the highly political content of most of Turgenev's works, the earliest Russian commentators tended to praise or disparage his writings along partisan lines. Similarly, many foreign critics of the nineteenth century were interested in Turgenev primarily for the light his prose shed on the political situation in Russia. Turgenev's works were quickly translated into French, German, and English, and he developed an overseas following. Many English and American readers considered Turgenev the most accessible of Russian writers and they—particularly American critics—took a lively, generally appreciative interest in his career beginning with the publication of *A Sportsman's Sketches*. Early Russian and English-language critics by no means neglected the aesthetic qualities of Turgenev's works, however, recognizing from the start that his fiction was more than simply the literal portrayal of the people and concerns of a particular country at a given historical moment.

Turgenev's literary reputation has remained generally stable over the years, with twentieth-century commentators echoing and amplifying the conclusions reached by their nineteenth-century counterparts. Critics agree that Turgenev's work is distinguished by solid literary craftsmanship, especially in the areas of description and characterization. Keenly observant, he infused his work with precise, realistic detail, bringing a natural scene or character into focus through the evocative power of his words.

Fathers and Sons Turgenev's 1862 novel *Fathers and Sons* remains perhaps his most studied work. Dmitry I. Pisarev, in a contemporary review of the book, states, "Turgenev's novel, in addition to its artistic beauty, is remarkable for the fact that it stirs the mind, leads to reflection, although, it does not solve a single problem itself and clearly illuminates not so much the phenomena depicted by the author as his own attitudes toward these phenomena." Novelist Henry James, in his *French Poets and Novelists*, states of the author, "His works savour strongly of his native soil, like those of all great novelists, and give one who has read them all a strange sense of having had a prolonged experience of Russia." James also notes that the author "is particularly unsparing of the new intellectual fashions prevailing among his countrymen," especially in *Fathers and Sons*, "for the figures with which he has filled his foreground are, with their personal interests and adventures, but the symbols of the shadowy forces that are fighting for ever a larger battle—the battle of the old and the new, the past and the future, of the ideas that arrive with the ideas that linger."

Responses to Literature

1. Research the circumstances surrounding Czar Alexander II's emancipation of the Russian serfs in 1861. What grounds do you find for the claim that *A Sportsman's Sketches* was an influential precursor to Alexander's decree?

2. Much has been made of the weakness of Turgenev's male heroes and the strength of his heroines. Script a conversation between Turgenev's Rudin and Shakespeare's Hamlet in which they discuss their inability to act. Include in this discussion their feelings about and perspectives of the women in their lives.

3. Write a short essay explaining how or if Turgenev's fiction reflects socialist realism in literature, a genre associated with Russian writers of the twentieth century.

4. Compare how Turgenev portrays the legacy of serfdom, and its impact on Russian society, to the treatment of Negro slavery in the works of prominent African American authors such as James Baldwin and Toni Morrison.

BIBLIOGRAPHY

Books

"Fathers and Sons by Ivan Turgenev." *Nineteenth-Century Literature Criticism*. Ed. Joann Cerrito. vol. 37. Detroit: Gale, 1993, pp. 353–452.

Freeborn, Richard. *Turgenev: The Novelist's Novelist*. London: Oxford University Press, 1960.

Gettman, Royal Alfred. *Turgenev in England and America*. Urbana: University of Illinois Press, 1941.

Lord, Robert. *Russian Literature: An Introduction*. New York: Taplinger, 1980.

Lowe, David A., ed. *Critical Essays on Ivan Turgenev*. Boston: G. K. Hall, 1989.

Magarshack, David, ed. *Ivan Turgenev: Literary Reminiscences and Autobiographical Fragments*. New York: Grove, 1958.

Moser, Charles A. *Ivan Turgenev*. New York: Columbia University Press, 1972.

Pritchett, V. S. *The Gentle Barbarian: The Life and Work of Turgenev*. New York: Random House, 1977.

Schapiro, Leonard. *Turgenev: His Life and Times*. New York: Random House, 1978.

Amos Tutuola

BORN: *1920, Abeokuta, Nigeria*

DIED: *1997, Ibadan, Nigeria*

NATIONALITY: *Nigerian*

GENRE: *Fiction*

MAJOR WORKS:

The Palm-Wine Drinkard and His Dead Palm-Wine Tapster in the Deads' Town (1952)

My Life in the Bush of Ghosts (1954)

Yoruba Folktales (1986)

Overview

Amos Tutuola was the first Nigerian writer to achieve international recognition. He spun adventure fantasies based on traditional Yoruba folktales, writing in an idiosyncratic, deliberately flawed pidgin English. His works are crudely constructed and restricted in narrative range, yet are highly imaginative. Tutuola is one of the most successful stylists in twentieth-century African literature.

Works in Biographical and Historical Context

Writing on the Job Tutuola was born in the western Nigerian town of Abeokuta in 1920, when Nigeria was ruled by the British as a part of the British Empire. Tutuola completed six years in missionary schools. When

Amos Tutuola *Tutuola, Amos, photograph. Harry Ransom Humanities Research Center, The University of Texas at Austin. Reproduced by permission.*

his father, a cacao farmer, died in 1939, he left school to learn a trade. Tutuola worked as a coppersmith in the Royal Air Force during World War II, but he lost his position in postwar demobilization. (In the postwar period, Nigeria demanded self-government from the British, resulting in a series of short-lived constitutions through the early 1950s.) He found employment as a messenger for the Department of Labor in Lagos. The job left him ample free time, and he took to writing English versions of stories he had heard old people tell in Yoruba.

In the late 1940s, he wrote to Focal Press, an English publisher, asking if they would consider a manuscript about spirits in the Nigerian bush. Several months later, *The Wild Hunter in the Bush of Ghosts* arrived, wrapped in brown paper and bound with twine. The mythological adventure story, clearly the work of a novice, would not be published until 1982. Had it been published earlier, it would not have generated the same excitement among readers overseas as did Tutuola's next narrative, a bizarre yarn with the improbable title *The Palm-Wine Drinkard and His Dead Palm-Wine Tapster in the Deads' Town* (1952).

The Palm-Wine Drinkard is a voyage of the imagination into a never-never land of magic and marvels. The prodigious drinker of palm wine appears at first to be an unpromising hero, but he cleverly circumvents numerous monsters and misadventures and settles the cosmic dispute between Heaven and Land, ending a catastrophic drought.

A Colonial Throwback? Tutuola was lucky to get this second story published and luckier still that it gained commercial success. The book might have sunk into obscurity had it not been enthusiastically reviewed by well-known poet Dylan Thomas. Within a year, an American edition won similar acclaim. It was eventually translated into fifteen languages.

In Nigeria, however, Tutuola's writing received an unfriendly reception. Educated Nigerians were shocked that a book written in substandard English by a lowly Lagos messenger was being lionized abroad. Tutuola's first books appeared at the close of the colonial era, when Africans were trying to prove to the outside world that they were ready to manage their own political affairs. For educated Africans, acutely conscious of their image abroad, the naive fantasies of Tutuola projected a primitive impression.

Despite the criticism from his countrymen, Tutuola pressed on, producing more adventure stories cut from the same cloth. *My Life in the Bush of Ghosts* (1954), opens as its hero, a boy of seven, abandoned by his stepmothers, is left to wander in the bush during a tribal war. He spends twenty-four years wandering in an African spirit world, until a "television-handed goddess" helps the young man escape. *Simbi and the Satyr of the Dark Jungle* (1955), in which a pampered only child defies her parents and undertakes a solitary journey, displays for the first time signs of formal literary influence. It is Tutuola's first book to be divided into numbered chapters, and it is written from the third-person point of view. Tutuola was becoming conscious of himself as an author and reading more widely. He continued to work as a messenger, writing in his spare time.

Imagination and Grotesque Fantasy As Tutuola continued his work as both a writer and a messenger, Nigeria was continuing to undergo political change. In the mid- to late 1950s, the country moved further into self-government and became a fully independent member of the British Commonwealth in 1960. In 1963, Nigeria became a republic, with Nnamdi Azikiwe serving as its first president. Internal unrest soon became a hallmark of Nigeria, with two military coups taking place in 1966 alone.

While Nigeria was going through these changes, Tutuola published such works as *Feather Woman of the Jungle* (1962). This book is Tutuola's most stylized work. The narrative frame is structured somewhat like the *Arabian Nights*: an elderly chief entertains villagers for ten nights with accounts of his past adventures. As with Tutuola's other works, the technique recalls devices from oral storytelling. Tutuola published nothing between *Ajaiyi and His Inherited Poverty* (1967) and *The Witch-Herbalist of the Remote Town* (1981), but the hiatus had no discernible impact on his chosen methods. In *The Witch-Herbalist*, a hunter goes on a quest to find a cure for his wife's barrenness. He survives bizarre and sometimes frightening encounters over six years, eventually reaching the Remote Town. He gets the medicine from the herbalist, sips some on his return to stave off hunger, and gives the rest to his wife, who promptly becomes pregnant. However, so does he, and he must undergo further trials and torments before being cured.

Evolved Late Works *Yoruba Folktales* (1986) is Tutuola's first effort at preserving, rather than retelling, the stories that are the communal literary property of his people. Tutuola remains faithful to tradition but occasionally adds some zaniness to spice up characterization and plot. The grammatical blunders and stylistic inventions found in Tutuola's earlier works are absent from *Yoruba Folktales*. The reason is not mysterious: The book was targeted at primary school classrooms, and one cannot address Nigerian schoolchildren in a fractured foreign tongue.

Tutuola's final publication, *The Village Witch Doctor, and Other Stories* (1990), contains eighteen stories based on traditional Yoruba fables. Like most of Tutuola's previous work, the stories deal with greed, betrayal, and tricksterism. After more than forty years, the same buoyant imagination and fascination with comically grotesque fantasy worlds were evident.

Tutuola resided in Ibadan and Ago-Odo, Nigeria, for most of his life. For several years, he worked for the Nigerian Broadcasting Corporation. He also traveled around Africa, Europe, and the United States, serving stints as a visiting fellow at the University of Ife, Nigeria (1979), and the University of Iowa (1983). He died in Ibadan in June 1997 from hypertension and diabetes.

Works in Literary Context

When *The Palm-Wine Drinkard* gained public attention abroad, some Nigerians were contemptuous of Tutuola's efforts because he had borrowed heavily from the well-known Yoruba novelist D. O. Fagunwa. Some Yoruba readers accused him of plagiarism. Indeed, the narrative devices, and much of the content of Tutuola's early writings, echo the work of Fagunwa rather precisely. Tutuola admitted as much in interviews and letters and never pretended that his stories were original creations. Rather, he was following in the norm of indigenous oral tradition. In oral art, what matters most is not uniqueness of invention but the adroitness of performance. A storyteller's contribution is to tell old, well-known tales in an entertaining manner. Thus, he was creatively exploiting, not pilfering, his cultural heritage.

Fagunwa was not Tutuola's only teacher. He had also read John Bunyan's *Pilgrim's Progress* (1678) and the *Arabian Nights* (c. 800–900), both classic adventure stories fabricated out of a chain of old tales loosely linked together. Events in Bunyan's narrative, such as Christian's visits to Vanity Fair, Doubting Castle, and the Celestial City, may have served as models for some of Tutuola's romantic adventures. However, unlike *Pilgrim's*

LITERARY AND HISTORICAL CONTEMPORARIES

Tutuola's famous contemporaries include:

Chinua Achebe (1930–): Nigerian novelist and essayist whose novel *Things Fall Apart* (1958) is the most widely read work of African literature.

Wole Soyinka (1934–): This Nigerian playwright, poet, and essayist was also a Nobel Prize winner. His plays include *A Dance of the Forest* (1960).

Fela Anikulapo-Kuti (1938–1997): This Nigerian musician and political activist sang in cunningly broken English. His albums include *Zombie* (1976).

Cheikh Anta Diop (1923–1986): This Senegalese anthropologist and historian studied ancient Africa and the origins of humanity. His books include *The African Origin of Civilization: Myth or Reality?* (1974).

James Baldwin (1924–1987): This African American novelist and essayist wrote *Go Tell It on the Mountain* (1953).

Gabriel García Márquez (1927–): This Colombian novelist wrote the Latin American epic *One Hundred Years of Solitude* (1967).

Italo Calvino (1923–1985): This Italian author of short stories and novels wrote modern fables, such as the *Our Ancestors* trilogy (1952–1959).

Progress—and Fagunwa's novels—Tutuola's narratives are not religious allegories. It is Yoruba oral tradition, not the Christian Bible, that influences Tutuola's works. Tutuola may have learned from Bunyan how to put an extended quest tale together, but in substance and spirit he was a thoroughly African storyteller.

The Heroic Quest Tutuola's storytelling method did not change much over the years. His stories typically concern a naive or morally weak character who is inspired or forced to embark on a spiritual journey. He or she encounters danger, confronts a tremendous variety of shape-shifting spirits from the underworld, and displays the heroic traits of the most popular folktale protagonists: hunter, magician, trickster, superman. Tutuola varies the quest pattern slightly from book to book, but never abandons it entirely. Because of their spiritual themes, allegorical characters, and symbolic plots, Tutuola's works have been called mythologies or epics rather than novels.

Ancestral, Yet Contemporary Tutuola employs many techniques associated with oral traditions in his novels and stories. The supernatural, fantastical, and grotesque are commonplace in Yoruba folklore. However, he embellishes ancestral tales with modern and Western elements, such as the "television-handed goddess" in *The Palm-Wine Drinkard*, which, in context, appear both exotic and in

COMMON HUMAN EXPERIENCE

The novels of Amos Tutuola represent a modern effort to preserve and revive folklore traditions. The following works of modern literature also invoke, update, or invent folktales:

The Robber Bride (1993), a novel by Margaret Atwood. This novel is loosely based on a fairy tale in the Grimm Brothers' collection, peppered with allusions to fairy tales and folklore.

Ceremony (1977), a novel by Leslie Marmon Silko. In this contemporary novel, a Native American returning from World War II delves into the ancient stories of his people to overcome despair.

Mules and Men (1935), a travelogue by Zora Neale Hurston. This unique anthropological travelogue documents the hoodoo practices of southern blacks, with many folktales thrown in.

The Wonderful Wizard of Oz (1900), a children's novel by L. Frank Baum. This celebrated fantasy book for children, the first of a long series, is a conscious attempt to create a modern American fairy tale, or "wonder tale."

The Jungle Book (1894), a story collection by Rudyard Kipling. This book of fables uses animals in an anthropomorphic manner to give moral lessons.

keeping with contemporary Nigerian changing culture. The result is a collage of borrowed materials put together in an eclectic manner by a resourceful raconteur working well within oral conventions.

Use of Language Perhaps the most unique aspect of Tutuola's novels is his unconventional use of the English language: skewed syntax, sometimes broken English, and idiosyncratic diction. For example, Tutuola wrote in *The Palm-Wine Drinkard*: "[If] I were a lady, no doubt I would follow him to wherever he would go, and still as I was a man, I would jealous him more than that." His usage of "jealous" as a verb reflects Yoruban grammatical constructs, in which adjectives and verbs are often interchangeable. Tutuola coins new words, incorporates Nigerian idiom and patois, and even spells with startling and charming inventiveness. In a unique way, he resolves the dilemma of the African writer representing his heritage authentically while working in the language of the colonizer.

Influence Most critics agree that Tutuola's literary style and method are highly personal and have had little influence on subsequent writers in Nigeria. However, his contribution—refashioning traditional Yoruba myths and folktales and fusing them with modern life—is increasingly appreciated. Tutuola retains a wide international readership, and his works are commonly read in Nigerian schools.

Students of African literature in Europe and the United States were also influenced by Tutuola and his writings.

Works in Critical Context

Audiences were sharply divided over Tutuola's work when it first began to appear in the 1950s. At first, Anglo-American commentators praised the style and content of Tutuola's fiction for its originality and imagination. Tutuola's later offerings were not as enthusiastically received in England and America as his first two. As new African voices reached the Western public, reviewers complained that Tutuola's writing seemed repetitive and rudimentary. His novelty had worn off, and the pendulum of critical opinion had begun to reverse direction. Later it would return to a more neutral position.

Early Nigerian critics expressed doubt about Tutuola's writing ability, but have since reclaimed him as a unique and innovative storyteller. In Nigeria, the pendulum started to swing in a more positive direction shortly after the nation achieved independence in 1960. The consensus of opinion today is that he is far too important a phenomenon to be overlooked.

The Palm-Wine Drinkard The appearance of *The Palm-Wine Drinkard* was greeted with hostility by Nigerian intellectuals. Some maintained that Tutuola's work was an unprincipled act of piracy, especially since he was writing in English for a foreign audience rather than in Yoruba for his own people, and that his obvious lack of proficiency in English would give readers overseas a poor opinion of Africans, thereby reinforcing their prejudices.

However, European and American readers found Tutuola an exotic delight. Dylan Thomas called the novel "bewitching." British critic V. S. Pritchett wrote in the *New Statesman and Nation* that "Tutuola's voice is like the beginning of man on earth." Perhaps Tutuola's Nigerian critics were right after all. To native speakers of English, his splintered style was an amusing novelty; to educated Nigerians who had spent years polishing their English, it was an abomination.

Responses to Literature

1. In a paper, identify some of the particular patterns of error or peculiarity in how Tutuola renders the English language. Assuming that these aberrations are purposeful, what purposes do they serve? Are they effective, and do they achieve what they are intended to?

2. Tutuola incorporates the phenomena of modern life into the fantasy worlds of his stories, yet he also seems to mourn the loss of ancient African traditions. How would you describe his attitude toward African modernity? Put your answer in the form of an essay.

3. What challenges did Tutuola confront in transmitting oral traditions into print? Would you think that these are challenges common to any writer facing this same

task within any culture, or is this exclusive to Tutuola's culture? Create a presentation with your findings.

4. As Nigeria struggled to overthrow colonialism, many of Tutuola's countrymen condemned him for disseminating a poor image of his people. Do you agree? Was his work a worthy representation of Nigerian culture? Write an essay that addresses these questions.

BIBLIOGRAPHY

Books

Asein, Samuel O., and Albert O. Ashaolu, eds. *Studies in the African Novel*. Ibadan, Nigeria: Ibadan University Press, 1986.

Collins, Harold R. *Amos Tutuola*. New York: Twayne, 1969.

Herskovits, Melville J., and Frances S. Herskovits. *Dahomean Narrative: A Cross-Cultural Analysis*. Evanston, Ill.: Northwestern University Press, 1958.

King, Bruce, ed. *Introduction to Nigerian Literature*. Ibadan, Nigeria: Evans Brothers, 1971.

Lindfors, Bernth, ed. *Critical Perspectives on Amos Tutuola*. Washington, D.C.: Three Continents, 1975.

Periodicals

Coates, John. "The Inward Journey of a Palm-Wine Drinkard." *African Literature Today* 11 (1980): 122–29.

Ferris, William R., Jr. "Folklore and the African Novelist: Achebe and Tutuola." *Journal of American Folklore* 86 (1973): 25–36.

Irele, Abiola. "Tradition and the Yoruba Writer: D. O. Fagunwa, Amos Tutuola and Wole Soyinka." *Odu* 11 (1975): 75–100.

Nkosi, Lewis. "Conversation with Amos Tutuola." *Africa Report* 9, no. 7 (1964): 11.

Obiechina, Emmanuel. "Amos Tutuola and the Oral Tradition." *Presence Africaine* 65 (1968): 85–106.

Tristan Tzara

BORN: *1896, Moinesti, Bacau, Romania*

DIED: *1963, Paris, France*

NATIONALITY: *Romanian*

GENRE: *Drama, poetry*

MAJOR WORKS:

The Gas Heart (1920)

Of Our Birds (1923)

Approximate Man (1931)

Conquered Southern Regions (1939)

The Escape (1947)

Overview

Tristan Tzara is a poet and essayist best known as one of the founders of the Dada artistic movement, which was

Tristan Tzara   *DEA Picture Library / drr.net*

focused primarily on protesting World War I and rejecting established traditions in art and literature. As a creator, chronicler, and critic, he wrote prolifically all his life. By the time of his death, he left behind numerous volumes of poetry, plays, essays on art and literature, critical commentary, unfinished studies on Rabelais and Villon, and an unfinished autobiographical novel titled *Place Your Bets*. Tzara's life journey westward from Romania to Switzerland, France, and briefly Spain constitutes a noteworthy example of the international character of the century's avant-garde movements and forms the background of his unceasing search for a genuine poetic language in conditions of war and human frailty.

Works in Biographical and Historical Context

Against Tradition Not much is known of Tzara's early life. He was born Samuel Rosenstock in Moinesti, in the Romanian province of Bacau, in 1896, the son of a prosperous forest administrator. Judging by his unfinished autobiography, *Place Your Bets*, it seems that from early on Tzara was a difficult, wayward youth battling against his traditional family, his father in particular. While studying mathematics and philosophy in Bucharest

LITERARY AND HISTORICAL CONTEMPORARIES

Tzara's famous contemporaries include:

André Breton (1896–1966): French writer and poet Breton is credited as the founder of the surrealist movement, writing the *Surrealist Manifesto* in 1924.

Ion Minulescu (1881–1944): Romanian avant-garde poet, novelist, journalist, critic, and essayist, Minulescu was strongly influenced by his stay in Paris during the 1920s. He returned to Romania, where he in turn became one of the major influences of modern Romanian literature.

Marcel Duchamp (1887–1968): French artist associated with Dada and surrealism whose provocative "found art" pieces challenged concepts of what constitutes art.

Fritz Lang (1890–1976): Austrian German film director and screenwriter whose silent films, including the classics *Metropolis* and *M*, continue to be highly influential for their visual power and imagery.

Philo Farnsworth (1906–1971): Holder of more than three hundred patents, Farnsworth is best remembered today as the inventor of the television and video camera. He transmitted the first experimental television pictures in 1927.

Henri Bergson (1859–1941): French philosopher and winner of the Nobel Prize in Literature in 1927; Bergson's ideas on metaphysics and the philosophy of language were highly influential in the first half of the twentieth century.

in 1912, he began to publish in his native language. His first postsymbolist poems appeared in the *Symbol*, a literary journal he had founded with Ion Vinea and Marcel Janco. Many of these poems, written in Romanian and influenced by French symbolist writers, appear in *Primele poeme: First Poems* (1965). Tzara derived the pseudonym he adopted in 1915 partly from the name of an esteemed predecessor, Tristan Corbière, and partly from *tara*, the Romanian word for country. He legally changed his name in 1925.

Dadaism Tzara immigrated to Switzerland from Romania in 1916. Together with Jean Arp, Hugo Ball, and others, Tzara founded Dadaism, a movement that emerged from their protest of artistic, social, and political convention and stylistically relied on the absurd or irrational. Tzara staged Dadaist performances at the Cabaret Voltaire in Zurich, but left Switzerland in 1919 to settle in Paris, where he engaged in Dadaist experiments with such literary figures as André Breton and Louis Aragon. Serious philosophical differences caused a split between Tzara and Breton in 1921; soon after, Breton founded

the surrealist movement, and by 1922 the Dada movement had dissolved. Tzara's early Dadaist verse, written between 1916 and 1924, utilizes clusters of obscure images, nonsense syllables, outrageous juxtapositions, ellipses, and inscrutable maxims to perplex readers and to illustrate the limitations of language. Volumes such as *Twenty-five Poems* (1918) and *Of Our Birds* (1923) display the propositions outlined in Tzara's manifestos and critical essays, often blending criticism and poetry to create hybrid literary forms.

Surrealism From 1929 to 1934, Tzara participated in the activities of the surrealist group in Paris. In this environment, he created a more sustained and coherent poetry that places less emphasis on the ridiculous than did his Dadaist verse. Tzara's works published during this period include *Approximate Man, and Other Writings* (1931), an epic poem that is widely considered a landmark of twentieth-century French literature. This work portrays an unfulfilled wayfarer's search for a universal knowledge and language. Art historian Roger Cardinal asserted: "[In] this apocalyptic explosion of language, Tzara finally approaches the primal seat of creativity, the point where the naked word reveals the naked truth about the world." This and Tzara's later surrealist volumes—*The Travelers' Tree* (1930), *Where Wolves Drink* (1932), *The Anti-head* (1933), and *Seed and Bran* (1935)—reveal his obsession with language, his vision of humanity's destiny of tedium and alienation, and his concern with the struggle to achieve completeness and enlightenment.

Communism In the 1930s, Tzara strove to bring about a reconciliation of surrealism and Marxism and began to turn away from aesthetic, surrealist revolt to political commitment. He became a member of the French Communist Party in 1936 and served as a delegate of the Second International Congress of Writers for the Defense of Culture to Spain during the Spanish Civil War. At this time, he joined the Republicans, or Spanish Loyalists, who championed democracy and liberty over tyranny and fascism, and also befriended Pablo Picasso. Later, forced into hiding during the Nazi occupation of France, Tzara participated in the Resistance. His clandestinely published poems were revolutionary and humanistic.

As his commitment to left-wing politics increased, his poetry included greater political content and stressed revolutionary and humanistic values while maintaining his lifelong interest in free imagery and linguistic experiments. *Conquered Southern Regions* (1939) focuses on Tzara's impressions of Spain during the country's civil war, while *The Escape* (1947) depicts the frantic German evacuation of Nazi-occupied France during World War II. The prose poems "Without a Need to Fight" (1949) and "Flame Out Loud" (1955) also address political topics related to World War II.

Tzara's embrace of communism, although by no means uncommon among European intellectuals in the late 1920s and early 1930s, remains somewhat of a surprise insofar as it comes from one of the most fiercely independent spirits among the Dadaists. No matter how much one would wish to excuse him, and in spite of a mostly discreet and possibly guarded allegiance, the fact remains that Tzara maintained his Communist Party membership with equanimity, if not enthusiasm, through the Stalinist purges and the Nazi-Soviet pact and into the cold war period until the very end of his life in 1963.

Works in Literary Context

Dadaism Tzara is remembered as a proponent and theoretician for Dadaism, an intellectual movement of the World War I era whose adherents espoused intentional irrationality and urged individuals to reject traditional artistic, historical, and religious values. In response to the alienation and absurdity of World War I and the staid, unimaginative art forms predominant in Europe during that era, Tzara and other European artists sought to establish a new style in which random associations would serve to evoke a vitality free from the restraints of logic and grammar. Tzara articulated the aesthetic theories of Dadaism in his seminal collection of essays, *Seven Dada Manifestos* (1924). This volume, in which Tzara advocates "absolute faith in every god that is the immediate product of spontaneity," represents a chaotic assault on reason and convention.

Works in Critical Context

Public and critical reaction to Tzara's work is difficult to evaluate using traditional measurements. As a Dadaist, the point of much of his early work was not to entertain or enlighten, but to evoke a reaction—typically a negative reaction due to the author's deliberate rejection of the familiar. In the decades since his death, however, scholars have been able to place Tzara's work in the context of the avant-garde movements of the time and judge its significance in the development of modern literature. Although his work often defies standard classification and is regarded by most contemporary English-speaking scholars as little more than a literary curiosity, Tzara is esteemed in France for his large and diverse body of poetry, which is unified by his critique of and search for a universal language and cosmic wisdom.

Approximate Man Hailed by surrealists upon its publication in 1931, the epic poem *Approximate Man* has continued to be viewed as one of Tzara's most significant works. Ruth L. Caldwell, in an essay for *Perspectives on Contemporary Literature*, calls the work his "masterpiece" and "his key poetical work, in which he sets forth the ideas which have occupied him for years." Mary Ann Caws, in *The Poetry of Dada and Surrealism:*

COMMON HUMAN EXPERIENCE

Tzara was the first to outline the tenets of Dada, but here are works by several other writers who are also credited with being early Dadaists, intentionally or not:

King Ubu (1896), a play by Alfred Jarry. This play is widely acknowledged as the forerunner of Dada, surrealist, and absurdist drama.

"Karawane" (1916), a poem by Hugo Ball. Composed by one of Tzara's collaborators at the Cabaret Voltaire, this work, written in German, consists of strings of nonsense words. The poem's very meaninglessness was one of the first formal expressions of Dada.

The Breasts of Tiresias (1917), a play by Guillaume Apollinaire. A two-act play that was one of the earliest recognized surrealist works.

Dada, Breton, Tzara, Éluard and Desnos, agrees with the label of "masterpiece" and notes that the "extremely diverse and unequally brilliant images" found in the work reinforce its theme of imperfection. However, not all readers sing the work's praises. Roger Cardinal, writing for the *Times Literary Supplement,* states, "Prolonged reading of the poem has left this reader unsatisfied that it succeeds in approximating a visionary grasp on cosmic realities. Much of [*The Approximate Man*] is too wordy, the modulation from chaos to confidence too sleekly *verbal.*"

The Gas Heart Critic Robert Varisco suggests that Tzara's play *The Gas Heart* represents "a form of anarchy against art or the theatre. Characters (body parts) have no spoken lines, personalities, names, real characters. The audience, meaning and authority are alienated—an initial step to overturn traditional theatre." Varisco also notes that Tzara, throughout the play, "elevates the realm of pointless verbiage." Varisco posits that the body parts, which are in fact the characters, express their resistance to (and by extension the author's resistance to) theatrical convention "in highly stylized and anti-symbolic philosophizing which always leads back to the prevalent feeling of 'lag' that they all share."

Responses to Literature

1. Read *Seven Dada Manifestos.* Then write a summary of what you think makes up this "philosophy of meaninglessness."

2. Read Tzara's *Approximate Man* and write an essay in which you describe what you think makes up his "philosophical driving force."

3. Choose a poem from Tzara's Dadaist period. Create an audio-visual presentation that illustrates Tzara's unique style and expression. Try to reflect the language and theme of the poem.

4. Read *Seven Dada Manifestos*. Then, using resources from your library and the Internet, research the varying styles of the pop art movement. Write a personal statement in which you discuss how you see Dadaist influences in pop art. Support your answer with examples from your research.

BIBLIOGRAPHY

Books

Ball, Hugo. *Flight Out of Time: A Dada Diary*. Viking, 1974.

Browning, Gordon Frederick. *Tristan Tzara: The Genesis of the Dada Poem, or from Dada to Aa*. Stuttgart: Akademischer Verlag Heinz, 1979.

Erickson, John D. *Dada: Performance, Poetry, and Art*. Boston: Twayne, 1984.

Harwood, Lee. *Tristan Tzara: A Bibliography*. London: Aloes Books, 1974.

Janco, Marcel. *Dada: Monograph of a Movement*. New York: St. Martin's 1975.

Ko, Won. *Buddhist Elements in Dada: A Comparison of Tristan Tzara, Takahashi Shinkichi, and Their Fellow Poets*. New York: New York University Press, 1977.

Lewis, Helena. *The Politics of Surrealism*. New York: Paragon House, 1988.

"Tristan Tzara (1896–1963)." In *Contemporary Literary Criticism*, vol. 47, edited by Daniel G. Marowski, Roger Matuz, and Sean R. Pollock, 384–96. Detroit: Gale Research, 1988.

"Tzara, Tristan (1896–1963)." In *Europe Since 1914: Encyclopedia of the Age of War and Reconstruction*, edited by John Merriman and Jay Winter. 5 vols. New York: Charles Scribner's Sons, 2007.

Miguel de Unamuno

BORN: *1864, Bilbao, Spain*

DIED: *1936, Salamanca, Spain*

NATIONALITY: *Spanish*

GENRE: *Drama, fiction, poetry*

MAJOR WORKS:

The Life of Don Quixote and Sancho (1905)

The Tragic Sense of Life in Men and in Peoples (1913)

Mist: A Tragicomic Novel (1914)

The Agony of Christianity (1925)

Overview

Miguel de Unamuno y Jugo is a crucially important figure in twentieth-century Spanish culture. Novelist, short-story

Miguel de Unamuno   *Popperfoto / Getty Images*

writer, poet, playwright, teacher, and commentator on politics, culture, and literature, he was appointed professor of Greek philology at the University of Salamanca at the age of twenty-six. By age fifty, he was rector of the university. Dismissed from his rectorship and later imprisoned and exiled for his public criticisms of the monarchy and the government, he went on to publish a study of the politics and philosophy of Christianity as well as other works. After a triumphant return to his native country, Unamuno remained a controversial figure: the Vatican placed his essay *The Agony of Christianity* (1925) on the Index of Prohibited Books twenty years after his death.

Works in Biographical and Historical Context

A Basque Youth   Unamuno was born in Bilbao in the Basque region of Spain and was raised in a traditional Catholic environment. He was profoundly affected during his childhood by political instability that ensued from attacks against the government by Catalan and Basque separatists; when he was nine years old, his native city was attacked by government troops, and one of their bombs destroyed a neighboring house. This civil war ended in

1876, the year Unamuno graduated from the Colegio de San Nicolas. He then entered the Instituto Vizacaino, where he became an advanced student in 1879 and revealed his aptitude for philosophy. The following year, Unamuno moved to the Spanish capital to continue his academic work at the University of Madrid, where he presented a dissertation on the Basque language and obtained a doctoral degree from the Faculty of Philosophy and Letters in 1884. For the following seven years, Unamuno unsuccessfully campaigned to obtain a university appointment; finally, in 1891, he was named professor of Greek at the University of Salamanca, the oldest and most revered university in Spain.

Religious Crisis In the 1890s, Unamuno's writings began to appear in periodicals, particularly the socialist *Class Struggle*. His first major work, *En torno al casticismo*, appeared as five separate essays in the journal *Modern Spain* in 1895. In these essays, Unamuno called upon Spain to cease its cultural isolation from the rest of Europe. Two years later, his novel *Peace in War* (1897) appeared, an event that coincided with a personal, intense religious crisis, from which Unamuno emerged without an orthodox faith in God. He subsequently expressed his struggle with the philosophical conflict between faith and reason in a series of acclaimed works: *The Life of Don Quixote and Sancho*, *The Tragic Sense of Life*, and *The Agony of Christianity*.

Political Conflicts In his essays, Unamuno attacked the policies of Spain's King Alfonso XIII, who ruled from 1902 until 1931, and the dictatorship of Primo de Riviera, the prime minister who effectively controlled the government from 1923 until 1930 during Alfonso's reign. Considered both a religious and political heretic, Unamuno was dismissed from the University of Salamanca in 1914 and exiled to the Canary Islands ten years later. Unamuno then moved to France, where he lived in Paris until settling in the frontier town of Hendaye on the border with Spain, near his Basque homeland. With the fall of the Riviera dictatorship, Unamuno returned to Spain in 1930 and resumed his university position, finishing his best-crafted work of fiction, *Saint Emmanuel the Good, Martyr* (1933).

In the early 1930s, Spain was a nation torn in two. Some citizens, including many in Unamuno's native Basque region, wished to become independent of the Spanish government based in Madrid and were known as republicans. These were regions traditionally viewed by their citizens as self-contained and autonomous despite the fact that they were all collectively referred to as Spain. Other republicans supported the creation of an effective democratic government. Opponents to this movement, known as nationalists and spearheaded by Francisco Franco, sought to keep Spain intact at any cost. Many nationalists also supported the return of the Spanish monarchy. While Unamuno was critical of the republicans, he ultimately became an outspoken critic of the nationalists as well,

primarily for their brutal tactics. After voicing his opposition to the nationalists, Unamuno was confined by military order to his house, where he died in 1936.

Works in Literary Context

Immortality and the Rejection of Religion Like his near contemporary José Ortega y Gasset, Unamuno was well versed in modern European literature and philosophy. Initially influenced by Georg Wilhelm Friedrich Hegel's dialectical method and the positivist worldview of Herbert Spencer, he later studied Søren Kierkegaard, Henri-Louis Bergson, and William James, especially for their perspectives on faith, reason, and intuition. Unamuno's philosophy reflected their fundamental skepticism: he defined man as an end in himself rather than as an agent of God's will, though he recognized humanity's innate desire for immortality, and he denied the validity of any autonomous philosophical system.

Works in Critical Context

Critic Enrique Fernandez suggested that Unamuno "dug deeper into the national spirit than any of his contemporaries,

COMMON HUMAN EXPERIENCE

Unamuno is regarded as an early existentialist writer, whose ideas were formulated a generation before existentialism emerged as a prominent intellectual movement in philosophy and literature. Here are some of the best-known works that deal with existentialist themes.

> *The Stranger* (1942), a novel by Albert Camus. Although Camus refused to be associated with existentialism, his philosophy of the absurd, expressed succinctly in this novel, led many to closely link him with other existentialist thinkers of his time.
>
> *Nausea* (1938), a novel by Jean-Paul Sartre. This novel functions as a sort of outline of existentialism, describing a main character who is suddenly struck by the realization of the indifference of his surroundings to his own existence.
>
> *Being and Time* (1927), a philosophical work by Martin Heidegger. Originally intended as the first part in an ultimately uncompleted larger project, this book has gone on to become one of the most influential works of philosophy of the twentieth century. Notably, it inspired Sartre to write *Being and Nothingness*, generally regarded as the first true existentialist philosophical work.
>
> *Waiting for Godot* (1953), a play by Samuel Beckett. This absurdist work about two men waiting for a third who never arrives is often singled out for its existentialist themes.

a generation whose collective project was the exploration of Spanishness." Unamuno's poetic emphasis and concern with human mortality has led many critics to characterize his work as distinctively Spanish. Salvador de Madariaga, who deemed Unamuno Spain's greatest literary figure, asserted that "Unamuno, by the cross which he has chosen to bear, incarnates the spirit of modern Spain." At the same time, Unamuno's eclecticism and experimental method have caused many critics to place him outside of the mainstream of modern Spanish literature. Fernandez also remarked, "Though he ravaged all genres, Unamuno is hard to classify as a writer—if he even is a writer." His fiction and poetry, "though powerful, [are] more philosophical than lyrical," Fernandez continued, and his philosophical writings "are emotional and personal" rather than logical or theoretical. "Too writerly to be a philosopher, too philosophical to be an artist," Fernandez concluded, "Unamuno is, as he deserves to be, a category unto himself."

Legacy "At his death in 1936," Arthur A. Cohen claimed in the *New York Times Book Review*, "Miguel de Unamuno was the most influential thinker in Spain, more renowned than his younger contemporary Ortega y Gasset and regarded by his own aficionados as the greatest stylist in the Spanish language since Cervantes." Fernandez posited in the *Voice Literary Supplement*, "Quixote incarnate, he lived out his nationality to its logical philosophical conclusions.... The soul-searching of the first Spanish moderns, who would be called the generation of 1898, found its fullest expression in Unamuno. In poems, plays, novels, and essays," the critic continued, Unamuno questioned "Spanishness, modernity, science, politics, philosophy, faith, God, everything."

The Tragic Sense of Life Unamuno's philosophical work *The Tragic Sense of Life* (1913) was, upon the publication of an English translation in 1921, a critical success. The book deals with the reconciliation of the logical mind with the spiritual, particularly regarding immortality. Salvador de Madariaga wrote in 1921, "This strife between enemy truths, the truth thought and the truth felt, or, as he himself puts it, between veracity and sincerity, is Unamuno's *raison d'être*. And it is because the *Tragic Sense of Life* is the most direct expression of it that this book is his masterpiece." Mark Van Doren, in a 1922 review for the *Nation*, wrote of Unamuno, "His masterpiece, [*The Tragic Sense of Life*] ... is modern Catholicism's richest, most passionate, most brilliant statement of the grounds that exist for faith in immortality, now that reason and science have done their worst." Van Doren noted the author's unorthodox but ultimately uplifting perspective: "Supremely intelligent, he never believes; religiously alive, he hopes. His book is very absurd, but it is tremendous work and fun for the mind." Ernest Boyd, in a 1925 essay, described the book as "a work which comes in direct line from the literature of the Spanish mystics.... The visionary passion of a mind which refuses to accept the denial of spiritual hopes and is yet conscious of the sovereignty of the reasoning faculties finds dramatic expression in this book."

Responses to Literature

1. Unamuno once said, "Realism is the coherence of mysticism." Write an essay in which you use Unamuno's work to comment on that quotation.

2. Read *El Cristo de Velazquez*. Then, create an audio-visual presentation that illustrates the religious themes and imagery evoked by the poem.

3. Write an informative essay that explains the Basque ideals that led to six years of exile for Unamuno.

4. Unamuno lived through many important events in the history of Spain. Research the following major events or eras in Spain's history: the Carlist Wars, the Spanish-American War, the dictatorship of Primo de Rivera, the Second Republic, or the Spanish Civil War. With other classmates who have read Unamuno, discuss how Unamuno's writings reflect the shifts in government and shifts in social concerns and attitudes toward the Catholic Church.

BIBLIOGRAPHY

Books

Altisent, Marta E., and Cristina Martínez-Carazo, eds. *Dictionary of Literary Biography.* Vol. 322: *Twentieth-Century Spanish Fiction Writers.* A Bruccoli Clark Layman Book. Detroit: Gale, 2006.

Barea, Arturo, and Ilsa Barea. *Unamuno.* Trans. I. Barea. Cambridge, U.K.: Bowes & Bowes, 1952.

Basdekis, Demetrios. *Unamuno and Spanish Literature.* Berkeley: University of California Press, 1967.

Bleiberg, Herman, and E. Inman Fox, eds. *Spanish Thought and Letters in the Twentieth Century: Miguel de Unamuno, 1864–1964.* Nashville: Vanderbilt University Press, 1966.

Ilie, Paul. *Unamuno: An Existential View of Self and Society.* Madison: University of Wisconsin Press, 1967.

Lacy, Allen. *Miguel de Unamuno: The Rhetoric of Existence.* The Hague, Netherlands: Mouton, 1967.

"Miguel de Unamuno (y Jugo) (1864–1936)." In *Twentieth-Century Literary Criticism,* vol. 9, edited by Dennis Poupard, 507–26. Detroit: Gale Research, 1983.

Mora, Jose Ferrater. *Unamuno: A Philosophy of Tragedy.* Trans. Philip Silver. Berkeley: University of California Press, 1962.

Perna, Michael L., ed. *Dictionary of Literary Biography.* Vol. 108: *Twentieth-Century Spanish Poets, First Series.* A Bruccoli Clark Layman Book. Detroit: Gale Research, 1991.

Rubia Barcia, Jose, and M. A. Zeitlin, eds. *Unamuno: Creator and Creation.* Berkeley: University of California Press, 1967.

Rudd, Margaret Thomas. *The Lone Heretic: A Biography of Miguel de Unamuno y Jugo.* Austin: University of Texas Press, 1963.

"Saint Emmanuel the Good, Martyr." In *Short Stories for Students,* vol. 20, edited by Ira Mark Milne. Detroit: Gale, 2005.

Wyers, Frances. *Miguel de Unamuno: The Contrary Self.* London: Tamesis, 1976.

◈ Sigrid Undset

BORN: *1882, Kalundborg, Denmark*

DIED: *1949, Lillehammer, Norway*

NATIONALITY: *Norwegian*

GENRE: *Drama, fiction, poetry*

MAJOR WORKS:

Jenny (1911)

Kristin Lavransdatter (1920–1922)

The Master of Hestviken (1925–1927)

The Wild Orchid (1929)

The Faithful Wife (1937)

Sigrid Undset   *Undset, Sigrid, photograph. AP Images.*

Overview

Norwegian author Sigrid Undset is a dominant figure among Scandinavian novelists and one of the foremost literary proponents of Christian ethics and philosophy. Her major works, *Kristin Lavransdatter* (1920–1922) and *The Master of Hestviken* (1925–1927), are skillfully rendered portrayals of medieval Norwegian life and have been praised as exemplary models of historical fiction, evidencing a detailed knowledge of and keen sympathy for their subject. On the strength of these works, she was awarded the Nobel Prize for Literature in 1928.

Works in Biographical and Historical Context

A Childhood Steeped in History   Born in Kalundborg, Denmark, in 1882, Unset was the eldest of three daughters of the renowned Norwegian archaeologist Ingvald Undset and his wife, Anna Charlotte. Ingvald Undset had come from Trondelag, an area of Norway articulately described in his daughter's masterpiece, *Kristin Lavransdatter.* Anna Charlotte Undset, a reserved and proud woman, inspired respect in her daughter but not the deep affection that the child felt for her father.

At the age of two, Unset moved with her family to the city of Christiania (now Oslo), where her father was associated with the archaeological section of the University Museum. As Ingvald Undset's health declined (he had caught malaria on an expedition to the Mediterranean), the family moved frequently, and Undset became intimately acquainted with many areas of the city of Oslo. As the daughter of an archaeologist, she acquired an acute sense of history. The Undset home was filled with books, and the child was encouraged by her father to read extensively, especially works of history and Old Norse sagas. When Undset was eleven years old, her father died, and the family experienced genuine poverty. Her autobiographical memoir, *The Longest Years* (1934), records memories of the first eleven years of her life. That she gave herself the name "Ingvild" in these memoirs suggests the strength of her attachment to and identification with her father.

Secretarial Work Although Undset attended the liberal school of Ragna Nielsen and had the opportunity to enroll in the university, she chose at the age of fifteen to prepare for a secretarial career at the Christiania Commercial College. Her certificate from this school a year later helped her to obtain a position in the local office of the German Electric Company, where she worked for ten years. Undset's intimate acquaintance with young working girls provided the material for many of her earliest works.

In her free time from her secretarial job, Undset turned her hand to writing. She submitted a historical novel to the Gyldendal publishing house in Copenhagen, only to be told that she should turn to modern themes that seemed more suited to her talents. Undset followed this advice, and her first contemporary social novel, *Mrs. Marta Oulie*, appeared in the fall of 1907. As Undset's career was taking off, Norway was undergoing political change as the country gained its independence from Sweden in 1905, after spending much of the nineteenth century in forced union.

After the publication of three additional works of moderate success, Undset felt secure enough to quit her job for a full-time career as a writer. In 1909 she received a travel grant from the Norwegian government and went to Rome, where she met her future husband, the painter Anders Svarstad. Married in 1912, the couple lived first in London and later in Norway, where Undset continued to produce fiction, nonfiction, and translations.

Contemporary Fiction Sparks Controversy The novel *Jenny* (1912), which caused a sensation in Scandinavian feminist circles, is the story of a promising young artist who commits suicide. Jenny has, along the way, had an affair with her fiancé's father, borne a child out of wedlock, suffered through the death of that child, and experienced frustration as a creative artist. Whether Jenny's suicide is caused by her failure as an artist or by her failure in erotic and maternal relationships is open to interpretation. In any case, the work is the most successful of all of Undset's social novels with contemporary settings. While her novels

featured concerns of the time, World War I was not a topic she focused on despite its importance in the 1910s. Though Norway remained neutral in the conflict, its merchant marine suffered losses.

As controversial as some of her novels of contemporary life may have been, none of them could compare with Undset's masterpieces of medieval life. Critics agree that it is the multivolume *Kristin Lavransdatter* and the *Olav Audunsson* series (*The Master of Hestviken*, 1925–1927), that have secured her place in literary history. Showing a mastery of style lacking in her novels of contemporary life, these works also reveal the understanding of vanished cultures and love of the past instilled in the writer by her father. Her intimate knowledge of the laws, culture, and history of earlier ages had given her a sense of the continuity of life. Despite the copious and meticulously accurate historical details that embellish these novels, there is nothing strange about the people who inhabit that distant world.

After the births of three children—Anders, Maren Charlotte, and Hans—Svarstad and Undset eventually became estranged, and their marriage was annulled when she converted to Catholicism in 1924.

Lillehammer and the War Exile Remaining in Lillehammer, Norway, until 1940, Undset devoted herself both to her work, for which she received the Nobel Prize for Literature in 1928, and to her children. Maren Charlotte, who was born handicapped, lived only to the age of twenty-three. Anders, Undset's eldest son, was killed in 1940 when German armies invaded Norway in 1940. While Norway had proclaimed its neutrality during the early days World War II, its waters were too strategically important for it to remain outside the war. Germany invaded in April 1940, and controlled the country by June. A government in exile was founded in England, led by King Haakon VII. With Hans, her only surviving child, Undset then made the long journey through Sweden to Russia, from there to Japan, and from there to San Francisco.

During the war, she channeled her considerable energies into the war effort, giving lectures, writing propaganda, and calling attention to the plight of occupied Norway. In August 1945, after the war's end, she returned to her homeland, and in 1947 King Haakon VII conferred upon her the Grand Cross of the Order of Saint Olav for service to her country. On June 10, 1949, Undset died in Lillehammer. Her life provided the impetus for her works: her religious faith, her pride in the past of her people, and her assessment of motherhood as woman's most important calling are all mirrored in her imaginative works and clearly stated in her nonfiction.

Works in Literary Context

Although there is no clear chronological division between Undset's novels of contemporary life and her works set in earlier historical periods (in 1909 she published a pastiche of the Icelandic saga, and contemporary social novels reoccur in the 1930s), most of her early writing was inspired by her knowledge of the working class of Oslo. Her interest in Scandinavian history and Norse legends primarily comes from the influence of her archaeologist father and his career. This influence compelled her to write accurate, compelling historical fiction.

Infidelity Undset is a moralist, first of all, though she is certainly not by temperament an ascetic. She has a profound, brooding awareness of the domination of the flesh in the average human life, the central place of passion in the average human destiny. *Mrs. Marta Oulie*, for example, treats of infidelity in marriage. The novel, which is written in diary form, begins with the confession, "I have been unfaithful to my husband." Undset's only play, *In the Gray Light of Dawn* (1958), is likewise concerned with adultery, and this theme is prominent in Undset's novels of the Middle Ages as well. Two collections of short stories, *The Happy Age* (1908) and *Poor Fortunes* (1912), address problems of adolescence, motherhood, and spinsterhood in the lower economic classes of Norwegian urban society.

Feminist Themes Several later works also realistically treat problems of sexual fidelity and parenthood, stressing the importance of forgiveness and presenting the child as the element that can weld the most disparate parents together. Through these novels, Undset was placed squarely at the head of the women's movement in Scandinavia, whether she wished to be in that position or not. An intelligent, creative working woman who also experienced marriage and motherhood, she could write eloquently of the problems that beset such women.

The question of whether Undset was a feminist or an antifeminist is a thorny one. Selective quoting can produce arguments for either side. Carl F. Bayerschmidt maintained that "Sigrid Undset was not a militant feminist, but neither was she an antifeminist. She believed that every woman should be free to practice an art or a profession or occupy herself in any form of work without losing the right to love and to establish a family."

Female Characters Undset was particularly interested in women, and she gives realistic descriptions of countless different women, descriptions marked by great psychological insight and understanding. The women we meet through Undset are seldom soft and obedient. Kristin, for example, is strong and resourceful, while her husband, Erlend, despite his high position in society, shows a weaker and more tender nature. Nevertheless, the strong woman is not a fixed pattern in Undset's books. There are strong women and weak women, hard women and soft, those who cannot cope with life, and those who surmount their difficulties and live full, rich lives. There are bitter women full of hate and revenge and women full of concern and thoughtfulness. As in life itself, Undset's books take in the whole spectrum of women—and of men. Throughout her fiction, we find the same theme we find in Undset's articles: woman is

---

LITERARY AND HISTORICAL CONTEMPORARIES

Undset's famous contemporaries include:

George V (1865–1936): King of Great Britain, Protector of Ireland, and Emperor of India, George ruled from 1910 to his death, guiding his country through the tumultuous days of World War I.

Vladimir Lenin (1870–1924): Lenin was a Russian political thinker and revolutionary who led the October Revolution of 1917, the uprising that led to the establishment of the Bolshevik regime. Lenin served as head of the Soviet Union until his death.

Joan Miró (1893–1983): Spanish painter and sculptor, Miró's modernist, surrealistic works, in particular his public sculptures, left their mark on his native Barcelona and other Spanish cities. His sculptures in Barcelona include *Woman and Bird* (1982).

Rudolph Valentino (1895–1926): Arguably the first male film idol, American actor Valentino's good looks in such films as *The Sheik* (1921) made him internationally famous. His funeral was attended by an estimated one hundred thousand people, including politicians and dignitaries.

Marcel Proust (1871–1922): French novelist and critic, Proust is best remembered today for his opus *In Search of Lost Time*, published over a fourteen-year period beginning in 1913. Many critics consider it the greatest literary work of the modern age.

George Gershwin (1898–1937): American composer who, with his brother Ira acting as lyricist, penned some of the most memorable musical pieces of the twentieth century. Their musical comedies included *Funny Face* (1927) and *Girl Crazy* (1930).

---

just as well endowed as man, she was not meant, by nature, to be a special carrier of "soft' values. Differences of this sort are culturally and socially conditioned.

Undset's heroines, after Jenny, are almost without exception not tragic characters. Most of them ultimately learn to adjust themselves to life, though only after a more or less severe struggle. This is true of Rose Wegner in *Springtime*, Undset's most important work in the decade between *Jenny* and the publication of *Kristin Lavransdatter*. This is true also of most of the women characters in the two collections of short stories *The Splinter of the Troll Mirror* and *The Wise Virgins*. And this is preeminently true of Kristin in *Kristin Lavransdatter*.

Works in Critical Context

Undset won a secure place in literary history as one of the foremost authors of historical novels and as the most prominent Catholic author Scandinavia has produced.

COMMON HUMAN EXPERIENCE

Although Undset's role as a feminist author remains debatable, she wrote at a time of great flowering among other women authors who most definitely were writing with an agenda in mind. Here are some works that address women's place in society.

> *The Awakening* (1899), a novella by Kate Chopin. This novella is the tale of an upper-class woman who longs to break free of the strict society she inhabits, and the price she must pay to do so.
> "The Yellow Wallpaper" (1892), a short story by Charlotte Perkins Gilman. Perhaps the first modern feminist text, this story, told in first person, concerns a woman confined to her room "for her own good" and her descent into psychosis as a result of her isolation.
> *Aurora Leigh* (1856), an epic poem by Elizabeth Barrett Browning. A nine-volume epic poem written in blank verse, this work chronicles the life and travels of its strong and capable heroine.

Carl F. Bayerschmidt, in his critical study *Sigrid Undset*, labeled the Norwegian novelist "one of the greatest realistic writers of the first half of the twentieth century." A. H. Winsnes, in *Sigrid Undset: A Study in Christian Realism*, called the author "the Christian realist *par excellence*." Critics believed that Undset's works are powerful not only because of their moral message but also because of her mastery of technique. Few other novelists have so accurately painted background and setting or so completely banned romanticism from their works.

Undset's critical reputation has waxed and waned over time. Her early works, especially *Jenny*, were well received upon their publication. By the 1930s and 1940s, on the strength of both her contemporary novels and historical fiction, she was regarded as one of the greatest realistic writers of the time. Because her writings are not particularly innovative stylistically or thematically, they became unfashionable, and critical interest lessened for a time. By the late twentieth century, interest was revived as critics reconsidered the value of the works of women writers. Undset's *Kristin Lavransdatter* and *The Master of Hestviken* have a secure reputation as masterpieces of the historical novel genre.

Historical Works In general, critics of Undset's era and of today have admired the sympathetic character portrayals and realism of her historical novels, especially the *Kristin Lavransdatter* and *The Master of Hestviken* series. In his presentation of the award at the ceremony in Stockholm, Nobel Committee chairman Per Hallström also praised Undset's depiction of the inner lives of her medieval characters. He noted briefly the concern of some critics that Undset had added fantasy to historical fact in her presentation of medieval psychological detail, but insisted, "the historian's claim is not absolute: the poet has at least an equal right to express himself when he relies on a solid and intuitive knowledge of the human soul." The critical reception of the Olav Audunsson novels was positive, but the main character was generally viewed as a less interesting personality than Kristin Lavransdatter.

As Winsnes pointed out, however, Undset has been called "the [Émile] Zola of the Middle Ages." Very few other writers have understood so fully the past and its connection with the present. Winsnes noted that "history is Sigrid Undset's muse. No one since [thirteenth-century Icelandic poet and historian] Snorri Sturluson has presented medieval Norway with such power."

Responses to Literature

1. From a young age, Undset was attracted to the Middle Ages. Why do you think she always felt more comfortable with that bygone era? Do you think she held a romanticized idea of the period? Why or why not? Use evidence from Undset's writings to support your assertion in essay form.

2. *Kristin Lavransdatter* has been hailed as an early feminist work. Do you agree with this assessment? What elements of the story, if any, do you think give it a feminist tone? Write an essay with your conclusions.

3. In a presentation, address these questions: How would you characterize the mother-daughter relationships in *At Eleven*? How do they relate to Undset's overall view of women and their relationships?

4. Discuss the role of religion and Catholicism in Undset's works in a paper. How did Undset's conversion to Catholicism influence her writing, and vice versa?

BIBLIOGRAPHY

Books

Bayerschmidt, Carl F. *Sigrid Undset*. London: Twayne, 1970.

Dunn, Margaret, Sister. *Paradigms and Paradoxes in the Life and Letters of Sigrid Undset*. Lanham, Md.: University Press of America, 1994.

McFarlane, James Walter. *Ibsen and the Temper of Norwegian Literature*. London: Oxford University Press, 1960.

Winsnes, A. H. *Sigrid Undset: A Study in Christian Realism*. Translated by P. G. Foote. Lanham, Md.: Sheed & Ward, 1953.

Luisa Valenzuela

BORN: *1938, Buenos Aires, Argentina*

NATIONALITY: *Argentine*

GENRE: *Fiction, nonfiction*

MAJOR WORKS:

Clara: Thirteen Short Stories and a Novel (1966)

Strange Things Happen Here (1976)

Other Weapons (1982)

Black Novel (with Argentines) (1990)

Bedside Manners (1990)

Overview

Luisa Valenzuela is an Argentine writer of both fiction and journalistic works. She is among her nation's most significant writers, best known for magic realism, a style of writing often associated with Latin American writers Gabriel García Márquez and Julio Cortázar, that blends magical and fantastic elements. Valenzuela is also one of the most widely translated female South American writers. Throughout her literary career, Valenzuela has focused on the themes of politics, language, and women. Valenzuela is renowned for her short stories, especially

Luisa Valenzuela   *Valenzuela, Luisa, photograph.© Jerry Bauer. Reproduced by permission.*

those collected in *Strange Things Happen Here* (*Aqui pasan cosas raras*) (1976) and *Other Weapons* (*Cambio de armas*) (1982).

Works in Biographical and Historical Context

The Liveliness of Words   Luisa Valenzuela was born November 26, 1938, in Buenos Aires, Argentina, to Pablo Francisco Valenzuela, a physician, and Luisa Mercedes Levinson, a writer. Valenzuela, an insatiable reader, attended a British school in her youth. Given her parents' place in society and the family's connections with academics, Valenzuela was able to meet writers, such as Jorge Luis Borges, Ernesto Sabato, and Peyrou, in her youth. While she originally hoped to become a painter or a mathematician, writing eventually won out over those early career aspirations.

Early Writing Endeavors   Valenzuela's first journalistic work appeared in magazines while she was still in her teens. Her first short story, "Ese Canto," was published in 1956. Valenzuela also worked for a time at the Biblioteca Nacional, where Borges was the library's director. She went on to earn a bachelor of arts degree from the University of Buenos Aires.

In 1958 Valenzuela married French merchant marine Theodore Marjak and moved with him to the Normandy region of France, where her daughter, Anna-Lisa, was born. It was while living in France that Valenzuela wrote her first novel, *Clara: Thirteen Short Stories and a Novel* (*Hay que sonreir*) (1966).

Journalism and International Attention   Divorcing her husband after five years of marriage, Valenzuela moved to Paris and began working as a writer for Radio Television Française. She returned to Buenos Aires in 1961 and worked as editor of *La Nación*'s Sunday supplement from 1964 to 1972.

A collection of short stories titled *The Heretics* (*Los Hereticos*) was published in 1967. Valenzuela was subsequently awarded a Fulbright grant in 1969 that allowed her to participate in the International Writers Program at the University of Iowa. The result of this fellowship award was the 1972 novel *Cat-o-Nine-Deaths* (*El Gato eficaz*). In 1970 Valenzuela began giving lectures about writing, and over the course of the next two years, she traveled to Spain, France, and Mexico on a grant from the National Arts Foundation of Argentina. Her journalistic work appeared in publications in the United States, Mexico, France, and Spain, as well as in various publications based in Buenos Aires.

Political Concerns   Returning to Buenos Aires in 1974, Valenzuela discovered that the political situation in Argentina following the death of Juan Perón—three-time president of Argentina, beloved by many but viewed as anti-intellectual by some writers and artists—had degenerated into a paramilitary dictatorship rife with violence and repression. Between 1976 and 1983, some twenty thousand Argentine citizens "disappeared" and were never heard

LITERARY AND HISTORICAL CONTEMPORARIES

Valenzuela's famous contemporaries include:

Juan Perón (1895–1974): Controversial yet popular, Perón was elected president of Argentina three times.

Peter Benenson (1921–2005): This English lawyer founded Amnesty International in 1961.

Gabriel García Márquez (1927–): García Márquez is a Colombian novelist and short-story writer who brought magic realism into the spotlight with his *One Hundred Years of Solitude*.

Margaret Atwood (1939–): This Canadian writer's themes involve women's issues, some told in the style of magic realism.

Laura Esquivel (1950–): Esquivel's magic realist romance novel *Like Water for Chocolate* was very successful in the United States.

from again. They were almost certainly the victims of abduction and murder by government forces. Continuing to work as an editor, Valenzuela was impelled to write fictional works under the repressive regime, resulting in another short story collection, *Strange Things Happen Here*. Valenzuela had been teaching at Columbia University periodically since 1973; in 1979 she was offered a writer-in-residence position and decided to move to the United States to escape political repression. At Columbia University she became a teacher in the school's writing division from 1980 to 1983, the year she was awarded a Guggenheim fellowship. The fellowship allowed Valenzuela to move across town to New York University, where she was appointed visiting professor in 1985. She held that post until 1990, traveling frequently to lecture, and was a guest speaker at writing conferences in locations throughout the world, including the Americas, Israel, and Australia. Valenzuela became a fellow at the New York Institute for the Humanities in 1982 and belonged to the Freedom to Write committee of PEN's American Center. Her concerns with human rights issues prompted her to join Amnesty International. In 1984, after the fall of Argentina's military regime, forensics specialists from the United States came to Argentina at the request of the government to help investigate the fate of the thousands of citizens who had disappeared. Hundreds of mass graves were found, and evidence uncovered by the forensics experts helped convict six out of nine leaders of the military junta of murder.

Return to Argentina With democracy restored to Argentina in April of 1989, Valenzuela returned to Buenos Aires. Occasionally visiting New York City, she continued to write prolifically, as evidenced by the publication of the novels *Black Novel (with Argentines)* (*Novela negra con argentinos*) (1990) and *Symmetries*

(*Simetrias*) (1993), as well as the 1990 short-story collection *Bedside Manners* (*Realidad nacional desde la cama*).

Valenzuela's works have been translated into English and have appeared in several anthologies. Much of her work has been published in translation outside the Americas, including Japan, and her books can be found in French, German, and Portuguese translations, leading to her acclaim as the most widely translated of the South American female authors.

Works in Literary Context

Since her earliest pieces, Valenzuela has concentrated on three interrelated topics: language, politics, and male-female relationships in patriarchal societies—societies in which the power is generally held and passed down from generation to generation by males. The power of Valenzuela's fiction lies both in the intrinsic interest of the themes it develops and in her constant search for a feminist discourse. Although she is not the only Latin American female writer to embark on such a project, her fiction undoubtedly has broken new ground for women's writing in Latin America.

The Power of Language Valenzuela's prose, often playful and humorous, underscores the fact that language is an untrustworthy means of expression and communication. Words not only can distort reality, but they can also contaminate social interactions. Most individuals are unaware of such contamination, and very few escape it. This idea constitutes a fundamental concern of the collection *Strange Things Happen Here*.

Characters in the stories of *Up Among the Eagles* (*Donde viven las aguilas*) (1983) explore language as a means to escape contemporary Western societies. Most of the tales are set in the Mexican highlands where vestiges of pre-Columbian cultures are still present. In these "upper worlds," reason and magic coexist; individuals experience closeness to nature, and the possibilities of communicating by interpreting pauses, intonations, facial expressions, and sighs allow the characters to pierce the boundaries of reason.

Politics and Women's Issues As critics have noted, Valenzuela's work usually revolves around themes of politics and women's issues. Also rooted within her work is the violence and suffering experienced in many Latin American countries under authoritarian regimes. For instance, in her novel *The Lizard's Tail* (*Cola de largartija*) (1983), the protagonist, a cruel sorcerer, is based on José López Rega, Isabel Perón's Minister of Social Welfare.

Strange Things Happen Here is Valenzuela's most overtly political work. Its stories were inspired by the "Dirty War" unleashed against the Argentinean population by that country's military dictatorship in the mid 1970s and early 1980s. The stories explore the psychological and social effects of sustained and systematic violence. One of their most immediate concerns is the effect of fear, which translates into people's unwillingness to recognize that strange things are happening, that nothing is normal anymore. The main character in "Who, Me a Bum?" for example, regards the cries of those being tortured that he overhears at night to be a mere impediment to his sleep. Also, while at a metro station, he comments on the anger of commuters because a suicide victim is holding up the train. Nobody questions the motives behind these incidents, and all continue about their business.

The five stories in *Other Weapons*—all of them narrated by a female voice—explore the ways women resist the codes of behavior imposed on them by the patriarchy. The title not only refers to the violence of the dirty war, of which women were often the main victims, but also to the recourses available to women in their struggle for freedom. In their struggle against a tradition of passivity, submission, and acquiescence, Valenzuela's women need to chart new ground and explore the untapped resources of their imaginations and erotic impulses.

Works in Critical Context

Called "the heiress of Latin American literature" by Mexican novelist Carlos Fuentes, Luisa Valenzuela is one of the most celebrated contemporary female authors in Latin America. Nearly all her novels and short stories have been translated into English, and some have been published as far abroad as Holland and Japan. Critic Evelyn Picon Garfield has described Valenzuela's prose as "critical and revolutionary."

Strange Things Happen Here The 1979 English publication of Valenzuela's story collection *Strange Things Happen Here* was marked by rather lackluster reviews. Fimie Richie, in a review for *Studies in Short Fiction*, states, "None of this is edifying nor pleasurable reading." Clara Claiborne Park, writing for *The Hudson Review*, asserts that most of the stories in the book are "finished before we know what they're up to," and therefore seem pointless. Park offers one possible explanation: "Maybe it's safer to stick to parable and mysterious vignette if you want to go on living and publishing in Argentina, where Valenzuela is a prominent journalist.... If this is the price of writing in Argentina it is a heavy one." Roger Sale, writing for the *New York Times Book Review*, acknowledges "moments of perkiness and whimsy in the stories." However, he calls the short novel "He Who Searches" (included in the collection) "unreservedly awful," and asserts that on the whole the author "is just playing around in a sandbox filled with trite words and events that she, and, one hopes, not very many others, find fascinating."

Responses to Literature

1. Why do you think magic realism seems to be so prevalent among South American writers? Is it popular in the literature of other cultures? Do you think the magic realism Valenzuela uses makes the violence she describes harder or easier to digest?

COMMON HUMAN EXPERIENCE

Valenzuela's works center around the power of language, especially when used to gain freedom for women or for the oppressed. Here are some other works that deal with similar themes:

Like Water for Chocolate (1989), a novel by Laura Esquivel. Each chapter of this novel begins with a Mexican recipe, symbolizing the main character's need to express herself the only way she has so far been allowed to: through cooking.

Evita (1978), a musical by Andrew Lloyd Weber and Tim Rice. This Broadway musical chronicles the life and death of Eva Perón, the much loved second wife of Argentine president Juan Perón.

Silkwood (1983), a film directed by Mike Nichols. This Academy Award–nominated film details the life of Karen Silkwood, an activist who mysteriously dies while investigating—and potentially disclosing—wrongdoings at a nuclear power plant.

The Handmaid's Tale (1985), a novel by Margaret Atwood. Set in a futuristic state, this novel deals with the subjugation and silencing of women and their attempts to regain freedom.

---

2. What do Valenzuela's works have in common with fairy tales you may have read or heard growing up? Would you recommend reading some of her stories to children?

3. Choose two different female characters from Valenzuela's works and two different male characters. Write a list of adjectives describing each. Are there any similarities among characters or genders?

BIBLIOGRAPHY

Books

Feminist Writers. Detroit: St. James Press, 1996.

Gazarian Gautier, Marie-Lise. *Interviews with Latin American Writers*. Elmwood, N.J.: Dalkey Archive Press, 1989.

"Luisa Valenzuela (1938–)." *Contemporary Literary Criticism*. Edited by Jean C. Stine and Daniel G. Marowski. Vol. 31. Detroit: Gale Research, 1985, pp. 436–441.

Marting, Diane E., ed. *Spanish American Women Authors: A Bio-bibliographical Source Book*. Westport, Conn.: Greenwood Press, 1990.

Medeiros-Lichem, Maria-Teresa. *Reading the Feminine Voice in Latin American Women's Fiction: From Teresa de la Parra to Elena Poniatowska and Luisa Valenzuela*. New York: Peter Lang, 2001.

Periodicals

Americas (January–February 1995).

Belles Lettres (January 1996).

Knight Rider/Tribune News Service (August 10, 1994).

Publishers Weekly (March 9, 1992); (November 21, 1994); (December 20, 1999).

World Literature Today (Winter 1984; Autumn 1995; Spring 2002).

Web sites

Interview with Luisa Valenzuela. Retrieved February 28, 2008, from http://alcor.concordia.ca/~matrix/excerpt3.html. Last updated January 3, 2008.

Paul Valéry

BORN: *1871, Cette (now Sete), France*

DIED: *1945, Paris, France*

NATIONALITY: *French*

GENRE: *Fiction, poetry*

MAJOR WORKS:

The Young Fate (1917)

Album of Old Verse, 1890-1900 (1920)

The Graveyard by the Sea (1920)

Songs; or, Poems (1922)

Paul Valéry *Valéry, Paul, photograph. Hulton Archive / Getty Images.*

Overview

Paul Valéry is widely regarded as one of the most important French poets and intellectuals of the twentieth century. He is best known for such highly introspective poems as *The Young Fate* and "The Graveyard by the Sea." His poetry reveals his concern with human consciousness, artistic form, and the creative process. Having endorsed Edgar Allan Poe's dictum that a poet should create solely from his powers of concentration and intellect (rather than depending on inspiration), Valéry developed a theory maintaining that literary composition, like science and mathematics, is valuable only as a mirror to the workings of the creative mind.

Works in Biographical and Historical Context

From Silence to Defining Voice Paul Valéry was born in the French Mediterranean coastal town of Cette. When he was fourteen, his parents moved to the nearby city of Montpellier, where he attended secondary school. After his graduation, he entered law school at the University of Montpellier. During this time he met the poet and novelist Pierre Louys, who introduced him to the circle of writers associated with the symbolist poet Stéphane Mallarmé. Mallarmé became the single most influential figure in shaping Valéry's aesthetic sensibility. Unlike Mallarmé, however, Valéry's principal interest lay in the process of poetic composition rather than the poem itself, which he considered necessarily imperfect due to the limitations of language and the artist's creative powers. After his initial appearances in French literary journals during the early 1890s, Valéry entered what many critics refer to as his "silent period," almost twenty years in which he wrote virtually no poetry and published very little prose. From approximately 1898 to 1917, he lived a quiet, studious life, investigating mathematics and psychology with the intent of developing a scientifically based theory of creative activity. He recorded his insights in personal notebooks, the *Cahiers*, or *Notebooks*, which were eventually published in twenty-nine volumes. He emerged from his silent period with the publication of *The Young Fate*, which established his reputation as France's most outstanding living poet and one of Europe's premier artists and intellectuals. In 1925 he was elected to the French Academy. Although he served as professor of poetry at the Collège de France from 1937 until his death in 1945, his literary work during the last twenty years of his life consisted primarily of prose.

Principal Works Valéry's three principal works of poetry are *Album of Old Verse, 1890–1900*, *The Young Fate*, and *Songs; or, Poems*. Published in 1920, *Album* is composed primarily of his early poetry and shows a tendency toward imitation, particularly of the rigorous formalism of Mallarmé's work. Valéry himself considered *Album* "an unsatisfactory collection, studies that do not exist as a harmonious whole." *The Young Fate* is a poem of some five hundred lines that took nearly five years to complete. By depicting a sequence of psychological states and emotions, the poem portrays the sensibility of a young woman who represents the universal self. An extremely complex work, the poem combines the external natural world with the woman's inner self through a series of interrelated images, and its movement is sustained by the shifting states of the protagonist's awareness. The poems in *Songs; or, Poems* feature a wide variety of forms and reflect the dominant concerns of Valéry's thought. Such poems as "Aurore" and "Palme," for example, concern the earliest stages of poetic creation, suggesting that a poem forms deep within the poet's mind and body. "Ebauche d'un serpent" ("Silhouette of a Serpent"), noted for its changing tone and rhyme schemes, focuses on intellectual activity, contrasting the perfection of pure thought with the imperfections of earthly existence. "The Graveyard by the Sea," which depicts a progression of moods as the poet meditates on the sea and light of the Mediterranean coast, addresses the theme of death and the compromise the individual must make between pure thought and the phenomenal world.

Nonpoetic Works In 1931 and 1934 Valéry collaborated with the composer Arthur Honegger to produce two short opera-ballets, *Amphion* and *Sémiramis*, both of which touched upon themes from similarly named poems Valéry had written previously. A third and final collaboration with another composer, Germaine Taillefer, gave rise in 1938 to *Cantate du Narcisse* (published 1939), yet another treatment of the Narcissus theme that had figured in both the *Album* and *Songs; or, Poems*.

Valéry served as a faculty member of the Collège de France, but lost this position as well as others he held after the German occupation of parts of France during World War II. The interim French government known as the Vichy regime, which collaborated with the German government in order to prevent occupation of the rest of France, objected to Valéry's lack of support. Paul Valéry died of a heart ailment on July 20, 1945. Even on the occasion of his death, the two worlds might be said to have been reconciled. He was given a lavish state funeral in Paris attended by thousands of mourners, but he was then buried in the quiet cemetery by the sea in Cette.

Works in Literary Context

Scholars generally concur that the central theme of Valéry's most accomplished poems, *The Young Fate* and "The Graveyard by the Sea," is the mind's struggle between total detachment from the world and total involvement. Commentators also agree on the important role that Valéry's appreciation of music played in the development of his style; for instance, the concept of modulation, which is a method for gradually changing key, tone, or mood in a musical work, plays a prominent role in the progression of psychological states depicted in *The Young Fate* and "The Graveyard by the Sea." In

---

---

discussing his theories of poetic composition scholars have focused on his aversion to the idea of poetry as a spontaneous expression and his claim that poetry should not evolve from ideas but from rhythms and words.

The Influence of Mallarmé and Poe A brief comparison of Valéry's famous poem *The Young Fate* to Mallarmé's "Herodiade" concretely illustrates the nature of the older writer's influence on the young one. Both poems depict a young woman engaged in narcissistic

COMMON HUMAN EXPERIENCE

Valéry's poetry is often linked to the symbolist movement due to his efforts to describe thoughts outside of a formal structure. What exactly comprised a symbolist poem can best be seen in the following works:

> *The Flowers of Evil* (1857), a poetry collection by Charles Baudelaire. Often called the father of the symbolist movement, Baudelaire faced legal action after the publication of the decadently erotic poetry in this, his most well-known collection.
>
> "The Afternoon of a Faun" (1876), a poem by Stéphane Mallarmé. Perhaps the definitive symbolist poem, this dreamlike, lyrical work describes the sensual experiences of a faun after waking up from a morning's nap.
>
> *Wisdom* (1880), a poetry collection by Paul Verlaine. One of Verlaine's later works, the subject matter of the poems in this volume, which focus on maturation, reflect the tumultuous life events experienced by the poet and the bitter lessons he had learned by that point.
>
> *A Season in Hell* (1873), a prose work by Arthur Rimbaud. Taking the sensuality of symbolism to deliriously nightmarish extremes, the *enfant terrible* of French poetry looked ahead to such twentieth-century movements as Dadaism and surrealism.

introspection, both embody a severely formal, musical prosody, and both deliberately reject any identifiable "content," or theme. Valéry's poem is, in fact, more obscure and less musical than Mallarmé's simply because it is more purely metaphysical.

Valéry's passion for "scientific speculation," which is how he preferred to label his metaphysical writing and that of others, was the reason for his lifelong fascination with American writer Edgar Allan Poe. In *The Tell-Tale Heart: The Life and Works of Edgar Allan Poe*, Julian Symons has described Poe as divided between two obsessive tendencies in his writings, a visionary one and a logical one. Although Mallarmé and French poet Charles Baudelaire had celebrated the visionary qualities in Poe, Valéry most fully admired his powers of reason, as revealed through Poe's pseudoscientific meditation on the nature of human knowledge, "Eureka," and through his brilliant practical logician, Auguste Dupin, the detective of "The Murders in the Rue Morgue" and "The Purloined Letter."

Valéry's unyielding positivism (rationalism) is thus another characteristic setting him apart from other French writers. In an early letter to André Gide, Valéry wrote: "Poe, and I shouldn't talk about it for I promised myself I wouldn't, is the only writer—with no sins. Never was he mistaken—not led instinctively—but lucidly and successfully, he made a synthesis of all the vertigoes."

Music and Letters In the highly formal, mannered musicality of Valéry's verse, the influence of Mallarmé is unmistakable. Valéry's *Notebooks* record his conviction that the subject of a poem was far less important than its "program": "A sort of program would consist of a gathering of words (among which conjunctives are just as important as substantives) and of types of syntactical moments, and above all a table of verbal tonalities, etc." Mallarmé had said something very similar in "Music and Letters": "I assert, at my own aesthetic risk, this conclusion: ... that Music and Letters are the alternate face here widened towards the obscure; scintillating there, with certainty of a phenomenon, the only one, I have named it Idea."

For Mallarmé, as for his younger disciple, Idea was not a theme that could be formulated in a sentence or two; it was not a thought but rather the ongoing process of thought within the mind. Yet although Mallarmé believed that the end product of thought had to be a poem, Valéry disagreed. In his view, thought was always an end in itself; poetry was simply a more or less desirable byproduct to be pursued as long as it stimulated the mental processes. As he put it in his *Notebooks*, "In sum, Mallarmé and I, this in common—poem is problem. And this, very important." But Valéry also declared: "For him: the work. For me, the self.... Poetry has never been an objective for me, but an instrument, an exercise." Responding to seventeenth-century poet and critic Nicolas Boileau's time-honored dictum that "my verse, good or bad, always *says* something," Valéry asserted in the *Notebooks*, "There is the principle and the germ of an infinity of horrors."

Symbolism Clearly Valéry was heir to the symbolist tradition of Mallarmé. On the other hand, he is understood as having broken away from symbolism, as having rejected the cult of poetry for its own sake in favor of a cult of the mind. These views need not be contradictory. Critics have focused on Valéry's relation to symbolism, the theme and style of his works, and his theories of poetic composition. Many early commentators, emphasizing his relationship to Mallarmé and the apparent similarity in technique and effect between Valéry's poetry and that of the Symbolists, interpreted Valéry's works as a direct extension of symbolism. Later critics, however, noting Valéry's rejection of the symbolist notion of art for art's sake, have argued that Valéry was attempting to move beyond symbolism and look at poetry in a new way.

Works in Critical Context

Paul Valéry occupies a position in the history of French letters that is at once strategic and highly problematic. Critics have affixed to him various labels, all of them partially correct. He has been called the last French symbolist, the first post-symbolist, a masterful classicist, an advocate of logical positivism, and a cerebral narcissist.

Critic Francis Scarfe stated in his essay "The Art of Paul Valéry": "I hesitate to say what estimate of Valéry could be made on the basis of his essays and aphoristic jottings alone. It is possible to rescue a critic and a critical system even from them.... But there are so many Valérys to be rescued, and when that is done a heap of unclassifiable Valérys still remain. Outside his poems, dialogues and libretti he left—as Leonardo left—nothing but a clutter of magnificent fragments. Only his poetry stands unchangeable and complete. Any final judgment on Valéry must be a judgment of his art and via his art."

The Young Fate The publication of *The Young Fate* (known as *La Jeune Parque* in French) in 1917 essentially marked a rebirth of Valéry's creative life. Reviews of the work were largely positive, despite the work's perceived difficulty. J. Middleton Murry, in a review for the *Times Literary Supplement*, writes, "French poetry and French symbolism have a message which we should understand—that the achievement of poetry, in whatever kind, is due to the exact probity with which it is pursued. Because of this *La Jeune Parque* is beautiful like an enchanted house set in a haunted garden. We could not live in it; but we enter, explore its darkest rooms with gratitude, peer through its windows as though they were our own, and go on our way comforted that someone should have so honourably labored on the mansion of his dream." According to scholar Alastair W. Thomson, the author himself stated of the work, "Its obscurity brought me into the light; neither one nor the other was the result of my wishes."

Responses to Literature

1. Analyze how Valéry's style differs among his prose, poetry, and drama. How is it similar? What messages does he convey through each?

2. Both Valéry and Edgar Allan Poe, whom he admired, are known for their gothic themes and images. Do they use these images and metaphors for the same purposes? Read a work by each writer and form an argument that explains why the authors are drawn to gothic imagery.

3. Stéphane Mallarmé exerted a strong influence on Valéry. Choose one of Valéry's works (such as *The Young Fate*) and discuss how Mallarme's style is apparent.

4. Valéry employed musical methods, most notably modulation, in his poetry. What other concepts of musical theory can be applied to poetry? Try writing a poem that integrates modulation or another musical technique into its structure.

BIBLIOGRAPHY

Books

Bertholet, Denis. *Paul Valéry, 1871–1945*. Paris: Plon, 1995.

Gifford, Paul, ed, *Reading Paul Valéry: Universe in Mind*. Cambridge, U.K.: Cambridge University Press, 1998.

Guerlac, Suzanne. *Literary Polemics: Bataille, Sartre, Valéry, Breton*. Stanford, Calif.: Stanford University Press, 1997.

Kluback, William. *Paul Valéry: Illusions of Civilization*. New York: P. Lang, 1996.

———. *Paul Valéry: The Continuous Search for Reality*. New York: P. Lang, 1996.

———. *Paul Valéry: The Realms of the Analecta*. New York: P. Lang, 1998.

Nash, Suzanne. *Paul Valéry's Album de vers anciens: A Past Transfigured* Princeton, N.J.: Princeton University Press, 1983.

"Paul Valéry (1871–1945)." *Poetry Criticism*. Ed. Drew Kalasky. Vol. 9. Detroit: Gale Research, 1994, pp. 344–404.

Putnam, Walter C. *Paul Valéry Revisitied*. London: Twayne, 1995.

Taylor, Benjamin.*Into the Open: Reflections on Genius and Modernity* . New York: New York University Press, 1995.

W. D. Valgardson

BORN: *1939, Winnipeg, Manitoba, Canada*

NATIONALITY: *Canadian*

GENRE: *Fiction, poetry*

MAJOR WORKS:

Bloodflowers (1971)

God Is Not a Fish Inspector (1975)

Gentle Sinners (1980)

W. D. Valgardson   *Photograph by Jan Magnusson*

Overview

During the 1970s, William Dempsey Valgardson established himself as one of Canada's foremost writers of short fiction. His forceful presentation of lives shaped by isolation and the brutal effects of a northern environment, his careful control of narrative method, and his respect for his audience have won him both a wide readership and high praise from critics and reviewers.

Works in Biographical and Historical Context

Isolated Childhood Born in Winnipeg, Manitoba, Canada, in 1939, Valgardson was the son of Dempsey Alfred Herbert and Rachel Iris Valgardson. His father was a fisherman of Icelandic descent. Valgardson grew up in Gimli, a fishing village on Lake Winnipeg which was originally known as New Iceland as it was settled in 1875 and 1876 by Icelandic settlers trying to get away from volcanic eruptions. Gimli retains a strong ethnic connection with Iceland and a sense of a collective Icelandic literary heritage. Valgardson says of the Gimli area: "In a sense, [it] was the Appalachia of Canada. The choices people had were incredibly restricted.... There was tragedy, poverty, foreignness, displacement and an idealization of the past." The Icelandic settlers to Gimli brought books with them as well as a tradition of interest in writers and writing. Thus both the community and his ancestry strongly influenced Valgardson's writing, providing him not only with settings and themes but also with a vision of human life.

Valgardson received his bachelor of arts degree from the University of Manitoba in 1960. He spent the next few years teaching English and art at various rural schools in Manitoba and earned a B.Ed. from the University of Manitoba in 1966. Valgardson then attended the Iowa Writer's Workshop at the University of Iowa, receiving a master of fine arts degree in 1969. In the early 1970s, Valgardson taught English at Cottey College in Missouri, where he was head of the department from 1971 to 1974. His writing career began in this period, but as would become a hallmark of his career, he worked slowly and always had a limited output. While teaching there, he began establishing his reputation as a short-story writer at home in Canada.

Short-Story Success After finding success in a number of writing contests, Valgardson published *Bloodflowers* (1971), a collection of ten short stories. The title story—which was originally published in a 1971 issue of *Tamarack Review* and won the President's Medal from the University of Western Ontario for best short story in a Canadian publication—depicts a young teacher from mainland Canada who comes to teach on an island off the coast of Newfoundland. Once there, he slowly begins to suspect that he is to be made the sacrificial victim in a ritual spring sacrifice. The sinister tone of this story is repeated in the others, which are pessimistic portrayals

of life in northern Manitoba; the moments of optimism that exist are brief and qualified.

While working on his second collection of stories, in 1974 Valgardson joined the faculty of the University of Victoria in British Columbia as a creative writing teacher. The following year, his second collection of short stories, *God Is Not a Fish Inspector* (1975), was published. Critics praised the book for its coherence and attention to the hardships of rural life. Following this volume, Valgardson published a collection of poetry that he had written in the late 1960s and early 1970s, *In The Gutting Shed* (1976). The collection received mixed reviews but nonetheless went into a second edition during its first year, a rarity in Canadian poetry. Returning to short stories, he published his third collection, *Red Dust*, in 1978. In this book, Valgardson continued to examine the poverty and violence that exists in portions of rural Canada, while showing newfound maturity and confidence as a writer. In "Red Dust," for instance, a man permits his niece to be raped in exchange for a hunting dog.

Continued Literary Success Valgardson's first novel, *Gentle Sinners*, was published in 1980 and won the *Books in Canada* award as the best first novel of the year. Somewhat different from his other work, *Gentle Sinners* suggested a limited form of redemption and happiness in its account of a boy who flees his authoritarian parents and finds a sense of community and ethnic identity with his uncle Sigfus. Two years after his first novel came out, Valgardson began his first stint as chair of the University of Victoria's Creative Writing Department. He held the post from 1982 to 1987. Also during this time, he served as the president of the Canadian Authors Association, from 1985 to 1986.

After publishing a second collection of poetry—*The Carpenter of Dreams* (1986)—Valgardson returned to short fiction with the collection *What Can't Be Changed Shouldn't Be Mourned* (1990) and the novel *The Girl with the Botticelli Face* (1992). Beginning in the mid-1990s, Valgardson began writing books for children. Valgardson revisits the setting of his early life in *Thor* (1994), a children's book that culminates in the unlikely heroism of a young boy named Thor. While visiting his grandparents in a small fishing village, Thor reluctantly abandons his favorite television programs to help his grandfather on Lake Winnipeg, where he discovers the selflessness and courage to save a drowning man. Though decidedly redemptive, Valgardson's evocative depiction of traditional Icelandic Canadian culture and engaging dialogue are consistent with his many other works. Valgardson published a number of other books for children, including the fairy tale–inspired *Sarah and the People of Sand River* (1995), the short-story collections *Garbage Creek, and Other Stories* (1997) and *The Divorced Kids Club, and Other Stories* (1999), and the young-adult novel *Frances* (2000). He continued to emphasize rural settings at a time when Canada's rural economy—

agriculture, fishing, and natural resources—were continuing to take a back seat to mechanization and an urban-based economy.

Valgardson remained with the faculty at the University of Victoria until 2004. Before his retirement, he also served his second stint as the chair of the Creative Writing Department, from 1999 until 2004. Valgardson continued to make his home in Victoria in retirement, though it was unclear if he could continue to write.

Works in Literary Context

As a writer, Valgardson found inspiration in his Icelandic ancestry as well as the rural Canadian landscapes where he grew up and taught. Thus, many of his books are set in harsh northern environments. In addition to being influenced by Icelandic storytelling traditions, Valgardson is often compared with Russian writers, and he admitted that Anton Chekhov was an influence on his work. While others have detected the impact of Thomas Hardy and William Faulkner on his writing, Valgardson also found inspiration in the stories of Ernest Hemingway and Somerset Maugham, the novels of Jane Austen, and the poetry of Al Purdy, James Dickey, Sylvia Plath, Anne Sexton, and Wallace Stevens. The author believes that his strong Lutheran, conservative background gave rise to an authoritative tone of voice in his writings.

Thematic Constancy Critics have noted that the themes of tragedy and isolation are typical of many of Valgardson's works, especially in books targeted at adults. While *Gentle Sinners* features some guarded optimism, the author's preferred themes dominate, and he also admitted that as a writer, theme is more important than plot to him. Even most of the poetry found in *In the Gutting Shed* is parallel, in setting and theme, to Valgardson's fiction. Many of his books for children focus on his dominant theme in a slightly different way. Books like *The Divorced Kids Club, and Other Stories* focus on the theme of the outsider.

When *Red Dust* was published, some reviewers of the book took Valgardson to task for not striking out in new directions stylistically and for not attempting to deal with new and different themes. Yet, as Margaret Atwood states in her discussion of this book for *Essays on Canadian Writing*, the author has deliberately chosen to develop his characteristic voice: "If you look at what most writers actually do, it resembles a theme with variations more than it does the popular motion of growth. Writers' universes may become more elaborate, but they do not necessarily become essentially different. Popular culture, based on the marketing of novelties, teaches us that change is desirable in and for itself. Valgardson is its antithesis."

Influence As an author, Valgardson stated once that his goal was to write stories that influence people and make them think. His short stories are so highly regarded

LITERARY AND HISTORICAL CONTEMPORARIES

Valgardson's famous contemporaries include:

Farley Mowat (1921–): Conservationist and author, Mowat was already well known in his native Canada when he shot to international fame with his documentary film about his work with wolf packs titled *Never Cry Wolf* (1983).

Queen Elizabeth II (1926–): Queen of the United Kingdom and other Commonwealth realms (including Canada, Australia, and New Zealand), Elizabeth is one of Britain's longest-reigning monarchs. Despite widespread personal support, her reign has seen an increasing dissolution of the respect and privacy normally afforded the royal family.

Richard Nixon (1913–1994): An American politician, Nixon made a name for himself as a staunch anti-Communist senator and vice president to Dwight Eisenhower. He was narrowly elected president in 1968, then reelected to a second term amidst a deep cultural war over America's involvement in Vietnam. Shortly after his reelection, stories began to surface of criminal activities during his campaign, eventually turning into the Watergate scandal. Rather than face certain impeachment, Nixon resigned in 1974.

Russell Means (1939–): A Lakota Sioux Indian, Means is one of the most recognizable activists for Native American rights. He rose to prominence as a leader of the American Indian Movement (AIM) and that group's nineteen-month occupation of Alcatraz Island in San Francisco Bay in 1969.

Leonid Brezhnev (1906–1982): Political leader of the Soviet Union from 1964 to 1982, Brezhnev reversed many of the domestic political reforms of his predecessor, Nikita Khrushchev, and pursued the policy of "détente" with U.S. presidents Nixon and Ford, seeking to end the Cold War arms race.

that he is regarded as a master of the form in Canada, an inspiration to others who write such stories in both his native country as well as in other English-speaking countries. Many of the stories have been translated into other languages, including Icelandic, Russian, Ukrainian, Danish, Dutch, Spanish, German, and French, ensuring Valgardson's influence abroad as well.

Works in Critical Context

Critical opinion of Valgardson has generally been positive, with some reviewers calling his work "prairie gothic" because of its unflinching depiction of the brutal aspects of rural life. Critics praise his works for their

COMMON HUMAN EXPERIENCE

Valgardson's repeated meditations on tragedy and isolation have strongly resonant analogs in some of the world's all-time literary classics, including:.

Frankenstein (1818), a novel by Mary Shelley. The Monster of Shelly's novel is not the semi-intelligent brute of film fame, but a thinking, rational creature, only too bitterly aware of his outcast status and consumed with both love and hatred for his creator.

Richard III (1591), a play by William Shakespeare. Essentially a work of propaganda, Shakespeare's take on the English monarch casts him as one of the all-time great villainous antiheroes—bitter, alone, and doomed.

Ethan Frome (1911), a novel by Edith Wharton. The story of a tragic love triangle, partly based on Wharton's own life, that ends with a cruel twist of fate for the title character and his would-be mistress.

craftsmanship, dedication, deep understanding of human motivation, and attention to detail in writing about such areas. While some critics, such as Sam Solecki, believe that Valgardson overwrites, relies too extensively on similes, and overrelies on a monotone style, they also praise his ability to movingly write about ordinary lives with respect.

God Is Not a Fish Inspector   Critics generally praised his second collection of short stories, *God Is Not a Fish Inspector*. Especially lauded was the collection's coherence and careful consideration of the hardships of life in a rural environment. Reviewing the collection, Adrian Vale of the *Irish Times* comments that Valgardson's "Manitoba countryside has close affinities with Egdon Heath. There is death and suicide and isolation. These elementals, however, are not dragged in to inflate a final paragraph; they come as hammer-blows, falling inevitably and with complete artistic rightness. Mr. Valgardson is an authoritative writer; he leaves the reader with no inclination to gainsay him or the truth of the events he describes."

Sarah and the People of Sand River   Valgardson's books for children are as highly regarded as his short-story collections targeted at adults. Critics regarded the novel he wrote for young readers, *Sarah and the People of Sand River*, as a tightly woven fairy tale with depth and meaning. Anne Louise Mahoney, writing for *Quill & Quire*, called the book a "haunting tale, skillfully written, and with a powerful ending." *Booklist*'s Carolyn Phelan believed that Valgardson's "taut narrative . . . transcends time." *Publishers Weekly* found the book poetic, writing

that "Wallace's . . . delicate, somber watercolors underscore the plaintive tone. Working in a subdued, pale palette, he diffuses the harshness of the heroine's experiences in a rush of gentle light."

Responses to Literature

1. Use the following questions as a basis for a small group discussion. Provide a definition, in your own words, for what you think the term "prairie gothic" means. Why do you think some critics have labeled Valgardson's work as such?

2. Valgardson's Icelandic heritage comes through in several of his stories. In an essay, examine the following questions: What role does his ancestral culture play in his narratives? How does it interact with Canadian culture?

3. Write a paper that addresses the following concerns: What major themes does Valgardson return to in his work? How effectively does he address these themes, in your opinion?

4. Valgardson hails from one of the "prairie provinces" of Canada. In a paper, compare his work with that of other Canadian writers from the central part of the country—Manitoba, Alberta, and Saskatchewan—and discuss common themes in the authors' works.

BIBLIOGRAPHY

Periodicals

Mahoney, Anne Louise. Review of *Sarah and the People of Sand River*. *Quill & Quire*, September 1994: 43.

Phelan, Carolyn. Review of *Sarah and the People of Sand River*. *Booklist*, November 1, 1996: 496.

Review of *Sarah and the People of Sand River*. *Publishers Weekly* 243, no. 39 (September 23, 1996): 76.

Vale, Adrian. Review of *God Is Not a Fish Inspector*. *Irish Times*, July 10, 1976.

▨ César Vallejo

BORN: *1892, Santiago de Chucho, Peru*

DIED: *1938, Paris, France*

NATIONALITY: *Peruvian*

GENRE: *Drama, fiction, poetry*

MAJOR WORKS:

The Black Messengers (1919)

Trilce (1922)

Spain, Take Away This Chalice (1937)

Poemas humanos (1939)

Overview

Peruvian author César Vallejo is known primarily for the highly original—almost postmodern—use of language in his poetry. His devastating vision of the world, coupled

César Vallejo   *Writer Pictures / drr.net*

with a hoped-for future utopia grounded in a Communist idealism, mark his writings as poignantly sensitive to the common man's struggles and ambitions. Deeply rooted in his mixed European and Peruvian Indian heritage, his poetry expresses universal themes related to the human condition. His literary production included essays, novels, short stories, plays, and a screenplay, but his reputation rests primarily on his poetry, much of which appeared posthumously.

Works in Biographical and Historical Context

Rural vs. City Life   Vallejo was born in Santiago de Chuco, a small village in the northern Andes Mountains of Peru in 1892. Raised Catholic and encouraged to become a priest, he discovered that he could not adhere to the requirement of celibacy. Though Vallejo's relationships with women were often complicated or stormy, he remained close and secure with his family. For a time, he was a clerk in his father's notary office. His mother's friendship, in particular, was a sustaining force in his life until her death in 1918. The comfort of this rural life set

for Vallejo a standard against which all later experiences seemed arduous and painful.

Early poems in his first collection, *The Black Messengers* (1919), relate Vallejo's bewilderment when struck with the harshness of city life in Trujillo and Lima, where he studied medicine, literature, and law. Introduced to the ideas of Marx, Darwin, and rationalist philosophers, Vallejo felt that the faith in which he was raised was no longer viable. Together with other intellectuals, he became actively interested in his pre-Columbian heritage and was anguished to learn of the suffering of aboriginals in his country.

Poems in *The Black Messengers*, like most Latin American poetry of the time, also follow the conventions of the *modernista* movement. The *modernistas* highlighted the melodic quality of language. Breaking a taboo, Vallejo added erotic lyrics to the descriptions of beautiful landscapes common to this style.

Personal Distress   Though Vallejo thrived in his studies in the city, his personal life was filled with turmoil. When his lover broke off their relationship due to pressure from her parents, Vallejo attempted suicide. Unable to replace the caring family he had lost, Vallejo felt alienated in the city. Alienation and the apparent senselessness of his suffering became his recurrent themes.

While Vallejo was writing and publishing this poetry, Peru was undergoing radical changes itself. While Peru had a constitutional democratic government and a stable economy, a military coup in 1919 changed the course of the country. Businessman Augusto Leguía y Salcedo, who had been the constitutionally elected president from 1908 to 1912, took power and began modernizing Peru along capitalistic lines. In opposition to Leguía's dictatorship Peruvian intellectual Victor Raúl Haya de la Torre founded the leftist political party the American Popular Revolutionary Alliance.

Political Persecution   After a number of years in Trujillo and Lima, Vallejo returned to his birthplace where, in 1920, he became involved in a political insurrection during which the town's general store was burned down. He was accused of instigating the conflict and was jailed for three months. The isolation and savagery of jail conditions, combined with the after effects of his mother's death, affected his mental health deeply. Accordingly, Vallejo's poems written in prison (collected in *Trilce*, 1922) are markedly different from the idyllic poems of *The Black Messengers*.

Marxism and Life Abroad   In the 1920s and 1930s, Vallejo became more engaged in politics. His three visits to the Soviet Union—the first in 1928—aided in the formulation of his political views, and he subsequently produced political tracts including the essay collected in *Rusia en 1931: Reflexiones al pie del Kremlin* (1931), first published in Spain and not printed in Peru until almost thirty years later. He also wrote the novel *Tungsten*

LITERARY AND HISTORICAL CONTEMPORARIES

Vallejo's famous contemporaries include:

Manuel González Prada (1844–1918): Director of the National Library of Peru, Prada was highly esteemed by his countrymen for his role in encouraging the development of the Peruvian intelligentsia and the Peruvian incarnation of the *modernismo*, or modernist movement.

Venustiano Carranza (1859–1920): One of the leaders of the Mexican Revolution, Carranza went on to become president of Mexico and presided over the creation of that country's current constitution. His reforms were considered too severe by some, too moderate by others, and he was assassinated while fleeing Mexico City after a previous, unsuccessful assassination attempt.

Benito Mussolini (1883–1945): A key figure in the formation of Fascism, a government philosophy promoting nationalism, expansionism, and anti-Communism. Mussolini (styled "Il Duce," or "the leader") was elected prime minister in 1922 and effectively ruled Italy until 1943. Although he was popular in the early years of his rule for his reforms, his decision to ally with Nazi Germany was seen by many Italians as dooming their country to the destruction and ruin of World War II.

Mustafa Kemal Atatürk (1881–1938): At the end of World War I and the dissolution of the Ottoman Empire, Atatürk was the founder and first president of the Republic of Turkey. Atatürk's policies and reforms led Turkey in a modern, secular, Westernized direction.

Albert Einstein (1879–1955): The German-born physicist became world famous for his revolutionary theories, which represented the most dramatic shift in scientific thought since Newton.

(1931), which condemns an American company for exploiting its Peruvian workers to get the element it needs to make weapons. (U.S. bankers had backed the dictatorship of Leguía, which lasted until 1930 when he was overthrown by Luis M. Sánchez-Cerro. Sánchez-Cerro was officially elected president in 1931, but assassinated in April 1933.)

Political statements emerged in his other works as well, but they did not dominate. Vallejo was an ambivalent Marxist. Scholar James Higgins finds evidence in *Poemas humanos* (1939) that Vallejo sometimes admired the single-mindedness of those who could submit themselves to "the cause," but again found it impossible to subject himself without question to Marxist or Communist ideals. He moved to Spain during its civil-war years to work as a journalist and lend support to his friends in defense of the Spanish republic. (Lasting from 1936 to 1939, the Spanish Civil War pitted fascist military forces, led by nationalist general Francisco Franco, against the supporters of the Second Spanish Republic. Franco won and controlled the country until his death in 1975.) At the same time, Vallejo admired the brotherhood achieved among the activists who gave their lives to serve what they believed was the improvement of life for the poor.

Having moved to Europe in 1923, Vallejo died in Paris in 1938 at the age of forty-six. After his death, his widow Georgette de Vallejo selected poems for publication in his last major poetry collection, *Poemas humanos* (1939).

Works in Literary Context

Vallejo's chief contribution to poetry is his innovative use of language to communicate intense, authentic emotion and to convey both personal and existential anguish. His verse is marked by a strong sense of compassion and filled with Christian imagery that in his later works is fused with Marxist ideology. In addition to being influenced by his Catholic/Christian background and his interest in Marxism and Communism, Vallejo was also inspired by *modernista* poets, especially Leopoldo Lugones and Julio Herrara y Reissig.

"Wrenched Syntax" *Trilce* is more difficult, more intense, and more original than Vallejo's first volume of poetry. Pared of all ornamental language, these poems convey the poet's personal urgency as he cries out against the apparent meaninglessness of his suffering. *Trilce* introduces the "wrenched syntax" that allows Vallejo to get beyond the constraints of linguistic conventions to a language that is true to his experience. Writing in *A History of Peruvian Literature*, Higgins catalogues the elements of Vallejo's diction:

> Vallejo confounds the reader's expectations by his daring exploitation of the line pause, which often leaves articles, conjunctions and even particles of words dangling at the end of a line, by his frequent resort to harsh sounds to break the rhythm, by employing alliterations so awkward as to be tongue-twisters. He distorts syntactic structures, changes the grammatical function of words, plays with spelling. His poetic vocabulary is frequently unfamiliar and 'unliterary,' he creates new words of his own, he often conflates two words into one, he tampers with clichés to give them new meaning, he plays on the multiple meaning of words and on the similarity of sound between words. He repeatedly makes use of oxymoron and paradox and, above all, catachresis, defamiliarising objects by attributing to them qualities not normally associated with them.

Vallejo's wrenched syntax is not a mere literary performance. It is the means necessary "to discover the man that has been hitherto hidden behind its decorative facades. The discovery is not a pleasant one, and the noise in the poems makes it consequently aggressive and not beautiful," D. P. Gallagher observes in *Modern Latin American Literature*. Out of Vallejo's self-discovery comes an "unprecedented, raw language" that declares Vallejo's humanness despite his confinement to make a statement "about the human problems of which Vallejo is a microcosm," Gallagher adds. *New York Review of Books* contributor Michael Wood explains, "With Vallejo [syntax] is an instrument—the only possible instrument, it seems—for the confrontation of complexity, of the self caught up in the world and the world mirrored in the self. It is an answer, let us say, to the simultaneous need for a poetry that would put heart into an agonizing Spain and for a poetry that will not take wishes for truths."

Influence Vallejo's poetry has influenced generations of Peruvian and other Spanish American poets to undertake further experiments with poetic language and technique.

Works in Critical Context

Although he published relatively little during his lifetime and received scant critical acclaim, Vallejo has come to be recognized as one of the most important and complex poets of the Spanish language, one of the foremost poets of Spanish America, and the greatest Peruvian poet of all time. "Vallejo created a wrenching Spanish poetic language that radically altered the shape of modernist imagery and the nature of the language's rhythms. No facile trend setter, Vallejo forged a new discourse in order to express his own visceral compassion for human suffering," Edith Grossman writes in the *Los Angeles Times Book Review*. "A constant feature of his poetry is a compassionate awareness of and a guilt-ridden sense of responsibility for the suffering of others," observes Higgins in *The Poet in Peru: Alienation and the Quest for a Super-Reality*.

In *Modern Latin American Literature*, D. P. Gallagher suggests that Vallejo was "perhaps the first Latin American writer to have realized that it is precisely in the discovery of a language where literature must find itself in a continent where for centuries the written word was notorious more for what it concealed than for what it revealed, where 'beautiful' writing, sheer sonorous wordiness was a mere holding operation against the fact that you did not dare really say anything at all."

Poemas humanos After its publication in 1939, *Poemas humanos* was well-regarded by critics over the next decades. In 1958, Xavier Abril saw a link between Vallejo's poems and the artistry of film comedian Charlie Chaplin. Abril writes in *Odyssey Review*, "Many of the pages of *Human Poems* have an indefinable Chaplinesque tint, especially those that are charged with the feeling of desolate misfortune or stark abandonment, in whish misery is like an X-ray of hunger and horror." M. L. Rosenthal and Clayton Eshleman see the poems in a different light. In the *New York Times Book Review*, Rosenthal

> ## COMMON HUMAN EXPERIENCE
>
> The first half of the twentieth century was an active time for poets with leftist or Communist sympathies. Like Vallejo, many poets were galvanized toward the left by the events of the Spanish Civil War. Poems that exhibit political views similar to those of Vallejo include:
>
> *Spain in My Heart* (1937), a poetry collection by Pablo Neruda. Already an ardent Communist, Chilean poet Neruda wrote this collection of poetry after the death of Federico García Lorca at the hands of the Fascist nationalists.
>
> *Between the Stone and the Flower* (1941), an epic poem by Octavio Paz. Although he would later denounce totalitarian Communism, Paz was an early Marxist sympathizer. This epic poem, his first of such length, concerns the proletarian struggles of Mexican peasants being exploited by greedy landlords.
>
> *Songs and Ballads of Absence* (1938–1942), a poetry collection by Miguel Hernández. A fervent supporter of the leftist republican forces in the Spanish Civil War, Hernández was imprisoned after the nationalist victory. He wrote this collection of poems, reflecting on the tragedy of civil war and his own personal loss, before his death from tuberculosis.

praises the poems, writing, "These are poems of cruel suffering, physical and mental, which yet have a kind of joy of realization in their singular music, harshness, humor and pain." Writing about the collection in *Tri-Quarterly*, Eshleman notes, "All solutions as such fade, in *Poemas Humanos*, before all-powerful death; it is as if man never dies but lives eternally at the edge of death; Vallejo is the great poet of the End."

Responses to Literature

1. In a paper, describe the body of poetry that was published after Vallejo's death. How does it compare with the poetry published before he died? How are the poems introduced or edited, and what does this say about Vallejo's posthumous reputation?

2. In a group, discuss these questions: How does Vallejo utilize emotions in *The Black Messengers*? What specific images or literary devices does he use to convey emotion? Why, do you think, did he make the artistic choices he did?

3. In an essay, discuss Vallejo's political beliefs as expressed in *Spain, Take Away This Chalice*. Can you compare these views with the views of other poets who appear in the "Common Human Experience" sidebar?

4. Vallejo's poetry has been categorized as both modernist and existentialist. What elements of modernism can you find in his work? How does his work compare with other existentialist poets of his day? Create a presentation with your conclusions

5. In an essay, address these questions: Why did Vallejo choose to leave Peru? How did his time abroad influence and change his poetry?

BIBLIOGRAPHY

Books

Adamson, Joseph. *Wounded Fiction: Modern Poetry And Deconstruction.* New York: Garland, 1988.

Niebylski, Dianna C. *The Poem on the Edge of the Word: The Limits of Language and the Uses of Silence in the Poetry of Mallarmé, Rilke, and Vallejo.* New York: Peter Lang, 1993.

Periodicals

Abril, Xavier. "Chaplin and Vallejo." *Odyssey Review* 2, no. 1 (March 1962): 172–90.

Eschleman, Clayton. "Translating César Vallejo: An Evolution." *TriQuarterly* 13/14 (Fall/Winter 1968/1969): 55–82.

Rosenthal, M. L. "Poems of Singular Music, Harshness, Humor and Pain." *New York Times Book Review,* March 23, 1969, 8.

◈ Mario Vargas Llosa

BORN: *1936, Arequipa, Peru*

NATIONALITY: *Peruvian*

GENRE: *Fiction, nonfiction*

MAJOR WORKS:

The Time of the Hero (1963)

The Green House (1966)

Conversation in the Cathedral (1969)

Aunt Julia and the Scriptwriter (1977)

The War of the End of the World (1981)

Overview

Few writers from South America have achieved the literary status and international recognition of Mario Vargas Llosa. A major figure in contemporary literature, Vargas Llosa is respected for his insightful examination of social and cultural themes and for the structural craftsmanship of his work. Vargas Llosa is best known for his novels, in which he combines realism with experimentation to reveal the complexities of human life and society. Never afraid of intellectual controversy, he has always been outspoken on Latin American cultural and political issues. He ran for the presidency of Peru in 1990, narrowly losing to Alberto Fujimori. In spite of his involvement

Mario Vargas Llosa *Vargas Llosa, (Jorge) Mario (Pedro), photograph. AP Images.*

in politics, literature remained his first passion, and it is in the art of storytelling that his talent has shone the most.

Works in Biographical and Historical Context

Brutal Discipline Shaped into Fiction Jorge Mario Pedro Vargas Llosa was born into a middle-class family on March 28, 1936, in Arequipa, Peru's second largest city. For the first ten years of his life he lived in Cochabamba, Bolivia, with his mother and grandparents. He returned to Peru in 1946 when his parents, who had divorced shortly before his birth, were reunited. Ernesto Vargas, disdainful of what he perceived as his son's unmanly personality, shipped the teenager off to the Leoncio Prado military academy. This experience marked the future writer's life; it was his first encounter with the institutional violence that affected the various social groups in Peru's ethnically diverse society. Vargas Llosa spent two years at the Leoncio Prado, then returned to his mother's suburban home to finish high school. Vargas Llosa worked for a local newspaper during that time and wrote a play, which was staged but never published.

In 1953, Vargas Llosa studied literature and law at the University of San Marcos in Lima. During these years, Peru was governed by the military dictator General Manuel Odría, who had overthrown the nation's democratic government in 1948. San Marcos was a stronghold for clandestine opposition to Odría's dictatorship. This proved crucial in Vargas Llosa's intellectual formation as he joined a student cell of the Peruvian Communist Party.

In 1959, Vargas Llosa left Peru to pursue doctoral studies at the Universidad Complutense of Madrid, Spain. His collection of short stories, *Los jefes* (*The Cubs and Other Stories*) (1959) was awarded the Leopoldo Alas Prize in Spain and published that year in Barcelona. Vargas Llosa later moved to Paris, where he worked as a journalist, taught Spanish, and continued to write. He became acquainted with several Latin American writers also living in Paris, including Julio Cortázar from Argentina and Carlos Fuentes from Mexico. In the 1960s, all three would be leaders of a literary "boom" that brought Latin American literature to international attention.

Vargas Llosa's painful experiences at Leoncio Prado were the basis for his first novel, *The Time of the Hero* (the title changed from the Spanish-language version *La ciudad y los perros*, meaning "the city and the dogs") (1963). The work gained instant notoriety when Peruvian military leaders condemned it and publicly burned one thousand copies.

Experiments in Social Narrative *The Green House* (*La Casa Verde*) (1966), Vargas Llosa's next novel, also won wide acclaim and established him as an important young writer. He followed up his success with *Conversation in the Cathedral* (*Conversacion en la catedral*) (1969), a monumental narrative exploring the moral depravity of Peruvian life under dictator Manuel Odría. In 1973, Vargas Llosa published his first satirical novel, *Captain Pantoja and the Special Service* (*Pantaleon y las visitadoras*). With biting wit, the novel demonstrates Vargas Llosa's disdain for military bureaucracy.

Fact and Fiction Four years later, Vargas Llosa published his autobiographical and most internationally popular novel, *Aunt Julia and the Scriptwriter* (*La tia Julia y el escribidor*) (1977). While this book is less complicated structurally than his earlier novels, Vargas Llosa's manipulation of point of view is of primary importance. Half the chapters in the book represent a fictionalized version of the author's short first marriage to his Aunt Julia. The alternate chapters are soap opera scripts composed by a radio scriptwriter, Pedro Camacho, whose stories of infanticide, incest, prostitution, religious fanaticism, and genocide keep his audience glued to the radio. Vargas Llosa stretches the limits of fact and fiction by using not only the historical real names of his main characters, but many historical events and characters from Peruvian public life as well.

Vargas Llosa produced an epic historical novel based on a true story, *The War of the End of the World* (*La guerra del fin del mundo*), in 1981. The plot concerns a rebellion in the Brazilian backlands late in the nineteenth century, reflecting

the plight of the poor throughout Latin American history. It received international acclaim and is considered by some to be Vargas Llosa's masterpiece.

Its huge success was only the beginning of an intense decade for Vargas Llosa, both as a writer and an influential public figure in Peru. In the 1980s he published a major anthology of his journalistic essays, *Against All Odds* (*Contra viento y marea*) (1983–1990). Its three volumes portray the shift in his political perspective, from his early admiration for socialism in the 1960s to his defense of free-market capitalism in the 1980s. This shift to a conservative position often placed him at the center of controversy both in Peru and abroad. After twelve years of progressive military rule, civilian rule was restored in 1980. Vargas Llosa maintained such close political ties to President Fernando Belaunde Terry that he was offered the post of prime minister, which he did not accept.

The Storyteller and the Candidate Vargas Llosa's political stands are present in his next novel, *The Real Life of Alejandro Mayta* (*Historia de Mayta*) (1985). Using real and imagined events, it tells the story of Alejandro Mayta, a Marxist revolutionary who organized a failed rebellion against the Peruvian government in the late 1950s and quickly faded from public view. At the same time, a contemporary novelist in the 1980s (like Vargas Llosa himself) is trying to track down information about the legendary Mayta, sometimes embellishing factual material with fiction to enhance the significance of his story. The novel is a politically charged inquiry into the relationship between representation and reality, fact and depiction.

In his 1987 work *The Storyteller* (*El hablador*), Vargas Llosa once again explores stories told from multiple points of view. *The Storyteller* concerns a Native American tribe, the Machiguengas, and in particular the community's storyteller, Saul Zuratas. The book energetically questions the multifaceted identity of Peruvian society, in which primitive and modern lifestyles are forced to coexist in conflict and contradiction. Peru has the largest Native American population in the western hemisphere: about half its population

COMMON HUMAN EXPERIENCE

Mario Vargas Llosa strove to write the "total novel," a sweeping view of society within the pages of a single work. Here are some other notable works that fit that definition:

The Sound and the Fury (1929), a novel by William Faulkner. The lives of the Compson family, expressed in stream-of-consciousness narrative, represent in microcosm the declining culture of the American South.

Madame Bovary (1857), a novel by Gustave Flaubert. In this novel that is credited as a founding text of literary realism, Flaubert uses the failing marriage of Emma and Charles Bovary to depict French bourgeois culture of the period.

Sister Carrie (1900), a novel by Theodore Dreiser. In this panorama of America at the turn of the century, a young country girl ascends in social class as mistress to a bar manager, finally becoming a well-known stage actress.

The Rules of the Game (1939), a film written and directed by Jean Renoir. This comedy of manners concerns a group of French aristocrats and the servants they employ.

of 28 million is Native American. More than 15 percent of Peruvians speak Quechua, an indigenous Peruvian language, and Native American storytelling traditions have had a marked effect on modern Peruvian literature.

Vargas Llosa believes that a Latin American writer is obligated to speak out on political matters. This belief led Vargas Llosa in 1987 to speak out against the reformist tendencies of Peruvian President Alan García. His protest quickly led to a mass movement against nationalization of Peru's banking industry, and the government was forced to back down. Vargas Llosa's supporters went on to create Fredemo, a conservative political party calling for democracy, a free market, and individual liberty. The novelist ran for the presidency of Peru in 1990 and, despite being heavily favored, lost in a second-round vote to the then unknown Alberto Fujimori.

Later Career Shortly before campaigning for the presidency, Mario Vargas Llosa published an erotic novel, *In Praise of the Stepmother* (*Elogio de la madrastra*; 1988), and followed it up with a work of literary criticism, *Lies That Tell the Truth* (or *A Writer's Reality*, 1991). He offers a critical look into his campaign in his 1993 memoir, *A Fish in the Water* (*El pez en el agua: Memorias*).

Since his political defeat, Vargas Llosa has lived in Europe and concentrated on his first love, literature. His novel *Death in the Andes* (*Lituma en los Andes*; 1993) was awarded Spain's prestigious Planeta Prize. His 1997

novel *The Notebooks of Don Rigoberto* (*Los cuadernos de don Rigoberto*) marked the first time any publisher had released a title in all Spanish-language markets on the same day. His most recent works of fiction are *The Way to Paradise* (*El paraíso en la otra esquina*; 2003) and *The Bad Girl* (*Travesuras de la niña mala*; 2006).

Works in Literary Context

As a teenager in the coastal town of Piura, Mario Vargas Llosa developed his affinity for literature, greatly admiring the works of a variety of authors, including Alexander Dumas and Fyodor Dostoyevsky. At the university, he was attracted by the rich narrative technique in the novels of William Faulkner, whose work he admired greatly.

The Total Novel Vargas Llosa's discovery of Faulkner was crucial in the experimental nature of many of his novels and his concept of the "total novel," an attempt to depict through writing as many facets of reality as possible. Another important source for Vargas Llosa's theory of the total novel is Gustave Flaubert, author of *Madame Bovary* (1857). For Vargas Llosa, Flaubert's writing is key to understanding realism and the modern novel. If the novel is a genre that captures all aspects of reality, the novelist should strive to represent all aspects of life with equal passion and persuasion, becoming the invisible creator of a fictional world, a god that holds the ultimate power over a given reality. In a later work of literary criticism, Vargas Llosa holds up *One Hundred Years of Solitude* (1967), by his contemporary Gabriel García Márquez, as a prime example of the total novel.

Jean-Paul Sartre and Political Prose At the same time, Vargas Llosa was also attracted to the way French author and philosopher Jean-Paul Sartre used literature as a tool to pursue a life of political commitment. Some of Vargas Llosa's early works, such as *The Time of the Hero*, are clearly inspired by Sartre's notion that the writer's role in any given society is to question the established social order relentlessly.

After the Boom Vargas Llosa's first two novels, with their innovations in narrative technique, established him as a major influence in Latin American literature, along with his fellow representatives of the "boom" generation. Vargas Llosa has continued to redefine the role of the writer in Latin American society, and, in that fashion, his work has remained contemporary. For example, *Aunt Julia and the Scriptwriter* is in tune with the works of the so-called post-boom generation of writers from the 1970s, including Manuel Puig and Isabel Allende, who immersed themselves in popular culture and expanded the Latin American genre of magic realism.

Works in Critical Context

Mario Vargas Llosa is one of a small handful of the most esteemed Latin American authors of the twentieth century.

His novels are widely acknowledged as path-breaking in their narrative complexity and in the social panorama they encompass. Some critics have found the labyrinthine structure of works like *Conversation in the Cathedral* difficult to comprehend. Others have objected to some of the stylistic pyrotechnics in Vargas Llosa's fiction, contending that they exist at the expense of character development.

Conversation in the Cathedral Llosa's 1969 novel *Conversation in the Cathedral*, first published in English in 1975, received a range of critical reactions typical of the author's work. Roger Sale, writing for *The Hudson Review*, notes that the book "is huge, almost a quarter of a million words, and it manages that bulk with often amazing skill." Although he claims the story would work better as a film, Sale concludes, "*Conversation in the Cathedral* is immensely knowing, and so it makes a reader feel knowing; it is an excellent rather than a moving novel, not great, but very good." Suzanne Jill Levine, in the *New York Times Book Review*, writes, "It would be a pity if the enormous but not insurmountable difficulties of reading this massive novel prevent readers from becoming acquainted with a book that reveals, as few others have, some of the ugly complexities of the real Latin America." Other critics were less enthusiastic. For example, Pearl K. Bell of *The New Leader* calls the book "such a tiresome, repetitious, logorrheic bore that only in the cruelest nightmare could I imagine myself reading [Vargas Llosa's] greatly praised earlier works."

Responses to Literature

1. Write an essay about the relationship between fact and fiction in *Aunt Julia and the Scriptwriter* and *The Real Life of Alejandro Mayta*.

2. Research the life story of Antonio Conselheiro and the bloody battle he and his followers provoked in Brazil. What interpretation does Vargas Llosa give to these events in *The War of the End of the World*?

3. What relationship do you discern between the evolution of Vargas Llosa's political views and the development of his literary concerns?

4. Which of Vargas Llosa's contemporaries had the greatest effect on his style of writing, and in which of his works do you see this being represented?

5. Is there an American author today whom you feel presents a similar biting look at politics in America? Explain your choice.

BIBLIOGRAPHY

Books

Booker, M. Keith. *Vargas Llosa among the Postmodernists.* Gainesville: University Press of Florida, 1994.

Cano Gaviria, Ricardo. *El buitre y el ave fénix: Conversaciones con Mario Vargas Llosa.* Barcelona: Anagrama, 1972.

Feal, Rosemary Geisdorfer. *Novel Lives: The Fictional Autobiographies of Guillermo Cabrera Infante and Mario Vargas Llosa.* Chapel Hill: University of North Carolina Press, 1986.

Gallagher, D. P. *Modern Latin American Literature.* Oxford: Oxford University Press, 1973.

Gerdes, Dick. *Mario Vargas Llosa.* Boston: Twayne, 1985.

Harss, Luis and Barbara Dohmann. *Into the Mainstream: Conversations with Latin-American Writers.* New York: Harper, 1967.

Lewis, Marvin A. *From Lime to Leticia: The Peruvian Novels of Mario Vargas Llosa.* Lanham, Md.: University Press of America, 1983.

"Mario Vargas Llosa (1936–)." *Contemporary Literary Criticism.* Edited by Carolyn Riley and Phyllis Carmel Mendelson. Vol. 6. Detroit: Gale, 1976, pp. 543–48.

Moses, Michael Valdez. *The Novel and the Globalization of Culture.* Oxford: Oxford University Press, 1995.

Oviedo, José Miguel. *Mario Vargas Llosa: La invención de una realidad.* Barcelona: Seix Barral, 1982.

Oviedo, José Miguel, ed. *Mario Vargas Llosa: El escritor y la crítica.* Madrid: Taurus, 1981.

Pereira, Antonio. *La concepción literaria de Mario Vargas Llosa.* Mexico City: Universidad Nacional Autonoma de Mexico, 1981.

Rodriguez Elizondo, José. *Vargas Llosa: Historia de un doble parricidio.* Santiago, Chile: La Noria, 1993.

Rossmann, Charles and Alan Warren Friedman, eds. *Mario Vargas Llosa: A Collection of Critical Essays.* Austin: University of Texas Press, 1978.

Standish, Peter. *Vargas Llosa: La ciudad y los perros.* London: Grant & Cutler, 1983.

Periodicals

Americas (March–April 1989): 22; (March–April 1995): 62.

Latin American Literary Review (1983): vol. 11 no. 22: 15–25; (January–June 1987): 121–31, 201–06.

New Yorker (February 24, 1986): 98, 101–04; (August 24, 1987): 83; (December 25, 1989): 103; (October 1, 1990): 107–10; (April 15, 1996): 84.

World Literature Today (Winter 1978) (Spring 1978).

◈ Vergil

BORN: *70 BCE, Andes, Cisalpine Gaul*

DIED: *19 BCE, Brundisium, Italy*

NATIONALITY: *Roman*

GENRE: *Poetry*

MAJOR WORKS:

Eclogues (42–37 BCE)

Georgics (37–30 BCE)

The Aeneid (31–19 BCE)

LITERARY AND HISTORICAL CONTEMPORARIES

Vergil's famous contemporaries include:

Augustus Caesar (63 BCE–14 CE): Born Gaius Octavius, grand nephew and adopted heir of Julius Caesar, Augustus rose to become the first Roman emperor.

Cleopatra VII (69 BCE–30 BCE): Hellenistic ruler of Egypt, Cleopatra was the last in a centuries-long dynasty of Greek-speaking pharaohs tracing their lineage back to the conquests of Alexander the Great.

Wang Mang (45 BCE–23 CE): Wang Mang led a palace coup in China, installing himself as emperor of the newly proclaimed Xin dynasty in place of the ruling Han dynasty, though his success was short-lived.

Strabo (64 BCE–24 CE): A Greek academic specializing in history, philosophy, and geography. His seventeen-volume *Geographica* described the peoples and history of the known world at the time.

Horace (65–8 BCE): Considered by his contemporaries and later historians as one of the greatest Latin poets, Quintus Horatius Flaccus specialized in lyric poetry and coined many famous Latin phrases such as *carpe diem* ("seize the day").

Overview

Vergil, or Virgil (both spellings are considered correct), was a Roman poet who wrote chiefly in the epic genre. His poems, written as the Roman republic was collapsing and the Roman Empire was taking shape under Augustus, reflect the concerns of his day as well as broader human emotions. They remain widely studied and admired both for their technical ability and thematic content.

Works in Biographical and Historical Context

Pastoral Beginning Publius Vergilius Maro was born on October 15, 70 BCE at Andes, in Cisalpine Gaul (now a part of northern Italy), thereafter a province in the expanding Roman Empire. His mother was the daughter of the small landowner who employed Vergil's father, Maro, a day laborer. The couple's marriage elevated Maro's social status, possibly enhancing the quality of his son's education. The boy received elementary schooling in Mantua and then studied rhetoric in Rome and philosophy under the Epicurean philosopher Siro in Naples. Vergil planned to practice law but proved too shy to speak comfortably in public.

Restoration of the Family Farm Returning to the small family farm his mother and father operated, he studied and wrote poetry until, in 41 BCE, the land was confiscated to compensate retiring soldiers. Friends urged

Vergil to appeal to Octavian (known as Augustus after 27 BCE), Julius Caesar's adopted son and eventual successor. Octavian restored the farm—perhaps, scholars speculate, because he was impressed by Vergil's work—but the poet soon moved to Naples.

Success in Naples While in Naples, between 42 and 37 BCE, he composed the *Eclogues*, whose title means "Selections." These ten poems, also referred to as the *Bucolics*, depict shepherds singing of unhappy loves in an idealized landscape, no doubt influenced by the rural region in which he grew up. Their publication attracted widespread praise and the sponsorship of Octavian's friend, the art patron Maecenas. Maecenas allegedly prevailed upon Vergil to compose his next work, the *Georgics*, as an agricultural paean to persuade Romans, then deserting the countryside in large numbers, to return to farming. Written in Naples between 37 and 30 BCE, the *Georgics*, or "Points of Farming," consists of four books that offer instruction in grain production, the cultivation of trees and vineyards, animal husbandry, and beekeeping. The work further enhanced Vergil's reputation upon its appearance in 29 BCE. Octavian, to whom Vergil read the completed poem, honored him with two villas and a generous stipend, and Octavian's friends asked Vergil to compose an epic honoring the emperor.

Deathbed Request Goes Unmet This project, which became *The Aeneid*, occupied the last ten years of Vergil's life. According to several of his friends, he first drafted the epic in prose, then laboriously reworked it in verse. Composition was slow and revision constant; Vergil responded to one of Augustus's many inquiries about the poem's progress by asserting that he "must have been just about mad to attempt the task." When he left Naples in 19 BCE to gather new material in Greece and Asia Minor, he planned to devote another three years to revisions, but caught fever at Megara and died soon after returning to Italy. His deathbed request was that his companions burn *The Aeneid*. However, Augustus countermanded the request, asking Vergil's friends, the writers Varius Rufus and Plotius Tucca, to edit the manuscript but specifying that they neither add, delete, nor alter significantly. Published in 17 BCE, the epic's resounding success assured Vergil's fame. More manuscripts of Vergilian works exist today than of any other classical author.

Works in Literary Context

Considered the greatest of Roman poets, Vergil is acclaimed for transforming the Greek literary traditions that provided Roman writers with material, themes, and styles. Latin authors, Joseph Farrell explains, were fully expected to imitate their Hellenic (Greek) precursors, and Vergil's three major works adapt the characteristics of numerous Greek models, although particular influences predominate. Vergil's pastoral poem, the *Eclogues*, is modeled after Theocritus's *Idylls*; his poetic treatise on the significance of human labor, the *Georgics*, after Hesiod's *Works and Days*; and his epic poem of Augustan Rome, the *Aeneid*, after Homer's *Iliad* and *Odyssey*. However, Farrell and numerous critics agree that surpassing the Greeks was far more esteemed than merely emulating them, and Vergil, synthesizing a more diverse array of literary examples than other Latin poets, reworked Hellenic influences so completely that he supplanted them.

Vergil's literary developments include populating a more idealized pastoral setting with contemporary figures, synthesizing vivid description with philosophical inquiry, increasing grammatical complexity, and enhancing psychologically realistic characterization. These technical innovations have informed all subsequent literature, yet Vergil is equally noted for his awareness of the uncertainties specific to the times in which he lived, as well as those inherent in the human condition. In addition, his work offers an insightful perspective on the anxieties of empire during the Augustan age.

The National Epic *The Aeneid* was composed at least in part to celebrate and promote the rebirth of the Roman way of life under Augustus. The epic poem also universalizes Roman experience, ideals, and aspirations. Critics have praised Vergil's ability to adapt a variety of traditions, motifs, ideas, and literary techniques to suit his poetic intentions in the work. As scholars have maintained, he forged a characteristically Roman epic from such disparate sources as archaic myths and mysteries, Homeric epic poetry, ancient beliefs such as reincarnation, and Stoic precepts. What makes *The Aeneid* so eminently Roman is its pervasive spirit of Augustan patriotism and imperialism, expressed through the idea of *pietas*, which, although formally denoting religious respect, in practice describes Augustus's strategy of using religion, history, and morality to create a Roman national identity with himself at the center.

Scholars have also carefully studied the formal structures of Vergil's epic. For example, Brooks Otis divides *The Aeneid* into symmetrical halves, each corresponding to one of Homer's epics. Thus, in the first six books, Aeneas's journey to what will eventually be Rome parallels Odysseus's homeward journey, while the last six books recount a Latin inversion of the Trojan War: the Greeks fought to destroy a city, while the Trojans fight to found one. This structural reading also supports the perception of some critics for whom the first six books constitute a spiritual journey that matures Aeneas so that he can lead the battles of Books VII–XII. Another popular approach to the epic's structure proposes that the books of the poem are alternately lighter and darker in tone. Viktor Poschl and George Duckworth perceive the poem as divided into three segments of four books each. The first four books they see as dark; the middle four, light; and the last four, dark. Such an interpretation of the poem's structure reinforces the critics' view of Vergil's attitude toward Augustan Rome—both believe that he stresses its human costs and moral ambiguity.

Poetic Innovations Vergil is credited with significantly refining narrative technique in *The Aeneid*. A characteristic reworking of Homeric episodes consists in shifting from an objective tone to the subjective perception of his characters. In addition to contributing to psychologically credible characterization, this narrative procedure enabled the poet to introduce ironic contrasts between different characters' interpretations of a particular event, and between the reader's wider and the characters' more limited knowledge. Vergil is also noted for developing the dactylic hexameter (a line consisting of six feet, with a predominance of dactyls—a long syllable and two short syllables), a typically Greek meter that such early Roman poets as Ennius used with questionable success, into an outstanding instrument of Latin poetry. Vergil was able to do this without unduly complicating his syntax, which generally remains straightforward.

Legacy Endures after Rome Falls Immensely popular in Augustan Rome, Vergil's poems became part of the standard curriculum in Roman schools within fifty years of his death, ensuring the production of numerous copies. After the collapse of the western Roman Empire in the fifth century CE, Vergil's works remained accessible to scholars through numerous manuscripts copied in monasteries throughout Christendom during the early Middle Ages. In particular, the surge of scholarly interest in classical literature during the reign of Holy Roman emperor Charlemagne (800–814) produced numerous cursive copies, many annotated and elaborately illustrated. Collectively, the four most reliable codices, so considered because they are the oldest, provide complete copies of Vergil's three major works; they are preserved in the Vatican library and the Church of San Lorenzo in Florence.

Works in Critical Context

Although critical reception of Vergil's works has fluctuated over the centuries, his themes and techniques have influenced virtually all subsequent Western literature, with Dante Alighieri, Geoffrey Chaucer, Edmund Spenser, John Milton, Percy Bysshe Shelley, and Matthew Arnold numbering among his prominent heirs. As centuries have widened the gulf between the present and pagan antiquity, scholars have increasingly appreciated the encyclopedic description of Greco-Roman culture Vergil's poetry provides.

The Aeneid Even in his own lifetime, Vergil's poetry had become a school text. Early Christian writers who attempted to reject Vergil could escape neither his style nor his attitudes. Christian thought assimilated them both. *The Aeneid* and the Bible were arguably the two most consistently read books in Western Europe for two thousand years. In that time, *The Aeneid* has been a pagan bible, a Latin style manual, a moral

COMMON HUMAN EXPERIENCE

The Aeneid is one of the great poetic national epics; other such works, that succinctly encapsulate the spirit and outlook of a people in verse form, include:

The *Kalevala*. Passed down via oral tradition for centuries, this national epic of Finland was compiled and put into print in the nineteenth century by Elias Lönnrot. Its length (more than twenty-two thousand verses) and narrative depth made an immediate impact on students of folklore and mythology; J. R. R. Tolkien claimed it as an inspiration for developing his own mythology for Middle Earth.

The Song of Roland. First appearing in the twelfth century and in other forms over the following two centuries, this epic poem of France describes the historical exploits, recast in a legendary, mythological mode, of Charlemagne and his paladin Roland, who fought a doomed battle against Spanish Moors. The poem's popularity was such that it launched an entirely new literary genre, the *chanson de geste* ("song of heroic deeds").

Mabinogion. A collection of prose and poetry, drawn from both oral and written sources, this is the medieval Welsh folkloric tradition encapsulated in a single volume. There is evidence that certain details may be rooted in pre-Christian, Iron Age society.

Beowulf. Dating from between the eighth and eleventh century, this Anglo-Saxon epic poem is the oldest work of English literature. Despite the fact that it describes events in the Saxon homeland of Scandinavia and Germany, it is often called England's national epic.

Responses to Literature

1. Define the difference between folk and literary epics. Into which category would you place *The Aeneid*? Why?
2. Roman civilization was strongly associated with the city, yet poets like Vergil were fond of writing about rural settings, describing them in the highest terms. Why do you think this was the case? Can you draw any parallels to our own modern, urban society?
3. Why do you think Vergil chose Aeneas as a hero for Romans to look up to? What was the significance of his Trojan heritage, and of his activities after the Trojan War? What were the personal traits of Aeneas that Romans might have looked up to?
4. How did the ongoing political situation during Vergil's lifetime affect his composition of *The Aeneid*? Was the work meant to stand above current politics, or did it address contemporary issues?

BIBLIOGRAPHY

Books

Bloom, Harold, ed. *Virgil*. New York: Chelsea House, 1986.

Commager, Steele, ed. *Virgil: A Collection of Critical Essays*. Englewood Cliffs, N.J.: Prentice-Hall, 1966.

Frank, Tenney. *Vergil: A Biography*. New York: Russell & Russell, 1965.

Knight, W. F. Jackson. *Vergil, Epic and Anthropology*. New York: Barnes & Noble, 1967.

Williams, R. D. *Virgil: His Poetry through the Ages*. London: British Library, 1982.

Dictionary of Literary Biography Vol. 211: *Ancient Roman Writers*. Edited by Ward W. Briggs. A Bruccoli Clark Layman Book. Detroit: Gale, 1999.

allegory, a document of European unity, a pacifist document—and one of the most-read and most-studied works of world literature of all time.

The Georgics Joseph Farrell has deemed the *Georgics* the most allusive poem of antiquity, and, though Hesiod's *Works and Days* is Vergil's most commonly cited model (perhaps because Vergil characterized his poem as "a Hesiodic song for Roman cities"), the influences of the *De Rerum Natura* of Lucretius, the *Odyssey* and the *Iliad* of Homer, the *De Re Rustica* of Varro, and the *Phaenomena* of Aratus are also significant.

The *Georgics* is widely considered the most polished of Vergil's works; John Dryden, who translated all of Vergil's works, called it "the best poem of the best poet." In the view of L. P. Wilkinson, "The *Georgics* is, in fact, the first poem in all literature in which description may be said to be the chief *raison d'être* and source of pleasure."

⬚ Paul Verlaine

BORN: *1844, Metz, France*

DIED: *1896, Paris, France*

NATIONALITY: *French*

GENRE: *Fiction, poetry*

MAJOR WORKS:

Saturnine Poems (1866)

Gallant Feasts (1869)

Wisdom (1880)

Love (1888)

Overview

A poet renowned for the fluidity and impressionistic imagery of his verse, Verlaine succeeded in liberating the musicality of the French language from the restrictions of its classical, formal structure. Highly influenced by the French painter Antoine Watteau, Verlaine was fascinated

Paul Verlaine   *Verlaine, Paul, photograph. Hulton Archive / Getty Images.*

by the visual aspects of form and color and attempted to capture in his poems the symbolic elements of language by transposing emotion into subtle suggestions. As a contributor to the French symbolists, who believed the function of poetry was to evoke and not describe, Verlaine created poetry that was both aesthetic and intuitive. Although his verse has often been overshadowed by his scandalous bohemian lifestyle, Verlaine's literary achievement was integral to the development of French poetry.

Works in Biographical and Historical Context

A Student of Life   Born in Metz to religious middle-class parents, Paul Marie Verlaine's youth was guarded and conventional until he became a student at the Lycée Bonaparte (now Condorcet). While he never truly excelled in his studies, Verlaine did enjoy a certain success in rhetoric and Latin. Despite winning a number of prizes in these areas, however, Verlaine was not a highly respected student—one of his instructors claimed he looked like a criminal and was the filthiest and most slovenly pupil in school—and he barely managed to obtain the baccalaureate. Upon gradu-

ation, Verlaine enrolled in law school, but because of his tendency to frequent bars and to associate with women of questionable morals, he was quickly withdrawn from his academic pursuits. His father secured a clerical position for his son at a local insurance company, and while the work was mundane, it allowed Verlaine time to patronize the Café du Gaz, a gathering spot for the literary and artistic community, and to develop his poetic talents.

The Parnassians   Verlaine made his literary debut with the publication of *Poèmes saturniens* (*Saturnine Poems*) in 1866. At this time, Verlaine began to associate with a group of young poets known as the Parnassians. This poetic movement, which had adopted Théophile Gautier's doctrine of "art for art's sake," included François Coppée, Charles Leconte de Lisle, and Charles Baudelaire. While Verlaine's *Saturnine Poems*, a volume true to the Parnassian ideals of detached severity, impeccable form, and stoic objectivity, was well received by his fellow poets, it took twenty years to sell five hundred copies, leaving Verlaine virtually unknown to general readers following its publication. Verlaine began to move away from the tenets of the Parnassians with his third volume, *Fêtes galantes* (*Gallant Feasts*). In this collection, Verlaine uses visual and spatial imagery to create poetry that has been described as "impressionistic music." According to many critics, this volume first revealed Verlaine's poetic talents in their pure form and later established Verlaine as a precursor to the symbolist movement.

While Verlaine's poetic style was taking shape and setting precedents, his personal life was slowly dissipating due to his increasing consumption of absinthe, a liquor flavored with wormwood that was believed to cause hallucinations. Despite his growing addiction and sometimes violent temperament, Verlaine's family encouraged him to marry, believing it could stabilize his raucous life. Verlaine sought out a young girl, Mathilde Maute, who was sixteen in 1869, the year of their engagement. Following their marriage in 1870, Verlaine published *La bonne chanson* (*The Good Song*), a volume that contains verse inspired by his young wife. This was Verlaine at his happiest; he seemed to truly believe that love and marriage would save him from his dangerous lifestyle.

Arthur Rimbaud   Verlaine's hopes and good intentions, however, were shattered when he received a letter from the then unknown poet Arthur Rimbaud in 1871. Verlaine urged Rimbaud, a precocious and unpredictable seventeen-year-old genius, to visit him in Paris. Tempted by the anarchic and bohemian lifestyle the young poet represented, Verlaine abandoned his wife, home, and employment for Rimbaud. The two poets traveled throughout Europe, a journey punctuated by drunken quarrels, until Verlaine shot and wounded Rimbaud during an argument in 1873. Verlaine was arrested and later sentenced to serve two years at Mons, a Belgian prison. During this time he wrote *Romances sans paroles* (*Songs Without Words*), a collection of verse strongly influenced by his affair with

LITERARY AND HISTORICAL CONTEMPORARIES

Verlaine's famous contemporaries include:

Arthur Rimbaud (1854–1891): A lasting influence on innumerable poets to follow, Rimbaud had given up poetry by the age of twenty-one, having already produced a handful of enduring classics.

Stéphane Mallarmé (1842–1898): A major French symbolist poet, Mallarmé was part of the Paris intellectual society in the latter half of the nineteenth century and hosted a weekly salon for writers and poets every Tuesday night.

Thomas Hardy (1840–1928): Though he considered himself a poet first and foremost, and his poetry has come to be highly regarded since his death, Hardy was best known in his lifetime for his novels, most of which were set in the semifictional county of Wessex.

Lafcadio Hearn (1850–1904): Born in Greece and raised in Ireland, Hearn moved to America to work as a journalist; this work took him to Japan, and his subsequent writings provided some of the West's first insights into Japanese culture.

Victor Emmanuel II (1820–1878): In 1861, Victor Emanuel, king of Piedmont, Savoy, and Sardinia, assumed the throne of Italy, becoming the first king of the newly unified state, despite the fact that several states, including Rome, would remain as holdouts over the next decade.

Anthony Trollope (1815–1882): Like Thomas Hardy, Trollope was a successful Victorian author who set many of his stories in a fictional county. His novels were notable for their sharp observations of political and social issues of the time.

Rimbaud. Verlaine's masterful use of ambiguities, the smoothness and economy of his verse, and his usage of "half-light," or vague but deeply suggestive visual imagery, led Arthur Symons to speak for many when he called this volume "Verlaine's masterpiece of sheer poetry."

While in prison, Verlaine turned from atheism to a fervent acceptance of the Roman Catholic faith into which he had been born. While some observers have questioned the sincerity of Verlaine's conversion, others have pointed to *Sagesse* (*Wisdom*), a volume of poems that depicts his religious crisis, as evidence of his depth of feeling and moral commitment. Critical response to *Wisdom* was somewhat mixed. Following *Wisdom*, Verlaine produced a trilogy exemplifying his religious genesis: *Amour* (*Love*) was to represent religious perseverance, *Parallelement* (*In Parallel*) moral relapse, and *Bonheur* (*Happiness*) repentance and consolation. In all three collections, Verlaine continued to develop his personal voice and to progress toward simple and graceful accentuations.

Later Life After being released from Mons, Verlaine traveled to Stickney and Bournemouth in England to become a teacher of French, Latin, and drawing. Although he called his stay in Stickney an *enchantement*, Verlaine decided in 1878 to take up a rustic life in the Ardennes with one of his former students, Lucien Letinois, whom he termed his adoptive son. Many of the elegies of *Love* refer to Letinois, who died in 1886 of typhoid, two years after the death of Verlaine's mother. For the remainder of his life, Verlaine lived in poverty and reverted to drink. Although he managed to publish a few works during this time, among them the tragic and brutal *Chansons pour elle* (*Songs for Her*), most critics contend that Verlaine's best and most original work can be found in his earlier volumes. After a number of hospital stays that allowed him to recuperate from his excesses, Verlaine died in humble lodgings in 1896.

Works in Literary Context

Symbolism While many critics consider Verlaine one of the harbingers of the French symbolists due to the impressionistic and evocative nature of his poetry, Verlaine denied belonging to any particular poetic movement. Instead of labeling himself a decadent or symbolist, Verlaine preferred to call himself a "degenerate," indicating his individualistic and anarchic tendencies. Much attention has been given to Verlaine's use of familiar language in a musical and visual manner and his ability to evoke rather than demand a response from his readers. Stéphane Mallarmé declared that "to name an object is to suppress three-fourths of the enjoyment of the poem … to suggest it, there is the dream." This statement, often considered the credo for the symbolist movement, can be used to describe much of Verlaine's poetry. As C. F. Keary suggests: "If there is one note which occurs more frequently than any other in [Verlaine's] poems, it is the longing for repose, a love of half-lights and the minor key."

Sensuous Beauty Out of the Ordinary Since the turn of the twentieth century, Verlaine has been noted for the sensuality and beauty he evokes with his poetic imagery and language. In 1922, Irène Dean Paul called Verlaine a "painter, a musician, and a remarkable philosopher" with the talent "to create out of old material new worlds, new sounds, new sights." Paul, like other critics to follow, praised Verlaine for his ability to take the reader along on his journeys; his detail is striking, vivid, and tangible. "Through his personality," Paul wrote, the reader sees landscape, and objects develop a "significance and personality of their own." Verlaine is known for his ability to draw the reader inside of everything he sees, touches, or experiences. With this technique, he takes the reader within himself, offering a new way in which to view and feel the world.

Works in Critical Context

Arthur Symons asserts that Verlaine's place in literary history rests on the fact that he "made something new of French—something more pliable, more exquisitely delicate and sensitive, than the language ever before has been capable of."

Verlaine's well-documented personal life has often overshadowed discussion of the merits of his numerous volumes of verse and his poetic genius. In Verlaine's work, as in his life, there was a constant struggle between the soul and the senses; between debauchery and repentance. This prompted critics to call him everything from a "propagator of moral cowardice" to "a victim of his own genius." Despite the many attacks on his character, Verlaine is considered a consummate poet whose extraordinary talents for fluid verse, figurative and suggestive language, and impressionistic imagery have assumed legendary stature. It was Verlaine, most critics agree, who was responsible for releasing French poetry from its technical severity and for bringing out the musicality inherent in the French language. "Remember," Anatole France wrote as early as 1891, "this lunatic has created a new art, and there is a chance that some day it will be said of him.... [']He was the greatest poet of his time.'"

"Art poetique" When Paul Verlaine wrote his "Art poetique" in 1874, he was protesting against two traditions firmly rooted in the poetry of the time: the tradition of pictorial description and the tradition of rhetoric. Some poets followed Verlaine in creating melodious verse in which the logical and intellectual content was reduced to a minimum and the outside world was used simply as a means of expressing by analogy the poet's inner world. For example, the first three lines of the last stanza are a good example of this kind of allusive imagery, in which the two terms of the comparison—"le vers" and "la bonne aventure"—are equated, while the reason for the equation is left unspoken. Other poets, with Mallarmé chief among them, took a more complex and more abstract view of music as a system of interlocking relationships of sound, on which poetry could superimpose a system of relationships of sense and imagery. A few, led by Rene Ghil, attempted to construct a theory of "instrumentism," which postulated rigorous correspondences between instrumental timbres, vowel sounds, and colors. Almost all of them would have agreed with Verlaine in shunning clear, direct statement and proceeding instead by allusion, suggestion, or symbol.

Jadis et naguère Hastily gathered, the poems of *Jadis et naguère* were born from the necessity for Verlaine to live on his writings and to capitalize on the poet's own growing fame. His sonnet "Langueur," published in *Le Chat Noir* (May 1883), became the poetic model of the decadents, a group of late-nineteenth- and early-twentieth-century writers who held that art was superior to nature and that the finest beauty was that of dying or decaying things, and who attacked the accepted moral, ethical, and social standards of their time. Arthur Symons

---

COMMON HUMAN EXPERIENCE

Verlaine preferred to refer to his work as "degenerate." Other works that have received a similar label, either from the authors themselves or from critics, include:

The Flowers of Evil (1857), a poetry collection by Charles Baudelaire. In this, the first volume of Baudelaire's poems, the decadent verses caused such a scandal that Baudelaire was brought up on criminal charges, even as they influenced countless other artists in France and abroad.

The Great God Pan (1890), a novella by Arthur Machen. A tremendous influence on later generations of horror writers, Machen used Pan as a symbol for the dark, forbidden power of nature in this novella.

The Torture Garden (1899), a novel by Octave Mirbeau. An allegorical attack upon the hypocrisy of European efforts to spread their idea of civilization, complete with its systematic institutions of murder and violence, around the world.

The Picture of Dorian Gray (1890), a novel by Oscar Wilde. The only novel published by the infamous wit Wilde, this book's themes of aesthetic decay and homoeroticism made it controversial upon its initial publication; it has gone on to be regarded as one of the great works of nineteenth-century literature.

---

wrote of the work in 1892 that "it makes no pretence to unity, but has something in it of every variety of his style, with certain poems, here and there, which rank among his special triumphs."

Legacy After his death in Paris on January 8, 1896, friends and admirers of Paul Verlaine—including François Coppée, René Sully-Prudhomme, José Maria de Heredia, Jean Richepin, Jean Moréas, Catulle Mendès, and Edmond Lepelletier—gathered to pay their respects to the poet they considered "the Master." Although Verlaine's literary reputation had declined later in his life—in part because of his scandalous behavior—in the 1890s he was closely identified with the younger poets of the symbolist movement, although he downplayed the association. Verlaine was also one of the models for the decadent movement that began in the 1870s. As much as for his literary reputation, however, his fame rests on his stormy personal relationship with fellow decadent Arthur Rimbaud.

Responses to Literature

1. Write a brief essay about how Verlaine views the past in *Gallant Feasts*. Discuss specific lines or imagery to support your ideas.

2. With a classmate, use resources from your library or the Internet to research Verlaine's life. Discuss the following: Why does Verlaine focus on remorse in *Wisdom*? What life events occurring around the time of his composing that volume would have led him to discuss such an emotion?

3. Read several selections from Verlaine's poetic canon. Write an essay explaining what role you think self-denial plays in Verlaine's poetry. Use specific examples from the poems you read to support your ideas.

4. Like many French poets, Verlaine's poetry often has a musical flow to it. Read a few selections of Verlaine's poetic work and have a classmate read a few selections of Charles Baudelaire's poetic work. Together, write an informal report in which you contrast the musicality of Verlaine's verse to that of Baudelaire. Cite examples from specific poems to support your opinions.

BIBLIOGRAPHY

Books

Adam, Antoine. *The Art of Paul Verlaine*, translated by Carl Morse. New York: New York University Press, 1963.

Carter, A. E. *Verlaine: A Study of Parallels*. Toronto: University of Toronto Press, 1969.

Coulon, Marcel. *Poet Under Saturn: The Tragedy of Verlaine*, translated by Edgell Rickwood. Port Washington, N.Y.: Kennikat Press, 1932.

Dictionary of Literary Biography, Volume 217: Nineteenth-Century French Poets. A Bruccoli Clark Layman Book. Ed. Robert Beum. Detroit: Gale Group, 1999.

Hanson, Lawrence, and Elizabeth Hanson. *Verlaine: Fool of God*. New York: Random House, 1957.

Nalbantian, Suzanne. *The Symbolist of the Soul from Holderlin to Yeats: A Study in Metonomy*. New York: Columbia University Press, 1977.

"Paul Verlaine (1844–1896)." *Poetry Criticism*. Ed. Robyn V. Young. Vol. 2. Detroit: Gale Research, 1991, pp. 411–34.

Richardson, Joanna. *Verlaine*. New York: Viking Press, 1971.

◈ Jules Verne

BORN: *1828, Nantes, France*

DIED: *1905, Amiens, France*

NATIONALITY: *French*

GENRE: *Fiction, drama*

MAJOR WORKS:

Extraordinary Voyages (1863–1910)

A Journey to the Center of the Earth (1864)

Twenty Thousand Leagues Under the Sea (1869–1870)

Around the World in Eighty Days (1873)

Jules Verne *Verne, Jules, 1904, photograph.*

Overview

Jules Verne is arguably one of the most underestimated writers of the entire French literary tradition. Although ranked as the fifth most-translated author of all time (behind Lenin, Agatha Christie, Walt Disney, and the Bible—according to a UNESCO poll), Verne and his *Extraordinary Journeys* (1863–1910) were until recently persistently denied any literary recognition in France. In America, Verne is largely unstudied but widely recognized as the father of science fiction.

Works in Biographical and Historical Context

Childhood in Nantes: The Art of the Sea and of the Machine Jules Verne was born on February 8, 1828, to a middle-class French family in the western port city of Nantes. His mother, Sophie (née Allotte de la Fuye), was the daughter of a prominent Nantes family of ship owners. His father, Pierre Verne, was a lawyer and the son of a Provins magistrate. Verne had three sisters—Anna, Mathilde, and Marie—and one brother, Paul, who eventually became a naval engineer and helped his older brother from time to time with the mechanical details of his imaginary technological marvels.

Verne was a good student. He repeatedly won awards, and he passed his *baccalauréat* easily in 1846. But he especially loved the sea. The small shipyard docks of nearby Île Feydeau and the bustling Nantes harbor itself never failed to spark his youthful imagination with visions of far-off lands and exotic peoples. And he also loved machines. Reminiscing about those formative years when interviewed by a British journalist in 1894, Verne compared the pastime of watching them to viewing the art of Raphael or Correggio.

Indentured to Law, Aspiring to Theater Intending that his son follow in his footsteps as an attorney, Verne's father sent him to Paris in 1848 to study law. Not distracted from his studies by the political turmoil that engulfed the city—The French Revolution of 1848 ended the reign of King Louis-Philippe and, ultimately, led to the creation of the Second French Empire—Verne took his education seriously. He completed his law degree in just two years. Perhaps most significantly, while at law school Verne discovered a new vocation, literature. The young Verne wrote plays, some of which were performed in local theaters. He even managed to become the secretary of the Théâtre Lyrique in 1852. Verne also composed poetry and penned several short stories, including "A Balloon Trip" (1851) and "Wintering in the Ice" (1855). He was, however, to become better known for his novels.

From the Stage to the Library Many years were to pass before Verne would reluctantly decide to abandon his theatrical aspirations and redirect those energies toward adventure stories. During those difficult years of 1850 to 1862, he spent more and more of his time writing lucrative short stories and nonfiction articles for popular journals, such as the *Musée des Familles*. This work was fascinating for Verne, but it required long days in the Bibliothèque Nationale researching geography, world history and popular science.

During these extended work sessions at the Bibliothèque Nationale, Verne first conceived of the possibility of writing a wholly new type of novel, what he first called a *roman de la science* (novel of science). This new form would fully incorporate the large amounts of factual material that he was accumulating in his library research, would combine scientific discovery, action and adventure, history and geography, and be patterned on the novels and tales of Sir Walter Scott, James Fenimore Cooper, and Edgar Allan Poe.

The Settled Life and the Mental Journey In 1857, Verne married Honorine Morel (*née* de Viane), a twenty-six-year-old widow with two daughters. With his new father-in-law's contacts in Paris and a monetary wedding gift from his own father, Verne reluctantly took a position as a stockbroker at the Paris Exchange with the firm Eggly & Cie and spent his early mornings at home writ-ing. When not writing or at the stock exchange, Verne spent his time either with his old theater friends or at the Bibliothèque Nationale. His long-contemplated ideas for a *roman de la science* soon crystallized into a rough draft of what would later be titled *Five Weeks in a Balloon* (1863)—the first novel of the *Extraordinary Journeys*.

After a heated dispute with the editor in chief of the *Musée des Familles* in 1856, Verne stopped contributing his writing to this journal. Still determined, however, to expand his short narratives into a full-length scientific novel, Verne discussed his ideas with his friends and colleagues. Then, in September 1862, Verne was introduced to Pierre-Jules Hetzel through a friend of both the publisher and Alexandre Dumas. Verne promptly asked Hetzel if he would consider reviewing for publication his manuscript, "An Air Voyage." Hetzel agreed to the request, and a few days later Verne and Hetzel began what would prove to be a highly successful author-publisher collaboration, lasting for more than forty years and resulting in more than sixty *romans scientifiques*. Soon after, Verne quit his job at the stock exchange and began to write full-time.

From the Earth to the Moon In 1864 Verne published *A Journey to the Center of the Earth*. The work proved to be one of his most popular *Extraordinary Journeys* volumes. Verne's famous *From the Earth to the Moon* (1865)—along with its sequel, *Round the Moon* (1870)—was the first "realistic" (that is, scientifically plausible) manned moon voyage in Western literature. Verne based his extrapolative tale on the lessons of modern astronomy and astrophysics. In 1868, Verne moved his family to the northern coast town of Le Crotoy. He purchased his first yacht, and, during his frequent voyages on the Somme River and along the coast of France, he began revising an early manuscript called "An Underwater Voyage." A year later, in early 1869, Verne put the finishing touches on his first novel of the sea, *Twenty Thousand Leagues under the Sea* (1869–1870).

During the summer of 1870, Verne received the Légion d'honneur (ironically, one of the last official acts of a corrupt government that the author despised). At the start of the short-lived Franco-Prussian War—the conflict that, ultimately, brought an end to the Second French Republic and established the modern German nation-state at its conclusion in 1871—he moved his family to Amiens to stay with his wife's relatives and joined the Le Crotoy home guard. After the ensuing German occupation and the Paris Commune (the socialist-anarchist self-rule of Paris in the wake of a revolt against the traditional authority that had driven the disastrous war just ended), Verne himself moved permanently to Amiens, where he spent the remaining thirty-three years of his life.

Around the World In 1873, Verne published his most commercially successful novel, *Around the World in Eighty Days*, a book inspired by rapid advances in transportation capabilities and communication technology in the late nineteenth century. For example, in the United States the

LITERARY AND HISTORICAL CONTEMPORARIES

Verne's famous contemporaries include:

Susan B. Anthony (1828–1906): An American civil rights leader, primarily responsible for creating and passing the Nineteenth Amendment.

Paul-Jacques-Aimé Baudry (1828–1826): A French painter who was awarded the *Prix de Rome* in 1850.

Solomon Loeb (1828–1923): An American banker and major philanthropist to Jewish charities.

Dante Gabriel Rossetti (1828–1882): An English poet, painter, illustrator, and translator who founded the Pre-Raphaelite Brotherhood.

Karl Marx (1818–1883): A German philosopher, economist, and visionary social thinker, Marx laid the intellectual groundwork for most socialist activity of the nineteenth and twentieth centuries.

transcontinental railroad was completed in 1869, linking the east and west coasts. In the early 1870s, advances in steamship design made international trade and travel much faster and economical. Also by the early 1870s, telegraph lines link ran virtually around the global, making rapid communication between places as distant from each other as Britain and India inexpensive and easy. The hardcover edition of Verne's book quickly set new sales records both in France and abroad, selling more than a half-million copies during the first year alone. Verne's growing celebrity correspondingly soared: in 1874 he was elected to the Académie d'Amiens, his *Extraordinary Journeys* were officially recognized by the Académie Française, and an extravagant stage adaptation of *Around the World in Eighty Days* proved to be a resounding success and would play uninterrupted at the Théâtre du Châtelet for a record-breaking fifty years. Verne's theatrical ambitions were finally satisfied. In 1877, Verne successively purchased two more yachts, and for the next few years he sailed to ever more distant ports of call. Not surprisingly, many of these locales found their way, sooner or later, into the settings of his subsequent *Extraordinary Journeys*.

During his final years, despite increasingly poor health, the death of his brother, Paul, in 1897, and annoying family squabbles, Verne continued diligently to churn out two to three novels per year. Verne fell seriously ill in early 1905, a few weeks after his seventy-seventh birthday. Lucid until the end, he told his wife Honorine to gather the family around him, and he died quietly on March 24, 1905. He was buried on March 28 in the cemetery of La Madeleine in Amiens. Two years later, an elaborate sculpture depicting the author rising from his tomb and engraved with the words "Toward immortality and eternal youth" was placed over his grave.

Works in Literary Context

Science Fiction In the history of literature, Verne's *Extraordinary Journeys* constitutes the birth of a unique, hybridized form of novel. This new brand of fiction was to be a forerunner of what would eventually evolve into the genre called science fiction. By any name, it represents the first successful attempt to incorporate science into literature by a delicate intertwining of fact with fantasy, mathematics with myth, and education with adventure—which constitutes the core of Verne's narrative recipe for the vast majority of his *Extraordinary Journeys* volumes.

A Dizzying Range of Contemporary Influences Perhaps more than most authors of fiction, Verne wrote in response to the perspectives and exploits of a wide range of his contemporaries. Among these were friends and colleagues including the famous explorer Jacques Arago, Verne's mathematician cousin Henri Garcet, and notorious daredevil balloonist Félix Tournachon, known to most Parisians by his popular pseudonym "Nadar." Nadar especially helped Verne, initiating him into the mysteries of air travel and bringing Verne into his own circle of friends, which included noted engineers and scientists who ultimately provided Verne with the technical knowledge that enabled him to write his first *roman scientifique*. A second influencing factor on the author was the list of current events themselves: stories about balloon travel and daily newspaper accounts of exotic new discoveries kept Verne informed about the world around him, and he saw in these ideal scenarios for his first scientific adventure novel.

Oppression, Animal Abuse, and Environmental Concern Two distinct thematic trends can be seen in the two different periods of Verne's writing life: in the first period, his outlook is more optimistic, some say shallowly so. In the post-1886 period, a variety of pro-environment and critical social themes emerge in his works. Readers can see the oppression of the Québécois in Canada in *A Family without a Name* (1889), the ignorance and superstition of humans in the world in *The Castle of the Carpathians* (1892), and a concern for the imminent extinction of whales in *An Antarctic Mystery* (1897), among many others.

Works in Critical Context

Literary criticism has taken a number of wild turns over Verne's work. In the early years of his career it was Verne's (or, more precisely, Hetzel's) English connection with the *Boy's Own Paper* that exacerbated the growing tendency among French literary scholars to categorize Verne as an author fit only for adolescents. There was also recently a controversy over how much of the posthumous novels of the *Extraordinary Journeys* Verne's son Michel altered prior to their publication. Close inspection has revealed that Michel, who frequently assisted and collaborated with his father during the latter's final years, is now known to have been the principal author of one posthumous and several other texts normally credited exclusively to Verne. Nevertheless, verified Jules Verne works enjoyed a renaissance long after the author's death.

Extraordinary Journeys (1863–1910) One hundred years after the publication of the first novel of the collection, Verne and his *Extraordinary Journeys* were the rage of Paris. Reprints of his novels appeared from a variety of prestigious French publishing houses. Universities began to analyze his works. Respected literary journals began to publish articles about him, with literary critics, for the first time, placing Verne "in a first-rank position in the history of French literature," according to scholar Marc Angenot. Outside of France, too, though it took a little longer, the Verne vogue caught on. With the growing academic respectability of science fiction and the sudden popularity of "new" French literary critics, such as Roland Barthes, Michel Foucault, and Jacques Lacan, on Western campuses, the study of Verne increased as well. After nearly a half-century of virtually no serious Anglo-American literary criticism on Verne, the period from 1975 to 1990 witnessed no fewer than two biographies, seven monographs, one primary and secondary bibliography, and dozens of scholarly articles in a wide variety of academic journals on this prolific French author who was for so long deemed unworthy of critical attention. And the Verne renaissance continues even today.

Although earlier responses to *Around the World in Eighty Days: The Extraordinary Journeys* tended to dismiss it as light entertainment, more recent scholarly responses have regarded it in both an analytical and historical light. Edmund Smyth, for instance, suggests that "it would be fair to state that in the popular imagination Verne and science fiction are largely synonymous, even if modern science fiction has moved far beyond the narratives of travel and endeavour which are found in *Voyage au centre de la terre*." He notes, too, that Verne's "writing is self-consciously wrestling with language itself, rather than being a vehicle for representation." Coming from another angle, literary critic Daniel Compere observes, "[Verne] also tried to use the poetic function in scientific discourse, emphasizing the formal aspect of language, something unheard of in discourse of this type."

Responses to Literature

1. The growing pessimism in Verne's private life between 1886 and 1905 had its counterpart in the French social climate of the 1880s and 1890s. Consider the factors of the severe long-term economic crisis from 1882 to 1895 in France. How was the mood of the time reflected in Verne's later work? Provide and analyze examples.

2. In the early 1990s, a Jules Verne manuscript was discovered, and newspapers all over the world chronicled the events leading up to the new find. In 1994 Random House published *Paris in the Twen-*

COMMON HUMAN EXPERIENCE

Here are a few works by writers who have also indulged in science-based schemes and themes:

"The Birth-Mark" (1843), a short story by Nathaniel Hawthorne. In this romantic piece, a scientist challenges nature for its imperfections—which are found on his wife's cheek.

The Moon Is a Harsh Mistress (1966), a novel by Robert A. Heinlein. In this science fiction work, the physical properties of humans are challenged by conditions on the surface of the moon where they are setting up a colony.

Strange Case of Dr Jekyll and Mr Hyde (1886), a novella by Robert Louis Stevenson. In this classic, a man fools with science by experimenting on himself—with very poor results.

The Time Machine (1895), a novel by H. G. Wells. In this work, the protagonist travels to the distant future where he meets the Eloi and Morlocks.

---

tieth Century. Research the discovery of this "lost" novel. Why was it not published during Verne's lifetime? Does it show the same optimistic outlook regarding technology that the author's other early work shows? How has this been changing scholarly opinion on how Verne's attitudes toward technology changed as he got older?

3. Jules Verne has been acknowledged as being brilliant in his careful predictions about the future, many of which accurately anticipated inventions and technologies not even sketched in any blueprint in his time: America's Apollo space program and the initial velocity necessary for escaping Earth's gravity; air conditioning; automobiles; television; and even the Internet. Did Verne's work—on your reading—simply predict the future, or did it also inspire it? Based on your examination of a specific technology, to what extent do you think each was the case?

4. Jules Verne is considered the "father of science fiction." Consider the genre: is science fiction really different from other fiction? If so, how is it different? Consider essays such as Isaac Asimov's "The Little Tin God of Characterization." What makes characters in science fiction any more or less believable than in other fiction?

BIBLIOGRAPHY

Books

Allot, Kenneth, *Jules Verne*. London: Crescent, 1940.

Angenot, Marc, "Jules Verne: The Last Happy Utopianist." In *Science Fiction: A Critical Guide*. Ed. Patrick Parrinder. New York: Longman, 1979.

Barthes, Roland. "The *Nautilus* and the Drunken Boat." In *Mythologies*. Trans. A. Lavers. New York: Hill & Wang, 1972.

Lemire, Charles, *Jules Verne*. Paris: Berger-Levrault, 1908.

Periodicals

Angenot, Marc, "Jules Verne and French Literary Criticism, Part 1." *Science-Fiction Studies* 1 (1973): 33–37.

Asimov, Issac, "The Little Tin God of Characterization." *Isaac Asimov's Science Fiction Magazine*, May 1985.

———"Jules Verne and French Literary Criticism, Part 2." *Science-Fiction Studies* 1 (1973): 46–49.

Hillegas, Mark R., "A Bibliography of Secondary Materials on Jules Verne." *Extrapolation* 2 (December 1960): 5–16.

"Jules Verne at Home, an Interview with Marie A. Belloc." *Strand* 9 (February 1895): 206–13.

Rose, Mark, "Filling the Void: Verne, Wells and Lem." *Science-Fiction Studies* 8 (1981): 121–42.

Winandy, André, "The Twilight Zone: Image and Reality in Jules Verne's Strange Journeys." *Yale French Studies* 43 (1969): 101–10.

Web Sites

Jules Verne Virtual Library. Retrieved March 10, 2008, from http://JV.Gilead.org.il/works.html.

Librivox. Audio *A Journey to the Interior of the Earth*. Retrieved March 10, 2008, from http://librivox.org/a-journey-to-the-interior-of-the-earth-by-jules-verne.

Smithsonian Institution Libraries. A Jules Verne Centennial. Retrieved February 14, 2008, from http://www.sil.si.edu/OnDisplay/JulesVerne100.

🏵 Alfred de Vigny

BORN: *1797, Loches, France*

DIED: *1863, Paris, France*

NATIONALITY: *French*

GENRE: *Drama, fiction, poetry*

MAJOR WORKS:

Cinq-Mars; or, A Conspiracy under Louis XIII (1826)

Stello: A Session with Doctor Noir (1832)

Chatterton (1835)

The Military Necessity (1835)

Overview

Alfred de Vigny is known for his philosophical plays, short stories, and poems, which are recognized as an important part of the French Romantic movement of the nineteenth century. In particular, his drama *Chatterton* contributed significantly to the development of the Romantic movement in French literature. Critics agree that Vigny is most admired

Alfred, Comte de Vigny   *Vigny, Alfred, Comte de, photograph. The Library of Congress.*

for his creative use of form, command of technique, innovative use of symbols, and philosophical themes.

Works in Biographical and Historical Context

Association with the Romantics   Vigny was born at Loches in the Touraine region of France to aristocratic parents who, though once wealthy, had lost their fortune during the French Revolution less than a decade before. The French Revolution had been a revolt of the working class against the rule and power of the nobility and the clergy; because of this, noble families such as Vigny's were stripped of much of their past prestige and wealth after the revolution. The family moved to Paris where Vigny was raised among the nostalgic survivors of the old nobility of prerevolutionary France. In 1814 he followed family tradition by joining the Royal Guard, where he served for thirteen years.

During this period he renewed his ties with his childhood friend Émile Deschamps; in 1820, he met through Deschamps the growing body of Romantics—including Antony Deschamps, Jacques Ancelot, Alexandre Soumet, Pierre Guiraud, Jules de Rességuier, and Gaspard de Pons—who belonged to the first Cénacle and met in the home of Charles Nodier. They soon gravitated toward Victor Hugo, with whom the aspiring poet Vigny became, for a while at least, the best of friends. Vigny made his poetic debut in the December 1820 issue of Victor, Abel, and Eugène Hugo's *Conservateur littéraire*.

Poetry   Vigny began his literary career by writing poetry. He wrote slowly and with difficulty, leaving less than three dozen "poèmes," long philosophical pieces of sustained verse on generally grandiose themes, on which his reputation primarily rests. Despite money worries, he was never constrained to live by his pen and could afford both the slow maturation of his poetry and the long delays during its composition and revision. He abandoned or destroyed a great deal of material. He regarded himself, as he wrote in his *Journal*, as "a sort of epic moralist." *Poèmes antiques et modernes*, which includes the ten works published in *Poèmes* and *Eloa; ou, La soeur des anges, mystère*, contains twenty-one poems that are divided into three groups according to their sources of inspiration: mystical, ancient, and modern poems. The ancient group is further divided into biblical and Homeric poems.

Novels, Drama, and Other Writings   *Cinq-Mars; or, A Conspiracy under Louis XIII* is Vigny's first significant novel. Influenced by the writings of Sir Walter Scott, this historical novel about the age of Louis XIII concentrates on the historical events of the period at the expense of its fictional scenes, which, according to critics, are flat and lack a genuine warmth and vitality.

Vigny's theatrical career began with his successful translation and adaptation of Shakespeare's *Othello* for the French stage. *Chatterton* followed, as a dramatic adaptation of Vigny's own short story "Chatterton," which depicts the fate of the poet Thomas Chatterton, who is eventually driven to suicide by a materialistic society that neither appreciates his talent nor offers him love. The play is classical in its taut construction, simple plot, and restrained emotion. Yet the attack on society, moral examination of the hero's soul, and impassioned defense of emotion over reason all contributed to its success as a Romantic drama.

Vigny's writings also include a significant collection of short prose works, including *Stello: A Session with Doctor Noir*, which represent his attempts to combine philosophy with storytelling. In these works, he consistently defended what he considered to be the outcasts of society: the poet, soldier, and visionary. The work testifies to Vigny's bitterness toward a society that, in his view, despises genius. *The Military Necessity*, similar in form and thought to *Stello*, consists of three stories unified by the author's personal comments on the role of the soldier, who is also a victim of society. Vigny depicted the struggle between the requirements of the soldier's conscience and the dictates of war; he contended that the soldier's greatness lies in his dignified and passive obedience to authority. Vigny began a third collection of stories on the suffering of the religious prophet, but he only completed one story, titled *Daphne*. In comparing these

LITERARY AND HISTORICAL CONTEMPORARIES

Vigny's famous contemporaries include:

Charles Darwin (1809–1882): An English naturalist, Darwin proposed and explained the processes of evolution and natural selection in such a satisfactory manner that his theories now form the basis of modern biology and evolutionary theory.

Antonio López de Santa Anna (1794–1876): Over four turbulent decades, Santa Anna held various military and political positions, rising as high as president and general; fighting both against and in favor of Mexican independence; and infamously leading the Mexican forces in an ill-fated attempt to suppress the Texan Revolution.

Hans Christian Andersen (1805–1875): A Danish author, Andersen penned several famous fairy tales, including "The Little Mermaid," "The Emperor's New Clothes," and "The Ugly Duckling," that are now considered international treasures.

Alexis de Tocqueville (1805–1859): French historian and political philosopher, de Tocqueville wrote the two-volume *Democracy in America*, a study of early American democracy and its effects on the average person.

Napoléon III (1808–1873): Born Louis-Napoléon Bonaparte, nephew to the legendary general, Napoléon III was an unlikely politician who rose to become president of the French Republic, then proclaimed himself emperor of the Second Empire, a title he held until he was deposed in the aftermath of the Franco-Prussian War.

Johann Wolfgang von Goethe (1749–1832): One of the true geniuses of the Enlightenment period, Goethe was an acclaimed author and poet, theologian, philosopher, and scientist. His two-part play *Faust* has been hailed as one of the greatest works of world literature.

stories with his earlier prose work *Cinq-Mars*, critics commend Vigny's improved literary technique. Both collections of stories are admired for their simple plots, especially the two stories, "Laurette; ou, Le cachet rouge," and "La vie et la mort du capitaine Renaud; ou, La canne de jonc," which are often cited as Vigny's best fiction.

Disillusionment and Isolation   Near the end of his military service, he married Lydia Bunbury, the daughter of a rich and eccentric Englishman who disapproved of Vigny and promptly disinherited her. Lydia became a chronic invalid shortly thereafter, and the marriage rapidly disintegrated. Vigny turned to other women for comfort, including the great Romantic actress Marie

COMMON HUMAN EXPERIENCE

Vigny was one of the leading lights of the Romantic movement in French theater; other works that touch upon Romantic themes include:

La Morte Amoureuse (1836), a short story by Théophile Gautier. Combining Gothic and Romantic themes, this short story by one of the acknowledged masters of Romanticism tells the story of a priest who falls in love with a woman who turns out to be a vampire.

Voyage to the Orient (1851), a nonfiction work by Gérard de Nerval. Perhaps the definitive Romantic poet, Nerval also penned this hallucinatory travel account of a drug-fueled trip through the Middle East in the 1840s. His work would prove a tremendous influence on later Symbolists and surrealists.

René (1802), a novella by François-René de Chateaubriand. Considered by many critics to be the first true work of French Romanticism, this novella—by the man who inspired Romantics as much through his lifestyle as through his writings—includes all the classic elements of Romantic drama, particularly in its sensitive young protagonist's rebellions against society.

Dorval. Disillusioned by politics, failed love affairs, and his lack of recognition as a writer, Vigny withdrew from Parisian society after 1840. In 1845 he was elected to the prestigious literary Académie française after several unsuccessful attempts. Three years later, Vigny retreated to the family home at Charente, for which the French critic Charles Augustin Sainte-Beuve coined the famous phrase a "tour d'ivoire," or ivory tower, where he lived quietly until his death.

Works in Literary Context

With his collection *Poèmes antiques et modernes* Vigny championed the *poème*, which he defined as a composition in which a philosophic thought is staged under an epic or dramatic form. Vigny's *poèmes* are characterized by their stoical pessimism, compact form, and visual imagery. Their principal themes include God's indifference to humanity, women's deceit, inexorable fate, and the poet's alienation from a mediocre world. According to many critics, "Moise" is one of the finest works in *Poèmes antiques et modernes* and an outstanding example of Vigny's use of the *poème* to dramatize a single idea through symbols. "Moise" has been described as his pronouncement on the nineteenth-century Romantic poet's position in society.

Isolation and Misunderstanding Virtually all of Vigny's work deals with the isolation of the individual

and his belief in values that bring him into tension with a society from which he stands apart. *Stello* is essentially a collection of stories about the isolation of poets as beings superior to the rest of society and again explores the Romantic theme of being true to a vocation, whatever the cost in comfort or happiness. The work contains a condemnation of all social and political illusion and especially of philistine materialism. It also affirms the individual's duty to allow himself to be destroyed by society rather than abandon his ideal. His three major plays share the same concerns as the novels.

The poems convey images of stoical superiority, silent isolation, and dignified suffering, which take self-dramatization no doubt too far for modern taste, but which convey the quintessential Romantic need to investigate the values of the individual, especially of the outcast, who needs to remain aloof and alone in order to be true to his inner self, sometimes disguised as destiny. Vigny's poetic output was slight in quantity but was clearly intended to be prodigious in depth and to make a claim for the leadership of the new school, a role that went in the end to Victor Hugo, whose *Odes et ballades*, published in 1826, overtook Vigny's *Poèmes* in prestige and popularity.

The Reform of French Theater As early as 1823, Vigny admired Shakespeare's adroit synthesis of styles that allowed him to capture both the prosaic and lyrical aspects of the totality of human expression and aspiration. He found such attributes to be conspicuously absent in the virtually moribund neoclassical dramas of the period. He became convinced that Shakespearean drama could serve as a model for the reform and modernization of French theater.

Vigny's sporadic career as a dramatist began precisely at the time the Shakespeare controversy erupted in France during the 1820s. When his collaboration in 1827 with Émile Deschamps on a French adaptation of *Romeo and Juliet* (1594) was neither produced nor subsequently published, he set to work alone to translate *Othello* as *The Moor of Venice*, first performed at the Comédie-française on October 24, 1829. Vigny wanted his adaptation to serve as a point of mediation between the neoclassical factions that resisted all change and the Romantic innovators who advocated a complete revamping of the French stage. His translation endeavored to show that a new style, crucially informed by a different worldview, could triumph over the arbitrary limitations imposed by neoclassicism. His adaptation of *Othello* succeeded in softening the diehard resistance of opponents of Shakespeare and may be justifiably credited with preparing the atmosphere that enabled the success of Hugo's *Hernani* in 1830 and other daring dramas later.

Works in Critical Context

Vigny's works have received significant critical acclaim but little popular support. Only *Cinq-Mars* was an immediate popular success, yet it is ignored today. While *Chatterton* influenced the course of French Romantic drama, it, too, has fallen into neglect. Of Vigny's collections of stories, *Stello* and *The Military Necessity* have enjoyed both popular and critical acclaim since their publication. Most critics also agree that Vigny conveys his philosophy most successfully in his poetry. For instance, *Les Destinées: Poèmes philosophiques* is generally considered to be Vigny's greatest poetic achievement, though some scholars have termed many of the poems uneven in quality. Nevertheless, Albert Thibaudet called *Les Destinées*'s tercets "the most lastingly luminous poems, the fixed stars of French poetry," and a further example of Vigny's substantial contribution to the development of nineteenth-century French literature.

Poèmes antiques et modernes The collection of poems elicited mixed popular and critical reaction. Critics point to Vigny's inconsistency, inauthenticity, and not-so-subtle moral lessons. Whatever else, *Poèmes antiques et modernes* attested to the significant accomplishment of a poet whose verse was intricately linked to the mood and tenor of the new civilization being fashioned in the aftermath of the French Revolution.

Cinq-Mars *Cinq-Mars* proved to be an immediate popular success in 1826. A second printing came out in June of the same year, and by 1827, Vigny counted thirteen printings in various formats—this despite glaring shortcomings in the novel. Charles-Augustin Sainte-Beuve criticized the work severely in the *Globe*, chiding Vigny for his outrageous falsification of historical personalities and events and for the irritating anachronisms that undermined the narrative at crucial intervals. He alluded to chapter 20, "The Reading," as a case in point. Vigny situates the episode in the salon of the celebrated courtesan Marion Delorme in 1642. Members of the audience listen distractedly to Milton as he reads from *Paradise Lost* (actually not written until 1665). In the background, a somewhat larger group listens in rapt attention to a libertine poet discuss Madeleine de Scudéry's "Map of Love" from *Clélie*, which she published between 1654 and 1661. Such anachronisms and sudden shifts in plot development were bound to disconcert the more discerning reader. Even the portrait of the main protagonist is, at times, skimmed over in rather cavalier fashion.

Legacy Alfred de Vigny, poet, novelist, and dramatist, was an influential figure in the Romantic movement, particularly as it developed in the late 1820s and 1830s. His influence on the direction of French theater was profound, despite the fact that his dramatic output was relatively small. He completed only three original plays, each of which he saw produced and published, and several translations of Shakespeare, only one of which was produced in his lifetime.

Responses to Literature

1. Read a selection of poems from the early years of Vigny's career and some from his later years. In an essay, compare and contrast how Vigny's philosophical views seem to change between his early and later writings. Use specific examples from the poetry to support your ideas.

2. The plays *Chatterton* and *Stello* share a similar focus. With a group of your classmates, discuss what you think that focus is. How are the two plays linked through this shared theme?

3. Write an informal essay in which you describe the sort of picture of military life Vigny paints in *The Military Necessity*. What do you think his motivation was for depicting military life in such a light?

4. Make a chart in which you list and define the attributes of French Romanticism in one column, and in the other, list the attributes of *Chatterton* that make it an exemplar of Romantic drama.

BIBLIOGRAPHY

Books

Dictionary of Literary Biography. Vol. 119: *Nineteenth-Century French Fiction Writers: Romanticism and Realism, 1800–1860.* Edited by Catharine Savage Brosman. A Bruccoli Clark Layman Book. Detroit: Gale, 1992.

Dictionary of Literary Biography. Vol. 192: *French Dramatists, 1789–1914.* Edited by Barbara T. Cooper. A Bruccoli Clark Layman Book. Detroit: Gale, 1998.

Dictionary of Literary Biography. Vol. 217: *Nineteenth-Century French Poets.* Edited by Robert Beum. A Bruccoli Clark Layman Book. Detroit: Gale, 1999.

Doolittle, James. *Alfred de Vigny.* New York: Twayne, 1967.

Whitridge, Arnold. *Alfred de Vigny.* New York: Oxford University Press, 1933.

Elio Vittorini

BORN: *1908, Syracuse, Sicily, Italy*

DIED: *1966, Milan, Italy*

NATIONALITY: *Italian*

GENRE: *Fiction*

MAJOR WORKS:
Petty Bourgeoisie (1931)
Conversation in Sicily (1941)
The Red Carnation (1948)
The Dark and the Light: Erica and La Garibaldina (1956)
Women of Messina (1949–1964)

Overview

Elio Vittorini is among Italy's most distinguished writers of the mid-twentieth century. Vittorini was both an artist and a cultural entrepreneur. He wrote six novels—of

Elio Vittorini *Vittorini, Elio, photograph. AP Images.*

which one is unfinished and another is a long fragment—and some fifty short stories, while his many articles on literature, fine arts, politics, culture, and book and movie reviews appeared in approximately forty newspapers, journals, and magazines. In addition, he translated works of English and American literature, founded two cultural reviews, and edited three anthologies.

Works in Biographical and Historical Context

Growing Up in Sicilian Train Stations Vittorini was born in Sicily and spent much of his childhood with his father, a railroad worker, at various train stations. After only eight years of schooling, Vittorini began working in construction. By his late teens, however, he was also producing short stories. He eventually became a regular contributor of stories to the cooperatively managed periodical *Solaria*, and in 1931 he published these tales in the volume *Piccola Borghesia*. By this time Vittorini was working as a proofreader for the newspaper *La Nazione*. There he developed a command of the English language (in part, so it is rumored, by reading and rereading Daniel Defoe's 1719 novel *Robinson Crusoe*); by the mid-1930s—after a severe bout of lead poisoning caused him to leave *La Nazione*—he was supporting himself with translations of American and British writers.

International Fame, Trouble at Home In the late 1930s Vittorini began publishing his first major work, the novel *Conversation in Sicily* (also translated as *Conversations in Sicily*), in serialization. This serial novel—produced as a book in 1941—concerns a young man whose father calls

him home after fifteen years to visit his mother, whom his father had earlier deserted. Once home, the main character meets various political figures, including both fascists and antifascists. This reflected Vittorini's own firsthand experiences with the growing importance—and criticism—of the Fascist Party in Italy during the 1920s and 1930s. On a more personal level, however, the main character also reunites with his mother and even converses with the ghost of his brother, who had perished in the Abyssinian War (fought between Ethiopia and Italy in 1885–1886, and ending in a decisive defeat for the Italians, making Ethiopia the only nation in Africa to successfully resist European colonialism with military strength). The novel ends with the return home of the father, who is forgiven by both his wife and his son.

With *Conversation in Sicily*, though, Vittorini ran afoul of Italy's Fascist leaders, who accused him of publishing subversive literature. A few years elapsed, but eventually the Fascists finally arrested him. Then, after less than a year of incarceration, he was freed as his country prepared for German occupation. Because Italy under Mussolini had been Nazi Germany's ally in World War II (1939–1945), Mussolini invited the Germans to occupy the country to protect it against the Allied forces (many Italian troops being occupied fighting in North Africa). After Mussolini was deposed by his own Grand Council of Fascism in 1943, Hitler set him up as a puppet ruler and continued using Italy as a military staging-point until Allied forces liberated the country in 1945. Living among the Italian underground (a group resisting the Germans), Vittorini wrote another novel, *Men and Not Men*. This work, which appeared in English translation in 1986, nearly forty years after its initial publication, details the often violent conflict between Italy's underground forces and the occupying Germans. In the *Los Angeles Times Book Review*, Eric Siggs notes the novel's "vivid, blow-by-blow account" of the "ugly, bitter contest."

Postwar Work After World War II ended, Vittorini resumed his multifaceted literary career and in the ensuing ten years produced many of his most important works. Perhaps foremost among his publications from this period is *The Twilight of the Elephant*, about an idle patriarch whose seemingly insatiable appetite threatens the remainder of his household with starvation. *The Red Carnation*, another of Vittorini's key works from this period, would have appeared several years earlier—in the mid-1930s—were it not for the then-ruling Fascists, who had prevented its publication. The novel tells of an adolescent boy who falls in love with a prostitute as he is simultaneously drawn to Fascism.

The novellas *Erica* and *La Garibaldina*, which were collected in English translation as *The Dark and the Light*, are probably the most important of Vittorini's remaining publications. Like *The Red Carnation*, *Erica* was actually written in the mid-1930s. Its heroine, an adolescent forced to fend for her younger siblings in an Italian slum, becomes an unlikely prostitute. The broader, more comical *La*

Garibaldina concerns a young soldier's encounters with hostile migrant workers and an aging camp follower.

During the 1950s and 1960s, Vittorini presided over the later period of Italian neorealism, editing and publishing new writers such as Italo Calvino, Leonardo Sciascia, and Beppe Fenoglio. He wrote little himself during his last ten years and died in Milan in 1966.

Works in Literary Context

It was while Vittorini worked as a proofreader that he "discovered" Cesare Pavese's early poetry. Vittorini used this as inspiration to incorporate "poetry" (in the sense of creative writing) into the essay material that had attached itself to the genre of the novel during the last century, and this technique is displayed in *The Red Carnation* and *Conversation in Sicily*.

Lyrical Rhythm, Allegory, and the Universe in the Past Having learned English by reading *Robinson Crusoe*, Vittorini had gone on to translate Edgar Allan Poe, William Faulkner, John Steinbeck, and William Saroyan into Italian. He read Ernest Hemingway and became friendly with him. From Saroyan and Hemingway he picked up and perfected a style based on rhythm and repetition, which went a long way to achieving his ambitions for the novel. *Conversation in Sicily* describes a journey back to his childhood roots by an autobiographical, near Dante-esque figure who is trying to make positive sense of his past and his present. Contemporary reality is superimposed on the past in symbolical and even allegorical terms. For instance, much importance is given to food: the bitter oranges of returning fruit pickers, his mother's herring, and the childhood memories of melons—a basic reality and yet symbolic of poverty, oppression, and resilience. The language used to re-create this experience is lyrical but sometimes unorthodox, and through the rhythmic repetition of certain key phrases such as "twice real" and "the extra now" the theme is raised to the level of the universal. Speaking of poetry in his postwar magazine *Il politecnico* in 1945, Vittorini said, "Poetry is poetry because it does not stay bound to its origins and if it is born of sorrow it can be linked to all sorrow."

The style and content of *Conversation in Sicily* gave the work a mythical quality and indeed, in his introduction to the novel, the author refers to its allegorical quality.

The New Italian Novel *Conversation in Sicily*—published in 1938–1939 during Mussolini's Fascist regime—was banned by government censors in 1943, although today it is unanimously regarded as one of the major achievements of Italian literature in the twentieth century. Indeed, Italo Calvino declared the novel to be the manifesto of modern Italian fiction on account of its stylistic innovations and the bold political agenda inherent in the work. *Conversation in Sicily* is one of the first examples of neorealist fiction.

Italian neorealism in the postwar period attempted to give an almost journalistic account of the stark, harsh realities of the working class. The south was a favorite

---

LITERARY AND HISTORICAL CONTEMPORARIES

Vittorini's famous contemporaries include:

Cesare Pavese (1908–1950): An Italian novelist, poet, and critic, Pavese was lionized after his death as one of Italy's great authors.

Agatha Christie (1890–1976): The pen name of Agatha Mary Clarissa, Lady Mallowan, this British author wrote romances, plays, and, most memorably, over eighty crime novels.

Eudora Welty (1909–2001): Starting out as a photographer during the Great Depression, Welty soon switched to literature, making a name for herself as a short-fiction writer with such works as "Why I Live at the P.O." and "A Worn Path."

Orson Welles (1915–1985): An iconoclastic American motion picture director, actor, and screenwriter who created *Citizen Kane*, often cited as the best film ever made.

Robert Frost (1874–1963): Perhaps the best-known American poet of the twentieth century, Frost's gentle, rural themes belied his deep philosophical explorations.

---

subject for neorealists because of the bleak situation in the rural areas of Italy. Vittorini's prose is simple and linear with brief sentences, balanced clauses, and extensive use of dialogue and repetition. The range of vocabulary is limited to the most everyday phrases and expressions, making the style the opposite of the heavy, ornate, and empty political rhetoric of Fascism.

Works in Critical Context

Vittorini's reception by readers and critics was hampered by the censorship his works were subjected to during Mussolini's rule. Often years passed between Vittorini's completion of a work and its publication in book form. Even so, the author was even then well regarded both in his native Italy and in other parts of the world where translations of his work were available. In the ensuing years, he has attained the status of a great figure in world literature, with references to his literature and critical works abounding in contemporary discourse.

Conversation in Sicily *Conversation in Sicily* became immensely popular upon translation into English in 1949. R. P. Warren, writing in the *Nation*, describes the novel as "remarkable, quite beautiful," and Bruce Taylor, in his *Chicago Sun* appraisal, notes its "positive freshness of purpose, of idea, of style." Similarly, Robert Pick hails *Conversation in Sicily* as "great" in the *Saturday Review of Literature* and adds, "To call [Vittorini] a master may be premature.... But you feel the master's hand at every page."

COMMON HUMAN EXPERIENCE

Allegory, or the representation of abstract concepts through concrete forms, was often employed by Vittorini, who was participating in a long and rich literary tradition. Here are some other works that employ allegory to achieve their emotional and conceptual effects:

The Divine Comedy (1308–1321), an epic poem by Dante Alighieri. Perhaps the best-known allegory in literary history, this epic three-part poem follows the author's journey from Hell to Purgatory and on to Heaven, neatly summarizing the entirety of the medieval worldview and critiquing contemporary political and religious leaders along the way.

The Trojan Women (415 BCE), a play by Euripides. In this early example of political allegory, Euripides sets his tragedy in the mythical Trojan War, but was using the play to comment directly upon Athenian policy during the then-ongoing Peloponnesian War.

Animal Farm (1945), a novella by George Orwell. By using barnyard animals in place of humans, Orwell weaves a harrowing tale of a populist rebellion that turns into tyranny, an allegorical condemnation of Stalinist communism in the Soviet Union.

The Lion, the Witch, and the Wardrobe (1950), a novel by C. S. Lewis. Lewis consciously injected his fantasy tales of Narnia, of which this novel is the first, with vivid Christian allegories—Aslan the Lion is a Christlike figure, for example.

Women of Messina Also notable among Vittorini's writings is *Women of Messina*, his novel of a Sicilian commune that slowly regains prosperity after World War II—only to consequently degenerate. In his *New Republic* review, Anthony Covatta deems *Women of Messina* Vittorini's "most extended and successful social statement." Similarly, Webster Schott, writing in *London*, describes *Women of Messina* as Vittorini's most ambitious work. "What we . . . have in *Women of Messina* is a novel of grand scale and ultimate ambition," Schott writes. "Vittorini wanted to tell us all he knew about how and why human beings behave as they do." Noting that Vittorini continually revised *Women of Messina* between its initial publication in 1949 and its reappearance in 1964, Schott called it "the kind of novel a man writes once in a lifetime, never finishes to his satisfaction, and surrenders rather than completes."

Responses to Literature

1. Vittorini wrote often of his childhood and of a longing for the land he grew up in. Find examples in his work of how he viewed his native region of Sicily.

Why do you think Vittorini left Sicily as a young man and never returned? How does that both fit and not fit with these portrayals?

2. Ernest Hemingway was an admirer of Vittorini, going so far as to write an admiring introduction to the American edition of *Conversation in Sicily*. Compare the two authors' writing styles. What similarities did they share? How were they different? Why do you think Hemingway admired Vittorini?

3. Discuss Vittorini's influence on postwar Italian writers like Italo Calvino. What elements of Vittorini's style did these writers integrate into their own work? Why do you think Vittorini has been so influential?

4. Read *Women of Messina* and comment on its implicit social theory. What idea of humanity, if any, is Vittorini espousing? Does this novel suggest a concept of human existence as a thing that may be improved, or is it guided by a darker vision? Structure your response as a thesis-driven essay, with detailed analysis of several specific passages from the novel.

BIBLIOGRAPHY

Books

Bonsaver, Guido. *Censorship and Literature in Fascist Italy*. Toronto: University of Toronto Press, 2007.

Brand, Peter, and Lino Pertile. *The Cambridge History of Italian Literature*. Cambridge: Cambridge University Press, 1999.

Büdel, Oscar. "Vittorini, Elio (1908–1966)." In *Encyclopedia of World Biography*. 2nd ed. Ed. Suzanne M. Bourgoin. Detroit: Gale Research, 1998.

Drake, Francis. *Apostles and Agitators: Italy's Marxist Revolutionary Tradition*. Cambridge, Mass.: Harvard University Press, 2003.

Guiat, Cyrille. *The French and Italian Communist Parties: Comrades and Culture*. London: Frank Cass, 2003.

Heiney, Donald. *Three Italian Novelists: Moravia, Pavese, Vittorini*. Ann Arbor: University of Michigan Press, 1968.

▨ Voltaire

BORN: *1694, Paris*

DIED: *1778, Paris*

NATIONALITY: *French*

GENRE: *Fiction, drama, nonfiction*

MAJOR WORKS:

Oedipus (1718)

The History of Charles XII, King of Sweden (1732)

The Elements of Sir Isaac Newton's Philosophy (1738)

Candide (1759)

Irene (1778)

Voltaire *Stock Montage / Getty Images*

Overview

For more than thirty years, scholars have been working to establish a definitive edition of Voltaire's works. Because of the vastness and variety of Voltaire's creative output as well as the seeming contradictions in his character and behavior, the story of his life is challenging and, at times, even perplexing. Voltaire wrote across genres as a poet-essayist-philosopher; he was known stylistically for his wit and thematically for his defense of civil liberties. An avid supporter of social reform in the face of strict censorship laws, he frequently used satire to criticize Catholic dogma and French institutions. The ideas Voltaire promoted in his work influenced important thinkers of both the American and French revolutions.

Works in Biographical and Historical Context

Forged by Class and Religion Voltaire was born François-Marie Arouet on November 21, 1694, to an upper-middle-class Parisian family. At birth he was a weak child whose parents held little hope for his survival. But, under the care of a nurse, he gained his strength and within two years became a healthy and mischievous boy. Voltaire's father was a successful notary whose clients were generally rich and aristocratic. Young Voltaire grew up surrounded by wealthy, influential people who were of a higher social class than his own. Still, he had no trouble impressing everyone with his brightness and comic antics.

Even at a very early age, he loved being the center of attention. When Voltaire was ten, he was sent to an exclusive Jesuit school for boys, where he quickly gained a reputation as a class clown. Although he loved learning, he was very resentful of authority and constantly argued with his teachers over religion. During his seven years at the school, Voltaire became increasingly anti-Catholic. He strongly believed in God and in moral responsibility but denied religious authority and divine revelation.

Youthful Folly In addition to his startling views on religion, Voltaire had a fondness for writing scandalous poems and stories. Upon his graduation, he announced to his father that he intended to be a writer. His father thought that literary pursuits were useless and encouraged him to become a lawyer instead. Voltaire reluctantly agreed but spent the next couple of years mostly jobless, and writing in his spare time. In 1713, when Voltaire was nineteen, his godfather's brother was named the French ambassador to The Hague, in Holland. Complying with his father's wishes, Voltaire went along as the ambassador's page, a nonpaying job. In The Hague, he fell in love and planned to elope, but the ambassador discovered the scheme and sent Voltaire back home in disgrace.

In 1715, King Louis XIV died. His successor, Louis XV, was only five years old at the time, so for a while France was ruled by a regent, the Duke of Orléans. The duke was a man of questionable morals, and rumors about him soon began to circulate around Paris. When an anonymous poem surfaced in 1717 accusing the duke of committing incest with his daughter, there was little doubt about the identity of its author. The duke imprisoned Voltaire in the Bastille for a year. He was released in the spring of 1718, under the condition that he would not live in Paris. This was Voltaire's first taste of exile, a form of punishment he would receive several times throughout his life. He went to England and stayed at his father's country house in Chatenay but longed to return to Paris. Meanwhile, a theater company accepted his first play, *Oedipus*, and by the time it opened in Paris, he had officially changed his name from Arouet to Voltaire. *Oedipus* was a tremendous success and by the age of twenty-four, the notorious Voltaire had become a literary sensation.

Enlightenment For the rest of his life, Voltaire worked tirelessly, writing plays, poems, novels, history books, philosophy texts, encyclopedia articles, and an endless list of pamphlets and letters. Through his works, he became known as the chief advocate of the Enlightenment, a philosophical movement rooted in the powers of human reason. Voltaire did not invent the Enlightenment; most of the views he preached had already been expressed by others. But Voltaire is regarded as a key Enlightenment thinker because—more than anyone else in his time—he helped to popularize the new philosophy in France and abroad. By exploiting every medium that existed in his day, Voltaire bombarded European culture with endless assaults against the status quo: Christianity and government practices were his primary targets. Voltaire's writings were distinctive and easily recognizable. Still, most were published anonymously, due to the constant threat of imprisonment their author faced.

Heavily influenced by the writings of the English philosopher John Locke, Voltaire approached the study of history with an Enlightenment theme. He viewed the evolution of history as the gradual victory of rationalism over ignorance and superstition. This theme also provided the basis for many of his fictional works, most notably *Candide*. This novel stands as an all-out attack on the philosophy of optimism, which states that everything that happens—no matter how horrible—is for the best. In its place, Voltaire offers a simple, practical solution to the world's problems: cooperation.

Ferney and Later Years In the mid-1700s Voltaire served as a royal historiographer for Frederick the Great, the king of Prussia, in Berlin. After quarreling with the king in 1751, he distanced himself from the monarchy and lived off and on at Ferney on the shores of Lake Geneva. Having accumulated considerable wealth through wise investment, Voltaire added to his money by building a watchmaking industry in competition with the Swiss manufacturers. While living at Ferney, Voltaire also adopted a noble but poor girl whom he called Belle et Bonne ("beautiful and good"). She later became the Marquise de Villete. During her time with Voltaire, she served as an important source of encouragement and helped to make the last twenty years of his life the most productive ever. Much of his writing from that time championed the rights of individuals who had been mistreated.

In 1778, after a lifetime of exile, Voltaire finally returned to Paris to see the production of his last play, *Irene*. He was given a hero's welcome and spent his final days receiving guests from around the world, including Benjamin Franklin. He died (of what was probably prostate cancer) on May 30 of that year, having lived long enough to see the first political outcome of the Enlightenment—the American Revolution. On his deathbed, he asked for paper and ink, with which he wrote: "I die adoring God, loving my friends, not hating my enemies, and detesting superstition." Following Voltaire's death, the Church refused to grant permission for a burial in holy ground; however, thanks to the intervention of his nephew, Voltaire's mortal remains were finally laid to rest in a monastery in Champagne.

Works in Literary Context

Philosophical Writings: Truth and Fiction Voltaire expressed his revolutionary views about political and religious freedoms through a myriad of genres. From the epistolary style of *English Letters* (1734)—in which he framed his opinions as a series of letters addressed to a friend in France—and the fictional *Candide* to his poetry and historical studies, Voltaire presented his Enlightenment philosophies in both direct and indirect ways. Voltaire is credited for inventing the philosophical *conte*, or story, a genre that expresses intellect through fantastical or absurd happenings. Stylistically speaking, he was as conscious about the fashion with which to best present his ideas as he was about fashion itself; he felt form was the key to expression. Interestingly enough, despite Voltaire's experimentation with many different genres, he had an affinity for the theater and his critical social commentary is reflected throughout a canon of more than twenty tragedies.

Social Influence Inside and outside his texts, Voltaire championed the fight against intolerance. This activism is best illustrated by his involvement in an event in which a man named Calas, a Protestant, had been unjustly condemned by the Parliament of Toulouse for having murdered his son because he decided to follow Catholicism. Voltaire described the case in *Treaty on Tolerance* (1763). Later, he wrote in *Commentary on Crime and Punishment* (1766) that punishment should fit the offense. He denounced the provincial parliaments for abusing power as well as particular laws in their jurisdictions. In this way, he inspired a multitude of social and civil improvements. Voltaire may rightly be called the father of the rationalism of the nineteenth century and even of the twentieth. The successive waves of anticlericalism that swept first through the French bourgeoisie and then through the masses, and the harsh measures taken against the Church, may possibly be traced to his influence.

Voltaire's Self-Contradictions A survey of Voltaire's work demonstrates his changeable opinions. For example, though he could be considered an optimist by his writing in *The World* (1736), as well as in *Discourse on Man* (1738), Voltaire uses cynicism to show his pessimistic side in *Poem about the Lisbon Disaster* (1756). Furthermore, while Voltaire presented himself as a defender of free will in

Treaty on Metaphysics, he plays the role of "apologist of determinism" in both *The Ignorant Philosophy* (1755) and in his *Philosophical Dictionary*.

Works in Critical Context

"The spirit of Voltaire"—to use the title of the classic work by Norman Torrey—remains vital and alive through his textual wit, the ironic verve of his commitments, and his sincere dedication to humanity in all of its global extent and variety. "Voltaire is a good vaccine against stupidity," writes Emmanuel Berl in an introduction to Voltaire's works, and that kind of protection is as crucial today as it was in Voltaire's day.

Candide   *Candide* is the most famous and widely read work by Voltaire. *Candide* was written in 1758, when Voltaire was exiled in Geneva, and published anonymously the following year. Voltaire consistently denied that he was the book's author and even called it a "schoolboy's joke." Although *Candide* was banned in Geneva and ordered destroyed, it was immensely popular and contributed to the demise of optimism as a serious philosophy. Not all agreed with Voltaire's criticisms, however; an unnamed reviewer writing for the *Gentleman's Magazine and Historical Quarterly* in 1759, took Voltaire to task for, "like other ignorant persons," either failing to understand the essence of the Optimists' argument or deliberately distorting it in order to prove it ludicrous. Still, James Boswell, writing in *The Life of Samuel Johnson* in 1791, noted that Voltaire had refuted Optimism "with brilliant success." It is perhaps an indication of Voltaire's success in this regard that scholars in the decades that followed spent a great deal of time analyzing not *Candide* but Voltaire's numerous other works. It has also been argued that because the work is ultimately a philosophical critique—albeit an effective one—it is not worthy of study as literature. More recent scholars have focused on the specifics of Voltaire's writing, such as the structure of his sentences (as in a 1959 Ira O. Wade essay), or on the political and philosophical context in which it was written.

Zadig   According to Andrée Maurois,

> Voltaire's contemporaries . . . attached little importance to frivolous stories in which what struck them most forcibly were numerous allusions to the author's personal enemies. 'It is easy to recognize Voltaire under the disguise of the sagacious Zadig. The calumnies and spite of courtiers . . . the disgrace of the hero are so many allegories to be interpreted easily enough. It is thus that he takes revenge upon his enemies.' The abbé Boyer, who was the Dauphin's tutor and a powerful ecclesiastic, took in very bad part the attacks on one whose identity was but thinly concealed behind the anagram Reyob. 'It would please me mightily if all this to-do about *Zadig* could be ended,' wrote Madame du Chatelet, and it was not long before

Voltaire disowned a book 'which some there are who accuse of containing audacious attacks upon our holy religion.'

Responses to Literature

1. Write a paragraph in which you describe the balanced religion of Eldorado as described in *Candide*.

2. Use resources from your library or the Internet to research the difference between Optimism and Enlightenment. Then, create an electronic or poster presentation in which you compare and contrast the two movements.

3. Read *Candide* and *Gulliver's Travels*. Make a chart in which you compare and contrast Gulliver and Candide.

4. Write an essay in which you explore whether you think Candide is an interesting character, or whether he is just important because of his travels and discoveries.

5. After reading selections from Voltaire's work, write an essay on how his fictional writing demonstrates influences from his historical writing.

BIBLIOGRAPHY

Books

Barr, Mary-Margaret H. *A Century of Voltaire Study: A Bibliography of Writings on Voltaire, 1825–1925*. New York: Institute of French Studies, 1929.

Besterman, Theodore. *Voltaire*. 3rd ed. Oxford: Voltaire Foundation, 1976.

Brooks, Richard A. *Voltaire and Leibniz*. Geneva: Droz, 1964.

Brumfitt, John Henry. *Voltaire, Historian*. London: Oxford University Press, 1958.

Desnoiresterres, Gustave. *Voltaire et la société française au dix-huitième siècle*. 8 Vols. 2nd ed. Paris: Didier, 1871–1876.

Hertzberg, Arthur. *The French Enlightenment and the Jews*. New York: Columbia University Press, 1968.

Lanson, Gustave. *Voltaire*. Paris: Hachette, 1960.

Mason, Haydn. *Voltaire*. Baltimore: Johns Hopkins University Press, 1981.

Pomeau, René. *D'Arouet à Voltaire, 1694–1734*. Oxford: Voltaire Foundation, 1985.

Torrey, Norman L. *The Spirit of Voltaire*. New York: Columbia University Press, 1938.

"Voltaire (1694–1778)." In *Literature Criticism from 1400 to 1800*, vol. 14, edited by James P. Draper and James E. Person Jr., 318–421. Detroit: Gale Research, 1991.

Wade, Ira O. *The Intellectual Development of Voltaire*. Princeton, N.J.: Princeton University Press, 1969.

▨ Andrei Voznesensky

BORN: *1933, Moscow, Soviet Union*

NATIONALITY: *Russian*

GENRE: *Fiction, poetry, nonfiction*

MAJOR WORKS:

Mosaic (1960)

Antiworlds (1964)

Voznesensky: Selected Poems (1966)

Nostalgia for the Present (1978)

Andrei Voznesensky © *Christopher Felver / CORBIS*

Overview

"The name of Voznesensky in Soviet poetry often becomes the centre of heated discussion," observed Vladimir Ognev. "The young poet leaves nobody indifferent. Widely differing estimations are given to his poetry—some call him a daring innovator, others a cold rhymester." Regardless of the more critical views of his work, Voznesensky warmed the hearts of his followers and heated the tempers of Soviet officials during his rise to international prominence in the 1960s. His swift, uncluttered, and often bold verse differed radically from the restricted poetry the Soviet Union had known in the Joseph Stalin years, and Russian audiences responded enthusiastically to the young poet's work.

Works in Biographical and Historical Context

Surrounded by Books As a child, Voznesensky was introduced to Russia's great literary tradition by his mother, who surrounded him with books by great authors such as Aleksandr Blok, Fyodor Dostoyevsky, and Boris Pasternak and read poetry to him as well. Voznesensky experimented a bit with writing when he was young, but devoted himself mainly to painting and drawing. After he received his degree from the Moscow Architectural Institute, however, his interest in architecture dropped. Some of his poems appeared in magazines at that time and two years later, in 1960, he published his first book, *Mosaic*.

As a teenager, Voznesensky had sent some of his poems to Pasternak, who consequently invited Voznesensky to visit. The poems were obvious Pasternak imitations. Later, though, Voznesensky sent some of his postgraduate poems to Pasternak, revealing an entirely different poet. In the 1980s, Voznesensky participated in the drive to reinstate Pasternak into the Soviet Writers Union, giving the writer official status in the Soviet Union for the first time since 1958.

Success and Change Several factors contributed to Voznesensky's "meteoric" rise from a developing poet to one of the Soviet Union's most prominent literary figures. To begin with, poetry is Russia's "national art," contends Voznesensky. In addition, his generation was financially and politically in a position to afford and appreciate poetry readings. By American standards, the audiences were stupendous. Typical crowds for readings by Voznesensky numbered more than fourteen thousand. Enthusiasm for the printed word matched the enthusiasm for the spoken word. Even today, Voznesensky's new books sell out within hours of publication.

Problems with Authority To Soviet government officials and heads of the Soviet Writers Union, Voznesensky was somewhat more of an individual than they would have liked. Many times during his career, he has been at the center of controversy. One especially noteworthy denunciation took place in 1963, when Soviet premier Nikita Khrushchev reprimanded Voznesensky and other Western-oriented intellectuals, accusing them of straying from the paths of "Soviet realism." The Soviet regime at the time subscribed to the notion of socialist realism, in which art was seen as a tool for expressing the ideals and praising the accomplishments of the Soviet people; art for any other purpose was viewed as nonproductive at best, and destructive to society at worst. Attacks continued in 1965 when the government-controlled Communist youth newspaper accused him of obscurity of content and experimenting with complicated poetic forms. By 1969, government suppression had erased Voznesensky's name from Soviet literary journals. A decade later, in 1979, Voznesensky and several other writers were chastised for their roles in the publication of *Metropol*, a new literary magazine that challenged the government's strict control of the arts.

One much publicized incident involving Soviet restrictions occurred in 1967, when a New York City reading had to be canceled. Two days before the scheduled reading, rumors circulated, suggesting that Voznesensky had been the target of governmental attempts to detain or restrict him. At first, messages from Moscow said Voznesensky was sick, yet later reports revealed that his passport had indeed been sent to the U.S. Embassy with a request for a visa. But renewed hope for Voznesensky's appearance faded when the poet himself phoned New York and canceled his visit.

Publications and Continuing Popularity His first two major translated volumes are *Antiworlds* and *Voznesensky: Selected Poems*, in which Voznesensky stresses the importance of human values through works of irony and eroticism. Voznesensky's later works have benefited from the increased artistic freedom permitted under the rule of Soviet premier Mikhail Gorbachev. Critics assert that Voznesensky's contemporary poems are more thoughtful, direct, and dynamic than his earlier

---

LITERARY AND HISTORICAL CONTEMPORARIES

Voznesensky's famous contemporaries include:

Mikhail Gorbachev (1931–): Last head of state of the former Union of Soviet Socialist Republics (USSR) and contributor to the end of the cold war.

Boris Yeltsin (1931–2007): First president of the Russian Federation after Gorbachev and the fall of Communism.

Yevgeny Yevtushenko (1933–): Voznesensky's peer and fellow poet; the two are often compared or confused with one another.

Bella Akhmadulina (1937–): Russian female poet whose works, despite the times, are decidedly antipolitical.

---

verse. Voznesensky also comments on such modern problems as Siberia's water pollution and the Chernobyl nuclear disaster, which resulted in the forced permanent relocation of over three hundred thousand citizens. *An Arrow in the Wall: Selected Poetry and Prose* (1987) probes humanity's pretensions through extensive use of irony. Reviewers lauded the volume's humor and sincerity, and he is regarded as one of Russia's finest to this day.

Works in Literary Context

Pop Culture A trademark characteristic of Voznesensky's work is its use of cultural references from around the world and throughout modern history. In one of his most celebrated poems, "I Am Goya," Voznesensky expounds on the destruction and wars that have ravaged Russia by utilizing the persona of Francisco de Goya (1746–1828), the Spanish painter whose works reflect the political and social upheavals of his time. Loss of identity is explored in "Monolog Merlin Monro" and "Oza" through two distinctly different techniques. The first poem, a discussion of ill-fated actress Marilyn Monroe, shows how the manipulative power of society can turn individuals into objects, while "Oza," a spoof of Edgar Allan Poe's "The Raven," examines the bewilderment of artists in a technocratic world.

Nationalism and Internationalism Despite his conflicts with Soviet authorities, Voznesensky maintains an intense love for his own country. In one poem, for example, "he exalted the ancient idea that Russia's mission is to save the world from darkness," reported the *New York Times*. Voznesensky has also admired the United States and, particularly, Robert Kennedy. The poet and the senator met in 1967 and discussed, among other topics, the youth of their respective countries. After Kennedy's death, Voznesensky published a poem paying tribute to his assassinated friend.

COMMON HUMAN EXPERIENCE

Voznesensky is concerned with political oppression, most likely inspired by the censorship of his own work in the Soviet Union. Though many of his peers chose to avoid being political for these reasons, he soldiered on and made an impact on the literary scene. Here are some other works that are defiantly—and often controversially—political.

The Prince (1532), an essay by Niccolò Machiavelli. This list of rules for a leader to follow has often been criticized as cruel, and it has a decidedly untrusting slant.

Uncle Tom's Cabin (1852), a novel by Harriet Beecher Stowe. Not only did this book portray the cruelty of slavery and advocate abolition, but some say it helped spark the American Civil War.

A Tale of Two Cities (1859), a novel by Charles Dickens. The basis for this famous, intricate book is the French Revolution.

1984 (1949), a novel by George Orwell. Though cloaked in the guise of fiction, this novel is obviously a warning against totalitarianism in England and Europe.

Works in Critical Context

Voznesensky has become a favorite of several distinguished American literary figures. Among the poets who have translated his work into English are Stanley Kunitz, Richard Wilbur, William Jay Smith, Robert Bly, W. H. Auden, Allen Ginsberg, and Lawrence Ferlinghetti. In his introduction to *Nostalgia for the Present*, playwright Arthur Miller assessed Voznesensky's efforts: "He has tried to speak, in these poems, as though he alone had a tongue, as though he alone had learned the news of today and tomorrow, as though the space taken up by his poem were precious and must not be used by counterfeit words." Another Voznesensky admirer, W. H. Auden, once gave these reasons for appreciating the poet: "As a fellow maker, I am struck first and foremost by his craftmanship.... Obvious, too, at a glance is the wide range of subject matter by which Mr. Voznesensky is imaginatively excited ... and the variety of tones, elegiac, rebellious, etc., he can command. Lastly, every word he writes, even when he is criticizing, reveals a profound love for his native land and its traditions."

Selected Poems Translations have been a difficulty with reviewers of Voznesensky's work, especially in some of the earlier volumes. Anselm Hollo's translations in *Selected Poems*, for example, disappointed Gibbons Ruark. Voznesensky's "work is clearly superior to Yevtushenko's," Ruark wrote in comparing the two poets. "Unfortunately, his excellence seldom shows through Anselm Hollo's translations." Critics agreed that Herbert

Marshall's translations in *Voznesensky: Selected Poems* surpassed Hollo's. "The volume of selections by Herbert Marshall is, on the whole, an improvement over Anselm Hollo," wrote the *Hudson Review*. "But it is still an awkward and in places a careless performance." Other translations of Voznesensky's work have received considerably more praise.

Antiworlds In his review of *Antiworlds*, Graham Martin noted "Voznesensky's main bogy is the 'cyclotron,' symbol of all the dehumanising pressures in the modern world, and in 'Oza,' a long difficult poem, he deploys all his satiric force against 'the scientist,' damn his eyes." Similarly, M. L. Rosenthal found in Voznesensky "a satirist ... who is against the computerization of the soul." As Auden pointed out, however, Voznesensky's focus can vary considerably. Miller Williams explained: "Voznesensky is an exciting writer who bangs and tumbles through his poems, knocking over icons and knocking down walls, talking with curiosity, anguish, and joy—in sharp and startling metaphor—about love and technology, science and art, the self and the soul and Andrei Voznesensky and people." Another admirer, A. Alvarez, praised Voznesensky, too, for "whatever direct, passionate thrust launches them [his poems in *Antiworlds*], they curve obliquely and brilliantly through layer after layer of experience before they land again."

Responses to Literature

1. Read two or three of Voznesensky's poems. With a classmate, discuss how Voznesensky's feelings toward technology are revealed in these works. Look specifically at language and imagery.

2. Using resources at your library or on the Internet, research Yevgeny Yevtushenko. Read one or two of Yevtushenko's poems. Then read one or two of Voznesensky's poems. Finally, using examples from the poems to support your opinions, write an essay in which you compare and contrast Yevtushenko's style with Voznesensky's.

3. Using resources at your library or on the Internet, research the Cold War. Then read one or two of Voznesensky's poems. Write an essay describing how the effects of the cold war are present in the poems you chose.

4. With a group of your classmates, discuss how political oppression could have actually helped Voznesensky's writing. Use examples from poems that you have read to support your ideas.

BIBLIOGRAPHY

Books

Carlisle, Olga. *Poets on Street Corners.* New York: Random House, 1969.

———. *Voices in the Snow.* New York: Random House, 1962.

W-Z

Derek Walcott

BORN: *1930, Castries, Saint Lucia*

NATIONALITY: *West Indian*

GENRE: *Poems, plays*

MAJOR WORKS:

Drums and Colours (1958)

In a Green Night (1962)

Another Life (1973)

The Star-Apple Kingdom (1979)

Omeros (1989)

Overview

For some forty years, Derek Walcott has been the leading poet and playwright of the West Indies. Winner of the 1992 Nobel Prize in Literature, Walcott is highly regarded for poetry and plays that focus on the mixed African and European influences of his Caribbean heritage. His poetic language reflects this cultural division, employing both the formal, structured language of Elizabethan verse and the colorful dialect of his native island, St. Lucia. His plays have ranged in subject matter from adaptations of classical Greek drama to topical explorations of everyday problems. While embracing the literary tradition of England, Walcott has frequently denounced the exploitation and suppression of Caribbean culture that resulted from British colonial rule.

Works in Biographical and Historical Context

Divided Loyalties   Derek Alton Walcott was born on January 23, 1930, on St. Lucia, a small island in the West Indies. His mother was a schoolteacher who encouraged his early education and love for reading. She was also involved in a community cultural group and got her son involved in local theater. His father, a civil servant, poet, and visual artist, died when Derek and his twin brother, Roderick, were only one year old. Walcott drew inspira-tion from the poems and watercolor paintings his father left behind and soon came to regard his own single-minded commitment to the artistic life as being a matter of completing what his father had begun.

Walcott has characterized his childhood as "schizo-phrenic," referring to the divided loyalties associated with his African and English ancestry as well as the fact that he grew up in a middle-class Methodist family in a society that was predominantly Roman Catholic and poor. This sense of divided identity would become one of the main themes of Walcott's writing.

The colonial education Walcott received exposed him to the heritage of English literature, for which he displayed an affinity. He began writing poetry at an early age, often imitating such writers as W. H. Auden, T. S. Eliot, James Joyce, and Dylan Thomas. When he was eighteen, he financed the publication of *Twenty-Five Poems* (1948), his first poetry collection. While studying literature at St. Mary's College in St. Lucia and at the University of West Indies in Jamaica, he completed two more volumes of poetry and wrote *Henri Christophe*, a historical play written in verse. The play was staged in 1950 by the St. Lucia Arts Guild, which he had helped to found earlier in the same year. He earned his bachelor of arts degree in 1953 in English, French, and Latin.

Creating a West Indian Theater   During his years in Jamaica in the 1950s, he became more locally popular, especially through the many productions of his plays, most of which he directed himself. In 1958, Walcott was commissioned to write a play for the opening of the first Federal Parliament of the West Indies. The result was *Drums and Colours*, a pageant that chronicles the history of the Caribbean in four episodes. Each episode centers on the story of a great historical figure: Christopher Columbus, Sir Walter Raleigh, Toussaint L'Overture, and the Jamaican nationalist George William Gordon, in chronological order.

Drums and Colors brought Walcott both critical rec-ognition and a Rockefeller Fellowship to study theater in

Derek Walcott   *Walcott, Derek, photograph. © Jerry Bauer. Reproduced by permission.*

the United States. He stayed less than a year, and upon his return to the Caribbean, became intensely involved in Trinidad's artistic community, writing reviews and organizing the Trinidad Theatre Workshop, where several of his plays were produced during the 1950s and 1960s.

Career Reaches New Heights *Dream on Monkey Mountain* (1967) is often considered Walcott's most successful play. The 1960s and the 1970s were also the period when Walcott gained international stature as a poet. *In a Green Night* (1962) included such soon-to-be-famous pieces as "A Sea Chantey," a litany of his love for the islands; "A City's Death by Fire"; "Ruins of a Great House," which wrestled with the understandable Caribbean rage at a history centered on slavery; and "A Far Cry from Africa," in which the poet captured the West Indian's dilemma with the lines, "The gorilla wrestles with the superman. / I who am poisoned with the blood of both, / Where shall I turn, divided to the vein?" The scope of Walcott's visibility widened when the New York publisher Farrar, Straus published his *Selected Poems* in 1964.

Revolution and Politics In *The Castaway, and Other Poems* (1965), Walcott used the iconic figure of

Robinson Crusoe to explore themes of alienation and isolation. The early 1970s were a time of political turmoil in the West Indies, as the socialist and "Black Power" movements confronted established governments. Walcott rejected radical platforms for social revolution, but was outspoken in his concern for the poor and his insights into the lasting legacies of colonial rule. From this period on, Walcott's political commitments became increasingly visible in his writing. He maintained a high literary output. Among his works of the 1970s are his autobiography in verse, *Another Life* (1973), two further volumes of poetry, *Sea Grapes* (1976) and *The Star-Apple Kingdom* (1979), and the musical play *O Babylon!* (1976), which concerns the Rastafarians of Jamaica. Rastafarianism is a fairly new religion that emerged in Jamaica in the 1930s; its combines Biblical teachings with the belief that Haile Selassie, the former emperor of Ethiopia, was God incarnate.

The Fortunate Traveler in the United States Derek Walcott received the lucrative and prestigious John D. and Catherine MacArthur Foundation Fellowship in 1981. Early in 1982, he accepted a position as visiting professor of English at Boston University. He has been teaching in American universities ever since. Although he relocated to the United States, he has continued to return to the Caribbean frequently to have plays produced there.

In the deepest sense, Walcott never left the Caribbean, even though he agonized about having left it, for his concerns remained exclusively with the legacy of Caribbean history. His poetry continues to delve into themes of division, whether in the form of inequality between rich and poor, as in "North and South" from *The Fortunate Traveller* (1981), or his own situation as a displaced exile, as in "Here" and "Elsewhere" from *The Arkansas Testament* (1987). His representation of the North, whether Europe or the United States, is always from the point of view of the Caribbean person.

Homeric Echoes Two highlights of Walcott's later career brought to a culmination his imaginative use of the classics, and more particularly, of Homer. In 1990, Walcott published his monumental *Omeros. Omeros* imagines West Indian fishermen, prostitutes, and landlords in such classical roles as Achilles, Helen, and Hector. It interweaves their story with its echoes of Homer, with the story of a retired British officer living in his adopted colonial home. The poet and narrator each appears as a character in his own fiction.

This achievement in poetry was doubled in the area of drama by Walcott's *The Odyssey*, which premiered in 1992. His epic, commissioned by the Royal Shakespeare Company, represented a fulfillment of Walcott's career. Like Odysseus himself, determined to return to his home of Ithaca and be reunited with his wife, Penelope, the playwright has consistently written of the wanderer, driven by the desire for home. He returned to the theme once again with *The Prodigal* (2004), a book-length poem that celebrates the happiness of homecoming and healing of the guilt of wandering. Walcott has said this will be his final book.

Works in Literary Context

Walcott was strongly influenced by his education within the British colonial system, which immersed him in classical and English literature. Some of his earliest works represent little more than imitations of modern poets such as Joyce and Eliot. He consciously absorbed and attempted to assimilate what he once referred to in the introduction to *Dream on Monkey Mountain and Other Plays* (1970) as "The literature of Empires, Greek, Roman, British." At the same time, staying true to his Caribbean roots and finding innovative ways to use language as a bridge between Afro-Caribbean and Western cultures have been the primary projects of his career.

Influence of Brecht Walcott's career in the theater illustrates this effort most vividly. His early efforts to forge a new type of West Indian theater led him to adapt traditional folk tales and incorporate such folklore elements as calypso music, carnival masks, and mime. In bringing these elements under artistic control, Walcott was aided by the influence of Bertolt Brecht, the German playwright and stage director. Brecht's theory of the "epic theater" provided the foundation for Walcott's assimilated techniques. Through Brecht, Walcott also discovered classic Asian theater and film. Akira Kurosawa's film *Rashômon* (1950), with its shifting perspectives on the reality of one event, is clearly a basis for Walcott's 1959 play *Malcauchon*.

Friends and Collaborators Walcott met and befriended the American poet Robert Lowell in Trinidad in 1962, not long after the publication of *In a Green Night*. Lowell enthusiastically praised Walcott's work, and Walcott has acknowledged Lowell's influence on his poetry. Walcott's commitment to the discipline of verse found encouragement in two literary friendships he developed on relocating to the United States: with Joseph Brodsky and Seamus Heaney, two of the most considerable poets of his time. All three were to become Nobel laureates (Brodsky in 1987, Heaney in 1995), and all three were published by Farrar, Straus, and Giroux. Additionally, the three men were all outsiders in the United States: Brodsky was an exiled Russian, and Heaney an Irish expatriate. The three poets collaborated on a book, published in 1996, celebrating the work of American poet Robert Frost.

Regional and Worldwide Influence Derek Walcott's artistic influence in the Caribbean is towering. He is a revered figure on his native islands. No writer has done more to fuse the Caribbean and European cultural traditions, while exploring the many tensions between them. His literary success has encouraged many younger Caribbean artists, many of whom have also spent time in

the United States or the United Kingdom. The success of his Trinidad Theatre Workshop has inspired new companies throughout the West Indies.

More broadly, Walcott has become a prominent voice in what has come to be called postcolonial literature, linking his work thematically with that of African and Asian authors. His international acclaim affirms the importance of small places, showing that writers from the outposts of world power who focus on the concerns of their place and people need not be dismissed as too regional or parochial.

Works in Critical Context

Even before receiving the Nobel Prize, Walcott enjoyed an international reputation placing him among the greatest of contemporary English writers. Although many of his plays are highly regarded, the strength of his reputation rests primarily on his lyric poetry. Throughout his career, though, he has had to contend with the charge that he is so deeply influenced by Western tradition that he has yet to achieve his own voice. Beginning in the 1960s with Walcott's first books, there were reservations about the artificiality of a West Indian using such "eloquent English." Some critics have charged that Walcott's written expression is so refined and technically intricate that it can obscure or overshadow his meaning. Such criticism arises in part from his efforts, some more successful than others, to blend Afro-Caribbean folk styles and classical European poetics. Over time, these critical voices have diminished somewhat, as his accomplishments are more widely recognized. Walcott offered a unique voice reflecting the cultural matrix of the New World.

Dream on Monkey Mountain (1967) The play *Dream on Monkey Mountain* was one of Walcott's first to receive international recognition from established critics. W. I. Scobie, writing for the *National Review*, called it "a superb play," as well as "a work of intense verbal and

COMMON HUMAN EXPERIENCE

Derek Walcott's poetry and plays are often categorized as postcolonial in their focus on the legacies of slavery and imperialism and the complications of clashing cultural inheritance. Here are some other important works in the postcolonial genre:

Midnight's Children (1980), a novel by Salman Rushdie. At the stroke of midnight on August 15, 1947, as India becomes an independent nation, two newborn infants—one from a wealthy Muslim family, one from a poor Hindu family—are switched.

In a Free State (1971), a novel by V. S. Naipaul. In these stories set in sub-Saharan Africa, the third world is a "free state" in which the characters can find nothing to belong to.

In the Skin of a Lion (1987), a novel by Michael Ondaatje. A fictional account of immigrants whose labor helped build the city of Toronto, several characters from this novel continue in the author's more widely known novel *The English Patient*.

Orientalism (1978), a nonfiction work by Edward Said. In this founding text of postcolonial studies, the author reveals the subtly demeaning codes Westerners use to discuss Arabs, Islam, and the Middle East.

The Shock of Arrival: Reflections on Postcolonial Experience (1996), a collection by Meena Alexander. This collection of poems and essays follows the author from her childhood in India and the Sudan to her present home in New York City.

visual beauty, and visionary insight." Edith Oliver, reviewing the play for *The New Yorker*, states, "Every line of it plays; there are no verbal decorations."

Another Life (1973) Walcott's long autobiographical poem *Another Life* divided many critics. "*Another Life* should make it clear," according to Roger Garfitt of *London Magazine*, "if it was ever in doubt, that Derek Walcott's superlative descriptions are far more than description, that they are the only feasible expression of his situation." Paul Smyth, in a review for *Poetry*, states, "It is a restless mixture of lyric and narrative, of the local and the European, of the evocative and the didactic; ultimately, its elements don't cohere or reconcile..." However, Smyth does recommend the book: "I urge everyone who cares for the wonders of fresh metaphor in the service of deep thought and feeling to sift *Another Life* for its triumphs." T. O'Hara offers a different opinion in *Best Sellers*, arguing that the poetry is too showy: "I was fascinated by his ingenuity but somewhat put off by the dazzling images and diction. The attention is violated in poetry like this rather than held as it should be."

O'Hara asserts that the book "suffers from a metaphor glut," and though the critic "[does not] doubt for a moment Mr. Walcott's abilities," his conclusion is that the book "doesn't work as a long poem."

Responses to Literature

1. Consider the use Walcott makes of classical references in *Omeros*. How is he asserting a connection between the heritage of ancient Greece and the present-day culture of the West Indies? Can you provide some specific examples from the text itself?

2. Do some research on the history of St. Lucia, the island nation where Derek Walcott was born. What light does this history shed on the multiple cultural traditions informing Walcott's literature?

3. Familiarize yourself with Bertolt Brecht's theory of dramaturgy, or stage direction. Which of his ideas do you think helped Derek Walcott integrate West Indian folklore with European traditions in the Trinidad Theatre Workshop, how were they used by Walcott and why were they successful?

BIBLIOGRAPHY

Books

Bloom, Harold, ed. *Derek Walcott*. Philadelphia: Chelsea House, 2003.

Breslin, Paul. *Nobody's Nation: Reading Derek Walcott*. Chicago: University of Chicago Press, 2001.

"Derek Walcott (1930–)." *Contemporary Literary Criticism*. Edited by Carolyn Riley. Vol. 4. Detroit: Gale Research, 1975, pp. 574–576.

"Derek Walcott (1930–)." *Contemporary Literary Criticism*. Edited by Carolyn Riley and Barbara Harte. Vol. 2. Detroit: Gale Research, 1974, pp. 459–460.

Hamner, Robert D. *Derek Walcott*. Boston: Twayne, 1981.

——. *Epic of the Dispossessed: Derek Walcott's Omeros*. Columbia: University of Missouri Press, 1997.

King, Bruce. *Derek Walcott and West Indian Drama*. Oxford: Oxford University, 1995.

——. *Derek Walcott: A Caribbean Life*. Oxford: Oxford University Press, 2000.

Olaniyan, Tejumola. *Scars of Conquest/Masks of Resistance: The Invention of Cultural Identities in African, African-American, and Caribbean Drama*. Oxford: Oxford University Press, 1995.

Parker, Michael, and Roger Starkey. *Postcolonial Literatures: Achebe, Ngugi, Desai, Walcott*. New York: St. Martin's Press, 1995.

Terada, Rei. *Derek Walcott's Poetry: American Mimicry*. Boston: Northeastern University Press, 1992.

Thomas, Ned. *Poet of the Islands*. Cardiff, Wales: Welsh Arts Council, 1980.

Periodicals

Agenda (Winter 2002–2003): 39.
Callaloo 28 (Winter 2005).
Verse 11 (Summer 1994): 93–170.

Edmund Waller

BORN: *1606, Coleshill, Hertfordshire, England*

DIED: *1687, Beaconsfield, England*

NATIONALITY: *British*

GENRE: *Poetry*

MAJOR WORKS:

"The Story of Phoebus and Daphne, Applied" (c. 1637)

"Go, Lovely Rose" (1645)

A Panegyrick to My Lord Protector, of the present greatness and joynt interest of His Highness, and this nation (1655)

Instructions to a painter, for the drawing of a picture of the state and posture of the English forces at sea (1665)

On the Park at St. James's (1660)

Edmund Waller © *Michael Nicholson / CORBIS*

Overview

Edmund Waller is considered a minor poet within the English canon. He is known less for his poetry than his political activism; specifically, the thwarted royalist conspiracy known as "Waller's Plot." In terms of his writing, he is best recognized for "Go, Lovely Rose" (1645), which has been widely anthologized as an excellent example of a Cavalier lyric.

Works in Biographical and Historical Context

Early Wealth Waller was born to Robert Waller and Anne Hampden Waller on March 3, 1606, in Coleshill, Hertfordshire, England. His mother was a cousin by marriage to Oliver Cromwell, who would later become Britain's ruler. Waller's father died when Waller was twelve, leaving him a significant allowance that made him independently wealthy.

Guided by his formidable mother to adulthood, Waller attended Eton College and King's College, Cambridge, but he never took a degree. He married Anne Banks, a wealthy heiress, on July 5, 1631. She died in 1634 while giving birth to their second child.

Parliamentarian and Middle-Aged Poet Royalist Edward Hyde, first Earl of Clarendon and a contemporary of the poet, once wrote that Waller was "nursed in parliaments." Although historians are uncertain about which parliament was his first, Waller himself asserted that he held his initial seat when he was only sixteen. Thus, most researchers surmise that Waller served in 1621 as a member for Agmondesham in the last parliament of King James I. In the parliament of 1624, he represented Ilchester and took a seat in the first parliament of Charles I.

Waller did not begin writing poetry until he was nearly thirty years old. He hired George Morley, who later became the bishop of Winchester, as his tutor. Waller's poetic talent was first widely noticed in his courtship poems. In addition to love lyrics, Waller also wrote poems to politicians and royalty and poems complimenting friends and private individuals.

Waller's Plot and Exile from England While the origins of Waller's 1643 plot against Parliament remain unclear, scholars have pieced together the actual events of the insurrection, the arrest of Waller and his coconspirators, and Waller's narrow escape from being executed. Essentially, Waller took the side of King Charles I against Parliament (the king and the parliament were at odds) and attempted to establish London as a stronghold for the king.

According to modern Waller critic George Thorn-Drury, Waller drew up a declaration of the conspirators' cause, but various indiscretions and leaks from those involved reached authorities in London and brought Waller and Tomkins under scrutiny. The two were arrested on

LITERARY AND HISTORICAL CONTEMPORARIES

Waller's famous contemporaries include:

René Descartes (1596–1650): French philosopher and mathematician, he is known as "The Father of Modern Philosophy" for his profound influences on subsequent generations of thinkers. His treatises include *Passions of the Soul* (1649).

John Milton (1608–1674): English poet and essayist, he is best known for his epic poem *Paradise Lost* (1667).

Blaise Pascal (1623–1662): French mathematician, physicist, and philosopher, Pascal contributed to such fields as fluid studies, the construction of calculators, and the theory of probability. His writings on mathematics include "Treatise on the Arithmetical Triangle" (1653).

Jan van Riebeeck (1619–1677): This Dutch colonial administrator founded Cape Town, South Africa.

Rembrandt van Rijn (1606–1669): A Dutch painter and etcher, he is considered one of the greatest artists in European history. His paintings include *Anatomy Lesson of Dr. Nicolaes Tulp* (1632) and *Night Watch* (1642).

May 31, 1643, and imprisoned in the Tower of London. When brought before the bar of the House of Commons to defend himself before being expelled from Parliament and remanded to a court-martial, Waller betrayed his fellow conspirators in order to attain a lenient ruling. He also appealed to his judges' interest in not setting too disgraceful and dangerous a precedent in the punishment of one of their own members of Parliament.

In addition, Waller tried to save himself by hypocritically accepting the spiritual help of nonconformist ministers, whose "ghostly assistance" he tried to buy with gifts. The leading members of the house were similarly solicited. What Waller undeniably bought—whether with his pathetic eloquence, his tactics of delay, his friends, or ready cash—was time, and thus eventually his life. After several interrupted preparations for court-martial, on September 23, 1644, a petition from "Edm. Waller, prisoner in the Tower" offered payment of a fine of ten thousand pounds and banishment from the realm. This was the judgment in fact finally handed down on November 4, 1644, giving Waller twenty-eight days from the 6th of November to leave England, not to return lest he incur the punishment both houses of Parliament saw fit.

Exile Revoked Waller's poems first found their way into print during his exile. Four editions were published in 1645, including an unauthorized volume published by Thomas Walkley in an attempt to cash in on Waller's notoriety. By the end of 1649, Waller and his second wife—Mary Bresse from the family of Thame, in Oxfordshire—had

settled in Paris, where, in contrast to the poverty and distress of most of the royalist exiles, he reportedly lived comfortably. On November 27, 1651, the House of Commons responded to "the humble petition of Edmond Waller" by revoking his sentence of banishment and ordering a pardon to be prepared for him.

Political Poems By this time, Great Britain had undergone extreme political changes. The English Civil War broke out in 1642 between Charles I, an absolutist believed to have Catholic leanings, and his royalist forces against the rising middle classes, primarily Protestant Puritans, who wanted to make Parliament superior to the monarchy. Charles was tried and executed in 1649, and Cromwell, a Puritan leader, took power as the Protector who ruled the newly created Commonwealth.

Waller ingratiated himself with Cromwell, writing in 1652, the year of his return to England, perhaps his best political poem, *A Panegyrick to My Lord Protector* (1655). In addition, Waller wrote two other poems voicing views favorable to the Protector's government, or promoting his success and greatness. Perhaps in recognition of this interest, Waller was appointed one of the commissioners for trade in December 1655. Almost immediately after another worshipful poem in 1658, his "Lord Protector" died. Waller responded with several elegies. Cromwell was succeeded by his son, Richard, who proved inept, and the monarchy was soon restored. In 1660, upon the succession of Charles II (the son of Charles I), Waller submitted his ingratiating *To the King, upon His Majesties happy return* (1660). Waller also returned to Parliament, serving again during Charles II's reign.

Final Writing Years According to the anonymous 1711 "Account of the Life and Writings," Waller dabbled in writing for the theater, though unsuccessfully. Nevertheless, as his eighteenth-century editor Elijah Fenton puts it, "He soon relaps'd into poetry" and continued to write verse to the end of his life. Toward the end, he focused on spiritual poetry. Waller died at his home at Beaconsfield on October 21, 1687.

Works in Literary Context

Unusual Influences Waller enjoyed many unusual personal influences. For instance, Waller followed a course of study guided by Dr. George Morley, an instructor at Christ Church, Oxford. Waller took Morley to live with him and oversee his reading at Beaconsfield. Morley was a member of the "college" of serious-minded intellectuals collected by Lucius Cary, Viscount Falkland, at his country house, Great Tew. According to Edward Hyde, first Earl of Clarendon, Waller was heavily influenced by the artistic and political ideas of Morley and his coterie, who rejected the ambiguous poetic style of the metaphysical poets. Morley's influence may be reflected in Waller's cultivation of what is determined by scholars as a cool, balanced Augustan classicism in virtually all his poetry. This style is one that intentionally returns to past models of writing.

Besides being informed by his social and intellectual connections, Waller's writing directly or indirectly reveals particular literary influences. In one of the sixteen Sacharissa poems, for instance, Waller refers specifically to Sir Philip Sidney's *Arcadia* (1590). The Sacharissa of the works is the Lady Dorothy Sidney, whom Waller was courting with the poems. Her uncle was the famous Sir Philip. In two other Sacharissa poems, Waller invokes Sidney's name and nobility. In the last poem of the series, in mock exasperation and despair, he charges that Sacharissa's refusal to be moved by his advances of love and poetry should deny her participation in such fine lineage as that of Sir Philip.

Three Styles of Poetry Waller's "essays" at verse may be categorized in three main groups: public panegyrics (formal speeches of praise), poems of compliment to private individuals, and love lyrics. First in the early collections and in the esteem of contemporaries are the panegyrics, poems of compliment with a political or larger public aspect. For example, with his "Of the Danger his Majesty (being Prince) escaped in the road at St. Andero," he turns a minor incident—Charles I's halted courtship of the Infanta of Spain while Prince of Wales—into a miniature heroic poem of 170 lines. The panegyrics aspire to a higher style—but the plain, urbane language of polished, sophisticated polite discourse is Waller's characteristic manner in most of his works.

The second type of poem composed by Waller were poems of compliment addressed to nonroyal personages or private friends and include commending verses for publications by other writers. They also include remarks on significant honors or trifling occurrences that befall the recipient; poems occasioned by illnesses; celebrations of marriages and births; funeral elegies; and epistles (or letters) of consolation. Examples include his 1665 "To His Worthy Friend, Sir Thos. Higgons, upon the Translation of 'The Venetian Triumph'" and *Instructions to a painter, for the drawing of a picture of the state and posture of the English forces at sea* (1665).

Lastly, the love lyrics embrace various Cavalier songs and the group of poems to "Sacharissa." This genre of poetry was particular to the seventeenth century Cavaliers—named for royalists during the civil wars who were supporters of King Charles I.

Influence To the generation of poets that succeeded him, Waller was one of the most important writers of the seventeenth century. Though he is now regarded as a minor poet, he anticipated the Augustan age in attitudes and diction. His versification was an important influence on John Dryden and Alexander Pope, among others.

Works in Critical Context

Waller's critical reputation has varied greatly over the past four centuries. Waller's contemporaries and the critics of

---

COMMON HUMAN EXPERIENCE

Here are a few works by writers who have also made dedication or courtship the focus of their poetic efforts.

"Ode I–XI Carpe Diem" (c. 20 BCE), an ode by Horace. In this work, the poet urges his listener to "pluck" or "seize the day."

"The Flea" (1683), a poem by John Donne. One tiny flea connects two lovers, the speaker suggests.

"since feeling is first" (1926), a poem by e.e. cummings. In this modern seduction poem, the speaker suggests that "kisses are a better fate than wisdom."

"Sonnet XVII" (1960), a poem by Pablo Neruda, from his *100 Love Sonnets*. Here, the poet speaks to convince his listener of his love.

"To His Coy Mistress" (1681), a poem by Andrew Marvell. Often called a seduction poem, the work attempts to convince a young woman to drop her coy stance and give in to the speaker's urgings.

---

the eighteenth century heaped praises on his poetic gifts, focusing on his political poems and panegyrics. By the eighteenth century, Waller was still highly regarded as a lyric poet, and "Go, Lovely Rose" was being seen as the perfect Cavalier poem. However, by the nineteenth century, his reputation suffered considerably, in part because the occasional nature of his poetry was regarded as unfashionable in this period. By the twentieth century, Waller was chiefly remembered for either his role in the royalist conspiracy or his poem "Go, Lovely Rose," which had appeared in many anthologies as an example of the ideal Cavalier lyric.

Current scholars and critics admire and comment on the political panegyrics and the poetry of social occasions—the poems that to readers from the Romantic period until recently have seemed the least likely to be revived of all Waller's literary efforts. In the last thirty years, literary scholars have begun again to discover in Waller a significant transitional figure, and a subtle and skilled minor poet.

Sacharissa Poems In more recent years, his so-called Sacharissa poems, those written to his poetic mistress, have gained the attention of critics. The Sacharissa poems, many critics argue, reveal a major problem in Waller's poetic achievement. The very politeness, the persistent optimism and unfailing pleasantness that we are told characterized his conversation and social manner ultimately weaken the picture of the world he presents in his verse. Comparing these poems of Waller with the work of French poet Vincent Voiture, Thomas Kaminski in *Philological Quarterly* wrote, "Waller in fact often displays a greater reticence and decorum, that is, often seems more typically precieux by our normal understanding of the term, than Voiture. And in his lyric poems Waller can achieve a unique poetic voice through the very quality that modern critics dislike in him—the restraint of his manner."

Responses to Literature

1. Investigate a significant historical event in Waller's time, such as Waller's Plot; the death of Oliver Cromwell, the "Lord Protector"; or the English civil wars (1642–1651). Find expressions and descriptions of the chosen event in Waller's poetry. What is the poet's general tone or attitude? What does his tone suggest about his political involvement? Put your conclusions in the form of a paper.

2. Consider a poem by Waller that discusses a woman's individual feminine traits (a poem such as "Go, Lovely Rose") for a presentation. Identify the gender characteristics, listing as many as you find. How do the descriptions inform readers of what was important to a "feminine" woman of the seventeenth century? What roles for women are suggested? What could be considered feminine values?

3. The practice of patronage in the arts has been common for centuries. In Waller's time, many poets' lives depended upon finding patrons to finance their poetry. Explore this practice further, first by finding examples of other writers, poets, and artists who relied on it in Great Britain, then by considering the practice as it existed in other cultures and periods—such as with the National Endowment for the Arts today. Write a paper with your findings.

4. You may be an artist or writer who will be considering funding soon, or you may imagine you will be. Come up with a "service" or offering and then consider a patron capable of supporting your art. (Oprah Winfrey, for example, is famous for taking solicitations for her donations). Write a "dedication" that will win your potential patron's favor.

5. Consider one of Waller's poems of courtship (such as "The Story of Phoebus and Daphne, Applied") and compare it with a contemporary song of seduction (such as Marvin Gaye's "Let's Get It On"). What elements make each a successful or convincing plea? Create a presentation with your findings.

6. While one of the genres Waller wrote in was Cavalier poetry, he is not considered among the most famous of Cavalier poets—generally, his writing is eclipsed by that of Thomas Carew, Robert Herrick, Ben Jonson, Richard Lovelace, Sir Walter Raleigh, Sir John Suckling, and Henry Vaughn. Research the elements of a Cavalier lyric and compare Waller's with one or more of the better-known poets of the seventeenth century in a paper.

BIBLIOGRAPHY

Books

Fenton, Elijah, ed. *The Works of Edmund Waller, Esqr. in Verse and Prose.* London: Jacob Tonson, 1729.

Steele, James Arthur. "A Biography of Edmund Waller." PhD diss., University of London, 1965.

Thorn-Drury, George. Introduction to *The Poems of Edmund Waller.* 2 vols. London: A. H. Bullen, 1901.

Periodicals

Aldington, Richard. "Notes on Waller's Poems." *Living Age* 312 (January 21, 1922): 179–81.

Kaminski, Thomas. "Edmund Waller: English Precieux." *Philological Quarterly* 79, no.1 (Winter 2000): 19–43.

Korshin, Paul J. "The Evolution of Neoclassical Poetics: Cleveland, Denham, and Waller as Poetic Theorists." *Eighteenth-Century Studies* 2 (December 1968): 102–37.

Larson, Charles. "The Somerset House Poems of Cowley and Waller." *Papers on Language and Literature* 10 (Spring 1974): 126–35.

Web Sites

"The Cavalier Poets." Luminarium. Retrieved April 25, 2008, from http://www.luminarium.org/sevenlit/cavintro.htm . Last updated on June 29, 2006.

"Edmund Waller (1606–1687)." *The Literary Encyclopedia.* Retrieved April 25, 2008, from http://www.litencyc.com/php/speople.php?rec=true&UID=4586. Last updated on October 28, 2000.

"Edmund Waller, 1606–1687." Project Gutenberg. Retrieved April 25, 2008, from http://www.gutenberg.org/browse/authors/w#a4510.

"Selected Poetry of Edmund Waller (1606–1687)." Representative Poetry Online (RPO). Retrieved April 25, 2008, from http://rpo.library.utoronto.ca/poet/341.html.

◈ Hugh Walpole

BORN: *1884, Auckland, New Zealand*

DIED: *1941, Cumberland, England*

NATIONALITY: *British*

GENRE: *Fiction, nonfiction*

MAJOR WORKS:

Fortitude (1913)

The Cathedral (1922)

Wintersmoon (1928)

Rogue Herries (1930)

Hugh Walpole *Walpole, Sir Hugh, photograph by Carl Van Vechten. Reproduced by permission of the Estate of Carl Van Vechten.*

Overview

Hugh Walpole was one of the most prolific writers of his day. He lived the sophisticated life of London to the fullest yet retained throughout his life a certain boyish enthusiasm and naïveté that are reflected in his writings.

Works in Biographical and Historical Context

Early Life as the Firstborn Child Hugh Walpole was born on March 13, 1884, the first of three children of George Henry Somerset and Mildred Barham Walpole in New Zealand, where his father was vicar of St. Mary's Church in Parnell, a suburb of Auckland. His family soon moved to New York, where his father taught at the General Theological Seminary, and in 1893, Walpole was sent to England to begin an English public school education; first, in Truro, then in Marlow and at King's School, Canterbury. In 1898, his family moved to Durham from the United States, and Walpole became a day student at Durham School, a place he heartily disliked.

A Born Storyteller Walpole attempted to write historical romances in his teens and seems to have been a born storyteller, although later in life he resented this designation and thought that he was stronger as a creator of intriguing characters than as a spinner of tales. In October 1903, he went to Emmanuel College, Cambridge, as a subsizar (receiving a yearly stipend because his parents could not pay the full fee); in September 1906, after graduation, he went reluctantly to Liverpool as a lay missioner on the staff of the Mersey Mission to Seamen. It soon became apparent that he was not cut out to be a lay missioner and certainly not a cleric as his father was. He seems to have had little doubt that he wanted a career in letters, and he began supporting himself by teaching in Germany and England until the publication of his first novel, *The Wooden Horse* in 1909. When the novel was published, Walpole was on the threshold of the London literary world—reviewing books for the *London Standard*, seeing Henry James, and communicating with other literary figures. He came to know many of the most prominent members of that world: James, Joseph Conrad, John Galsworthy, Arnold Bennett, Virginia Woolf, John Buchan, Maurice Hewlett, J. B. Priestley, Dorothy Richardson (who called him "eminently a humanist, a collector of people"), and many others.

Experiences in Revolutionary Russia Just after the start of World War I, Walpole went to Russia to write newspaper articles for the *London Daily Mail*. Soon he was put in charge of the British propaganda bureau in Petrograd, then capital of Russia, but the enterprise degenerated into a rather farcical operation in which all secrecy was lost, and the office of propaganda became almost useless. He witnessed the first revolution of 1917 in Petrograd and left Russia just as the Bolsheviks were taking over in November 1917. This series of events marked the transfer of governing power from the Tzarist autocracy to the Soviet Union and the end of the Russian Empire. The material for two novels came out of Walpole's Russian experiences—*The Dark Forest* (1916) and *The Secret City* (1919), the latter the winner of the first James Tait Black Memorial Prize for the best work of fiction in 1919.

Return to London Back in London, Walpole worked for a short time in the Foreign Office of the Department of Information under novelist John Buchan and was awarded the CBE (Commander of the Order of the British Empire) after the war. *The Green Mirror* was published in England in 1918, again to generally good reviews and only one or two dissenting voices. In 1919 *Jeremy*, the first of a series of books, was published, and Walpole left on the first of several lecture tours of America. On these tours, over the years, he met many American writers. In 1921, *A Hugh Walpole Anthology* was published with a short prefatory note by Joseph Conrad, one of Walpole's close friends.

The Revenge Novel In 1922, the year of the publication of T. S. Eliot's *The Waste Land* and James Joyce's *Ulysses*, Walpole produced *The Cathedral*. Walpole's biographer, Sir Rupert Hart-Davis, suggests that in this

LITERARY AND HISTORICAL CONTEMPORARIES

Walpole's famous contemporaries include:

Sylvia Beach (1887–1962): Famous American expatriate who owned and ran the influential Shakespeare and Company Bookstore in Paris in the 1920s.

Sir Winston Churchill (1874–1975): Twice prime minister of the United Kingdom, this statesman and acclaimed orator was also a Nobel Prize–winning author.

Georgia O'Keeffe (1887–1986): Famous American artist, she is best known for her Southwest themes and her radical defiance in both her art and her life.

T. S. Eliot (1888–1965): Poet whose most famous works, "The Love Song of J. Alfred Prufrock" (1915) and *The Waste Land* (1922), exhibit the modernist ideas and techniques that Walpole famously critiqued.

George Cukor (1899–1983): American film director who helmed the 1935 adaptation of *David Copperfield* coscripted by Walpole. Cukor went on to direct film classics such as *The Philadelphia Story, Born Yesterday,* and *My Fair Lady.*

novel Walpole hits back at the cathedral clique and the snobbishness of which he and his family were the victims in their years in Durham. The fictional town of Polchester in this novel was also to be the setting for *Jeremy, Harmer John* (1926), and *The Inquisitor* (1935).

The Critique Novel In 1924, Walpole purchased Brackenburn, a home in Cumberland. He also kept a flat in London and divided his time between the two locations for the rest of his life. Throughout his career, Walpole felt a simultaneous respect for and distrust of the modernists. In 1928 he produced *Wintersmoon*, in which he sets forth his ideas on the new "modern" temperament as opposed to the traditional English one and, by extension, his ideas on modernist writers as opposed to traditionalist writers. The coldness, detachment, and scorn for traditional values—personal, societal, literary— that Walpole believed characterized the moderns are manifested in *Wintersmoon*'s characters Rosalind and Ravage. Their foils, or opposites, are Janet Grandison and the members of her husband's aristocratic family.

The Popular Herries Novels The Herries novels, beginning with *Rogue Herries* in 1930 and continuing with *Judith Paris* (1931), *The Fortress* (1932), and *Vanessa* (1933), reflect something of Walpole's interest in Sir Walter Scott and his own adopted Cumberland. *Rogue Herries* is about an outcast from society. The novel is set around Cumberland, and its action skirts the events of the 1745 rebellion. In 1934 Walpole went to Holly-

wood, where he wrote the scenario for the film version of *David Copperfield* (1935). He became friends with director George Cukor and producer David Selznick and had a small part in the film. He also worked on other screenplays, including one for *Little Lord Fauntleroy* (1936).

Hugh Walpole never married. He was knighted in 1937, died at Brackenburn, his Cumberland home, on June 1, 1941, and was buried in St. John's churchyard, Keswick, Cumberland.

Works in Literary Context

Influences Walpole was an avid reader and early on was influenced by Nathaniel Hawthorne and his ideas of evil. Walpole said later in life that there were "two strands—say Hawthorne and Trollope—from which I am derived." Walpole also acknowledged what he considered the superior genius of Virginia Woolf and contrasted it with his own mere talent. Sometimes he felt that he would have liked to have been a more modern writer but realized that he was hopelessly old-fashioned: "verbose, over-emphasized, unreal in many places, sometimes very dull" was his critical self-evaluation on one occasion. He felt that his connection with Virginia Woolf helped him "to get over a little of my sententiousness and sentimentality"—a change he welcomed while at the same time not wanting to surrender too much to her influence.

Romantic Style It is difficult to see any change in his writing because of his friendship with Virginia Woolf, but two years after *Wintersmoon*, Walpole did depart from traditional realistic fiction with an escape into historical romance. Having become something of an authority on nineteenth-century Scottish author Sir Walter Scott, Walpole's later works reflect the Romantic Scott and not the experimental Woolf. The Romantic movement in literature emphasized the transcendant power of nature and privileged the imagination over reason and emotion over intellect. These elements may have seemed ordinary for readers of Walpole's works.

Interest in Walpole's books, intimately tied to the author himself, dropped off sharply after his death in 1941. The advent of World War II and subsequent changes in literary styles also contributed to a decline in critical and popular attention to his works. Nevertheless, his books are still read, and his position as a prominent twentieth-century novelist remains secure.

Works in Critical Context

Most of Walpole's novels were well received, each one outselling its predecessor. Critics, however, were not impressed. After publication of *The Bright Pavilions* (1940), for instance, a reviewer commented that Walpole might have been a serious artist but had settled instead for being "a very good entertainer." But Walpole answered, "This is the old regular 'highbrow' attack. How sick I am though of this long-continued attempt to make the novel a solemn, priggish, intellectual affair, removed from the ordinary reader." This resistance to meet the highbrow demands of the literary experts is demonstrated in novels such as *Fortitude*, *The Duchess of Wrexe*, and *Rogue Herries.*

***Fortitude* (1913)**   With *Fortitude*, Walpole achieved widespread recognition in the literary world of London. The novel is a bildungsroman (a novel of self-cultivation) of sorts with a slow but steady narrative pace and a deadly serious tone. Its young hero, Peter Westcott, displays a toughness in facing bullies, and his emergence as a victor in school struggles suggests a bit of wishful thinking on Walpole's part—what he himself may have wished to accomplish in his unhappy days at school. Some critics, however, objected to the novel's mystical elements. Peter hears voices enumerating a new set of beatitudes at the end of the novel. Walpole saw no problem with the inclusion of the mystical in an otherwise realistic novel.

***The Duchess of Wrexe* (1914)**   *The Duchess of Wrexe* was published to generally favorable reviews. This book is discussed by Walpole's contemporary Henry James in his essay "The Younger Generation." He praises Walpole's enthusiasm but looks forward to the time when "form" or "a process" will be manifest in Walpole's writings. Indeed, this kind of criticism—again, that he was careless and failed to impose upon his novels some controlling sense of form—was made of Walpole's work throughout his career. He himself realized his lack of a distinguished style, but he recognized and emphasized his strong points—his goodwill, enthusiasm, and verve in storytelling. In a letter to Arnold Bennett (one of the many mutually chiding letters that these two exchanged), Walpole wrote, "I know that I am sentimental, romantic and slipshod," but, he insisted, this combination of traits represented the essential Hugh Walpole, take it or leave it.

***Rogue Herries* (1930)**   *Rogue Herries* is lively but promises more than it delivers. Walpole develops the tic of saying "he would remember this incident years later," and then allows allegedly unforgettable events to come to nothing. But *Rogue Herries* is a good story (one that Virginia Woolf herself enjoyed); and with the other three novels gathered into one volume in 1939, *The Herries Chronicle*, the story was popular for years. Walpole's own evaluation of the entire series might be applied to his fiction as a whole: "It carries the English novel no whit further but it sustains the tradition and has vitality."

Responses to Literature

1. A unique contribution to the literature of the 1700s and 1800s, gothic fiction shares elements with horror. Research the two genres, identifying the characteristics of each. Then, consider what the two have in common. Find examples of gothic, horror, and gothic horror fiction, explaining how each demonstrates the genre you decide it fits.

2. Walpole made it clear that he thought entertainment was the most important purpose his novels served.

COMMON HUMAN EXPERIENCE

Here are a few works by writers who also wrote in nineteenth-century Romantic or gothic styles:

Frankenstein (1818), a novel by Mary Shelley. In this gothic novel, the elements set the pace not only for nineteenth-century literature that challenges science but for the gothic horror genre that developed after it.

The Scarlet Letter (1850), a novel by Nathaniel Hawthorne. In this Romantic and gothic work, Puritan values are closely examined and challenged.

Wuthering Heights (1847), a novel by Emily Brontë. This work is often considered not only a classic but one of the most profound romances of all time.

What other purposes can novels serve? Think about your favorite book. Is entertainment value the most important quality it possesses? If not, what is its most important quality? Do you think all novels should have at least some entertainment value? In your opinion, are novels that emphasize entertainment less artistically important than other, more literary novels? Explain your answer using examples.

3. Walpole acknowledged being influenced by Virginia Woolf. Woolf's style was predominantly a stream-of-consciousness technique: her narrations were done through the ongoing thought processes of her characters. Find examples of stream-of-consciousness writing (in Walpole, Woolf, Jamaica Kincaid, Henry James, or others) and then try imitating this style. Can you turn ordinary observation into interesting interior monologue?

BIBLIOGRAPHY

Books

Hart-Davis, Rupert. *Hugh Walpole, a Biography.* New York: Macmillan, 1952.

James, Henry. *Notes on Novelists with Some Other Notes.* New York: Scribner's, 1914.

Steele, Elizabeth. *Hugh Walpole.* New York: Twayne, 1972.

———. *Hugh Walpole: His World of Fiction.* Ann Arbor, Mich.: University Microfilms, 1967.

Strong, L. A. G. *Personal Remarks.* London: Nevill, 1953.

Web Sites

Fantastic Fiction. Hugh Walpole, 1884–1941. Retrieved March 10, 2008, from http://www.fantasticfiction.co.uk/w/hugh-walpole.

Spartacus Educational. Hugh Seymour Walpole. Retrieved March 10, 2008,from http://www.spartacus.schoolnet.co.uk/Jwalpole.htm.

Taormina, Agatha. "The Nineteenth-Century Novel." Retrieved March 10, 2008, from http://nvcc.edu/home/ataormina/novels/history/19thcent.htm.

Evelyn Waugh

BORN: *1903, West Hampstead, London*

DIED: *1966, Somerset, England*

NATIONALITY: *British*

GENRE: *Fiction, nonfiction*

MAJOR WORKS:

Decline and Fall (1928)

A Handful of Dust (1934)

Brideshead Revisited (1945)

The Loved One (1947)

Overview

Evelyn Waugh ranks as one of the outstanding satiric novelists of the twentieth century. During a four-decade-long career, Waugh was thought by many critics to be England's most prominent man of letters. Savage wit and an enviable command of the English language were hallmarks of his style. He was admired by critics and the reading public alike for his portrayal of the attitudes, foibles, and virtues of the British aristocracy, but the author also wrote short stories, travel narratives, biographies, and one volume of an unfinished autobiography.

Evelyn Waugh *Waugh, Evelyn, photograph by Mark Gerson. Reproduced by permission of Mark Gerson.*

Works in Biographical and Historical Context

Religion a Prominent Part of Education at Lancing Evelyn Arthur St. John Waugh was born on October 28, 1903, in Hampstead, England. He grew up in a comfortable middle-class London suburb, the son of Arthur Waugh, a well-known literary critic and publisher, and Catherine Charlotte Raban Waugh. Reading and writing were a daily part of the Waugh household, and books were always a major topic of discussion. When Evelyn was seven, he wrote a short story that was published in an adult collection of narratives.

In addition to literature, Waugh showed an early interest in religion. He attended Lancing preparatory school, known for educating sons of Anglican clergymen. At Lancing, chapel attendance every morning and evening was compulsory, and on Sundays, attendance at three services was required. Waugh later recalled that he never thought this requirement excessive. As his education continued, however, Waugh came in contact with more rebellious and undisciplined schoolmates. He and his artistically and literarily inclined companions began to dominate Lancing school life. Before he left Lancing, Waugh realized he had ceased being a Christian. This occurred because of his association with more freethinking companions, because of his considerable reading of philosophy, and, ironically, because one of his Anglican clergyman-instructors instilled in him serious doubts about religious orthodoxy.

Oxford and a True Calling After Lancing, Waugh continued his studies in 1921 at Oxford. There, Waugh soon became associated with a different crowd, an arty, well-established group at the university that engaged in a considerable amount of socializing, party-going, and drinking. Because Waugh did only a minimal amount of studying at Oxford, he was forced to leave the university in his third year (1924) without a degree and saddled with debts.

After Oxford, Waugh decided to become a schoolmaster, but he was fired from three schools in less than two years, drank heavily, and gradually became so depressed about his lack of success that he attempted suicide. He noted many years later that during this period of his life, he was really avoiding the vocation that had been his since childhood. In 1927, however, he began to write steadily, and after the publication of a few short

pieces, he published his first novel, *Decline and Fall*, which gained him much attention.

Waugh's fame as a humorist and prose stylist developed thereafter in the period between the two World Wars. During this time, he produced many of his most well-regarded books written in the same vein of farce and burlesque, including *Vile Bodies* (1930), *Black Mischief* (1932), *Scoop* (1938), and *The Loved One* (1948). In a more serious mode, he published *A Handful of Dust* (1934) and *Helena* (1950).

Conversion to Catholicism   Catholicism, in particular, influenced Waugh's works after he became a convert in 1930. The conversion created so much fanfare in London society at the time that Waugh responded by writing an article entitled "Converted to Rome: Why It Happened to Me," in which he claimed his conversion was not about religious orthodoxy but about making a choice between Christianity and chaos. Waugh's choice had come during his unhappy marriage to aristocrat Evelyn Gardner that lasted from 1928 to 1930. Although Waugh himself denied that his divorce had been an important catalyst behind his conversion, many critics and commentators feel that Waugh's conversion was a direct result of the end of his first marriage and the personal life crisis that his wife's adultery (which prompted the divorce) caused him.

After the divorce, Waugh searched for life circumstances in which marriage vows would be taken seriously and moral values constantly emphasized. In 1936, after many years of frustration, he secured an annulment of his first marriage, and then married Laura Herbert, a young woman from a staunch Roman Catholic family. (Roman Catholics are not permitted to marry people who have been divorced; an annulment is a retroactive cancellation of a marriage.)

Patriotism and Disillusionment   Always patriotic, no matter how much he may have satirized and ridiculed British follies, Waugh took the earliest opportunity when war broke out in 1939 to join the military and defend his country. Although his age was against him (he had passed his midthirties), Waugh finally succeeded in getting the Royal Marines to accept him in December 1939. He saw service in West Africa and Crete, and as a British liaison officer he parachuted into Yugoslavia, where he narrowly escaped death in the crash of a transport plane. Later, during a period of leave and transition, he completed the most controversial of his novels, *Brideshead Revisited* (1945), and it immediately made him famous. The book became a best-seller in England and the United States, but by this time, Waugh had become severely disillusioned by the war and deeply disturbed by the evil he saw in contemporary society. He grew unhappy and introverted, characteristics that lasted until his death of a heart attack on April 10, 1966.

LITERARY AND HISTORICAL CONTEMPORARIES

Waugh's famous contemporaries include:

D. H. Lawrence (1885–1930): A prolific and diverse writer whose collected works illustrated the vile effects of modernity and industrialization.

Virginia Woolf (1882–1941): Regarded as one of the foremost modernist literary figures of the twentieth century, Woolf's novels explored the nature of history, identity, and gender.

Pablo Picasso (1881–1973): As one of the most famous figures in twentieth-century art, this Spanish painter, draftsman, and sculptor is best known for having helped establish the Cubist movement and for the wide variety of styles embodied in his work.

Albert Einstein (1879–1955): This German-born, Nobel Prize–winning theoretical physicist is best known for his theory of relativity.

Winston Churchill (1874–1965): This Nobel Prize–winning author, orator, and statesman is best known for his leadership of Great Britain as the nation's Prime Minister during World War II.

Works in Literary Context

Many critics declared Waugh's first book, *Decline and Fall*, to be central to the modern movement in literature. Modernism was a cultural and artistic movement affirming the power of human progress, often through scientific knowledge and practical experimentation. Other modernists were more pessimistic, but as a group, they embraced the idea that the World Wars clearly meant that it was now time to disrupt old approaches and replace them with new ones. Waugh's brand of modernism manifested as cynicism, savage fantasy, and satire. Critics past and present have described his novels as funny, witty, and inventive in their attacks on vice and hypocrisy.

Satire

Satire is a form of writing in which the author criticizes elements of society or human nature, often in a way that on the surface seems to support the very thing the author is criticizing. Satirists usually rely on humor as a way to make their criticisms entertaining and therefore more likely to be accepted by readers. *Decline and Fall* is a good example of Waugh's satiric prose style. Through the novel's innocent main character, Paul Pennyfeather, Waugh draws a comic portrait of British high society in the 1920s. Pennyfeather is expelled from Oxford because of a lack of aristocratic connections and money to pay a fine he does not deserve, while those who committed a

COMMON HUMAN EXPERIENCE

A major theme common to many of Waugh's novels is the horror of twentieth-century amorality and the modern "wasteland," where people give only lip service to principles. Here are some other works that share this theme:

> *In Our Time* (1925), a collection of stories and vignettes by Ernest Hemingway. This collection was American author Ernest Hemingway's breakthrough work. The story "Big Two-Hearted River" is about a man looking for consolation in the world that to him seems wrecked and desolate.
> *The Waste Land* (1922), a poem by T. S. Eliot. This highly influential modernist poem is about personal isolation and decaying contemporary life.
> *Endgame* (1957), a play by Samuel Beckett. This play is about four characters locked in a room in a postapocalyptic world and how they deal with their mundane existence.
> *Less than Zero* (1985), a novel by Bret Easton Ellis. Easton's debut novel examines the empty lives of rich, spoiled young college students.

dishonorable act against him are wealthy students who can easily afford to pay their fines. Pennyfeather's discoveries during his subsequent tenure as a schoolmaster emphasize that most of the teachers are either not interested in their profession or are unqualified for their jobs. The glorious tradition of sports as a character-building occupation that induces fair play is disgraced by a track-and-field day dominated by cheating, injury (even an eventual death), arguments, and racial hostilities. As the novel progresses, old burglars are transformed into members of Parliament, hypocrisy abounds, and the wealthy owe their fortunes to their corruption.

Authorial Influence

Throughout the presentation of disorder and evil in *Decline and Fall*, Waugh added two additional features to the detachment of his prose: black humor and disjointed dialogue, which years later became identified with the theater of the absurd. Indeed Waugh is one of the first, if not the first, to blend these two elements successfully in one book. Yet, as several scholars have noted, Waugh drew his inspiration from an earlier, lesser-known author named Ronald Firbank. Firbank had been effective in using fragmentary and exceptionally concise dialogue in a fresh, comic way. He was also talented in handling sly innuendos and revelations of characterization presented in a cold, detached manner so that no moral judgment appeared to be operative. Waugh took

Firbank's techniques, perfected them, and added his own ingredients. Influenced as well by Charles Dickens, William Thackeray, John Ruskin, and Saki (H. H. Munro), Waugh added a polished classical style, a greater subtlety of phrasing than Firbank was capable of, and a rare flamboyant comic touch.

Catholicism

The other great influence on Waugh's writing was Catholicism following his conversion in 1930. This newfound religious purpose is first reflected in *A Handful of Dust* (1934). Largely autobiographical, the novel traces the collapse of Tony and Brenda Last's marriage after Brenda has an affair with John Beaver. Brenda's affair is encouraged by her sophisticated London friends. The novel ends in tragicomedy. A despairing Tony travels to the Brazilian jungle to forget his troubles but is taken prisoner by Mr. Todd. Todd, a devotee of Charles Dickens, forces Tony into reading to him from Dickens's novels, presumably for the rest of his life. On a deeper level, the novel is an intense and bitter examination of humanism and modern society. The wild satire of Waugh's previous novels has gone; in its place is a more subtle satire and biting irony. Critics noted that the novel deals with the horror of modern amorality, calling it a classic portrayal of contemporary savagery. While *A Handful of Dust* was strongly Catholic in tone, it was not until *Brideshead Revisited* that Waugh wrote an overtly Catholic novel.

Brideshead Revisited, Waugh's most successful novel, chronicles twenty years in the lives of the Marchmains, a wealthy English Catholic family. It is narrated by Charles Ryder, who befriends Sebastian Marchmain while attending Oxford University in the 1920s and is later engaged to Sebastian's sister, Julia. Sebastian is an alcoholic; Julia has her first marriage annulled; and their father, long separated from his wife, returns to the Church only on his deathbed.

Works in Critical Context

In addition to some who do not relate well to his often sardonic comic touches, there are those critics who fault Waugh for not having a "social consciousness" and for being too conservative. His emphasis on religion in his later works has also not been well received in secular humanistic circles. Nevertheless, Waugh's overall literary achievement is considerable. He has presented an arresting historical portrait of British society and manners from the early 1920s to the end of the World War II era.

Decline and Fall

It is difficult to imagine a novel today that publishers would require the author to preface with a disclaimer such as Waugh's: "Please bear in mind throughout that it is meant to be funny." Yet *Decline and Fall* was so detached in its presentation of injustice and immorality and outrageous occurrences that parts of the book were censored and the prefatory note was required before publication could be permitted. It did appear that Waugh was allowing all seven deadly sins to hold sway and was enjoying the triumph of evil and decadence in the novel with the most carefree attitude possible.

Critic Anthony Burgess argued that *Decline and Fall*'s continuing power is due to its underlying moral purpose. "Waugh's humour," Burgess wrote, "is never flippant. *Decline and Fall* would not have maintained its freshness for nearly forty years if it had not been based on one of the big themes of our Western literature—the right of the decent man to find decency in the world."

Brideshead Revisited

Because of its essentially Catholic message and its alleged idealization of the English upper classes, *Brideshead Revisited* proved to be Waugh's most controversial novel. Many critics attacked the book for its sentimentality and seeming affection for English gentry. According to L. E. Sissman in the *New Yorker*, the Catholicism and conservatism in *Brideshead Revisited* made the book nearly unpalatable to critics. Critic Bernard Bergonzi attacked the book because, as he wrote, "the aristocracy—particularly the Catholic aristocracy—were seen as the unique custodians of the traditional values in a world increasingly threatened by the barbarians." At the same time, other important critics rejected such statements and lauded the book as Waugh's greatest. Brad Leithauser of the *New Republic*, for example, argued that Waugh's Catholicism "gives *Brideshead Revisited*, the most unfairly denigrated of his novels, its submerged power: *Brideshead* was...the book in which Waugh invested the most of himself: in some ways, it was the book of his life."

Responses to Literature

1. Waugh was a harsh critic of the upper-class youth of his time. What do you think his opinion would be of today's youth? What about today's youth might he satirize?

2. Waugh was one of many British writers who lived for a time in Los Angeles and worked for the film industry. Many expatriate Brits belonged to the Hollywood Cricket Club, which Waugh satirizes in *The Loved One*. Using your library and the Internet, find out more about the Hollywood Cricket Club. Write a paper tracing its history.

3. Waugh was hurt by his first wife's adultery and seems almost preoccupied with the idea of adultery in some of his novels. Do you think general attitudes toward adultery have changed since Waugh's time? If so, how?

BIBLIOGRAPHY

Books

Doyle, Paul A. *Evelyn Waugh: A Critical Essay*. Grand Rapids, Mich.: Eerdmans, 1969.

Hastings, Selena. *Evelyn Waugh: A Biography*. Boston: Houghton Mifflin, 1995.

Lodge, David. *Evelyn Waugh*. Columbia Essays on Modern Writers 58. New York: Columbia University Press, 1971.

Pryce-Jones, David, ed. *Evelyn Waugh and His World*. London: Weidenfeld & Nicolson, 1973.

Stannard, Martin. *Evelyn Waugh: The Early Years 1903–1939*. New York: Norton, 1987.

———. *Evelyn Waugh: The Later Years 1939–1966*. New York: Norton, 1992.

Stannard, Martin, ed. *Evelyn Waugh: The Critical Heritage*. London: Routledge & Kegan Paul, 1984.

Stopp, Frederick J. *Evelyn Waugh: Portrait of an Artist*. London: Chapman & Hall, 1958.

Web sites

Four BBC Audio Interviews with Evelyn Waugh. Retrieved February 17, 2008, from http://www.bbc.co.uk/bbcfour/audiointerviews/profilepages/waughe1.shtml.

Pearce, Joseph. *Evelyn Waugh*. Retrieved February 17, 2008, from http://www.catholicauthors.com/waugh.html.

John Webster

BORN: *c. 1580, London, England*

DIED: *c. 1634*

NATIONALITY: *British*

GENRE: *Drama, poetry*

MAJOR WORKS:

The Malcontent (1604)

The White Devil (1612)

Three Elegies on the Most Lamented Death of Prince Henrie (1613)

The Duchess of Malfi (1614)

The Devil's Law-Case (c. 1619)

Overview

Critics often rank British author John Webster second only to William Shakespeare among Jacobean tragedians. His two major works, *The White Devil* (1612) and *The Duchess of Malfi* (1614), are more frequently revived on stage than any plays of the period other than Shakespeare's. Webster is considered a somewhat difficult dramatist to appreciate, especially on the first reading of his plays.

Works in Biographical and Historical Context

Limited Information   Little is known about Webster's life. He was born around 1580 in London, the

LITERARY AND HISTORICAL CONTEMPORARIES

Webster's famous contemporaries include:

René Descartes (1596–1650): A French philosopher and mathematician, he is nicknamed "The Father of Modern Philosophy" for his profound influences on subsequent generations of thinkers. His treatises include *Discourse on Method* (1637).

Galileo Galilei (1564–1642): Though known as an Italian physicist, he was also a mathematician, philosopher, and astronomer who was instrumental in the scientific revolution. His treatises include *Dialogue Concerning the Two Chief World Systems* (1632).

Ling Mengchu (1580–1644): Chinese writer of the Ming dynasty, he is best known for his short-story collection, *Astonished Slaps upon the Desktop*.

Saint Vincent de Paul (1581–1660): A French patron saint, he founded several charitable organizations, including the Congregation of the Daughters of Charity and The Congregation of Priests of the Mission.

William Shakespeare (1564–1616): Primarily a playwright and poet, Shakespeare is typically referenced as the greatest writer of all time. His plays include the tragedy *Hamlet* (c. 1601).

eldest son of a prosperous coachmaker and member of a prestigious guild, the Merchant Taylors' Company. Given his father's status, Webster was probably educated at the highly respected Merchant Taylors' School. Noting the prominence of legal concerns in Webster's dramas, scholars speculate that he may have also had some legal training. Records indicate that, like his father, Webster was a respected member of the community, and upon the elder Webster's death, he assumed his membership in the Merchant Taylors' Company.

From his birth to early adulthood, Webster lived during a relatively stable time in British history. Elizabeth I had taken the throne in 1558 and ruled until her death in 1603. During her reign, England acquired its first colony (Newfoundland) in 1583 and defeated the Spanish Armada in 1588, ensuring England's freedom. Elizabeth also oversaw the beginnings of a golden age of drama, literature, and music, of which both Shakespeare and Webster played a part.

Respected in the Theater Webster's career in the theater began with collaborative work for Philip Henslowe, a man perhaps best known as the proprietor of London's Rose Theatre. Henslowe's *Diary*, which provides an invaluable view of English drama of the time, records in May 1602 that he paid Webster, Anthony Munday, Michael Drayton, Thomas Middleton, and Thomas Dekker for the now lost *Caesar's Fall, or The Two Shapes*. In October 1602, Henslowe paid Webster, Dekker, Heywood, Henry Chettle, and Wentworth Smith for a play called *Lady Jane*. Also in October, Webster and Heywood were advanced money for a play called *Christmas Comes but Once a Year*.

Although Webster appears to have had no further connection with Henslowe, he continued to collaborate on dramatic works, and towards the end of 1604, he and Dekker wrote *West-ward Hoe*, a scandalous comedy. This satire spurred John Marston, George Chapman, and Ben Jonson to respond with the even more scandalous *Eastward Hoe*. Dekker and Webster returned with *Northward Hoe* in 1605, which many critics consider to be the better of the two Dekker-Webster comedies.

Webster's first independent work was *The White Devil*, apparently performed in 1612. This play, with Webster's next drama, *The Duchess of Malfi* (1614), established a reputation for the dramatist that has sustained itself for four centuries. Most scholars note a significant decline in Webster's dramaturgy following the composition of *The Duchess of Malfi*. Most also agree that his next play, the tragicomic *Devil's Law-Case* (publication date is said to be between 1619 and 1622), is the most difficult of Webster's works to assess because of its nearly incoherent plot. In fact, it has only been performed once—in 1980—since Webster's time.

Last Known Contributions Webster also contributed thirty-two character sketches to the sixth edition of Thomas Overbury's *New and Choice Characters, of Several Authors* (1615). In addition, Webster continued to collaborate on plays, including *Appius and Virginia*, perhaps written with Heywood around 1634. Other plays attributed either wholly or partially to Webster include several lost works and *A Cure for a Cuckold* (1624 or 1625), which survives only in a carelessly printed edition.

Thus, much of Webster's most active writing period was during the reign of Elizabeth's successor, James I, and his son, Charles I, the first two Stuart kings who oversaw a country becoming intensely disillusioned with the national life. While both James and Charles favored the notion of absolutism—that is, that the monarch holds all the political power—the rising middle classes, especially Puritans, believed Parliament should rule over the monarch. This conflict eventually led to the English Civil War, a few years after Webster's death. Scholars usually date Webster's death around 1634, the year that Thomas Heywood referred to him in the past tense in his *Hierarchie of the Blessed Angels* (1635), but it could be as late as 1638.

Works in Literary Context

Influence or Plagiarism? To his peers, Webster was a slow, careful writer who "borrowed" lines from his fellow playwrights and used them to create powerful scenes. Scholars are certain that he lifted many sentiments, images, and even whole sentences from such authors as Michel de Montaigne, William Shakespeare, and Scottish dramatist William Alexander. Such borrowing was not uncommon during the Jacobean era, but Webster made use of the material of others to such a degree that he was even satirized by such fellow writers as Henry Fitzjeffrey—who mocked the "Crabbed Websterio" for not writing one word of his own and not caring whether he would be misunderstood and obscure. Thus it is quite clear from Webster's writings that he was influenced by, and alert to, the work of his contemporaries. The legal training he probably received also influenced the imagery and scenarios in a number of his plays.

Varying Levels of Difficulty Some of Webster's works, such as *The Devil's Law-Case* (1619–1622?), are difficult to understand. This particular play, unlike the others that follow the period's model for tragicomedy, has an incoherent plot full of actions that are both absurd and shocking. Other plays, however, are highly accomplished. Both *The White Devil* and *The Duchess of Malfi*, for example, are based on Italian history, have a clearly established tragic outcome, and express well-defined themes that are accessible to audiences.

Dark and Severe Themes Both *The White Devil* and *The Duchess of Malfi*, as period tragicomedies, express the influence of a pessimistic worldview. Both reflect a sense of darkness encompassing human existence and a profound consciousness of evil and suffering in the world. *The White Devil* relates a complex tale of love, adultery, murder, and revenge. It centers on the adulterous passion between the Duke of Brachiano and Vittoria Corombona, who together plot and direct the murders of their spouses. Some scholars and critics maintain that the absence of any positive, truly moral figure makes the world presented in the play one of unrelieved bleakness.

The Duchess of Malfi offers no more relief. The widowed duchess, against the wishes of her brothers, secretly marries her servant Antonio. The brothers—the fanatical Ferdinand and the scheming Cardinal—plant a spy, Bosola, in their sister's household. When Bosola uncovers the truth about the duchess's marriage, her brothers ruthlessly harass her, drive her from her home, and eventually imprison her. In a famous scene, she is tormented by madmen performing a stylized dance around her, and she is ultimately murdered. Scholars agree that the duchess herself is one of the greatest tragic heroines of the period. As she resigns herself to a Christian stance in the face of her brothers' vicious cruelty, she is filled with a profound dignity: the depiction of her murder is commonly judged one of the most moving scenes in all of Jacobean drama.

Works in Critical Context

The great number of printings and revivals of Webster's plays during the seventeenth century attest to their pop-

> # COMMON HUMAN EXPERIENCE
>
> Here are a few works by writers who also present themes of good exposed to evil.
>
> *A Clockwork Orange* (1962), a novel by Anthony Burgess. In this futuristic work, the powers that be devise select ways for treating the truants and thugs in the small gang called the Droogs.
>
> *Crime and Punishment* (1866), a novel by Fyodor Dostoyevsky. This novel of good and evil presented through a plot that turns on moral dilemmas was first published in serial form.
>
> *The Darkness and the Light* (2001), a poetry collection by Anthony Hecht. In this work, the Nobel Prize–winning American exposes the technical, intellectual, and emotional terrors of the Holocaust and World War II.
>
> *Othello* (1604), a tragedy by William Shakespeare. This play includes a character whom many scholars have named the most evil in all of literature: Iago.

ularity. In the eighteenth century, however, his reputation was eclipsed by a growing interest in Shakespeare. Increasingly, Webster was known only among bibliographers and scholars who considered his plays scarcely more than period pieces, fine examples of the drama of the past but with little to offer contemporary audiences. In fact, his tragedies were performed only five times during the eighteenth century.

From his own time to the present, some critics have praised the poetic brilliance of Webster's tragic vision, while others have scorned his plays as confusing and excessively violent. While undeniably horrifying, his depictions of people struggling to make sense of their lives in an apparently meaningless world possess a curiously modern sensibility. This is demonstrated in such plays as *The Duchess of Malfi*.

The Duchess of Malfi *The Duchess of Malfi* is widely acclaimed as Webster's masterpiece. Initial response to the play was strong. For decades, the play was one of those commanded by royalty, and it has been performed throughout the centuries. Algernon Charles Swinburne maintained that it "stands out among its peers as one of the imperishable and ineradicable landmarks of literature." Many subsequent critics have echoed his opinion, and the play retains a vitality that continues to appeal to actors, audiences, and critics.

For example, John Russell Brown has suggested that *The Duchess of Malfi* offers a rich variety of interpretive possibilities for the stage, allowing it to retain its relevance for modern audiences. Literary scholars have focused their attention on both the form and the themes of the play. Webster's talent as a technician has been a matter of some debate. In his study of Webster's dramatic art, Charles R. Forker has described Webster as one of the first playwrights to successfully create distinct psychological portraits of his characters, a claim with which later critics have concurred. Forker also notes the connection to Shakespeare, concluding that "the Duchess of Malfi not only appropriates some of Richard II's tragic self-consciousness; she also has a "mirror scene" of her own—one as fully theatrical and thematically suggestive as his."

Responses to Literature

1. The practice of patronage in the arts has been common for centuries. In Webster's time, his life depended upon finding patrons to finance his work. Using your library and the Internet, find out more about the relationship between a famous artist or writers and his or her patron. Write an essay in which you examine the impact of patrons on the lives and artistic decisions of artists.

2. The revenge tragedy—developed in the Elizabethan period—is often referred to as "the tragedy of blood." This genre includes common elements: a quest for vengeance (often at the, sometimes repeated, prompting of the ghost of a loved one); scenes involving real or feigned madness; scenes in graveyards; and/or scenes of carnage or mutilation. Using either *The White Devil* or *The Duchess of Malfi*, find examples that define the play as a tragedy of blood. Then, find contemporary comparisons by identifying the same revenge elements in a movie—for example, *Gladiator*, *Mystic River*, or *Payback*. Write about your findings in an essay, while answering the following questions: How is the movie you chose a modern revenge tragedy? How could one explain the popularity of the Jacobean and the modern-day tragedies of blood?

3. Consider all of the parallels between Queen Elizabeth and the Duchess of Malfi in an essay. Where does the duchess differ in her ruling style? Argue in agreement with or argue against Cyran's suggestion that the duchess's choosing love destroys her.

BIBLIOGRAPHY

Books

Archer, William. *The Old Drama and the New*. London: Heinemann, 1923.

Brown, John Russell. "Techniques of Restoration: The Case of *The Duchess of Malfi*." In *Shakespearean Illuminations: Essays in Honor of Marvin Rosenberg*. Jay L. Halio and Hugh Richmond, eds. Newark: University of Delaware Press, 1998.

Forker, Charles R. "*The Duchess of Malfi*." In *Skull Beneath the Skin: The Achievement of John Webster*.
Carbondale: Southern Illinois University Press, 1986.

Schuman, Samuel. *John Webster: A Reference Guide*. Boston: G. K. Hall, 1985.

Swinburne, Algernon. *The Age of Shakespeare. The Complete Works of Algernon Charles Swinburne*. Vol. 11 (Prose Works vol. 1). Sir Edmund Gosse, C.B., and Thomas James Wise, eds. London: Heinemann, 1926.

Periodicals

Bennett, Robert B. "John Webster's Strange Dedication: An Inquiry into Literary Patronage and Jacobean Court Intrigue." *English Literary Renaissance* 7 (Autumn 1977): 352–67.

Chillington, Carol A. "Playwrights at Work: Henslowe's, Not Shakespeare's, Book of Sir Thomas More." *English Literary History* 11 (1981): 439–79.

Web Sites

"An Analysis of *The Duchess of Malfi* by John Webster." Retrieved April 25, 2008, from http://virtual.park.uga.edu/~cdesmet/sabrin/7home.htm.

"John Webster (1580?–1685?)." Luminarium. Retrieved April 25, 2008, from http://www.luminarium.org/sevenlit/webster. Last updated on July 18, 2006.

"Learn About Jacobean Style." Vam British Galleries. Retrieved April 25, 2008, from http://www.vam.ac.uk/vastatic/microsites/british_galleries/bg_styles/Style01b/index.html.

"John Webster." *The Age of Shakespeare: The Complete Works of Algernon Charles Swinburne*. The Swinburne Project. Retrieved April 25, 2008, from http://www.letrs.indiana.edu/cgi-bin/acs-idx.pl?type=section&rgn=level1&byte=1613585.

"Webster, John, 1580–1625." Project Gutenberg. Retrieved April 25, 2008, from http://www.gutenberg.org/browse/authors/w#a857.

"What Is Tragedy?" BBC h2g2 Guide. Retrieved April 25, 2008, from http://www.bbc.co.uk/dna/h2g2/A873858.

▣ Simone Weil

BORN: *1909, Paris, France*

DIED: *1943, Kent, England*

NATIONALITY: *French*

GENRE: *Poetry, nonfiction*

MAJOR WORKS:

The Need for Roots: Prelude to a Declaration of Duties toward Mankind (1949)

Oppression and Liberty (1955)

Simone Weil © *Photo12 / The Image Works*

Overview

A French political activist and religious mystic, Simone Weil was a renowned and enigmatic Christian thinker. Her ambivalence toward the Catholic Church and her life of rigorous self-discipline and self-denial have become as well known and as much a part of her influence as her written works, most of which were collected from her notebooks and published after her death. Often paradoxical and contradictory, Weil's writings convey her intense compassion for the suffering of others, her disdain of nihilism (the belief that there is no meaning or purpose in existence), and her longing to be united with God.

Works in Biographical and Historical Context

The Beginnings of Activism Simone Adolphine Weil was born in Paris on February 3, 1909, the daughter of a prosperous doctor and his wife. Her childhood was marked by intellectual precociousness and a sensitivity to human suffering. At the age of five, for example, she refused to eat sugar because none could be supplied to the soldiers at the front during World War I; at the age of six, she was able to quote passages of seventeenth-century French dramatist Jean Racine from memory. Although she earned her high school degree at fifteen, she felt extremely inferior to her brother, who was a mathematical prodigy. Consequently, she seriously considered sui-

cide and nearly suffered a nervous breakdown early in her life. Between 1925 and 1928, Weil studied at the Henri IV Lycée under the philosopher Alain (Émile-Auguste Chartier), whose influence intensified Weil's self-questioning search for truth.

Following the completion of her École Normale studies in 1931, Weil taught philosophy for several years in various provincial girls' schools. These were years of severe economic depression and great political upheaval in Europe, and Weil's interest in the common worker and her passionate concern for social justice led her to devote all of her time outside of teaching to political activism in the French trade-union (syndicalist) movement. She taught classes for workingmen, took part in meetings and demonstrations, and wrote for a variety of leftist periodicals that supported a workers' revolution and the establishment of a communist society.

At first Weil shared her comrades' belief that a workers' revolution was in the near future. Soon, however, both her experience with the revolutionary movement and her observation of the international political situation led her to the following conclusions: What had developed in the 1930s was different from anything Karl Marx (author of the foundational text of the communist movement, *The Communist Manifesto*, 1848) had expected, there were no signs of the working-class revolution, and a new oppressive class was emerging—the managerial bureaucracy. Though Weil was an admirer of Marx himself, she became a critic of Marxism. In the last half of 1934, she wrote a lengthy essay, *Oppression and Liberty* (1955), in which she summed up the inadequacies of Marxism, attempted her own analysis of social oppression, and outlined a theoretical picture of a free society.

Experiences in Factories and the Spanish Civil War Between 1934 and 1935, Weil's intense sympathy for the working class led her to take a leave of absence from teaching to spend eight months as an anonymous worker in three Paris factories. This experience reinforced her conviction that political revolution without a total transformation of the methods of production—which depended on the subordination of the worker both to the machine and to managerial bureaucracy—would do nothing to alleviate working-class oppression.

When the Spanish Civil War broke out in July 1936, Weil, hoping that a genuine working-class revolution was under way in Spain, went immediately to Barcelona. The Spanish Civil War was a conflict between the ultra-nationalist forces of General Francisco Franco and the Republican forces. Many foreigners, including large number of artists and writers, volunteered to serve on the side of the Republicans. Weil was accepted into a militia unit, but she had to be hospitalized after only a week when her foot and ankle were badly burned in a camp accident. Her experiences in Spain further disillusioned her; she observed so much brutality on both sides of the conflict

LITERARY AND HISTORICAL CONTEMPORARIES

Weil's famous contemporaries include:

Dietrich Bonhoeffer (1906–1945): German Lutheran theologian and founder of the Confessing Church, he participated in the German Resistance movement and was centrally involved in Abwehr (German Military Intelligence) plots to assassinate Adolf Hitler.

Charles de Gaulle (1890–1970): A French general and leader of the Free French Forces, de Gaulle founded the French Fifth Republic and became its first president.

Edith Stein (1891–1942): A Carmelite nun and German philosopher, she became a martyr of the Catholic Church upon losing her life at Auschwitz.

Anne Frank (1929–1945): Frank was a German-Jewish teenager who kept a journal while her family was in hiding during the Holocaust.

John Dos Passos (1896–1970): This American's bitter novels attacked the hypocrisy and materialism of the United States between the two world wars.

that she concluded that violence for any purpose could never be justified.

After Weil returned to France, ill health kept her from returning to teaching. Her burn was slow to heal, she was anemic, and her debilitating migraine headaches became worse. She spent the last of the 1930s reflecting and writing about war and peace, at the same time beginning to formulate her thoughts on the nature of force, on the human spirit's tragic subjection to it, and on mankind's temptation to worship it. These reflections found expression in early 1940 in two essays, "The Iliad, or the Poem of Force" and "The Great Beast," which was a long essay on the rise of Adolf Hitler.

Conversion Experience In 1937, Weil underwent a spiritual conversion, complete with mystical experiences. For instance, at the chapel of St. Francis in Assisi, Weil was so overwhelmed by the presence of "something stronger than [herself]" that she was forced to her knees. She memorized George Herbert's poem "Love," and used it as a meditation when she had migraines. Because she had previously believed that God did not directly reveal himself to individuals, Weil was convinced that her mystical encounters were authentic. This religious transformation led to a change in Weil's political views: She turned from political and social action to a search for spiritual truth.

Time in Marseilles during World War II Following the German occupation of Paris in June 1940, Weil and her parents fled to the south of France, residing in Marseilles from September 1940 until May 1942. Marseilles was located in a part of the country that remained "free" under a provisional government approved by the Germans and based in the city of Vichy. During the time she spent in Marseilles, Weil was productive in her writing. She wrote essays on problems in modern science, a number of essays on religious subjects, and her Marseilles *Notebooks*. Though reluctant to leave France, Weil was persuaded to accompany her parents to New York in May 1942. Before she left, she gave her notebooks to Gustave Thibon, a noted Catholic philosopher and writer, urging him to use her ideas in his own writing.

Once in New York, Weil hoped to interest the U.S. government in a plan she had to organize a corps of nurses who would go into battle with the soldiers in order to give immediate aid, thereby saving lives that would otherwise be lost due to shock and loss of blood. Weil's proposal was turned down, and after five months in New York City, she traveled to London to work for the French Resistance, which fought back against the German forces in occupied France. Believing she was called by God to experience the perils of war, she asked to be parachuted into France to disrupt the war effort; instead, she was given a desk job and asked to develop her own ideas about how France should be reconstructed after the war. The result was *The Need for Roots: Prelude to a Declaration of Duties Toward Mankind* (1949), a treatise on both the causes of modern man's loss of roots in the sacred and her suggestions for a solution.

Reported Suicide Limiting her food to the amount that the French were allowed during rationing, Weil was overcome by stress and malnourishment, and in April 1943 she was hospitalized with tuberculosis. Even in the hospital, she was either unwilling or unable to eat more than meager amounts. She died in a sanatorium in Ashford, Kent, on August 24, 1943, at the age of thirty-four. The local newspaper described her death as a "voluntary suicide." The story that she died because of her solidarity with the starving French captured the popular imagination, and Weil was widely seen as a kind of crazy secular saint, admirable but ludicrous in her intensity and impractical idealism. As her writings were published and translated in the 1950s and 1960s, this image gave way to serious study of her work.

Works in Literary Context

Weil's writing reflects the paradoxes of her life: Profound faith with intellectual skepticism, deep compassion for the suffering of others with a disregard for her own suffering, and a logical mind with a mystical spirit. Even though Weil's theories were not consistent and did not adhere to the conventions of traditional philosophical argument, they contain several recurring concepts essential to understanding much of her work.

Destruction of Self One of Weil's most basic concepts was that the self must be destroyed in imitation of Christ's self-sacrifice. Weil did not see the crucifixion of Jesus as a sacrifice that relieved mankind of its burden of sin, but rather as an inspirational model that the believer should follow. The experiences of abandonment and self-sacrifice, the ache of the absence of God, were, for Weil, necessary preludes to redemption by God's love.

Weil considered *The Iliad* to be the perfect example of pacifism because it presented the absolute futility of the Trojan War. In her essay on Homer's epic, Weil concluded that violence degrades both the victim and the victor; violence makes people selfless "things." To Weil, a soul destroyed externally was the ultimate sin because then the soul could not be sacrificed to God. This sacrifice was the key to atonement and redemption.

Manichaeism Another fundamental belief found in Weil's writing is related to Manichaeism, an ancient religious doctrine based on the separation of matter and spirit and of good and evil. Weil expressed this duality as the tension between "gravity" and "grace." The physical universe is drawn downward by gravity; Weil considered these physical laws inherently evil because God is absent in the physical world. Since God is absent, man cannot be near to God. The only hope for mankind is to wait for a visit from God, who will uplift man's soul to himself. This is grace.

Universal Faith Weil also believed that some elements of Christian faith, including the possibility of redemption, exist in all religions. Moreover, they existed in myths long before the birth of Christ. Weil's studies revealed these elements in many ancient religions, illustrated, for example, by ancient Greek writers such as Sophocles, Plato, and Homer. In fact, within Platonic philosophy, Greek tragedy, Hindu Upanishads, and ancient Egyptian and Chaldean writings, she believed she had found the basis for an ideal society: a truly Christian civilization that would be hierarchical yet non-oppressive.

Influences Weil published only magazine articles and poems during her lifetime. The bulk of her work was collected from her notebooks by J. M. Perrin and G. Thibon and published after her death. Nevertheless, Weil's limited writings have affected everyone from philosophers to filmmakers. Albert Camus, after winning the Nobel Prize in Literature, spent an hour meditating in the deceased Weil's room before boarding the plane for Stockholm. Iris Murdoch's writings are marked by Weil's intellectualism. Even writer Mario Puzo and director Francis Ford Coppola are reported to have turned to Weil for inspiration when working on the script for *The Godfather III*.

Works in Critical Context

Weil wrote on both her secular thoughts and spiritual beliefs. Her works were intellectual and enthusiastic, eliciting mixed reviews from critics who focused on her

COMMON HUMAN EXPERIENCE

Here are a few works by other writers who have examined the intersection of politics and religion:

The Human Condition (1958), a philosophical work by Hannah Arendt. This work examines activities in realms most important to her "labor, work, action"in the context of society, politics, and the public and private sectors.
Homo Sacer: Sovereign Power and Bare Life (1998), a philosophical work by Giorgio Agamben. This work is an exhaustive study by the Italian philosopher focusing on the place of the individual in society.
Working (1974), a book by Studs Terkel. In this collection, the social historian examines the work blue collar workers and investigates how such work gives or does not give their lives meaning.

mental instability or praised her philosophical insight and literary prowess.

Genius and Madness At the time of Weil's death, she was generally regarded as a crazed fanatic who exaggerated her interests in human salvation; however, she eventually earned a favorable reputation as one of the most original thinkers of her era. Eminent figures like Charles de Gaulle, who, as the leader of the Free French knew Weil slightly, considered her mad. Others who knew and respected her honored her genius. French existentialist playwright Gabriel Marcel admired her greatly, and T. S. Eliot described her as "a woman of genius, of a kind of genius akin to that of the saints." Had Weil been better appreciated in her time, she might have contributed much more than she did posthumously to political and social thought. She had visions and awakenings that prevented her from being taken seriously, but she also had premonitions and theories that might be regarded today as uncanny in their foreshadowing.

Other critics have decided that while, as scholar Jean Amery says, "the prestige of her death has shielded her from criticism," Weil's work must be examined in global terms. Weil has been harshly criticized for being a Jewish anti-Semite and for what critics have called misguided political suggestions. She denied the presence of any divine revelation in the Jewish religion, but found it in many other faiths besides Christianity. She advocated sacrificing Czechoslovakia to Hitler in the 1930s, writing in her 1943 notebook that the French ought to have used Gandhi-like passive resistance against the Nazis.

The Need for Roots: Prelude to a Declaration of Duties Toward Mankind According to a reviewer for the *Times Literary Supplement*, *The Need for Roots* examines "politics in the widest Aristotelian understanding of the term, and the treatment is of exceptional originality and breadth of human sympathy." Weil wrote the volume at the request of the French in London, who were curious about her thoughts on the potential of France's reconstruction after World War II. Or, as Jenny Turner in the *New Statesman* remarked, Weil specifically wrote the piece for General de Gaulle, and "it was intended to provide a philosophical foundation for the Fifth Republic." However, as the *Times Literary Supplement* reported, "the [book] is of equal interest and appeal . . . no matter what country." Indeed, Weil's words seem to have been portentous: "What a country calls its vital economic interests are not the things which enable its citizens to live, but the things which enable it to make war. Gasoline is much more likely than wheat to be a cause of international conflict."

S. M. Fitzgerald of the *New Republic* judged that the intended audience or target would not benefit from her thought: "[Weil's] thinking is sometimes idiosyncratic in the extreme, displaying a lack of objectivity that seems almost willful, and some of her outbursts are so emotional as to be almost altogether untrustworthy." In general, as the reviewer for the *Times Literary Supplement* said, the "provocation to agree with her, and more often to disagree, is . . . strong." Although dissent and controversy surround her work, most critics concede that Weil demonstrated penetrating insight and unquestionable integrity in all of her writings.

Responses to Literature

1. Research people who have gone on hunger strikes as a form of protest. Choose one individual whose story intrigues you. Prepare a speech that you would give on behalf of that individual, stating his/her cause and including comparisons to Weil's situation.

2. Some critics relate Weil's religious writing to the work of Blaise Pascal and Ludwig Wittgenstein. What commonalities does Weil have with these two writers? Are there any contemporary figures whose religious writing compares to that of Weil's?

3. Define "radical humanism." Create a timeline of individuals whom you think have demonstrated radical humanism. Each person on your timeline should have a picture of him or her and a short description of what makes this person's actions an example of radical humanism.

BIBLIOGRAPHY

Books

Cohen, Arthur A., ed. *Arguments and Doctrines: A Reader of Jewish Thinking in the Aftermath of the Holocaust*. New York: Harper, 1970.

Milosz, Czeslaw. *Emperor of the Earth: Modes of Eccentric Vision*. Berkeley: University of California Press, 1977.

Petrement, Simone. *Simone Weil: A Life*. New York: Schocken Publishing, 1976.

Rosenfeld, Sidney, and Stella P. Rosenfeld, eds. *Radical Humanism: Selected Essays*. Bloomington: Indiana University Press, 1984.

Twentieth-Century Literary Criticism, Volume 23. Detroit: Gale, 1987.

Weil, Simone. *The Notebooks of Simone Weil*. London: Routledge, 1984.

Periodicals

Fitzgerald, S. M. *New Republic* (August 18, 1952): 18; (July 2, 1977): 33–37.

Times Literary Supplement (July 28, 1989): 821; (July 13, 1990): 747; (August 23, 1991): 7.

Turner, Jenny. *New Statesman* (August 28, 1987):24; (September 4, 1987).

Web sites

The American Weil Society Colloquy at the University of Notre Dame. Retrieved February 14, 2008, from http://www.nd.edu/~weilaws.

Thomas, Brian. *Introducing Simone Weil through the Internet*. Retrieved February 14, 2008, from http://www.rivertext.com/weil.html.

———. *Rivertext: Simone Weil in the Godfather*. Retrieved February 14, 2008, from http://www.rivertext.com/weil1c.html.

H. G. Wells

BORN: *1866, Bromley, England*

DIED: *1946, London, England*

NATIONALITY: *British*

GENRE: *Fiction, nonfiction*

MAJOR WORKS:

The Time Machine (1895)

The Island of Doctor Moreau (1896)

The Invisible Man (1897)

The War of the Worlds (1898)

The Shape of Things to Come (1933)

Overview

Herbert George Wells is best remembered today as an author of several enduring science fiction classics, among them *The Time Machine, The War of the Worlds, The Invisible Man, The First Men in the Moon* and *The Island of Doctor Moreau*. He was also a vocal advocate of socialism and wrote a large volume of political philosophy and history in addition to his "science romances."

H. G. Wells *Wells, Herbert George, photograph. AP Images.*

Works in Biographical and Historical Context

An Early Love of Science Born in Bromley, Kent, on September 21, 1866, Wells was the third son of Joseph Wells, a shopkeeper, and Sarah Wells. The family's lower-middle-class status was not helped by the fact that Wells's father preferred playing cricket to working as a shopkeeper. When he was injured in Wells's childhood, Wells's mother became the primary breadwinner, working as a housekeeper. While the young Wells inherited his mother's capacity for hard work, he did not share her religious nature. Wells later commented that he found religion of little use during a period of painful convalescence after breaking his leg in 1874. What he did find useful, he said, was the opportunity to read voraciously at this time, particularly science books. Wells later identified his reading as a turning point in his life.

Wells struggled to gain an education and finally succeeded in studying the natural sciences under the well-known proponent of evolution T. H. Huxley. Wells also became associated with the *Science Schools Journal* as a writer and editor.

A Prolific Writer In 1887 Wells and his cousin Isabel Mary Wells fell in love while he was living with her family as a student. They married in 1891, though the couple divorced by 1895 and Wells soon married another woman named Amy Catherine Robbins. Not content to

write only for periodicals, Wells turned his attention to books, and a good indication of how prolific he was at this time can be seen in the fact that in 1895 he published four books, including *The Time Machine*.

Largely on the basis of *The Time Machine*, which was popular during its 1895 serialization in William Ernest Henley's *New Review* and even more popular when published in book form, Wells became an overnight celebrity and was compared to a host of other writers. As he notes in his autobiography, he was variously called the next Jonathan Swift, the next Jules Verne, the next Robert Louis Stevenson, the next Rudyard Kipling, the next J. M. Barrie, and so on. While his next novel, *The Island of Doctor Moreau*, was less well received than *The Time Machine*, Wells nonetheless was on his way up the literary ladder.

The year 1898 was a difficult one for Wells, as several years of overwork resulted in a serious breakdown of his health, with the problem variously diagnosed as tuberculosis and kidney trouble. To recuperate, he and his wife spent much of the year in different seaside resorts on the Kentish coast. Here he met and befriended both Henry James and Joseph Conrad, who lived nearby. This year also saw the publication of Wells's novel *The War of the Worlds*, a story of the invasion of Earth by Martians.

Moving Away from Science Fiction In 1900 Wells clearly saw the need to branch out from science fiction. That year he published *Love and Mr. Lewisham*, his first successful realistic novel, which deals with the conflicts between academic ambition and sexual desires in a protagonist much like Wells during his undergraduate years and early teaching career. Wells continued to be a prolific writer, producing science fiction such as *The First Men in the Moon* (1901) and increasingly writing about politics and science's impact on society.

Prior to World War I, such works as *A Modern Utopia* (1905) and *The New Machiavelli* (1911) established Wells as a leading proponent of socialism, world government, and free thought. During the period of widespread disillusionment that followed World War I, Wells revised his essentially optimistic vision of the future. For example, his volume of essays *The War That Will End War* (1914), published shortly after the outbreak of World War I, inadvertently gave the world, through its title, a cynical catchphrase for obstinate naiveté in the face of widespread corruption. But throughout the 1920s and 1930s Wells wrote social and political criticism and prognostications about the future that were increasingly pessimistic. His last book, *Mind at the End of Its Tether* (1945), predicts the destruction of civilization and the degeneration of humanity. Wells died in 1946.

Works in Literary Context

Wells's critical and popular reputation rests primarily on his early works of science fiction. Wells's science fiction was profoundly influenced by his adaptation of Huxley's philosophical interpretation of Darwinian evolutionary

LITERARY AND HISTORICAL CONTEMPORARIES

Wells's famous contemporaries include:

Jules Verne (1828–1905): French author of *Twenty Thousand Leagues Under the Sea* and *Journey to the Center of the Earth*, and widely considered to be the first modern science fiction author.

Rabindranath Tagore (1861–1941): Bengali poet, playwright, and philosopher, Tagore was the first Asian Nobel laureate, winning the 1913 Prize for Literature.

T. H. Huxley (1825–1895): English biologist nicknamed "Darwin's bulldog" for his vigorous defense of the new science of evolution.

George Bernard Shaw (1856–1950): Irish playwright who wrote of society's ills and the exploitation of the working classes and women. A lifelong socialist and early advocate of vegetarianism, Shaw is also the only person to win both the Nobel Prize and an Oscar.

theory, contending that the course of life on earth, like that of any organism, follows a pattern of quickening, maturation, and decadence. Writing at a time when the notion was seriously advanced that "everything had been discovered"— that only refinements of existing scientific and technological advances remained to be made—Huxley's "cosmic pessimism" was deeply disturbing, implying that humankind faced inevitable decline. Wells adopted this chilling notion in the stories and novels that he wrote in the 1890s, such as *The Time Machine* (1895), *When the Sleeper Wakes* (1899), and *The First Men in the Moon* (1901).

Cosmic Insignificance Wells's first published novel presents some of the major themes that recurred throughout his works, fictional and nonfictional. "The Time Machine," said Frank McConnell and Samuel Hynes in their essay "The Time Machine and The War of the Worlds: Parable and Possibility in H. G. Wells," "is a parable of [a] late-Victorian state of mind—a parable in which science is used as the vehicle for meanings that are profoundly anti-scientific." By the end of the nineteenth century, the reviewers argued, industrialization and scientific advances had created as many, if not more, problems than they had solved. The ultimate expression of Wells's despair of human progress can be found in the climactic scene of the distant future, after the Time Traveller has fled the Morlocks who have taken Weena. "Escaping on the recovered time machine into the infinite future," explained fellow science fiction writer and critic Jack Williamson in *H. G. Wells: Critic of Progress*, "he finds mankind extinct and the solar system itself near death, the earth spiraling inward toward the dying sun."

By the time Wells published *The War of the Worlds*, dozens of future-war stories had been read by audiences at first as cautionary tales and later for their vivid scenes of mass destruction. *The War of the Worlds* is also a future-war novel with many scenes of mass destruction; Wells's innovation here consisted of the fact that this was one of the first, if not the first, such works to describe an invasion by beings from another planet. Like *The Time Machine* with its suggestion that the extinction of the human race is possible if not in fact likely, the result is a questioning of humanity's confidence in its supremacy. Wells reinforces this theme with the conclusion of the novel: While some people have fought valiantly against the Martian onslaught, it is not human ingenuity or power that defeats the aliens, but rather microbes.

Evolution and Devolution In *The Island of Doctor Moreau* Wells presents a microcosm both of the dark side of scientific progress and the inherent savagery of evolution. If Moreau is a twisted God figure, the Beast Folk offer a savage satire of humanity and civilization similar to that found in *Gulliver's Travels* by Jonathan Swift, one of Wells's favorite authors. When he returns to Europe, much like Gulliver after his experience with the Houyhnhnms, the protagonist cannot help seeing his fellow human beings as essentially animals. Despite all our seeming civilization, *The Island of Doctor Moreau* tells readers that because of our evolutionary heritage we are more like the Beast Folk than we would care to admit.

The novel *The Time Machine* also explores the implications of human evolution over the long term. In it, society has divided cleanly between the privileged Eloi and the laboring Morlocks. With the elimination of basic societal ills, the Eloi are humans that have evolved but not progressed; along with eliminating disease, crime, and other types of conflict, they no longer have a need for art or science. The Morlocks, with no chance of achieving anything greater than serving the machinery that provides the Eloi their comfortable existence, have also reached an evolutionary dead end.

Works in Critical Context

In his lifetime Wells was frequently criticized not only by those who disagreed with his socialist and agnostic tendencies but by those—such as Virginia Woolf and Henry James—who focused instead on his work's occasional lack of polish and its tendency to drift into propaganda. In some academic quarters, Wells, in many ways so much the antithesis of the widely admired Woolf and James, continues to be regarded with condescension. In his review of David Smith's 1986 biography of Wells, Stanley Weintraub, for example, asserts that Wells "was not a great artist, nor was he a major prophet. He was an undersized boy from the working class who, after a Dickensian childhood, heightened the imaginations of readers all over the world and in the process became rich, famous, self-indulgent, and sloppier as a writer."

Those who admired Wells in his lifetime included Anatole France, who described Wells as "the greatest force in the English speaking world." Though he deplored the propagandistic streak in Wells's later novels, H. L. Mencken greatly admired the strength and vigor of Wells's mind, calling it "one of the most extraordinary that England has produced in our time." In 1941—five years before Wells's death—Sinclair Lewis suggested that "there is no greater novelist living than Mr. H. G. Wells." More recent biographies and critical studies by Smith, Patrick Parrinder, John R. Reed, and John Batchelor reveal that a sympathetic interest in Wells and his work continues to grow. "Wells," Batchelor suggests, "is a great artist, and those of us who enjoy his work need not feel ashamed of the pleasure we take in reading him."

To the end of his life, Wells considered his scientific romances as inconsequential. Most contemporary critics agreed with him, including his distinguished colleague, the French science fiction writer Jules Verne. Verne told interviewer Gordon Jones in *Temple Bar*, "The creations of Mr. Wells . . . belong unreservedly to an age and degree of scientific knowledge far removed from the present, though I will not say entirely beyond the limits of the possible." Verne does state, however, "I have the highest respect for his imaginative genius."

The War of the Worlds Many critics have interpreted *The War of the Worlds* as an assault on Victorian imperialism and complacency. "Wells repeatedly compares the Martians' brutal treatment of their victims to civilized man's treatment of animals and supposedly inferior races," declared Michael Draper. "The overdeveloped brains, lack of emotions, and artificial bodies of the Martians parody the characteristics of modern man and suggest his evolutionary destiny." "The germs that kill the Martians appear at first glimpse to be coincidental, simply a convenient *deus ex machina* invented by the author to bring about a pleasing conclusion," Jack Williamson said. "A second glance, however, shows this solution arising logically from the theme that progress is controlled by biological laws—which bind Martians, no less than men. Meeting a competing species of life against which they have no biological defenses, the Martians are eliminated. Ironically, their lack of defenses is probably the result of their own past progress."

Responses to Literature

1. What parallels in Wells's *The Time Machine* can be drawn between the Morlocks and the Eloi and contemporary society? How does the author's depiction of these two societies reflect his political views? What do you think Wells's ideal future society would look like?

2. If Jules Verne was the father of science fiction, it could be said that H. G. Wells was the father of science romance. Define science romance; what differentiates it from science fiction? What recent movies or books do you think could be classified as science romance?

3. H. G. Wells was a pacifist, but he also wrote a set of war-game rules called *Little Wars*, designed for

playing with toy soldiers. Do you think Wells was being hypocritical? What are your own views of pacifism? Do you think being against war in real life means that you cannot be interested in military matters at all?

4. Wells wrote about scientific discoveries and inventions that, for modern readers, are in many cases already history. Humans have already ventured to the Moon, for example, and unmanned exploration of Mars has revealed no vengeful alien race ready for attack. Despite this, Wells's work remains popular, especially among younger readers. What do you think accounts for the continuing popularity of Wells's work? Be specific in your answer.

BIBLIOGRAPHY

Books

Batchelor, John. *H. G. Wells.* Cambridge, U.K.: Cambridge University Press, 1985.

Bloom, Robert. *Anatomies of Egotism: A Reading of the Last Novels of H. G. Wells.* Lincoln: University of Nebraska Press, 1977.

COMMON HUMAN EXPERIENCE

Wells was a master of integrating biting social and political commentary into supposedly fantastic tales, making his far-out tales eerily relevant to his readers. The following are some other works that share these themes and reflect similar mastery of mixing contemporary relevance into tales of imagination.

Slaughterhouse-Five (1969), a novel by Kurt Vonnegut. This story of a man who has become "unstuck in time" uses time travel as a vehicle for exploring its protagonist's personal relationships.

Brave New World (1932), a novel by Aldous Huxley. Set in the far future, Huxley describes a utopia free from war and disease, but purchased at the price of many things considered central to the human condition, such as love, family, and art.

Atlas Shrugged (1957), a novel by Ayn Rand. This magnum opus expounds on Rand's philosophy of objectivism by presenting a world in which artists and intellectuals cease to contribute to the world's welfare, to the detriment of all.

Neuromancer (1984), a novel by William Gibson. Gibson imagines a near-future time dominated by corporations and advanced technology in one of the first popular works to examine genetic engineering, artificial intelligence, virtual reality, and worldwide computer networks.

Dictionary of Literary Biography, Volume 34: British Novelists, 1890–1929: Traditionalists. A Bruccoli Clark Layman Book. Ed. Thomas F. Staley, University of Tulsa. Detroit: Gale Group, 1984.

Dictionary of Literary Biography, Volume 70: British Mystery Writers, 1860–1919. A Bruccoli Clark Layman Book. Eds. Bernard Benstock, University of Miami, and Thomas F. Staley, University of Tulsa. Detroit: Gale Group, 1988.

Dictionary of Literary Biography, Volume 156: British Short-Fiction Writers, 1880–1914: The Romantic Tradition. A Bruccoli Clark Layman Book. Ed. William F. Naufftus, Winthrop University. Detroit: Gale Group, 1996.

Dictionary of Literary Biography, Volume 178: British Fantasy and Science-Fiction Writers Before World War I. A Bruccoli Clark Layman Book. Ed. Darren Harris-Fain, Shawnee State University. Detroit: Gale Group, 1997.

Dilloway, James. *Human Rights and World Order.* London: H. G. Wells Society, 1983.

Gill, Stephen. *The Scientific Romances of H. G. Wells.* Cornwall, Ont.: Vesta, 1975.

Parrinder, Patrick. *Shadows of the Future: H. G. Wells, Science Fiction, and Prophecy.* Syracuse, N.Y.: Syracuse University Press, 1995.

"Study Questions for H(erbert) G(eorge) Wells." *DISCovering Authors.* Online ed. Detroit: Gale, 2003.

"The Time Machine." *Novels for Students.* Ed. David A. Galens. Vol. 17. Detroit: Gale, 2003.

"The War of the Worlds." *Novels for Students.* Eds. Ira Mark Milne and Timothy Sisler. Vol. 20. Detroit: Gale, 2005.

"Wells, H(erbert) G(eorge) (1866–1946)." *DISCovering Authors.* Online ed. Detroit: Gale, 2003.

"Wells, H(erbert) G(eorge) (1866–1946)." *UXL Junior DISCovering Authors.* Online ed. Detroit: UXL, 2003.

Wood, James Playsted. *I Told You So! A Life of H. G. Wells.* New York: Pantheon, 1969.

Wykes, Alan. *H. G. Wells in the Cinema.* London: Jupiter, 1977.

⬧ Rebecca West

BORN: *1892, London, England*

DIED: *1983, London, England*

NATIONALITY: *British*

GENRE: *Fiction*

MAJOR WORKS:

The Return of the Soldier (1918)

Harriet Hume (1929)

Black Lamb and Grey Falcon (1941)

The Fountain Overflows (1957)

The Birds Fall Down (1966)

Rebecca West   *West, Rebecca, 1953, photograph. Baron / Hulton Archive / Getty Images.*

Overview

Rebecca West's career as a writer spanned more than seventy years. She excelled in writing novels and short stories, literary theory and criticism, biography, political analysis, and persuasive rhetoric for various causes (socialist, feminist, anti-Fascist, and anti-Communist). Both her fiction and nonfiction are notable for their penetrating psychological analyses of motivation and behavior, and her nonfiction demonstrates her ability to research and to synthesize her findings on historical eras and sociological issues.

Works in Biographical and Historical Context

An Impoverished Beginning Rebecca West was the pseudonym of Cicely (the spelling later changed to Cicily) Isabel Fairfield, born in London in 1892. The youngest of three daughters born to Charles and Isabella Fairfield, she had a childhood filled with intellectual stimulation but marred by instability. Her father abandoned the family when West was eight, and her mother, a Scotswoman, moved the family to Edinburgh. West's schooling was interrupted in 1907 when she feel ill with tuberculosis.

In her teens, West became active in the women's suffrage movement. In England, the push to gain women the right to vote became especially vigorous. Emmeline Pankhurst, the most famous of the British suffragists, had founded a militant political action group in 1903 that staged numerous protests to draw attention to the cause. Pankhurst was arrested more than a dozen times, and she inspired thousands of women to join her struggle. British women finally gained full voting rights in 1928.

Although West harbored an early ambition to be an actress, she only attended the Royal Academy of Dramatic Art in London for three terms before deciding it was not the profession for her. She remained there long enough, however, to play the role of Rebecca West in Henrik Ibsen's *Romersholm*, a play she later characterized as "the 'Hamlet' of the revolutionary intellectual movement," in a 1919 *London Daily News* article. Thus, she found the name she made her own. The first published piece bearing this pen name appeared in the *Freewoman* in February of 1912. West made light of her decision to launch a literary career: "At home," she said, "we all wrote and thought nothing of it."

Feminist Writings: Wit, Audacity, and Savage Criticism

It was as a book reviewer and journalist that West initially established her reputation, writing for a growing number of prominent publications in Britain and the United States. She joined the staff of the *Freewoman*, a militantly feminist publication, as a reviewer of books known for her wittily savage criticisms. Mrs. Humphrey Ward, a formidable member of the literary establishment and a foe of the suffragists, was one of her first targets. H. G. Wells was another, but he was so intrigued by her clever audacity that he sought her out. This marked the beginning of a ten-year relationship between Wells and West—an affair that resulted in the birth of their son Anthony West in August of 1914.

Support of Women's Suffrage

Many of West's early pieces were written in support of the women's suffrage movement. For example, "The Life of Emily Davison" is an angry and moving essay on the suffragette who threw herself in front of the king's horse at Ascot. West had the ability to write passionate controversial prose, but she was also adept at the acidic aside, a technique she employed to devastating effect in her literary reviews. Although she claimed in her essay "Mr Chesterton in Hysterics" that "I myself have never been able to find out what Feminism is; I only know that people call me a Feminist whenever I express sentiments that differentiate me from a doormat or a prostitute," her adherence to a broadly feminist point of view is clear.

Career as a Novelist

West's first book—a study of the American writer Henry James, published in 1916— was an extended example of the same kind of literary criticism for which she was known. In it, West condemns James for portraying women only as "failed sexual beings" and accuses him of lacking intellectual passion. While it also shows West to be a great admirer of James, the book came in for criticism from those who regarded it as unseemly for a twenty-three-year-old woman to criticize the work of such an esteemed writer.

West's first work of fiction was *The Return of the Soldier*, published in 1918. It employs amnesia from shellshock and an unusual perspective on the war: that of those who waited at home. These elements permit West to explore the reactions of three women to a returning soldier who, though married, remembers only an earlier, idyllic love for another woman. This is the shortest of West's novels, and although it may be "composed entirely of the fictional clichés of its time," as Martin Green declared in a 1977 *Saturday Review* essay, it went into a second printing within a month. When her second novel, *The Judge*, was published in 1922, it inspired Somerset Maugham to write, "I do not think there is anyone writing now who can hold a candle to you."

Studies of Nazism and Treason

West married banker Henry Maxwell Andrews in 1930, and after the publication of her fifth novel, *The Thinking Reed*, in 1936, she wrote no more fiction for nearly twenty years. In 1937, she and her husband undertook a trip to Yugoslavia that resulted in a mammoth volume on the history of the region and the threat of Nazism, *Black Lamb and Grey Falcon* (1941). Yugoslavia entered World War II, when Hitler—aided by Italian, Hungarian, and Bulgarian forces—invaded, bombing Belgrade and other major cities in April of 1941. After World War II, she wrote *The Meaning of Treason* (1947), a book that grew out of her coverage of the Nuremberg war crime trials for the *New Yorker. The Fountain Overflows* (1957) is a semi-autobiographical evocation of West's Edinburgh childhood. It was the first part of an intended trilogy, the second two books of which, *This Real Night* and *Cousin Rosamund*, were published posthumously. *The Birds Fall Down*, which appeared in 1966, was described by West as a study of treachery and can perhaps be seen as the working out in fictional form of themes that appeared in *The Meaning of Treason*.

West's last book, *1900* (1982), provides a compact social history of a single year, as well as a perspective from which that year can be seen as pivotal between the nineteenth and the twentieth centuries. The book might be viewed as a nonfiction sequel to *The Fountain Overflows*, as if Rose had returned at the age of ninety to look back at her life in 1900. The episodic situation, the whimsical selection of anecdote, the swiftly sketched personalities, and the ranging interests of that novel all reappear, as does the vitality one identifies with the youthful narrator of that book and with the essays in *The Young Rebecca*,

LITERARY AND HISTORICAL CONTEMPORARIES

West's famous contemporaries include:

Charlie Chaplin (1889–1977): English actor and director who has been hailed as one of the greatest comic minds of the modern age. His iconic "Little Tramp" character is recognizable the world over and has influenced generations of comedians and actors since the character's screen debut in 1914.

H. G. Wells (1866–1946): Along with Jules Verne, Wells is often cited as the father of modern science fiction. Like Verne, his futuristic visions have had a tremendous influence on popular culture as well as legitimate scientific thought.

Mickey Spillane (1918–2006): Starting his literary career in the 1940s, Spillane churned out a series of "hard-boiled" detective novels featuring his signature hero, Mike Hammer.

Haile Selassie I (1892–1975): Emperor of Ethiopia from 1930 until his death; Selassie's speeches to the League of Nations protesting Italy's invasion and use of chemical weapons in 1936 were some of the most eloquent words spoken against the brutality of modern war.

Amelia Earhart (1897–1937): An early aviation pioneer, Earhart was the first woman to fly solo across the Atlantic and the first woman to receive the Distinguished Flying Cross. She disappeared somewhere over the Pacific Ocean while attempting to circumnavigate the globe.

Howard Hughes (1905–1976): An aviation pioneer, Hughes went on to a career as a successful film director in Hollywood before becoming one of the world's most famous eccentric recluses.

1911–1917 (1982). In *1900*, the substantial text is accompanied by excellent photographs.

In her last years, West remained articulate and thoughtful on public issues and figures. Two years before her death, she appeared in the film *Reds*, commenting upon the Russian revolution. In May 1980, when the Iranian embassy, adjacent to her home in Kensington, was under siege, she was reluctant to be evacuated. A month before her death her last article was published in *Vogue*, describing with sharp observation and gentlest wit the changes that age was producing in her sensory and mental processes—changes she found not only frustrating but sometimes intriguing. Her final illness was brief; she died on March 15, 1983, and was buried at Brookwood Cemetary, Woking.

Works in Literary Context

Heavily influenced by her youth in a household of fervent intellectual discussion and, later, by her relationships with many prominent writers of her day, West was one of the leading intellectual figures of the twentieth century. Though her varied and long career makes it difficult to generalize about her work, certain philosophical views do underlie and unify her writing. After World War II, one theme emerged as a key element in much of West's work, both fiction and nonfiction: the nature of treason and betrayal.

Treason and Betrayal West wrote much on treason and related topics in various periodicals. Some of this material she collected in two books, *A Train of Powder* (1955) and *The Vassall Affair* (1963). The courtroom atmosphere of *The Meaning of Treason* is present again in *A Train of Powder*. Although it contains two essays on the development of political awareness in postwar Germany, the book focuses primarily on trials: for war crimes at Nuremberg, for a racially motivated murder in South Carolina, for a greed-inspired killing in London, and—again—for treason of various kinds. West's ability to bring these courtroom dramas to life, to make their participants live on the page, enhanced her reputation as one of the greatest journalists of her period. *The Vassall Affair*, her report on a young Englishman who spied for the Soviets, can be read as an addendum to *The New Meaning of Treason*. The report primarily illustrates how demoralizing the discovery of these spies was to the British government's confidence in its own integrity and its ability to function in the country's best interests.

A final example of West's interest in treason's many faces is her novel *The Birds Fall Down* (1966). Instead of using an example from the gallery of traitors she had observed in the British courtrooms, she drew upon the story of a double agent from tsarist Russia, Ievno Azeff, who was both an informant for the secret police and a leader of a terrorist band. The novel West creates out of this double betrayal concludes with the deaths of both the traitor and a friend he betrayed. Told through the consciousness of a young girl, the story is as much about how her innocent involvement in events affects her as it is about the entanglement of loyalties and betrayals among the adults.

Influence through the Power of Observation West's literary production was so varied and at times so unorthodox that attempting to restrain her within any conventional category would do her an injustice. She did have a large reading audience, though its composition shifted from book to book. As a novelist she was popular, but her wider influence came through her feminist writings and journalism, which are now receiving renewed attention from newer generations of readers. These works all carry a trademark power of observation that remains relevant. Thus William Shawn, editor of the *New Yorker*, could comment in the *New York Times*: "No one in this century...looked at the intricacies of human character and the ways of the world more intelligently."

Works in Critical Context

The Judge While she was writing *The Judge* (1922), West entered a period of personal loss that may have negatively impacted her creative process. H. G. Wells insisted in an angry letter that he must be honest about how much she had failed in this novel, saying that *The Judge* was "an ill conceived sprawl of a book with a faked hero and a faked climax, an aimless waste of [her] powers." Fortunately for West, none of the published evaluations were as negative. Most of those in the prominent publications praised her writing, but they ended with reservations about the aesthetic value of the work. Its length, its slow pace, and the lack of unity between its two large sections clearly damaged the novel in the minds of the critics.

Harriet Hume In *Harriet Hume* (1929), an experiment in fantasy, West also experiments with the form of the novel. In contrast to his critiques of her earlier novels, H. G. Wells wrote West a note of praise, stating that the love-antagonism of Harriet and Arnold illustrated Swiss psychiatrist Carl Jung's "ideas about the persona, anima, and animus." The novel gained neither popular nor critical attention, but Wells could still be positive about this work, although his note implied disparagement of her other books: "It is just as though you were coming awake and alive after years in a sort of intellectual trance."

While critics agree that Rebecca West may be the most consequential journalist of the twentieth century and one of the best modern essayists, one finds less agreement as to the permanence of her fiction in literary history. Most critics who have sought to generalize about her contribution to fiction since her death have stressed her style, wit, and facility with language, her tremendous intellectual powers, and her understanding of the intricacies of the human mind and emotions. Diana Trilling judged her to be "one of the major literary figures of this century" and celebrated the rigor of an intellect that "was never taken in by any of the easy pieties of the literary or political culture." William F. Buckley, acknowledging her liberal persuasion as different from his own, acclaimed her as "a great literary figure," "the literary virtuoso of immense learning... who was... *forever* capable of marshalling her incomparable energies to make the case for human decency."

Responses to Literature

1. Review modern definitions of feminism. Do Rebecca West's writings reflect any contemporary views? How do her views differ?

2. In West's travelogue of Yugoslavia, *Black Lamb and Grey Falcon*, how does she portray the native populations? Does she take sides between the Serbs and Croats?

3. What do you think West meant when she said "I only know that people call me a Feminist whenever I express sentiments that differentiate me from a doormat or a prostitute"?

COMMON HUMAN EXPERIENCE

Rebecca West was a notable feminist journalist, critic, and author. Works by other well-known feminist writers include:

The Feminine Mystique (1963), a book by Betty Friedan. Often cited as having launched the modern women's movement, Friedan's book condemned the widely held belief that women's lives existed solely to cook, clean, and raise children.

A Room of One's Own (1929), an extended essay by Virginia Woolf. Based on a series of lectures, this work examines women's capabilities as authors and the obstacles they face.

The Bell Jar (1963), a novel by Sylvia Plath. Although not explicitly a feminist work, this novel, closely based on Plath's own life and struggles with mental illness, strikes several strongly feminist chords, as in the famous quote, "What I hate is being under a man's thumb."

---

4. Do you agree with West's assertion in *The New Meaning of Treason* that there *are* secrets of science—such as nuclear weapons—that should not be shared with enemy nations? Why or why not?

BIBLIOGRAPHY

Books

Deakin, Motley F. *Rebecca West*. London: Twayne, 1980.

Dickinson, Lovat. *H. G. Wells: His Turbulent Life and Times*. New York: Atheneum, 1969.

Hammond, J. R. *H. G. Wells and Rebecca West*. New York: St. Martin's, 1991.

Marcus, Jane. *The Young Rebecca*. New York: Viking, 1982.

Packer, Jean Garrett. *Rebecca West: An Annotated Bibliography*. New York: Garland, 1991.

Redd, Tony. *Rebecca West: Master of Reality*. Columbia: University of South Carolina Press, 1972.

Wolfe, Peter. *Rebecca West: Artist and Thinker*. Carbondale: Southern Illinois University Press, 1971.

Patrick White

BORN: *1912, London, England*

DIED: *1990, Sydney, Australia*

NATIONALITY: *Australian*

GENRE: *Fiction, poetry*

MAJOR WORKS:

The Tree of Man (1955)

Voss (1957)

Riders in the Chariot (1961)

The Vivisector (1968)

Patrick White   *Patrick Riviere / Getty Images*

Overview

Best known as the author of such novels as *The Tree of Man* (1955) and *Voss* (1957), Patrick White remains a central figure in Australian literature. The Nobel Academy awarded him the Nobel Prize in Literature in 1973 for "an authentic voice that carries across the world," but his unflattering portrayal of Australian society denied him the stature within his homeland that he enjoyed elsewhere. White's novels are stylistically complex explorations of isolation, often featuring unstable and eccentric characters who attempt to forge some semblance of normalcy in a banal and often cruel environment.

Works in Biographical and Historical Context

Educated in England   The first child of a wealthy Australian couple, White was born while his parents were visiting London in 1912. He began writing plays at an early age and attended schools in Australia until the age of thirteen, when his parents sent him to Cheltenham College, a boarding school near Gloucester, England. After graduating in 1929, White returned to Australia and worked for two years as a jackeroo, or ranch hand.

During this period, he published a small volume of poetry—*Thirteen Poems* (1930)—and began writing novels. In 1932, White returned to England and entered Cambridge University, where he studied French and German.

Receiving his bachelor's degree in 1935, White remained in London but frequently traveled throughout the United States and the European continent. He published another volume of poetry, *The Ploughman, and Other Poems* (1935), contributed several short stories in the *London Mercury*, and put out his first serious novel, *Happy Valley* (1939). Awarded the gold medal of the Australian Literary Society in 1941, *Happy Valley* takes place in a fictional rural region of Australia during the mid-1930s and chronicles the events leading up to the murder of an adulteress and the subsequent death of her killer.

Served in World War II   During World War II, White served in the Royal Air Force as an intelligence officer from 1940 to 1945. World War II began in Europe in 1939 when Great Britain declared war on Germany after the Nazis invaded Poland. Britain and its allies sought to contain German leader Adolf Hitler's territorial and military ambitions, but Germany was able to control much of continental Europe for much of the war and heavily bombed Great Britain in preparation for an invasion that never happened. Great Britain's casualties reached seven hundred thousand over the course of the conflict. Australians fought alongside the British during the conflict, primarily in the Middle East theater from 1940 to 1942, then in the Pacific theater after the Japanese attack on Pearl Harbor.

While serving in the military during the war, White published one novel. *The Living and the Dead* (1941) centers on a middle-aged bachelor who reflects upon his childhood and family history. This work is chiefly noted for its development of stream-of-consciousness narration and its use of flashbacks. After World War II ended, White returned to Australia, where a period of intense immigration had just begun. There, he focused primarily on writing and soon became a literary success. White's third novel, *The Aunt's Story* (1948), is generally considered his first major work.

International Recognition   After moving to a six-acre property known as Dogwoods, where he grew fruit and flowers, gathered farm produce, and bred goats and schnauzers, White published his fourth novel. He received international recognition for *The Tree of Man* (1955), which concerns a pioneering Australian couple who establish a farm at the turn of the twentieth century. The eponymous protagonist of White' next novel, *Voss* (1957), is modeled after Ludwig Leichhardt, a German explorer who disappeared while attempting to cross the interior of the Australian continent during the 1840s.

Contrasting the experience of outsiders in Australian society with those of the well-established middle class, much of the narrative alternates between Voss's expedition across the outback and the daily life of Laura Trevelyan, a young woman living in Sydney with whom Voss shares an intuitive emotional bond that some commentators have described as telepathic.

The author continued to write challenging books in the 1950s. *Riders in the Chariot* (1961) concerns the persecution of four social outcasts by the inhabitants of Sarsaparilla, a fictitious suburb of Sydney. Critics have frequently noted White's satirical condemnation of the stifling conformity of suburbia in his portrayal of the residents of Sarsaparilla. White's seventh novel, *The Solid Mandala* (1966), is also set in Sarsaparilla.

Nobel Prize White's output was unabated in the 1970s. In *The Vivisector* (1970), he examines the relationship between the artist and society through his portrayal of the artistic and emotional development of a fictional Australian painter. White was awarded the Nobel Prize for his realistic portrayal of Australian society shortly after the publication of his ninth novel, *The Eye of the Storm* (1973). The author's life changed after he won the award as he was compelled to become a public figure. White became more outspoken on national and international issues, speaking out against Australian conscription for the war in Vietnam and the power brokers in Sydney, for example. He also used his Nobel Prize money to fund a grant for Australian writers.

By the end of his life, White resided on a duck farm in New South Wales, where he lived off the produce he raised there. During his last decade, he published his third short-story collection, *Three Uneasy Pieces* (1987). Like his previous two collections—*The Burnt Ones* (1964) and *The Cockatoos* (1974)—many of these stories feature the Sarsaparillan settings and themes found in his novels and are often noted for their harsh satirizing of middle-class life and politics. White also published another novel, *Memories of Many in One, by Alex Xenophon Demirjian Gray* (1986), his last work of fiction; *Three Uneasy Pieces* (1987); and his autobiography, *Flaws in the Glass: A Self Portrait* (1981), which focuses primarily on his early life and relates his experiences as a writer and homosexual in Australian society. As he had for many years, White continued to point out corruption in the Australian government as well as its inhumane treatment of aborigines. White openly boycotted the 1988 celebrations commemorating the two hundredth anniversary of white settlement in the country. He died after a long illness on September 30, 1990, in Sydney, Australia.

Works in Literary Context

As a writer, White found much of his inspiration in the way people lived and thought in the varied, harsh Aus-

LITERARY AND HISTORICAL CONTEMPORARIES

White's famous contemporaries include:

Sidney Nolan (1917–1992): One of the best-known Australian painters, Nolan made a name for himself with an iconic series of paintings of the outlaw hero Ned Kelly.

Tennessee Williams (1911–1983): One of the most successful and influential playwrights of the twentieth century, the American Williams specialized in writing emotionally charged character studies set in his native South. Many of his plays, such as *A Streetcar Named Desire* (1947) and *Cat on a Hot Tin Roof* (1955), were adapted into successful films.

Dwight D. Eisenhower (1890–1969): Known as "Ike," American general Eisenhower became a national hero during World War II when he led the Allied forces in Europe to victory. He rode this popularity to a two-term presidency in the 1950s, a decade often remembered as the "Eisenhower era."

Yuri Gagarin (1934–1968): Soviet cosmonaut Gagarin became the first man in space and the first to orbit the earth on April 12, 1961, beating the Americans in the space race by twenty-three days.

Ernest Hemingway (1899–1961): An American novelist and journalist, Hemingway's rugged, globe-trotting lifestyle was almost as noteworthy as his distinctive prose stylings. Winner of the Nobel and Pulitzer prizes, Hemingway's writings, such as *The Old Man and the Sea* (1952), are still widely read and highly influential.

Groucho Marx (1890–1977): Perhaps the best known of the Marx Brothers comedy troupe, Groucho was famed for his distinctive look—greasepaint eyebrows and moustache, and a porkpie hat—and his razor-sharp wit. His films include *Animal Crackers* (1930).

tralian landscape as well as his own sexual identity and interest in spirituality. Other authors also affected his works, and he was influenced by and compared with Russian novelist Leo Tolstoy for his psychological perceptions, the epic nature of his works, and his variety of characters. In addition to being influenced by D. H. Lawrence and Thomas Hardy, White's modernist tendencies can be linked to his interest in James Joyce's *Ulysses* (1922) and the abstract paintings of Australian painter Roy de Maistre.

Spirituality and the Search for Meaning White examined a variety of religious attitudes to attain the philosophies he needed to explore his overriding concern: man's search for meaning in an apparently meaningless society. Inherent in White's consideration of spirituality in a mechanical and materialistic world was the concept of man's isolation in a crowded society. Even within the most basic societal structures man is alienated, alone; man's need for meaning is ultimately to be found in the interior world, the world of the imagination and the soul. Robert Phillips said, "White's thesis...is simply this: We are all alone in a chaotic world and only we ourselves can help ourselves during our brief tenure." Often White's theory of the duality of man was exhibited through characters decayed in body but whole in spirit. When asked in an interview if there were any continuing theme running through his work, White told Andrew Clark in the *New York Times Book Review* that his "dominant obsession" was the search for "some meaning and design" in what he described as "the tragic farce of life—to find reason in apparent unreason, and how to accept a supernatural force which on the one hand blesses and on the other destroys."

Isolation White's frequent use of the isolation theme in his fiction was rooted in his personal feelings of alienation from his fellow countrymen. Several periods of expatriation preceded his ultimate return to Australia. As he explained to Ingmar Bjoerksten in *Patrick White: A General Introduction*: "It was eighteen years before I dared to come back to Australia for the third time.... I couldn't do without the countryside out here. I don't believe in a final break with the place one originates from. Only a temporary break...to get perspective. You are shaped by the place you have your roots in; it has become part of you. Outside places don't shape you in the same way. This has nothing to do with nationalism. People are always the same. This is what my compatriots find so difficult to understand." Bjoerksten explored another possible cause of White's feelings of alienation: "For a long time he was dismissed as peculiar, pretentious, and irrelevant by his countrymen, whose restricted vision and whose limited experience of what human life has to offer he exposes time after time, while simultaneously attacking the holy cow that they so deeply revere: an uncritical materialism that never questions itself." White's 1973 Nobel Prize has gained him greater acceptance among Australians, although he is still more widely read in other countries.

White's Homosexuality White saw no need to write the "great Australian homosexual novel" although he was urged to do so. He despised those who surrounded themselves with fellow homosexuals, yet he made no apologies about his own sexual orientation, which he thought to be the source of his creativity. For him, homosexuality meant a blending of masculine and feminine, and he credited his feminine side with the insight that enabled him to depict so accurately the spiritual and psychological inner beings of his characters. Although there are few overtly homosexual figures in his novels, and they are often singled out and criticized for shallowness, there are many substantial, almost mystical friendships, such as that between Voss and Harry Robarts. His "heroes" are mystics, driven to pursue the meaning below the surface of everyday life.

Influence As a leading author in twentieth-century Australian literature, White affected the generations of Australian novelists who followed him in the late twentieth and early twenty-first centuries. While all Australians have not always appreciated the way White has depicted them or their culture and society, his Nobel Prize brought greater attention and worldwide recognition of his power and influence as an author. He also helped financially support Australian writers through the grant program he established with the money that accompanied the Nobel Prize.

Works in Critical Context

White's reputation as a writer rests primarily on his novels, though his short stories, plays, and poetry have received increasing critical attention. With the publication of *The Aunt's Story* and *The Tree of Man*, he achieved international recognition as a novelist with a distinctive, if somewhat disturbing, literary style and vision of life. But such praise was almost exclusively outside his home country. In Australia, critics and readers initially found White's work harsh and difficult to read. This view changed with the publication of such masterworks as *Voss*, *Riders in the Chariot*, and *The Solid Mandala* in the late 1950s and early 1960s. White is now generally recognized as one of

Australia's most important writers, perhaps its greatest novelist of the twentieth century. Many critics have found that his writing is "unreadable" and convoluted, that his symbolism is sometimes heavy-handed, and that his characterizations are restrictive or uneven. Others, however, have argued that within White's cynicism is a recipe for wisdom and redemption, and that his brutally honest depictions of the sinister aspects of human life contain hints, if not confirmations, of a higher reality to our mundane existence.

The Twyborn Affair   One novel by White that exemplifies critical division is *The Twyborn Affair*, a modern rendering of the Tiresias myth set in the early twentieth century. While some reviewers found this work repugnant and degrading, others commended White's compassionate view of homosexuality. Many critics were impressed with White's achievement in finding new expression of a longtime major theme in his work—the infinite possibilities of a single personality. In the *New Leader*, Betty Falkenberg praised *The Twyborn Affair* as "an extraordinary novel of quest, an odyssey through place, time and especially gender—all three of which, by virtue of their boundaries, delimit and even alienate the individual from his possible selves." While the *New York Times Book Review*'s Benjamin DeMott believed that the book was "a case study of sexual proteanism and the thematic core is the mystery of human identity," he also believed that "the problem is the book's too unremitting scorn of human attachment." More impressed was William Walsh. Reviewing *The Twyborn Affair* for the *Times Literary Supplement*, Walsh wrote, "The novel is impressive in its conception, astonishing in its concreteness, sharp in its sardonic social discriminations, and rich in its use of the resources of language."

Responses to Literature

1. White's unique style has drawn as many negative critiques as encomiums. Write an essay in which you explore this question: Do you feel his style interferes with the message of his writing or supports it?

2. Despite feeling his whole life that he was a "Londoner" and not an Australian, White set all his novels in Australia. In a small group, discuss these questions: How does this ambivalence manifest in White's writing? Why do you think White chose to write about Australia if he felt so disconnected from it?

3. *Voss* centers on the real-life nineteenth-century attempts to cross the Australian outback. Research the life of Ludwig Leichhardt and other outback explorers and write a paper that includes your findings and answers these questions: What were some of the hardships they faced? Does White do an effective job of communicating these difficulties?

4. Create a presentation that answers these questions: How does White view organized religions? How does he address theological questions in his work? Does White think religion is relevant in modern society?

BIBLIOGRAPHY

Books

Bjoerksten, Ingmar. *Patrick White: A General Introduction*. Queensland, Australia: University of Queensland Press, 1976.

Dyce, J. R. *Patrick White as Playwright*. Queensland, Australia: University of Queensland Press, 1974.

Giffin, Michael. *Arthur's Dream: The Religious Imagination in the Fiction of Patrick White*. Sydney: Spaniel, 1996.

Morley, Patricia A. *The Mystery of Unity, Theme, and Technique in the Novels of Patrick White*. Montreal: McGill-Queen's University Press, 1972.

Williams, Mark. *Patrick White*. New York: St. Martin's, 1993.

Elie Wiesel

BORN: *1928, Sighet, Romania*

NATIONALITY: *Romanian, Jewish, American*

GENRE: *Novels, essays*

MAJOR WORKS:

Night (1958)

Dawn (1961)

The Accident (1961)

Elie Wiesel   *Wiesel, Elie, 1986, photograph. AP Images.*

Elie Wiesel   *Wiesel, Elie, photograph. AP Images.*

Overview

A survivor of the Nazi concentration camps and the winner of the 1986 Nobel Peace Prize, Elie Wiesel is one of the most important authors of Holocaust literature and an eloquent spokesperson for contemporary Judaism. Throughout his work, he has attempted to comprehend the horror of the concentration camps and the apparent indifference of God, thereby reaffirming his life and faith. Although Wiesel seemingly focuses on exclusively Jewish concerns, the relevance of his work lies in his ability to speak for all persecuted people, and, by extension, for humanity itself.

Works in Biographical and Historical Context

Eliezer Wiesel was born on September 30, 1928, in Sighet, Romania, a town situated in the Carpathian Mountains in northern Transylvania. He was the third of four children and the only son born to Shlomo and Sarah Feig Wiesel. Sighet, which passed from Romanian to Hungarian rule during World War II, is described under various guises in several of Wiesel's novels. As Wiesel recalled in *From the Kingdom of Memory: Reminiscences* (1990), Sighet was a typical Jewish town, "rambunctious and vibrant with beauty and faith," whose inhabitants prayed in Hebrew, spoke Yiddish among themselves, and responded to outsiders in Romanian, Hungarian, or Ruthenian. Jews had lived there since the seventeenth century, developing synagogues, day schools and yeshivas, and various communal institutions, as well as newspapers. Sighet inspired Wiesel's profound sense of Jewish identity and particularly his belief in the Jewish people and God.

A Terror Never to Be Forgotten Wiesel's formal education began when he was three years old in traditional Jewish *kheder* (elementary religious school). His parents encouraged his interest in Hebrew and Yiddish as well as in the teachings of the Hasidic masters and the traditions of the Torah, Talmud, and Kabbala.

In the spring of 1944, the Nazis raided Sighet and deported Wiesel, then fifteen years old, and his family to the concentration camps at Birkenau and Auschwitz. Wiesel's descriptions of the traumatic end of Sighet's Jewish community capture not only his personal tragedy but the total destruction of Central and Eastern European Jewish life during the Holocaust. The Holocaust was the systemic arrest and murder of millions of European Jews and other populations deemed "undesirable" by the racist Nazi regime. Separated from his mother and sisters upon arrival, he was sent with his father to Auschwitz. When Soviet troops neared the concentration camp in 1945, the captives were forced to march to Buchenwald, another camp. Wiesel's father died in Buchenwald just days before the United States Army liberated the camp on April 11, 1945. Upon liberation, Wiesel learned that his mother and younger sister had perished in the gas chambers. His older sisters, however, had survived, and years later they and Elie were reunited.

Wiesel was evacuated with other child survivors from Germany by the American military, but their train was diverted to France on orders from Charles de Gaulle, head of the French provisional government after World War II. Wiesel was sent to a home for Jewish child survivors in Normandy. Later, in Paris, he found his eldest sister, Hilda.

Breaking the Silence About the Concentration Camps In Paris, Wiesel studied literature at the Sorbonne. Beginning in 1947, he became a journalist, writing for the French-Jewish periodical *L'Arche* and for the Israeli newspaper *Yediot Akharonot*. In 1949 he traveled to Israel to cover the War of Independence. His experience as a journalist provided Wiesel with the rigorous discipline he employed in his subsequent writing. But he could not quite bring himself to write about what he had seen at Auschwitz and Buchenwald. Doubtful of his—or of anyone's—ability to convey the horrible truth without diminishing it, Wiesel vowed never to make the attempt.

The young journalist's self-imposed silence came to an end in 1954, after he met and interviewed the Nobel Prize–winning novelist François Mauriac. Deeply moved upon learning of Wiesel's tragic youth, Mauriac urged him to tell the world of his experiences, to "bear witness" for the millions of men, women, and children whom death had silenced. That meeting set Wiesel on his life-long career as a Holocaust witness, writer, lecturer, and educator. Over the next year, Wiesel wrote an 800-page

Yiddish memoir, *And the World Kept Silent*, which was published in Argentina in 1956. On Mauriac's counsel, Wiesel revised, shortened, and translated the Yiddish text into French, giving it the title *Night* (1958). *Night* would come to be recognized as one of the most powerful works in Holocaust literature.

Life in America Wiesel moved to the United States in 1955. He followed up *Night* with *Dawn* (1961) and *The Accident* (1962). The three books together are known as the "Night Trilogy." Wiesel applied for and received U.S. citizenship in 1963, when his French travel papers expired. In 1969, he married Marion Ester Rose, a fellow Holocaust survivor who is now the primary English translator of his works.

With the success of his writings, Wiesel has emerged as an important moral voice on issues concerning religion and human rights, as well as one of the most significant witnesses to the Holocaust. From 1972 to 1976, Wiesel held a full-time position as distinguished professor at City College of New York, where he taught Hasidic texts, Holocaust-related subjects, and Talmud. Throughout this period, Wiesel produced several works about Jewish history and scripture.

In 1976, Boston University appointed Wiesel the Andrew W. Mellon Professor Chair in the Humanities. President Jimmy Carter invited Wiesel to chair the President's Commission on the Holocaust in November 1978. Wiesel's work helped create the United States Holocaust Memorial Museum in Washington, D.C., and the annual "Days of Remembrance" to recall and honor the millions who lost their lives in the Holocaust. During the 1980s, Wiesel spoke out on many international issues, including the maltreatment of Soviet Jews, the suffering of African tribes, the injustice of apartheid in South Africa, and the perils of nuclear weapons. In 1985 President Ronald Reagan awarded Wiesel the United States Congressional Gold Medal. In 1986, the Nobel Committee conferred the Nobel Peace Prize on Wiesel.

Memoirs Wiesel produced two volumes of memoirs: *All Rivers Run to the Sea* (1995), spanning the years from his childhood to the 1960s, and *And the Sea Is Never Full* (1996), bringing his story to the present. The author devotes only twenty pages of the first book to his concentration camp experiences. The emphasis is not on those specific events, but on how he has spent the remainder of his life in their shadows.

Works in Literary Context

The major literary influences in the life of Elie Wiesel come from his early immersion in study of Jewish texts such as the Torah and Talmud, as well as Jewish history and the lives of the Hasidic masters. A great proportion of Wiesel's literary output has been Jewish in its overriding occupation with ethical and religious

---

LITERARY AND HISTORICAL CONTEMPORARIES

Wiesel's famous contemporaries include:

Jacques Chirac (1932–): served as the president of France from 1995 to 2007
Harold Pinter (1930–): English playwright
Derek Walcott (1930–): West Indian poet and playwright
Desmond Tutu (1931–): South African religious leader and Nobel peace laureate

---

questions. Later, when he studied at the Sorbonne, his teacher Francois Wahl played a significant role in his life, conveying to him the subtleties of French literature.

Memory and Shaping Events Thematically, the writing of Elie Wiesel has been consistent, even single-minded, in its emphasis on the power of shaping events—most crucially, the experience of the concentration camps—to dominate the lives not only of their survivors, but of their children, and entire communities. His writings serve as rituals of collective memory for the Jewish people, and for the world: reminders not to forget the tragedy of the Holocaust. Not surprisingly, then, the issue of memory, and the limits of its power, is another touchstone in Wiesel's literary work. Wiesel has been an influential force in the ever-expanding literature of the Second World War, as well as twentieth-century Jewish writing. His intense confrontation with the meaning of the concentration camps, and his willingness to speak from a moral perspective on a range of issues, have influenced survivors of war and ethnic violence worldwide to testify publicly about their experiences.

Works in Critical Context

Night has been universally acclaimed as one of the most powerful works of literature to come out of World War II, although questions have at times been raised as to the veracity of some of the incidents and images recorded in the memoir. The remainder of Wiesel's work has been open to a range of critical assessments. He has his detractors, who dismiss many of his plots and characters as mere vehicles for his political and social concerns, and question whether his fiction is art or polemic. Some find that his prose occasionally turns trite. Others take issue with some of his political stances, such as his alleged lack of concern for the plight of the Palestinians. However, most commentators praise his sensitive insight into human behavior, his moral candor, and his status as the virtual living embodiment of Holocaust memory.

COMMON HUMAN EXPERIENCE

Here are some important works of postwar literature that, like the novels of Elie Wiesel, grapple with the epic tragedies of the war years:

Doctor Faustus (1947), by Thomas Mann. An elaborate reworking of the legend of Faust, set against the spiritual and intellectual disaster of the Third Reich.

The Thin Red Line (1962), by James Jones. A fictional account of the Battle of Guadalcanal, describing the alienation and horrors of American servicemen in the Pacific.

Black Rain (1965), by Masuji Ibuse. A novel based on records of the atomic bombing of Hiroshima in 1945 and its aftermath.

Slaughterhouse-Five (1969), by Kurt Vonnegut. A tragicomedy of time travel that opens with the firebombing of Dresden.

Responses to Literature

1. What do you think explains Elie Wiesel's consuming interest in the Holocaust and its aftermath? How has this interest affected other great humanitarian voices around the world? Describe two other such figures and talk about their influences as well.

2. Elie Wiesel's life has differed immensely from the life he imagined for himself as he grew up in the Romanian-Jewish shtetl of Sighet. Do some research on Sighet, and try to express some specific ways that Wiesel was shaped by his religious upbringing there.

3. Find three passages in Weisel's works that you feel demonstrate his most powerful rhetoric and describe how they reflect his postwar passions.

BIBLIOGRAPHY

Books

Berenbaum, Michael. *Elie Wiesel: God, the Holocaust, and the Children of Israel.* Springfield, N.J.: Behrman House, 1994.

Cargas, Harry James, ed. *Responses to Elie Wiesel: Critical Essays by Major Jewish and Christian Scholars.* New York: Persea Books, 1978.

Chmiel, Mark. *Elie Wiesel and the Politics of Moral Leadership.* Philadelphia: Temple University Press, 2001.

Cohen, Myriam B. *Elie Wiesel: Variations sur le silence.* La Rochelle, France: Rumeur des ages, 1988.

Davis, Colin. *Elie Wiesel's Secretive Texts.* Gainesville: University Press of Florida, 1994.

Lazo, Caroline Evensen. *Elie Wiesel.* New York: Macmillan, 1994.

Pariser, Michael. *Elie Wiesel: Bearing Witness.* Brookfield, Conn.: Millbrook Press, 1994.

Rosen, Alan, ed. *Celebrating Elie Wiesel: Stories, Essays, Reflections.* Notre Dame, Ind.: Notre Dame University Press, 1998.

Rosenfeld, Alvin. *Confronting the Holocaust.* Bloomington: Indiana University Press, 1978.

Schuman, Michael. *Elie Wiesel: Voice from the Holocaust.* Berkeley Heights, N.J.: Enslow, 1994.

Sibelman, Simon P. *Silence in the Novels of Elie Wiesel.* New York: St. Martin's Press, 1995.

Stern, Ellen Norman. *Elie Wiesel: A Voice for Humanity.* Philadelphia: Jewish Publication Society, 1996.

Periodicals

New Yorker (March 18, 1961); (January 9, 1965); (August 20, 1966); (July 6, 1970); (July 12, 1976).

New York Times Book Review (July 16, 1961); (April 15, 1962); (July 5, 1964); (January 21, 1979); (April 12, 1981); (August 15, 1982); (April 30, 1989); (April 19, 1992): 8; (December 17, 1995): 7.

Publishers Weekly (April 6, 1992); (October 16, 1995): 49; (October 23, 1995): 33; (January 15, 1996): 320; (May 20, 1996): 245.

■ James Alfred Wight

SEE *James Herriot*

◈ Oscar Wilde

BORN: *Dublin, Ireland, 1854*

DIED: *Paris, France, 1900*

NATIONALITY: *Irish, British*

GENRE: *Drama, fiction, poetry, essays*

MAJOR WORKS:

The Picture of Dorian Gray (1890)

Lady Windermere's Fan (1892)

An Ideal Husband (1895)

The Importance of Being Earnest (1895)

The Happy Prince, and Other Tales (1888)

Overview

There is a temptation to treat British author Oscar Wilde's work lightly in large part due to his flamboyant and notorious lifestyle, which is often better known than his writings. He posed as an aesthete and a decadent—a follower of literary movements of the late Victorian age that argued for "art for art's sake." Nevertheless, Wilde advocated reform through social critique in his plays,

Oscar Wilde   *Wilde, Oscar, photograph.*

short stories, novels, essays, and poems, and he challenged Victorian morality with his work and his lifestyle.

Works in Biographical and Historical Context

Influenced by Creative, Flamboyant Mother Wilde was born in Dublin, Ireland, in 1854. At the time, Ireland was part of the United Kingdom, and controlled by the British. Outside of the six counties of the north that were predominantly British and Protestant— commonly known as Ulster—absentee British landlords controlled much of the land in the remaining twenty-six counties that were predominantly Catholic, rural, and poor. There was long-standing tensions between the British and Irish, as the Irish agitated for more control and home rule. Wilde's family was Anglo-Irish, and he was raised a Protestant.

His father, Sir William Wilde, was a well-known surgeon. Wilde likely learned sympathy for the poor from his father, who would collect folklore instead of fees from the peasants he treated. Wilde's mother, Jane, wrote popular poetry and prose under the pseudonym Speranza. She was a writer and poet with a flair for the dramatic not only in her writing but also in her appearance. She dressed up in increasingly outlandish costumes,

complete with headdresses and bizarre jewelry. Wilde shared both her literary taste and fashion flamboyance.

Jane Wilde created a salon society in Dublin, and her large Saturday-afternoon receptions included writers, government officials, professors, actors, and musicians. After her husband died in 1876, she moved her salon to London. Her poetry was inflammatory and pro-nationalist, and in 1849 during the sedition trial of a magazine editor, she stood up in court and claimed authorship of the offending articles (a mother taking responsibility for someone else's failings to save their reputation is a theme in Wilde's play, *Lady Windemere's Fan*, 1892). She became famous for this incident and, many years later, encouraged Wilde to stand trial rather than run away, no doubt imagining another famous court victory for the Wilde family.

In general, Wilde's childhood appears to have been a happy if unconventional one. He had an older brother, Willie, and a younger sister, Isola, who died at the age of eight in 1867. The family was devastated by Isola's death. Wilde, who regularly visited her grave, wrote the poem "Requiescat" (1881) in her memory. His father's three illegitimate children, fathered before he married Jane, were also included in the family, and all of the children spent their holidays together.

Early Literary Attention For three years, Wilde was educated in the classics at Trinity College, Dublin, where he began to attract public attention through the eccentricity of his writing and lifestyle. At the age of twenty-three, Wilde entered Magdalen College, Oxford. In 1878, he was awarded the Newdigate Prize for his poem "Ravenna" (1878). He attracted a group of followers who became a personal cult, self-consciously effete and affected. His iconoclasm contradicted the Victorian era's easy pieties (the Victorian era was marked by romantic, evangelical, and humanitarian impulses, but with moral, insular overtones), but this was one of his aims. Another was the glorification of youth.

Wilde published his well-received *Poems* in 1881. He lectured in the United States and in England, and he applied unsuccessfully for a position as a school inspector. In 1884, he married Constance Lloyd, and their children were born in 1885 and in 1886. He encouraged his wife's political activity, including her involvement in the women's liberation and suffrage movements.

Challenging Societal Norms Wilde was also a reformer in support of women's liberation. He took over the editorship of the *Lady's World: A Magazine of Fashion and Society* in 1887 and reconstituted it. Discussion of fashion was relegated to the end of each issue, and serial fiction and articles on serious topics, such as the education of women, were moved to the front. Wilde also insisted the magazine be renamed the *Woman's World*, because he regarded "lady" as a pejorative term. Wilde remained editor for two years, but his involvement lessened as his other writing activities increased. His first

LITERARY AND HISTORICAL CONTEMPORARIES

Wilde's famous contemporaries include:

Bram Stoker (1847–1912): This Irishman was a theater manager and agent for twenty-seven years, but his part-time career as a fiction writer brought him immortality as the author of *Dracula* (1897).

Paul Gauguin (1848–1903): This French postimpressionist painter spent most of his life in Tahiti and the South Pacific, creating highly original and influential paintings of scenes and people there. His paintings include *Where Do We Come From? What Are We? Where Are We Going?*

George Eastman (1854–1932): This American inventor founded the Eastman Kodak Company and helped bring photography into the mainstream.

George Bernard Shaw (1856–1950): This British writer and playwright wrote more than seventy plays during his career, including *Pygmalion* (1916, later adapted as the musical *My Fair Lady*).

Emilia Pardo Bazàn (1852–1921): This Spanish novelist described the degeneration of aristocratic families in novels like *Los Pazos de Ulloa* (1886).

popular successes in prose were fairy tales: *The Happy Prince, and Other Tales* (1888) and *The House of Pomegranates* (1892).

Wilde became a practicing homosexual in 1886. He believed that this subversion of the Victorian moral code was the impulse for his writing. Wilde considered himself a criminal who challenged society by creating scandal, and his works often explore the criminal mentality. "Lord Arthur Savile's Crime," from *Lord Arthur Savile's Crime, and Other Stories* (1891), is a comic treatment of murder and its successful concealment. The original version of *The Picture of Dorian Gray*, published in *Lippincott's Magazine*, emphasized the murder of the painter Basil Hallward by Dorian as the turning point in Dorian's disintegration.

Dramatic Success Between 1892 and 1895 Wilde was an active dramatist, writing what he identified as "trivial comedies for serious people." His plays were popular because their dialogue was clever and often epigrammatic, relying on puns and elaborate word games for their effects. *Lady Windermere's Fan* was produced in 1892, *A Woman of No Importance* in 1893, and *An Ideal Husband* and *The Importance of Being Earnest* in 1895.

The years 1889 to 1895 were prolific ones for Wilde, but during these years he led an increasingly double life that ended in his imprisonment in 1895. This secret life was also featured increasingly in his work, especially in the novella *The Picture of Dorian Gray* (1891). This novella's

themes were also an example of the aesthetic movement, of which Wilde was a part. This late nineteenth century European arts movement centered on the doctrine that art existed for the sake of its beauty alone. The movement began as a reaction to prevailing utilitarian social philosophies and to what was perceived as the ugliness and philistinism of the industrial age.

On March 2, 1895, Wilde initiated a suit for criminal libel against the Marquis of Queensberry, who had objected to Wilde's relationship with his handsome young son, Lord Alfred Douglas. When his suit failed, countercharges followed, and after a sensationalistic public trial, Wilde was convicted of homosexual misconduct and sentenced to two years in prison at hard labor. (Until 1861, the punishment for men convicted of having sexual intercourse with men was death, while a lesser offense of attempted "buggery" was punishable by at least two years in jail. The 1885 Labouchere Amendment to the Criminal Law Amendment Act prohibited gross indecency between men. Gross indecency was interpreted to be any type of male homosexual behavior. Wilde was convicted under this amendment and received the harshest possible punishment under the law.)

Imprisonment Prison transformed Wilde's experience as radically as had his 1886 introduction to homosexuality. In a sense, he had prepared himself for prison and its transformation of his art. "De Profundis" is a moving letter to his former lover that Wilde wrote in prison and that was first published as a whole in 1905. His theme was that he was not unlike other men and was a scapegoat. "The Ballad of Reading Gaol" (1898) was written after his release.

After his release from prison in May 1897, Wilde went to France. He attempted to write a play in his earlier witty style, but the effort failed. He died in Paris on November 30, 1900.

Works in Literary Context

Wilde's early education generated an admiration for John Keats, Percy Shelley, Benjamin Disraeli, and Honoré de Balzac. In college, he was influenced by the writings of Walter Pater, who in his *Studies in the History of the Renaissance* (1873) urged indulgence of the senses, a search for sustained intensity of experience, and stylistic perfectionism in art. Wilde adopted this as a way of life, cultivating an extravagant persona that was burlesqued in the popular press and music-hall entertainments, copied by other youthful rebels, and indulged by the literary and artistic circles of London where Wilde was renowned for his intelligence, wit, and charm.

Reaction to Victorian Values *The Importance of Being Earnest*, Wilde's last and most brilliant play, is a hysterical comedy but also a serious critique of Victorian society. Wilde anticipated modern writers such as Samuel Beckett in his use of farce to comment upon serious issues. The Victorian upper classes are presented as enclosed characters more intent on social surface in a world where form replaces emotion. Victorian stuffiness and hypocrisy in marriage, education, and religion are all critiqued, but always through the sparkle of Wilde's biting satirical wit.

Readers familiar only with Wilde's plays and conversation may be surprised by his poetry, which demonstrates an expertise in classical literature and the mainstream Victorian influences of Matthew Arnold, Dante Rossetti, and Alfred Lord Tennyson. In *Poems* (1881), Wilde experimented with form and touched on many of the themes he would develop in his later works as a social and cultural reformer. He commented on what he regarded as the decline of civilization from the ancient Greeks to modern-day Europe. Decline became a recurrent theme in Wilde's later poetry, which he used to attack Victorian ruling-class values. He refused to see the Victorian age as one of glory, writing instead about the seedy, usually unmentioned side of Victorian life.

Aestheticism Wilde saw art as a vehicle for moral and social reform; what was not beautiful was not good, including poverty. The idea of poverty as dehumanizing ran counter to accepted middle-class views, both secular and religious, for by implication the ruling classes were responsible for this oppression. The value of domesticity, pride in industrialization, and the ennobling quality of poverty were popular Victorian literary themes. In his lectures and essays, Wilde preached a new program of social reform through art and beautification projects. Wilde criticized the false glamour of Victorian upper-class society, but Wilde was also attracted to that world. He viewed Victorian ideals of art, reflected in the ornate and orderly decor of upper- and middle-class homes, as a sham. During his aesthetic phase, he set about to reform rigid notions of art and decorated his home and his person as exhibits of this new modern art.

Wilde's critical essays and dialogues in *Intentions* (1891) defined his artistic philosophy. For example, "The Critic as Artist" developed his deeply held belief that originality of form is the only enduring quality in a work of art, a quality transcending its age. "The Decay of Lying" insisted on the superiority of art to nature and put forth the paradox that "nature imitates art," using this thesis to work out an ingenious line of argument revealing insights into the relationship between the natural and aesthetic worlds. "Pen, Pencil, and Poison" examined the relationship between art and morality, concluding that in fact there is none.

Influence Wilde has remained one of the most admired, read, and performed writers of all time. His poetry, essays, and children's books are reprinted regularly. *The Importance of Being Earnest* remains his best-known stage play, and is regularly performed all over the globe. Wilde's influence can be seen in a number of authors's writings, including E. M. Forester (who explores homosexuality in his novel *Maurice*) and, more recently, Stephen Frye, an actor/novelist/amateur Wilde scholar.

Works in Critical Context

Wilde's lasting literary fame resides primarily in his plays, one of which—*The Importance of Being Earnest*—is a

classic of comic theater. His only novel, *The Picture of Dorian Gray* (1891), while artistically flawed, gained him much of his notoriety during his life time. This book gives a particularly 1890s perspective on the timeless theme of sin and punishment.

Upon his release from prison, however, Wilde was generally either derided or ignored by literary and social circles. At the time of his death in 1900, the scandal associated with Wilde led most commentators to discuss him disrespectfully, if at all. While critical response no longer focuses so persistently on questions of morality, Wilde's life and personality still attract fascination. Biographical studies and biographically oriented criticism continue to dominate Wilde scholarship. After his death came a renewed critical interest in him, but it is only within the last thirty years that his work has received serious scholarly attention.

COMMON HUMAN EXPERIENCE

Wilde was a famous conversationalist. His sharp, witty observations seemed to come out of his mouth perfectly formed, precisely balanced, and always apt. Legend has it that Wilde's dying words were "Either that wallpaper goes, or I do." The following works celebrate the art of witty conversation.

The Life of Johnson (1750), a biography by James Boswell. Samuel Johnson was a leading author and critic in the eighteenth century, and much of his considerable literary authority came from the forcefulness and genius of his conversation. Boswell recorded a great deal of it, real or reconstructed, in what became the first great biographical study.

Annie Hall (1977), a film written and directed by Woody Allen. This film established the comic pattern that Allen would follow in many of his later comedies: an effete, clumsy intellectual encounters beautiful women and his own insecurities, and the result is a long string of witty exchanges and sharp, self-deprecating one-liners.

The Bonfire of the Vanities (1987), a novel by Tom Wolfe. Wolfe is a conservative dandy, usually decked out in a white suit, florid tie, and spats, playing the role of bemused and devastatingly witty social critic. This best-selling novel is set in New York and takes an ironic look at American culture of the 1980s.

A True Relation of My Birth, Breeding, and Life (1656), a memoir by Margaret Cavendish. In an era when intellectual pursuits were reserved only for men, Cavendish was a poet, philosopher, playwright, and author of one of the earliest science fiction novels. In her autobiography, she describes herself as extremely shy, but in public she made a space for a new kind of brave female writer through her eccentricity and extravagant dress.

Both Wilde's sincerity and his integrity have long been issues in criticism of his works. His conception of artistic beauty was often considered a superficial taste for ornament, though some critics have acknowledged that this conception of beauty additionally demands, as Wilde's character Gilbert states, "thought and passion and spirituality." Commentators on Wilde have also come to stress the intellectual and humanist basis of his work. Traditionally, critical evaluation of Wilde has been complicated, primarily because his works have to compete for attention with his sensational life. Wilde himself regarded this complication as unnecessary, advising that "a critic should be taught to criticize a work of art without making reference to the personality of the author. This, in fact, is the beginning of criticism."

Poetry The general critical reaction to Wilde's poems at the time of their publication was condemning and dismissive. Most reviewers were eager to denounce Wilde on the grounds of imitation of various writers and on his ornate language. The audacity of Wilde, an unknown in the literary world, perhaps triggered the critical attack when he published a collection of poetry. But in spite of the generally hostile reaction, within a year, five editions of Wilde's *Poems* had been sold.

An Ideal Husband While audiences thoroughly enjoyed the play *An Ideal Husband* when it was first produced, critics were more ambivalent. Many did not know how to respond to Wilde's treatment of his subject matter. That number included Henry James, who disliked the play so much that he wrote in a letter to his brother William about his own play *Guy Donville*, which was opening in London at the same time, "How can my piece do anything with a public with whom that is a success?" Even critics who had praised Wilde's previous work began to question his use of the epigram and criticized him for relying too heavily on his trademark device without providing substance to support his witticisms. However, the play did have its supporters, including George Bernard Shaw, who was so moved after seeing it that he described Wilde as "our only thorough playwright." In a review of the New York production of *An Ideal Husband*, William Dean Howells called the play "an excellent piece of art."

Recent critics of *An Ideal Husband* have generally accepted the conventional elements in the play at face value. Such elements include the melodramatic characters, the sentimental plot, the improbable twists, the witticisms, and the tidy resolutions, all of which make it a "well-made play." Instead, such critics focus on the core issues such as Wilde's social commentary on morality, the nature of political ambition, the disconnect between external appearances and the hidden lives of men and women, and the redeeming power of love. Thus, what has emerged is a view of the play as one in which Wilde developed markedly as a comedic playwright, providing, in addition to his biting social commentary, characters and themes that transcend the conventions of his theater. As Alan Bird stated in 1977, *An Ideal Husband* "marks yet another stage in [Wilde's] evolution as a dramatist while retaining its intrinsic value as a comedy which entertains, delights, intrigues, and amuses audiences of today as much as it did the first-night audience in 1895."

Responses to Literature

1. Identify and summarize melodramatic scenes from *The Picture of Dorian Gray*. What is their thematic purpose, if any? Put your answer in the form of a presentation.

2. What are "aphorisms" and "epigrams"? Locate some of Wilde's most famous examples. Can Wilde's conversation rightly be seen as part of his lasting artistic achievement? Do the characters in his plays speak in much the same way? Write an essay with your conclusions.

3. Read "The Ballad of Reading Gaol" and/or "De Profundis," and research the events in Wilde's life that led up to it for a paper. Are you convinced by Wilde's account of his motives and actions?

4. In a small group, look over the broad scope of Wilde's life and work. Discuss such questions as: Could you say that one phrase that sums up most of it could be "the importance of being earnest"? Why or why not?

BIBLIOGRAPHY

Books

Bird, Alan. "*An Ideal Husband.*" In *The Plays of Oscar Wilde*. London: Vision Press, 1977.

Ellmann, Richard. *Oscar Wilde*. New York: Knopf, 1988.

Foldy, Michael S. *Feasting with Panthers: Social and Cultural Dimensions of the Wilde Trials*. New Haven, Conn.: Yale University Press, 1997.

Horan, Patrick M. *The Importance of Being Paradoxical: Maternal Presence in the Works of Oscar Wilde*. Madison, N.J.: Fairleigh Dickinson University Press, 1997.

Howells, William Dean. "William Dean Howells on *An Ideal Husband.*" In *Oscar Wilde: The Critical Heritage*. Edited by Karl Beckson. New York: Barnes & Noble, 1970.

James, Henry. "Henry James' Letter to William James on the 'Triumphant Oscar.'" In *Oscar Wilde: The Critical Heritage*. Edited by Karl Beckson. New York: Barnes & Noble, 1970.

Miller, Robert Keith. *Oscar Wilde*. New York: Ungar, 1982.

Morley, Sheridan. *Oscar Wilde*. New York: Holt, Rinehart and Winston, 1976.

Nassaar, Christopher S. *Into the Demon Universe: A Literary Exploration of Oscar Wilde*. New Haven, Conn.: Yale University Press, 1974.

O'Connor, Sean. *Straight Acting: Popular Gay Drama from Wilde to Rattigan*. Washington, D.C.: Cassell, 1997.

Raby, Peter, ed. *The Cambridge Companion to Oscar Wilde.* Cambridge: Cambridge University Press, 1997.

San Juan, Epifanio. *The Art of Oscar Wilde.* Princeton, N.J.: Princeton University Press, 1967.

Shewan, Rodney. *Oscar Wilde: Art and Egotism.* New York: Barnes & Noble, 1977.

Worth, Katharine. *Oscar Wilde.* New York: Grove, 1984.

Web Site

The Official Web Site of Oscar Wilde. Retrieved April 28, 2008, from http://www.cmgworldwide.com/historic/wilde.

⊠ Charles Williams

BORN: *1886, Holloway, North London, England*

DIED: *1945, Oxford, England*

NATIONALITY: *British*

GENRE: *Fiction, poetry, nonfiction, drama*

MAJOR WORKS:

Outlines of Romantic Theology (1908)

Descent into Hell (1937)

Taliessin through Logres (1938)

The Region of the Summer Stars (1944)

All Hallows' Eve (1945)

Overview

British author Charles Williams was in many ways a paradox. He was a working-class man who lectured at Oxford University. He was a devoted Christian whose novels explore black magic. He was an eloquent philosopher of human and divine love whose own romantic life was often deeply troubled. Williams's talents were evident in many genres, including poetry, drama, fiction, biography, poetic theory, theology, literary essays, and book reviews.

Works in Biographical and Historical Context

Family Finances Affect Life Williams was born in London on September 20, 1886, to a middle-class family in financial straits. Raised in the Anglican faith, Williams loved the city of London and the Church of England throughout his life, and both are central elements in much of his fiction.

Forced in 1908 by his family's lack of money to curtail his education at the University of London after only two years, Williams secured an editorial position at the London office of the Oxford University Press—where he worked for the rest of his life. During the same year,

he met Florence Conway, whom he later married and to whom he wrote many love poems.

Professional Poet, Eternal Mystic Throughout his professional writing life, Williams considered himself to be primarily a poet, and during the early years of his career, published only poetry. In his late twenties, he became interested in magic and Rosicrucianism—a view based on Western traditions of mystery that is concerned with inner worlds, mysticism, and spirituality. At this time, he also joined the Hermetic Order of the Golden Dawn, a secret society devoted to the acquisition of occult knowledge. Although he did not remain with the group, Williams later drew upon his acquired knowledge of *Magia* (white magic) and *Goetia* (black magic) for subject matter in his novels.

By 1930, when the first of these novels, *War in Heaven*, was published, Williams had established himself as a minor poet and critic, as well as an outstanding lecturer on the major English poets at evening literature classes in London. His "supernatural thrillers," as his novels were called, attracted a wide audience at the time and introduced the author to two notable admirers: T. S. Eliot, who as a director of Faber and Faber published several of Williams's novels; and C. S. Lewis, whose own *Allegory of Love* (1936) delighted Williams and initiated the two writers' friendship.

Oxford With the outbreak of World War II and the Nazi bombing of Great Britain, the staff of the Oxford University Press's London office was evacuated to Oxford. World War II began when Great Britain declared war on Nazi Germany after the latter country invaded Poland in 1939. While Britain, as well as the rest of Europe, had tried to appease the territorial and military ambitions of Adolf Hitler by allowing him to take over certain territories in the late 1930s, the Nazi leader's actions in Poland were deemed unacceptable. France and other countries joined Britain as allies against the Germans and their allies, including Italy and, initially, the Soviet Union. Germany was soon in control of much of continental Europe and launched massive air attacks, known as the Blitz, against Great Britain in September 1940 that lasted till May 1941. Bombing attacks continued off and on until the end of the war.

At Oxford, Williams was soon introduced by Lewis into the Inklings—a group that gathered for discussions that ranged across politics, art, religion, and above all, fellowship. During one period of several months, members listened as the group's three principals read aloud from works in progress: C.S. Lewis from *Perelandra* (1943), J.R.R. Tolkien from *The Fellowship of the Ring* (1954), and Williams from *All Hallows' Eve* (1945)— novels that are recognized today to be among their authors' most accomplished works.

Charles Williams *Used by permission of the Marion E. Wade Center, Wheaton College, Wheaton, Il.*

Through the offices of Lewis and Tolkien, Williams was able to serve at Oxford as a lecturer on English poetry, attracting enthusiastic audiences at each appearance and receiving an honorary MA from the university in 1943. When he died suddenly after a seemingly minor operation in 1945, fellow Inkling Warren Lewis noted in his journal that "the black-out has fallen, and the Inklings can never be the same again."

Works in Literary Context

Many and Varied Influences When Williams took on theology and literary analysis, his work reflected his study of and interest in other famous writers like Dante and noted mystic/writer Evelyn Underhill. During the early years of his career when he published only poetry, much of it showed influences of Dante and, in its style, of G. K. Chesterton. *The Figure of Beatrice* (1943), for instance, was highly influenced by Williams's growing interest in Dante and the stories of the Grail, seminal influences on his thought that increased in power as the years passed. Some other works, such as *Divorce* (1920), were inspired by models ranging from Robert Herrick

and other seventeenth-century poets to the pre-Raphaelites and William Butler Yeats.

Mystical, Supernatural Style Williams's first Grail poetry, *Taliessin through Logres* (1938), demonstrates his mystical interests. He may have been drawn to the tragedy of Arthur, Guinevere, and Lancelot, but more central was the story of the Grail and the quest to establish God's kingdom, orderly and just, in England. The poems in the book are complex. Williams uses diagrammed associations to develop the narrative. For example, he connects characters to animals, and associates cities and their roles with parts of the human body and their functions.

But the religious, the magical, and the mythical make the most impact in his works as they reflect his devout Anglicanism and lifelong interest in all aspects of the supernatural. Williams's novels, such as *War in Heaven* (1930), *All Hallows' Eve*, and *The Place of the Lion* (1931) depict the earth as a battleground in a cosmic struggle between the forces of good and evil. These novels present the author's notion of the natural and supernatural realms as spheres separated by a penetrable boundary.

In *War in Heaven*, for example, Williams establishes one hallmark of his fiction: realistic depictions of common people encountering supernatural forces in and through everyday English life. In one set of critical terms, this type of fantasy is "low fantasy," supernatural but taking place in this world, as opposed to the otherworldly "high fantasy" of Tolkien's *The Hobbit* or *The Lord of the Rings*. In this way Williams is an ancestor to, though rarely a direct influence on, the supernatural-horror genre of the later twentieth century.

Influence Though Williams rarely influenced later horror, he was instrumental for fellow writers in another way. During the tenure of his friend C. S. Lewis as a fellow at Oxford's Magdalen College, Williams became a guiding force of the Oxford Christians or "Inklings," a group of like-minded writers who met weekly in Lewis's rooms to discuss literature and to read works in progress to each other for critical advice and mutual enjoyment. Although his works are not today as well known as those of his fellow Inklings Lewis and Tolkien, Williams was an important source of encouragement and influence among the group, and his death brought about its demise.

Williams's influence is most markedly evident, for example, in the work of Lewis, whose controversial *Preface to "Paradise Lost"* (1942) and apocalyptic novel *That Hideous Strength* (1946) advance ideas held by Williams. Such theological books as *He Came Down from Heaven* (1938) and *The Descent of the Dove: A Short History of the Holy Spirit in the Church* (1939) are important for their explicit statements of the author's spiritual beliefs. *The Descent of the Dove* was a key influence in poet W. H. Auden's conversion to Christianity, which affected that author's output.

Works in Critical Context

Concerning Williams's fiction, William Lindsay Gresham has remarked that "reading him we feel like the blind man who was given his sight and saw people like trees walking," referring to the Gospel of Mark 8:24. But despite their interesting plots and elements of the supernatural, the novels have never attracted a wide audience. Because of Williams's difficult style, they require closer attention than most readers are willing to devote to them. Critics have praised Williams's novels for their ability to portray spiritual truths. They have condemned them for their sensationalism. They have analyzed the precision and delicacy with which Williams writes. They have also complained of the author's obscurity. However, most critics agree that Williams's strength as a fiction writer grew throughout his career: this is demonstrated by the success he achieved with his last works, including *Descent into Hell.*

Descent into Hell Generally seeing it as one of Williams's two or three best novels, critics regard *Descent into Hell* as his most structurally satisfying novel, mapping the crossed ascent and descent of two characters. The ascending character is Pauline Anstruther, a young woman terrified by appearances of her doppelgänger—an eerie exact double. She is taught the truths of doubling and substitution by Peter Stanhope, a playwright who is her mentor. Since doubling is limited by neither space nor time, Pauline is eventually able to substitute herself for a martyred ancestor during his burning, thus ending her own haunting. Conversely, the title refers to the path of Lawrence Wentworth, a man of small vices and smaller virtues, who falls willing victim to a succubus because true love—or even true companionship—is too irritatingly demanding for him. With *Descent into Hell*, as Charles Moorman points out, Williams was shifting away from "adventure" and increasingly "toward an attempt to picture salvation and damnation as they exist among the people of Williams's own time."

Poetry Williams's verse is often difficult for readers. Anne Ridler wrote, "It is not a poetry for all moods; it is one, also, to which you must wholly submit in order to enjoy it. But I am sure that his cycle has its place in the tradition of English visionary poetry." Agnes Sibley, agreeing with Ridler's appraisal, added that "to all of Williams's writings 'you must wholly submit'." Though not as well known as his novels, Williams's Arthurian *Taliessin through Logres* (1938) and *The Region of the Summer Stars* (1944) are determined by some critics to

be among the most original works in twentieth-century English poetry. This Arthurian—or, more accurately, Grail—poetry is, as Roma A. King Jr. writes, "the poetical creation of a coherent mythical vision of man and his place in the larger creation of which he is a part."

Responses to Literature

1. In Williams's novels and dramas, common, unsuspecting characters from the natural world encounter beings from the supernatural realm. The reader is likewise intended to be startled by these strange and unexpected confrontations, and thereby awakened to their symbolic value. Consider one of the most important objects in your life. Write a personal essay in which you explain why you chose this object. What did it make you think of? What feelings come from the object/image for you? What does your choice say about who you are? How does your choice represent your personality?

2. Think about how natural and supernatural characters in Williams's works are caught up together in the struggle between good and evil. In *War in Heaven*, for example, the opposing forces converge on a humble church, each seeking to possess the Holy Grail, which has long stood unnoticed among the church's ornaments. Using either the Grail, the church, or another item from a Williams novel, consider all of the possible associations. Write a

COMMON HUMAN EXPERIENCE

As ancestor to the supernatural-horror genre, Williams can be said to have pioneered it to some degree. Here are a few works that later established the genre as best-seller material and developed it further.

The Exorcist (1971), a novel by William Peter Blatty. Evil takes possession of a little girl's body and soul and leaves several dead in its wake.

Flowers in the Attic (1977), a novel by V. C. Andrews. In the first of a series of novels, the children lose their parents and are taken in by a malicious, abusive grandmother.

Rosemary's Baby (1967), a novel by Ira Levin. The biggest problem Rosemary has in the new apartment building, the Bramford, is the devil-worshipping elderly couple next door.

The Shining (1977), a novel by Stephen King. A winter caretaker and his family have other worldly experiences in the Overlook Hotel.

Lost Boy, Lost Girl (2003), a novel by Peter Straub. In this novel, a house is haunted, there is a serial killer on the prowl, and people are missing.

paragraph in which you discuss how the item is a symbol and explore what it might represent.

3. In his poetry, Williams celebrates a vision he shared with Dante, one which reflects his major belief: that love is a sacrament enabling fellowship with God. With a group of your classmates, survey a few of Williams's poems and find evidence of love and of one's connection with God through love. Use examples from the texts to further your understanding of Williams's philosophy.

4. Williams did not fail to perceive suffering and ugliness in the world, but he believed that God's purposes are accomplished in spite of and with the seeming agency of evil. This concept derived from one of his major influences, the Scottish fantasist George MacDonald. Consider the instances of evil in a Williams work. With another classmate, discuss how good prevails, or how God's purposes are accomplished.

BIBLIOGRAPHY

Books

King, Roma A., Jr. *The Pattern in the Web: The Mythical Poetry of Charles Williams*. Kent, Ohio: Kent State University Press, 1990.

Lewis, C. S. "The Novels of Charles Williams." In *On Stories*. Ed.Walter Hooper. New York: Harcourt Brace Jovanovich, 1982.

Moorman, Charles. *Arthurian Triptych: Mythic Materials in Charles Williams, C. S. Lewis, and T. S. Eliot*. Berkeley: University of California Press, 1960.

Sibley, Agnes. *Charles Williams*. Boston: Twayne, 1982.

Williams, Charles. *The Image of the City, and Other Essays*. Ed. Anne Ridler. London: Oxford University Press, 1958.

Periodicals

Auden, W. H. "Charles Williams: A Review Article." *Christian Century*, January–June 1956, 552–54.

Eliot, T. S. "The Significance of Charles Williams." *Listener*, December 19, 1946, 894–95.

Web Sites

The George MacDonald Informational Web. "Charles Williams." Retrieved April 25, 2008, from http://georgemacdonald.info/williams.html.

The Lost Club Journal. "The Novels of Charles Williams." Retrieved April 25, 2008, from http://homepages.pavilion.co.uk/users/tartarus/williams.html.

Project Gutenberg Australia. "Charles Williams (1886–1945)." Retrieved April 25, 2008, from http://gutenberg.net.au/plusfifty-n-z. html#letterW.

Sturch, Dr. R. L. "The Charles Williams Society." Retrieved April 25, 2008, from http://www.geocities.com/charles_wms_soc.

Emlyn Williams

BORN: *1905, Mostyn, Wales*

DIED: *1987, London, England*

NATIONALITY: *British*

GENRE: *Drama, nonfiction, fiction*

MAJOR WORKS:
A Murder Has Been Arranged (1931)
The Corn Is Green (1935)
Night Must Fall (1936)
Someone Waiting (1956)
Beyond Belief (1967)

Overview

British author Emlyn Williams is primarily recognized for his achievements after the late 1920s, as an actor-playwright in London's West End and on New York's Broadway. He has been credited with establishing the psychological thriller on the modern stage and was well-respected for one-man shows in which he portrayed Charles Dickens and Dylan Thomas. In addition,

Emlyn Williams   *Williams, Emlyn, photograph. © Jerry Bauer. Reproduced by permission.*

Williams wrote several studies of the criminal mind that have since become models for the mystery and documentary novel genres.

Works in Biographical and Historical Context

Interest in Death Sparked by Tragedies George Emlyn Williams was born on November 26, 1905, near Mostyn, Flintshire (now Clwyd), Wales, to Richard and Mary Williams. Formerly a stoker in a coal mine, at the time of Williams's birth his father was an unsuccessful greengrocer. (Coal and iron mining were primary industries in Wales in the eighteenth and nineteenth century, turning south Wales, especially, into a very industrialized area.) In 1906, the family moved to Pen-y-maes, Glanrafon, Wales, where Williams's father became the landlord of a pub. In Wales, the childhood experiences of death—when a village girl died and when a neighboring farmer committed suicide—prompted the young Williams to develop a fascination with the macabre. This would impact his writings for the rest of his life.

Early Scholarship Williams received his earliest education at a convent of French nuns and at a council school. He then earned a scholarship at Holywell County

School. He was eleven years old when he met Sarah Grace Cooke, the teacher who both inspired his interest in education and provided moral and financial support for him to continue. She encouraged his interest in language and sent him to St. Julien, France, when he was fifteen to study French with a teacher of her acquaintance. Williams describes the relationship with Miss Cooke in his two autobiographical books, *George* (1961) and *Emlyn* (1973). It also served as a source of inspiration for his play *The Corn Is Green* (1938).

Early Theatrical Inclinations Williams earned a scholarship to Oxford and entered the university in 1923. While he did well in school, it soon became clear to him that he was not a scholar. His main interest was in theater, and he became a member of the Oxford University Dramatic Society. At Oxford, he decided to drop his first name in favor of his unusual middle name. Also at Oxford, he expressed his first tendencies towards the "sinister"—in a one-act drama, *Vigil*, which was produced in 1925. Successful on the stage, it was published in 1954.

Williams's first full-length play, *Full Moon*, was produced at Oxford in 1927. Later that year, he received his degree and moved to London to seek a career in the theater, making his professional acting debut as Pelling's Prentice in J. B. Fagan's *And So to Bed* in 1927. A series of other roles followed, including Jack in his own *Glamour* in 1928.

Williams's next venture in the realm of the mystery genre was *A Murder Has Been Arranged*, which began its run at London's St. James's Theatre on November 26, 1930, with Williams as director. Combining a story of murder with the supernatural, the play received favorable reviews, which emphasized William's command of atmosphere and sense of the theater, but it was not a commercial success. From April 1930 to January 1931, Williams played the role of the Chicago gangster Angelo in Edgar Wallace's *On the Spot*. When the play concluded its run, he went to Germany to research the mass murders of Fritz Haarman, the "Butcher of Hannover." (Haarman was a prolific serial killer who targeted young men in that small city in the late 1910s and early 1920s. It is believed he killed at least twenty-four people.) In August 1931, he opened in Wallace's crime drama *The Case of the Frightened Lady* in the role of Lord Lebanon.

Personal Relationships and Dramatic Success Williams's next play, *Port Said* (1931), was, like *A Murder Has Been Arranged*, a failure. It was no more successful when it was renamed and revised in 1933 as *Vessels Departing*. Williams went on to appear as a young Frenchman in another crime drama, *The Man I Killed*, by Reginald Berkeley, in 1932. Three years later,

LITERARY AND HISTORICAL CONTEMPORARIES

Williams's famous contemporaries include:

Josephine Baker (1906–1975): This expatriate dancer and singer became an international star as the first African American woman to star in a major motion picture.

Pablo Neruda (1904–1973): This Chilean author and Communist politician won the Nobel Prize for Literature in 1971 and created controversy because of his Communist political leanings. His poetry collections include *Twenty Poems of Love and a Song of Despair* (1924).

B. F. Skinner (1904–1990): An American psychologist, he made a great impact on the field with his theories on operant conditioning, his science of Radical Behaviorism, and his school of experimental research into and analysis of behavior. His books include *Beyond Freedom and Dignity* (1971).

Hiroshi Inagaki (1905–1980): A Japanese filmmaker, he is best known for his *Samurai* trilogy (1954–1956).

Jean-Paul Sartre (1905–1980): A French philosopher, writer, and critic, he is credited with pioneering modern existentialism. He explored this philosophy in plays like *No Exit* (1944).

Williams married Molly O'Shann, whom he had known since 1930; they had two children together. In the autobiographical *Emlyn* (1973), Williams frankly discusses his relationships with several men prior to his marriage to Molly, including the actor Bill Wilson and a younger man named Fess Griffiths. The latter is thought to be the model for the character Dan in *Night Must Fall* (1935), Williams's first successful play using a mystery motif.

Night Must Fall established Williams as a playwright, and his portrayal of Dan furthered his reputation as an actor. The play opened at the Duchess Theatre in London on May 31, 1935, and ran for 435 performances, then moved to the Ethel Barrymore Theater in New York. It was filmed in 1937 with Robert Montgomery as Dan and again—less successfully—in 1964, with Albert Finney in the role. Williams toured in the part in 1943 and for the armed forces in the Middle East in 1944. By this time, World War II was nearing its end. While the war had begun in Europe and later extended to Asia, the Middle East theater of war was primarily active from 1940 to 1943. The Middle East theater included northeast Africa (such as Tunisia, Libya, Egypt) and southwest Asia (such as the Arabian Peninsula, Iraq, Iran, and Tur-

key). The British Middle East Command was based in Cairo and took charge of operations in these areas for such military campaigns as the Middle East Campaign in 1940 and 1941.

In 1945, as the war was reaching its end, Williams wrote a crime sketch, *Thinking Aloud*, about the thoughts of an actress who has murdered her husband. It was performed at the Stage Door Canteen in London in July 1945, published in 1946, and revived in New York in 1975.

Final Transition to "Nonfiction Novels" In 1953, Williams completed *Someone Waiting*, his last play to study the psychology of a criminal. It opened at the Globe Theatre in London on November 25, with Williams in the role of Fenn. Williams then turned to "nonfiction novels"—works that are documentary but read like exciting fiction. His first was *Beyond Belief* (1967), a nonfiction novel similar to Truman Capote's *In Cold Blood* (1966). His second work in this new genre, *Dr. Crippen's Diary*, was published in 1978 in *Great Cases of Scotland Yard* and separately in 1988. Williams would not see its second printing. He died of cancer on September 25, 1987, in London.

Works in Literary Context

Influences Although Williams used a modern form for his documentary novels, the form of his plays is dated and appears artificial to contemporary audiences. According to Don Dale-Jones, "His acknowledged influences are [W. Somerset] Maugham, [Henrik] Ibsen, [J. M.] Barrie and [John] Galsworthy, writers of 'well-made' plays."

Criminal Psychology Much of William's literary achievement derives from his interest in criminal psychology. Williams is more concerned with the psychology of the killer and those associated with him than with presenting the crime as a puzzle to be solved. For example, while *A Murder Has Been Arranged* (1930) portrays a fatal birthday celebration in a haunted theater, *Night Must Fall* (1935) concerns a homicidal psychopath stalking an elderly woman and her young niece in a huge, old home. Williams's nondramatic works, *Beyond Belief* (1967) and *Dr. Crippen's Diary* (1988), are based on actual crimes. The former recounts a series of torture-killings of children in 1963 and 1964. The latter purports to be the diary kept by convicted wifemurderer Dr. Crippen, who was executed in 1910. These "nonfiction novels" also explore the background and psychology of the criminals, Ian Brady and Myra Hindley.

Solo Performance Though known for his psychological thrillers on both the page and stage, Williams was also celebrated for his one-man shows. His portrayal of

Charles Dickens, for example, made him a success as a solo performer. Williams did not simply read Dickens' work. Instead, he depicted the famous author as he was during his famous reading tours. Though some critics did not like the mode of one-man plays and refused to view them as legitimate theater, Williams persisted in experimenting with the genre. In 1955, he performed in a solo act based on the poetic writings of Dylan Thomas. Unlike his performance of Dickens, however, this play focused on interpreting Thomas' words, rather than inhabiting Thomas himself.

Influence Williams' long and distinguished career influenced generations of writers who followed. Like *In Cold Blood*, Williams's documentary novels anticipated the popularity of true crime books in the late 1950s. The emphasis on the psychology of criminals in many of his plays also provided a model for crime dramas that followed.

Works in Critical Context

While many of Williams's plays were not box office successes when originally introduced, critics found more to like. Plays like *A Murder Has Been Arranged* were embraced more by critics than by audiences; however, most critics concur that Williams will be best remembered as a writer of psychological thrillers, particularly *Night Must Fall*, and as the author of the more traditionally dramatic *The Corn Is Green*. Both plays were extremely popular in Great Britain and the United States.

Summarizing Williams's achievement as a playwright, Richard B. Gidez concludes in the *Dictionary of Literary Biography* that "his plays are often entertaining, his plotting ingenious [,] his ability to create atmosphere sure, his sense of theater consummate." As for Williams's nondramatic works, Nelson observes that "he is a good storyteller, and he is always entertaining. His contribution to the crime story is in his penetrating studies of the personality and psychology of the criminal."

Night Must Fall According to Gidez, *Night Must Fall* "is one of the most successful and chilling psychological thrillers of the modern stage." Audiences responded to the story as well as Williams's chilling portrayal of a homicidal psychopath stalking an elderly woman and her young niece in a huge old home. Of the London production, the *Spectator*'s Derek Verschoyle wrote: "In comparison with this play, all other modern plays with murder as their theme . . . seem in retrospect as flat as the proverbial pancake." When *Night Must Fall* was staged in New York City, critics were similarly impressed. The *New York Times* concluded: "When he is at his best as an author and actor, Mr. Williams can be morbidly terrifying, and enough of *Night Must Fall* is just that."

COMMON HUMAN EXPERIENCE

Here are a few works by writers who have also shown interest in the psychology of criminals.

Brighton Rock (1938), a novel by Graham Greene. A chance meeting between a sociopath and a newsman has gruesome consequences in this thriller.

A Darker Justice (2004), a novel by Sallie Bissell. Abduction and psychopathology run in parallel stories in this crime fiction thriller.

Rules of Prey (1989), a novel by John Sandford. This first in the thriller series introduces readers to one of the more acclaimed detective characters in popular fiction.

The Straw Men (2002), a crime novel by Michael Marshall. Serial killers on the loose start their spree at an innocuous small-town McDonald's.

Thinner (1984), a novel by Stephen King. In this thriller, an overweight executive appears to get away with vehicular manslaughter of an old man. The man's surviving son, a traveling gypsy, touches the killer's cheek and utters a curse: "Thinner."

The Corn Is Green The more personal play, *The Corn Is Green*, attracted kudos from audiences and critics. The story focuses on the efforts of a schoolteacher, based on his own mentor, Cook, to found a school for the children of Welsh miners in the late nineteenth century and her efforts to help a boy, based on and played by Williams, win a scholarship. Although citing the sometimes overly theatrical nature of the play, Stark Young in the *New Republic* nonetheless found that Williams had given the play "something deeply felt, and perhaps personal, that gives it more life, refinement and intensity." Writing in *The Amazing Theatre*, James Agate commented, "The simplicity of the story can be relied on to throw the spectator into a mood of acceptance of make-believe from which he need make very occasional sorties to admire this bit of pathos pressed home but not too far home." Erik Johns concludes, "In the entire history of Wales [Williams] is the one solitary figure on the plane of first-rate dramatists to write a play in English that is essentially Welsh in essence."

Responses to Literature

1. While a playwright named Eugène Scribe is credited with creating the theater genre known as the well-made play, Williams was known as a playwright who met the conventions of that genre. Research the elements that make up this kind of play and match the list of criteria against one of Williams's works. Report back to a group of your classmates to discuss

Williams's important techniques of action, characterization, and plot.

2. The psychological thriller model is a specific subgenre of the larger thriller genre. However, where thrillers focus on plot over character, psychological thrillers put more importance on character (and characters' minds, mentality, and mental manipulation) than on plot. Consider a Williams work such as *Night Must Fall*. Write an essay that explains what makes the work a psychological thriller. Focus on such key elements as how the characters' minds work, the use of stream-of-consciousness, what the first-person narration reveals, and any history (or back-story) that adds suspense and psychological intensity.

3. Several contemporary directors are masters of the psychological thriller—including Alfred Hitchcock, David Lynch, and Takashi Shimizu. Taking into consideration such directors and their techniques, choose one Williams work that would best lend itself to movie production. To gain a greater appreciation of the elements of the novel as a psychological thriller, meet with a group of peers and draft plans to turn the story (or one scene) into a movie. Consider the following possibilities:

What are the components of the character's psyche that are important to the storyline?

What is the "thrill" experienced by readers that could be translated to film to thrill viewers? For example, where does Williams put his protagonist at greatest risk, and how is this exciting? How would a favorite director illustrate this peak excitement?

What is important to the story that affects the characters' mentally? How would you script mental threats, abuse, fear, or other Williams issues so they translate to the screen? Would you use interior monologue? Voiceover narration? Dialogue between characters that reveals the necessary details?

What theme is expressed in Williams's play that needs to be expressed in the movie/scene? For example, is there an obsessive preoccupation with or fixation on something—identity, reality versus the unreal or untrue, or a problem to be solved? How would this best be filmed—by character behavior, quirks, dialogues, flashback devices, or special lighting or other special effects?

BIBLIOGRAPHY

Books

Agate, James. *The Amazing Theatre*. London: Harrap, 1939.

Dale-Jones, Don. *Emlyn Williams*. Cardiff: University of Wales Press, 1979.

Findlater, Richard. *Emlyn Williams*. New York: Macmillan, 1956.

Taylor, John Russell. *The Rise and Fall of the Well-Made Play*. London: Methuen, 1967.

Williams, Emlyn. *Emlyn: An Early Autobiography, 1927–1935*. London: Bodley Head, 1973.

Periodicals

Heath, Tony. "Obituary: Emlyn Williams." *London Independent*, July 20, 1995.

King, Florence. "Misanthrope's Corner." *National Review*, June 11, 2001.

Mintz, S. L. "Less Isn't More." *American Theatre* 10 (April 1993).

Web Sites

"Emlyn Williams." *BBC—North East Wales Arts*. Retrieved April 25, 2008, from http://www.bbc.co.uk/wales/northeast/guides/halloffame/arts/emlyn_williams.shtml.

"Emlyn Williams (I)." Internet Movie Database. Retrieved April 25, 2008, from http://www.imdb.com/name/nm0930539.

"Emlyn Williams (1905–1987), a Fan Tribute." Retrieved April 25, 2008, from http://www.mooncove.com/emlynwilliams.

Raymond Williams

BORN: *1921, Llanfihangel Crocorney, Monmouthshire, Wales*

DIED: *1988, Cambridge, England*

NATIONALITY: *British*

GENRE: *Nonfiction, fiction*

MAJOR WORKS:
Culture and Society, 1780–1950 (1958)
The Country and the City (1973)
Television: Technology and Cultural Form (1974)
Keywords: A Vocabulary of Culture and Society (1976)
People of the Black Mountains (1989; 1990)

Overview

British author Raymond Williams ranks as one of the most influential post–World War II cultural theorists in the English-speaking world. A prolific writer, he made significant contributions to intellectual history, literary criticism, and historical linguistics (language studies). His work includes the critical and historical examination of the novel, the popular press, drama, television, and the cinema. He also wrote novels, short stories, and plays. Williams is perhaps best remembered as one of the creators of cultural studies, a discipline that has profoundly reshaped scholarship in the humanities since the mid-1970s.

Works in Biographical and Historical Context

Welsh Origins   Raymond Henry Williams was born in Wales on August 31, 1921, the only child of Henry Joseph Williams, a railway signalman and active supporter of the labor movement, and Esther Gwendolene Williams. At age eleven, Williams received a scholarship that allowed exceptional working-class children to attend the King Henry VIII Grammar School for Boys in Abergavenny. He received outstanding examination scores, and his headmaster arranged for him to attend Trinity College, Cambridge, on a full-tuition scholarship, plus a stipend.

By the time he arrived at Cambridge to study literature in 1939, Trinity College was the scene of a vibrant left-wing intellectual atmosphere. Already a socialist, Williams joined the Communist-dominated Socialist Club, became a Communist Party member for a short time, and wrote for various left-wing magazines and journals. In the 1930s, such left-leaning political beliefs were popular in Great Britain as well as the United States among those who rejected Fascism and wanted to improve the lives of working-class people through political change.

Service in World War II   Williams's education was interrupted in 1941 by military service in World War II. This war had broken out in Europe in 1939 when Nazi Germany, led by Adolf Hitler, invaded Poland. Great Britain, allied with France and other countries, had allowed Germany's territorial ambitions to go unchecked until this point. Realizing Hitler wanted to conquer Europe, if not the world, Great Britain and its allies declared war. While Hitler soon came to control much of continental Europe and began intensely bombing Britain in preparation for an invasion, Britain and its allies, which later included the United States, were able to defeat Germany. During the war, Williams achieved the rank of captain, but the war experience, he later said, caused him to feel as if he had lost the most significant dimension of his humanity. On leave in June 1942, he married Joy Dalling, a student at the London School of Economics. They had three children: Merryn in 1944, Ederyn in 1947, and Gwydion Madawc in 1950.

Critical Inquiry   When the war ended, Williams returned to an England in which public opinion had begun to tilt toward the left. The millions of soldiers coming home from the war were eager for change. Their support resulted in the Labour Party's victory over Winston Churchill's Conservatives in 1945. The Labour government failed to bring about the ideal community for which Williams and other socialists had hoped, but he viewed the creation of a mixed economy and a welfare state as a substantial step forward.

Graduating from Cambridge with a degree in English in 1946, Williams became a tutor for the Oxford Delegacy for Extra-Mural Education of the Workers' Educational Association (WEA). The WEA had been founded in 1903 to extend educational opportunities to working people by offering courses that developed their intellectual skills while drawing on their practical experience. As a WEA teacher, Williams found himself mediating disputes between his Labour and Communist colleagues.

Published Culture and Society   Although a committed socialist, Williams was attracted to the conservative ideas of F. R. Leavis and his followers. He appreciated Leavis's perspective: that critics were the guardians of the "great tradition" of literature. Literature was being produced for a passive and uncritical mass audience and was under siege by a debased popular culture. Yet, Williams objected to Leavis's elitist politics and disdain for the masses. This view prompted the launch of the journal *Politics and Letters*, which he edited from 1947 to 1948. *Politics and Letters* attempted to merge Leavis's critical methods with a leftist political outlook. Williams also respected Leavis's defense of cultural standards and agreed with him that language and literature played critical roles in cultural transmission, but rejected the notion that literature represents the entire cultural heritage and that intellectuals are its only guardians. To express these and other positions, in 1958 Williams published *Culture and Society, 1780–1950*, the book for which he is best known.

Williams was an original member of the editorial board of the *New Left Review*, founded in 1960 through the merger of *Universities and Left Review* and *The New Reasoner*. In 1961, he left his position with the WEA to become a lecturer in English and a fellow of Jesus College at Cambridge. That same year, he published *The Long Revolution*, in which he examines the economic, political, social, and cultural transformations of the previous two hundred years. Williams was always ambivalent about his career at Cambridge. He was critical of the university's conservatism, hierarchy, and pretension: scholar Terry Eagleton quotes him as describing it as "one of the rudest places on earth...shot through with cold, nasty and bloody-minded talk." Despite such criticisms, Williams apparently enjoyed the prestige that his position carried.

Left Labour Party   When prime minister Harold Wilson condemned the leaders of the 1966 strike by the National Union of Seamen as "a tightly knit group of politically motivated men," Williams resigned from the Labour Party in response. In 1967 and 1968, he contributed to the building of an alternative politics with the *May Day Manifesto* movement, which sought to reconstitute and expand the agenda of the original New Left. Williams was so disenchanted with Labour politics that he actually welcomed the election of the Conservative Edward Heath as prime minister in June 1970.

LITERARY AND HISTORICAL CONTEMPORARIES

Williams's famous contemporaries include:

Dylan Thomas (1914–1953): Welsh poet famous as much for his writing as for his distinctive recorded readings of his own work. His best known work is *Under Milk Wood* (1953).

Richard Burton (1925–1984): Eminent Welsh actor who was at one time the highest-paid actor in Hollywood. Famous for his tumultuous relationship with actress Elizabeth Taylor, Burton was celebrated for both his stage and film work.

Toni Morrison (1931–): An African American Pulitzer Prize– and Nobel Prize–winning author, she wrote such novels as *The Bluest Eye* (1970) and *Beloved* (1987).

Ernest "Che" Guevara (1928–1967): Marxist revolutionary leader from Argentina. Guevara was a hero of the countercultural movement of the 1960s.

His disillusionment with the Labour Party coincided with a new openness toward Marxism, or its variant, "Western Marxism." His attitude is reflected in "Literature and Sociology: In Memory of Lucien Goldmann" and "Base and Superstructure in Marxist Cultural Theory," published in the *New Left Review* in 1971 and 1973, respectively, and anthologized in *Problems in Materialism and Culture* (1980).

Taught in United States Also in 1973 was the publication of his *The Country and the City*. In this work, Williams traced ideas of the urban and the rural in the English literary tradition from the early modern era to the contemporary period—critiquing early seventeenth-century poems he said celebrate the paternalistic culture of the landlords while ignoring the people of the countryside whose labor made the culture possible. The year this work was published, Williams was teaching at Stanford University in California, though he had previously refused to teach in the United States because of the country's involvement in the Vietnam War.

For the cultural theorist, his stay in California was highlighted by his exposure to American television. Throughout his career, he had demonstrated a scholarly and critical interest in popular cultural forms, and from 1968 to 1972, he had written a weekly column on television for the BBC publication the *Listener*, collected in *Raymond Williams on Television: Selected Writings* (1989). Thus, watching American television did not create an interest where none had existed; rather, it forced him to see television from a fresh perspective. The result was his best-known critical work, *Television: Technology and Cultural Form* (1974).

Returning to "Welshness" Cultural studies, the field Williams had helped to found, had developed in multiple directions in the 1960s and 1970s. Williams became professor of drama at Cambridge in 1974. In 1977, he published *Marxism and Literature*, a definitive statement of the position he called "cultural materialism." Following his retirement from Cambridge in 1983, Williams devoted most of his energy to a multivolume novel encompassing all of Welsh history, *People of the Black Mountains*. The work remained unfinished at his death in London on January 26, 1988.

Works in Literary Context

Williams's work was influenced by or prompted by his responses to other theory. For example, based on his critiques of the elitist view of culture held by F. R. Leavis and based on Marxist views of class consciousness, he created a new theoretical space he called "cultural materialism." He rejected the distinction between high culture and popular culture. Instead, he saw cultural representations—whether epic poetry or workers's cooperatives—as "ordinary." He saw these representations not in the sense of being common but as giving meaning to everyday life.

Antielitist Theory of Culture *Culture and Society*, for another example, is an act of historical recovery that fleshes out a tradition whose scope was not understood at the time he wrote the book: the "culture and society" tradition. This tradition includes, in addition to Leavis, the inspiration of T. S. Eliot and his influential *Notes Towards the Definition of Culture* (1949). Williams rejected both Leavis's and Eliot's theories, considering them culturally elitist. He refuted the idea that culture is incompatible with democracy, socialism, and popular education. He argued that the capitalist social order that underpins Eliot's cultural elite must be held responsible. He also rejected the conventional distinction between "high" and "low" culture, and argued for a more encompassing view: culture as "the whole way of life."

Influence Instrumental in creating cultural studies, Williams's influence can be seen in each academic who studies in this intellectual area. His influence can similarly be seen in sociology and intellectual history as well as modern, popular analyses of culture like literature, television, radio, drama, and film. Williams's left-leaning political and social beliefs also affected authors who followed him.

Works in Critical Context

Cultural studies has developed in directions that Williams could never have imagined, but the growth of the field is in large part indebted to his pioneering work. Speaking at a memorial service for Williams, former student and, later, friend and colleague Stephen Heath said, "To remember Raymond Williams here today is to pay tribute to a thinker whose work transformed our understanding of society and culture." Several scholars have since agreed. Yet, Williams is not without his critics. Some have charged him with having such an unshakable certitude in the truth of his own experience that his work borders on being preachy. Nevertheless, his creation of cultural studies as a field of study remains of the greatest importance, and the origin and continued inspiration he has left are forever reflected in his body of writings. This is demonstrated in such works as *The Country and the City.*

The Country and the City (1973) According to the Marxist philosophy of the period, the logical progression of history requires that industrial production displace agricultural society. In *The Country and the City*, Williams opposes—among other things—mainstream Marxism. He acknowledges the accelerating spread of modernization, but also claims that the developmental process entails the growing rather than the shrinking of the agrarian sector.

The Country and the City was received enthusiastically by the British intellectual Left. Scholar E. P. Thompson echoed the general reception when he described the book as "part of that stubborn, uncompromising clarification of socialist thought which historians will come to see as more important and more lasting in influence than better advertised products of the international new left." He concluded: "There is something in the unruffled stamina of this man which suggests a major thinker."

Responses to Literature

1. Williams expressed a profound interest in culture and the language of culture in such works as *Culture and Society, The Long Revolution*, and *Keywords*. He regarded culture in his and the previous eras by considering the development of ideas. He studied culture as a kind of response—revealed in the political and social changes that came about because of the Industrial Revolution. Williams offered three kinds of culture:

   In anthropology, *culture* signifies the meanings, values, and institutions of a society, or what he called a "whole way of life";

   The term *culture* also refers to the intellectual and imaginative work associated with the arts and humanities;

   Ideal culture includes that intellectual and imaginative work that is what Matthew Arnold called "the best that has been thought and written."

2. To come to a better understanding of at least one of Williams's approaches to the term "culture," imagine you are an ambassador of your society who has been called to travel to another planet to characterize and demonstrate what your culture involves. Choose one of the above definitions/forms of culture. Go out in the world (or online) and "collect" artifacts that will

---

COMMON HUMAN EXPERIENCE

Here are a few works by writers who also critiqued culture in general or some specific aspect of culture.

Amusing Ourselves to Death: Public Discourse in the Age of Show Business (1985), critical nonfiction by Neil Postman. The author analyzes the cultural medium of television.

Civilization and Its Discontents (1929), critical nonfiction by Sigmund Freud. The author studies culture versus the individual.

Critique of Dialectical Reason (1960), critical nonfiction by Jean-Paul Sartre. The author challenges definitions of class and social methods of grouping.

Women, Culture, and Politics (1990), critical nonfiction by Angela Davis. The author discusses her notions of class with regards to minority, working, and gender groupings.

---

best demonstrate your culture for the new planet. Justify your choices, whether they include foods, arts, writings, technologies, rituals, costumes, or any other elements you think will illustrate your culture, by writing a brief speech that points out each item you collected.

3. How does *The Country and the City* argue in favor of the natural world (country) or the progressive world (city) as vital for a person's moral growth? What descriptions, scenes, dialogue, or other elements suggest this? What does the comparison say about personal preferences, values, and beliefs?

4. In the early 1970s, Williams focused on his "Welshness." This increasing interest found its way into his critical works, such as *People of the Black Mountains*, and it appears in his fiction, such as *Border Country*, *Second Generation*, and *The Fight for Manod*. To better appreciate Williams's persistent "return to Welshness," consider your own nationality and/or ethnicity for a paper. Make note of all that makes up who you are—including values, orientations or preferences, community concerns, family histories, and anything else that contributes to how you identify yourself.

5. Consider Williams's comment about King Henry VIII Grammar School for Boys in Abergavenny, found in his *Politics and Letters: Interviews with* New Left Review (1979): "What I did not perceive at the time but I now understand is that the grammar schools . . . in the towns of Wales . . . imposed a completely English orientation, which cut one off

thoroughly from Welshness." With a small group of your classmates, share similar experiences you have had regarding an institution or group that has disturbed your identity.

BIBLIOGRAPHY

Books

Eagleton, Terry, ed. *Raymond Williams: Critical Perspectives* Cambridge: Polity, 1989.

Inglis, Fred. *Raymond Williams.* New York: Routledge, 1995.

Thompson, E. P. "Country and City." In *Making History: Writings on History and Culture.* New York: New Press, 1994.

Web Sites

Milligan, Don. "Raymond Williams: Hope and Defeat and the Struggle for Socialism." Retrieved April 25, 2008, from http://www.studiesinanti-capitalism.net/StudiesInAnti-Capitalism/RaymondWilliams.html.

Museum of Broadcast Communications. "Williams, Raymond: British Media Critic." Retrieved April 25, 2008, from http://www.museum.tv/archives/etv/W/htmlW/williamsray/williamsray.htm.

The Raymond Williams Society. Retrieved April 25, 2008, from http://www.raymondwilliams.co.uk. Last updated on February 5, 2008.

Williams, Raymond. Excerpts from *Keywords.* Retrieved April 25, 2008, from http://pubpages.unh.edu/~dml3/880williams.htm#N_1_.

◨ Angus Wilson

BORN: *1913, Bexhill-on-Sea, East Sussex, England*

DIED: *1991, Bury St. Edmunds, Suffolk, England*

NATIONALITY: *British*

GENRE: *Fiction, nonfiction*

MAJOR WORKS:

Hemlock and After (1952)

Emile Zola: An Introductory Study of His Novels (1952)

A Bit Off the Map (1957)

The Middle Age of Mrs. Eliot (1958)

No Laughing Matter (1967)

Overview

Angus Wilson was one of the leading British authors to emerge in the post–World War II era. Wilson is best known as a chronicler of the postwar social revolution in England and for his ability to successfully combine the techniques of modernist fiction with the traditional novel.

Angus Wilson   © Sophie Bassouls / CORBIS SYGMA

Although often extremely funny, his novels also contain serious critiques of British society. Wilson's subjects are usually failed or wasted lives, individuals whose crises reflect the disintegration of a larger way of life.

Works in Biographical and Historical Context

Isolated Childhood Angus Frank Johnstone Wilson was born in Bexhill, Sussex, a small town on the southeastern coast of England, on August 11, 1913. His father, William Johnstone-Wilson, was of Scottish origin, and his mother, Maude Caney Johnstone-Wilson, was from South Africa. Wilson was the youngest of five sons, thirteen years younger than the fourth child. Consequently, Wilson spent a somewhat lonely childhood with adults as companions, and this isolation from other children was further compounded by his parents' frequent moving. Wilson took refuge in his imagination, in role-playing and reading.

Becoming Politically Active In 1932, Wilson went to Merton College, Oxford, to study medieval history. At Oxford, he met friends with different backgrounds and political ideas. Wilson adopted several left-wing causes and converted to socialism. In the 1930s, such left-leaning political beliefs were popular in Great Britain as well as the United States among those who rejected fascism and wanted to improve the lives of working-class people through political change.

After graduating, Wilson took a variety of jobs, including tutoring and secretarial work. In 1936, he took a position in the Department of Printed Books at the British Museum, where he worked for almost twenty years. During this period, he was politically active, mixing with intellectuals of the left, who recur in his work. This experience, as well as his education, made him interested in the use and abuse of power.

Affected by World War II   In 1939, Great Britain declared war on Germany after the Nazis invaded Poland, beginning World War II in Europe. Britain and its allies sought to contain German leader Adolf Hitler's territorial and military ambitions. Germany, however, was able to control much of continental Europe for much of the war, and heavily bombed Great Britain in preparation for an invasion which never happened. Great Britain's casualties reached seven hundred thousand over the course of the conflict.

During the war years, Wilson worked in the Foreign Office doing intelligence work. He had to leave the busy city life and move to a small village where he was housed with a widow and her daughter. His sense of loneliness and alienation at work and at his lodgings, together with an unsuccessful love affair, brought him to the point of a nervous breakdown. Per his therapist's suggestion, Wilson began writing short stories, and during the following seven years, he published two collections of short stories and two novels. His first short-story collection, *The Wrong Set and Other Stories*, appeared in 1949. By this time, he held a new post.

From 1947 to 1955, Wilson was deputy superintendent of the Reading Room, where he was in charge of replacing three hundred thousand volumes lost in the bombings of World War II. His work in the museum and the Foreign Office provided him with important insights into the world of the cultural establishment and into the workings of bureaucratic administration, both of which he frequently criticizes in his stories.

Writing and Teaching   In 1955, Wilson resigned his job at the British Library to become a full-time writer. During the next ten years, he produced four novels and one more collection of short stories. Wilson's novels in this time period include *The Middle Age of Mrs. Eliot* (1958) and *The Old Men at the Zoo* (1961). He also became an active reviewer and literary biographer.

From 1966 to 1978, Wilson was a professor in the School of English and American Studies at the University of East Anglia in Norwich, but he continued to travel and lectured extensively all over the world. In 1978, at age sixty-five, Wilson retired from his teaching post, though he continued to take guest professorships at various universities in the United States.

He was knighted in 1980 for both his literary achievements and his contributions to the arts and service

LITERARY AND HISTORICAL CONTEMPORARIES

Wilson's famous contemporaries include:

William Golding (1911–1993): Golding was a British novelist and poet best known for his novel *Lord of the Flies* (1954).

Richard Nixon (1913–1994): Nixon was an influential American politician and thirty-seventh president of the United States (1969–1974).

Ernest Hemingway (1899–1961): Hemingway was an American Nobel Prize–winning author, one of the most celebrated and influential literary stylists of the twentieth century. His novels include *The Old Man and the Sea* (1952).

Irwin Shaw (1913–1984): Shaw, an American writer best known for his novel *Rich Man, Poor Man* (1970), was considered a master of modern short fiction in the years between World War II and the Vietnam War.

Ralph Ellison (1914–1994): Ellison was an American author best known for his novel *Invisible Man* (1953), which won the National Book Award.

Doris Lessing (1919–): Lessing is a British novelist who won the Nobel Prize in Literature in 2007. Her novels include *The Golden Notebook* (1962).

organizations. His last novel, *Setting the World on Fire* (1980), explores the influence of place on human character and is largely constructed of dramatic dialogue. Wilson died of a stroke on May 31, 1991, at a nursing home in Bury Saint Edmunds, where he had spent his last few years.

Works in Literary Context

Wilson's stories fictionalize much of his childhood and experiences during the war. Childhood and the family form the deepest autobiographical layers in Wilson's fiction. In a 1972 interview with Frederick P. W. McDowell, Wilson describes his stories as being "s little bits of my life which I had transformed into stories."s Wilson's work at the museum gave him an understanding of the management of English high culture that also informed and influenced his work. In his stories, Wilson describes and criticizes simultaneously, mixing nostalgia and sarcastic wit. His prime targets are old-fashioned middle-class aspirations and traditional liberal values.

Family Relationships   Most of the stories in *The Wrong Set* take place in the 1930s, and Wilson uses jargon and fashions to place the characters and their backgrounds. In Wilson's fiction, language is the most important indicator of a character's sincerity and self-awareness, or lack thereof. Many of the stories focus on

COMMON HUMAN EXPERIENCE

Wilson never preaches or moralizes. Instead, he allows the characters to reveal and condemn themselves. Here are some works that take a similar approach to character development:

Something Happened (1974), a novel by Joseph Heller. This work is a darkly humorous treatment of the work and home life of a corporate man living the American Dream.

American Beauty (1999), a film directed by Sam Mendes. This Academy Award–winning film tells the story of a cynical forty-two-year-old man attempting to find meaning and purpose in his life.

The Seagull (1895), a play by Anton Chekhov. The story centers around the conflicts between four characters working in the theater.

the uncertainties and clashes caused by the postwar unsettling of class barriers. *The Wrong Set* explores the diametrically opposed political and social values that split a family. Wilson's pointed titles are frequently clichés taken from conversations in the stories, as he explains in the interview with Michael Millgate: "I take a platitude—'the wrong set,' for example: the point is that no one knows what the wrong set is, and one person's wrong set is another's right set. And you get the pay-off, which is something I like."

Middle-Class Values In many of Wilson's stories, he interweaves the effects of a shifting class structure with individual hopes. He portrays how "getting ahead" means that sacrifices and compromises must be made. Social and material "success" are bought dearly, at the price of displacement and loneliness. The tone is often somber and disillusioned as characters must sort out the predicament of his society. The old world and its ways are in decline, but there are no new alternatives to replace it.

In *A Flat Country Christmas*, Wilson explores the social problems of the suburbs. The flatness of the landscape is reflected in the dullness of the human life it supports. The new housing estates flatten out class differences and facilitate the gathering of an amorphous collection of people without common values. The two couples celebrating the season are connected only by the men's work, and they adopt party personas in order to get through the evening without dissension and boredom. However, their masks are shattered by a seemingly harmless party game. One of the men confronts his own nothingness in the mirror, yet this vital self-revelation is typically brushed under the rug in order to maintain appearances.

Influence Wilson's influence extends beyond his fiction, for he was a respected critic, reviewer, and biographer. These writings, together with his work as a professor and international public lecturer, have had a profound effect on the shape of English literature from the 1940s onward. Wilson is regarded by many literary historians as a transitional figure from the modernist to the postmodernist era because of his unusual melding of traditional subjects with experimental methods. No other writer at the time so clearly dramatized the collapse of the upper middle class in England, and his social satire opened the way for the works of social protest by the angry young men in the 1950s.

Works in Critical Context

Wilson's position as a major novelist and, perhaps more important, as a distinguished man of letters for the period after World War II, is eminently secure. In *Critical Essays on Angus Wilson*, Malcolm Bradbury called him "one of four or five great English post-war writers," placing him in the company of William Golding, Graham Greene, Doris Lessing, and Iris Murdoch.

When Wilson's first stories were published, reviewers were impressed with the technical skill displayed by the fledgling author. They praised his work for its attention to detail, expert mimicry, and accurate representation of the English social scene. While some critics reacted negatively to the violence in his fiction, it was also understood that it reflected the condition of the postwar period. Wilson's reputation grew with the publication of several popular novels, but his experimentation with nontraditional form in subsequent works drew mixed reactions. Some of his later novels were deemed inaccessible, but renewed interest in—and appreciation of—his work was sparked shortly before his death in 1991. At that time, his books began being reissued in paperback. The television version of *Anglo-Saxon Attitudes* (1956) put the book on the best-seller lists, where it had never been during Wilson's lifetime.

Hemlock and After When Wilson's first novel *Hemlock and After* was published, it was very well received. Evelyn Waugh wrote in praise of it in the Catholic journal *Month*, noting what he considered its defects but stressing that it was "a thing to rejoice over." The *Times Literary Supplement* gave it a full-page review, praising it highly for its representation of contemporary English life. Even Ernest Hemingway had some good words for it, remarking that Wilson was a writer worth watching. If the novel has subsequently become overshadowed by his other, more ambitious works, it is nevertheless a very significant achievement, revealing Wilson's ability right at the start to handle important ideas and themes in a novelistic way.

Responses to Literature

1. After reading Wilson's work, determine what kind of social observation Wilson is making. In a group, discuss Wilson's view of the working middle class.

2. Read several stories from *The Wrong Set and Other Stories*, noting Wilson's treatment of violence. Write a short critical essay in which you argue whether the violence in the stories is gratuitous or necessary to enhance the theme.

3. Wilson wrote several important literary biographies on authors who influenced his style and themes. Read one of these biographies and write a brief report on the author.

4. Wilson makes use of a mixture of subjective and experimental first-person accounts with more traditional third-person narrative. Write a story that uses both of these narrative techniques.

BIBLIOGRAPHY

Books

Drabble, Margaret. *Angus Wilson: A Biography*. London: Secker & Warburg, 1995.

Faulkner, Peter. *Angus Wilson: Mimic and Moralist*. London: Secker & Warburg, 1980.

Fletcher, John. *Claude Simon and Fiction Now*. London: Calder & Boyars, 1975.

Gardner, Averil. *Angus Wilson*. Boston: Twayne, 1985.

Grandsden, K.W. *Angus Wilson*. London: Longmans, Green, 1969.

Halio, Jay L. *Angus Wilson*. Edinburgh: Oliver & Boyd, 1964.

———, ed. *Critical Essays on Angus Wilson*. Boston: G. K. Hall, 1985.

McSweeney, Kerry. *Four Contemporary Novelists*. Montreal: McGill-Queen's University Press, 1983.

Periodicals

Bradbury, Malcolm. "The Short Stories of Angus Wilson." *Studies in Short Fiction* (Winter 1966).

Cox, C.B. "The Humanism of Angus Wilson: A Study of *Hemlock and After*." *Critical Quarterly* (Autumn 1961).

Scott-Kilvert, I. "Angus Wilson." *Review of English Literature* (April 1960).

Shaw, Valeria. "*The Middle Age of Mrs. Eliot* and *Late Call*: Angus Wilson's Traditionalism." *Critical Quarterly* (Spring 1970).

◈ Colin Wilson

BORN: *1931, Leicester, England*

NATIONALITY: *British*

GENRE: *Fiction, nonfiction*

MAJOR WORKS:

The Outsider (1956)

Ritual in the Dark (1960)

Adrift in Soho (1961)

Man Without a Shadow: The Diary of an Existentialist (1963), published in the United States as *The Sex Diary of Gerard Sorme*

Necessary Doubt (1964)

Overview

Colin Wilson shot to fame in 1956 with his first book, *The Outsider*, a lively and wide-ranging survey of social and spiritual alienation. The book quickly became a best seller in Britain and the United States and made its previously unknown author, a self-educated twenty-four-year-old from the English Midlands, into an international celebrity. But Wilson soon fell from grace, and critics savaged his second book, *Religion and the Rebel* (1957). Since then, however, he has produced more than one hundred books on topics such as philosophy, psychology, literature, murder, sexuality, and the occult.

Works in Biographical and Historical Context

Eclectic Early Years   Colin Henry Wilson was the first child of Arthur Wilson, a boot and shoe salesman, and Annetta Jones Wilson. Although he learned to read relatively late (at age seven) and only read a weekly comic until he was ten, he started to read more widely at that

Colin Wilson   *Getty Images*

LITERARY AND HISTORICAL CONTEMPORARIES

Wilson's famous contemporaries include:

Issac Asimov (1920–1992): One of the most prolific writers of all time, having written or edited more than five hundred books on a wide array of subjects, especially science and science fiction.

Tom Wolfe (1931–): A best-selling American author and journalist who was a founder of the New Journalism movement of the 1960s and 1970s.

The Beatles (1957–1969): A rock group from Liverpool, England—featuring Paul McCartney, John Lennon, Ringo Starr, and George Harrison—that became one of the most commercially successful and critically acclaimed bands in the history of popular music.

John Kennedy (1917–1963): President of the United States from 1961 until his assassination in 1963. He was the initiator of the Peace Corps and the Apollo space program, and the figurehead (alongside his wife Jackie) of an era that came to be called "Camelot."

Neil Armstrong (1930–): A former American astronaut, test pilot, university professor, and naval aviator. He was the first person to set foot on the Moon.

age, consuming thrillers, science fiction, true crime, romance magazines, and books of science. In his early teens he picked up the classics of English literature. This eclectic mix of reading material was later mirrored by Wilson's wide-ranging choice of subjects to cover in his works. At age eleven, he won a place at the Gateway Secondary Technical School in Leicester, and while he was not an outstanding pupil, he further developed his interests in science and writing.

After a brief stint in the Royal Air Force, Wilson went back to Leicester. He worked at a fairground, at building sites, and on a farm. He then went to Paris for three months. Returning to Leicester, he took an office job in a factory, where he met the company nurse Betty Dorothy Troop, whom he married in June 1951. They moved to London, where their son Roderick was born. Wilson continued to work on a novel, for which he now had ambitious plans: As he wrote in *Voyage to a Beginning*, "[i]t was to possess the power of *Crime and Punishment*, and the length and technical complexity of *Ulysses*." He would use the Egyptian *Book of the Dead* for a design, as James Joyce had used the *Odyssey* for the design of his novel *Ulysses*. But life in London was often difficult. Wilson went through eighteen months of factory jobs and periods on unemployment benefits, moving frequently; finally, his wife moved back to Leicester, and the marriage effectively came to an end. Having finished

the first part of his novel, he decided to dash off an account of his own ideas; this account became *The Outsider* and changed his life.

Rise and Fall Published in 1956, *The Outsider* was immediately acclaimed and became a best seller, first in England and then in the United States. Wilson briefly became a celebrity intellectual, but his provocative remarks—his assertions of his own genius, his attack upon William Shakespeare as second-rate, his praise of the former British fascist leader Sir Oswald Mosley—combined with growing reservations among critics about the quality of *The Outsider*. Wilson's critical downfall was hastened by adverse publicity about his personal life that culminated in scandal when the father of his second wife, having received a garbled report of the contents of one of Wilson's journals, tried to horsewhip him. Wilson's next book, *Religion and the Rebel*, which developed the themes of *The Outsider* in relation to religious experience, met a largely hostile response. The collapse of Wilson's reputation was summed up by a caption in *Time* (November 18, 1957): "Egghead, scrambled."

Such abuse might have broken some writers, but as writer Hilary Corke observed, "Wilson turned out to be a much tougher egg." The notion that he was destined for recognition had sustained him since the time before he was published. While still in his early teens he had begun to feel superior to the "vegetable mediocrity" of his working-class Leicester background. After settling down in Cornwall, he remained there, apart from lecture tours of the United States in 1961 and of Japan and Australia in 1986 and periods as a visiting professor at various universities.

Works in Literary Context

The Evolution of the Mind Essentially just a single idea drove all of Wilson's work: people can elevate themselves to a new stage of evolutionary development by using their intelligence and willpower to achieve higher levels of consciousness. He believed that his task as a writer was to develop the conceptual and imaginative frameworks that foster this "evolutionary leap." The novel, Wilson feels, has a vital role to play in this task since it can depict the complexity of experience more fully than abstract philosophy. His body of work includes nonfiction, novels, biographies, plays, and encyclopedic investigations of crime and the occult, but many of his best-known novels fall into the science fiction and fantasy categories, including *The Mind Parasites*, *The Philosopher's Stone*, and *The Space Vampires*. Wilson claimed George Bernard Shaw was an important early influence on his science fiction writing, especially Shaw's long science fantasy play *Back to Methuselah*, which became a mainspring for Wilson's own science fiction works. In *Colin Wilson: The Outsider and Beyond*, Clifford P. Bendau wrote: "The essence of Wilson's position is that man can and must expand the present modes of consciousness . . . . The phenomenon of man's resignation to littleness is used to show the reader that man is perceptually aware of very little; but that man is conscious or unconsciously *choosing* not to be aware."

Views Outside the Mainstream Wilson published *The Outsider* at the age of twenty-four. His writings after that expanded upon the theme he introduced in that work: With the arrival of the Romantic movement in art at the end of the 1700s, there were outstanding writers and thinkers who remained unsatisfied afterwards by the emptiness of scientific and philosophic thought. In his later nonfiction works, including *Religion and the Rebel*, *The Stature of Man*, and *Beyond the Outsider: The Philosophy of the Future*, Wilson posited a kind of "optimistic existentialism" that places importance on intuition and visionary experiences. According to John A. Weigel, Wilson deserves "to be credited with the courage to rebel against deterministic philosophies and to insist that man is free to improve himself and his community *if he wants to.*"

Works in Critical Context

Wilson has authored over one hundred books, plus many plays and articles, and he supported himself primarily by writing for over four decades. During that time he maintained a high degree of confidence in his talent and ideas, even in the face of severe criticism. Initially, however, critics gave him reason to be confident. His first book, *The Outsider*, was at first an unqualified success. Only later was there backlash regarding the work and its creator.

Wilson claimed in *Voyage to a Beginning* that after his second book, *Religion and the Rebel*, was "hatcheted to death" by the critics, his name got mentioned "if someone needed a symbol of intellectual pretentiousness, or unfounded generalization, or an example of how hysteria can make a reputation overnight."

Wilson has continued, without apology, to make the kinds of claims for his own abilities that helped to arouse such hostility at the time of *The Outsider*. In his 1986 interview with Diana Cooper-Clarke, while claiming he no longer cared about his literary reputation, he nonetheless said: "I suspect that I probably am the greatest writer of the twentieth century." This judgment may never be widely shared, but Wilson's novels are a stimulating contribution to postwar fiction, and some of them, especially *Ritual in the Dark*, are likely to endure.

The Outsider *The Outsider* was immediately acclaimed in the Sunday newspapers by the two most influential English reviewers of the day, Cyril Connolly and Philip Toynbee. *Observer* contributor Philip Toynbee called *The Outsider* "an exhaustive and luminously intelligent study of a representative theme of our time . . . truly astounding . . . a real contribution to an understanding of our deepest predicament." Other reviewers offered similar

---

COMMON HUMAN EXPERIENCE

Wilson believed that people could, and should, develop and sustain an intensity of consciousness to realize their full potential. Wilson was drawing upon Romantic thought, a movement that began around the time of the French Revolution in the 1790s, which emphasized the imagination and the powers of the individual mind. Here are some works that explore similar ideas:

The Prelude (1805, revised in 1850), a poem by William Wordsworth. This long narrative poem focuses on the importance for an artist of sensitivity, memory, and the powers of imagination.

"A Theory of Human Motivation" (1943), a paper by Abraham Maslow. For this influential psychology paper, Maslow studied remarkable people such as Albert Einstein, Frederick Douglass, and Eleanor Roosevelt to determine what makes a person fully "self-actualized," or able to reach their maximum potential.

The Electric Kool-Aid Acid Test (1968), a nonfiction work by Tom Wolfe. In this pioneering work of "New Journalism," Wolfe followed the author Ken Kesey and his group of "Merry Pranksters" as they drove around the country in a painted school bus following the band the Grateful Dead and philosophizing about what they considered to be spiritual and philosophic insights through the regular use of LSD and other hallucinogenic drugs.

In the Buddha's Words: An Anthology of Discourses from the Pali Canon (2005), a philosophical work edited by Bhikkhu Bodhi with a foreword by the Dalai Lama. An overview of the teachings of Siddhartha Gautama, who lived in India during the fifth and sixth centuries BCE and is recognized by millions around the world as the Supreme Buddha.

---

praise, and the book achieved best-seller status in both England and the United States.

Wilson, who had long labored in poverty and anonymity, was accorded celebrity status, but the publicity was not always of a positive nature. He was misquoted on several occasions, and a domestic dispute with his fiancée's family provided a scandal that was "of exactly the right palate for the popular Press," in critic and writer Kenneth Allsop's words. Within six months of its publication, critics began to reevaluate *The Outsider* and its author with less-than-flattering results. Wilson was called to task for his excessive quotations from other sources, for his disregard of formal philosophical method, and for the stridency of his assertions. Dismayed by the change in the critical climate, Wilson moved to a cottage in Cornwall and continued to write. Kenneth Allsop described

Wilson's career as having occurred "from out of nowhere (or, to be precise, from out of a sleeping bag on Hampstead Heath) up through a dizzying arc of fame and fortune, with a steep nose-dive into disfavour."

Ritual in the Dark One of Wilson's most enduring novels was called *Ritual in the Dark*. It traced the main character's fascination and partial identification with a killer. The initial reception of *Ritual in the Dark* ran from dismissal to qualified praise. The *London Times* reviewer (March 3, 1960) condemned the book's "nugatory thinking, clumsy progress and unkempt style," and Paul West in the *New Statesman* of March 5, 1960, summed up the novel as a "farrago of vision and vastation, chips and psychopathology, self-regarding sexuality and Victorian earnestness." Both Anthony Quinton in *London Magazine* (May 1960) and Frank Kermode in the June 1960 *Encounter* acknowledged that the novel was "readable," but Quinton found it "written without distinction" and Kermode felt it was held together by "an immature arrogance." A more sympathetic response, however, came from P. N. Furbank in the *Listener* (March 3, 1960); he found the book clumsy but commended its "well thought out and original plot" and its "excellent and subtle dramatic surprises," and observed that Wilson "could one day be a novelist to reckon with."

Responses to Literature

1. Wilson has written fiction, philosophy, true crime stories, books about the occult, and other topics. Do you think it is possible to write equally well on a wide range of subjects and in different styles? Can you think of any examples of an author who does this?

2. If Wilson had never written *The Outsider*, or if he had written it or some of his other books under a different name, do you think the criticism of his later novels would have been so harsh? Why or why not? Do you think it is fair for a critic to judge a writer's work by what he or she says and does outside the work, as well as the content inside?

3. Which, if any, of Wilson's characters live up to the ideals he valued in the real world of the human mind's realizing its full potential?

4. Wilson wrote about the Kabbalah, a brand of Jewish mysticism, which has received much recent attention from singer Madonna and actress Demi Moore. Using your library and the Internet, find out more about the Kabbalah and write a paper summarizing your findings.

BIBLIOGRAPHY

Books

Allsop, Kenneth. *The Angry Decade: A Survey of the Cultural Revolt of the Nineteen-Fifties.* Wendover, England: Goodchild, 1985.

Bendau, Clifford P. *The Outsider and Beyond.* San Bernardino, Calif.: Borgo Press, 1979.

Bergstrom, K. Gunnar. *An Odyssey to Freedom: Four Themes in Colin Wilson's Novels.* Uppsala, Sweden: University of Uppsala Press, 1983.

Campion, Sidney. *The World of Colin Wilson: A Biographical Study.* London: Muller, 1962.

Dossor, Howard F. *Colin Wilson: The Man and His Mind.* Shaftesbury, England: Element, 1990.

Stanley, Colin, ed. *Colin Wilson, a Celebration: Essays and Recollections.* London: Woolf, 1988.

Tredell, Nicolas. *The Novels of Colin Wilson.* London: Vision, 1982.

Weigel, John A. *Colin Wilson.* Boston: Twayne, 1975.

Web sites

Colin Wilson World. Retrieved March 10, 2008, from http://colinwilsonworld.co.uk/default.aspx. Last updated on March 10, 2008.

Jeanette Winterson

BORN: *1959, Manchester, England*

NATIONALITY: *British, English*

GENRE: *Fiction, nonfiction*

MAJOR WORKS:

Oranges Are Not the Only Fruit (1985)

Sexing the Cherry (1989)

The PowerBook (2000)

Lighthousekeeping (2004)

The Stone Gods (2007)

Overview

Provocative and talented, Jeanette Winterson has influenced both popular and literary culture in England. Whether writing newspaper articles or novels, she is unafraid of controversy and never apologizes for her moral stances on topics ranging from women's rights to global politics. By challenging such institutions as marriage and family, Winterson aims to transcend established boundaries of gender and sexual identity with her presentation of a feminine perspective of passion, romantic love, and the search for self-knowledge. Inspired by the modernists, Winterson writes fiction that combines intriguing characters with postmodern self-consciousness, at the same time exploring unconventional concepts of reality and dimension.

Works in Biographical and Historical Context

Adoption and Missionary Training Winterson was born in Manchester, England, on August 27, 1959. Adopted in infancy by Pentecostal evangelists John and Constance Winterson, she grew up in Lancashire, in northern England. Winterson's father worked in a local television factory. Her mother, a religious zealot, oversaw her education, limiting the literature available in their household to the Bible as she trained her daughter to become a missionary. At the age of eight, Winterson was composing sermons, a practice that sharpened the rhetoric skills she would later use in her career as a writer. During her teenage years, she became a voracious reader when, in a public library, she discovered the wide worlds of literature and history beyond the Bible.

On Her Own: Leaving Home After being scorned by her family and rejected by the church for having an affair with one of its female converts, Winterson left home when she was sixteen, supporting herself by working odd jobs as a makeup artist in a funeral parlor, an ice cream vendor, and an orderly in a psychiatric hospital. During this time, Margaret Thatcher was the prime minister of the United Kingdom, a leader not popular among many people in the working class, most particularly for her emphatic stance against trade unions. In 1981, Winterson received a master's degree in English from St. Catherine's College, Oxford. After an editor, who was interviewing Winterson for a position at Pandora Press in 1985, admired her gift for language and storytelling, Winterson began writing creatively.

Reinventing Life in Fiction Winterson began her literary career by reinventing her life in fiction. When *Oranges Are Not the Only Fruit* debuted in 1985, it was an immediate critical and popular sensation and won the 1985 Whitbread First Novel Award, despite its openly lesbian theme and its controversial view of family and religious values. At once sardonic and comedic, *Oranges Are Not the Only Fruit* remains noteworthy as Winterson's most overtly autobiographical and structurally conventional work.

Although Winterson's second novel, *Boating for Beginners* (1985), a satiric rendition of the biblical story of Noah, was less successful, her next two novels garnered important literary awards: the John Llewellyn Rhys Prize for *The Passion* (1987) and the E. M. Forster Award for *Sexing the Cherry*. She also won a British Academy of Film and Television Arts award for her 1990 screenplay adaptation of *Oranges Are Not the Only Fruit.*

Human Possibility and Truth In 1992, a major change in Winterson's writing emerged: She was moving away from magical realism. That year, *Written on the Body* was published. The novel is mostly a plotless narrative that explores gender and sexual identity while addressing the problems involved in conveying a love story without succumbing to romantic cliché. *Art and Lies* followed in 1994. This novel is another deviation from her earlier work in that it uses Handel, Picasso, and Sappho as characters who examine not only sexuality, but also art, music, and philosophy. Winterson's message here concerns the responsibility of art to transcend what is known, thereby revealing human possibility and life's truths.

Although Winterson's next work of fiction, *Gut Symmetries* (1997), contains allusions to such disparate subjects as fairy tales and quantum physics, it defies

categorization as fantasy or science fiction. Similarly, *The PowerBook* (2002) cannot be considered science fiction, despite delving into the possibilities of technology by investigating the impact of e-mail and the Internet on writers, as well as the whole of literature. In 2002, Winterson adapted *The PowerBook* for the Royal National Theatre London and the Theatre de Chaillot, Paris.

Artistic Versatility and Personal Life An author of many talents, Winterson has also written children's stories, including *The King of Capri* (2003), *Lighthousekeeping* (2004), and *Tanglewreck* (2006). *The Stone Gods* (2007) is a return to fantasy and science fiction. Currently, Winterson divides her time between a cottage in the woods of Gloucestershire and an apartment in London, located above Verdes, a natural foods shop she owns. In addition to writing regularly for various newspapers in the United Kingdom, Winterson is at work on a series of Internet films with the BBC.

Works in Literary Context

Magical Realism Winterson's early exposure to the stories, characters, poetic rhythms, and morality of the

COMMON HUMAN EXPERIENCE

Many of Winterson's novels feature what literary scholars call "unreliable narrators": voices that may or may not be telling the truth. Other authors have used the device of the unreliable narrator to great effect. Their works include:

As I Lay Dying (1930), a novel by William Faulkner. Written as a series of interior monologues from different characters, this work presents events from a variety of perspectives. The characters, all deeply flawed, often shape their telling of the story to suit themselves.

"My Last Duchess" (1842) and "Soliloquy of the Spanish Cloister" (1842), poems by Robert Browning. In both of these dramatic monologues, the speakers gradually reveal aspects of their true character of which they themselves are not aware.

Vantage Point (2008), a film directed by Pete Travis. In this movie, five witnesses recount what they saw during an assassination attempt on the president of the United States.

"The Tell-Tale Heart" (1842), a short story by Edgar Allan Poe. The narrator of this tale insists he is not mad, declaring that his calm telling of the story is evidence of his sanity.

Bible has left its mark on her work since the beginning of her career. Even more influential, however, have been literary classics and modernist writers, including T. S. Eliot, Virginia Woolf, Ezra Pound, and Gertrude Stein, writers whose ideas have motivated Winterson to create new realms for fiction. Winterson's caustic satire is frequently compared to that of Jonathan Swift, her magical realism to that of Gabriel García Márquez, her textual experimentation and adaptation of myth and fairy tale to that of Italo Calvino. Some critics have even attributed Winterson's comedic abilities to the influence of Monty Python.

Supported by a strong narrative drive, works of magical realism blend elements of dreams, myths, or fairy tales with everyday occurrences; what is realistic merges with what is inexplicable. Because of her ability to combine historical events with the mythical elements of fairy tales, Winterson has found a place in the school of magical realism alongside such storytellers as Angela Carter and Jorge Luis Borges. For Winterson, who masterfully manipulates narrative forms and storytelling, play between the fantastic and the real is meant to contradict readers' expectations and reveal the power of imagination. This intention is clear in the "Book of Deuteronomy" in *Oranges Are Not the Only Fruit*: "People like to separate storytelling which is not fact from history which

is fact. They do this so that they know what to believe and what not to believe." By rewriting fairy tales and myths, along with creating new ones of her own, Winterson confronts the absurdity that passes for truth in traditional history.

Literary Legacy   Most likely a result of her unwavering belief in the power of literature to transform one's life, Winterson's body of work exhibits many different themes. The nature of love, the discovery of one's sexual identity, the implications of time, the search for self, the functions of art—all are themes that Winterson explores, at the same time continuing to challenge literary and social standards. In her diligent pursuit of new possibilities for the genre of fiction, Winterson reveals a commitment to linguistic and artistic experimentation that will surely benefit generations of writers to come.

Works in Critical Context

Because she is simultaneously one of the most original and controversial voices to have emerged in British fiction during the late twentieth century, Winterson evokes deeply divided critical response. In *The New York Times*, Michiko Kakutani praised Winterson as a writer who "possesses an ability to dazzle the reader by creating wondrous worlds in which the usual laws of plausibility are suspended." Many critics also commend Winterson's finesse in infusing feminist beliefs into the traditional fairy-tale form. Others, however, consider her to be a writer who lacks the talent to repeat the brilliance of her debut novel. These are the same people who claim that Winterson's subsequent work is self-absorbed and resorts to sentimentality and superficial devices to gain attention.

Oranges Are Not the Only Fruit   Most reviewers agree that *Oranges Are Not the Only Fruit* demonstrates exceptional humor, talent, and skill. Critic Jonathan Keates remarks, "[The] comic detachment with which the narrator beats off the grotesque spiritual predatoriness surrounding her is matter for applause." Certainly, the manner in which Jeanette interacts with her mother is one of deadpan wit. Some critics contend that the humorous parables interjected into the narrative of *Oranges Are Not the Only Fruit* reflect Jeanette's sexual identity crisis and spiritual confusion. As such, the novel is considered a work of unparalleled originality. Others, like critic Lyn Pykett, prefer the "gritty realism" of this work to her later efforts.

Personal Criticism   Winterson the individual has earned the same degree of divisive criticism as her work. While many readers regard Winterson to be a fresh, innovative literary voice, detractors believe she is conceited, so much so that her self-importance overshadows her work. Without a doubt, Winterson is proud of her accomplishment and gift for the written word. In fact, she offended many people by nominating herself as the greatest living writer in the English language and by choosing her *Written on the Body* as Book of the Year in 1992. Because of such hubris, she has been deemed too arrogant and self-aggrandizing for the literary world.

Responses to Literature

1. Many writers have based their fiction on actual events in their lives. Anne Sexton and Sylvia Plath, for example, wrote confessional poetry that revealed intimacies not previously seen in poetry. What do you think about these writers who "bare their souls" in their work? What is the tradition of this style? How does talk-show television perpetuate the confessional trend?

2. Consider the characters' perspectives on evolution versus creation in *Oranges Are Not the Only Fruit*. What statement do you think Winterson is making about the debate between religion and science? How does this statement relate to religious debate today? In your own belief system, how do you reconcile the fundamentals of religion with scientific advancement?

3. In an interview, Winterson said, "Always in my books, I like to throw that rogue element into a stable situation and then see what happens." How does having knowledge of this technique affect your reading of Winterson's work? What are some examples of rogue elements that you might use when writing a short story or novel?

4. The settings for love stories portrayed in Winterson's novels have ranged from the French Revolution to cyberspace. When you considered her fiction as an ongoing whole, what truth, potential, and resolution do you believe Winterson offers in regard to love?

BIBLIOGRAPHY

Books

O'Rourke, Rebecca. "Fingers in the Fruit Basket: A Feminist Reading of Jeanette Winterson's *Oranges Are Not the Only Fruit*." In *Feminist Criticism: Theory and Practice*. Edited by Susan Sellers. Toronto: University of Toronto Press, 1991.

Periodicals

Anshaw, Carol. "Into the Mystic: Jeanette Winterson's Fable of Manners." *Village Voice*, June 12, 1990, 516–17.

Gerrard, Nicci. "The Prophet." *New Statesman and Society* 2 (September 1, 1989): 12–13.

Hind, Hilary. "*Oranges Are Not the Only Fruit*: Reaching Audiences Other Lesbian Texts Cannot Reach." *New Statesman and Society* 2 (September 1, 1989): 12–13.

Marvel, Mark. "Jeanette Winterson: Trust Me, I'm Telling You Stories." *Interview XX* 10 (October 1990): 162, 168.

Web Sites

Kakutani, Michiko. "Books of The Times: A Journey Through Time, Space and Imagination." Retrieved April 14, 2008, from http://query.nytimes.com/gst/fullpage.html?res=9C0CE FDF1031F934A15757 C0A966958260&sec=&spon=&pagewanted=2#.

Smith, Jules. "Jeanette Winterson." Retrieved April 4, 2008, from http://www.contemporarywriters.com/authors/?p=auth100".

P. G. Wodehouse

BORN: *1881, Guildford, England*

DIED: *1975, Southampton, New York*

NATIONALITY: *English, American*

GENRE: *Fiction, drama*

MAJOR WORKS:
Piccadilly Jim (1918)
Mulliner Nights (1933)
Thank You, Jeeves (1934)
Blandings Castle (1935)
Young Men in Spats (1936)

P.G. Wodehouse   *Wodehouse, P.G., photograph. AP Images.*

Overview

P. G. Wodehouse (pronounced like "Woodhouse") is an anomaly in twentieth-century fiction. In an age of relentless artistic experimentation, he wrote fiction firmly rooted in the Edwardian world of his childhood. In an age of rapidly changing moral and sexual values, he created characters and situations remarkable for their purity and innocence. In an age of seriousness, he wrote fiction designed solely for amusement. In an age of artistic anxiety and alienation, Wodehouse wrote novels and short stories that succeeded in pleasing his readers, his critics, and himself.

Works in Biographical and Historical Context

A Dulwich Impression Pelham Grenville Wodehouse was born on October 15, 1881, the third of four sons of Henry Ernest Wodehouse, a member of the British civil service in Hong Kong, and Eleanor Deane Wodehouse, the daughter of Rev. Deane of Bath. Sent back to England for schooling in 1884 with his older brothers, Wodehouse began his education at Bath. Wodehouse told *Paris Review* interviewer Gerald Clarke, "I was writing stories when I was five. I don't remember what I did before that. Just loafed, I suppose." Wodehouse attended Elizabeth College in Guernsey before enrolling in Malvern House, a navy preparatory school, in Kearnsey. His most important educational experience began at the age of twelve when he began attending Dulwich College, where he studied for six years. During his last year there, he received his first payment for writing "Some Aspects of Game Captaincy," an essay that was a contest entry published in the *Public School Magazine.* Wodehouse recognized the important influence of Dulwich College on his life and later wrote to friend Charles Townsend that "the years between 1896 and 1900 seem[ed] like Heaven" to him.

Oxford Detour Wodehouse could not proceed to Oxford University—the usual path for a boy of his background—because his father's pension was paid in rupees, the value of which fell so drastically at the time that the family could not afford another son at the university, even if a scholarship had been available. Wodehouse already knew he wanted to write and suggested that he become a freelance writer, but his father would not hear of such impracticality. Wodehouse became a clerk at the London branch of the Hong Kong and Shanghai Bank, a training post for those to be sent to the Far East. His time as a clerk proved not entirely unproductive: During his tenure at the bank he sold eighty stories and articles, primarily sports-related articles for the *Public School Magazine.*

American Humor Wodehouse always recalled that a "total inability to grasp what was going on made me something of a legend" in the bank, and he soon entered the more congenial profession of journalism. He was first a substitute writer for the "By the Way" column in *The Globe*, and by August 1903 he was employed full-time by the paper. Fascinated with boxers and wanting to meet James J. Corbett and other fighters, Wodehouse fulfilled a longtime ambition by making his first trip to America, arriving in New York in 1904. After a short stay, he returned to England as editor of the "By the Way" column, but his love for America, and for the possibilities he felt it promised writers, remained with him. In a 1915 *New York Times* interview with Joyce Kilmer, Wodehouse predicted that the years following World War I would "afford a great opportunity for the new English humorist who works on the American plan."

Wodehouse eventually seized this opportunity and exploited it so well that years later one reviewer of *Young Men in Spats* (1936) remarked that Wodehouse was "the only Englishman who can make an American laugh at a joke about America." The reviewer reasoned that the real secret of Wodehouse's American popularity was that he really liked Americans. One American whom Wodehouse particularly liked was Ethel Newton Rowley, a widow with one child named Leonora. Wodehouse had met Ethel on one of his visits to America, and he married her on September 30, 1914.

Minor Hollywood Scandal In 1904, Wodehouse ventured into theatrical writing when Owen Hall asked him to compose lyrics for a song in the show *Sergeant Bruce*. Wodehouse responded with "Put Me in My Little Cell," sung by three crooks. In 1906 Sir Seymour Hicks hired Wodehouse as lyricist for his Aldwych Theatre shows, the first of which, *The Beauty of Bath*, also marked his initial collaboration with Jerome Kern. When Kern introduced Wodehouse to Guy Bolton in 1915, the three men shared ideas about a new kind of musical comedy and decided to join forces to create what became known as the Princess Theatre shows. The Kern-Bolton-Wodehouse team set new standards for musical comedy.

Throughout the 1920s Wodehouse's work as a journalist, lyricist, and fiction writer made him increasingly famous and wealthy, and his success inevitably attracted the attention of Hollywood. In 1930, after being subjected to the typically shrewd business negotiations of Ethel Wodehouse, Samuel Goldwyn offered Wodehouse two thousand dollars a week for six months, with a further six-month option. Wodehouse's contribution amounted to little more than adding a few lines to already-completed scripts, and this caused him to tell an interviewer for the *Los Angeles Times* that "They paid me $2000 a week—$104,000—and I cannot see what they engaged me for. They were extremely nice to me, but I feel as if I cheated them."

Wodehouse's remarks caused a minor scandal and were said to have caused New York banks to examine studio expenditures more closely. That he actually negatively impacted Hollywood finance seems doubtful, especially since three years after the *Los Angeles Times* interview, he was asked to return to Hollywood. His final film project in 1937 was not a success, and that year

Wodehouse left Hollywood for good. Film scripts constitute the only type of writing Wodehouse attempted without success, but the Hollywood experience did give him abundant material for his later fiction.

The Hollywood experience aside, the 1920s and 1930s were remarkably productive and successful years for Wodehouse. It was also during these years that he wrote some of his best short stories, especially the Mr. Mulliner tales, which are driven by a golf theme and told by "The Oldest Member." Wodehouse's best-known short stories, however, are those devoted to his beloved characters Bertie Wooster and Jeeves, his valet. In each of these tales, Jeeves must rescue the ridiculous Bertie from various absurd situations.

American Broadcasts   Shortly after Wodehouse was honored by being made a doctor of letters by Oxford University in 1939, he was unable to escape Le Touquet, France, where he was living at the time that France fell to the rapidly advancing Nazi German army. On July 21, 1940, Germany decreed that all male aliens were to be interned, and Wodehouse was imprisoned in Tost (now Toszek), Upper Silesia. In June 1941, when Wodehouse was to be released, CBS correspondent Harry Flannery arranged for Wodehouse to broadcast to America from a script Flannery had written.

It was not long before the German Foreign Office asked Wodehouse to make a series of broadcasts to America using his own scripts. He agreed and broadcast a series of talks called "How to Be an Internee in Your Spare Time Without Previous Experience." These talks treated his experiences in prison camp with his usual humor, and what he read today seems harmless enough. However, the reactions of British press and government approached hysteria at the time. William Connor of the *Daily Mirror* accused "the elderly playboy" of broadcasting Nazi propaganda, though Connor never mentioned what Wodehouse actually said in the broadcasts. Ironically, the U.S. War Department used recordings of the broadcasts as models of anti-Nazi propaganda in its intelligence school, but members of the British government remained unforgiving.

After this bitter experience, Wodehouse left England for New York in 1947. He seldom spoke of the broadcasts later and, at least publicly, held no grudges. He became an American citizen in 1955 and never returned to England, although he frequently discussed doing so, especially when he was granted a knighthood on New Year's Day 1975. He remained on Long Island, New York, where he lived a happy life "just writing one book after another." He was working on another novel, *Sunset at Blandings*, when he died on February 14, 1975.

Works in Literary Context

Comic Wordplay   In his school stories, Wodehouse used materials from conventional novels, enhancing his

LITERARY AND HISTORICAL CONTEMPORARIES

Wodehouse's famous contemporaries include:

Scott Joplin (1867–1916): This famous American composer was innovative in Ragtime music.
Louis B. Mayer (1882–1957): Mayer, an American film producer, cofounded one of the first film studios, Metro-Goldwyn-Mayer (MGM).
George Orwell (1903–1950): This celebrated English author and journalist concerned himself with government, politics, language, and the oppression of censorship.
Frank Sinatra (1915–1998): Sinatra was a popular American singer and award-winning actor known as "Ol' Blue Eyes."
James Thurber (1894–1961): Thurber was an American writer, humorist, and cartoonist.

stories with literary allusions and quotations that became characteristic features of his later work. In his work of the 1920s and 1930s, he introduced his most characteristic devices: a mixture of convoluted plots; comic timing; stereotypical characters; and above all, his own invented language. Such language consists of odd personifications, a thorough confusion of vocabulary, an abundance of puns, and wild similes and metaphors that transport both characters and readers far beyond the bounds of logical discourse.

One way Wodehouse manipulates language to achieve comic effect is by adding and omitting prefixes and suffixes. For example, he takes the prefix de-, as in debunk or delouse, and adds it to proper names. The effect is witty and humorous, as seen in *Uncle Dynamite* when Pongo Twistleton gets Elsie Bean out of a cupboard: "His manner as he de-Beaned the cupboard was somewhat distrait." Another example can be observed in *Jeeves in the Offing* when Bobbie Wickham has left Kipper Herring alone: Herring was "finding himself de-Wickhamed."

Wodehouse's use of language to evoke humor can also be seen in the Jeeves and Bertie stories. Even though Bertie is a highly educated person, he has a limited vocabulary and either haltingly tries to remember the "right" word or depends on Jeeves to complete his thoughts for him by providing the appropriate word. For instance, in *Stiff Upper Lip*, Bertie says, "I suppose Stiffy's sore about this...what's the word?...Not vaseline...Vacillation, that's it." In *Jeeves and the Feudal Spirit*, Bertie says, "Let a pluguly young Thos loose in the community...[is] inviting disaster and...what's the word? something about cats." Jeeves replies, "Cataclysms, sir?" The results are amusing.

COMMON HUMAN EXPERIENCE

Wodehouse's incomparable wit was his trademark. Other works known for their comic appeal include:

Barrel Fever (1994), a collection of stories by David Sedaris. Noted humorist David Sedaris won widespread acclaim and attention with this collection.

The Importance of Being Earnest (1895), a play by Oscar Wilde. In this comedy of manners, misunderstandings and misinformation create a comic situation akin to Wodehouse's later Jeeves and Wooster tales.

Gentlemen Prefer Blondes (1925), a novel by Anita Loos. This comic novel about the substantial power of a gold-digging blonde was turned into a successful 1953 movie starring Marilyn Monroe.

Influences The enormous influence of Dulwich College in Wodehouse's work has long been recognized. J. B. Priestley voiced the sentiment that Wodehouse remained "a brilliant super-de-luxe schoolboy" throughout his life, a belief that explains the sexless young women, terrifying aunts, and eccentric aristocrats who fill his pages. Another great influence on Wodehouse's fiction, especially his short stories, was his theatrical writing. In *Over Seventy* (1956), Wodehouse names several other humorists he greatly respected, including Alex Atkinson, A. P. Herbert, and Frank Sullivan.

Works in Critical Context

Wodehouse Collaborated Musicals As early as 1935, Frank Swinnerton offered a remark that is surely the best praise a humorist can receive: Wodehouse was so popular because "in a period when laughter has been difficult, he has made men laugh without shame." Wodehouse did not receive much critical attention during his career, and he described himself as "a pretty insignificant sort of blister, not at all the type that leaves footprints on the sands of time," because "I go in for what is known in the trade as 'light writing' and those who do that—humorists they are sometimes called—are looked down upon by the intelligentsia and sneered at." Other writers, however, not to mention millions of readers, have found in Wodehouse's world a wonderful escape from their own. Evelyn Waugh, in a broadcast of July 15, 1961, explained Wodehouse's continuing attraction: "For Mr. Wodehouse there has been no Fall of Man, no aboriginal calamity.... Mr. Wodehouse's world can never stale."

The Kern-Bolton-Wodehouse team of 1915 set new standards for musical comedy. The *Oxford Companion to the American Theatre* asserts that Wodehouse "may well be considered the first truly great lyricist of the American musical stage, his easy colloquially flowing rhythm deftly intertwined with a sunny wit." The Princess Theatre shows, though highly successful and influential in their time, are now seldom-revived period pieces. Their real and lasting influence was not only on audiences but on Wodehouse's fiction, which he subsequently began to structure in the fashion of the musical comedy. According to scholar David Jasen, Wodehouse himself "described his books as musical comedies without the music."

Responses to Literature

1. Using your library and the Internet, find out more about the roles of household servants to upper-class British families in the nineteenth and twentieth centuries. What roles were fulfilled by such servants as the housekeeper, the butler, and the valet? How many servants did the typical household employ? Do upper-class families in England continue to employ such servants today?

2. Gentleman's clubs feature prominently in Wodehouse's fiction. Using your library and the Internet, find out more about one of London's historic gentleman's clubs and write a short summary of its history.

3. Wodehouse's Jeeves stories were adapted for television in the Independent Television series *Jeeves and Wooster* (1990–1993), which starred Stephen Fry and Hugh Laurie. Watch some of the episode of this series. Do you think the television shows capture the humor of Wodehouse's writing? Are the portrayals of antics of British aristocrats affectionate or critical?

BIBLIOGRAPHY

Books

Bordman, Gerald. *Oxford Companion to American Theatre*. New York: Oxford University Press USA, 2004.

Jasen, David A. *A Bibliography and Reader's Guide to the First Editions of P. G. Wodehouse*. Peoria, Ill.: Spoon River Press, 1986.

Wodehouse, P. G. *Life With Jeeves (A Bertie and Jeeves Compendium)*. New York: Penguin, 1983.

———. *Over Seventy*. London: Herbert Jenkins Press, 1957.

———. *Uncle Dynamite*. New York: Overlook Press Hardcover, 2007.

Periodicals

Clarke, Gerald. *Paris Review* (Winter 1975).

Kilmer, Joyce. *New York Times* (February 15, 1975); (October 18, 1981); (November 12, 1984); (November 7, 1985); (October 20, 1987); (March 23, 1989).

Los Angeles Times (June 7, 1931).

Web sites

Books and Writers. *Sir P(elham) G(renville) Wodehouse (1881–1975)*. Retrieved February 14, 2008, from http://www.kirjasto.sci.fi/pgwod.htm.

Lawrie, Michael. *Cassandra [William Connor] and P. G. Wodehouse*. Retrieved February 14, 2008, from http://lorry.org/cassandra.

The Wodehouse Society (TWS). *Official P. G. Wodehouse Website*. Retrieved February 14, 2008, from http://www.wodehouse.org. Last updated on May 17, 2007.

Virginia Woolf

BORN: *1882, London, England*

DIED: *1941, Lewes, Sussex, England*

NATIONALITY: *British*

GENRE: *Fiction, nonfiction*

MAJOR WORKS:

Mrs. Dalloway (1925)

To the Lighthouse (1927)

Orlando (1928)

A Room of One's Own (1929)

Virginia Woolf *Hulton Archive / Getty Images*

Overview

One of the most prominent literary figures of the twentieth century, Virginia Woolf is chiefly renowned as an innovative novelist. She also wrote book reviews, biographical and autobiographical sketches, social and literary criticism, personal essays, and commemorative articles treating a wide range of topics. Concerned primarily with depicting the life of the mind, Woolf revolted against traditional narrative structures and developed her own highly individualized style of writing.

Works in Biographical and Historical Context

Early Life in an Unconventional and Literary Atmosphere Born in London, Virginia Woolf was the third child of Julia and Leslie Stephen. Although her brothers, Thoby and Adrian, were sent to school, Virginia and her sister, Vanessa, were taught at home by their parents and by tutors. Theirs was a highly literary family. Woolf received no formal education, but she was raised in a cultured atmosphere, learning from her father's extensive library and from conversing with his friends, many of whom were prominent writers of the era.

Formation of the Bloomsbury Group Following the death of her father in 1904, Woolf settled in the Bloomsbury district of London with her sister and brothers. Their house became a gathering place where such friends as J. M. Keynes, Lytton Strachey, Roger Fry, and E. M. Forster congregated for lively discussions about philosophy, art, music, and literature. A complex network of friendships and love affairs developed, serving to increase the solidarity of what became known as the Bloomsbury Group. Here she met Leonard Woolf, the author, politician, and economist whom she married in 1912. Woolf flourished in the unconventional atmosphere that she and her siblings had cultivated.

Financial Need Catalyzes Literary Output The need to earn money led her to begin submitting book reviews and essays to various publications. Her first published works—mainly literary reviews—began appearing anonymously in 1904 in the *Guardian*, a weekly newspaper for Anglo-Catholic clergy. Woolf's letters and diaries reveal that journalism occupied much of her time and thought between 1904 and 1909. By the latter year, however, she was becoming absorbed in work on her first novel, eventually published in 1915 as *The Voyage Out*.

The Hogarth Press In 1914, World War I began, a devastating conflict that involved carnage on an unprecedented scale. It involved nearly every European country and, eventually, the United States. About twenty million people were killed as a direct result of the war. Nearly a million British soldiers died (similar losses were experienced by all the other warring nations). In 1917, while England was in the midst of fighting World War I, Woolf

LITERARY AND HISTORICAL CONTEMPORARIES

Woolf's famous contemporaries include:

Henry James (1843–1916): James was an American-born novelist who became a British citizen and was highly influential in both British and American literary circles.

Sigmund Freud (1858–1939): Freud was an Austrian psychologist who founded the school of psychoanalysis and pioneered theories of the unconscious mind.

James Joyce (1882–1941): Joyce was an Irish writer who is widely considered one of the literary giants of the twentieth century, particularly because of his master-work, *Ulysses*.

Katherine Mansfield (1888–1923): Mansfield was a prominent New Zealand modernist short-fiction writer.

T. S. Eliot (1888–1965): Eliot was an American-born poet and dramatist who became a British citizen at the age of thirty-nine. He won the Nobel Prize in Literature in 1948.

William Faulkner (1897–1962): Faulkner was an American novelist widely regarded as one of the most influential authors of the twentieth century. He was awarded the Nobel Prize in Literature in 1949.

Simone de Beauvoir (1908–1986): De Beauvoir was a French author and philosopher best known for her 1949 treatise *The Second Sex*, an analysis of women's oppression and one of the most important texts of modern feminism.

and her husband cofounded the Hogarth Press. They bought a small handpress, with a booklet of instructions, and set up shop on the dining room table in Hogarth House, their lodgings in Richmond. They planned to print only some of their own writings and that of their talented friends. Leonard hoped the manual work would provide Virginia a relaxing diversion from the stress of writing.

It is a tribute to their combined business acumen and critical judgment that this small independent venture became, as Mary Gaither recounts, "a self-supporting business and a significant publishing voice in England between the wars." Certainly being her own publisher made it much easier for Virginia Woolf to pursue her experimental bent but also enabled her to gain greater financial independence from what was at that time a male-dominated industry. Like Woolf, many British women joined the professional work force in an increased capacity during World War I, capitalizing on England's need for heavy industry to support its armed forces.

Successful Experiments This philosophy of daring and experimental writing is shown in her self-published works. While the novel *Night and Day* (1919) is not a stylistic experiment, it deals with the controversial issue of women's suffrage, or right to vote—a right championed by Woolf. At the time of its publication, English women over the age of thirty had just finally received voting rights; it would still be another decade before women held the exact same voting rights as men. Where Woolf might have had difficulty finding another publisher for a book dealing with such a subject, access to Hogarth Press left her free to deal with whatever subject matter she saw fit.

This freedom expressed itself more in stylistic terms in her following works. The novel *Jacob's Room* (1922), for example, tells the story of a character who is never directly introduced to the reader, but only revealed through the recollections of others. *Mrs. Dalloway* (1925) takes place over the course of a single day and presents the thoughts of characters in a free-flowing way meant to mimic actual consciousness. This description of her characters's "inner life" continued with *To the Lighthouse* (1927), and both novels earned Woolf the esteem of critics and readers. These novels, despite being experimental in style, directly reflect the author's own literate and well-heeled upbringing in their characters and settings.

Circumventing Censorship in Orlando Woolf drew upon her own relationships in *Orlando* (1928) a book characterized by Woolf as a biography but by most readers as a novel. The main character, who does not grow old and changes genders, is directly inspired by the female author Vita Sackville-West, a bisexual member of the Bloomsbury Group with whom Woolf had an intimate relationship. Many scholars and critics have viewed the main character's gender-switching as a clever device meant to suggest—but not directly depict—a lesbian relationship, since such topics were the subject of censorship at the time.

Depression and Suicide Woolf fought an ongoing battle against depression for most of her life. After her mother's death in 1895, she had a nervous breakdown, the first of four periods of depression and emotional trauma. Woolf had a second breakdown nine years later when her father died. A third episode of mental illness began early in 1912, became acute in September of 1913 (when she attempted suicide), and lasted into 1916.

In 1941 Woolf published her last novel, *Between the Acts*. She suffered another emotional breakdown in February of 1941, likely brought on by the escalation of World War II. After the horror of World War I, many people felt there could not possibly be another conflict of that type in Europe. That Europe could descend into violence once again so soon after World War I shocked and saddened Woolf deeply. Fearing that she lacked the stamina needed to weather further bouts of depression, Woolf drowned herself in a pond near Monks House, the Woolfs' home in Sussex, on March 28, 1941.

Works in Literary Context

Stream of Consciousness Woolf grew up in an environment rich in Victorian literary influences. Although she lacked the formal education afforded to men of her day, Woolf acquired extensive knowledge of the classics and English literature in the family's enormous home library. In addition, many influential literary figures visited her childhood house, including George Eliot, Henry James, George Lewes, Julia Cameron, and James Lowell, who was named Woolf's godfather. Proximity to influential writers of her day continued into her adulthood with the formation of the Bloomsbury group and creation of the Hogarth Press. With the freedom to create and publish her own work, Woolf largely avoided traditional narrative structures or plots. Her novels are noted for their subjective exploration of character and theme and their poetic prose. Woolf is chiefly renowned as an innovative novelist and in particular for her contribution to the development of the stream-of-consciousness narrative technique.

The stream-of-consciousness technique is found in much of Woolf's fiction. This technique, which emerged in the late nineteenth and early twentieth centuries, is meant to reflect the way in which a character's thoughts flow freely, often without formal sentence structure or punctuation. Famous writers that popularized this technique included James Joyce and Marcel Proust. Examples of Woolf's stream-of-consciousness style can be found in many of her works but are especially notable in *Mrs. Dalloway* (1925).

Writing for "the Common Reader" Woolf also wrote book reviews, biographical and autobiographical sketches, social and literary criticism, personal essays, and commemorative articles treating a wide range of topics. Her essays are commended for their perceptive observations on nearly the entire range of English literature, as well as many social and political concerns of the early twentieth century. She maintained that the purpose of writing an essay was to give pleasure to the reader, and she endeavored to do this with witty, supple prose, apt literary and cultural references, and a wide range of subjects. Aiming to identify closely with her audience, she adopted a persona she termed "the common reader": an intelligent, educated person with the will and inclination to be challenged by what he or she reads.

Influence Because of her importance as an innovator in the modern novel form, and as a commentator on nearly the entire range of English literature and much European literature, Woolf's life and works have been the focus of extensive study. In addition to occupying the attention of scholars, Woolf has inspired experimental works in a variety of artistic genres including author Michael Cunningham's Pulitzer Prize–winning novel *The Hours* (1998), in which Woolf appears as a character,

---

COMMON HUMAN EXPERIENCE

Woolf's fiction reveals an ongoing concern with subjective exploration of character and incident, which she accomplishes with frequent use of a stream-of-consciousness narrative style. Here are some other works that are constructed with a stream-of-consciousness style:

Ulysses (1922), a novel by James Joyce. This work, widely considered to be one of the most important works of modern literature, chronicles its main character's passage through Dublin during an ordinary day.

Steppenwolf (1927), a novel by Hermann Hesse. This work explores the duality of human nature as exemplified by the inner and outer struggles of its main character.

As I Lay Dying (1930), a novel by William Faulkner. This work tells the story of the death of Addie Bundren from the point of view of fifteen different narrators.

On the Road (1957), a novel by Jack Kerouac. This highly autobiographical work is based on the author's recollections of spontaneous road trips across mid-twentieth-century America.

---

and playwright Edward Albee's work *Who's Afraid of Virginia Woolf?* (1962) among many others.

Works in Critical Context

The writings of Virginia Woolf have always been admired by discriminating readers, but her work has suffered, as has that of many other major authors, periods of neglect by the literary establishment. She was, as she herself put it, always a hare a long way ahead of "those hounds my critics." It was difficult to find copies of her books during the 1950s and 1960s, and they were rarely included on syllabi for literature classes. The extensive and serious treatment given Virginia Woolf's novel *To the Lighthouse* in Erich Auerbach's much-esteemed book *Mimesis* (translated into English in 1953), presaged and perhaps helped cause the turnaround.

The advantages of the recent critical and popular attention are manifold. Her novels are now in print again, in a variety of editions, often with introductions in homage by today's writers. They have been translated into more than fifty languages. Her essays, reviews, and short stories have been collected. And then there is the vast delight of the many volumes of letters and diaries, all scrupulously edited, copiously footnoted, and indexed. Even her reading notes are being published.

Mrs. Dalloway When *Mrs. Dalloway* was published in 1925, Woolf received the immediate critical attention her earlier fiction failed to find. In a review for the *New York*

Times, John W. Crawford wrote that, despite the inventiveness of other contemporary authors, "Virginia Woolf is almost alone . . . in the intricate yet clear art of her composition." Edwin Muir, in *Transition: Essays on Contemporary Literature*, compares the novel favorably to her earlier *Night and Day*, stating, "[I]t is infinitely more subtle in its means, and it has on all its pages, as *Night and Day* had not, the glow of an indisputable artistic triumph."

To the Lighthouse   The critical success Woolf achieved with *Mrs. Dalloway* raised expectations for the 1927 release of her next novel, *To the Lighthouse*. Critical opinion of the book was mixed, with many noting the author's obvious skill at turning a phrase and offering credit for the stylistic and structural difficulties she tackled with the work. Edwin Muir, in a review for *Nation and Atheneum*, states that the book is "difficult to judge" because of this, and he credits Woolf as "a writer of profound imagination." Muir concedes, "Yet as a whole, though showing an advance on many sides, it produces a less congruous and powerful effect than *Mrs. Dalloway*." In his review for the *New York Times*, Louis Kronenberger agrees: "It is inferior to *Mrs. Dalloway* in the degree to which its aims are achieved; it is superior in the magnitude of the aims themselves." Orlo Williams, in a review for the *Monthly Criterion*, offers praise wrapped in criticism: "Her mastery increases with each book, but, I fear, it will always fall short of her vision." Despite these reviews, modern scholars have devoted much attention to the novel as one of Woolf's most complex and masterful works.

Responses to Literature

1. Because Woolf and her husband operated a press, she was free to write without worrying about rejection by a publisher. In today's world, the Internet allows nearly anyone to publish their views easily and cheaply. Does the Internet provide the same kind of freedom that Woolf enjoyed as a writer? Are there differences in the way that online writers make use of their freedom? Do readers today approach online writings differently than they approach printed texts?

2. In *Mrs. Dalloway*, Woolf presents the suicidal character of Septimus Smith, a shell-shocked World War I veteran. Veterans of World War I commonly exhibited mental health problems, but they were largely misunderstood by doctors. Today, someone like Septimus Smith would probably be diagnosed with post-traumatic stress disorder. Using your library and the Internet, research the history of medical treatment for post-combat mental illnesses. Write an essay summarizing your findings.

3. Woolf famously argued in her long essay *A Room of One's Own* that in order for women to succeed as writers of fiction, they needed to have a reliable means of income and a private space in which to work. Why do you think having "a room of one's own" would be important for women writers of the early twentieth century? In your opinion, are these still important factors for allowing women to succeed as writers? Why or why not? Do these same prerequisites also apply for male writers? Why or why not?

4. Woolf frequently employed a stream-of-consciousness narrative style to explore the inner lives of her characters. Write a short story or essay using the stream-of-consciousness style.

BIBLIOGRAPHY

Books

Auerbach, Erich. *Mimesis: The Representation of Reality in Western Literature*, translated by Willard R. Trask. Princeton, N.J.: Princeton University Press, 1953.

Bell, Quentin. *Virginia Woolf: A Biography*. New York: Harcourt Brace Jovanovich, 1972.

Bennett, Joan. *Virginia Woolf: Her Art as a Novelist*. Cambridge, U.K.: Cambridge University Press, 1964.

Edel, Leon. *Bloomsbury: A House of Lions*. Philadelphia and New York: Lippincott, 1979.

Fleishman, Avrom. *Virginia Woolf: A Critical Reading*. Baltimore: Johns Hopkins University Press, 1975.

Freedman, Ralph, ed. *Virginia Woolf: Revaluation and Continuity*. Berkeley: University of California Press, 1980.

Gaither, Mary. "A Short History of the Press," in *A Checklist of the Hogarth Press*, by J. Howard Woolmer. Andes, N.Y.: Woolmer / Brotherson, 1976.

Goldman, Mark. *The Reader's Art: Virginia Woolf as Literary Critic*. The Hague: Mouton, 1976.

Gorsky, Suan Rubinow. *Virginia Woolf*. Boston: Twayne, 1978.

Kirkpatrick, B. J. *A Bibliography of Virginia Woolf*, 3rd ed. Oxford: Clarendon Press, 1980.

Latham, Jacqueline E. M., ed. *Critics on Virginia Woolf*. London: Allen & Unwin, 1970.

Leaska, Mitchell A. *The Novels of Virginia Woolf: From Beginning to End*. New York: John Jay Press, 1977.

Lehmann, John. *Virginia Woolf and Her World*. New York: Harcourt Brace Jovanovich, 1975.

Noble, Joan Russell, ed. *Recollections of Virginia Woolf by Her Contemporaries*. New York: Morrow, 1972.

Spater, George and Ian Parsons. *A Marriage of True Minds*. New York: Harcourt Brace Jovanovich, 1977.

Web Sites

Crawford, John W. "The Perfect Hostess (review of *Mrs. Dalloway*." *New York Times* (May 10, 1925). Reprinted on the *New York Times* Web site at http://www.nytimes.com/books/97/06/08/reviews/woolf-dalloway.html. Accessed May 27, 2008.

Kronenberger, Louis. "Virginia Woolf Explores an
English Country Home (review of *To the Lighthouse*."
New York Times, May 8, 1927. Reprinted on the *New
York Times* Web site at http://www.nytimes.com/
books/97/06/08/reviews/woolf-lighthouse.html.
Accessed May 27, 2008.

University of Alabama in Huntsville Web site.
Contemporary Reviews of To the Lighthouse.
Retrieved May 27, 2008 from http://www.
uah.edu/woolf/lighthousecontemprev.html.

◈ William Wordsworth

BORN: *1770, Cockermouth, Cumberland,
England*

DIED: *1850, Ambleside, England*

NATIONALITY: *English*

GENRE: *Poetry, nonfiction*

MAJOR WORKS:

Lyrical Ballads (1798)

Poems (1807)

The Sonnets of William Wordsworth (1838)

The Prelude (1850)

William Wordsworth *Wordsworth, William, photograph.*

Overview

Asserting in the preface to his *Lyrical Ballads* that poetry
should comprise "language really used by men," William
Wordsworth challenged the prevailing eighteenth-
century notion of formal poetic diction and thereby profoundly affected the course of modern poetry. His major
work, *The Prelude*, a study of the role of the imagination
and memory in the formation of poetic sensibility, is now
viewed as one of the most seminal long poems of the
nineteenth century. The freshness and emotional power
of Wordsworth's poetry, the keen psychological depth of
his characterizations, and the urgency of his social commentary make him one of the most important writers in
English.

Works in Biographical and Historical Context

Tranquility, Tragedy, and Revolution William
Wordsworth was born in Cockermouth, England, the
second son of John and Anne Cookson Wordsworth.
An attorney for a prominent local aristocrat, John
Wordsworth provided a secure and comfortable living
for his family. But with his wife's death in 1778, the
family became dispersed: The boys were enrolled at a
boarding school in Hawkeshead, and Wordsworth's sister, Dorothy, was sent to live with cousins in Halifax. In
the rural surroundings of Hawkeshead, situated in the
lush Lake District, Wordsworth early learned to love
nature, including the pleasures of walking and outdoor
play. He equally enjoyed his formal education, demonstrating a talent for writing poetry. The tranquility of his
years at Hawkeshead was marred by the death of his
father in 1783. Left homeless, the Wordsworth children
spent their school vacations with various relatives, many
of whom regarded them as nothing more than a financial
burden. Biographers have pointed out that Wordsworth's frequently unhappy early life contrasts sharply
with the idealized portrait of childhood he presented in
his poetry.

After graduating from St. John's College in Cambridge in 1791, Wordsworth lived for a short time in
London and Wales and then traveled to France. The
French Revolution was in its third year, and although
he previously had shown little interest in politics, he
quickly came to advocate the goals of the revolution.
Along with a heightened political consciousness, he experienced a passionate affair, the details of which were kept
a family secret until the early twentieth century. During
his stay in France, he fell in love with a French woman,
Annette Vallon, and in 1792, they had a child, Anne-
Caroline. Too poor to marry and forced by the outbreak
of civil war to flee France, Wordsworth reluctantly
returned alone to England in 1793.

LITERARY AND HISTORICAL CONTEMPORARIES

Wordsworth's famous contemporaries include:

Ludwig van Beethoven (1770–1827): German composer and virtuoso pianist who, despite his eventual loss of hearing, became famous for his concertos, symphonies, and chamber music.

Napoleon Bonaparte (1769–1821): Famous general during the French Revolution who eventually became ruler of France.

Samuel Taylor Coleridge (1772–1834): Wordsworth's longtime friend and author of "The Rime of the Ancient Mariner" and "Kubla Khan."

Jane Austen (1775–1817): English realist novelist famous for *Pride and Prejudice* and *Sense and Sensibility*.

Writing Habits and Lifelong Friends   Following a brief sojourn in London, Wordsworth settled with his sister at Racedown in 1795. Living modestly but contentedly, he now spent much of his time reading contemporary European literature and writing verse. An immensely important contribution to Wordsworth's success was Dorothy's lifelong devotion: She encouraged his efforts at composition and looked after the details of their daily life. During the first year at Racedown, Wordsworth wrote *The Borderers*, a verse drama based on the ideas of William Godwin and the German Sturm und Drang writers, who emphasized emotional expression in their work. The single most important event of his literary apprenticeship occurred in 1797 when he met the poet Samuel Taylor Coleridge. The two had corresponded for several years, and when Coleridge came to visit Wordsworth at Racedown, their rapport and mutual admiration were immediate. Many critics view their friendship as one of the most extraordinary in English literature. The Wordsworths soon moved to Nether Stowey in order to be near Coleridge. In the intellectually stimulating environment he and Coleridge created there, Wordsworth embarked on a period of remarkable creativity.

In 1802, Wordsworth married Mary Hutchinson. Realizing that Wordsworth now required a more steady source of income, Coleridge introduced him to Sir George Beaumont, a wealthy art patron who became Wordsworth's benefactor and friend. Beaumont facilitated the publication of the *Poems* of 1807; in that collection, Wordsworth once again displayed his extraordinary talent for nature description and infusing an element of mysticism into ordinary experience. Always fascinated by human psychology, he also stressed the influence of childhood. Most reviewers singled out "Ode: Intimations of Immortality from Recollections of Early Childhood" as perhaps Wordsworth's greatest production.

Later Life   The remaining years of Wordsworth's career are generally viewed as a decline from the revolutionary and experimental fervor of his youth. He condemned French imperialism in the period after the revolution, and his nationalism became more pronounced. The pantheism of his early nature poetry, too—which celebrated a pervasive divine force in all things—gave way to orthodox religious sentiment in the later works. Such admirers as Percy Bysshe Shelley, who formerly had respected Wordsworth as a reformer of poetic diction, now regarded him with scorn and a sense of betrayal. Whether because of professional jealousy or because of alterations to his personality caused by prolonged drug use, Coleridge grew estranged from Wordsworth after 1810. Two works, *Yarrow Revisited and Other Poems* (1835) and *The Sonnets of William Wordsworth* (1838), received critical accolades upon their publication and evoked comparisons of Wordsworth's sonnets with those of William Shakespeare and John Milton. In 1843 he won the distinction of being named poet laureate. After receiving a government pension in 1842, he retired to Rydal. When he died in 1850, he was one of England's best-loved poets.

Works in Literary Context

Romantic Movement   Wordsworth was a quintessential Romantic poet. The Romantic Movement in literature, which began in the late eighteenth century, was a reaction against what was seen as the cold rationality of the Enlightenment period. During the Enlightenment, developments in science and technology ushered in the massive social changes in western society. The Industrial Revolution brought about population explosions in European cities while the works of political scientists and philosophers laid the groundwork for the American and French Revolutions. The Romantics viewed science and technology skeptically, and stressed the beauty of nature and individual emotion in their work.

Works in Critical Context

Critics of Wordsworth's works have made his treatment of nature, his use of diction, and his critical theories the central focus of their studies. Early response to his poetry begins with Francis Jeffrey's concerted campaign to thwart Wordsworth's poetic career. His reviews of the works of the Lake poets—Wordsworth, Coleridge, and Robert Southey—and of Wordsworth's poetry in particular, were so vitriolic that they stalled public acceptance of the poet for some twenty years but brought many critics to his defense. To Jeffrey, Wordsworth's poetic innovations were in "open violation of the established laws of poetry." He described Wordsworth's stylistic simplicity as affectation. Like Jeffrey, many readers may have believed Wordsworth "descended too low" in his writing, as an advertisement printed with the *Lyrical Ballads* in 1798 warns. The advertisement recognizes that the familiar tone Wordsworth uses may not be what poetry readers prefer and tries to frame Wordsworth's poetic inclusion of ordinary language as an "experiment" that attempts "to ascertain how far the language of conversation in the middle and lower classes of society is adapted to the purposes of poetic pleasure." Despite this public hesitation, Wordsworth's poetry eventually gained acceptance. By the 1830s, Wordsworth was England's preeminent poet.

The Excursion In 1978, Annabel Patterson wrote in a journal called *The Wordsworth Circle* that *The Excursion* "has a history of disappointing its readers." Patterson goes on to describe how Wordsworth's literary contemporaries reacted negatively to the volume and expected far more. Yet other critics have viewed *The Excursion* like other Wordsworth works, as poetic song or even a "song of daily life," in the words of scholar Brian Bartlett. Bartlett remarks on Wordworth's distinct combination of "man's music and nature's music." William Wordsworth is considered the preeminent poet of nature, though he claimed his main subject was "the Mind of Man—/ My haunt, and the main region of my song." Wordsworth portrays suffering humanity in many of his poems, showing a variety of causes: poverty, separation, bereavement, neglect. As Geoffrey Hartman has written, "those famous misreaders of Wordsworth who say he advocates rural nature as a panacea should be condemned to read *The Excursion* once a day."

The Prelude Wordsworth's *The Prelude* was published shortly after his death. Begun some fifty years earlier, the poem was completed in 1805 and then drastically revised over time. Greeted with uneven praise at its first appearance, the poem is now hailed as Wordsworth's greatest work. Scholar Alan Richardson notes that because of the work's autobiographical slant, many literary critics view *The Prelude* through a variety of lenses, particularly psychoanalytic. Wordsworth, or the poet, becomes the subject, while the critic becomes amateur analyst. At the same time, some critics tend to explore the poem through historical criticism, preferring, as David Miall suggests, to see how "Wordsworth engages with contemporary events…at the local level and…on a broader canvas." In this vein, scholars like to analyze the way Wordsworth may "position himself as a historical figure." In general, critics laud *The Prelude's* blending of autobiography, history, and epic, its theme of loss and gain, its mythologizing of childhood experience, and its affirmation of the value of the imagination.

Responses to Literature

1. Wordsworth was good friends with the poet Samuel Coleridge. Write a one- to two-page essay that describes their friendship as illustrated in Wordsworth's *Lyrical Ballads*.

COMMON HUMAN EXPERIENCE

Wordsworth was keenly interested in depicting idealized portraits of rural people. Here are some other works that champion or examine "common" rural, hardworking lives:

So Big! (1924), a novel by Edna Ferber. Ferber's Pulitzer Prize–winning novel shows a moral contrast between the hardworking farm woman and her city-dwelling architect son.

The Grapes of Wrath (1939), a novel by John Steinbeck. This novel set during the Great Depression follows Tom Joad and his family on their journey to the promised land of California.

Let Us Now Praise Famous Men (1941), a book by James Agee with photographs by Walker Evans. Agee and Evans photographed and detailed the real lives of sharecropper families in the U.S. South. Their portraits are a far cry from Wordsworth's idealized visions.

2. Read a selection of Wordsworth's early poems. Write an essay on how these poems demonstrate how Wordsworth was influenced by the French Revolution.

3. Research the literary movements of naturalism, realism, romanticism, and transcendentalism. Make a chart that describes each movement in detail. Then write a paragraph about which literary style you think Wordsworth followed and why.

4. One of Wordsworth's most quoted lines is "The world is too much with us." In an informal essay written from a first-person point of view, explain how the title statement might apply to today's world.

5. Compare Wordsworth's "My Heart Leaps Up" with Walt Whitman's "Leaves of Grass." With a classmate, discuss how the language and imagery might reveal that one poet is from England and one from America.

BIBLIOGRAPHY

Books

Abrams, M. H., ed. *Wordsworth: A Collection of Critical Essays.* Englewood Cliffs, N.J.: Prentice-Hall, 1972.

Batho, Edith. *The Later Wordsworth.* Cambridge, UK: Cambridge University Press, 1933.

Bewell, Alan J. *Wordsworth and the Enlightenment: Nature, Man, and Society in the Experimental Poetry.* New Haven, Conn.: Yale University Press, 1989.

Hartman, Geoffrey. *Wordsworth's Poetry: 1787–1814.* New Haven, Conn.: Yale University Press, 1964.

Jones, John. *The Egotistical Sublime: A Study of Wordsworth's Imagination.* London: Chatto & Windus, 1954.

Onorato, Richard. *The Character of the Poet: Wordsworth in "The Prelude".* Princeton, N.J.: Princeton University Press, 1971.

Perkins, David. *Wordsworth and the Poetry of Sincerity.* Cambridge, Mass.: Harvard University Press, 1964.

Roe, Nicholas. *Wordsworth and Coleridge: The Radical Years.* Oxford: Oxford University Press, 1988.

Simpson, David. *Wordsworth's Historical Imagination.* New York: Methuen, 1987.

Woodring, Carl. *Wordsworth.* Boston: Houghton Mifflin, 1965.

◈ Judith Wright

BORN: *1915, Armidale, New South Wales, Australia*

DIED: *2000, Canberra, Australia*

NATIONALITY: *Australian*

GENRE: *Poetry, nonfiction, fiction*

MAJOR WORKS:
The Moving Image (1946)
Woman to Man (1949)
The Gateway (1953)
The Two Fires (1955)
The Other Half (1966)

Judith Wright   *Wright, Judith, photograph. Coward of Canberra Photography. Reproduced by permission of Judith A. Wright.*

Overview

While Australian poet Judith Wright may be recognized nearly as much for her passionate involvement in social and environmental causes as she is for her literary work, that should not be seen as mitigating the importance of her contribution to Australian letters. One of the country's most celebrated poets, she has been lauded by even the notoriously difficult-to-please poet and critic Robert Lowell and is a significant influence on the contemporary generation of Australian poets.

Works in Biographical and Historical Context

Raised by the Land Judith Arundell Wright was born on May 31, 1915, at Thalgaroch Station near Armidale, New South Wales, to pastoralist Phillip Arundell Wright and Ethel Mabel Bigg Wright. Ethel became an invalid after the birth of the second of Judith's two brothers, and she died when Judith was twelve. Often left to her own devices, young Judith spent much of her time outdoors. The land became for her a presence that was almost maternal; that land also became the primary source of her poetry.

Wright was educated first at home and then as a boarder at the New England Girls' Grammar School, where her English teacher recognized and encouraged her talent. A serious riding accident kept her in the hospital for three months during her last year at school and pre-

vented her from matriculating at Sydney University, but she went on to the university after a year at home—supported by a legacy from her grandmother. There she followed her interests, studying English, history, philosophy, and anthropology and spending time in the library reading widely to prepare herself for a writing career.

World War II and the Birth of a Frightened Patriotism In 1937, with the last of the legacy from her grandmother, Wright went to England, where she met some of her relatives. She then toured Europe, witnessing Nazism firsthand in Germany. On her return to Australia, she settled in Sydney. Not long afterward, World War II broke out in Europe. Two years later, in 1941, the Japanese attack on Pearl Harbor and rumblings throughout Southeast Asia brought the threat dangerously close to home. Wright returned to New South Wales to help her father run the family properties while her two brothers were in the army. On the train trip there she became "suddenly and sharply aware" that Australia was "my country" but now in a different, more threatened, way.

When her elder brother was released from the army after the Allied victory in the Pacific Theater had been achieved—to some extent through the humanitarian catastrophe of the U.S. bombing of the Japanese cities Hiroshima and Nagasaki with atomic weapons—Wright went north to Brisbane to work as an unpaid secretary for

C. B. Christesen, at his newly founded literary magazine, *Meanjin Papers.* At one of Christesen's gatherings in 1945, she met Jack Philip McKinney. Wright found in McKinney an integrity, a "certainty, passion and peace" she had not encountered before, and he became her partner—and, in 1962, her husband.

Poetry of Power Wright's reputation was made by a series of poems about the land and the people who pioneered it—which she published first in the *Bulletin* and *Meanjin Papers* and later collected in her first volume, *The Moving Image* (1946). These poems transformed the bush tradition of rural Australia, even as she wrote about and from within it.

Wright's second work, *Woman to Man* (1949), celebrated the power of womanhood; it was to become for critics one of her most profound works. Her next two collections—*The Gateway* (1953) and *The Two Fires* (1955)—moved away from personal and anecdotal material toward more metaphysical and universal subject matter. Amidst such solemn works, Wright also produced *Birds* in 1963, a collection of poems that commented on the characteristics of Australia's winged wildlife. In her next collection, *Five Senses* (1963), human figures returned, and the poems, less impersonal, again expressed Wright's feeling for and delight in the earth.

Working and Writing to Empower Wright returned to metaphysical issues in many of her poems written in the mid-1960s, with *The Other Half* (1966) addressing the mystic relationship between the conscious and unconscious mind—despite the fact that her energies were increasingly taken up by activist concerns. At this time, Wright was heavily involved with lectures and critical writing, and was also making great efforts to save the Australian rain forest. More and more of her time and energy also went into battles to save the Great Barrier Reef; to oppose the new supersonic aircraft, the Concorde (because of the threat it posed to the environment); to preserve the rain forests; and, increasingly important, to support the aboriginal people of Australia in their struggles for recognition and restitution. Like the Native Americans in the United States, the aboriginals in Australia had been systematically stripped of their land and their customs, even of their language. Thousands of aboriginal children had been kidnapped and forced to live with white families of European descent, in an effort to assimilate them into the dominant white culture. As in the U.S., where the situation is in many ways even more grim (still today), aboriginal peoples lived, at best, in colonial relationships to the Australian government; a good part of Wright's energy was devoted to helping aboriginals change this situation.

Losing McKinney and Leaving Queensland When McKinney died in 1966, Wright's poetic output reflected her grief; *Collected Poems, 1942–1970* (1971) includes poems devoted to her love for her mate and

LITERARY AND HISTORICAL CONTEMPORARIES

Wright's famous contemporaries include:

Aleksandr Solzhenitsyn (1918–2008): A Russian author and dissident famous for his novels depicting the harsh conditions in Soviet labor camps.

Heinrich Böll (1917–1985): A German author who was respected for his post–World War II writings as much as for his successful resistance to joining Hitler's Youth.

William S. Burroughs (1914–1997): An American avant-garde writer known as one of the central members of the Beat generation.

Edith Piaf (1915–1963): A French songstress who was so popular that, when she died, the streets of Paris closed down, and thousands upon thousands mourned her passing.

Frank Sinatra (1915–1998): The American popular singer and award-winning actor known as "Ol' Blue Eyes."

her pain at losing him. Many of the poems in the "Shadow" section of the book describe McKinney moving away from her as he grew increasingly frail with age and illness; but they also celebrate the journey she and her husband had made together.

As an activist elated by the 1972 electoral success of the Labor Party under Gough Whitlam—which led to a government that seemed to be concerned with the same issues about which she felt passionately—Wright decided to leave Queensland. She moved south to a block of land she bought near the Shoalhaven River in southeastern New South Wales, where she built the house in which she hoped to spend her last years in the midst of nature. *Alive: Poems, 1971–1972* appeared in 1973. This collection continued her emphasis on the natural beauty of her Queensland home, however, contrasting that with urban ruin—using this comparison to comment on the destruction of the Australian wilderness.

The Conscience of the Nation After a lengthy break from publishing poetry collections, Wright published *Phantom Dwelling* in 1985. Also in 1985, on her seventieth birthday, she announced that she would write no more poetry, instead focusing on the causes in which she so passionately believed. When she died on June 25, 2000, at the age of eighty-five, she was not only arguably Australia's best-known poet but had also come to be regarded by many as the conscience of the nation.

Works in Literary Context

In her earliest years it was Miles Franklin's novel *My Brilliant Career* (1901) that inspired Wright's determination to become a writer. In turn, it was her fascination

COMMON HUMAN EXPERIENCE

Wright was particularly concerned with the issue of identity for those from whom identity had been systematically stripped: in Australia, the aboriginal people. Here are a few works by writers who also focused on themes of authentic identity for indigenous peoples:

Cry, the Beloved Country (1948), a novel by Alan Paton. In this acclaimed novel, South African apartheid is encroaching—against the social protests of select individuals and subcultures.

Once Were Warriors (1990), a novel by Alan Duff. Later adapted into a power film, this novel closely examines Maori cultural struggles in the setting of urban New Zealand and by way of the impoverished, undereducated Heke family.

Things Fall Apart (1959), a novel by Chinua Achebe. This novel is the story of colonialism and its invasive and destructive impact on Nigerian tribal culture.

The World of Malgudi (2000), a collection of novellas by R. K. Narayan. In this collection, the author expresses the values and mores of domestic life and explores what it means to be (East) Indian in modern times.

with Jack McKinney and her desire to partner and have children with him that inspired poems such as "Woman to Man" and "Woman to Child," collected in *Woman to Man* (1949). And it was the influence of such esteemed writers as William Blake and T. S. Eliot that informed Wright's works such as *The Gateway* (1953)—in its consideration of love, creation, and eternity. But it was her childhood at Wallamumbi, her family's sheep ranch in New South Wales, that drove Wright's interest in the Australian land itself. At one point, Wright explained this influence, saying, "As a poet you have to imitate somebody, but as I had a beautiful landscape outside that I loved so much and was in so much...it was my main object from the start."

Identity and Power In works as late as *Phantom Dwelling* (1985), Wright brings new light to bear on the themes that dominate so much of her poetry, particularly humanity's relationship with nature and death. Wright also depicts nature and birth: she portrays pregnant and birthing mothers as elemental forces like floods, fires, and droughts—all of which figure as the enemy in the bush tradition. Such poems, expressions, and images also establish the woman as a figure of power, however. This power extended to Australia's people and land as well; it was of major importance to Wright to make her people indigenes—natives—to give them their rightful connection to their true history. Poems in several vol-

umes address this focus, with themes on the struggle to attain permanence and security and the need to overcome transience through love. Ultimately, for Wright, poetry was "a means of regaining faith in man" as well as "a way of finding a difficult balance" between internal and external reality.

Works in Critical Context

With few exceptions, critical response to Wright's poetry has been positive. From her first two collections onwards, she was almost invariably lauded for her fresh treatments of the subject matter with which she dealt.

The Moving Image (1946) In this first collection, Wright uses lucid, graceful lyrics to evoke a mythic dimension in her subjects. In the process, she conveys a vivid sense of the landscape and history of the New England region of Australia. Appraising *The Moving Image*, Vincent Buckley argues that "Judith Wright surpasses all other Australian poets in the extent to which she...reveals the contours of Australia as a place, an atmosphere, a separate being." Such praise was echoed by many other critics, as *The Moving Image* established Wright as one of Australia's major poets.

Woman to Man (1949) Wright's second volume of verse is a celebration of womanhood. Often regarded as her most profound work, critics have found *Woman to Man* notable for its striking imagery and focus on love and chaos, and they credit Wright with giving a uniquely female perspective to poems dealing with love, creation, and the universe. Elizabeth Vassilieff, an activist in the Fellowship of Australian Writers (FAW), contends that with these poems Wright exhibits "the ability to re-create the meanings of common words with every new usage; to refresh, deepen and invigorate the language.... And in this power I think she has no equal among Australian poets."

On the collections published after *Woman to Man* the critics are divided. Many contend that her increasingly metaphysical focus and her forays into rather literal protest poetry dilute her ability to draw universal and poetic images from common events. Her departure from the more traditional style of her early verse has also been scorned by some observers. Others, however, have characterized her politics and mysticism and her stylistic experiments with free verse as the explorations of a serious poet, who, not content to rest on her laurels, continued ever to redefine herself and her subject matter as she matured. Nela Bureu, for example, describes Wright's poetry in its style and content as a "deep meditation on the meaning and value of life."

Responses to Literature

1. Investigate Australia—its history, geography, culture, and people. Where is Australia prominent in Wright's poetry, and what differences do you find between her

treatments of "different Australias" (that is, Australia as a historical state, as a piece of land, as a national idea, etc.)? Structure your thoughts in a thesis-driven essay, explaining your understanding of Wright through detailed analysis of specific passages.

2. While several of Wright's works push beyond historical fact into the world of myth, her experiences and studies of significant events influenced the poet and affected her poetry.

3. Study the functions of The Department of the Environment in at least four different countries. Analyze how each country's respective federal agency contributes to the destruction of the environment in some way, even as they also help to protect it. Write a protest poem modeled on Wright's later work that addresses this situation at large or some particular environmental issue.

4. In her preface to *Preoccupations in Australian Poetry* Wright comments that "the true function of an art and a culture is to interpret us to ourselves, and to relate us to the country and society in which we live." Consider what this means by regarding several forms of art in your own culture—pottery, sculpture, painting, poetry, a television program, or Internet medium. How does each help (or fail to help) you to interpret who you are? What does each tell you about the culture you live in?

BIBLIOGRAPHY

Books

Barfield, Owen. *Poetic Diction: A Study in Meaning.* New York: McGraw-Hill, 1964.

Buckley, Vincent. "The Poetry of Judith Wright." In *Essays in Poetry, Mainly Australian,* edited by A. K. Thompson, 158–76. Melbourne: Melbourne University Press, 1957.

Wright, Judith. *Half a Lifetime.* Edited by Patricia Clarke. Melbourne: Text, 1999.

———. *Preoccupations in Australian Poetry.* Oxford: Oxford University Press, 1965.

Periodicals

McKinney, Meredith. Review of *Birds. National Library of Australia News* 14, no. 6 (March 2004): 7–10.

Shapcott, Tom. "With Love and Fury: Selected Letters of Judith Wright." *Sydney Morning Herald,* March 10, 2007.

Stewart, Douglas. Review of *The Moving Image. Bulletin,* October 16, 1942.

Web Sites

Books and Writers. "Judith Wright (1915–2000)." Retrieved May 16, 2008, from http://www.kirjasto.sci.fi/jwright.htm.

Brady, Veronica. National Library of Australia. *Judith Wright's Biography: A Delicate Balance between Trespass and Honour.* Retrieved May 16, 2008, from http://www.nla.gov.au/events/doclife/brady.html.

World Socialist Web Site. *Australian Poet Judith Wright (1915–2000): An Appreciation.* Retrieved May 16, 2008, from http://www.wsws.org/articles/2000/aug2000/wrig-a31.shtml. Last updated on August 31, 2000.

◈ William Wycherley

BORN: *c. 1640, Hampshire, England*

DIED: *1715, London, England*

NATIONALITY: *British*

GENRE: *Drama, poetry*

MAJOR WORKS:

Love in a Wood (1671)

The Country-Wife (1675)

The Plain-Dealer (1677)

Miscellany Poems: as Satyrs, Epistles, Love-Verses, Songs, Sonnets, etc. (1671)

William Wycherley *Wycherley, William, photograph. © Michael Nicholson / Corbis.*

Overview

One of the foremost dramatists of the Restoration period, British author William Wycherley combined irreverent social satire and complex verbal wit to create comedies of lasting interest and appeal. His comedies ridiculed the manners and morals of sophisticated ladies and gentlemen who delighted in illicit intrigue. Wycherley's plays have attracted much controversy over the years for their candid treatment of moral—particularly sexual—attitudes and behavior, with the result that Wycherley has been alternately hailed as a force for moral regeneration and denounced as a purveyor of moral indecency.

Works in Biographical and Historical Context

Social-Climbing Father Wycherley was born in Hampshire, England, c. 1640, into an established Shropshire family. His father, David Wycherley, was a steward and deputy for a local aristocrat, and he spent his entire adult life hoarding money, trying to climb the social ladder, and entering into lawsuits. Such activities became prime targets of his son's satire in later years, and Wycherley was believed to have modeled several unattractive characters after his father.

Royalist Exile Less than two years after Wycherley's birth, the English civil war began. Oliver Cromwell led a coalition of Puritans and supporters of parliamentary rule against the forces of King Charles I. At issue were the questions such as the king's right to sole autocratic power and the position of the Anglican church as the official church of England. Cromwell's victory was complete in 1649 when he proclaimed himself Lord Protector for Life and had Charles I's head cut off at the guillotine. Before his death, Charles wisely had his son, also named Charles, sent out of the country to France, where he received support and recognition from the king and aristocratic families there.

France became a safe haven for "Royalist" families such as Wycherley's who supported the king and his dynasty. At the age of fifteen, Wycherley was sent to Angoulême where he began his remarkable education. Wycherley became associated with the brilliant intellectual Julie d'Angennes, the wife of the province's governor, who was at the center of a fashionable group of writers and thinkers who demonstrated "la préciosité": exquisitely refined manners, morals, and verbal elegance. One of their codes was that passionate love refines the soul and lifts it above the constraints of marriage. (At the time, marriages were usually arranged for financial advantage among the aristocratic class or those who aspired to it). This theme appears often in Wycherley's works, although sometimes in a bawdy comic form that is anything but "précieuse."

Return to England There is little evidence of Wycherley's activities between the ages of fifteen and thirty. All we know for sure is that he, along with many other Royalists, returned to England in 1660 when Parliament—the same group who fought with Cromwell to depose King Charles I—tired of the restrictions of Puritan rule and voted to invite Charles's son back from France to claim the English throne as King Charles II a few years after the death of Cromwell. Wycherley had converted to Roman Catholicism while he was in France, but after he had begun studying at Queens College, Oxford, he converted back to Protestantism. In November of 1660, Wycherley enrolled as a law student in London, but it is doubtful that he ever completed his training or practiced law. It is more likely that Wycherley took some part in the naval battle against the Dutch in 1665, and it is certainly true that throughout his writing career he associates aristocratic bravery with heroism at sea.

Wycherley's first play, *Love in a Wood*, premiered in London in 1671 and made him famous overnight. It attracted the attention of Charles II's mistress, the Duchess of Cleveland, who introduced Wycherley to court circles. His second play, a comedy titled *The Gentleman Dancing Master*, was performed later that year, but it was not as well received. Shortly after this, Wycherley probably served as a naval officer in the Dutch War.

Wrote Last Plays *The Country-Wife*, Wycherley's best-known play, was first performed in 1672 or 1673 and centers on the attempts of a jealous husband named Pinchwife to keep his young and naive wife out of society because of his fear that she will be unfaithful. This play was a great success and is still performed today. The next year *The Plain Dealer* was performed with equal success. After *The Plain Dealer*, Wycherley stopped writing for the stage.

Wycherley fell ill in 1678, and Charles II sent him to France to recuperate. When Wycherley returned, the king entrusted the education of his illegitimate son, the duke of Richmond, to Wycherley, but he lost the appointment a year later because of Charles's displeasure at his absence from court. This absence was occasioned by Wycherley's secret marriage to the countess of Drogheda, who died about a year later. Litigation over her estate proved so expensive that Wycherley was imprisoned for debt. About seven years later, King James II secured his freedom, paid his debts, and gave him a pension.

In 1697, Wycherley succeeded to his father's estate. In 1704 he published *Miscellany Poems*, which caught the attention of young Alexander Pope, who later helped Wycherley to revise and edit his poetry. Wycherley died on January 1, 1716.

Works in Literary Context

Wycherley was both a product and an exponent of the "Restoration," a period from 1660 to 1700 marking Charles II's "restoration" to the British throne. After his father was executed in 1649, Charles II left England to be protected in the opulent palace of King Louis XIV of France, where he learned the pleasures of fast living and enjoyed the attention of fine ladies. When Charles returned to England, the London court culture seemed to explode with new life after a long period of repressive Puritan rule. Cromwell had closed all of the theaters (bringing the rapid advancements that William Shakespeare had introduced to a sudden halt), but under Charles II, they opened with a full agenda of witty, satirical, and highly sexualized plays that seemed designed to offend Puritans as much as possible.

Restoration Themes In his comedies, Wycherley both celebrated the live-for-the-day immorality of aristocratic London society and satirized its hypocrisies and follies. His plays helped to establish the subjects and structures that would come to define "Restoration comedies": sharp and smart dialogue, elaborate plots full of mistaken identities and overheard speeches, sexual intrigue, and conclusions that often go easy on the villains and ridicule the morally prudent. Another common feature of Restoration comedies was a plot involving a woman forced to disguise herself as a man, as seen in *The Country-Wife*. The Restoration was the first time women were allowed to perform on stage, and a play always sold tickets if the plot gave men in the audience an excuse to leer at women in tight men's breeches.

Restoration Characters Amply represented in Wycherley's work are such stock Restoration characters as the roguish wit; the deceived cuckold (a clueless husband whose wife is cheating on him); the conceited, ineffectual fop (or social-climbing, fashion-conscious man); and the falsely pious hypocrite.

Wit Wycherley's plays are replete with wit, a quality very highly prized during the Restoration. "Wit" meant not just humor or irony but a keenness of perception that recognized the relationship between seemingly dissimilar things, an ability to cut straight to the heart of a matter in an original way, and an ability to express all of this with cleverness and quick improvisation. Such verbal dexterity is a famous feature of Wycherley's work, and he incorporates it brilliantly into how characters compete with and evaluate one another. Wycherley has even been faulted for being *too* clever, for occasionally sacrificing consistency of characterization for the sake of a witty exchange.

Influence Wycherley greatly influenced other Restoration dramatists as well as a number of British authors who followed him. Later in the eighteenth century, for example, David Garrick adapted his own version of *The Country-Wife* as *The Country Girl* in 1766, which became the preferred version through the end of the nineteenth century. Outside of drama, Wycherley's young friend Alexander Pope was influenced by his mentor's verse.

Works in Critical Context

Wycherley's reputation as a playwright and his place in the literary tradition have always been problematic

---

LITERARY AND HISTORICAL CONTEMPORARIES

Wycherley's famous contemporaries include:

Alexander Pope (1688–1744): British poet Pope attracted serious critical attention at the age of twelve for his remarkably mature and polished poetry. He continued to refine his art until he was widely acknowledged as the greatest poet of his day.

Oliver Cromwell (1589–1658): British political leader Cromwell was a Puritan who helped raise an army to rebel against King Charles I. He ruled as Lord Protector and engaged in a brutal oppression of the Irish in order to enforce British claims on the island and to stamp out Catholicism.

Aphra Behn (1640–1689): Behn was one of the first Englishwomen to be a professional writer. Her works include the short novel *Oroonoko: Or, the Royal Slave* (1688). She also worked as an actress and as a spy, and spent time in debtor's prison.

Christopher Wren (1632–1723): Briton Wren was a brilliant architect, designer, engineer, and astronomer whose mark can be seen all over London to this day. In 1666, London suffered a terrible fire that destroyed much of the city. Charles II, who was interested in design and architecture himself, gave Wren free reign to rebuild the city on a more logical and elegant plan.

John Dryden (1631–1700): Dryden was the first poet laureate in England, but long before that honor, he was regarded by other writers of the era as their leader, model, and patron.

---

because the history of Wycherley studies hinges upon a bitter paradox. In his own day, Wycherley was considered to be a moral satirist of the seriousness and stature of the classical writers Horace and Juvenal. Yet from the nineteenth century to the present, he has been thought successively to be a monster of moral depravity, a writer of artificial comedies of manners, and a writer of mere sex farces. From the mid-nineteenth to the mid-twentieth century, the history of Wycherley criticism was one long contention between critics who dismissed his best plays—*The Country-Wife* and *The Plain Dealer*—as immoral and those who sought to clear them of that charge. It was not until 1965, in Rose A. Zimbardo's *Wycherley's Drama: A Link in the Development of English Satire*, that a serious, book-length study was devoted to placing Wycherley, the satirist, firmly back into English literary history.

The Country-Wife Wycherley's reputation as a playwright was immediately enhanced by the production of *The Country-Wife*. It was an extremely popular play in the seventeenth century, deemed a hilarious comedy for its

COMMON HUMAN EXPERIENCE

Wycherley's work often satirizes the hypocrisies and immoralities of London high society. Here are some other works that poke fun at the rich and mighty:

The Rape of the Lock (1712), a narrative poem by Alexander Pope. Pope was asked by some friends to mend fences between two aristocratic families after a man cut off a lock of hair, without permission, from a young woman he admired. Pope turned it into a mock-epic satire full of sparkling wit, stinging satire, and obvious affection for an elegant society that he could observe but never fully join himself.

Vile Bodies (1930), a novel by Evelyn Waugh. Waugh uses his trademark black humor to expose the shallowness of the "bright young things" of post–World War I British society.

Shampoo (1975), a film directed by Hal Ashby. This satire on the sexual and social mores of the rich in the late 1960s starred Warren Beatty as a hairdresser who makes housecalls, allowing him to use his charms to cuckold all the husbands who are at work earning the money their wives are spending on their selfish pleasures.

jeers at adulterers who claim virtue. By the eighteenth century, changing values and social norms led to censorship of the play as it was judged offensive and dissolute. This trend continued into the nineteenth century as changing views on how drama affects audiences changed the reception of Wycherley's plays. A play that in the eighteenth century exposed audiences to instances of immoral behavior, offering up such behavior to denounce it, was seen in the nineteenth century as providing audiences immoral behavior to emulate. Today, critics remain distressed with the morality of the play, but with different rationale. With central characters that seem to exemplify the vices of lust and hypocrisy, critics question exactly which values Wycherley was condoning at the time of publication and against what the satire is actually directed. Reviewing a 2007 London production of *The Country-Wife*, Lloyd Evans wrote in the *Spectator*, "William Wycherley's 332-year-old sex romp is about as entertaining as I would be if I were 322. The plot is dazzlingly crass.... The characters are as crude and oafish as the storyline. Only the elegance of the script delivers the occasional joy."

Responses to Literature

1. In an essay, consider the following questions: Do you think a play is "immoral," if it is trying to accurately reflect or satirize immoral times? Was the Restoration court under Charles II as "immoral," as it is usually assumed to be?

2. In a presentation, consider the following questions: What is the role of women in one or more of Wycherley's plays? What stereotypes do they embody, or do you think they run counter to stereotypes? How does Wycherley use the plot in order to get his female actors into sexually alluring costumes or provocative situations?

3. Consider the names of some of Wycherley's comic characters. How are they meaningful? Do you think the satire is subtle or heavy-handed? Discuss your opinions in a group.

BIBLIOGRAPHY

Books

Hume, Robert. *The Development of English Drama in the Late Seventeenth Century.* Oxford, U.K.: Oxford University Press, 1976.

Rogers, Katharine M. *William Wycherley.* New York: Twayne, 1972.

Vernon, P. F. *William Wycherley.* London: Longmans, Green, 1965.

Wilson, John Harold. *A Preface to Restoration Drama.* Boston, Mass.: Houghton Mifflin, 1965.

Zimbardo, Rose A. *Wycherley's Drama: A Link in the Development of English Satire.* New Haven, Conn.: Yale University Press, 1965.

Periodicals

Evans, Lloyd. "Losing the Plot (*The Country Wife* and *Rent.*" *Spectator* (November 3, 2007): 84.

Rump, Eric. "Theme and Structure in Wycherley's *Love in a Wood.*" *English Studies* 54 (August 1973): 326–33.

Web sites

William Wycherley. Retrieved March 13, 2008, from http://www.imagi-nation.com/moonstruck/clsc95.html

Gao Xingjian

BORN: *1940, Ganzhou, China*

NATIONALITY: *Chinese*

GENRE: *Drama, fiction, nonfiction*

MAJOR WORKS:

Bus Stop (1983)

Soul Mountain (1990)

One Man's Bible (1999)

Gao Xingjian   *Evan Agostini / Getty Images*

Overview

Playwright, novelist, and artist Gao Xingjian was a prominent leader of the avant-garde artistic movement that emerged following the Cultural Revolution (1966–1976) in China. In 2000 he received the Nobel Prize in Literature, the first winner to write in the Chinese language. Gao is the author of several experimental plays as well as two highly acclaimed autobiographical novels, *Soul Mountain* and *One Man's Bible*. Gao's works are banned in the People's Republic of China, and he is now a French citizen.

Works in Biographical and Historical Context

Childhood in a Time of War Gao was born in Ganzhou, Jiangxi Province, on January 4, 1940, during the Japanese occupation of China. This was part of the Second Sino-Japanese War, during which Japan attempted to claim parts of China as its own; this conflict ultimately merged into the greater conflict known as World War II, and it ended with Japan's surrender in 1945. Gao received his formal education in the Communist People's Republic of China, established in 1949. Gao, however, had grown up in a liberal family with a sizable library of Chinese literature, as well as many volumes on Western literature and art. His mother, an

actress in local productions, fostered in her son her love of the arts. Sometimes Gao and his mother staged plays in the house for Gao's father, a banker.

The Cultural Revolution From childhood, Gao wanted to be an artist and planned to enroll in art school after graduating from high school. In Communist China, however, the role of the artist was limited to works that glorified the state and its ideals. When he realized that being an art student would mean painting propaganda posters, he decided to study French at the Beijing Foreign Languages Institute. This choice proved a great influence on his development as a writer: As more and more Chinese books were banned by the Communist regime beginning in the 1950s, Gao continued reading his way through the shelves of French works at the Institute library.

Following his graduation in 1962, Gao worked as a translator and editor at the Foreign Languages Press in Beijing. He continued reading in French until all books in foreign languages were banned during the Cultural Revolution initiated by Communist Party chairman Mao Zedong. Gao had obsessively kept a diary, and, though he knew such self-expression did not conform to Mao's guidelines, he wrote many works of fiction, though he burned most when he became concerned he would be arrested or imprisoned if his work was discovered.

Freedom and "Spiritual Pollution" In 1970, along with countless other artists and intellectuals, Gao and his colleagues at the press were sent to a rural labor camp for "reeducation." He remained for nearly six years. When he came under investigation for leading a "rebel" group against the "revolutionary pedigree" group that was beating and torturing older workers from the Foreign Languages Press, Gao escaped into the mountains and began living the life of a peasant, working in rice paddy fields. Eventually, Gao was chosen to teach in a village school.

The Cultural Revolution ended with Mao's death in 1976. Subsequently, the amount of artistic freedom in China increased. Gao was able to return to his position with the Foreign Languages Press in Beijing and to write openly. His short stories, essays, and literary criticism began to appear regularly in literary magazines. He published a collection of his essays titled *A Preliminary Discussion of the Art of Modern Fiction* (1981), which daringly stressed that effective fiction requires freedom—for the author, the reader, and the characters as well. His argument established his credentials among Chinese intellectuals, but authorities of the state frowned on his embrace of decadent ideas from the capitalist West.

Gao's play *Warning Signal* was staged in Beijing in 1982. The experimental piece challenged decades of established socialist-realist practices in the theater. Gao's innovative techniques, such as flashbacks, different perspectives, and his focus on the psychological dimensions of his characters, were enormously appealing for audiences, but government authorities found the play subversive.

LITERARY AND HISTORICAL CONTEMPORARIES

Gao's famous contemporaries include:

Deng Xiaoping (1904–1997): Leader of the Chinese Communist Party from 1978 to the early 1990s, Deng introduced free-enterprise elements into China's economy.

Dario Fo (1926–): An Italian theatrical satirist who is often censured for social agitation, Fo won the Nobel Prize in Literature in 1997.

Tenzin Gyatso (1935–): The fourteenth Dalai Lama is an exiled Tibetan spiritual leader who won the 1989 Nobel Peace Prize.

Jimmy Carter (1929–): Carter was the forty-ninth U.S. president and is the author of over twenty books that include everything from collections of poems and meditations to discourses on how to solve the Israeli-Palestinian problem.

Derek Walcott (1930–): This West Indian poet and playwright won the Nobel Prize in Literature in 1992 for work that revolves around myth and culture.

Bus Stop, staged the following year, caused more controversy. The play depicts people waiting at a bus stop, watching buses pass without stopping, as the years pass by as well. Chinese audiences thought the play a refreshing change from the overtly didactic plays of past decades. Authorities shut down the production after three weeks, banned all of Gao's works, and demanded that the playwright apologize in public for his "spiritual pollution." Gao refused to do so.

Soul Mountain   During these anxious times, Gao was diagnosed with lung cancer and was convinced his death was imminent. Weeks later, a second X-ray determined that the diagnosis had been a mistake. Gao felt reborn and resolved to be free, defying all authority except his own inner voice. Hearing that the regime intended to incarcerate him again, he took an advance royalty from an editor and fled into the forests of Sichuan Province. During the time he was gone, the Oppose Spiritual Pollution Campaign of 1983 was born, and Gao was blacklisted for promoting capitalist Western literature.

Gao traveled more than fifteen thousand kilometers along the Yangtze River for five months, observing remainders of early civilization and ancient folk practices that provided material for his reflections on human existence and the function of language, song, and storytelling. The solitude of his long journey also provided time for him to examine his own life, both his present predicament and the fragments of forgotten memories that had surfaced during his confrontation with death. The writing he did during this time became the basis for his groundbreaking novel, *Soul Mountain*.

At the end of 1983, Gao returned to Beijing, and continued to submit works for publication, despite intermittent campaigns of repression. Even with careful self-censorship, his writings continued to cause troubles for him. His play *Wild Man*, staged in 1985 at the Beijing People's Art Theater, was the last of his plays performed in China. In 1987, the opportunity arose for Gao to travel to Germany. Frustrated by near-constant harassment in his homeland, he remained in Europe and took up residence in Paris. In 1989, following the Chinese government's attack on student protesters in Tiananmen Square, Gao quit the Communist Party and applied for political asylum. He became a French citizen in 1998.

In Paris, Gao completed his novel *Soul Mountain*, a massive experiment in language and narrative form. The novel dramatizes one man's quest to come to terms with nature, society, and the self. Exploring the landscapes and legends in the Chinese hinterlands, the narrator laments the immense destruction wrought by the Cultural Revolution. Storytelling and imagination, including the unfolding of multiple personalities within the individual "I," relieve the narrator from the loneliness of the human condition. Gao's second autobiographical novel, *One Man's Bible*, returns to the years of the Cultural Revolution. Gao depicts the drastic distortion of human behavior created by tyrannical individuals such as Mao Tsetung and his followers, and insightfully explores the dynamics of power at various levels of all human relationships.

Theatrical Visions and Sudden Celebrity   Gao's next major play, *Fugitives* (1990), is a tragic love story set against the backdrop of the Tiananmen Square protests. Chinese authorities published *Fugitives* as a showcase of immoral literature by Chinese living abroad. Starting in the late 1980s, eminent directors have produced Gao's plays on five continents. Gao's play *Interrogating Death* was presented in Marseilles, France as one of the events for "Gao Xingjian Year," declared by the city in 2003.

When Gao received the Nobel Prize in Literature in 2000, his reclusive life in Paris was suddenly interrupted by publicity. It was the first time that his writings had brought him significant financial rewards. Prior to that, he had supported himself by selling his Chinese ink paintings. No Chinese writer had ever been awarded the prize, and Gao's works were officially blacklisted in his home country. The Chinese government imposed a media blackout on the Nobel ceremonies that year.

After collapsing while directing rehearsals in 2002, Gao underwent two operations for heart trouble. His health has improved significantly since then, and he continues to derive pleasure from writing poetry and painting.

Works in Literary Context

Gao was exposed at an early age to classics of both Chinese and Western literature and recalled reading Honoré de Balzac, Émile Zola, and John Steinbeck from the shelves of his family home. As a student of French literature, he became even more widely read. His own artistry was particularly influenced by avant-garde European dramatists, such as Samuel Beckett and Eugene Ionesco, whose work he later translated for the Beijing Foreign Languages Press. Elements of surrealism and the "Theater of the Absurd" abound in his works for the stage. At the same time, his drama incorporates traditional Chinese aesthetics.

Tripartite Actor   Concerned that theater had lost its appeal, Gao called for a return to what he considers to be the essence of theater: its "theatricality," the very thing that distinguishes drama from other literary forms. To address modern theater's deficit in theatrical elements, Gao formulated his idea of the "tripartite actor:" the actor as a person, the neutral actor, and the character. To achieve neutrality, the actor casts his everyday self aside in order to observe his own acting from a distance. Based on his observations, the actor would then modify his acting accordingly. In other words, the actor is asked to identify psychologically with the audience.

Pronouns as Characters   One intriguing aspect of Gao's exploration of individuality is his experimentation with pronouns. Many of his stories alternate between first-person, second-person, and third-person narration. *Soul Mountain*, a novel of considerable length, impressively sustains this technique as Gao uses the pronoun "I" to represent the narrator's physical journey through China. In his loneliness, "I" creates "you," who is in fact a reflection of the narrator. Naturally, being a reflection of "I," "you" also experiences loneliness and creates "she" for a companion. "You" flirts with "she," who finally succumbs, and the two gratify their lust. Traveling together to Snow Mountain, "you" tells "she" a number of fascinating tales. "She" becomes tired and depressed during the never-ending journey to the mountain, and in a fit of hysteria "she" attacks "you" with a knife, though "you" is able to fend off her assault. "She" finally departs, leaving "you" to travel alone to Soul Mountain. As "you" walks away, the back of "you" becomes "he". Such shifts in perspective reflect the author's dissection of the self and its essential multiplicity.

Works in Critical Context

Gao was largely unknown by the world's reading public until his Nobel selection in 2000. In his home country, his writings have been banned for years, and none of his books was readily available in the United States at the time he received the prize, though that soon changed. He has readers in Hong Kong and Taiwan, but few in the West; however, he has a small but devoted following in Sweden. A small scandal broke out among the Swedish

---

COMMON HUMAN EXPERIENCE

Gao's controversial plays, such as *Bus Stop* and *Snow*, are influenced by the surrealist tradition in drama, often called the theater of the absurd. Here are some other notable titles in the absurdist genre:

Six Characters in Search of an Author (1921), a play by Luigi Pirandello. In this early exploration of meta theater, the characters appear on stage out of the imagination, all demanding to tell their stories.

The Bald Soprano (1950), a play by Eugene Ionesco. In this play, two families engage in a nonsensical conversation that seems to demolish language itself.

The Birthday Party (1958), a play by Harold Pinter. Influenced by Beckett, this work is an early "comedy of menace" by one of England's leading playwrights.

Film (1965), a film with a screenplay written by Samuel Beckett. The only work of cinema by the leading absurdist playwright starred Buster Keaton, whose masterpieces of silent film comedy influenced the absurdist genre.

Rosencrantz and Guildenstern Are Dead (1966), a play by Tom Stoppard. Two minor characters wander in existential confusion on the outskirts of William Shakespeare's *Hamlet*.

Academy when it was discovered that a Swedish translator served on the Nobel selection committee. Although some detractors accused the translator of a conflict of interests the committee refused to deem any of the action involved inappropriate.

Very, Very Average   In October of 2000, the Nobel Prize committee awarded its literature prize to Gao for his "oeuvre of universal validity, bitter insights, and linguistic ingenuity, which has opened new paths for the Chinese novel and drama." Because no Chinese writer had ever received the Nobel Prize in Literature and because Gao was a blacklisted exile, many assumed that his selection was a political gesture intended to rile the Chinese government. (In fact, following the Nobel committee's announcement, a spokesman for the Chinese Writer's Association stated that all other Chinese writers found his work to be "very, very average," according to Jonathan Mirsky in the *International Herald-Tribune*.) However, Gao's work is more appropriately viewed as individual self-expression rather than political expression. In his Nobel Prize speech, Gao warned that "once literature is contrived as the hymn of the nation, the flag of the race, the mouthpiece of a political party or the voice of a class or a group, it can be employed as a mighty and all-engulfing tool of propaganda."

The Nobel committee singled out *Soul Mountain* and *One Man's Bible* for particular praise. In the *Wall Street Journal*, Peter Hessler described *Soul Mountain* as "mostly about uncovering layered tales deep in the countryside of the Chinese interior." It is a far-reaching blend of narratives, styles, and characters, with a constantly changing viewpoint, while *One Man's Bible* is an autobiographical recollection of Gao's years during the Cultural Revolution. When asked if he would go back to China, Gao remarked to Rekdal in the *New York Times Magazine*, "I don't consider myself to have cut myself off from my roots. But China remains an authoritarian state, and I don't plan on returning while I'm alive. That said, China is still in my blood. I have my own personal China; I don't need to go there."

Western Reach Some Western reviewers have noted that Gao's experiences in the Cultural Revolution and its aftermath may remain beyond the understanding of readers in the liberal West. Overseas productions of Gao's plays, strongly Chinese in their production values, have provoked similar concerns about the difficulties of translating the subtle traditions of an alien culture. Recent criticism, however, has noted Gao's achievements in bridging Eastern and Western elements. By invoking the European techniques of absurdist theater, while grounding his dramas in Chinese aesthetic traditions derived from Taoism and Zen Buddhism, Gao developed a way to surpass the limitations of socialist realism and rejuvenate Chinese literature.

Responses to Literature

1. Gao's writing often seems to be a tool for uncovering past events that have been obscured by political forces, such as the Cultural Revolution. Consider his use of Chinese history and folk traditions in *Soul Mountain*. Would you say that the preservation of the past through art is a driving motivation of the book? If so, why does it matter? If not, then what is Gao's preoccupation with stories of the past, both ancient and recent?

2. Using your library and the Internet, find out more about the Taoist philosophy. Do you think Gao's ideas of human dignity and freedom are related to ancient Chinese Taoism?

3. Find out more about China's Cultural Revolution by watching *China: A Century of Revolution* (2007), a three-DVD documentary on twentieth-century China.

BIBLIOGRAPHY

Books

Draguet, Michel. *Gao Xingjian: The Taste of Ink*. Paris: Hazan, 2002.

Goldblatt, Howard, ed. *Worlds Apart: Recent Chinese Writing and Its Audiences*. New York: M. E. Sharpe, 1990.

Lovell, Julia. *The Politics of Cultural Capital: China's Quest for a Nobel Prize in Literature*. Honolulu: University of Hawaii Press, 2006.

Luk, Yun-Tong, ed. *Studies in Chinese-Western Comparative Drama*. Hong Kong: Chinese University Press, 1990.

Ren, Quah Sy. *Gao Xingjian and Transcultural Chinese Theater*. Honolulu: University of Hawaii Press, 2004.

Tam, Kwok-kan, ed. *Soul of Chaos: Critical Perspectives on Gao Xingjian*. Hong Kong: Chinese University Press, 2001.

Zhao, Henry Y. H. *Towards a Modern Zen Theatre: Gao Xingjian and Chinese Theatre Experimentalism*. London: SOAS Publications, 2000.

Periodicals

Hessler, Peter. *Wall Street Journal* (December 15, 2000): W10.

Larson, Wendy. "Realism, Modernism, and the Anti-'Spiritual Pollution' Campaign in Modern China." *Modern China* 15 (1989): 37–71.

Lee, Mabel. "Pronouns as Protagonists: Gao Xingjian's *Lingshan* as Autobiography." *China Studies* 5 (1999): 165–83.

Lin, Sylvia Li-chun. "Between the Individual and the Collective: Gao Xingjian's Fiction." *World Literature Today* (Winter 2001): 20–30.

Mirsky, Jonathan. *International Herald-Tribune* (October 10, 2000).

Moran, Thomas. "Lost in the Woods: Nature in *Soul Mountain*." *Modern Chinese Literature and Culture* (Fall 2002): 207–36.

Rekdal Paisley. *New York Times Magazine* (December 10, 2000): 51.

◈ Lu Xun

BORN: *1881, Shaoxing, China*

DIED: *1936, Shanghai, China*

NATIONALITY: *Chinese*

GENRE: *Fiction, nonfiction, poetry*

MAJOR WORKS:
"Diary of a Madman" (1918)
The True Story of Ah Q (1927)
Selected Stories of Lu Xun (1954)
Dawn Blossoms Plucked at Dusk (1976)

Overview

Chinese writer Lu Xun is widely regarded as the founder of modern Chinese literature. His writings addressed

Lu Xun   © *Bettmann / CORBIS*

emy in Nanking in 1898, he transferred to the School of Railways and Mines, graduating in 1901. He then won a government scholarship to study medicine in Japan. After two years of Japanese language study in Tokyo, he entered the Sendai Provincial Medical School in the summer of 1904.

In the early twentieth century, China was a country in the midst of great transformation. Beginning with the Boxer Rebellion of 1900 (in which the peasantry revolted against foreigners), and moving on to the Russo-Japanese War, the Revolution of 1911 (which ended the Ch'ing Dynasty), the New Culture Movement (which spurned traditionalism and embraced social democracy), and the May Fourth Movement of 1919 (which sought national independence and individual freedoms), China was redefining itself in many ways. It was this shifting political and social landscape that inspired and colored Lu Xun's writing.

Thus, after witnessing the humiliation of China in the Russo-Japanese War of 1904–1905, Lu Xun turned his attention to writing as a means of awakening the Chinese people to the need for revolution. The major essays of his early period were published in 1908 in *Henan*. In one essay, he analyzes the rise and problems of the West, drawing conclusions relevant to China's modernization process. In another he criticizes China's gentry for blaming the country's backwardness on the "ignorance and superstition" of the peasants, rather than admitting their own responsibility. *Henan* was banned by the Japanese government at the request of the Qing authorities before Zhou could publish a sequel.

Disappointed by the failure of the masses to respond to his writings, however, and discouraged by the failure of the Revolution of 1911, Lu Xun abandoned his crusade and spent most of the years 1909 to 1919 publishing studies of traditional Chinese literature and art.

important political and cultural issues associated with communism and the modernization of China. His story "Diary of a Madman" was published in 1918, and is one of the more famous stories in the canon of Chinese literature.

Works in Biographical and Historical Context

A Strong Mother   Lu Xun was the pen name of Zhou Shuren, who was born September 25, 1881, into a poor but educated family in the Zhejiang province of China. He and his two younger brothers received a classical Chinese education based on Confucian texts. His family's financial situation deteriorated during his early years because of his grandfather's imprisonment for bribery; family resources were exhausted in appeals for clemency for his grandfather. Then his father died during his teenage years. Lu Xun's mother, educated and independent, held the family together during Lu Xun's first seventeen years and had a powerful influence on him throughout his life.

Education and Loss of Heart   As was typical of many intellectuals of his generation, Lu Xun chose other educational paths after his early grounding in Confucianism. After studying briefly in the Jiangnan Naval Acad-

Writing Success   After Lu Xun's return to China, he took a job teaching in his hometown. When the 1911 revolution began, Zhou was teaching in a middle school in Shaoxing. He was among the first to realize that though the Qing Dynasty had been overthrown, little else had changed. In fact, warlords, old-style gentry, and opportunists of every sort took over the government at the national and local levels, and the weak, far from being liberated, became victims. He addresses the failure of the revolution in several of his short stories and particularly with the black humor of his novella "A Q zheng zhuan" (1923), translated as "Our Story of Ah Q," (1941).

In April 1918, Lu Xun began to contribute stories to *Xin qingnian* (New Youth), a liberal magazine with a nationwide circulation; it was a principal mouthpiece of the New Culture movement, which was closely allied with the May Fourth Movement. He first used the pen name Lu Xun for the story "Kuangren riji" (translated as "Diary of a Madman," 1981) in the May 1918 issue of

LITERARY AND HISTORICAL CONTEMPORARIES

Lu Xun's famous contemporaries include:

Zhu De (1886–1976): Chinese statesman who founded the Chinese Red Army.

Hu Shi (1892–1962): Essayist who promoted the Vernacular Chinese style, which made writing accessible to the less educated.

Mao Zedong (1893–1976): Controversial Communist leader of the People's Republic of China.

Allen Ginsberg (1926–1997): Famous American Beat poet who openly idealized China and praised communism.

Xin gingnian. In keeping with the New Culture movement, the short story was critical of traditional Confucian ideas. It was the first significant Chinese literary effort that was written in the vernacular, as opposed to the elevated prose of traditional literature, and for this reason, Lu Xun is regarded as the father of modern Chinese literature.

Impact on China   Lu Xun went on to write many more major short stories, essays, poems, and literary criticism in the vernacular style. Among the most celebrated of these were "The True Story of Ah Q," and "The New Year's Sacrifice," (1924), which looked at the oppression of women. His influence was such that by the turn of the twenty-first century, Lu Xun's works had been translated into approximately fifty languages and published in over thirty countries.

Lu Xun's politics were decidedly leftist throughout his life, although he declined to ever formally join the Chinese Communist Party. His support for the 1926 Beijing student rebellion forced him to leave the city, and he settled in Shanghai in the late 1920s. There he continued to write and work, while serving as the head of the League of Left-Wing Writers. He founded a magazine, the *Torrent,* in 1928 and edited others. On October 19, 1936, Lu Xun died of tuberculosis, a highly contagious disease that affects the lungs.

Works in Literary Context

Lu Xun wrote poetry, short stories, and essays. While his essays tend to be dry and sardonic, his prose is introspective. In addition to writing about his characters—their appearance, personality traits, and actions—Lu Xun delved into the inner conciousness of his characters. He wrote extensively about what his characters were thinking and feeling. One of Lu Xun's most memorable characters is Ah Q.

The Everyman   Ah Q is a peasant who views himself as a winner. He is a new Everyman, an international symbol of human folly whose penchant for self-delusion is evident: Whenever he is humiliated by a rival, he quickly turns the experience around in his mind and imagines himself to have come out on top. "The True Story of Ah Q" is often read as a national allegory, though when it was published, several individuals thought themselves to be the butt of the satire; some wrote letters to the newspaper in protest.

Tradition and Superstition   In "The New-Year Sacrifice," (1981), Lu Xun confronts the May Fourth movement, which rejected traditional literature and applauded modern prose. The narrator is an intellectual who has come home for a visit and worries about a peasant woman, a widow whose son was carried off by a wolf. She presses the narrator with the question, "When people die, do their souls live on?" Not knowing the context of her question and hoping to comfort her, he suggests that there may, indeed, be life after death. The answer only increases her anxiety. The story ends with a passage describing the narrator's reaction to the Lunar New Year celebration immediately after her death.

Much of the story has to do with the narrator's inability to communicate meaningfully with the townspeople; thus, it encapsulates the tragedy not only of the peasant woman but also of China's modern intelligentsia and their inability to change, or even influence, conditions in the country.

Works in Critical Context

Lu Xun's initial fame rested on a series of sometimes bleak, sometimes humorous, often satirical short stories written in the modern Chinese vernacular. He gained renewed fame and influence as a master of the feuilleton, which he wielded as a rhetorical dagger first against the warlord government in Beijing in the late 1920s and then in the 1930s against the Nationalist Party. He was not afraid to use his pen against oppression and express his ideological concerns.

Commenting on the author in a *Xinhua News Agency* article, Kitaoka Masako noted: "Without a thorough understanding of Lu Xun, it's impossible to know about China." In the same article, Maruyama Noboru commented that "The works of Lu Xun and the spirit they carried have transcended every impediment on ideology and last far beyond his age."

"Diary of a Madman"   Lu Xun's first short story, "Diary of a Madman," was written in modern Chinese. This groundbreaking story is considered one of the first Western-style stories in China. The story established the theme with which Lu Xun became identified by most of his Chinese readers: the denunciation of traditional ethical codes as hypocritical cant formulated by the oppressors to justify an inhumane order that permits the strong to prey on the weak.

A contributor to the Pegasos Web site noted: "The narrator, who thinks he is held captive by cannibals, sees the oppressive nature of tradition as a 'man-eating' society." The writer added that the author's "tour de force helped gain acceptance for the short-story form as an effective literary vehicle" in China. Lu Xun later wrote that he had used cannibalism in this story as a metaphor for exploitation and inhumanity.

"The True Story of Ah Q" Lu Xun's most famous story, "The True Story of Ah Q," tells the tale of a poor, uneducated farm laborer who not only suffers but seems to readily accept a series of humiliations that finally end in his execution during the 1911 revolution. Throughout his ordeals, the protagonist blames himself for his troubles or holds on to a misguided belief that it all must be for the better. "It is a mentality that people recognize as universal," commented Sue Fan in an article by Sandy Yang in the *Daily Bruin* of the University of California at Los Angeles. "By looking at human nature, we all have our way of rationalizing our actions. It is a survival mechanism to look at the brighter side of things even when you're being humiliated."

In a critical essay in *East Asia: An International Quarterly*, Rujie Wang called the tale "a brilliant satire" and went on to note: "In Lu Xun's text, everybody, Ah Q as well as the villagers of Weizhuang, prefers existing knowledge to anything new and original. No one in the village is bothered with finding the truth of what really goes on." Wang added, "As an absurd hero whose tragedy has absolutely no redeeming qualities, Ah Q exists to ridicule the views and values the anti-traditionalist intellectuals have gladly declared bankrupt, values which have been affirmed in the past by many tragic heroes confronted with similar calamities."

Responses to Literature

1. Compare and contrast "Diary of a Madman" and "Upstairs in a Wine Shop." In your analysis, consider how traditions and modernism are viewed by the characters. Explain the meaning of Lu Xun's line "Save the children."

2. After reading "The True Story of Ah Q," discuss Ah Q's view of his situation. What message do you think the author is making about Chinese traditions?

3. Lu Xun often chose to write satirically. Discuss why satire is a suitable approach when writing about politics.

BIBLIOGRAPHY

Books

Hsia, Tsi-an. *The Gate of Darkness: Studies on the Leftist Literary Movement in China*. Seattle: University of Washington Press, 1968.

Huang, Songkang. *Lu Hsün and the New Culture Movement of Modern China*. Amsterdam: Djambatan, 1957.

Kowallis, Jon Eugene von. *The Lyrical Lu Xun: A Study of His Classical-Style Verse*. Honolulu: University of Hawaii Press, 1996.

Lu Xun. *Dictionary of Literary Biography*, Volume 328: *Chinese Fiction Writers*, 1900–1949. A Bruccoli Clark Layman Book. Middlebury College. Ed. Thomas Moran. Detroit: Gale, 2007, pp. 129–50.

Lyell, Jr., William A. *Lu Hsün's Vision of Reality*. Berkeley: University of California Press, 1976.

Wang, Shiquing. *Lu Xun: A Biography*. Beijing: Foreign Languages Press, 1984.

Periodicals

Duke, Michael S. "The Lyrical Lu Xun: A Study of His Classical-Style Verse." *World Literature Today*, (Winter 1998): 203.

Wan, Rujie. "Lu Xun's 'The True Story of Ah Q' and Cross-Writing." *East Asia: An International Quarterly*, (Autumn 1998): 5.

Xinhua News Agency, (April 21, 2001); (October 7, 2001); (October 28, 2001); (December 20, 2001).

Yang, Sally. "Tale Cues in Essence of Individuality; Performance: 'Ah Q' Combines Dance, Theater to Critique Human Nature." *Daily Bruin* (University of California, Los Angeles), (December 3, 1998).

■ Koizumi Yakumo

SEE *Lafcadio Hearn*

◈ William Butler Yeats

BORN: *1865, Dublin*

DIED: *1939, Roquebrune, France*

NATIONALITY: *Irish*

GENRE: *Poetry, plays, essays*

MAJOR WORKS:

The Wind Among the Reeds (1899)

The Wild Swans at Coole (1917)

A Vision (1925)

The Tower (1928)

*The Winding Stair and
    Other Poems* (1933)

Overview

William Butler Yeats was an Irish poet and playwright closely associated with Irish nationalism. He received the 1923 Nobel Prize in Literature "for his always inspired poetry, which in a highly artistic form gives expression to the spirit of a whole nation," as the citation read.

William Butler Yeats *Howard Coster / Hulton Archive / Getty Images*

Works in Biographical and Historical Context

An Anglo-Irish Protestant Upbringing Yeats belonged to the Protestant, Anglo-Irish minority that had controlled the economic, political, social, and cultural life of Ireland since at least the end of the seventeenth century. Most members of this minority considered themselves English people who merely happened to have been born in Ireland, but Yeats staunchly affirmed his Irish nationality. Although he lived in London for fourteen years of his childhood (and kept a permanent home there during the first half of his adult life), Yeats maintained his cultural roots by featuring Irish legends and heroes in many of his poems and plays. He was equally firm in adhering to his self-image as an artist.

Yeats was born in the Dublin suburb of Sandymount on June 13, 1865. He was the oldest of the four surviving children of the painter-philosopher John Butler Yeats and his wife, Susan Pollexfen Yeats. The poet was proud to belong to the Anglo-Irish Protestant minority in both strains of his blood. His mother's family were ship owners and millers in and about Sligo. The hills and lakes and fens about the busy West of Ireland seaside town became Yeats's spiritual home in childhood and remained so all his life. The young Yeats was dreamy and introspective but by no means housebound. He rode about the Sligo countryside on a red pony and began to immerse himself in the fairy lore of the local peasants. His formal education, however, was not so enriching. He was so slow in learning to read that he was thought to be simple

The Influence of Maud Gonne on Yeats's Nationalism and Spiritualism The year 1885 was important in Yeats's early adult life, marking the first publication of his poetry (in the *Dublin University Review*) and the beginning of his important interest in the occult. At the end of 1886, Yeats moved to London, where he composed poems, plays, novels, and short stories—all with Irish subjects, characters, and scenes. In addition, he wrote book reviews, usually on Irish topics. The most important event in Yeats's life during these London years, however, was his acquaintance with Maud Gonne, a beautiful, prominent young woman passionately devoted to Irish nationalism—the establishment of an Irish nation independent of British rule. Irish nationalism had grown in fits and starts since 1800, when Ireland was forcefully joined with Great Britain in the British Act of Union. In the 1880s and 1890s, Irish politician Charles Stewart Parnell managed to introduce two bills on Irish Home Rule in British Parliament, but both were defeated. It became clear to the Irish that they would not find independence through negotiation alone.

Yeats soon fell in love with Gonne and wrote many of his best poems about her. With Gonne's encouragement, Yeats redoubled his dedication to Irish nationalism and produced such nationalistic plays as *The Countess Kathleen*, dedicated to Gonne, and *Cathleen ni Houlihan* (1902), which featured Gonne as the personification of Ireland.

Gonne also shared Yeats's interest in occultism and spiritualism. In 1890 he joined the Golden Dawn, a secret society that practiced ritual magic. The society offered instruction and initiation in a series of ten levels, the three highest of which were unattainable except by magi, who were thought to possess the secrets of supernatural wisdom and enjoy magically extended lives. Yeats remained an active member of the Golden Dawn for thirty-two years and achieved the coveted sixth grade of membership in 1914, the same year that his future wife, Georgiana Hyde-Lees, joined the society. Yeats's 1899 poetry collection *The Wind Among the Reeds* featured several poems employing occult symbolism.

The Abbey Theatre   The turn of the century marked Yeats's increased interest in theater, an interest influenced by his father, a famed artist and orator. In the summer of 1897, Yeats enjoyed his first stay at Coole Park, the County Galway estate of Lady Augusta Gregory. He, Lady Gregory, and her neighbor, Edward Martyn, devised plans for promoting an innovative, native Irish drama. In 1899 they staged the first of three annual productions in Dublin, including Yeats's *The Countess Kathleen*. In 1902 they supported a company of amateur Irish actors in staging both George Russell's Irish legend *Deirdre* and Yeats's *Cathleen ni Houlihan*. The success of these productions led to the founding of the Irish National Theatre Society, of which Yeats became president. With a wealthy sponsor volunteering to pay for the renovation of Dublin's Abbey Theatre as a permanent home for the company, the theater opened on December 27, 1904, and featured plays by the company's three directors: Lady Gregory, John M. Synge (whose 1907 production *The Playboy of the Western World* would spark controversy with its savage comic depiction of Irish rural life), and Yeats, who opened that night with *On Baile's Strand*, the first of his several plays featuring the heroic ancient Irish warrior Cuchulain.

The Easter Rising   While Yeats fulfilled his duties as president of the Abbey Theatre group for the first fifteen years of the twentieth century, his nationalistic fervor waned. Maud Gonne, with whom he had shared his Irish enthusiasms, had moved to Paris with her husband, exiled Irish revolutionary John MacBride, and the author was left without her important encouragement. His emotion was reawakened in 1916's Easter Rising, an unsuccessful, six-day armed rebellion of Irish republicans against the British in Dublin. MacBride, who was now separated from Gonne, participated in the rebellion and was executed afterward. Yeats reacted by writing "Easter, 1916," an eloquent expression of his feelings of shock and admiration. The Easter Rising contributed to Yeats's eventual decision to reside in Ireland rather than England, and his marriage to Georgianna Hyde-Lees in 1917 further strengthened that resolve. Once married, Yeats traveled

LITERARY AND HISTORICAL CONTEMPORARIES

Yeats's famous contemporaries include:

Madame Blavatsky (1831–1891): A world-renowned psychic medium, Blavatsky founded the Theosophical Society.

Isabella Augusta, Lady Gregory (1852–1932): Lady Gregory was one of the founders of the Abbey Theatre, as well as Yeats's lifelong benefactor.

John MacBride (1865–1916): This Irish Nationalist married Maud Gonne, the love of Yeats's life, and was executed for his part in the Easter Rebellion of 1916.

John Millington Synge (1871–1909): Synge was an Abbey Theatre playwright who wrote *The Playboy of the Western World* (1907).

James Joyce (1882–1941): A famous Irish novelist, Joyce is most known for the modern epic *Ulysses* (1922) and the autobiographical *A Portrait of the Artist as a Young Man* (1916).

with his bride to Thoor Ballylee, a medieval stone tower where the couple periodically resided.

In the 1920s, Ireland was full of internal strife. In 1921 bitter controversies erupted within the new Irish Free State over the partition of Northern Ireland and over the wording of a formal oath of allegiance to the British Crown. These issues led to the Irish Civil War, which lasted from June 1922 to May 1923. Yeats emphatically sided with the new Irish government in this conflict. He accepted a six-year appointment to the senate of the Irish Free State in December 1922, a time when rebels were kidnapping government figures and burning their homes. In Dublin, where Yeats had assumed permanent residence in 1922, the government posted armed sentries at his door. As senator, Yeats considered himself a representative of order amid the new nation's chaotic progress toward stability. He was now the "sixty-year-old smiling public man" of his poem "Among School Children," which he wrote after touring an Irish elementary school. But he was also a world renowned artist of impressive stature; he received the Nobel Prize for Literature in 1923.

Old Age and Last Poems   The poems and plays Yeats created during his senate term and beyond are, at once, local and general, personal and public, Irish and universal. The energy of the poems written in response to these disturbing times gave power to his collection *The Tower*, which is often considered his best single book. Another important element of these later poems is Yeats's keen awareness of old age. His romantic poems from the late 1890s often mention gray hair and weariness, though those poems were written while he was still a young

COMMON HUMAN EXPERIENCE

Yeats's ideas and themes, while varied, were mired in his love for Ireland, and his imagery was often centered around Irish landscape and folklore. Here are some other works with significantly nationalistic themes.

Dr. Zhivago (1956), by Boris Pasternak. This torrid love story is set during the turbulent Russian Revolution of 1917.

One Hundred Years of Solitude (1967), by Gabriel García Márquez. Set in the fictional town of Macondo, this novel is an extended metaphor about Colombian and South American history.

The Journals of Susanna Moodie (1970), by Margaret Atwood. Chronicles the trials and tribulations of a woman living in the Canadian wilderness in the late nineteenth century.

Disgrace (1999), by J.M. Coetzee. The protagonist of this novel set in Cape Town must confront a number of difficult issues in post-apartheid South Africa.

man. When Yeats was nearly sixty, his health began to fail, and he faced what he called "bodily decrepitude" that was real, not imaginary. Despite the author's keen awareness of his physical decline, the last fifteen years of his life were marked by extraordinary vitality and appetite. He continued to write plays, including "The Words upon the Window Pane," a full-length work about spiritualism and the eighteenth-century Irish writer Jonathan Swift. In 1929, as an expression of thankful joy after recovering from serious illness, he also wrote a series of brash, vigorous poems narrated by a fictitious old peasant woman, "Crazy Jane."

Yeats faced death with a courage that was founded partly on his vague hope for reincarnation and partly on his admiration for the bold heroism that he perceived in Ireland in both ancient times and the eighteenth century. He died, after a series of illnesses, in 1939, and after a quick burial in France, was exhumed and reburied in his beloved Sligo. His epitaph, one of the most famous of tombstone inscriptions, comes from his own poem "Under Ben Bulben": "Cast a cold eye / On life, on death. / Horseman, pass by!"

Works in Literary Context

Yeats was, from first to last, a poet who tried to transform the concerns of his own life by embodying them in the universal language of his poems. His brilliant rhetorical accomplishments, strengthened by his considerable powers of rhythm and poetic phrase, have earned wide praise from readers and from fellow poets, including W.H. Auden (who praised Yeats as the savior of English lyric poetry),

Stephen Spender, Theodore Roethke, and Philip Larkin. It is not likely that time will diminish his achievements.

Ireland's Writer In 1885 Yeats met John O'Leary, a famous patriot who had returned to Ireland after twenty years of imprisonment and exile for revolutionary activities. O'Leary had a keen enthusiasm for Irish books, music, and ballads, and he encouraged young writers to adopt Irish subjects. Yeats, who had preferred more romantic settings and themes, soon took O'Leary's advice, producing many poems based on Irish legends, Irish folklore, and Irish ballads and songs. He explained in a note included in the 1908 volume *Collected Works in Verse and Prose of William Butler Yeats*: "When I first wrote I went here and there for my subjects as my reading led me, and preferred to all other countries Arcadia and the India of romance, but presently I convinced myself...that I should never go for the scenery of a poem to any country but my own, and I think that I shall hold to that conviction to the end." Indeed, Yeats turned almost exclusively to the folklore, culture, history, and landscape of Ireland for his inspiration.

Works in Critical Context

For many years, Yeats's intent interest in subjects that others labeled archaic delayed his recognition among his peers. At the time of his death in 1939, Yeats's views on poetry were regarded as eccentric by students and critics alike. This attitude held sway in spite of critical awareness of the beauty and technical proficiency of his verse. Yeats had long opposed the notion that literature should serve society. As a youthful critic he had refused to praise the poor lyrics of the "Young Ireland" poets merely because they were effective as nationalist propaganda.

In maturity, he found that despite his success, his continuing conviction that poetry should express the spiritual life of the individual estranged him from those who believed that a modern poet must take as his themes social alienation and the barrenness of materialist culture. As Kathleen Raine wrote of him: "Against a rising tide of realism, political verse and University wit, Yeats upheld the innocent and the beautiful, the traditional and the noble," and in consequence of his disregard for the concerns of the modern world, was often misunderstood. As critics became disenchanted with modern poetic trends, Yeats's romantic dedication to the laws of the imagination and art for art's sake became more acceptable.

Indeed, critics today are less concerned with the validity of Yeats's occult and visionary theories than with their symbolic value as expressions of timeless ideals.

The Winding Stair and Other Poems The *Winding Stair and Other Poems* (1933) includes sixty-four poems in a wide range of form and tone. The volume opens with the beautiful romantic rhapsody "In Memory of Eva Gore-Booth and Con Markiewicz," addressing the horse-riding Gore-Booth sisters of his Sligo youth, remembered as "Two girls in silk kimonos, both / Beautiful, one a gazelle," but now "withered old and skeleton-gaunt" with time and political passion. The poem ends in an ecstasy of acceptance and defiance of tragic reality in which Yeats does not separate his own history from theirs.

The emblems of the tower and Sato's sword keep recurring in this volume. In the tiny poem "Symbols" the tower carries its usual connotations of withdrawal, contemplation, and arcane study, and the sword blade is violently active, "all-destroying." Yeats is both the tower's "blind hermit" and the "wandering fool" who carries the sword. But the tower is also the house of the marriage bed, and the phallic sword's housing is the feminine "gold-sewn silk" of the scabbard. So the final couplet couples the coupling of all the emblems: "Gold-sewn silk on the sword-blade / Beauty and fool together laid."

In "Blood and the Moon" Yeats abruptly alters the symbolic value of the tower, making it "my symbol" and emblematic of a self that is specifically Irish, involved in historical time and in the conflicting spiritual values that divide real personalities. "Quarrel in Old Age" of this volume describes Dublin offhandedly as "this blind bitter town," and "Remorse for Intemperate Speech" puts in capsule form the compacted bitterness that Yeats had long seen as genetic in Irish character: "Great hatred, little room, / Maimed us from the start." In "Blood and the Moon" his scene is contemporary Ireland, against which he erects his roofless tower: "In mockery of a time / Half dead at the top." Yeats's verse swoops and soars with his mind: "I declare this tower is my symbol; I declare / This winding, gyring, spiring treadmill of a stair is my ancestral stair; / That Goldsmith and the Dean, Berkeley and Burke have travelled there."

"The Second Coming" Based in part on his ideas in *A Vision*, "The Second Coming" has resonance today. The poem moves with a confident mastery, but here the vision is sweeping and apocalyptic, the rhetoric formal, grand, full of power, the structure that of two stately violent blank-verse paragraphs. In it, Yeats dramatizes his cyclical theory of history: that whole civilizations rotate in a "gyre" of about two thousand years, undergoing birth, life, and death and preparing all the while for the life of its opposing successor. The critical period of the "interchange of tinctures," when one era struggles to die and its "executioner" struggles to be born, will be violent and dreadful. Yeats's poem remembers war and revolution and inhabits an apocalyptic climate in which man has lost touch with God, with any center of order.

Essayist Joan Didion borrowed from the poem the title of her 1968 collection *Slouching Towards Bethlehem* and this is generally regarded as one of Yeats's most important and most widely anthologized poems.

Responses to Literature

1. Study Yeats's "The Second Coming" and construct a version of his gyres for today. What sorts of events and people do you think might be caught in the inter-secting cones? If Yeats were alive today, which political events do you think he would choose to include?

2. Read W.H. Auden's "In Memory of W.B. Yeats" and connect this eulogy to any five of Yeats's poems. Do you think Yeats would have felt "honored" by Auden's poem?

3. Read "Adam's Curse," "No Second Troy," and "When You Are Old" and determine 1) why you think these poems could be about Maud Gonne specifically and 2) whether Yeats was truly in love with her or merely obsessed with the idea of her.

BIBLIOGRAPHY

Books

Alldritt, Keith. *W.B. Yeats: The Man and the Milieu*. New York: Clarkson Potter, 1997.

Allen, James Lovic. *Yeats's Epitaph: A Key to Symbolic Unity in His Life and Work*. Washington, D.C.: University Press of America, 1982.

Bloom, Harold. *Yeats*. New York: Oxford University Press, 1970.

Brown, Terence. *The Life of W.B. Yeats: A Critical Biography*. Malden, Mass.: Blackwell, 1999.

Chaudhry, Yug Mohit. *Yeats, the Irish Literary Revival, and the Politics of Print*. Cork, Ireland: Cork University Press, 2001.

Doggett, Rob. *Deep-Rooted Things: Empire and Nation in the Poetry and Drama of William Butler Yeats*. Notre Dame, Ind.: University of Notre Dame Press, 2006.

Finneran, Richard J. ed., *Critical Essays on W. B. Yeats*. Boston: G.K. Hall, 1986.

Fletcher, Ian. *W.B. Yeats and His Contemporaries*. New York: St. Martin's Press, 1987.

Hall, James, and Martin Steinmann, eds.,*The Permanence of Yeats*. New York: Collier, 1961.

MacBride, Maud Gonne.*A Servant of the Queen*. Dublin, Ireland: Golden Eagle, 1950.

Marcus, Phillip L. *Yeats and the Beginning of the Irish Renaissance*. Ithaca, N.Y.: Cornell University Press, 1970.

Robinson, Lenox. *Ireland's Abbey Theatre: A History 1869-1951*. London: Sidgwick & Jackson, 1951; Port Washington, N.Y.: Kennikat Press, 1968.

Vendler, Helen H. *Yeats's "Vision" and the Later Plays*. Cambridge, Mass.: Harvard University Press, 1963.

A. B. Yehoshua

BORN: *1936, Jerusalem, Palestine (now Israel)*

NATIONALITY: *Israeli*

GENRE: *Fiction, nonfiction, drama*

MAJOR WORKS:

Over against the Woods (1968)

Three Days and a Child (1970)

Between Right and Right (1981)

A Late Divorce (1983)

Five Seasons (1989)

Overview

A. B. Yehoshua is one of Israel's foremost contemporary fiction writers. He is a member of "the generation of the state," the first generation to come of age after Israel was proclaimed an independent state in 1948. One of Israel's most important social critics, his political and social commentaries appear both in his fiction and as essays in Israeli newspapers and magazines. Yehoshua's works have been translated into numerous languages and eight of his works have been adapted for film and television.

Works in Biographical and Historical Context

Childhood in the New Jewish State Abraham B. Yehoshua was born on December 9, 1936, in Jerusalem, Palestine, to Yakov and Malka Rosilio Yehoshua; he was a member of the fifth generation of a Sephardic Jerusalemite family. A child during World War II (1939–1945) and the Nazi-directed Holocaust of six million Jews throughout Europe, he was eleven years old when the nation of Israel was formed from a portion of what had

A. B. Yehoshua *Yehoshua, A.B., photograph. AP Images.*

once been Palestine, an event that both fulfilled Jewish dreams of a permanent homeland and brought resistance from Arab Muslims. The largely Muslim Palestinians had fought for independence of these same lands from Turkish rulers three decades before. This led to decades of conflict between Israelis and their Arab neighbors, conflict that remains far from resolved; it is this tension more than any other that has shaped the work of Yehoshua and other Israeli writers of his generation.

A Background in Hebrew Literature and Philosophy After serving in the Israeli Army as a paratrooper in the Nachal unit from 1954 to 1957—during the Suez Crisis of 1956, in which Britain, France, and Israel fought to eject Egyptian forces from the Suez Canal region, which Egypt had decided to nationalize—Yehoshua attended the Hebrew University in Jerusalem. There he studied Hebrew literature and philosophy. He graduated in 1961, a year after marrying Rivka Kirsninski, a psychoanalyst, on June 14, 1960. They had three children: Sivan, Gideon, and Naum. Yehoshua then began a high school and university teaching career, starting in Paris, where he lived and worked from 1963 to 1967. In 1972 Yehoshua took a position with the University of Haifa in Israel, where he is currently a professor of literature.

A "New Wave" Writer Yehoshua began publishing fiction after his military service. He gained his first critical attention with short-story collections such as *The Death of an Old Man* (1962) and *Over against the Woods* (1968) and an early novella, *Early in the Summer of 1970* (1972). By the early 1970s he had become a notable figure in the "new wave" generation of Israeli writers and had collected several awards to testify to this—including the 1961 Akum Prize, second prize in the 1964 Kol-Yisrael Competition for his radio script *The Professor's Secret*, the 1968 Municipality of Ramat-Gan Prize for his short-story collection *Over against the Woods*, and the 1972 Prime Minister Prize. Yehoshua also earned a University of Iowa fellowship in the international literature program, which he took in 1969. Throughout this period, Israel was periodically at war with its neighbors—Egypt, Lebanon, Syria, and Iran, especially—and much of Yehoshua's fiction includes responses to this state of near-perpetual war, the ongoing Arab-Israeli conflict.

Multiple and Prestigious Literary Awards Yehoshua's first novel, *The Lover* (1977), was controversial in Israel because of its criticisms of Israeli society, but this was not representative of the author's reception at home. Yehoshua's second novel, *A Late Divorce* (1982), was praised for its critical depiction of a Jew who leaves Israel to start a new life in America. That same year Yehoshua was awarded the Brener Prize by the Hebrew Writers Association. A year later, Yehoshua was awarded the Alterman Prize (1986), and a year before he was to receive the Bialik Prize (1988), he published his third novel, *Five Seasons* (1987; published in the U.S.A. in 1989). The work was equally well received, while his next novel, *Mr Mani* (1990), earned the author one of England's highest accolades as it was named Best Novel of the Year.

The 1990s continued to prove successful for Yehoshua: As he garnered ever more accolades for his writing in both reviews and honorifics, he moved away from political and social morality issues and looked to history in *A Journey to the End of the Millennium* (1997), a historical novel set in the year 999. With *A Late Divorce* Yehoshua told the *New York Times Book Review*'s Laurel Graeber that he had "wanted to understand the present by digging through the layers of the past." With *A Journey to the End of the Millennium* he uses an intricate tale of a medieval merchant's travels and marriages to illuminate a rich moment in Jewish history.

A Controversial Success Yehoshua has continued to publish novels and short-story collections in the 2000s. His 2006 novel *A Woman in Jerusalem* won the Los Angeles Times Book Prize of the same year, but has also attracted much criticism for its controversial message that the only authentic Jewish identity to be found today must be found in Israel and in Zionism, in the promise and practice of a Jewish state. He also continues to teach and to write from his home in Haifa—to the pleasure of readers, critics, and scholars alike. According to the Institute for the Translation of Hebrew Literature, his 1989 novel *Five Seasons* is one of the ten most important books since the creation of the State of Israel.

Works in Literary Context

Influences According to David Wiley at the *Minnesota Daily*, Yehoshua names Shmuel Yosef Agnon, William Faulkner, and Franz Kafka as his influences. It therefore makes sense that he is described by the *New York Times* as "a kind of Israeli Faulkner," and that critics have compared him with Franz Kafka—because of the abstract nature of his stories.

Abstract Fables? Many of Yehoshua's stories—such as *The Death of an Old Man* (1962) and *Over against the Woods* (1968)—are modern fables that are not necessarily set in any particular time or place; instead Yehoshua uses allegory to comment on contemporary Israel and humanity in general.

For example, *A Late Divorce* (1983) concerns an Israeli who has immigrated to the United States and later returns home to obtain a divorce. The man finds his family in a state of decay, which some critics considered a symbol for the decline of Israel. Yehoshua explained, "I don't claim the family is a symbol of Israel, but there is a layer of allegory—the imbalance between the father and mother, which does not create proper relations for the health of the family. Like the father, who gives up his responsibilities and goes to America, Jews who leave Israel for America are escaping their responsibility."

Jewish and Generational Themes Yehoshua's fiction treats concerns that have arisen in his generation: such political problems as the ongoing Arab-Israeli conflict; such moral dilemmas as the danger of clinging to the Zionist dream without facing the reality of Palestinian demands; and such social issues as the emigration from Israel of the younger generation and its loss of faith in the Zionist ideology that created Israel. For instance, for the story "Facing the Forests," which appeared in *Three Days and a Child* (1970), scholars and critics have offered a variety of interpretations. A frustrated and disaffected Israeli graduate student takes a job as a forest ranger. He ultimately acts as a silent accomplice when an Arab burns down the forest that had displaced his village. In the context of the Arab-Israeli conflict, the story has been seen as an illustration of the younger generation's ambivalence and lack of faith in Israel. On a more universal level, the story has been interpreted as a commentary on humanity's tendency toward unmotivated evil and isolation.

Works in Critical Context

Critics of Yehoshua's early story collections such as *The Death of an Old Man* (1962) and *Three Days and a Child* (1968) compared him with Franz Kafka because of the abstract or surrealistic nature of his stories. And such novels as *A Late Divorce* (1983)—a family saga that employs a series of different narrators to explore psychological and moral questions—they compare to William Faulkner's *The Sound and the Fury* (1929). And though

COMMON HUMAN EXPERIENCE

Although much of Yehoshua's work is centered on Israeli concerns, certain characteristics give his fiction universal significance: his underlying theme of the alienation and isolation of humankind and the careful development of the psychological state of his characters, for example. Here are a few works by writers who have also concerned themselves with the psychology of the alienated or isolated human:

Man's Search for Meaning (1946), a nonfiction work by Viktor Frankl. In this powerful work, the Austrian neurologist and psychiatrist retells his experiences as a Holocaust survivor, putting forth a philosophy of alienation and suggesting a therapy of existential healing.

"The Metamorphosis" (1915), a short story by Franz Kafka. Kafka's classic investigation of man as an alienated being is conducted through the person/bug of Gregor Samsa, a traveling salesman who wakes one morning to find he cannot move because he has turned into a giant cockroach in the night and is stuck on his back in bed.

"A Rose for Emily" (1930), a short story by William Faulkner. In this story, Emily Grierson is alienated from her immediate society and is isolated in her aging, eccentric, and "spinster" years.

The Stranger (1942), a novel by Albert Camus. In this existentialist novel, the protagonist, Meursault, is less than sympathetic from the start as an alienated, damaged soul.

Lengthening Silence of a Poet," from his *Three Days and a Child* (1970), he portrays the impotence of the older generation and the lack of inner resources of the younger one. Consider one or more works by Yehoshua that reveal a commentary on the generations as contrasting groups. To what extent is each to blame for the problems faced by both?

2. Of Yehoshua's works critic Jerome Greenfield writes, "In the existential despair, the pessimism, the sense of dislocation and alienation that pervade his work, Yehoshua establishes a bridge between modern Israeli writing and a dominant stream of some of the best Western literature of our age . . . without abandoning . . . the everyday reality of Israeli life." Search the Internet for examples of everyday Israeli life—considering the culture, religion, government and politics, science, medicine, education, or other components. Then, find evidence of this "everyday reality" in one or more of the author's works. Does Greenfield's depiction ring true, based on your research?

3. In an effort to gain understanding of one of Israel's greatest political problems—the Arab-Israeli conflict—create a time line of events in Israeli history. Pick three of these events and discuss Yehoshua's response to these in two or more of his works, supporting your arguments with detailed analysis of passages from his writings.

4. Yehoshua's early short-story collections, such as *The Death of an Old Man* (1962) and *Three Days and a Child* (1968), have been labeled "modern fables." What does it mean for a fable to be "modern," and is this an appropriate description of Yehoshua's work?

BIBLIOGRAPHY

Books

Bloom, Harold. *A. B. Yehoshua*. London: Chelsea House, 1992.

Horn, Bernard. *Facing the Fires: Conversations with A. B. Yehoshua*. Syracuse, N.Y.: Syracuse University Press, 1997.

Periodicals

Ben-Dov, Nitza. "In the Back Yard of Agnon's House: Between the *Liberated Bride* by A. B. Yehoshua and S. Y. Agnon." *Hebrew Studies* 46 (2006): 237–51.

Graeber, Laurel. "Six Generations in Search of an Author." *New York Times Book Review*, March 1, 1993: 3.

Greenfield, Jerome. General Review, *Midstream* 25, no. 7 (August/September 1979): 48–54.

Shaked, Gershon. "Gershon Shaked Interviews A. B. Yehoshua." *Modern Hebrew Literature* 3 (Fall 2006): 157–69.

Wiley, David. "Talkin' 'bout His Generation: Israeli Writer A. B. Yehoshua on the Waning Art of the Democratic Novel." *Minnesota Daily*, 1997.

the extensive use of symbolism in Yehoshua's works is a characteristic some critics have found overwhelming, critical reaction as a whole has often focused more on the ideas Yehoshua presents than on his literary style.

Between Right and Right While being commended for his storytelling abilities, the psychological depth of his characters, his precise and evocative use of language, and for his structural innovations, Yehoshua is also acknowledged as one of Israel's most important social critics. Eminent literary critic and scholar Harold Bloom, describing *Between Right and Right* (1981) as "a polemic against the Diaspora," asserts that the essays within are important "efforts to reformulate the terms of identity, Jew, Zionist, Israeli." As the Jewish Virtual Library recounts the comments of *The Village Voice*, "Yehoshua's stories find their way right into the unconscious. Nobel prizes have been given for less."

Responses to Literature

1. In several of his stories Yehoshua positions one generation against another; for example, in "The

Web Sites

The Department for Jewish Zionist Education. "Yehoshua, A. B. (1936–)." Retrieved May 16, 2008, from http://www.jafi.org.il/education/100/people/BIOS/ab.html.

The Institute for the Translation of Hebrew Literature. "Abraham B. Yehoshua." Retrieved May 16, 2008, from http://www.ithl.org.il/author_info.asp?id=286.

Jewish Virtual Library. "Avraham B. Yehoshua (1936–)." Retrieved May 16, 2008, from http://www.jewishvirtuallibrary.org/jsource/biography/yehoshua.html.

Yevgeny Yevtushenko

BORN: *1933, Stanzia Zima, Siberia, USSR (now Russia)*

NATIONALITY: *Russian*

GENRE: *Poetry, fiction, drama, nonfiction*

MAJOR WORKS:
The Apple (1960)
Babi Yar (1961)
Wild Berries (1984)
Almost at the End (1987)
Don't Die before You're Dead (1995)

Yevgeny Yevtushenko   *Yevtushenko, Yevgeni, 1994, photograph. AP Images.*

Overview

Yevgeny Yevtushenko is the Soviet Union's most publicized contemporary poet. He became the leading literary spokesman for a generation of Russians in the post-Stalin era, and he is often considered one of the first dissident voices to speak out against Stalinism. His 1987 prose and poetry collection *Almost at the End* established him as a prominent spokesman for Soviet president Mikhail Gorbachev's glasnost campaign of political liberalization.

Works in Biographical and Historical Context

Born under the Sign of Stalin Yevgeny Yevtushenko was born on July 18, 1933, in Stanzia Zima, Siberia. His father Gangnus was a geologist, and his mother, Zinaida, was also a geologist, as well as being a singer. Yevtushenko's family was of mixed Ukrainian, Russian, and Tatar heritage. His maternal grandfather, Ermolai, was a Red Army officer during the Russian Revolution and the civil war; both Ermolai and Yevtushenko's paternal grandfather were accused of being "enemies of the people" and were arrested in 1937 during Stalin's purges. Estimates of the number of deaths associated with the Great Purge, the most significant of these, range from the official Soviet number of 681,692 to close to 2 million.

Spokesman for a Liberal Youth Yevtushenko began writing early, and crafted his first verses and song lyrics by the time he was seven years of age. After his parents divorced in the early 1940s, the young Yevtushenko spent his early childhood in Moscow with his mother and sister, Yelena, and in the late 1940s traveled with his father on geological expeditions to Kazakhstan and Altai, Siberia.

Yevtushenko was attending Gorky Literary Institute in Moscow when he published his first volume of poetry, *The Prospectors of the Future* (1952). Following the Twentieth Communist Party Congress of 1956—during which Soviet premier Nikita Khrushchev publicly enumerated the crimes of former leader Joseph Stalin—Yevtushenko emerged as a prominent spokesman for Russian youth and for the new regime's commitment to more liberal policies. At about the same time he published his next work, *Winter Station* (1956), a highly acclaimed long poem first published in the Soviet journal *Oktiabr.*

Political and International Attention In 1955, his third poetry collection, *Third Snow*, was published, followed by *Highway of the Enthusiasts* in 1956, *Promise* in 1957, and *The Bow and the Lyre* in 1959. During the late 1950s, Yevtushenko emerged as a leading nationalist proponent of the Cold War "thaw" between the Soviet Union and the United States. This thaw was envisioned

LITERARY AND HISTORICAL CONTEMPORARIES

Yevtushenko's famous contemporaries include:

Sawako Ariyoshi (1931–1984): A Japanese novelist whose works concern significant social issues, such as environmental pollution and treatment of the elderly.

Jean-Luc Godard (1930–): A French/Swiss filmmaker best known for being one of the pioneers of the French New Wave in film.

André Previn (1930–): A German-born American award-winning pianist, composer, and conductor known for such film scores as *Porgy and Bess*, *Gigi*, and *My Fair Lady*.

Aleksandr Solzhenitsyn (1918–2008): A Russian author and dissident famous for his novels depicting the harsh conditions in Soviet labor camps.

Mikhail Gorbachev (1931–): The final leader of the Soviet Union, who partially engineered its collapse in 1991 and who was awarded the Nobel Peace Prize in 1990.

as a way for the two cultures to better the chances of a peaceful future through cultural exchanges with one another. Granted permission by government authorities to deliver poetry readings in both countries in 1960, Yevtushenko soon became Russia's best-known living poet.

While new volumes of his verse—including *The Apple* (1960), *Tenderness: New Poems* (1962), and *A Wave of the Hand* (1962)—appeared in the Soviet Union, Yevtushenko's early verse was introduced to English readers through such collections as *Selected Poems* (1962) and *Selected Poetry* (1963). In one of his most controversial poems of this period, "Stalin's Heirs," Yevtushenko describes a fictional reawakening of Stalin following a brief interment in the tomb of Communist leader Vladimir Lenin, implying that Russians should beware the reemergence of Stalinism. Such a warning was not entirely without merit, as the rise to power of Leonid Brezhnev signaled a movement away from the reforms of his predecessor, Khrushchev, and the reconstitution of a Stalinesque authoritarian state (culminating first in the crushing of the anti-Soviet Prague Spring in 1968 and then in the invasion of Afghanistan in 1979).

Russian Reprimand While Yevtushenko was on tour reading from his latest works, the publication in France of his *A Precocious Autobiography* (1963) was arranged without Soviet permission. With this volume—combining his political views with memoirs of his youth—Yevtushenko was reprimanded for his personalized interpretation of Russian history. He was, however, permitted to continue publishing, and he again attracted

international recognition for his next volume, *New Works: The Bratsk Station* (1965), in which the poet praises Russian workers by contrasting them with earlier, ancient civilizations. That same year Yevtushenko received the USSR Commission for the Defense of Peace award.

Diversified Work Yevtushenko's poetry of the early 1970s was collected in several books, including the particularly successful *Stolen Apples* (1971). It was also in these years that Yevtushenko began working on plays. His drama *Under the Skin of the Statue of Liberty* (1972), a series of revue sketches set in the United States, was originally produced by Yuri Lyubimov, a leader in the Soviet avant-garde theater. *Under the Skin* achieved popular success in Russia, though it was faulted for Yevtushenko's inability to impart his concerns to Western audiences.

Yevtushenko followed his dramatic work with two more poetry collections, *The Face behind the Face* (1979) and *Ivan the Terrible and Ivan the Fool* (1979). In 1979 he also expanded his repertoire to include acting for the cinema. He appeared in such Soviet films as *Take-Off* (1979) and *The Kindergarten* (1983). In the early 1980s, Yevtushenko gradually moved away from poetry to experiment with various prose forms, including *A Dove in Santiago: A Novella in Verse* (1982).

A Celebrated Novelist, a Politician, and a Traveling Poet-Teacher Yevtushenko's first novel, *Wild Berries* (1984), was originally published in 1981 in the Soviet periodical *Moskva*, and is likened to an American thriller with its emphasis on action, sex, and exotic locales. Despite that work's mixed reception—Soviet critics faulting it for focusing on war miseries instead of triumphs; Western critics praising its sincerity—*Wild Berries* made Yevtushenko a 1985 finalist for the Ritz Paris Hemingway Award for best 1984 novel published in English. That same year also saw him receiving the esteemed USSR state prize and publishing his second novel, *Ardabiola*.

In the waning moments of the Soviet Union and the fall of the Iron Curtain (under Gorbachev), Yevtuskenko served from 1988 to 1991 in the first freely elected Russian parliament since the revolution, where he fought against censorship and other restrictions. Yevtushenk's more recent works, both then and in the post-Soviet era, have focused on problems in human interaction with the natural environment; but he has—to the surprise and chagrin of many observers—been less than critical of autocratic president Vladimir Putin. Today, Yevtushenko divides his time between Russia and the United States, teaching at both the University of Oklahoma at Tulsa and at Queens College of the City University of New York. He has also served as an artist in residence at a number of other institutions. His more recent works include the film *Stalin's Funeral* (1990) and the novel *Don't Die before You're Dead* (1995), which is a satirical retelling of the 1991 events that ended the Soviet Union and lifted Boris Yeltsin to power.

Works in Literary Context

Lyrical Style for Political and Personal Themes
Long prescribed by scholars of Russian poetry is a favoring of emotion over principles, and it is a prescription Yevtushenko follows. He makes use of a lyrical style that many critics have compared with early twentieth-century poet Vladimir Mayakovsky for its rage against hypocrisy and passivity. In all of his works Yevtushenko presents nationalistic and critical views on political, civic, and personal themes.

The long poem *Winter Station* (1956) is Yevtushenko's attempt to resolve personal doubts as well as moral and political questions raised by Stalin's regime. In the title piece of *New Works: The Bratsk Station* (1965), Yevtushenko contrasts the use of slaves to construct the Egyptian pyramids with the willingness of Russian workers to build a hydroelectric complex in Siberia. In his drama *Under the Skin of the Statue of Liberty* (1972), Yevtushenko condemns American violence while praising the idealism of the nation's youth. In *Ivan the Terrible and Ivan the Fool* (1979), he returns to nationalistic concerns to contrast the abused working class with the dreaded autocrat who transformed Russian culture and society during the sixteenth century. In *Ardabiola* (1984), composed of chapters written in diverse styles and combining elements from several genres, he takes the opportunity to satirize Soviet culture and government and to address the influence of American materialism on Russian youth. And *Almost at the End* (1987—and it came indeed almost at the end of the Soviet Union) features as its centerpiece the poem "Fuku," a long work in which Yevtushenko uses a cinematic style and combines traditional poetry, free verse, and prose to comment on such characteristic concerns as history, tyranny, and justice.

Works in Critical Context

Eastern-bloc and Western critics alike have often vacillated in their opinions of Yevtushenko's work, in part because he tends to embrace opposing ideologies and he tends to alternately celebrate and censure elements of both Communist and capitalist approaches to civilization. Yet his poems are often commended for their political significance, optimism, and explosive use of language. Representative of the wide array of criticism are responses to two works, *Babi Yar* and *Wild Berries*.

Babi Yar (1961) Originally published in the periodical *Literaturnaya gazeta*, *Babi Yar* garnered international acclaim. The title of this long poem refers to a ravine near Kiev, where historians estimate that between thirty-four thousand and one hundred thousand Jews were massacred by the Nazis during World War II. *Babi Yar* was ridiculed by many Soviet critics for its accusation that many Russian people harbor anti-Semitic sentiments—a claim that, Yevtushenko asserted, was corroborated by public indifference to erecting a memorial on the site. Contemporary critics have often read Yevtushenko through the lens of Holocaust studies, as seen

---

COMMON HUMAN EXPERIENCE

In its way, Yevtushenko's work is concerned not only with depicting, but also with understanding, the working of politics in culture. Here are a few other works by writers who have addressed the cultural impacts of politics in their writing:

The Great Game: The Struggle for Empire in Central Asia (1992), a political study by Peter Hopkirk. This nonfiction survey closely considers the "great game" played between Tsarist Russia and Victorian England for supremacy in Central Asia.

Mourning Dove: A Salishan Autobiography (1994), a cultural history by Mourning Dove (Christine Quintasket). In this sprawling narrative, the Native American author recounts life with the Colville Confederated Tribes of the Pacific Northwest at the dawn of the twentieth century.

Red Azalea (1994), a memoir by Anchee Min. In this autobiographical work the author recounts her biggest challenge, in which she was forced to choose between self-will and the will of the Chinese Communist Party.

The Republic of Poetry (2006), a book of poems by Martín Espada. These poems explore the politics of Latin American loyalty and freedom.

This Earth of Mankind (1991), a novel by Pramoedya Ananta Toer. Indonesian political dissident Toer offers an intriguing story of love and colonialism in turn-of-the-century Java.

---

in historian Dagmar Herzog's argument that Yevtushenko's political victory with the poem *Babi Yar* "was a hollow one," because the memorial erected after the poem's success refers to those massacred not as Jews but simply as "citizens of Kiev and prisoners of war."

Wild Berries (1981) Yevtushenko's first novel, *Wild Berries*, is said to celebrate Russian philosophy and existence but at the same time is similar to an American thriller. The book was faulted by Soviet critics for its emphasis on the miseries of war rather than past military triumphs and for its treatment of Stalin's deportation of the kulaks (landowning peasant farmers) in the 1930s. *Wild Berries* was praised by many Western reviewers for Yevtushenko's sincerity of purpose. Critic Susan Jacoby further expressed the multiple views on the author when she commented, "In American terms, [Yevtushenko] might best be imagined as a hybrid of Walt Whitman and Norman Mailer—with all the extravagant enthusiasms, risk-taking, self-promotion, blundering and talent that might be expected from such a creature."

Responses to Literature

1. According to Russian writer and fellow dissident Andrei Sinyavsky, Yevtushenko seeks in his work "to

---

communicate the experience of the modern age and to connect this with the experience of the past, with Russian history." Consider how one of Yevtushenko's works seeks to connect past with present, structuring your thoughts as a thesis-driven essay.

2. In 1952, Yevtushenko joined the USSR Union of Writers, also known as the Union of Soviet Writers. What differences do you find in his writing from after this time. Does this joining appear to have had a significant impact on his style? Why or why not?

3. In 1957 Yevtushenko was expelled from the Literary Institute for displaying "individualism." Research different definitions of "individualism." Why do you think Yevtushenko's brand of individualism was seen as a threat to Soviet culture? Support your position with detailed analysis of passages from his work.

4. With the novel *Ivan the Terrible and Ivan the Fool* (1979), Yevtushenko returned to nationalistic concerns: he contrasts Ivan the Fool, the ill-used but unstoppable working-class folk hero, with Czar Ivan the Terrible, the autocrat who oversaw extensive changes in Russian culture and society during the sixteenth century. Do a Web search for background information on Ivan the Terrible (Ivan IV). Summarize the leader's personality and how he came to earn the "terrible" moniker. Then, consider how he is contrasted with the working-class citizen in the novel.

BIBLIOGRAPHY

Books

Blair, Katherine Hunter. *A Review of Soviet Literature*. Port Townsend, Wash.: Ampersand, 1966.

Brown, Edward James. *Russian Literature Since the Revolution*. New York: Collier, 1963.

Yevtushenko, Yevgeny. *A Precocious Autobiography*. New York: Dutton, 1963.

Periodicals

Brownjohn, Allen. "Travellers Alone." *Poetry* 89 (October 1956): 45.

Jacoby, Susan. "Shostakovich; 'Babi Yar' Troubles." *New York Times*, March 19, 2000.

Web Sites

Aytmatov, Chingis. Spin Tongues. *The Sail of Poetry*. Retrieved May 16, 2008, from http://spintongues.msk.ru/aytmatov.html.

Bedford/St. Martin's Lit Links. "Yevgeny Yevtushenko, b. 1933." Retrieved May 16, 2008, from http://bcs.bedfordstmartins.com/litlinks/Pages/Main.aspx.

Nation, Brian. Boppin a Riff. *Three Poems by Yevgeny Yevtushenko*. Retrieved May 16, 2008, from http://www.boppin.com/poets/yevtushenko.htm. Last updated on May 7, 2008.

Russian Culture Navigator. "A Poet in Russia" (Marking the 65th birthday of Yevgeny Yevtushenko). Retrieved May 16, 2008, from http://www.vor.ru/culture/cultarch30_eng.html. Last updated on July 18, 1998.

Charlotte Yonge

BORN: *1823, Otterbourne, Hampshire, England*

DIED: *1901, Otterbourne, Hampshire, England*

NATIONALITY: *British*

GENRE: *Fiction*

MAJOR WORKS:

The Heir of Redclyffe (1853)

The Little Duke; or, Richard the Fearless (1854)

The Daisy Chain; or, Aspirations (1856)

Aunt Charlotte's Stories of English History for the Little Ones (1873)

The Pillars of the House; or, Under Wode Under Rode (1874)

Charlotte Mary Yonge   *Hulton Archive / Getty Images*

Overview

British author Charlotte Mary Yonge may be placed in literary history as the leading novelist of that Anglo-Catholic revival known as Tractarianism, or the Oxford Movement. However, this classification cannot explain why her domestic novels have always been enjoyed by many readers to whom her religious views are a matter of indifference or even hostility. Firmly opposed to crudely didactic fiction—especially for children—she had the ability to extract dramatic tension from almost any family situation and relationship and to develop it with delicate moral and psychological notation.

Works in Biographical and Historical Context

Life Spent in Otterbourne Yonge was born in Otterbourne, England, in 1823, and she lived all her life in the village of her birth. Her father, William Yonge, had sacrificed his military career, his beloved Devonshire home, and many of his artistic tastes in order to gain the consent of his mother-in-law, a woman considered narrow by her own contemporaries, to his marriage to Frances Mary Bargus. He and his wife settled down on Mrs. Bargus's small estate in Otterbourne, near Winchester.

Here, he made a new life for himself out of village interests, church building, and the education of his daughter. He and his wife taught her Latin, French, German, history, and mathematics, in addition to giving her religious instruction. In the nineteenth century, there were limited educational opportunities for young girls in Great Britain. Few schools focused on such academic topics, and many girls were educated in some fashion at home. At the age of seven, Yonge attended the Otterbourne Sunday School. She went on to teach in the school, seldom missing more than a few weeks each year, until her death seventy years later.

Religion and Friendship In 1836, John Keble became rector of the neighboring parish of Hursley and would be, after her father, her greatest influence. In preparing Yonge for confirmation, he recognized her brilliant mind and passionate love of history. She absorbed all he had to teach her about the doctrine of the Church of England, and in her later life, neither the claims of the Roman Catholic Church on the one hand nor the prevalence of religious doubt on the other seemed ever to have troubled her faith. Keble's support of her intellectual interests was unusual in this time period. In nineteenth-century Britain, women were treated as inferior. Stereotypes and prejudices portrayed women as weak and incapable in most areas. Most professions and occupations were closed by statute to women, and the only professions that were socially acceptable were those of teacher, secretary, or homemaker.

Yonge's circle also included the family—which eventually numbered fifteen children—of George Moberly, headmaster of Winchester College. The Kebles, Moberlys, Yonges, and the Yonges' Coleridge relations formed a close circle of mutual interests and stimulation. In 1850, Marianne Dyson, an invalid friend, suggested that Yonge develop a story that would contrast two characters, the essentially contrite and the essentially self-satisfied. The result, finished late in 1851, was *The Heir of Redclyffe* (1853). Shortly after the publication of *The Heir of Redclyffe* in January 1853, Yonge found herself famous. Her family initially had disapproved of her desire to become a writer, as it was considered socially improper for a woman to profit from her own labor. They only agreed to let Yonge continue as long as the proceeds were contributed to missionary activities.

Continuing Success While working on *The Heir of Redclyffe*, Yonge was also writing her best children's book, *The Little Duke* (1854), about the tenth-century Richard of Normandy, and beginning two series, *Cameos from English History* (1868–1899) and *Conversations on the Catechism* (1859). All three were serialized in the magazine she founded in 1851 and edited until 1894, the *Monthly Packet of Evening Readings for Members of the Church of England*. The magazine, which probably never had more than fifteen hundred subscribers, was thoroughly an expression of her personality and interests: fiction, history, literary history, theology, and botany were the leading subjects. Later, more scientific material

COMMON HUMAN EXPERIENCE

Throughout her life, Yonge was concerned with issues of spirituality and faith. She attended church regularly, and emphasized loyalty to God in her works. Here are a few other works that deal with issues of religion.

> *Poems of Gerard Manley Hopkins* (1918), a poetry collection by Gerard Manley Hopkins. This posthumous collection is concerned with God's presence.
> *Siddhartha* (1922), a novel by Herman Hesse. This novel centers around the worldly and spiritual trials of a man named Siddhartha, who may or may not be the Buddha.
> *Four Quartets* (1943), poems by T. S. Eliot. This book of four poems uses mysticism, Hindu philosophy, and Christian imagery to get its message across.

was added, and British author Lewis Carroll (*Alice in Wonderland*, 1865) contributed some mathematical puzzles.

After the death of her father, Yonge and her mother moved in 1858 to the nearby Elderfield Cottage, which remained Yonge's home until her death. The 1860s were a difficult time in Yonge's life. Both of the Kebles died in 1866, and the Moberlys left Winchester the next year. Her mother began a decline into senility, possibly through a series of small strokes, which Yonge found all the more difficult to bear because she and her mother had been such inseparable companions. Her novels of this period share a depressed tone, but her output remained as high as ever.

Old Age The early 1870s saw Yonge at the height of her powers. In addition to beginning the series of "nursery histories" known as "Aunt Charlotte's Stories" and a series of religious pamphlets to be used in preparing young people for confirmation, she serialized in the *Monthly Packet* her tribute to John Keble. In 1870, she also began to serialize in the *Monthly Packet* a novel called *The Pillars of the House* which, along with *The Daisy Chain*, represents the summit of her achievement as a domestic novelist.

Yonge was occupied with her writing and her village pursuits until March 1901, when she was overtaken by bronchitis and pneumonia. She died on March 24, 1901.

Works in Literary Context

In her writings, Yonge was greatly influenced by her faith and religious beliefs as a member of the Oxford Movement. Her life in the village of Otterbourne as well as her intellectual grounding in history also informed her works. In addition, Yonge reflected the Victorian era in which she lived by exploring the middle-class domestic life she

knew so well. She was personally mentored by her father and Keble in her literary pursuits.

Women in Society The religious, moral, educational, and social standards Yonge sets for her gentlewomen are so high that only superior men could surpass them. She inveighs against the double standard because she believes that men and women should be equally chaste. Women should work outside the home only when they must and be always "strong-minded," to speak out against improprieties at home and evils abroad. That the married woman's noblest role lies in making her home a center of refuge, repose, and stimulation for her family is a conventional view of the time; but Yonge also insists that the unmarried woman has a vital role to play in society, provided she does so as a "daughter of the Church."

Struggles with Spirituality Like Flora May's in *The Daisy Chain*, Philip's punishment for his worldliness in *The Heir of Redclyffe* is the attainment of his wishes: a seat in Parliament, the Redclyffe estate, and marriage to his cousin Laura. Like Flora, the self-righteous Philip has a harsh measure of mental and spiritual suffering meted out to him because Yonge sees in him the ability to benefit and change. The spiritual awakening of Philip, with his self-deception, his thwarted career, and his despair at the self-inflicted poverty that makes him an ineligible suitor for his cousin, reflects Yonge's need to chronicle the destiny of her characters. She drew into *The Heir of Redclyffe* characters she would use in varied forms throughout her works: the ineffective father who must nonetheless be obeyed, the invalid, and the pert younger sister. As one anonymous reviewer for *Fraser's Magazine* reported: "When we bid her characters farewell, it is ever hereafter to recall them to our affectionate remembrance as friends whom we have known and loved on earth, and whom we may hope to one day meet in heaven."

Influence Yonge's domestic novels and family sagas influenced at least two generations of girls and young women about their roles in life. Authors like Christabel Coleridge, Florence Wilford, and Frances Peard followed in Yonge's footsteps by being submissive and writing for children. In later decades of the twentieth century, Yonge's early Victorian-focused message came to seem outdated as society's attitude towards women—and their education—changed.

Works in Critical Context

In Yonge's time, her domestic novels were admired by novelist Henry James, poet Alfred Lord Tennyson, and a wide public of discriminating reviewers and readers. In the twentieth century, her enormous output of over two hundred books—historical novels; histories; biographies; children's stories; tales of village life; and volumes on religion, geography, and names—tended to be held against her. Despite her varied career, her claim to importance rests on her domestic fictions. In those long chronicles of large, middle-class Victorian broods, family life is presented, in the phrase of her admirer C. S. Lewis, as an "arduous vocation."

The Heir of Redclyffe An oblique retort to Queenie Leavis's charges that doctrinal rigidity and provincialism are the dominant qualities in Yonge's domestic novels comes from Kathleen Tillotson. Writing in 1953 for a centenary broadcast on the BBC about *The Heir of Redclyffe*, she claims that "the moral content of *The Heir of Redclyffe* is easily disengaged from the social content and is not seriously out of date." After praising Yonge's use of symbols in this novel, Tillotson notes that the final chapters trace the progress of the heroine after Guy Morville's death; "It was, I think, Charlotte Yonge's keen sense of [domestic] life that kept her from vapid sentimentality ...." Also contributing to the argument, Barbara Dennis asserts that Yonge's work is weakened by "her inability to come to terms with the movement of mind in the nineteenth century" and the lack of sympathy she displays toward manifestations of religious doubt.

Among the best-known admirers of *The Heir of Redclyffe* were William Morris and his friends, the artists Edward Burne-Jones and Dante Gabriel Rossetti. They appreciated Guy's love of the Middle Ages and Malory, of English cathedrals, and of de La Motte-Fouqué's romance *Sintram* with its hero's appreciation of the value of symbols. The reviewer for the *Times* remarked of Guy that "never before did the beauty of holiness appear more beautiful or more winning."

Responses to Literature

1. Write an essay explaining what is meant by a "domestic" novel. Describe, using examples from Yonge's work, how Yonge's writing fits into this category.

2. Lead your class in an exploration of Guy Morville in *The Heir of Redclyffe*. Is he admirable? What are his faults?

3. Create a poster or electronic presentation in which you compare Yonge's children's fiction with C. S. Lewis's *Narnia* series. Why do you think the latter was more successful?

4. With a small group of your classmates, discuss what might be the best way to present a doctrine of religion or ideology to children. What would or wouldn't you want to hear or read? Come up with a brief proposal to present to the rest of your class.

BIBLIOGRAPHY

Books

Battiscombe, Georgina. *Charlotte Mary Yonge: The Story of an Uneventful Life*. London: Constable, 1943.
Brownell, David B. "The Two Worlds of Charlotte Yonge." In *The World of Victorian Fiction*.
Cambridge, MA: Harvard University Press, 1975, pp. 165–78.
Coleridge, Christabel Rose. *Charlotte Mary Yonge: Her Life and Letters*. London: Macmillan, 1903.
Lewis, C. S. *God in the Dock: Essays on Theology and Ethics*, ed. Walter Hooper. Grand Rapids, Mich.: Eerdmans, 1970.
Romanes, Ethel. *Charlotte Mary Yonge: An Appreciation*. London: Mowbray, 1908.
Tillotson, Kathleen, *Mid-Victorian Studies*. London: Athlone Press, 1965.

Periodicals

Dennis, Barbara, "The Two Voices of Charlotte Yonge." *Durham University Journal* 65 (1973): 181–88.
Leavis, Queenie Dorothy. "Charlotte Yonge and 'Christian Discrimination.'" *Scrutiny* 12 (Spring 1944): 152–60.
Mitchell, Sally. "Sentiment and Suffering: Women's Recreational Reading in the 1860s." *Victorian Studies* 21 (Spring 1977): 29–45.
Sturrock, June. "A Personal View of Women's Education 1838–1900: Charlotte Yonge's Novels." *Victorians' Institute Journal* 7 (1979): 7–18.

▨ Marguerite Yourcenar

BORN: *1903, Brussels, Belgium*

DIED: *1987, Mount Desert Island, Maine, United States*

NATIONALITY: *Belgian, French, American*

GENRE: *Drama, fiction, poetry, nonfiction*

MAJOR WORKS:
Alexis (1929)
Fires (1936)
Coup de Grâce (1939)
Memoirs of Hadrian (1951)
Dear Departed (1974)

Overview

Marguerite Yourcenar was the first woman elected to the prestigious Académie française. A self-taught scholar, novelist, poet, dramatist, essayist, and translator, widely traveled and well read, Yourcenar brought a broadly based sensibility to her literary work. Her writings treat the dawn of time and the future; the physical and the spiritual worlds; characters ranging from peasants to emperors, courtesans to Hindu gods; nature and civilizations; and the arts and religion. Although she frequently ignored or defied literary styles, the advice of critics, and the conventions of Parisian literary life, Yourcenar managed to reach and appeal to a wide audience in France and throughout the world. A woman who worked for conservationist and ecological causes, consumer

Marguerite Yourcenar   *DEA Picture Library / drr.net*

protection, and civil rights, as well as a writer whose scholarship, command of her craft, and far-ranging knowledge in many fields were very striking, she occupies a privileged place in twentieth-century letters.

Works in Biographical and Historical Context

Life without a Mother, but in a Lovely World
Marguerite Antoinette Jeanne Marie Ghislaine Cleenewerck de Crayencour was born on June 8, 1903, to a French father, Michel, and a Belgian mother, Fernande de Cartier de Marchienne, both of whom came from old and influential families in Belgium—from Flanders and the Walloon section of the country, respectively. Because of her mother's wish to be near her relatives, Yourcenar was born in Brussels, although she was immediately registered as a French citizen.

Following her mother's death (ten days after Yourcenar was born), Yourcenar was brought to Mont-Noir, the ancestral home of the Crayencour family, where she spent the summers during her childhood; winters were spent in Lille for the first two years and afterward in the south of France. At Mont-Noir Yourcenar made contact with the land, with country people, and with animals—all of which

had an influence on her life. When she was nine, Yourcenar and her father moved to Paris, where the world of books, museums, and art expanded her environment.

Fleeing War, an Invitation to India, and the Death of Her Father   Yourcenar's first contact with war and exile came in 1914 when, while visiting Ostende, Belgium, she and her father had to flee from the advancing German armies across the channel to England. There, they lived for a year before making their way to southern France for the remainder of World War I (1914–1918) and beyond. During these years at Aix-en-Provence, Yourcenar completed her early education. By the age of sixteen, she had already begun to write. Her first publication, privately printed, came in 1921, and for it she and her father invented the pen name Yourcenar, a near anagram of Crayencour. *The Garden of Chimeras* proved her able to interpret and expand myths in order to express her own views. This work shows the aspirations of a young person, as Icarus is drawn to Helios, in contrast to the archetype of the wise old man, Daedalus. The volume had a certain caché, attracting the attention of the Nobel laureate Rabindranath Tagore, who wrote to the young poet, inviting her to visit him in India.

In 1929, three events occurred that would alter the course of Yourcenar's life. The first, in January, was the death of her father after a long illness. The second was the Wall Street crash, which caused Yourcenar to lose most of the fortune she inherited from her mother and signaled the approaching end of the privileged existence she had enjoyed. The third, and perhaps most important, was the publication of her first novel, *Alexis*; in desperate times, she had been confirmed as a member of that mythical tribe: she was a writer.

The Touch of Grace and a New Life in the States
The 1930s were the period in which Yourcenar's life and talents took on new dimensions and found new means of expression. During this decade Yourcenar, although in the orbit of Paris as much as any young French writer, spent much of her time living and traveling in Italy, Germany, and, especially, Greece. This was a time of challenge, a time to try new methods, to publish what she had already written, to discover herself as she discovered the world she had loved in books.

In 1939, Yourcenar completed her novel *Coup de Grâce*, considered by many to be among her finest, but when World War II (1939–1945) began, she once again found herself trapped. Low on funds, unable to find a position, and prevented from returning to Greece as she had planned, she accepted the invitation of her American friend and translator Grace Frick to join her in the United States. Although Yourcenar would subsequently travel abroad for periods as long as two years, she established her permanent home in the States at that time.

The break with her past around 1940 was profound. Not only did she suffer, as did many exiles, from a forced separation from the places and people that had been part of her life, but she was also obliged for the first time to earn a living, taking jobs in journalism and commercial translation before accepting a position as a part-time instructor at Sarah Lawrence College in 1942. In 1947 she became an American citizen and, at the same time, took Marguerite Yourcenar as her legal name. This shift in identity was further reinforced in 1950 when she, with her long-time partner Grace Frick, moved to Mount Desert Island in Maine, where she lived until her death.

Finding a Home in Activism In 1951, the publication of *Memoirs of Hadrian* brought unexpected international success and served to establish Yourcenar firmly in the line she would follow over the next decades. During this decade also, Yourcenar became ever more concerned about social evils and involved herself in groups and programs aimed at combating them. She joined both American and European societies fighting for civil rights, world peace, protection of the environment, endangered or mistreated animals, and consumer protection, as well as groups against nuclear proliferation and overpopulation.

Following the death of Grace Frick in 1980, Yourcenar embarked once more on her world travels, this time accompanied by Jerry Wilson, an American. She traveled often: to France, England, the Low Countries, Denmark, North Africa, Spain and Portugal, Italy, Egypt, Greece, Canada, Japan, Thailand, India, and Kenya, visiting some more than once. Throughout these travels, she was ever concerned with the plights of the oppressed, and her contact with different cultures broadened the scope of her social concerns.

Struggling against Illness, for Justice During a stop in Nairobi in 1983, the year after Yourcenar was elected to the American Academy of Arts and Letters, she and Wilson were hit by a police car. The next year the flu interrupted her work for a considerable time. In 1985 Wilson was diagnosed as having tuberculosis, and, in September, Yourcenar suffered a heart attack, necessitating surgery. She recovered, but Wilson died of viral meningitis in February of 1986.

Yourcenar maintained her activist and scholarly interests to the end. In the last three months of her life she gave two speeches, one in Canada on "superpollution" and one at Harvard on Jorge Luis Borges. She had planned to travel to Paris and from there to India and Nepal, but on November 8, 1987, she suffered a stroke, which led to her death on December 17. Her grave, near the memorials to Grace Frick and Jerry Wilson, is in the cemetery at Somesville, Maine, close to the first house where she lived on Mount Desert Island.

Works in Literary Context

The Many Forms of Love *Fires* (1936) illustrates or underscores most of Yourcenar's themes. It was written in part to get over an unhappy love affair with the nameless "man I loved." Passages from her diary alternate with

---

LITERARY AND HISTORICAL CONTEMPORARIES

Yourcenar's famous contemporaries include:

Vladimir Nabokov (1899–1977): A Russian American novelist most famous for his extremely controversial novel *Lolita*.

Pablo Neruda (1904–1973): A Chilean poet and writer and political Communist; his 1971 receipt of the Nobel Prize in Literature caused much controversy.

Erich Fromm (1900–1980): A renowned German American social psychologist.

René Magritte (1898–1967): A Belgian surrealist painter known for his plays on words and pictures, particularly *The Treachery of Images*.

James Baldwin (1924–1987): An African American writer who lived in France and explored issues of homosexuality and politics; Yourcenar translated one of his plays into French.

---

prose poems whose protagonists are primarily mythical women. Mary Magdalene goes beyond physical love to a love for Christ, while Antigone devotes herself to an ideal. Sappho closes this collection, and she is saved from her suicide attempt by the safety net of her art. Her lover, Attys, leaves her; and she begins to prefer a young man, who has just enough feminine qualities to be attractive. This blend of the sexes is very common in Yourcenar's work and may reflect Yourcenar's own romantic experiences.

History Rewritten *Memoirs of Hadrian* (1951) is an imagined first-person narrative in epistolary, or letter form, written by the Roman emperor Hadrian shortly before his death, when action has had to yield to contemplation and analysis of his accomplishments. Yourcenar's attempt to "redo [history] from within" shows Hadrian primarily as good; his meditations on classical art, dreams, destiny, religions, women, freedom, and so forth make him an extremely well-rounded character. Similarly, the events of his life in politics, love, and war are documented, chronicling the self-improvement that allows him to realize his own potential and his plans for the Roman Empire.

Yourcenar frequently used historical or legendary events and figures as the basis for her creative works. This is also seen in *Fires*, which includes figures such as the ancient poet Sappho, and *The Abyss* (1968), a tale that takes place in sixteenth-century France.

Works in Critical Context

Despite Yourcenar's prediction that *Memoirs of Hadrian* would find an audience of "a few students of human

COMMON HUMAN EXPERIENCE

Yourcenar draws on history to add density to her works. With the help of actual events, her fiction becomes richer and more complex. Here are a few other works that use real occurrences to emphasize their central themes and embellish their characters:

A Tale of Two Cities (1859), a novel by Charles Dickens. Beginning with 1775, this novel explores the events leading up to the French Revolution.

The Name of the Rose (1980), a novel by Umberto Eco. Set in a monastery during the middle ages, this story, in which a murder takes place and must be solved, is among Eco's most famous.

The Remains of the Day (1989), by Kazuo Ishiguro. An English butler struggles to maintain his professionalism at the expense of his humanity in this novel set during the tense times prior to World War II.

Braveheart (1995), a film directed by Mel Gibson. Set in the thirteenth century, this film focuses on William Wallace, a Scot who attempted to overthrow King Edward I of England.

destiny," it is her best-known work. But for several reasons, recognition as one of the leading figures of modern French literature was a long time coming for Yourcenar. She refused to be lionized; she lived from 1939 until her death in 1987 in the United States and ignored popular trends in order to write about what seemed important to her.

Dear Departed A series of autobiographical books published by Yourcenar focus less on herself than on her family. *Dear Departed* (1974) chronicles the story of Yourcenar's mother, Fernande de Crayencour, and her family, tracing them back over several centuries in Belgium. Of her effort, Harold Beaver writes in the *New York Times Book Review*: "Anyone who has ever tried to sort out boxes of family effects will be astounded at what Yourcenar has achieved. For she reoccupies the past, as it were, nourishing it with her own substance to bring it alive once again." But for *New York Review of Books* contributor John Weightman, the series is disappointing in its lack of information on Yourcenar herself. He concludes, "In her family saga, she traces the strands which crisscrossed to form…her unique identity and then, almost perversely, leaves that identity unexplained, presumably for all time."

Memoirs of Hadrian In the *Spectator*, Miranda Seymour calls *Memoirs of Hadrian* "arguably the finest historical novel of this century." Likewise, *New York Herald Tribune Book Review* contributor Geoffrey Bruun notes

that *Memoirs of Hadrian* "is an extraordinarily expert performance…. It has a quality of authenticity, of verisimilitude, that delights and fascinates." Mavis Gallant feels that Yourcenar "stands among a litter of flashier reputations as testimony to the substance and clarity of the French language and the purpose and meaning of a writer's life." The author continued to write, travel, and contemplate historical and philosophical issues central to the human condition into her eighties. In his *Saturday Review* essay, Stephen Koch concludes:

As an artist and thinker—for Yourcenar's novels must be regarded as simultaneously art, scholarship, and profound philosophical meditation—Marguerite Yourcenar writes squarely in defense of the very highest standards and traditions of that enlightened humanism which Hadrian promulgated for an empire and to the agonized rebirth of which her Zeno dies a martyr. It is, to say the least, heartening to find a writer so deeply committed to that humanism who is producing major art at this moment in our own history. It is, in fact, inspiring.

Responses to Literature

1. Yourcenar was the first woman to be in the Académie française. Research the institution and explain why you think she, unlike any women writers before her, received this honor.

2. Yourcenar lived in and traveled to many different places. How do these different landscapes show up in her works? Does she seem attached to any one sort of place?

3. Yourcenar spent many years working on *Memoirs of Hadrian*. What can this fictional treatment of history tell us about history itself? Are there ways in which fiction can communicate more truth than nonfiction? If you think so, how and why? If you think not, what is the value of doing historical research to write fiction? Or is this valuable? Support your position with detailed analyses of specific passages from *Memoirs of Hadrian*.

4. Consider Yourcenar's treatment of her family in *Dear Departed*. What stylistic techniques does she use to evoke an emotional response from readers, and what is that response? How does this emotional charge affect the overall message of the work itself?

BIBLIOGRAPHY

Books

Farrell, C. Frederick, Jr., and Edith R. Farrell. *Marguerite Yourcenar in Counterpoint*. Lanham, Md.: University Press of America, 1983.

Horn, Pierre. *Marguerite Yourcenar*. Boston: Twayne, 1985.

Howard, Joan E. *From Violence to Vision: Sacrifice in the Works of Marguerite Yourcenar*. Carbondale: Southern Illinois University Press, 1992.

Savigneau, Josyane. *Marguerite Yourcenar: Inventing a Life*. Translated by Joan E. Howard. Chicago: University of Chicago Press, 1993.

Periodicals

Royer, Jean-Michel. "Marguerite Yourcenar." *Actualité*, March 1972: 64–72.

Rutledge, Harry C. "Marguerite Yourcenar: The Classicism of *Fires* and *Memoirs of Hadrian*." *Classical and Modern Literature* 4 (Winter 1984): 87–99.

Soos, Emese. "The Only Motion Is Returning: The Metaphor of Alchemy in Mallet-Joris and Yourcenar." *French Forum* 4 (January 1979): 3–16.

Watson-Williams, Helen. "Hadrian's Story Recalled." *Nottingham French Studies* 23 (October 1984): 35–48.

Whatley, Janet. "*Memoirs of Hadrian*: A Manual for Princes." *University of Toronto Quarterly* 50 (Winter 1980/1981): 221–37.

■ Tao Yuanming

SEE *T'ao Ch'ien*

▨ Émile Zola

BORN: *1840, Paris, France*

DIED: *1902, Paris, France*

NATIONALITY: *French*

GENRE: *Fiction, drama, nonfiction*

MAJOR WORKS:

The Markets of Paris (1873)

Germinal (1885)

The Masterpiece(1886)

The Earth (1887)

Émile Zola   Zola, Emile, photograph. AP Images.

Overview

Émile Zola is one of the most important nineteenth-century French novelists, along with Stendhal, Victor Hugo, Honoré de Balzac, and Gustave Flaubert. *The Rougon-Macquarts*, the series of twenty novels that Zola published between 1870 and 1893, is a major monument of French fiction. Zola also wrote short stories, plays, and opera librettos and had already established himself by the age of thirty as one of France's leading literary figures.

Works in Biographical and Historical Context

Early Years and Paris   Émile-Edouard-Charles-Antoine Zola was born in Paris on April 2, 1840. His father, Francesco Zola (originally Zolla, meaning in Ital-

ian "a clod of earth"), developed pleurisy and died when Émile was just six years old, leaving his wife and son with debts of more than ninety thousand francs. The family moved a total of five times in ten years, always to cheaper quarters, ending up in two sordid rooms on a street inhabited by poor working-class people. Although his mother and her aged parents did everything possible to shield Émile from the effects of these misfortunes, the boy was affected by them as he grew older. They help explain his lifelong compassion for the poor, his longing for social justice, his rejection of what usually passes for charity, and his hatred of middle-class hypocrisy, cupidity, and pride. His fictionalized portrayals of Aix (represented in his novels by the town of "Plassans") teem with scheming, avaricious middle-class characters reminiscent of those who had stolen his mother's and his inheritance.

In many respects, however, Zola's childhood years in Aix were among the best of his life. He, Paul Cézanne (the future painter), and another schoolmate, Baptistin Baille, made frequent excursions into the countryside—reflected in Cézanne's idyllic Provençal landscapes and portrayals of bathers as well as in some of the most delightful pages of Zola's novels. During these jaunts Zola acquired the love of nature and respect for the forces of life that pervade his writings.

Zola's grandmother Aubert died in the fall of 1857. Once again, the boy, temperamentally somber, nervous, high-strung, terrified even by thunder, had to face the awful reality of death—which would turn, as the years passed, into one of his most obsessive literary themes. Then misfortune struck another blow. The family's increasingly desperate financial situation forced them to move to Paris, where Zola's mother would be in a better position to try to enlist the support of her husband's powerful friends. She managed, with help from one of them, to obtain a scholarship for Émile at the Lycée Saint-Louis.

French Idealism Zola wrote during the intellectual and spiritual crisis brought on by the eighteenth-century Enlightenment, the French Revolution, and the rise of modern science. Zola's Paris, like the Roman Empire in the first century, was a boiling cauldron of philosophical and religious ideas. Like thousands of other thoughtful mid-nineteenth-century Frenchmen, the young writer spent hours wrestling with great eternal questions about the nature of reality, the problem of evil, and the meaning of life.

By January 1866 Zola could often be observed meeting with a group of young revolutionary artists, including several of the future impressionists, at the Café Guerbois. Cézanne, Camille Pissarro, and Claude Monet showed up occasionally. The author, then in his late twenties, rightly sensed that the time was ripe at last to write his masterpiece, *Les Rougon-Macquart*. Throughout 1868 he spent every moment that he could working on his plans for his magnum opus, which, as it turned out, would largely take up the next twenty-five years of his career. Consisting of twenty novels (instead of the ten he had originally foreseen), the series studies human nature through the Rougons, a wealthy family, and their illegitimate, less affluent counterparts, the Macquarts. The epic cycle spans from the reign of Napoleon III (in the 1850s) through the Franco-Prussian War of 1870–1871.

Death and Political Conflicts 1880 was the year of one of Zola's greatest literary triumphs, but also a year of bereavements. His friend Louis Duranty, an older writer who had been one of the leaders of the realist school in the 1850s, died that April. A month later a telegram arrived from Guy de Maupassant announcing Gustave Flaubert's death. In October, Zola's mother died. Zola tried to suppress his sorrows by working, but he was continuously haunted by the specter of death. In October 1882 he had a nervous breakdown. He longed vainly for the comfort of the old religion and mumbled prayers despite his skepticism.

During the final period of Zola's life, he became caught up in "The Dreyfus Affair," which divided French society into two violently opposed camps. In December 1894 Captain Alfred Dreyfus, a Jewish officer in the French army, was convicted by a court-martial of having sold military secrets to Germany and was imprisoned on Devil's Island. At first Zola paid scant attention to the affair, but finally, convinced by his conversations with Dreyfus's defenders that the man was innocent, he decided to intervene. Persuaded that a direct challenge to the government and military authorities was necessary to keep Dreyfus's case alive, he published in a Parisian newspaper an instantly world-famous open letter to the president of the republic. A tremendous uproar ensued, and Zola became a spokesperson for legal justice. After creating what historian Barbara Tuchman referred to as "one of the great commotions of history," Zola was arrested for libel.

In a celebrated trial conducted by a biased judge, Zola was found guilty and sentenced to a year in prison and a fine of three thousand francs. He promptly appealed. A second trial took place but he fled to England without waiting for the result. The verdict this time would have been without appeal. He remained in England, writing *Fecondite*, until 1899, when, having heard that there was to be a review of the first Dreyfus trial, he returned to Paris.

On September 28, 1902, Zola and his wife Alexandrine took up their autumn and winter quarters on the Rue de Bruxelles. It was chilly, so a fire was lit in their bedroom. It burned badly, and the room filled with carbon monoxide while they slept. The next morning one of the servants, after knocking repeatedly on their bedroom door, became frightened, broke it down, and found Alexandrine lying unconscious and Zola dead. The public mourned the death of Zola at an enormous public funeral held on October 5, 1902. On June 4, 1908, Zola's coffin was removed from its tomb in the Montmartre Cemetery and transported to the Paris Pantheon, the resting place of some of France's greatest heroes. After a second funeral, his remains were placed close to the sarcophagi of Voltaire and Jean-Jacques Rousseau. They are still there today, sharing a small vault with the remains of Victor Hugo.

Works in Literary Context

Impressionism Zola spent much of his childhood in the countryside and was friends with many impressionist painters. His third novel of the *Les Rougon-Macquart* series, *The Markets of Paris*, is set in the picturesque central food market of Paris, and is the object of powerful descriptions that recall impressionist paintings. Zola intended the market to stand for the belly—the belly of Paris, the belly of humanity, and, by extension, the belly of the empire. Though the novel was often distasteful to middle-class readers—for the middle class is reviled for their imperial allegiance throughout the novel—critics of the time praised the work highly. This fusion of impressionist aesthetics with liberal politics would become Zola's stylistic trademark.

Pieces into Wholes The overall structure of Zola's fiction largely resulted from the interplay of opposing forces. In terms of aesthetic ideas, Zola championed unity, clarity, and simplicity. However, he also wanted to burst through the bounds of the novel, and transform traditional literary genres: the realistic novel, tragedy, comedy, farce, melodrama, epic, idyll, biography, history, scientific dissertation, and other forms. He aspired to be both realistic and visionary at the same time. He wanted his novels to reflect his centerless, chaotic vision of reality—hence his tendency to group his novels together into series rather than independent works. He built frames within frames, complex structures in which everything—a character, a setting, an action—represents the larger whole of which it is a part: the working class, the priesthood, capital, humanity, or life itself.

Works in Critical Context

During much of the early twentieth century, Zola was relegated to a kind of critical limbo. The public at large continued to read his works, but literary critics who had positive things to say about his writings were few and far between. On July 17, 1932, André Gide noted in his journal that he considered the discredit of Zola at that time as a monstrous injustice that said little for the literary critics of the day. Since the 1950s, however, Zola has been the object of a new critical reevaluation. Between 1952 and 1980 alone, more than twenty-six hundred new books and articles about him were published. His works lend themselves extraordinarily well to most of the new critical approaches that have flourished since the middle of the twentieth century. The old myths and prejudices that blinded many earlier critics have been largely dispelled.

L'Assommoir *L'Assommoir*, Zola's first great international success, has lost none of its influence more than a century after it was written. In its own day it was also one of the most controversial of Zola's works. Its impact is due in part to its sociological subject: working-class reality. The French bourgeoisie eyed the novel with a mixture of curiosity, contempt, guilt, and fear. Hugo and other Romantics had written novels about the suffering of the poor of their day, but their depictions had been sentimental and, by realistic standards, quite false. Zola, who knew the Parisian working class as well as any other author of his time, made no attempt to idealize it. On the contrary, he was the first major French author to portray it comprehensively. Henry James, in his *Notes on Novelists, with Some Other Notes*, writes, "*L'Assommoir* is the nature of man—but not his finer, nobler, cleaner or more cultivated nature; it is the image of his free instincts, the better and the worse.... The whole handling makes for emphasis and scale, and it is not to be measured how, as a picture of conditions, the thing would have suffered from

timidity." James also asserts about Zola's personal vision, "Of this genius *L'Assommoir* is the most extraordinary record."

The Earth By the time Zola's novel *The Earth* appeared in 1887, a negative reaction to naturalism, which had begun several years earlier, was rapidly gaining strength in the younger generation. Even some writers, including Maupassant and Huysmans, who had fought alongside Zola in his campaign to promote Naturalism, were now heading in new directions. Zola's own fame, however, continued to grow, and it was clear that he had lost none of his creative power. *The Earth* sold thousands of copies when it first appeared, and it has remained one of Zola's most popular and highly regarded novels. While some critics immediately sensed the work's greatness, many others were rudely shocked. All aspects of life, no matter how revolting or horrible, are recounted in Homeric detail. The widely respected novelist Anatole France accused Zola of trying to exploit a perverted popular taste for obscenity in fiction. A group of five younger writers, Paul Bonnetain, J.-H. Rosny, Lucien Descaves, Paul Margueritte, and Gustave Guiches, took advantage of the occasion to fire off a long, indignant, and highly scurrilous attack directed not only at the novel but also at Zola. Accusing him of moral depravity, they violently and publicly rejected him as their literary master.

Responses to Literature

1. Zola is perhaps best known for his treatment of the working class within his novels. What do you think Zola achieved by using naturalism to describe the

conditions of the poor? Can you compare his methods to those of other authors that write about similar subjects, such as Victor Hugo and Charles Dickens?

2. Why do you think Zola made his famous series twenty novels long? How does the concept of time function in this series?

3. Research Zola's interest in the Dreyfus affair, and read the open letter that was published under the headline "J'accuse!" Why do you think Zola championed Dreyfus with as much zeal as he did?

4. Explain this quote from Henrik Ibsen, the playwright, with a specific reference from one of Zola's works: "Zola descends into the sewer to bathe in it, I to cleanse it."

5. How is naturalism different from realism? Explain this using examples from both Zola's work and the works of other authors of the time period.

BIBLIOGRAPHY

Books

Alexis, Paul. *Émile Zola: Notes d'un ami*. Paris: Charpentier, 1882.

Baguley, David. *Naturalist Fiction: The Entropic Vision*. Cambridge, U.K.: Cambridge University Press, 1990.

"Émile Zola (1840–1902)." *Twentieth-Century Literary Criticism*. Edited by Dedria Bryfonski and Phyllis Carmel Mendolson. Vol. 1. Detroit: Gale Research, 1978, pp. 585–98.

Hemmings, F. W. J. *Émile Zola*. Oxford: Clarendon, 1966.

Hilton, Guieu, and Alison Hilton, eds. *Émile Zola and the Arts*. Washington, D.C.: Georgetown University Press, 1988.

Knapp, Bettina. *Émile Zola*. New York: Ungar, 1980.

Nelson, Brian. *Émile Zola: A Selective Analytical Bibliography*. London: Grant & Cutler, 1982.

Niess, Robert J. *Zola, Cézanne, and Manet: A Study of "L'Ouvre"*. Ann Arbor: University of Michigan Press, 1968.

Richardson, Joanna. *Zola*. London: Weidenfeld & Nicolson, and New York: St. Martin's Press, 1978.

Wilson, Angus. *Émile Zola: An Introductory Study of His Novels*. London: Secker & Warburg, 1964.

Xau, Fernand. *Émile Zola*. Paris: Marpon et Flammarion, 1880.

Periodicals

Yale French Studies, no. 42 (1969).

◈ Mikhail Zoshchenko

BORN: *1895, Poltava, Ukraine*

DIED: *1958, Leningrad, USSR*

NATIONALITY: *Russian*

GENRE: *Fiction, nonfiction*

MAJOR WORKS:

The Stories of Nazar Ilich, Mister Sinebriukhov (1922)

Youth Restored (1933)

Before Sunrise (1943, 1972)

Overview

Mikhail Zoshchenko is relatively unknown outside of Russian literature, but he was the most popular satirist in the Soviet Union from the early 1920s until 1946, when he was expelled from the Union of Russian Writers and his works banned. Zoshchenko incisively examined the cultural confusion that followed the Bolshevik Revolution, using a traditional Russian literary technique known as *skaz*, which establishes a comic narrator distinct from the author. Central to Zoshchenko's satire was the singular language his *skaz* narrators employed, blending slang, Marxist jargon, and humorous distortions of common usage.

Works in Biographical and Historical Context

Privileged Upbringing Mikhail Mikhailovich Zoshchenko was born on July 28, 1895, in Poltava, Ukraine, then part of the Russian Empire. His father, Mikhail Ivanovich Zoshchenko, was a painter and landowner, while his mother had been an actress and had published a few short stories. He was drawn to writing at a young age, composing poetry by 1902 at the age of seven and

Mikhail Zoshchenko   *akg-images, London / RIA Nowosti*

attempting his first prose in 1907, the year his father died. At seventeen, he began studying law at the University of St. Petersburg.

A Soldier during World War I

When World War I began, Zoshchenko abandoned his studies and joined the Imperial Army. World War I began when the heir to the throne of Austria-Hungary, Archduke Franz Ferdinand, was assassinated by a terrorist in Sarajevo, Serbia, in June 1914. Austria-Hungary soon declared war on Serbia and its allies. Entangling alliances brought nearly every European country into the conflict. Austria-Hungary allied with Germany, Turkey, and, until 1915, Italy, against France, Russia, Great Britain, and, after 1917, the United States. Zoshchenko became a lieutenant in the grenadiers and was decorated twice for bravery. During the war, he suffered gas poisoning, which left him in chronic ill health.

As World War I was being fought, Russia was facing internal challenges. During the reign of Tsar Nicholas II, which began in 1894, numerous opposition groups formed that opposed the autocratic nature of his rule. Such groups gained power when the tsar's forces were defeated in the 1905 Russo-Japanese War. While Nicholas tried to hold on to power by allowing elected Dumas (legislatures), he allowed only limited reforms while retaining control of the government. Further defeats in World War I to the Germans led to the end of Nicholas's reign. He was forced to abdicate in March 1917, leading to another conflict over who would run the country. The Bolsheviks (Communists), led by Vladimir Lenin, ultimately emerged victorious in 1918, and Lenin immediately agreed to a peace treaty with Germany.

Soviet Russia's Best-Selling Humorist

After the Russian Revolution, Zoshchenko held a number of different jobs, from bootmaker to patrolman. He briefly joined the Red Army, though he never joined the Communist Party and in fact remained politically uncommitted throughout his life. He settled down in St. Petersburg (then called Petrograd), married and had a child, and began his first serious efforts at writing. He helped found a group called the Serapion Brothers, who were mostly socialists but opposed restrictions on artistic expression. His first *skaz* sketches assumed the voice of a poor soldier named Sinebriukhov, who narrates his mishaps in a nonsensical mishmash of slang, dialect, and bureaucratic jargon. The first collection of Zoshchenko's stories, *The Stories of Nazar Ilich, Mister Sinebriukhov* (1922), was an instant success. Twenty more followed over the next four years, selling millions of copies and quickly establishing him as the most popular humorist of the time.

The Sinebriukhov stories gave Zoshchenko his signature style. His narrators took on various pseudonyms, but his work was instantly recognizable by its uniquely zany diction and its tragicomic portrait of Soviet society. Satirizing the everyday hardships facing the Soviet citizen, he avoided the romantic or grandiose tone of many of his peers. To him the new society was nothing heroic or inspiring but instead a series of petty frustrations and defeats.

Reflection of Changes in Society

Zoshchenko's humor captured the social chaos in Russia after 1917. The collapse of the monarchy and aristocracy brought acute disruption and dislocation. Public discourse was suddenly full of a strange Marxist vocabulary—language itself had undergone a revolution. Massive literacy campaigns produced millions of newly educated readers. Zoshchenko spoke to them, ironically contrasting revolutionary ideals with the reality of Soviet life, in prose that replicated oral storytelling. In "The Woman Who Could Not Read," for example, a woman fails to respond to the party's literacy drive—until she finds a scented letter in her husband's pocket.

Some of Zoshchenko's stories underscore the deprivation and hardship of contemporary life. The much lauded introduction of electric light, in the story "Poverty" (1924), only reveals how poorly the people truly live. Zoshchenko's narrators typically live in collective apartments, divided among several families who share

LITERARY AND HISTORICAL CONTEMPORARIES

Zoshchenko's famous contemporaries include:

Mikhail Sholokhov (1905–1984): This Soviet novelist wrote *And Quiet Flows the Don* (1928–1940). He was the winner of the 1965 Nobel Prize in Literature.

Isaac Babel (1894–1984): This Jewish Soviet journalist, playwright, and short-story writer published such books as the short-fiction collection *The Odessa Tales* (1927) and the play *Zakat*.

Nathanael West (1903–1940): This American author, screenwriter, and satirist was best known for his darkly humorous *The Day of the Locust* (1939).

Robert Benchley (1889–1945): This American humorist was known for his work as a newspaper columnist, film actor, and member of the Algonquin Round Table.

Aldous Huxley (1894–1963): This English novelist, essayist, poet, and short-story writer is best known for his 1932 classic *Brave New World*.

the kitchen and bathroom. In "The Crisis" (1925), a man and his wife live in a bathroom, giving their newborn a bath every day, while their thirty-two roommates also want to use the facilities. A series of longer, darker stories, collected as *What the Nightingale Sang: Sentimental Tales* (1927), plays on literary conventions as well as motifs from classic Russian works, such as those of Nikolai Gogol and Aleksandr Pushkin.

Youth Restored Zoshchenko, as well as Soviet society as a whole, faced challenges in the mid-1920s. After the death of Lenin in 1924, a power struggle ensued for control of the Communist Party. By 1928, Joseph Stalin had eliminated all his rivals and achieved full power. His rule was harsh and included forced industrialization and collectivization of agriculture. During Stalin's so-called Cultural Revolution on the establishment, Zoshchenko felt pressure to bring his work into line with more orthodox Soviet literature. The gray area in which uncommitted artists could work was closing. At the same time, Zoshchenko had a personal impulse to clarify his writing. His health had become an obsession that soon overshadowed his work. Zoshchenko was a hypochondriac and chronically depressed. At the end of one severe bout of ennui in the early 1930s, he felt he had found the secret to health and longevity, which he set out to share with his readers. The result, a novella called *Youth Restored* (1933), became Zoshchenko's most controversial work.

What Zoshchenko envisioned as a straightforward, didactic work came out as something quite the opposite. The story of *Youth Restored* concerns an aging, depressed professor who embarks on a rigorous program of self-help,

which succeeds to the point where he courts and marries his neighbor's nineteen-year-old daughter. In the margins of this ludicrous *skaz* narrative, however, one hundred pages of footnotes present Zoshchenko's newfound views on wellness. The juxtaposition creates an unsettling experience for the reader: Is this a sophisticated satire, an earnest self-help treatise, or could it conceivably be both?

Survival without Ambiguity The intentions of his next work, *The Blue Book* (1935), were similarly opaque. It also blends fiction and documentary, parody and ideological correctness. *The Blue Book* surveys human history, with dramatized historical episodes or concise bulletins of facts linked by a common theme. Confounding critics, the work could be seen as either a simplistic historical romp or a clownish mockery.

Producing such unorthodox literature was risky under Stalin. In the later 1930s, after socialist realism had become the official doctrine for Soviet literature, Zoshchenko modified his style. In his short pieces, the language is demonstrably clearer, and the narrator has a clear grasp of the story and the lesson to be drawn from it. Several documentary works seemed to demonstrate his ability to write without irony or ambiguity. If the world Zoshchenko created in the 1920s was chaotic and frustrating, now it was relatively efficient and welcoming. Because of the manifest changes in his work, Zoshchenko's official standing reversed itself. Stalin's purges claimed the lives of millions and devastated the ranks of experimental writers, but Zoshchenko was not subject to persecution nor was his work suppressed.

Wrote Before Sunrise During World War II (a global military conflict involving sixty-one countries that ultimately left 55 million people dead), Zoshchenko contributed antifascist propaganda work, as did nearly all Soviet writers. He also completed his most ambitious and autobiographical work, *Before Sunrise* (1943).

Denounced and Silenced Zoschenko's message was too idiosyncratic and egocentric for Stalin's Soviet Union. Publication of *Before Sunrise* was interrupted after the first half appeared in the journal *October*. The second half would not see print until 1972, long after Zoshchenko's death. The censorship of *Before Sunrise* crushed Zoshchenko.

Two years later came a worse blow. In 1946, one of Zoshchenko's stories for children was republished in an adult periodical, and out of context it seemed provocative and politically suspicious. Andrei Zhdanov, the leading literary hatchet man of the Stalinist era, heaped devastating criticism on Zoshchenko, calling his writings "rotten, vulgar, and empty." Zoshchenko was kicked out of the Writers' Union, deprived of his ration card, and even forced to return to shoemaking. His career as a satirist was essentially over, his long contribution to Soviet literature dismissed. The cultural thaw following Stalin's death did not restore his reputation. His health deteriorated, and he died in Leningrad in 1958.

Works in Literary Context

Zoshchenko's satirical prose is often compared with that of the nineteenth-century Russian master Nikolai Gogol. Zoshchenko shares with Gogol a highly inventive verbal expressiveness and a similar trajectory from ironic humor and absurdism to attempts to write highly didactic texts. Some critics also believe that Zoshchenko's humor was influenced by two other Russian writers, Nikolai Leskov and Anton Chekhov. In addition, Zoshchenko's writings were affected by the challenges of day-to-day existence in the Soviet Union.

Skaz Gogol was also one of the most notable practitioners of the *skaz* technique, whose most recognizable feature is the oral quality that the written text exhibits. A *skaz* author seems to have turned over the storytelling to a newcomer, often a barely literate one. Zoshchenko exploited the comic potential of this device, often to absurd effect, thereby increasing the ambiguity inherent in any *skaz* text. Since the author openly passes responsibility to a fictional narrator, the question is always open as to whether the narrator's comments reflect the character's ideas or those of the author. Thus, Zoshchenko's use of *skaz* created a certain anonymity, which vexed those Soviet critics who judged literature purely on ideological grounds. The technique won him a notable degree of free expression.

Class Conflict and the Party Line In terms of content, Zoshchenko's stories belonged to a rich satirical tradition that played up the petty foibles of daily life in Soviet society. His fresh, modern subject matter seemed in tune with the revolutionary spirit of the times. He adopted the viewpoint of the newly triumphant proletariat, yet often mocked notions of class conflict. In "Philistines" (1926), the narrator is outraged when a fellow worker is tossed off a tram for improper attire, when in truth, the worker had entered the tram covered in wet paint. His protagonist usually aspires to cultural sophistication while behaving in ways that undermine his pretensions. His satire extends to Communist Party doctrine. Typically his narrator would faithfully express the party line but in an ignorant or farcical way. No subversive views would appear in the text, but astute readers could enjoy the parody.

A Hornet's Nest of Language Zoshchenko's narrators speak in an unforgettable jumble of slang, working-class idiom, Bolshevik lingo, and sheer nuttiness. The brilliance of this verbal humor is difficult to capture in translation. Passages take dizzying, unexpected twists as language escapes the narrator's control. Tangled in a snarl of words, the moral of the story eludes the narrator or gets turned on end, delightfully frustrating the reader's expectations for a clear-cut, didactic tale.

Influential Comic Master Despite Zoshchenko's detours into the self-help genre, and his subsequent trou-

---

COMMON HUMAN EXPERIENCE

Zoshchenko was one of the first to satirize life in the new Soviet society. Here are some other works sending up Soviet socialism:

Heart of a Dog (1925), a novel by Mikhail Bulgakov. In this banned Soviet novel, a professor implants human organs into a dog, who grows into a version of the "New Soviet man."

The Twelve Chairs (1928), a novel by Ilia Il'f and Evgenii Petrov. In this book, a confidence man and a dispossessed aristocrat pursue some contraband jewelry hidden in a dining room chair.

Ninotchka (1939), a film directed by Ernst Lubitsch. This comedy starring Greta Garbo contrasted the dull gray of Soviet life with the romantic decadence of Paris.

Animal Farm (1945), a novella by George Orwell. The most famous allegorical satire of the Russian Revolution and the rise of Stalin.

Moscow 2042 (1986), a novel by Vladimir Voinovich. Time travel reveals the bleak future of the Soviet Union, in a dystopian parody written during the glasnost (openness) period.

---

ble with the regime, his popularity with readers has ensured his lasting influence. His contributions to Russian literature, in terms of humor, language, narrative persona, and the genre of the short story, cannot be denied.

Works in Critical Context

Zoshchenko wrote for the "mass reader" with great success. By virtue of his popularity, he could be considered among the most democratic writers in Soviet history. Furthermore, his appeal bridged normally distinct readerships, since it could be read and appreciated at different levels. The virtuosity of his comic language, and the humanity that shines through his work, have won many admirers.

Shifting Reception His critical reception in the Soviet Union, however, was politically fraught. As his popularity peaked in the 1920s, the critical establishment viewed him suspiciously: some found his work too grim and pessimistic, even anti-Soviet. In the 1930s, as he trimmed the ambiguity from his stories and clarified their edifying intent, he gained more critical acceptance. At the same time, critics reevaluated his earlier work, reaching consensus that Zoshchenko should be seen as distinct from the proletarian narrators he created. The critics, in effect, had finally caught up to the readers in their judgment.

Before 1946, Zoshchenko's name was generally unrecognized outside the Soviet Union. Upon his persecution, Western scholars promoted him as anti-Soviet, placing him in the canon of dissidents who bravely told the bitter truth of Soviet life. Ironically, a contrary process took place in the Soviet Union after his death. He was rehabilitated, and collections of his stories were republished, though carefully edited on ideological grounds. In the 1970s, three critical books resurrected his standing as a pro-Soviet satirist, generally on the same terms he enjoyed in the 1930s. With the fall of the Soviet Union, he came to be seen as a martyr, and his works gained still further attention and appreciation.

The Blue Book Zoschenko's largest work *The Blue Book* received a mixed response from critics from its first serial publication in *Krasniaia nov'*. This story features a tour through human history that focuses on four constants—money, love, treachery, and misfortune—balanced by a section titled "Amazing Events," which highlights revolutionaries and the achievements of the Soviet Union. Depending on which section or narrative voice a critic focused on, *The Blue Book* could be seen either as an optimistic, albeit simplified, survey of history or a ludicrous, clownish mockery. In *Pravda*, Aron Gurshtein dismissed the book as a cheap vulgarization that suffered from the very present authorial "smirk" whether topics were tragic or uplifting. Alternately, Aleksandr Dymshits in the proletarian journal *Rezets* praised Zoshchenko for producing a book which was strong and optimistic.

Responses to Literature

1. Write an essay comparing Zoshchenko's use of *skaz* narrative with the comic writings of Nikolai Gogol.

2. In a presentation, address how the *skaz* technique allowed Zoshchenko an expanded freedom of expression.

3. Write a research paper on how Zoshchenko's lifelong health concerns affected his literary career.

4. Make a careful study of the types of verbal humor in Zoshchenko's stories and in a detailed essay describe as precisely as you can the elements that make his work funny.

5. Based on his short fiction, how would you summarize Zoshchenko's attitude toward the Soviet revolution? Was he pro-Soviet, anti-Soviet, or does neither label apply? Share your opinions in a small group setting.

BIBLIOGRAPHY

Books

Carleton, Gregory. *The Politics of Reception: Critical Constructions of Mikhail Zoshchenko*. Evanston, Ill.: Northwestern University Press, 1998.

Chudakova, Marietta Omarovna. *The Poetics of Mikhail Zoshchenko*. Moscow: Nauka, 1979.

Harris, Jane Gary, ed. *Autobiographical Statements in Twentieth-Century Russian Literature*. Princeton, N.J.: Princeton University Press, 1990.

Hicks, Jeremy. *Mikhail Zoshchenko and the Poetics of Skaz*. Nottingham, U.K.: Astra, 2000.

Popkin, Cathy. *The Pragmatics of Insignificance: Chekhov, Zoshchenko and Gogol*. Stanford, Calif.: Stanford University Press, 1993.

Scatton, Linda Hart. *Mikhail Zoshchenko: Evolution of a Writer*. Cambridge: Cambridge University Press, 1993.

Simmons, Edward, ed. *Through the Glass of Soviet Literature: Views of Russian Society*. New York: Columbia University Press, 1953.

Periodicals

Dymshits, Aleksandr. Review of *Blue Book*. *Rezets* (1936).

Gurshtein, Aron. Review of *Blue Book*. *Pravda*, May 9, 1936.

Hodge, Thomas P. "Freudian Elements in Zoshchenko's *Pered voskhodom solntse[BA1]* (1943)." *Slavonic and East European Review* 1 (1989): 1–28.

Titunik, Irwin. "Mikhail Zoshchenko and the Problem of Skaz." *California Slavic Studies* 6 (1971): 83–96.

Von Wiren, Vera. "Zoshchenko in Retrospect." *Russian Review* 4 (1962): 348–61.

Glossary of Literary Terms

The glossary contains terms found in various entries throughout the *Gale Contextual Encyclopedia of World Literature*. This glossary includes: terms for various literary components or techniques relevant to the work of the authors; terms for important artistic movements or groups discussed in relation to the authors; and terms for social, political, or philosophical ideas that profoundly impacted world literature. Definitions for more basic literary terms, such as "figurative language," have not been included.

ACMEISM: A Russian literary movement in which writers focused on concrete imagery and description of the physical world. Acmeism (derived from "acme," a Greek term meaning "peak") was seen largely as a reaction to Russian Symbolism. Acmeist writers mentioned in this encyclopedia include Osip Mandelstam and Anna Akhmatova.

ALLEGORY: A work in which the entire narrative serves as a symbol for something beyond the surface-level story. For example, George Orwell's *Animal Farm* (1945), aside from being a tale about a group of farm animals revolting against their master, is acknowledged by the author to be a criticism of Stalinist Russia in which each animal represents a real historical figure.

ANACHRONISM: A thing or idea mentioned in a work of art that occurs outside its normal place in time. In William Shakespeare's play *Julius Caesar*, for example, the author mentions the striking of a clock to indicate time passing—even though no such clocks existed in ancient Rome, the time period in which the play is set.

ANGRY YOUNG MEN: A group of British writers in the mid-twentieth century defined by their expression of discontent for traditional social and political institutions. Writers associated with this loosely-defined

movement include Kingsley Amis, Harold Pinter, and John Osborne.

ANTI-HERO: A main character in a literary work whose actions and ideals would not generally be regarded as heroic, though the character may still be portrayed sympathetically by the author. Raskolnikov, the protagonist of Fyodor Dostoyevsky's novel *Crime and Punishment*, is an example of an anti-hero.

AUTOMATIC WRITING: A method of writing, often employed by Surrealists such as André Breton, in which the hand is allowed to write freely without being guided by conscious thought. The novel *The Magnetic Fields* (1920) by Breton and Philippe Soupault was reportedly written using this technique.

AVANT-GARDE: Meaning "advance guard" in French, a term used to describe artists or artistic works that are considered innovative or pushing the boundaries of tradition. The term has been applied to writers of all manner of literary movements, including Surrealism, Expressionism, Symbolism, and Futurism.

BALLAD: A poetic work written in the form of a traditional song that commonly relates a folk tale, myth, or legend. Ballads are often written in four-line stanzas with alternating lines of eight and six syllables, in which the lines with six syllables contain end-rhyme. "The Rime of the Ancient Mariner" (1798) by Samuel Taylor Coleridge is a famous example of a ballad.

BILDUNGSROMAN: Taken from a German term meaning "novel of formation," a novel that documents the maturation of the protagonist. The bildungsroman is also commonly known as a "coming of age" novel.

BLANK VERSE: A type of poetry which follows a set pattern of stressed and unstressed syllables in each line, but does not feature consistent rhyme. Playwrights William Shakespeare and Ben Jonson created many of their works in blank verse, as did poet John Milton.

BLOOMSBURY GROUP: A group of London artists and intellectuals formed in the early twentieth century, named after the central London area in which many of them lived. Notable members included Virginia Woolf and E. M. Forster.

CLASSICAL UNITIES: A set of parameters for drama, originally derived from Aristotle and followed by neoclassicists, that were believed to be necessary for creating ideal dramatic works. According to the classical unities, a play should: focus on a single story (unity of action); take place in a single location (unity of place); and cover a period of time no longer than twenty-four hours (unity of time).

CLASSICISM: A term applied to several artistic movements in which the artists emphasized structures and styles similar to those found in ancient Greek and Roman art. For literature, this included an emphasis on the observable world and aesthetic beauty.

CLOSET DRAMA: A dramatic work that is not meant to be performed on stage. Closet dramas may be read aloud among a small group, or may be read silently as with non-dramatic literature. *Samson Agonistes* (1671) by John Milton is a famous example of a closet drama.

COMEDY: In classical Greek drama, a play that ends happily for its major characters; many ancient comedies poked fun at political figures or cultural stereotypes, which inspired the laughter modern audiences now associate with the term.

COMEDY OF ERRORS: A dramatic work in which the characters are subject to misunderstandings and coincidences that lead to humorous conflicts, but which are ultimately resolved without tragic consequences. William Shakespeare's *A Midsummer Night's Dream* (c. 1596) is an example of a comedy of errors.

COMEDY OF MANNERS: A dramatic work that points out the unique behaviors of a certain social class or group in order to derive humor at their expense. Oscar Wilde's play *The Importance of Being Earnest* is an example of a comedy of manners.

COMMEDIA DELL'ARTE: Meaning "comedy of artists" in Italian, a type of street drama that relies heavily on improvisation and physical comedy built around a traditional storyline.

DADAISM: A European artistic movement that flourished during World War I and was characterized by opposition to the war, as well as a rejection of logic and traditional definitions of art. Poet and playwright Tristan Tzara was a key figure in Dadaism.

ELEGY: A written work, generally a poem, that expresses mourning over the death of a person or some other profound loss. Percy Bysshe Shelley's poem "Adonaïs" (1821) is an example of an elegy.

ENJAMBMENT: In poetry, the splitting of a continuous phrase or sentence into two or more lines. The result is that a single line may appear to express an incomplete thought, though the work as a whole is afforded a more complex rhythm and structure. William Shakespeare made frequent use of enjambment in his later plays.

EPIC: A literary work, originally a work in poetic form, that focuses on large-scale events and themes, and often takes place over a long period of time. *The Odyssey*, an ancient Greek epic by Homer, is one of the earliest examples.

EPIGRAM: A short, clever statement—often in the form of a couplet—intended to impart humor and insight.

EPISTOLARY NOVEL: A novel in which the story is told through letters written by one or more characters. Samuel Richardson was an early practitioner of the epistolary novel, with works such as *Pamela* (1740) and *Clarissa* (1748).

EXISTENTIALISM: A philosophical movement that gained popularity in the first half of the twentieth century, thanks to literary works by Jean-Paul Sartre and Simone de Beauvoir, among others. Existentialism is characterized by the idea that life does not have a greater meaning or purpose beyond that which people choose to create for themselves.

EXPERIMENTAL NOVEL: A work which defies the traditional structure or subject matter of a novel, and emphasizes style or technique over content. Though the term can be used to describe any number of nontraditional works, Laurence Sterne's *The Life and Opinions of Tristram Shandy, Gentleman* (1759) is an oft-cited example of an early experimental novel.

EXPRESSIONISM: An artistic movement characterized by an emphasis on expressing emotion and psychological states instead of objective realism. Playwright August Strindberg is often considered one of the first to bring Expressionist ideas to drama.

FABLE: A short tale whose purpose is to impart a message or lesson, usually featuring animals as characters. "The Tortoise and the Hare" is a well-known example of a fable.

FARCE: A dramatic work characterized by characters being put into comedic situations that are unlikely or improbable, as in Georges Feydeau's *A Flea in Her Ear* (1907).

FLASH FICTION: Short fiction, usually under one thousand words, that despite its length contains all the traditional elements of story such as a protagonist and conflict that is somehow resolved.

FRAME NARRATIVE: A literary device in which the main story being told to the reader is presented as a story being told by one of the characters within the work, such as in *Heart of Darkness* (1899) by Joseph Conrad. Frame narratives often contain several stories and multiple storytellers, as in Geoffrey Chaucer's *The Canterbury Tales* (written in the fourteenth century).

FUTURISM: A literary movement of the early twentieth century, primarily in poetry, meant to express the dynamic nature of the modern world. Futurist poetry was characterized by onomatopoeia, unusual word order, and unexpected juxtaposition of objects and images. Vladimir Mayakovsky was one of the best-known Russian Futurists.

GENERATION OF '27: A loose collective of Spanish poets and artists active during the 1920s who became known, despite their differing styles, for their avant-garde approach. The Generation of '27 included members such as Federico García Lorca, Luis Cernuda, and Jorge Guillén.

GENERATION OF '98: A group of Spanish writers active during and after the Spanish-American War, known for their interest in forging a Spanish cultural identity. Members of the Generation of '98 included Antonio Machado and Ramón del Valle Inclán.

GOTHIC FICTION: A literary sub-genre that emerged in the last half of the eighteenth century and was characterized by eerie atmosphere, melodrama, mystery, and romance. Ann Radcliffe was an important figure in the development of Gothic fiction.

GRAND GUIGNOL: A French theater founded in 1894 and known for its plays depicting horrifying and graphically violent events, most of which were written by André de Lorde; the term "Grand Guignol" is still used to describe tales of grisly horror.

GROUP 47: A German literary group established to cultivate and advance German literature in the wake of World War II. Though membership was often private and ever-changing, notable members included Günter Grass and Heinrich Böll.

HAIKU: A Japanese poetic form whose English equivalent consists of only three lines, the first and third containing five syllables and the second containing seven. Matsuo Bashô was an early master of this poetic form.

HEROIC COUPLET: An English poetic form which consists of a rhyming pair of ten-syllable lines. Geoffrey Chaucer and Alexander Pope were both known for their use of the heroic couplet.

HUMANISM: A philosophical notion that emphasizes the inherent goodness and rationality of all people, as well as the encouragement of artistic creation among people of all levels of society. François Rabelais and Thomas Mann were both notable supporters of humanism.

IMAGISM: A poetic movement of the early twentieth century that emphasized direct expression through concise imagery and non-standard structure. Ezra Pound was instrumental in the development of the Imagist movement.

IMPRESSIONISM: An artistic movement that emerged during the latter half of the nineteenth century, and focused on artistic impression over realistic representation. In literature, impressionism was characterized by a focus on the depiction of the interior, mental landscapes of characters, and was associated with other literary movements such as Symbolism.

IRONY: A literary device in which a character's perception of reality differs from actual reality, or in which a character's words do not express their true feelings. Sarcasm is a well-known form of irony. Dramatic irony occurs when an audience is given information that is not known by one or more characters in the play.

LIBRETTO: A text for the vocal portion of an opera or other musical work, often written in verse form. Famous composers frequently employed well-known poets to write libretti for their works, and writers such as William Congreve, Victor Hugo, and Gertrude Stein have worked as librettists.

LOST GENERATION: A term used to describe a loosely defined group of American writers who spent time in Europe—especially Paris—following World War I. These writers, including Ernest Hemingway, F. Scott Fitzgerald, and Sherwood Anderson, were notable for themes of disillusionment in their works.

MAGIC REALISM: A literary style developed primarily in South America in which fantastic or supernatural elements are woven into otherwise realistic tales. Writers commonly associated with magic realism include Jorge Luis Borges, Alejo Carpentier, Gabriel García Márquez, and Carlos Fuentes.

MASQUE: A theatrical pageant performed for royalty and nobility during the sixteenth and seventeenth centuries. Masques were generally written and performed for special occasions. Ben Jonson and Sir Philip Sidney were well-known writers of masques.

MELODRAMA: A literary work which contains heightened or exaggerated emotions from the characters. The term originally applied to theatrical productions in which music (or melody) was used to accentuate the drama occurring on the stage.

MODERNISM: An artistic movement during the early twentieth century influenced by the rapid industrialization, scientific advancements, and devastating warfare of the time. Modernist writers were noted for their radical departure from traditional literary forms, with notable Modernist works including T. S. Eliot's poem "The Waste Land" (1922) and James Joyce's novel *Ulysses* (1922).

NATURALISM: A literary movement from the late nineteenth century that focused on realistic portrayals of people and situations, and specifically dealt with the effects of heredity and environment on a character's personality and development. Émile Zola is widely regarded as a Naturalist.

NEOCLASSICISM: A literary movement during the first half of the twentieth century that marked a movement away from romanticism and sought inspiration in ancient Greek and Roman art.

NIHILISM: A philosophical movement that first appeared in the nineteenth century and is characterized by the belief that life has no objective purpose, moral code, or value. Writers associated with nihilism include Ivan Turgenev, whose novel *Fathers and Sons* (1862) described the Russian Nihilist movement and popularized the concept.

NOUVEAU ROMAN: Also known as an "anti-novel" (the term itself is French for "new novel"), a literary work in which traditional storytelling elements are absent or altered, so that the reader cannot determine with certainty the correct order or reality of events depicted. Alain Robbe-Grillet was instrumental in defining the *nouveau roman*.

PARABLE: A short tale meant to impart a message or lesson to the reader. Parables are similar to fables, but do not include supernatural or fantastic elements such as talking animals.

PARODY: A literary work designed to mock or criticize another, usually well-known literary work or genre. An early example is *Shamela* (1741), Henry Fielding's parody of the successful Samuel Richardson novel *Pamela* (1740).

PASTORAL: Literature that depicts rural life, nature, and the people of the region in a highly idealized way. *Eclogues* (c. 40 B.C.E.) by the ancient Roman poet Virgil are among the oldest examples of pastoral poetry.

PICARESQUE: A type of novel first developed in Spain that focuses on the adventures of a rogue, or clever anti-hero. Among many others, George MacDonald Fraser's *Flashman* novels exhibit the key traits of the picaresque.

POSTMODERNISM: A post-World War II literary movement characterized by nonlinearity, or a nonstandard narrative timeline, as well as metafiction, in which the author shows awareness of the story as a work of fiction and may even appear as a character within it.

PSEUDONYM: An alternate name used by a writer, often to hide the writer's identity. For example, Charles Dodgson used the pen name Lewis Carroll when writing *Alice's Adventures in Wonderland* (1865) and *Through the Looking-Glass* (1871).

PSYCHOLOGICAL NOVEL: A type of novel in which a great deal of attention is paid to the thoughts and feelings of the characters, as opposed to external action. Stendahl's 1830 novel *The Red and the Black* is often cited as an early example of the psychological novel.

REALISM: An artistic movement characterized by a desire to portray characters and environments as objectively, or as close to reality, as possible. Realism relies heavily upon physical descriptions, and Gustave Flaubert's novel *Madame Bovary* (1856)—with its almost grotesque precision to detail—is considered a landmark work of realism.

ROMAN À CLEF: A literary work containing fictionalized depictions of real people and events. The work may be autobiographical, as in Sylvia Plath's *The Bell Jar* (1963), or it may refer to thinly-disguised versions of well-known figures, as in George Orwell's depiction of Stalin and other Soviet politicians in *Animal Farm* (1945).

ROMANTICISM: An artistic and philosophical movement that developed throughout Europe in the late eighteenth and early nineteenth centuries. Romantic literature is notable for its expression of powerful emotions and use of natural settings. Poets associated with the Romantic movement include Lord Byron, William Wordsworth, and John Keats.

SAMIZDAT: A secret distribution method used by Soviet dissident writers for literary works that could not be published within their own country. *Samizdat* involved the manual copying of manuscript pages to be distributed among small groups of readers who could be trusted not to reveal the source of the work. Writers whose work appeared in *samizdat* form included Aleksandr Solzhenitsyn and Joseph Brodsky.

SATIRE: A type of literature intended to attack a person, group, institution, or idea through parody or irony. Very often, the satirist exposes the shortcomings of its subject by ironically expressing a position in support or praise of the subject. A famous example of satire is Jonathan Swift's "A Modest Proposal," (1729) in which he skewers England's mistreatment of Ireland by enthusiastically proposing to the Irish that they sell their children for food.

SERIAL PUBLICATION: The printing of consecutive portions of a novel or other lengthy work of literature in successive issues of a periodical. Serial publication was especially popular in England during the nineteenth century, and many of Charles Dickens's novels were first printed through serial publication.

SOCIAL REALISM: An artistic movement of the nineteenth century defined by sympathetic yet realistic depictions of the working class and the poor conditions in which they lived.

SOCIALIST REALISM: The official art style of the Soviet Union of six decades, socialist realism was defined by its glorification of the working class and Soviet leaders, as well as its depiction of common scenes and avoidance of fanciful subject matter. Artists and writers who did not fit this style were typically deemed unproductive or disruptive, and sent to one of many government-run labor camps.

SONNET (ELIZABETHAN): A poetic form popular in England during the sixteenth and seventeenth centuries (during the reign of Queen Elizabeth I), typically consisting of fourteen ten-syllable lines and an alternating rhyme scheme. William Shakespeare is perhaps the most famous practitioner of the Elizabethan sonnet.

STREAM OF CONSCIOUSNESS: A literary technique meant to emulate the flow of thought in a character's mind. This is sometimes expressed through disjointed or run-on sentences, repetitions of words or phrases, or tenuous associations between different subjects. Notable works that use the stream of consciousness technique include *Mrs. Dalloway* (1925) by Virginia Woolf and *Finnegans Wake* (1939) by James Joyce.

STURM UND DRANG: A German artistic movement that arose in the late eighteenth century and was characterized by free expression of emotion—often negative emotion such as torment or greed. Literary works of the *Sturm und Drang* movement often end tragically or violently for their characters. Writers associated with the *Sturm und Drang* movement include Johann Wolfgang von Goethe and Friedrich Schiller.

SURREALISM: An artistic movement of the early twentieth century noted for its embrace of the irrational. Surrealist literary works often contained jarring juxtapositions of unrelated things, seemingly random or nonsensical phrases, and dreamlike situations. Poet André Breton was a founding figure in Surrealism.

SYMBOLISM: A late nineteenth century artistic movement noted for its rejection of realism and description of the physical, in favor of using words to evoke the metaphysical, emotional, and spiritual. Maurice Maeterlinck was a key figure in the development of Symbolist drama.

THEATER OF CRUELTY: A view of theater conceived by playwright Antonin Artaud in which audiences are exposed to painful truths by being centrally involved in the play's action.

THEATER OF THE ABSURD: A dramatic movement linked with Existentialism in which characters often find themselves at the mercy of an incomprehensible universe. A rejection of realism and typical story structure, Theater of the Absurd dramas often had no discernible purpose or message.

TRAGEDY: In classical Greek drama, a play that focuses on themes such as love, fate and betrayal, does not end happily for one or more of the main characters. The play *Antigone* (c. 442 B.C.E.) by Sophocles is a typical Greek tragedy.

VERNACULAR: The casual and natural speech of a group of people or culture. Up until the Middle Ages, European literature was typically written in Latin instead of the commonly spoken language of the region; the development of literature written in the vernacular allowed audiences of almost any social level to enjoy such works.

Index

U

Nationality Index